Criminal Justice

To my wife, Julie, and my daughters,
Emmeline and Eleanor

Criminal Justice

An introduction to crime and

the criminal justice system

Peter Joyce

WILLAN
PUBLISHING

Published by

Willan Publishing
Culmott House
Mill Street, Uffculme
Cullompton, Devon
EX15 3AT, UK
Tel: +44(0)1884 840337
Fax: +44(0)1884 840251
e-mail: info@willanpublishing.co.uk
website: www.willanpublishing.co.uk

Publishing simultaneously in the USA and Canada by

Willan Publishing
c\o ISBS, 920 NE 58th Ave, Suite 300
Portland, Oregon 97213-3786, USA
Tel: +001(0)503 287 3093
Fax: +001(0)503 280 8832
e-mail: info@isbs.com
website: www.isbs.com

Paperback
ISBN-13: 978-1-84392-182-0
ISBN-10: 1-84392-182-0

Hardback
ISBN-13: 978-1-84392-183-7
ISBN-10: 1-84392-183-9

British Library Cataloguing-in-Publication Data

A catalogue record for this book is available from the British Library

Typeset by Pantek Arts Ltd, Maidstone, Kent
Project management by Deer Park Productions, Tavistock, Devon
Printing and bound by Cromwell Press, Trowbridge, Wiltshire

Contents

List of abbreviations

ABC	Acceptable Behaviour Contract
ACPO	Association of Chief Police Officers
APA	Association of Police Authorities
ASBO	Anti-Social Behaviour Order
BCS	British Crime Survey
BCU	Basic Command Unit
BVPI	Best Value Performance Indicator
CARATS	Counselling, Assessment, Referral, Advice and Throughcare Services
CCRC	Criminal Cases Review Commission
CCTV	Closed-Circuit Television
CDRP	Crime and Disorder Reduction Partnership
CHE	Community Home (with Education)
CJA	Commission for Judicial Appointments
CPM	Community Panel Member
CPS	Crown Prosecution Service
CRE	Commission for Racial Equality
CSO	Community Service Order
CSU	Community Safety Unit
DAT	Drug Action Team
DCA	Departmemt for Constitutional Affairs
DHSS	Department of Health and Social Security
DLP	Discretionary Lifer Panel
DPP	Director of Public Prosecutions
ECP	Enhanced Community Punishment
GCHQ	Government Communications Headquarters
GIS	Geographic Information System
HDC	Home Detention Curfew
HMIC	Her Majesty's Inspectorate of Constabulary
ICCP	Intensive Change and Control Programme
IEP	Incentives and Earned Privileges Scheme
IP	Intensive Probation
IPCC	Independent Police Complaints Commission
ISM	Intensive Supervision and Monitoring
ISSP	Intensive Supervision and Surveillance Programme
IT	Intermediate Treatment
LAG	Legal Action Group

LSB	Legal Services Board
LSC	Legal Services Commission
LSP	Local Strategic Partnership
MACC	Mutual Aid Coordination Centre
MDT	Mandatory Drug Test
MPA	Metropolitan Police Authority
MPS	Metropolitan Police Service
NACRO	National Association for the Care and Resettlement of Offenders
NAFIS	National Automated Fingerprint Identification System
NCIS	National Criminal Intelligence Service
NCRS	National Crime Recording Standard
NCS	National Crime Squad
NIC	National Information Centre
NIM	National Intelligence Model
NOMS	National Offender Management Service
NOMIS	National Offender Management Information System
NPIA	National Policing Improvement Agency
NPS	National Probation Service
NRC	National Reporting Centre
OASys	Offender Assessment System
OCJR	Office for Criminal Justice Reform
OLC	Office for Legal Complaints
OSS	Office for the Supervision of Solicitors
PAC	Public Accounts Committee
PACE	Police and Criminal Evidence Act 1984
PAT	Policy Action Team
PCA	Police Complaints Authority
PCB	Police Complaints Board
PCSO	Police Community Support Officer
PDR	Performance Development Review
PNC	Police National Computer
PND	Penalty Notice for Disorder
POA	Prison Officers' Association
POP	Problem-oriented Policing
PPAF	Policing Performance Assessment Framework
PRT	Prison Reform Trust
PSIA	Private Security Industry Authority
PSNI	Police Service of Northern Ireland
PSU	Police Standards Unit
PSU	Police Support Unit
QC	Queen's Counsel
RIC	Regional Intelligence Cell

SARA	Scanning, Analysis, Response and Assessment
SEARCH	Selection Entrance Assessment for Recruiting Constables Holistically
SEU	Social Exclusion Unit
SGC	Sentencing Guidelines Council
SIA	Security Industry Authority
SIS	Schengen Information System
SITO	Security Industry Training Organisation
SOCA	Serious Organised Crime Agency
SOTP	Sex Offender Treatment Programme
STOP	Straight Thinking on Probation programme
UKADCU	UK Anti-Drug Coordination Unit
VOM	Victim–Offender Mediation
VORP	Victim–Offender Reconciliation Program
YOI	Youth Offenders Institution
YOP	Youth Offender Panel
YOT	Youth Offending Team

Table of cases

do so as this matter was a policy decision by the chief constable with which he felt the court should not interfere.

This case concerned the secrecy of jury deliberations. Here the House of Lords ruled that jury deliberations should remain secret after a verdict had been given and that not even an Appeal judge could inquire into jury deliberations.

These two cases were concerned with constabulary independence and especially in connection with law enforcement. In the first of these judgements (which related to the failure to prosecute for gaming offences), Lord Denning stated that the responsiblity for law enforcement rested on the chief constable who could not be told how to act by ministers or police authorities. In the second (which concerned the enforcement of the 1959 Obscene Publications Act) Lord Denning re-affirmed the principle of constabulary discretion in prosecution matters).

This case arose in connection with police misbehaviour towards a black 17-year-old youth. The Police Complaints Board declined to press for disciplinary charges to be brought against the errant police officers on the grounds that as the DPP had considered prosecuting these officers for a criminal offence it would constitute double jeopardy to latterly insist that a disciplinary charge should be brought using the same evidence. Here the Appeal Court queried this definition of double jeopardy then used by the Police Complaints Board.

This case was concerned with the sentencing power of the courts in connection with racially motivated crimes of violence. Here Lord Chief Justice Taylor ruled that although the law did not then contain any specific offence of racial violence, judges could exercise their discretion and award an increased sentence in cases where a racial motive had been proven.

This was an example of the ability of judges to effectively act as law-makers. Here Lord Simmonds proclaimed the existence of the common law offence of 'conspiracy to corrupt public morals' in the 'Ladies' Directory' case.

Preface

The book provides an account of the operations of the criminal justice system in England and Wales, devoting particular attention to reforms introduced by Conservative and Labour governments after 1979. It anticipates little or no prior knowledge of the subject area, and seeks to provide an introductory text for those commencing their studies in the disciplines of criminology, politics, public sector studies and law for whom crime, law and order and the criminal justice system form important areas of study. For this reason the book includes a considerable amount of factual material which is designed to form the basis of more detailed and evaluative studies at later stages of study. The book will also be of interest to general readers and practitioners in the criminal justice system.

Each chapter contains some questions that are designed both to test the reader's understanding of the subject area and to encourage further investigation, perhaps drawing upon contemporary issues discussed in newspapers and journals. Each chapter also includes a date chart that is designed to highlight the main issues that have been raised and identifies some of the more specialised literature that can be consulted to obtain a more detailed understanding of the subject areas.

Chapters 1 and 2 provide the context for an examination of the criminal justice system, discussing the various explanations which have been put forward to explain why crime occurs, how it can be measured and what might be done to prevent it. Chapter 2 further considers the contemporary importance attached to community safety.

Chapters 3–8 are concerned with the role, functions and working practices of the main agencies that operate within the criminal justice system. Chapter 3 evaluates the methods that have evolved to deliver policing and analyses the reasons for changes that have been made to its structure and organisation. These have created a more centralised service since 1945, and resulted in some police responsibilities being delivered by private bodies. Chapter 4 examines changes to the control and accountability of the police service, analysing the key changes introduced by Conservative governments between 1979 and 1997 and by Labour governments after 1997.

Chapters 5 and 6 provide an account of the operations of the legal system. Chapter 5 discusses the workings of the prosecution system. It investigates the functioning of agencies that include the Crown Prosecution Service and the Criminal Cases Review Commission and the rationale for proposals to reform important aspects of the prosecution service such as trial by jury. Chapter 5 also examines the extent to which gender bias operates in the prosecution process and analyses the importance of discretion to its workings.

Chapter 6 focuses on the role of the judiciary. It examines the structure of the courts and the legal profession, discusses the role performed by judges in the judicial process and considers contemporary issues affecting the appointment of judges.

Chapters 7 and 8 are concerned with the punishment of offenders. Chapter 7 examines the concept of punishment and the diverse aims that punishment may serve. Significant attention is devoted to restorative justice which has been introduced into the juvenile justice system but which has the potential for adoption throughout the criminal justice process. It also evaluates sociological approaches to punishment that seek to explain why societies introduce changes to the methods that they employ. The final section of this chapter considers sentencing policy in contemporary England and Wales.

Chapter 8 focuses on the role of prisons. It examines the purpose of prisons and in particular assesses the problems that such institutions face in seeking to secure the rehabilitation of offenders. The contemporary significance of community-based penalties is also discussed, and the changing role performed by the Probation Service is examined. This chapter also discusses the rationale and implications of merging the prison and probation services into a unified correctional service.

Chapter 9 deals with the topic of juvenile justice, seeking to highlight the tensions inherent in this system between the welfare of juveniles and the punishment of those who offend. This chapter analyses in detail the proposals put forward by the 1997 Labour government to respond to juvenile crime (particularly the introduction of Youth Offending Teams and Youth Offender Panels and the policies which have been put forward to tackle its social causes).

Chapter 10 tackles a key issue affecting the operations of the entire criminal justice system, that of racial discrimination. This chapter concentrates on the background to the reforms put forward by Sir William Macpherson in his 1999 report, and the progress that has subsequently been made to implement them.

This book has explored a number of issues related to contemporary criminal justice policy and the operations of the agencies within the criminal justice process. The final chapter identifies a number of key themes that have been discussed in the book.

The book includes a brief section that is headed 'Keeping up to date'. This contains information on a number of organisations that play an important role in formulating or implementing criminal justice policy. Readers are encouraged to consult these organisations in order to keep abreast of the changes that are constantly being made to the delivery of criminal justice policy.

The idea for this book originated in connection with a course I have taught for some years in Criminal Justice Policy at Manchester Metropolitan University. I would like to record my appreciation to the students who have taken this course and also to my colleagues in the Criminology team with whom I have worked – Sandra Walklate (who now occupies the Eleanor Rathbone Chair of Sociology at Liverpool University), Helen Jones, Dan Ellingworth, Wendy Laverick, Jo Massey, Eileen Berrington, Graham Smyth, Ron Wardale and John Houghton.

I would also like to record my appreciation to my publisher, Brian Willan, for his constant support during the production of this work and also to the two reviewers of the manuscript (Rob Mawby at the University of Central England and the other who was anonymous). Both made detailed and helpful suggestions that have considerably improved the content of the book. All errors and omissions that remain are, of course, my responsibility.

1 The causes of crime and deviancy

There is no universally accepted explanation of why people carry out criminal acts, and as a result there are many different theories. This chapter seeks to analyse the main perspectives that have been adopted within criminology to explain the causes of crime and deviant behaviour.

In particular it will:

- discuss the key features associated with classicist criminology and identify the reforms associated with this approach;
- distinguish between classicist and positivist approaches to the study of crime: a more detailed consideration of the theories and theorists associated with positivism will be considered in the following sections dealing with biological, psychological and sociological explanations of crime;
- consider the wide range of biological explanations for crime dating from the findings of Cesare Lombroso in the late nineteenth century to more recent attempts to identify the existence of a criminal gene;
- examine psychological explanations for crime and deviance, particularly focusing on the contributions made by Sigmund Freud and Hans Eysenck;
- evaluate a wide range of sociological theories related to the causes of crime and deviance which seek to locate the causes of crime and deviance in the social environment in which it occurs;
- analyse the approaches associated with theories which place the operations of the state and the power structure underpinning it at the forefront of explanations for behaviour that is depicted as criminal: these approaches include new deviancy, Marxist, left idealist, left realist and critical criminologies;
- discuss conservative and new right opinions concerning the occurrence of crime;
- identify the key contributions made by feminist criminologies to the study of crime and deviance.

Classicism

Classicism developed out of the Enlightenment movement of late eighteenth-century Europe. Its political expression was liberalism that viewed society as a contract voluntarily entered into by those who were party to it rather than being a structure handed down by God. Government emerged as the result of a rational choice by those who subsequently accorded their consent to its operations, and this belief ensured that the rights of the individual were prominent concerns of liberal and classicist thinking. Crime was viewed as an act that infringed the legal code whose rationale was to safeguard the interests of those who were party to the social contract, especially the preservation of their personal safety and privately owned property. In such a contractual society, the equality of all citizens before the law and the presumption of the innocence of a person accused of criminal wrongdoing were viewed as cardinal principles to safeguard individual rights and liberties. The state was entitled to intervene in the lives of its citizens only when this would promote the interests of the majority.

A key exponent of classicist criminology was Cesare Beccaria, who put forward several views concerning crime and how the state should respond to it (Beccaria, 1764). These included the following:

- *Crime was an act undertaken by a rational being.* Individuals possessed free will and the decision to commit crime was viewed as the consequence of a logical thought process in which a person calculated the benefits to be derived from a criminal action compared to the personal costs it might involve. Classicists assumed that rational beings sought to maximise their pleasure and avoid inflicting pain on themselves. Accordingly, they advocated measures that guaranteed that crime would inevitably result in sanctions.

- *Crime required a uniform and consistent response.* Classicists argued that the most appropriate solution to crime was a clearly defined and consistently applied legal code and a criminal justice system that was predictable (and also swift) in its operations. This would ensure that potential criminals were aware of the inevitable personal cost of committing crime. In the United Kingdom, uniformity was promoted by giving central government an important role in the criminal justice system that it discharged through the process of inspection.

- *Discretion was to be avoided.* The emphasis on a uniform and consistent approach to crime inevitably rejected the exercise of discretion by professionals such as magistrates and judges. Beccaria argued that punishments laid down in law should never be exceeded and that the role of judges was to apply, but never to interpret, the law (or what a judge might subjectively view as the spirit of a law).

- *Punishments should fit the crime.* The harm which a particular criminal action did to society was the classicist yardstick by which they judged the appropriateness of punishments. Classicism focused on the act and not the person who carried it out, thus intent was deemed irrelevant. It was further argued that the degree of punishment to be inflicted on a wrongdoer should be no more than what was required to outweigh any advantage which the criminal action might bring.

- *Deterrence.* The main aim of state intervention against crime was to deter persons from committing wrongdoings rather than to punish them after they had transgressed.

In Britain, Jeremy Bentham was a leading classicist criminologist. The reforms with which he and his followers were identified included the following:

- *Reform of the penal code.* Classicists were opposed to the contemporary penal code in Britain which provided the death penalty for a very wide range of offences. They sought to adjust penalties to reflect the seriousness of the crime in the belief that the application of the criminal law was frequently disregarded because the penalties it prescribed were seen as unreasonable. The Criminal Law Commissioners (who were appointed in 1833) sought to limit the use of judicial discretion in sentencing: although their Draft Codes were not enacted, Parliament did remove the death penalty from a considerable number of offences in the early decades of the nineteenth century (Thomas, 2003: 52).

- *Police reform.* This entailed the abolition of the historic 'parish constable' system of policing which had been rendered ineffective by urbanisation following the agricultural and industrial revolutions. Towns were viewed as havens of crime and disorder, and classicists sought to introduce a more efficient and standardised policing system to increase the likelihood that those who broke the law would be apprehended.

These two reforms were underpinned by the principle of general deterrence: the belief that the certainty of arrest and subsequent conviction would enable citizens to make informed decisions not to offend. However, classicists accepted that some human beings failed to make these rational choices, so they sought to bring about the reform of the individual through the use of prisons in which those who committed crime would be encouraged to avoid such actions in the future through the development of rational thought processes. Accordingly, prison reform was also a major interest of classicist criminologists, emphasising the utilitarian belief that punishment was not an end in itself but the means to an end.

Prison reform

Classicists viewed prisons as institutions where convicted prisoners could learn to make rational choices. The way in which this was to be achieved was based upon Bentham's 'pleasure-pain' principle whereby rewards became associated with conformity and sanctions (in the form of severe prison conditions) were linked with rebellion. The harsh environment within prisons was intended to act as machines which would 'grind rogues honest' by encouraging inmates to transform themselves into rational beings who were capable of performing useful tasks in developing capitalist society. Thus work and reflection were key aspects of the prison environment.

Surveillance played an important role in bringing about personal transformation. The possibility that an inmate's every action was being observed by prison guards was designed to bring about a transformation in their attitudes and behaviour. The 'internalisation' of controls affecting their behaviour resulted in the development of self-discipline that would transform them into conforming individuals able to perform a useful role in society upon release.

This approach was compatible with the view subsequently expressed that the power of prisons was the power to exert discipline over inmates in order to secure social conformity through subjugation (Foucault, 1977).

There are some advantages associated with the views of classicist criminology, in particular the way in which the dispassionate application of the law would avoid bias or stereotyping by those who worked in the key agencies of the criminal justice system. However, the approach put forward by classicists could be challenged on a number of grounds. These included the following:

- *There was no proof to support their ideas*. Their views concerning the commission of crime and the way society should respond to it were based on philosophic speculation rather than being derived from the result of social scientific enquiry. There was no 'hard' evidence, therefore, to justify their beliefs.
- *There was an overemphasis on rationality*. There were two problems associated with rationality. Some people were mentally incapable of making rational choices, and, additionally, factors such as poverty might override logical considerations and induce the commission of crime. The classicists' emphasis on individual responsibility led them to underplay the role of environment or social pressures on criminal behaviour.
- *Equality before the law*. Although Beccaria emphasised that the law should show no distinction between rich and poor this ideal was undermined by social divisions which ensured that access to the law was unequal.
- *The importance of discretion was underemphasised*. The classicist belief in the importance of a criminal justice system which operated in a consistent manner downplayed the importance of discretion. By tempering the dispassionate application of the law, discretion could help to secure popular approval for the criminal justice system when its operations (or the social relations which underpinned them) were not universally viewed as being fair. Discretion subsequently became a prized skill of practitioners such as police officers, magistrates and judges.

Neoclassisicism

This approach made some adjustments to classicist criminology without destroying its basic tenets, in particular its doctrine of human nature (Vold et al.,1998: 22). Some concessions were, however, made to acknowledge that the actions of some people were not based on free will and that rationality 'might be constrained by factors such as poverty, enfeeblement, madness or immaturity' (Pitts, 1988: 8): 'in the neo-classical schema man is still held to be accountable for his actions but certain minor reservations are made, the past history and the present situation of the actor are held to affect his likelihood to reform' (Taylor et al., 1973: 8). The existence of 'small ghettos of irrationality' in an otherwise rational social world was responded to by the 'administrative manipulation of penalties' thereby setting in train a movement away from penalties which fit the crime to penalties which fit the criminal (Pitts, 1988: 8–9).

Positivism

A major difficulty associated with classicism was its insistence that crime was the result of rational calculation based on an individual's freedom of choice. This assumption was challenged during the nineteenth century by positivism. This approach argued that criminals did not possess free will, but were instead motivated by factors over which they had no control. This meant that punishing people for their wrongdoings was inappropriate but it justified removing criminals from society and where possible offering treatment (and sometimes inflicting it on them).

Positivists placed the notion of causality at the heart of the criminological enterprise (Cohen, 1988: 4). Unlike classicism, positivism utilised scientific methods (or what has been referred to as the search for 'facts') (Walklate, 1998: 18) in an attempt to quantify and predict human behaviour. The evidence on which positivist assumptions were based was largely derived from quantitative research methodologies. Its key features included the following:

- *Focus on the offender*. As in classicism, all forms of positivist criminology concentrate attention on the behaviour of the individual. However, positivism sought to gain an understanding of the person who committed the offence rather than focusing on the crime which had been committed.
- *Crime was viewed as an act which breached society's consensual values*. A common store of values was assumed to exist within all societies. The criminal, therefore, was an undersocialised individual who failed to adhere to these standards of behaviour. The reasons for such undersocialisation, however, were the subject of much debate within positivist criminology. Positivism embraced biological, psychological and sociological explanations of crime, which are discussed in greater detail below.

Positivist criminology has been subject to a number of criticisms. These include the following:

- *Determinism*. Positivism suggested that individuals were not responsible for their actions. This implied a total absence of free will and the ability to control one's actions.
- *Undersocialisation*. Positivism defined crime in relation to consensual values, but the extent to which universally accepted standards of behaviour exist within any society may be questioned. Marxism, for example, referred to human behaviour being shaped according to dominant values that reflected the power relationship within society.
- *Crime as a working-class phenomenon*. The identification of crime as an activity primarily associated with the undersocialised resulted in a tendency to associate criminal behaviour with those at the lower end of the social scale. This provided no explanation for the criminal actions of those in a superior social position.

● *Over-concentration on the offender*. The focus on the individual who committed crime rather than the nature of the crime itself could lead to injustices in the form of penalties reflecting personal circumstances rather than the severity of the offence.

> Identify the key differences between classicist and positivist criminologies regarding the causes of, and solutions to, crime.

Biological explanations of crime

In the late eighteenth and early nineteenth centuries Joseph Gall explored the view that physical traits were related to behaviour. He popularised phrenology that sought to equate the shape of a person's skull with the structure of their brain which in turn was deemed to influence their behaviour. Cesare Lombroso developed the belief that it was possible to identify criminals by their biology.

In the first edition of his book *L'Uomo Delinquente* (Lombroso, 1876) he came to two main conclusions:

● *Criminals were those individuals who had failed to evolve*. In keeping with the Darwinian background to his work he perceived criminals to be primitive biological freaks who possessed characteristics appropriate to earlier, primitive man. This view is commonly referred to as the concept of atavism.
● *Criminals could be identified by their physical features*. His studies of executed criminals led him to assert that the 'criminal type' could be identified by distinguishing physical features (such as the shape of the skull or facial characteristics) which he referred to as 'stigmata'. Many of these were inherited, reflecting biological inferiority which indicated that the person had a propensity for committing crime. These physical traits were frequently reinforced by other non-hereditary features such as tattoos.

These views are compatible with the view that criminals were 'born bad'. Lombroso's ideas were subsequently modified by Ferri. He asserted that there were three categories of criminal – those who were born bad, those who were insane and those whose actions were the consequence of a particular set of circumstances in which they found themselves (Ferri, 1917). In his later writings Lombroso modified his 'born bad' stance by including factors extraneous to the individual (such as climate or education) as explanations of criminal behaviour.

Although Lombroso's methodology has been subsequently criticised (for reasons which included the unrepresentative nature of his subjects), he is nonetheless viewed as an important figure in criminology. He shifted attention away from the criminal law by making individual offenders the focus of his studies, and rejected the classicist view that punishment should fit the crime by asserting that the rationale of state intervention should be that of protecting society. His belief that those who broke the law were physically different from law-abiding members of society was reflected in later approaches, in particular that of somatotyping (which suggested that the shape of the body was a guide to behaviour). One study suggested that there were three basic body types – endomorphic, mesomorphic and ectomorphic – and associated criminal and delinquent behaviour with mesomorphy, which was characterised by a muscular body build (Sheldon, 1949).

Biological explanations for criminal behaviour have been subsequently developed in a number of different directions that are discussed below. Their common approach rejects free will and personal responsibility for this behaviour in favour of predestination.

The search for the criminal gene

The perception that crime sometimes 'runs in families', has given rise to a view that this is due to a genetic abnormality which overrides free will and propels a person to commit crime. Medical science accepts a wide range of illnesses are caused by genes and has sought to develop this into explanations for criminal behaviour, especially uncontrollable violence and aggression.

Initial research in this field was based on the existence of chromosome deficiencies that may affect the chemistry of the brain. An early attempt to reveal the existence of a 'criminal chromosome' was the XYY syndrome – the belief that males with an extra Y chromosome were predisposed to commit violent or antisocial actions (Jacobs et al., 1965). However, this failed to provide a universal explanation of crime since many persons with this abnormality did not commit actions of this nature.

Chromosome deficiencies were not inherited, but arose at the moment of conception. Subsequent research has centred on genes that reside on chromosomes. There are a large number of genes that are active in the brain and mutated genes may result in a person being unable to control his or her emotions. This condition is inherited.

The origins of arguments related to the existence of a criminal gene can be traced to studies that sought to establish the hereditary nature of criminality. These included the study of family trees (Dugdale, 1877), although this research emphasised that criminality which seemed to 'run in families' could be successfully countered by environmental changes. Attempts to prove the existence of a criminal gene subsequently developed in various ways, which included studying the behaviour of twins (Lange, 1931), especially those who were adopted (Hutchings and Mednick, 1977). As is discussed below, attempts have also been made to apply genetic explanations to the crime patterns of minority ethnic groups (Wilson and Hernnstein, 1985; Hernnstein and Murray, 1994).

The most important research that provided a possible genetic explanation for violent behaviour was provided by Han Brunner. His study of a Dutch family some of whose members exhibited extreme violent behaviour that stretched over several generations revealed a deficiency in several of the males of monoamine oxidase A (MAOA) (Brunner et al., 1993). However, the assumption that MAOA was *the* criminal gene (or at least the gene responsible for violent and aggressive crime) was not universally endorsed, even by Brunner himself who contended that it was unlikely that there was a direct causal relationship between a single gene and a specific behaviour (Brunner, 1995). At best it might be concluded that genetic deficiencies may exert some influence on an individual's behaviour but are not the sole cause of his or her actions.

The belief that crime is caused by inherited genetic disorders is subject to further criticisms:

- *The 'nature versus nurture' debate.* Crime may 'run in families' not because of inherited genetic disorders but, rather, because of environmental factors which include bad parenting, deficient role modelling and social and economic deprivation. This view might suggest that the children of violent or criminal parents are themselves likely to commit crime, especially when social immobility results in successive generations experiencing social and economic deprivation. However, when a multiplicity of circumstances exist that potentially affect an individual's behaviour, one of them cannot be isolated and held solely responsible for that person's conduct.

- *Minimises the extent of free will.* A genetic explanation for crime implies that a person is not responsible for his or her actions since uncontrollable impulses override freewill.

- *Justifies pre-emptive action.* If it is accepted that crime is genetically transmitted, state intervention directed against those who are deemed to be at risk – whether or not they have actually committed any offence – may be employed to protect the remainder of society. It is compatible with eugenics which sought to improve the quality of the human race by eliminating its 'undesirable stock' before they could inflict economic or moral hardships on the rest of the country (Conrad and Schneider, 1992: 219). This approach (which might involve measures such as pre-emptive imprisonment or compulsory sterilisation) contravenes the human rights and civil liberties of those who are subjected to this treatment.

Criticisms of this kind have resulted in biological theorists referring to biological dispositions to commit crime and focusing less on the search for one specific criminal gene in favour of research into whether combinations of normal genes can explain criminal behaviour (Williams, 2001: 160).

Biochemical explanations of crime

Biological explanations of crime have embraced explanations other than genetic ones to explain criminal behaviour. It has been suggested that biochemical factors may explain criminal behaviour. Hormonal explanations (which include the impact of pre-menstrual tension on female behaviour and excess testosterone on actions performed by males) have been put forward to account for some forms of criminal activity. Biochemical explanations also centre on neurotransmitters, one aspect of which is the argument that abnormally low levels of serotonin (a chemical found in the brain which regulates mood) can result in violent behaviour. Other biochemical explanations for crime focus on diet. These include assertions that behaviour may be adversely affected by factors that include a deficiency of glucose in the bloodstream, excessive amounts of lead or cobalt in the body or an insufficiency of vitamin B.

Other studies associated with biology have considered problems associated with the central nervous system as explanations for criminal activity. These include excessive amounts of slow brain activity and cerebral dysfunctions. The latter embraces learning disabilities and brain disorders that may arise from factors such as drug or alcohol abuse by a mother during pregnancy, difficulties in connection with the delivery of the child (such as being deprived of oxygen at birth), or by accidents that occur in later childhood.

Attention Deficit Hyperactivity Disorder is an important aspect of brain dysfunction that causes irrational and often violent behaviour, an inability to concentrate and poor short-term memory. Attention Deficit Disorder is a similar illness but without hyperactivity. Both have been linked to higher than average rates of delinquency (Farrington et al., 1990). Although anti-social behaviour arising from these conditions does not inevitably lead to delinquent or criminal activity, the potential link between hyperactivity and crime has been used to justify interventions to treat children before any criminal tendencies can be realised. Low arousal levels in the frontal cortex of the brain where emotions are controlled can be scientifically measured and treatments involving the use of drugs and intensive counselling may then be initiated to normalise behaviour.

Biological explanations which emphasise that crime is based on brain disorders may be used in an attempt to medicalise a social problem, perhaps also indicating the growing power of the medical profession as an agent of social control on post-industrial societies (Conrad and Schneider, 1992) whereby 'medical intervention as social control seeks to limit, modify, regulate, isolate and eliminate deviant behaviour with medical means in the name of health' (Zola, 1972). Suggestions that anti-social behaviour arises from brain disorders (ignoring any contribution from social or economic circumstances) may give rise to a 'quick-fix' approach when those who engage in activity of this nature are subjected to drug treatments which are far cheaper than social reform programmes. There may also be moral objections to drug therapy, especially if this became compulsory.

Pre-emptive action directed at those with brain disorders may further be criticised for labelling a child perhaps as young as four or five as a potential criminal before any action of this nature has occurred. Another problem is concerned with defining a child as 'hyperactive', using this to justify examining arousal levels in the brain and then (if this test is positive) initiating remedial action. The negative self-perception that may arise from this initial act of labelling may result in exactly the type of criminal behaviour that the action was designed to prevent.

An alternative course of action is possible for juveniles and adults suffering from brain disorders who have actually committed crime. Termed 'biofeedback', this treatment seeks to train such a person to change their own arousal levels without the use of drugs.

Using sources additional to those in this chapter, write a critical account of the contribution made by Cesare Lombroso to an understanding of the cause of crime.

Psychological explanations for crime

The psychological approach to the study of crime focuses on the mind of criminals: this may be affected temporarily by the use of substances such as alcohol or drugs or it may be more permanently damaged. The psychological approach is particularly concerned with the latter, viewing crime as an action that is symptomatic of internal neurological disorders or deeply hidden personality disturbance within an individual (Bynum and Thompson, 1996: 129). It embraces the study of individual characteristics that include 'personality, reasoning, thought, intelligence, learning, perception, imagination, memory and creativity' (Williams, 2001: 192).

The belief that human behaviour is governed by processes which occur in the mind was based upon the pioneering work of Freud, who shifted attention away from innate biological or genetic explanations of human behaviour and towards unconscious conflicts or tensions which took place within the psyche of an individual. In particular, he asserted the importance of childhood experiences in repressing desires in the unconscious mind as explanations for later personality disorders. His approach gave rise to psychoanalysis as the means to uncover the underlying forces governing human behaviour (Freud, 1920; 1930). The aim of this approach was to unlock and bring to the surface unconscious mental processes thereby revealing repressed experiences and traumatic memories. It was designed to give the patient a clear insight into his or her illness and, hopefully, to provide the basis for a corrective emotional experience (Conrad and Schneider, 1992: 53). Although Freud's approach was compatible with many aspects of the positivist approach to the study of criminology, psychoanalysis involved an element of interpretation that went beyond the normal positivist reliance on scientific observation.

Sigmund Freud and the study of crime

Criminal behaviour was not a prime concern of Sigmund Freud who was especially interested in explaining how the early parent–child relationship shaped the formation of sexuality and gender in adulthood. However, his ideas could be adapted to explain criminal behaviour.

Freud was concerned with the way in which the adult personality developed. In his view, there were three aspects to the human mind – the id, the superego and the ego. We were born with the id and the other two developed at different stages of our lives. The id drove humans to carry out activities, and was especially motivated by the advancement of pleasure based on primitive biological impulses; the superego was associated with control and repression, seeking to constrain (or repress) human actions on the basis of social values which were developed during early childhood, especially in interactions with parents. If the demands of the id and inhibitions of the superego were effectively balanced by the ego, or conscious personality, an individual would perform actions which society approved of (Freud, 1923).

Criminal behaviour could arise from deficiencies affecting either the ego or superego. An individual with an overdeveloped superego might commit crime because of an excess of guilt and the desire to seek punishment to relieve it. Alternatively, crime might be the product of an underdeveloped superego, arising from an id that was insufficiently regulated. Research by Bowlby (1946; 1953), which suggested that maternal deprivation affected a child's mental development and could lead to criminal behaviour, was developed by Aichorn (1963) who suggested that lack of parental love or supervision could result in the underdevelopment of the child's superego resulting in his or her subsequent delinquent behaviour.

These approaches were deterministic and viewed crime as the irrational consequence of conflicts occurring within the subconscious mind of the individual. Freud depicted mental symptoms as the 'intelligible but distorted results of the individual's struggle with internal impulses' (Conrad and Schneider, 1992: 52). Inner turmoil did not, however, explain all crime that might arise from factors extraneous to the individual such as the environment.

Unlike Freud, Hans Eysenck believed that personality was fashioned by biological and social factors rather than childhood experiences. He asserted that innate physiological characteristics were of more importance than learning theory as an explanation of human behaviour.

His ideas on the criminal personality were a synthesis of research conducted by Jung (who discussed extrovertism and introvertism) and Pavlov (who examined excitation and inhibition) (Pavlov, 1927). Eysenck believed that individuals had two key dimensions to their personality – extrovertism and neuroticism, which were measured on the E and N scales respectively. He believed that those whose personalities were placed on the upper end of both scales were difficult to condition and experienced the most difficulty in social learning. A criminal was thus viewed as being typically extrovert, with an enhanced desire for stimulation and a lower level of inhibitory controls. This made for a personality which was difficult to condition and hence to socialise (Eysenck, 1960), and which was directed to the pursuit of excitement and pleasure regardless of the punishment which may arise in consequence.

He later included the P scale (pyschoticism), and asserted that those on the upper end of this scale were likely to be deviant, and that those at the top end of this scale were likely to commit the most serious offences. He further argued that there were two components to extrovertism – impulsiveness and sociability – and that the former was of most importance in determining an individual's behaviour (Eysenck, 1970). Although he accepted that not all criminals were located at the upper end of these three scales, other studies (for example, Farrington, 1994) observed a link between offending and impulsiveness.

Personality testing

Personality can be assessed and evaluated through ways other than psycho-analysis. One alternative method of doing this is through the use of personality tests (such as the Minnesota Multiphasic Personality Inventory (MMPI) and the Interpersonal Maturity Test (I-L)). These assume the existence of a core personality and seek to establish differences between criminal and non-criminal personalities. The evidence provided in these tests can justify the use of corrective treatment for those whom the data indicate to be criminal types. Psychological assessment of this nature can further be used to assess the risk which dangerous offenders pose to society. This assessment may provide the basis of decisions regarding the release of those serving prison sentences for violent offences and it may be used pre-emptively against those who have committed no crime at all.

Aspects of a criminal personality may also be revealed through outward manifestations such as the type of crime committed, the circumstances under which it was carried out and the methods that were used to conduct it. The practical use to which this may be put is offender profiling which involves 'teasing out the characteristics of the offender from a detailed knowledge of the offence and other background information' (Williams, 2001: 210) with the aim of constructing offender types. The use of this approach was pioneered by the American Federal Bureau of Investigation in the 1970s and in the United Kingdom was subsequently popularised by the television programme *Cracker*.

Intelligence and criminality

Psychological explanations of crime have also focused on intelligence and a link has been asserted between low intelligence (as measured in IQ tests) and criminal and delinquent behaviour (Hirschi and Hindlelang, 1977: 571). Low intelligence could be attributed to a variety of causes that include brain disorder, environment and heredity.

The alleged hereditary basis of low intelligence has been developed in America to explain the criminality of minority ethnic groups. It has been argued that low IQ is a feature of race and an explanation for the apparent high level of crime carried out by minority ethnic groups (Hernnstein and Murray, 1994). However, claims that low intelligence is mainly inherited (Jensen, 1969: 1) downplay the importance of environment and the impact which racial discrimination has on opportunities (which is a constant factor operating across many generations). Further, the suggestion that low intelligence is an explanation for criminality ignores white collar, corporate and middle-class crime. It may be the case, however, that low intelligence is a feature of unsuccessful criminals (namely those who are caught).

New psychology

Psychological approaches to an understanding of crime were subsequently developed by the 'new' psychology of the 1970s and 1980s. The determinism associated with positivist criminology was replaced by a humanist approach that concentrated on the meaning of deviance for those who committed these actions. Crime was viewed as an activity that occurred as the result of a rational person making choices (Kelly, 1955). This approach was criticised for its tendency to romanticise criminal actions and (in common with all psychological positivism) for concentrating on the individual and ignoring the wider social system which exerted influence over an individual's behaviour.

Stress theory

Stress theory suggested that stress among young people might result in crime and other disorderly activities. Factors that included the breakdown of family stability and the growth of an autonomous youth culture outside parental control may generate pressures (such as whether to take drugs). Unemployment among young people could also result in stress by ensuring that children remain under their parents' control for longer than they wish, and also for making it difficult either to fulfil the expectations which the individualist creed emphasised by Conservative governments between 1979 and 1997 placed upon them (Rutter and Smith, 1995) or to conform to the idealised images offered by advertising and the media (Women's Unit, 2000).

Crime and its social setting

Sociologists turned attention away from the human body or mind as the explanation for behaviour. They focused on the social context in which human behaviour occurred. This approach emphasised factors such as the operations of the social system as an explanation for criminal behaviour.

This section focuses on theories which emphasise the social setting in which crime occurs. It is argued that adverse social circumstances have a direct or indirect bearing on the behaviour of individuals or groups committing crime. There is, however, no agreement as to the nature of these circumstances nor to the response that they provoke.

Emile Durkheim and anomie

Durkheim was a leading figure in sociological positivism in which crime was depicted as the consequence of social upheaval. Durkheim developed the concept of anomie to describe a state of social indiscipline affecting the way in which individuals seek to achieve their personal goals. His theory of crime was devised 'in the context of an overall theory of modernisation' (Vold et al., 1998: 132) whereby societies progressed from feudalism to capitalism (which Durkheim referred to as a transition from a mechanical to an organic society). He asserted that all societies were in the process of transition with none being totally one or the other (Vold et al., 1998: 125).

Durkheim's concept of anomie was initially put forward in 1893 and was subsequently developed in 1897. Anomie occurred in two separate sets of circumstances. The first was in the initial period of transition from one society to another, when the old social order and its methods of enforcing social control broke down but the new social order and rules to regulate the behaviour of its members were not fully developed. In such periods of transition a diversity of behaviour was tolerated, and punishment was characterised by its relative lack of severity.

The second period of social development in which anomie occurred was in an organic society undergoing rapid social change or upheaval, which Durkheim associated with the boom and slump of capitalist economies. In these situations of social disintegration, the law was unable to maintain social cohesion (in the sense of regulating the relationships between the diverse parts of society – differences which were based upon the division of labour). Anomie described the situation in which personal aspirations or ambitions were not constrained by societal restraints on behaviour for which were substituted an 'every man for himself' attitude in the pursuit of his or her goals.

Durkheim also considered whether crime played a useful or harmful role in society. His view on this matter was influenced by the key positivist concept of consensual values.

He believed that social cohesion was influenced by the division of labour and consequent specialisation of tasks within it. He argued that a mechanical society was characterised by little division of labour and consequent uniformity in the work and beliefs of most of its members. The solidarity of this society was maintained by the pressure for uniformity exerted by the majority against the minority who held different standards. In a society in which consensual values were adhered to by most of its members – which was the feature of a mechanical society, although it might also arise in stable organic societies whose characteristics could thus be described as 'tending towards the mechanical' – diversity was inevitable. Crime was both normal in such a society and also useful in that it was a spur to progress, challenging the status quo.

The situation was, however, different in an organic society. Here social cohesion arose not from the existence of consensual values but from 'a complex system of interdependence which recognises the pursuit of individual goals, provided they are legitimate and socially sanctioned' (Pakes and Winstone, 2005: 4). The law played an important role in reconciling differences and in providing a mechanism to promote social solidarity through the affirmation of social values.

However, rapid social change could destroy the vigour of mechanisms that were maintaining social equilibrium. In societies experiencing this form of upheaval anomie was viewed as a pathological state, giving rise to crime that, in extreme cases, could result in anarchy and the total destruction of that society.

As a positivist, Durkheim focused attention on the individual whose actions could be influenced by social processes, and was especially concerned with suicide. However, his emphasis on the social origins of crime gave impetus to a new approach that directed attention at the operations of the social system and how these influenced criminal behaviour. Durkheim's focus on the operations of society was adapted by other theorists whose work is discussed below.

> Assess the contribution made by Emile Durkheim to the study of crime.

The Chicago School, social disorganisation and environmental criminology

Some aspects of biological positivism suggested explanations as to why crime appeared to run in families. The Chicago School of sociology focused on a different issue, that of environment, and gave birth to the concept of social disorganisation. It sought to explain why crime seemed perennially endemic to certain neighbourhoods or localities.

Shaw and McKay (1942) were especially concerned to map the areas of a city that were inhabited by juvenile delinquents aged between 10 and 16 years. To study this, they employed methodologies that combined official data, such as crime statistics, with information from other alternative sources such as life histories and participant observation. Life histories had been previously employed by Shaw (1930; 1938) who demonstrated that the difference between delinquents and non-delinquents lay in the opportunities provided in neighbourhoods and in their personal attitudes that were shaped by environmental factors.

They concluded that there was a definite spatial pattern based on concentric circles affecting the residence of juvenile delinquents. These were concentrated in the inner-city zones of cities and this pattern was constant despite frequent changes to the make-up of the population that resided in this area, resulting in the existence of perennial high crime areas (Shaw and McKay, 1942). These ideas were influenced by studies of cities that were conducted during the nineteenth century (such as Mayhew, 1862) that drew attention to the manner in which urban development had produced attendant problems such as poverty and crime. However, these studies largely failed to explain the nature of the link between crime and environment.

Shaw and McKay also drew heavily on earlier work conducted by other members of the Chicago School, in particular the concept of human ecology (Park, 1925) and the zonal model of urban development (Burgess, 1925). The first theory viewed the city as an ecological system, a social organism. 'Natural' social processes shaped the development of the city (so that the poorest lived in the zone of transition from where the more affluent inhabitants migrated) and people adapted to the circumstances of the area in which they resided. Burgess built upon this theory and suggested that the cities grew out from the centre in a series of concentric 'zones'. Five were identified, each with its own economic and social characteristics (Burgess, 1925).

Shaw and McKay concluded that juvenile delinquency was particularly identified with a specific geographic area within a city. This was what Burgess had earlier termed 'zone two' or the 'zone of transition', which circled the non-residential business zone (zone 1 or the 'loop'). It was characterised by rapid population change, dilapidation and conflicting demands made upon land use which was evidenced by housing being pulled down to make way for new businesses. New immigrants would initially settle in this zone (or ghetto) as rented residential property was cheapest here, but would move outwards into the other residential zones when their material conditions improved, being replaced by further immigrants (Burgess, 1925). The development of the city was viewed as operating according to the process of evolution, and delinquency was thus the 'natural outcome of economic competition for desirable space' (Bursik, 1986: 61). It was argued that crime rates were determined by distance from the city centre.

Population changes in the zone of transition were rapid and it housed a wide range of social problems, including crime and immorality. In these circumstances it was impossible for institutions such as the family or church to effectively uphold society's conventional values. The social solidarity of the neighbourhood was eroded and those who lived in it were subjected to a multiplicity of values. Thus a climate that was conducive to the commission of (or tolerance towards) crime and delinquency was created which arose from the absence of an established set of values to guide the actions of those who lived there. The ineffectiveness of informal methods of control to shape communal behaviour was referred to as 'social disorganisation', a concept which developed out of Durkheim's theory of anomie (and which was later built upon by control theorists) (Williams, 2001: 320). It was this situation (and not poverty per se) that was put forward as the explanation for crime.

It was not made exactly clear, however, whether the constant absence of neighbourhood stability and communal values was the source of crime in high delinquency areas, or whether this problem arose out of the existence of criminal subcultures in the affected areas and the cultural transmission of these delinquent values across the generations (Bottoms and Wiles, 1994: 590–1). Later applications of the concept of social disorganisation, especially within conservative criminology (which is discussed below), emphasised the significance of the decline of the family unit in socially disorganised neighbourhoods as a symptom of moral decline and as an explanation for crime and delinquency.

Practical applications

Shaw was especially concerned to develop the practical application of his theories by setting up the Chicago Area Project in 1932. This set up neighbourhood centres in a number of areas that were designed to redress social disorganisation by creating a sense of community feeling. This was compatible with later applications concerned with community justice which 'is concerned with a struggle to develop and improve communities, and to promote a better quality of community living with more cooperation, more mutual aid and more collective problem-solving. It points to an improved standard of social conduct and pro-social opportunities, and it promotes forms of criminal justice practice which are seen as consistent with these' (Raynor and Vanstone, 2002: 112).

The mapping of crime zones has a number of practical applications, in particular the targeting by the police of 'high crime' areas. However, the definition of a 'crime zone' is problematic since the areas in which crime occurs are not necessarily the same places where those who commit them reside. This might suggest that attempts to map where crimes occur would be of greater practical benefit to agencies such as the police service than would mapping the spatial distribution of offenders which was the focus of early studies conducted by Shaw and McKay (Coleman and Moynihan, 1996: 7–8). Thus subsequent applications of environmental criminology focused attention on the places where crimes were committed and what has been termed the 'rediscovery of the offence' (Bottoms and Wiles, 1994: 592) gave rise to a number of practical methods of situational crime prevention that are discussed in Chapter 2.

However, there are certain difficulties associated with plotting areas with high offence rates and translating this information into effective measures of crime prevention. In particular, this approach fails to devote sufficient attention to studying offenders, in particular why they commit crime in particular areas and whom or what they target for their illicit activities. It has been suggested that offences were most likely to occur where criminal opportunities intersected with areas that were cognitively known to the offender (Brantingham and Brantingham, 1984: 362). Thus studying the routine activities of offenders might produce a more useful insight into where crime is likely to occur than will the plotting of areas in which offenders reside. A further problem is the 'ecological fallacy' that assumes that the identification of areas with high levels of offenders further identifies those who offend (Bottoms and Wiles, 1994: 598). This may result in the delivery of a coercive style of policing underpinned by stereotypical assumptions that those on the receiving end may deem to constitute harassment, thus resulting in a breakdown of police–public relationships.

Criticisms of the Chicago School

There are several problems with the work of the Chicago School. Their reliance on crime statistics to provide information on the distribution of crime within a city focused their attention on lower social classes and thus ignored criminal activities committed by persons in higher social categories. This methodology also disregarded the manner in which control agencies such as the police service could construct crime.

Immigration was viewed by Shaw and McKay as an important factor affecting population change in the zone of transition. As delinquency rates remained constant in this area, it was implied that all immigrant groups had similar crime rates – although it was emphasised that this was due not to race per se but the environment in which new immigrants settled. However, this is not invariably the case since immigrant groups frequently exhibit different crime rates (Jonassen, 1949), perhaps reflecting the varying strengths of traditional controls, especially the extent to which the family unit could continue to act as a constraint on behaviour even in inhospitable environments. Further, it will be argued in Chapter 2 that crime statistics do not necessarily give an accurate picture of the true level of crime from which crime zones (based on offences or offenders) can be mapped. It has also been asserted that the concept of social disorganisation was overly deterministic and over-predictive of crime (Matza, 1964), in this respect reflecting a positivist influence affecting the work of Shaw and McKay (Williams, 2001: 307).

The belief that offender rates followed a pattern of concentric circles was especially questioned. In Britain, it was argued that the free market affecting housing provision had been subverted by local authority allocation policies so that areas containing high numbers of offenders were found in local authority-owned estates outside the zone of transition (Morris, 1957: 130). A later study in Sheffield confirmed these findings (Baldwin and Bottoms, 1976), from which it was concluded that there was no tidy zonal model but that 'areas with high and low offender residence rates were distributed throughout the city in apparently haphazard fashion' (Brantingham and Brantingham, 1984: 322).

The implication of this research was that crime zones did not occur as the result of the natural evolution of the city but were artificially created. This idea was further developed to suggest that the character of an area was shaped by the operations of the local housing market. Decisions by local authorities (for example, to create 'sink' estates) and building societies (to refuse granting mortgages in certain 'red-lined' areas) served to create areas in which a disproportionate number of criminals and delinquents lived. The prevalence of offenders in these areas was explained both by the operations of the housing market but also by a range of secondary social effects that included the relationships constructed and developed in the area and the attitude taken by outsiders towards it (Bottoms et al., 1992: 120). It was the interaction between the workings of the housing market and these other social processes that influenced the behaviour of those who lived there (Bottoms and Wiles, 1994: 638).

A final criticism is that the ecological approach utilised by the Chicago School discussed the relationship of people and the urban environment. The study of rural crime was neglected. Instead certain assumptions were (and continue to be) made regarding this problem which include the assertion that stronger social bonds exist in rural areas and that the opportunities to commit crime in these places are relatively limited (Williams, 2001: 304–5).

Later applications

Explanations of crime that focus on cultural tensions have been adapted to explain the crime rates of minority ethnic communities. Children of first-generation immigrants were likely to experience tensions between the values of their parents (derived from their previous country of abode) and those of the host community. Those caught in this situation were unable to adopt either culture fully, and became caught in a cultural 'no man's land' that was deemed to be conducive to criminal and delinquent behaviour. In addition, problems which included clashes within families between those adhering to 'traditional' values and those wishing to adopt 'Westernised' lifestyles eroded the strength of the family unit and the discipline imposed by it which meant that children were not effectively controlled or socialised because of the absence of stable standards of behaviour (Park, 1928).

Criminal activity may also be exacerbated by racial discrimination that denies immigrants conventional opportunities to obtain economic rewards and status. The higher rates of crime sometimes found among first-generation settlers have been attributed to this combination of cultural conflict and other sociological factors (Sellin, 1938). High crime rates among such communities is not universal, however: some studies in Britain indicated relatively low levels of crime within Asian communities (Mawby et al., 1979), perhaps reflecting the vigour of family control. The pattern may be influenced by the age profile of such communities, changes to which may also affect patterns of crime.

> To what extent is the concept of social disorganisation a useful one in accounting for the causes of crime?

Social strain

Strain theory developed from the functionalist perspective that human behaviour was determined by the social structure. Robert Merton was a leading social strain theorist who concentrated on explaining deviancy. His ideas were originally put forward in 1938. He asserted that anomie arose from a mismatch between the culturally induced aspirations to strive for success (which he asserted in Western societies was the pursuit of wealth) and the structurally determined opportunities to achieve it. The 'differential application of opportunity' (Williams, 2001: 345) imposed a strain on an individual's commitment to society's success goals and the approved way of attaining them and resulted in anomie which was characterised by rule-breaking behaviour by those who were socially disadvantaged. Unlike Durkheim (who believed that an individual set his or her own success goals subject to the constraints imposed by society), Merton contended that these and the means to achieve them were set by society. Merton further asserted that social inequality was the key reason for deviancy. It was not, as Durkheim contended, dependent on social disintegration but was an endemic condition that was particularly associated with the working class.

Robert Merton and strain theory

Merton suggested that there were a number of behavioural patterns which individuals could exhibit in reaction to the culturally approved goals of the society in which they lived and the institutionalsed ways of achieving them (Merton, 1938: 676). These were:

- *Conformity*. This entailed accepting society's success goals and the approved means to attain them. Merton believed that most people behaved in this conforming way and conformity was a feature of stable societies.
- *Ritualism*. An individual could adhere to the culturally accepted goals of society, even though intuition suggested that these were unlikely to be attained through conventionally approved ways. A person in this situation continued to adhere to the approved means to attaining these goals but was likely to experience feelings of despair (although he or she did not necessarily turn to crime).
- *Innovation*. An individual prevented from obtaining society's success goals by legitimate means might attempt to achieve them by abandoning the 'rules of the game' and attain them by criminal methods.
- *Retreatism*. In this case an individual abandoned both the culturally accepted goals of society and the conventional means of securing them. Behaviour that embraced the use of drugs or alcohol might be taken up by a person who adopted a negative form of deviancy and effectively decided to 'opt out' of society.
- *Rebellion*. An individual unable to achieve society's success goals and the approved means to achieve them might reject them and replace the goals with new objectives which were achievable. These were often associated with a cause or an ideal. This form of positive deviance was associated with the activities of street gangs or terrorists (Williams, 2001: 346).

Relative deprivation

Relative deprivation describes a situation whereby 'the feeling of deprivation may arise when an individual compares his situation with that of others or with that of himself at an earlier time' (Williams, 2001: 350). The strain that is experienced refers to a mismatch between goals defined in relation to what others are achieving and an individual's means to attain them. This gives rise to feelings of unfairness or injustice. The root cause of (and solution to) this is the unequal distribution of wealth, which has led to suggestions that high crime is especially likely to occur in periods of recession (Box, 1987) when the gap between rich and poor grows making it hard for economically marginalised groups to attain the consumerist goals associated with market economies.

Agnew's general strain theory

Strain theory was traditionally associated with economic disadvantage and the manner in which this undermined an individual's commitment to attaining conventional goals through legitimate means. This approach tended to view crime as a lower-class phenomenon, thus ignoring delinquency committed by those in a higher social bracket, and also disregarded the way in which a disposition towards crime could be constrained by factors that included the quality of family relationships (Agnew, 1985: 152–3).

This resulted in an attempt to broaden the scope of strain theory beyond Merton's emphasis on economic factors and to incorporate the strain imposed on an individual's commitment to the law arising from other forms of goal blockage, in particular his or her inability to avoid situations that they found painful or aversive. This version of strain theory was put forward as an explanation for adolescent delinquency. It was argued that 'the blockage of pain-avoidance behaviour frustrates the adolescent and may lead to illegal escape attempts or anger-based delinquency (Agnew, 1985: 154).

According to this approach, delinquency is derived from the frustration of being unable to adopt pain-avoidance behaviour to escape from a wide range of aversive situations (which may include school, family or neighbourhood), even if this situation does not directly affect the individual's ability to attain intermediate or long-term goals. One difficulty with this argument is that it suggests that the origins of strain are internal to an individual, thus downplaying the importance of structural factors to criminal and delinquent behaviour.

Subcultural theorists

Subcultural theorists combined Merton's strain theory (which explained individual deviancy) with the Chicago School's ecological theory (which was concerned with collective deviancy). Whereas Merton argued that delinquency arose from a mismatch between goals and the means to achieve them, subculturalists focused on group responses to goal blockage and asserted that this situation resulted in the emergence of deviant values that constituted a delinquent subculture.

Albert Cohen was a leading exponent of subcultural theory. He argued that working-class boys experienced inner tensions in a society that was dominated by middle-class values. The school was seen as an important forum in which this 'status frustration' occurred. They could chose to conform to these values (either by seeking to achieve middle-class success goals or to exploit the limited opportunities with which they were presented as fully as they could – characteristics which Cohen identified with the college boy and corner boy respectively) or they could rebel against middle-class norms of behaviour and engage in delinquent actions. Cohen labelled this reaction as the response of the delinquent corner boy. This situation resulted in the emergence of a delinquent subculture in which society's values were rejected and new ones were substituted in their place. These new values formed the basis of a delinquent subculture – 'a system of values that represented an inversion of the values held by respectable, law-abiding society' and it was in this sense that it was asserted 'the world of the delinquent is the world of the law-abiding turned upside down' (Matza and Sykes, 1957: 664).

The delinquent actions which arose from the deviant subculture were not necessarily designed to advance material goals but were especially concerned with achieving status and prestige amongst the delinquent's peers which resulted in him acquiring self-esteem which mainstream society denied them (Cohen, 1955).

In America, subcultural theories were put forward as the basis of the behaviour of delinquent gangs. In the United Kingdom, however, subcultural theories have generally been applied to more loosely organised juvenile associations such as peer groupings.

Learning theories

Aspects of subcultural theory were evident in social learning theory and opportunity theory. According to learning theory:

> Antisocial behaviour and the attitudes and beliefs supporting antisocial behaviour are most likely to develop when a child is surrounded by 'models' (in real life and in the media) who engage in antisocial behaviour, when antisocial cues (unlearned cues such as guns; or learned cues such as oppressive authority) are common in a child's environment, and when the child receives reinforcements for behaving antisocially (such as obtaining tangible goods). (Huesmann and Podolski, 2003: 59)

Expressed more simply, committing crime is a learned response.

Learning theories are rooted in the disciplines of psychology and sociology. Psychological learning theories are based on the work of Pavlov (1927) who sought to demonstrate that behaviours could be learned by association.

Differential association

The most important social learning theory applied to criminal behaviour was the concept of differential association (Sutherland, 1939; 1947). This has been associated with explaining white-collar crime but could be applied to similar activities carried out by persons of lower social status. It was influenced by the ecological and social disorganisation theories associated with the Chicago School and based on Tarde's theory of imitation (that is, that humans copy each other's behaviour) (Tarde, 1876). Differential association theory argued that the techniques of committing crime and the motives and rationalisations of attitudes which were favourable towards violating the law were aspects of a normal learning process and occurred when people were subject to an excess of definitions favourable to the violation of the law over definitions which supported rule-abiding behaviour (Sutherland, 1947; Sutherland and Cressey, 1955: 77–80). This theory emphasises the importance of socialisation, and suggests that inadequate socialisation from parents will result in the behaviour of children being fashioned by other role models such as peer groups. Crime is thus behaviour that is learned 'during the process of growing up' (Ainsworth, 2000: 78).

This theory asserted personal contact to be the fundamental source of criminal behaviour and further implied that the actions of an individual were the determined product of their personal experiences. However, other social learning theorists emphasised the importance of individual choice in deciding whether to identify with a criminal subculture, thus giving rise to a theory of differential identification (Glaser, 1956). This helped to explain why, in areas of social inequality, some people embraced deviant forms of behaviour whereas others did not. Sutherland subsequently stated that opportunity and the presence or absence of alternative behaviours influenced whether a person who had learned an excess of definitions favourable to crime would perform such actions (Sutherland, 1973).

Social learning theory has also been applied to examining the impact that external influences such as books, films and television have on an individual's learned behaviour. This approach has formed the basis of accusations (albeit supported by little 'hard' evidence) alleging that the violent and sensational depiction of crime by the media has resulted in similar actions occurring in real life. The fear of imitation of this nature taking place has formed the basis of voluntary or compulsory censorship.

Social learning theory embraces the concept of deterrence and bears many similarities to rational choice theory – 'the basic idea and central propositions of deterrence and rational choice theory … have already been captured in the social learning approach to deviant and criminal behaviour' (Akers, 1990: 675). However, rational choice theory tends to ignore social learning theory in favour of economic theory which views the decision to commit crime as a 'function of the balance of rewards and costs for crime and its alternatives' (Akers, 1990: 669).

There are difficulties associated with the concept of differential association, including the inability to test the theory empirically and vagueness concerning the content of definitions which are favourable to crime which are likely to vary across historical periods and which are unlikely to justify all forms of criminal activity (Matsueda, 1988: 284 and 296). Social control theorists reject differential association theory in favour of an approach that alleges that factors such as attachment to parents and peers influence criminal behaviour directly without being derived from any process of imitation or learning (Kornhauser, 1978).

Differential reinforcement

The theory of differential association has been subsequently modified in a number of ways.

Differential reinforcement theory accepts that most behaviour is learnt, but takes account of a wide range of factors that influence whether such behaviour will be repeated (positive reinforcers) or shied away from (negative reinforcers). Thus behaviour is determined by a calculation that estimates 'the balance of rewarding and aversive stimuli' (Akers, 1990: 658), and is repeated when there is strong positive reinforcement for it (Williams, 2001: 286).

The development of differential reinforcement theory was influenced by social learning theory. This argued that the factors that influenced behaviour went beyond operant learning and embraced cognitive experiences. This new approach is particularly associated with the psychologist Albert Bandura, who sought to explain aggression. He argued that people behave in a violent manner mainly because they see others acting in this way, and thus learn that such behaviour is appropriate (Ainsworth: 2000: 79). It was concluded that the behaviour of individuals was based on their learning experiences, derived from observing and imitating the behaviour of others (whether in the family or outside of it) *and* being rewarded or punished for certain actions (Bandura, 1977).

> Thus social learning incorporates reward and punishment in the explanation of crime, and the concept of differential reinforcement applies to the balance of the full range of formal and informal rewards and punishments, from the most 'rational' calculation of this balance to the most irrational responses to it. (Akers, 1990: 670)

Opportunity theory

Strain and subcultural theories were developed by 'opportunity theory' (Cloward and Ohlin, 1960). This drew on Merton's strain theory and Sutherland's concept of differential association and was concerned with the legitimate and illegitimate ways of achieving success in society. According to this theory, the legitimate opportunity structure was mainly available to upper- and middle-class youths whereas working-class juveniles, finding the legitimate route to success blocked, were more likely to rely on illegitimate ways to achieve it. Unlike Cohen, opportunity theory did not involve any psychological explanations for delinquent behaviour. Instead, this behaviour was viewed as arising from an objective/quasi-rational assessment that it was impossible to achieve success through legitimate means. This strain resulted in lower-class youths banding together with others in a similar position.

However, opportunity theory also attempted to explain why varying forms of delinquent subculture were evidenced in different areas. The explanation centred on the balance struck in particular communities between the legitimate and illegitimate ways to achieve success in society. It was asserted that lower-class juveniles who were denied the possibility of achieving success through legitimate means would form gangs whose behaviour was dependent on the kind of illegitimate opportunities that were available to them. Three scenarios were identified:

- *The crime orientated gang*. This consisted of a juvenile gang whose main activities were stealing. It was associated with an area in which there was a high degree of tolerance towards crime, thus existing alongside (and perhaps orchestrated by) more hardened adult criminals who served as role models for disaffected youths and could arrange for the disposal of goods that had been stolen by them. In these areas, juvenile crime was characterised by a relatively high level of organisation.

- *The conflict gang*. This gang was especially characteristic of socially disorganised neighbourhoods. The absence of effective restraints on the behaviour of young people (including the lack of criminal opportunity structures which were found in areas in which juvenile criminal gangs operated) resulted in violence that might take the form of warfare in which rival gangs vied with each other for control (and the status which derived from this) of an area. This conflict was similar in nature to territorial explanations of football hooliganism (Marsh et al., 1978) that were applied to outbreaks of inter-community rivalry (such as that which occurred between West Indians and Asians in Handsworth in 1985).

- *Retreatism*. Those who failed to achieve success in society through legitimate or illegitimate means might embrace a more passive rejection of society and its values which was characterised by drug-taking. This activity was more loosely structured than the delinquency of crime and conflict gangs, and could entail individual as opposed to group responses to the inability to achieve success.

Strain and subcultural theories – criticisms

Strain theory focused on economic causes of crime. This approach viewed the deviant as neither sick nor acting on immoral impulses but sought to explain it by concentrating on factors external to the individual. Deviancy was depicted as a logical response by those whose social position denied them the opportunity to achieve commonly held objectives such as 'making money'. The solution to deviancy put forward by social strain theorists involved reforms to improve social equality, thus reducing the strain between aspirations and the means to achieve them.

However, strain theory has been criticised for making assumptions that a high level of agreement existed within society about desirable objectives, and a tendency to ignore the deviancy of those who did not suffer from inequality. As has been argued above, this latter objection was responded to in Agnew's general strain theory.

A more significant objection, however, concerned whether social strain did, in fact, give rise to deviant subcultures that indicated a rejection of society's mainstream values. One argument that sought to refute the existence of a subculture of deviant values asserted that it was not possible for juveniles to totally cut themselves off from society and its values. It was alleged that delinquents were committed to society's mainstream values but justified actions which were in breach of them by applying the concept of mitigating circumstances as an explanation of their behaviour. This was referred to as the 'techniques of neutralisation' that sought to explain or excuse delinquent juvenile behaviour and thus offset the negative views which society might otherwise adopt towards such action (Sykes and Matza, 1957). Thus 'rather than standing in opposition to conventional ideas of good conduct, the delinquent is likely to adhere to the dominant norms in belief but render them ineffective in practice by holding various attitudes and perceptions which serve to neutralize the norms as checks on behavior' (Matza and Sykes, 1961: 712–13).

There were five of these techniques. These were a denial of responsibility for an action, a denial that injury had been caused to a victim, a denial that the victim was, in fact, a victim, an assertion that those who condemned the action were hypocritical, and seeking to explain a delinquent action by reference to higher loyalties (such as to friends or a gang). It was concluded that these techniques (applied before or after a delinquent act) 'are critical in lessening the effectiveness of social controls and … lie behind a large share of delinquent behavior' (Sykes and Matza, 1957: 669).

A further critique of subcultural theory argued that the values underpinning juvenile delinquency were not totally dissimilar from attitudes embraced by law-abiding, conforming members of society. It was suggested that delinquent behaviour commonly displayed traits that included the search for excitement or thrills, a disdain for routinised work in favour of 'making easy money' and aggression. Although these characteristics seemed at variance with the dominant values of society, it was argued that this was not the case since they were also espoused by respectable middle-class persons, in particular in connection with their pursuit of leisure, and thus coexisted alongside society's dominant values. These 'alternative' values were labelled 'subterranean', consisting of values 'which are in conflict or in competition with other deeply held values but which are still recognised and accepted by many' and in this sense were 'akin to private as opposed to public morality' (Matza and Sykes, 1961: 716). There was thus no separate delinquent subculture: delinquents adopted one aspect of the dominant values of society but their behaviour was more regularly governed by them. This view also accounted for delinquency not committed by lower-class juveniles, since 'some forms of juvenile delinquency … have a common sociological basis regardless of the class level at which they appear' (Matza and Sykes, 1961: 718).

A further difficulty with the approach of subcultural theorists was that many delinquents did not consistently behave in this manner (they might grow out of delinquency as they entered adulthood, for example) that ought to be the case if the middle-class standards that they were rebelling against remained constant. It was thus asserted that juvenile delinquents did not adhere to a body of subcultural values but, rather, drifted between delinquency and conformity. This 'drift' occurred when social controls were loosened enabling a person to pursue their own responses to whatever situations arose. Most juveniles committed delinquent acts, but those who did it most often were those who were able to successfully explain their delinquent behaviour away through the application of the techniques of neutralisation (Matza, 1964). The decision to adopt one or other of these two courses of action was primarily seen as a personal one, thus reintroducing the concept of individual choice into the discussion of the causes of crime.

The strain theorists' argument that deviancy was the product of lower-class conflict with middle-class values was further challenged by some cultural transmission theorists. These asserted the existence of a defined body of lower-class values, and delinquency was attributed to the acting out of these standards of behaviour (Miller, 1958) whose origins were thus 'natural' as opposed to being derived from social strain.

> Citing relevant theorists whose work is considered above, consider arguments for and against the proposition that 'juvenile criminals exhibit an attachment to subcultural values'.

Hirschi's social bond theory

A further critique of strain and cultural transmission theories was offered by social bond theory (Hirschi, 1969). This developed from control theory whose focus was conformity rather than criminality. Control theory asserted that all individuals had the innate capacity to break the law and thus crime was natural. Thus they inverted strain theory's focus on why people committed crime and instead sought to explain law-abiding lives. It was concluded that this behaviour was the product of social control. Control theory seeks to explain the 'mechanics' of this control and establish the factors that induce people to abide by the rules of the society they inhabit.

There is no consensus in control theory as to the nature of controls that produce social conformity. Psychological accounts emphasise factors internal to an individual (such as a healthy superego) (Reiss, 1951) that may be supplemented by external forces (Reckless, 1967; 1973). Social control theories emphasise the importance of controls that are external to an individual. Social bond theory holds that conformity derives from the process of sociali- sation in which the family plays a crucial role in instilling self-control in children that helps them to withstand pressures (for example, from peer groups) to engage in criminal or deviant behaviour when the opportunity to do so arises.

Hirschi held that the social bond which restrained an individual's criminal propensities consisted of the interplay between four elements – emotional attachment to other people, ideological commitment derived from pursuing conventional objectives, the time and effort expended through involvement in conventional activities, and a personal belief in the moral validity of soci- ety's norms (Hirschi, 1969). This approach tended to view the factors which produce control as 'largely external and structural' (Williams, 2001: 369) but later accounts emphasised the interplay of factors internal to an individual whereby criminality was influenced by both self-control fashioned during childhood and the opportunity to commit crime (Gottfredson and Hirschi, 1990). It was proposed that those with low self-control were more likely to yield to inducements to commit crime when they presented themselves. This approach is compatible with proactive interventions by the state into the lives of very young children because what is perceived to be defective parent- ing may produce inadequate self-control in the child, thus heightening the prospects of him or her committing crime in the future.

One important development of control theory was that of control balance theory. This explained crime in relation to the power wielded by individuals in their relationships with others. Those with too little power might resort to crime as a means to rectify the deficit and those with too much power might violate the law out of greed, in order to enhance the scale and scope of their domination. In both sets of circumstances, however, criminal activity is set in motion by a trigger, and also requires both the opportunity to commit an illicit act and the absence of constraints to deter it (Tittle, 1995; 2000).

> Compare and contrast the explanations offered by strain and control theo- ries concerning the causes of crime.

The state and criminality

This section discusses a range of theories whose common features include rejecting the assumption that society is based on consensual values and which focus not on the behaviour of criminals but on the power relationships in society and how these are maintained by the process of criminalisation.

New deviancy

Key aspects of strain theory were developed by a new criminological school that emerged during the 1960s: that of new deviancy (or interactionism). This moved attention to the various factors which were involved in determining whether an act was judged to be deviant rather than on the nature of the act itself. The key features of this approach are discussed below.

Concentrate on the operations of the social system

Attention was focused on the social system rather than those engaged in acts of crime or deviancy. New deviancy rejected the existence of consensual values within society, and asserted that it functioned in the interests of the powerful who were able to foist their attitudes throughout society because of the control they exerted over the state's ideological apparatus (such as religion, education and the mass media), its political system and its coercive machinery (especially the police and courts). Thus the moral, cultural and political values of the dominant class(es) became adopted throughout society – creating an illusion of consensual values which in reality did not exist.

Focus on the social construction of deviancy

Deviancy was viewed as behaviour that was defined as 'bad' or 'unacceptable' by a powerful group of people who controlled the operations of the state, and who were able to utilise their power to stigmatise actions of which they did not approve. The definition of deviancy was thus rooted in the power structure of society. New deviancy theory thus concentrated on social intervention and social reaction to activities which were labelled as 'deviant' rather than seeking to discover their initial causes.

This aspect of new deviancy was based upon symbolic interactionism associated with George Herbert Mead (Mead, 1938) and developed by the Chicago School. An important new deviancy theorist was Howard Becker, who argued that the 1937 Marijuna Tax Act led to the creation of a new category of deviant marijuana sellers and users (Becker, 1963: 145). This led him to suggest that deviancy was the consequence of the application by others of rules and sanctions directed at an 'offender': the deviant was a person 'to whom that label has successfully been applied, deviant behaviour is behaviour that people so label' (Becker, 1963: 9).

Emphasise the impact of labelling on those to whom it was applied

New deviancy was concerned with the negative reaction adopted by an individual whose behaviour had been labelled as 'deviant'. This aspect of new deviancy had initially been put forward by Edwin Lemert (1951). Individuals who were labelled became stigmatised and a self-fulfilling prophecy arose whereby they might seek to live up to their designation by engaging in activities which they would have otherwise avoided. In this sense, therefore, 'social control leads to deviance' (Lemert, 1967: v). This was opposed to the conventional assertion that crime or deviancy led to social control.

Crime as a social construct

Interactionism underpinned the view that crime (and also deviance) were social constructions. This suggested that crime and deviance were based upon subjective considerations and value judgements – 'deviance is not a property *inherent* in any particular kind of behavior; it is a property *conferred upon* that behavior by the people who come into direct or indirect contact with it' (Erikson, 1966: 6). Several important considerations derive from this viewpoint.

The first implies that crime and deviance are activities which are 'natural' or 'normal' to those who carry them out, possessing no inherent negative qualities until these are bestowed upon them by the processes of making and enforcing rules to prohibit such behaviour.

The second concerns who in society has the power to define actions as 'criminal' or 'deviant'. There are several views concerning this. Phenomenological explanations emphasise that reality is constructed out of social reaction. Thus definitions of crime or deviance arise as the product of a dialectic process whereby individuals interact with their social world. Liberal explanations view definitions of crime and deviance as consensual, reflecting popular perceptions of right and wrong. Alternatively, conflict theorists suggest that definitions of crime and deviance are the outcome of a process of political and social conflict. Pluralists root this conflict in the competition between interest groups seeking control of the policy-making agenda, whereas Marxists see it as the inevitable product of inequality born of the class structure in capitalist society whereby actions which pose a threat to the economic dominance and political power of the bourgeoisie are labelled 'criminal'.

The third is that crime and deviance are not permanent designations but change over periods of time. This may result in criminalising actions that were formerly tolerated, or the decriminalisation of those which were previously disapproved of. Prohibition between 1920 and 1932 in America is an example of the former and the United Kingdom's 1968 Abortion Act (which legalised abortions under certain circumstances) an example of the latter.

Labelling theory

Labelling theory was based upon aspects of early twentieth-century social psychology that argued that an individual's self-evaluation was primarily a reflection of how other people reacted to him or her (Cooley, 1902). This gave rise to the argument that society has the ability to create hardened criminals through the way it treats offenders (Tannenbaum, 1938).

Lemert distinguished between primary deviance (an act labelled as deviant) and secondary deviance (caused by labelling the primary act). He suggested that social reaction was the prime factor producing deviance, since an individual's internalisation of the social stigma attached to the label of 'deviant' had an adverse effect on that person's self-perception and subsequent patterns of behaviour, possibly forcing them to associate with others who had been similarly stigmatised (Lemert, 1951). The argument that the process of social reaction was formulated by the agencies of social control, which identified deviants and proceeded against them, was developed to suggest that justice was a process of negotiation between them and the individual (Cicourel, 1968).

New deviancy viewed criminalisation as a mechanism of social control that entailed 'the power to have a particular set of definitions of the world realised in both spirit and practice' (Conrad and Schneider, 1992: 8). It further gave rise to suggestions that certain types of activity identified as criminal should be decriminalised to avoid the negative consequences associated with labelling. The argument that the actions of an individual were of less importance than how society reacted to them emphasised that similar acts might be treated differently, determined by factors such as who committed them and where. This was compatible with the view that crime was ubiquitous and not an activity primarily carried out by the working class.

However, this approach was also criticised. Its emphasis placed on why and how individuals were defined as deviant and how the application of such a label affected their subsequent actions was applied at the expense of a failure to discuss the initial causes of their behaviour. Additionally, the fact that it viewed behaviour as deviant only when it was officially labelled as such implied that there was no consensus whatsoever within society on values and standards of behaviour. New deviancy also assigned a passive role to those who were labelled as deviant, whereas they may regard their actions as positive protests directed against society and its values. There was also very little objective evidence to support the theories of new deviancy: it could be, for example, that recidivism among many ex-offenders was largely due to lack of skills or opportunities rather than the stigma of the label.

Write a critical account of new deviancy theory.

Conflict theories

Labelling theory focused on the way in which crime was produced and aggravated by the reaction to the behaviour of those who were identified as offenders. However, labelling theorists failed to offer any detailed investigation of the way in which social reaction was influenced by political interests and political power. 'Whether labels can be made to stick and the extent to which those labelled can be punished may depend essentially on who has power.' Conflict theory focuses attention on the struggles between individuals or groups in terms of power differentials (Lilly et al., 1989: 137). This section identifies some of the key aspects of conflict theory.

Marxism

Marxists agreed with the new deviancy school that society did not operate in a consensual manner but tried to explain why this was so. They concentrated on the issue of the law as an instrument of ruling-class power, an issue neglected by new deviancy that had been accused of being apolitical (in the sense that they avoided structural considerations in their analysis) (Taylor et al., 1973). According to Marxists, society was comprised of classes. Social relationships were viewed as reflecting the 'relations of production' that entailed a minority owning the means of production and a majority selling their labour. Exploitation and social inequality were seen as inevitable features of capitalist society. The economy was thus the basis on which all other institutions were constructed: the state and its institutions were primarily concerned with serving the interests of those who owned or controlled the means of production and in particular to ensure that conditions existed for the accumulation of capital which was needed both to buy labour and to invest.

Traditionally Marxists displayed little attention to crime since they believed that criminal activity had no major contribution to make to the class struggle. An early Marxist criminologist, Willem Bonger, asserted the relevance of the capitalist economic system in promoting values which promoted greed and selfishness as opposed to altruism (Bonger, 1916), but this approach was not pursued, and Marxist criminology 'virtually disappeared from the English-speaking world' until the 1960s (Vold et al., 1998: 264).

There are two key aspects of Marxist criminology that are discussed below.

The maintenance of social order through criminalisation

Marxists directed attention to the mechanisms of state control that ensured the continuance of what they asserted was an essentially unjust social system. It was argued that the existing power relationships in society were maintained by the related processes of indirect and direct coercion. The former ensured compliance through people's incorporation into the labour market, in which wages were received as the result of 'honest' labour. Direct coercion referred both to the ideological control exerted by institutions such as the media which regulated behaviour, and the sanctions which might be applied by the agencies of the criminal justice system to compel obedience. These were especially directed against those who threatened to subvert the principles on which capitalist society operated.

Thus the criminal whose actions challenged private property ownership and threatened to undermine the work ethic, the striker whose actions eroded profit margins or the rebellious underclass which jeopardised social harmony were examples of groups whose actions were likely to become criminalised by the law, subjected to special attention by the police and treated harshly by the sentencing policy of the courts. This view rested on the belief that law was a function of the class and power structure of society, and emphasised the manner in which those in positions of power could apply the label of 'criminal' to whole groups of people who posed a threat to the existing social order. According to such an analysis, criminalisation was primarily directed against the lower classes and actions such as white-collar crime that do not essentially threaten the underpinnings of the capitalist state were likely to be viewed more leniently.

These two forms of coercion are related: the existence of a reserve army of labour served to control the actions of those in employment (perhaps to accept depressed levels of wages in order to avoid the stigma of unemployment) while incorporation into the labour market provided a model of respectability to which the workless might aspire.

Crime is based on economic inequality

Marxist criminology viewed the law as a mechanism designed to serve the interests of the bourgeoisie and perpetuate a situation of economic inequality. It was accepted, however, that legitimacy was accorded to the law from a wider segment of society. The defence of private property ownership, for example, applied to all property regardless of ownership and thus provided a wide degree of support for this cardinal principle of capitalism. Because material equality was not evenly spread, however, the law essentially served the interests of those who gained most from its operations.

Marxists viewed the economic system and the unequal property relations that this generated as the root cause of crime, although there were diverse views as to why crime emerged in situations of economic inequality. These included arguments that crime was an inevitable expression of class conflict based upon the exploitive nature of class relations (Chambliss, 1975), that crime was a protest or incipient rebellion by the poor against the social conditions which prevented them from acquiring goods, and that in a capitalist society the poor and powerless were forced into crime in order to survive (Quinney, 1980). Additionally, delinquency among lower-class juveniles has been attributed to various forms of frustration (such as lack of money or failure to achieve respect) derived from economic disadvantage (Greenberg, 1977).

Marxist criminology has been criticised for failing to encompass crime that is not obviously underpinned by economic motives. However, it has been suggested that juvenile aggression manifested in ways including violence and sexual assault could be explained by underlying economic factors such as unemployment. Problems of this nature prevent young males from fulfilling their socially constructed gender roles (especially that of provider) causing them to display their masculinity through acts of aggression (Greenberg, 1977). Marxist criminology has also been criticised for tending to glamorise criminal actions by depicting them as subversive acts directed against capitalism and its underlying values, in particular the work ethic and the sanctity of private property ownership. What is more, Marxist criminology is also compatible with the view of crime as a mechanism of wealth redistribution, imbuing the criminal with the characteristics of Robin Hood, who is said to have robbed the rich to give to the poor. In reality, however, much crime is not of this nature but is directed against members of the working class.

Radical and critical criminology

Marxism provided the ideological underpinning for radical (sometimes referred to as 'new') criminology that emerged during the 1960s. This first arose in America against a background of popular protest in connection with issues such as civil rights and opposition to the Vietnam war, which highlighted the lack of power and alienation of the lower classes. In the United Kingdom, radical criminology was initially most forcefully expressed in *The New Criminology* by Taylor, Walton and Young (1973), and whose second work (published in 1975) was entitled *Critical Criminology*.

Critical criminology

Radical criminology provided a synthesis of labelling theory and Marxist criminology to provide a comprehensive conflict theory. It rejected attempts (especially those associated with psychological criminology) to locate the cause of crime within the individual. Instead, it directed attention at the impact of wider social processes on the behaviour of individuals, asserting that the root causes of crime were located 'in the class-based and patriarchal nature of contemporary societies'. This approach 'also locates crime in the nature of market capitalism: in its unequal class structure and in the rampant individualism that the market engenders' (Mooney, 2003: 101). Radical criminology highlighted the manner through which the state maintained the rule of the elite by its ability to define conflicting actions or values as 'criminal'. An important aspect of radical criminology was its focus on the process of criminalisation.

The terms 'radical' and 'critical' are frequently used interchangeably but the term 'critical' has become more widely used. The main concern of critical criminology is the power structure of society and how this is maintained rather than why people committed crime. Critical criminology was based on the premise that capitalist society was not consensual but, rather, was 'rooted in conflict' (Walklate, 1998: 32) based upon social and economic inequalities, and it sought to provide an understanding of society's underlying power relationships. It has been observed that politically, critical criminology has a strong socialist rather than a liberal reformist orientation and 'its analytical focus emphasises the causal significance of capitalism in the generation of and responses to "crime"' (White and Haines, 2004: 197).

Although critical criminology seeks to expose the nature of society's underlying power relationships there is no single view as to the source of power. What has been described as the structuralist approach views power as 'ingrained in social structures' (White and Haines, 2004: 202) which give rise to a range of oppressive social relations based upon class division, sexism and racism (White and Haines, 2004: 203).

Alternatively, a postmodernist perspective of critical criminology viewed the world 'as replete with an unlimited number of models of order each generated by relatively autonomous and localised sets of practices which are incapable of being explained by any "scientific" theory' (Muncie, 1999: 151). The postmodernists' rejection of a totalising social theory meant that they rejected the existence of any single explanation for crime. This led them

towards seeking to explain the meanings that became attached to social phe-
nomena such as crime, rather than the causes of them. The postmodernist
focus on the way in which meanings were defined and constructed led them
to concentrate particular attention on the control of the language systems,
arguing that language can privilege some points of view and disparage others
to the extent of establishing dominance relationships (Vold et al., 1998: 270
and 282). That is, 'those who control the means of expression are seen to
hold the key to controlling and exercising power over others', and the 'key to
social transformation … lies in analysing the languages that construct social
relationships in a particular way, to the advantage of some and to the disadvantage of others' (White and Haines, 2004: 207). One way to redress this
imbalance is to ask those who have committed crime to account for their
behaviour and to base an understanding of the problem on their testimonies.

Left realism

This term was coined by Jock Young and represented a left-wing attempt to
wrest the initiative away from the right – especially Conservative governments that dominated British politics after 1979 – in connection with
popular worries concerning the escalation of crime and disorder and the
apparent inability of society to stem this tide. It represented a division in critical criminology between those termed 'left realists' and those described as
'left idealists'.

Left realism rejected the arguments based upon Marxist criminology that
placed emphasis on criminalisation as an essential activity utilised by the
capitalist state to sustain itself (a view which tended to glamorise criminal
activity as a form of political protest). Whereas left idealism emphasised the
essentially coercive way in which the state secured conformity by all of its
citizens, left realism asserted that most of the problems arising from criminal
behaviour were experienced by the poor, which justified the left taking this
problem seriously. Left realism placed considerable reliance on obtaining evidence of people's experiences of crime, especially through the use of social
surveys (such as the Islington crime surveys, the results of which were published in 1986 and 1990) in order to design practical policies to reduce the
level of crime, especially as it impacted on working-class communities.

The response to crime put forward by left realism has been described as a
'holistic approach' (Williams, 2001: 467) which sought to identify the four
main elements of the crime problem – offenders, victims, formal control
(exercised by agencies such as the police and educational system) and informal control (carried out by the general public) and to study the
interrelationships between these key aspects of what is referred to as 'the
square of crime'.

A number of problems arose from the approach adopted by left realism.
These included the extent to which it is possible, or desirable, to formulate
public policy on the basis of the response of a number of individuals to
unstructured questions. The public were unlikely to possess either unity or
consistency in their responses to crime-related issues, and the 'true picture'
articulated by the public was likely to be contaminated by values which were

socially constructed. Further, while social surveys which focused on victims of crime might unearth problems which did not previously figure on the policy agenda (such as violence towards women and children in the home), it did not follow that this 'democratic' approach to tackling crime based on people's experiences would produce progressive policies which the left could endorse.

The process of criminalisation

Conflict theory viewed criminalisation as a key mechanism for securing the maintenance of the existing social order. It was the means to ensure the acquiescence of those who adopted a rebellious stance towards the values or institutions of capitalist society, and the targeting of these rebels helped to divert attention from the inherent unfairness of that system. This enabled inequalities in the distribution of wealth and power to be perpetuated, and ensured the continuance of conditions that were required for the accumulation of profit. The removal of inequalities in the distribution of wealth and power and 'the practices of the powerful, both the seen and the unseen' (Walklate, 1998: 32) were thus viewed as legitimate concerns of criminology.

However, in a liberal democratic political system, social control achieved through punitive actions would only be successful if these had a considerable degree of public support. Drawing from a number of criminological perspectives, in particular labelling and conflict theories, the concept of moral panics has been advanced to explain how widespread popular endorsement for a law and order response to social problems that threatened the position of the ruling elite could be created.

Moral panics

Moral panics describe a situation whereby 'a condition, episode, person or group of persons emerges to become defined as a threat to societal values and interests' (Cohen, 1980: 9). Moral panics generally occur in periods of rapid social change. Problems such as recession, unemployment or the growth of monopoly capitalism lead many members of the general public to become disquieted concerning the direction society is taking, especially those whose interests or values seemed directly threatened by these changes. Those affected by feelings of social anxiety were especially receptive to the simplistic solutions provided by scapegoating a segment of the population and depicting them as the physical embodiment of all that was wrong with society. It has been argued that such persons tended to be especially drawn from the lower-middle-class who were excessively concerned with status (Holdaway, 1996: 80) and who frequently supported right-wing extremist politics in eras of adverse social change (Scott, 1975: 226). It was these members of the general public who were most susceptible to the appeals generated through moral panics.

The manufacturing of a moral panic involved two key processes:

- *The marginalisation of specific groups of citizens.* A key purpose of this was to legitimise the use of discriminatory practices against them. This could be achieved by a campaign of denigration or vilification to establish in the public mind that these groups constituted a social problem.

- *The institutionalisation of prejudice towards these marginalised groups.* This aimed to ensure the subsequent perpetuation of prejudice towards the groups which had been marginalised by seeking to establish a linkage in the public mind between the targeted group and deviant or criminal behaviour. The resulting level of popular prejudice was one explanation why similar activities performed by different groups of people were viewed in contrasting ways by both public opinion and the criminal justice system.

The behaviour of young people (often, but not exclusively, of working-class origin) is frequently the subject on which moral panics are based. Examples of moral panics included the clashes between 'mods' and 'rockers' at South Coast holiday resorts in the 1960s (Cohen, 1972) and mugging in the 1970s where it was argued (by Hall et al., 1978) that this term (which embraced a number of forms of street crime) was socially constructed by the media and utilised in a political way to divert attention from other problems of a structural nature that were then facing society. Subsequent examples of moral panics included activities associated with the 'underclass' (particularly urban disorder and juvenile crime) in the 1980s and 1990s. A particularly significant event was the abduction and murder of James Bulger by two ten-year-old boys in 1993 which became the flashpoint 'which ignited a new moral panic and led to further demonization of young people and, increasingly in the 1990s, also of lone mothers' (Newburn, 1997: 648).

Panics rooted in middle-class fears of a threat to their social position have allegedly surfaced on a regular basis (approximately every twenty years): it has been asserted that these have sought to resurrect the social values of what was seen as a previous 'golden age' but which in reality was based upon a blinkered and over-romanticised view of the past (Pearson, 1983).

The media enables the powerful to exert ideological control throughout society and was accorded a crucial role in the production of a moral panic. It was initially responsible for making people feel uneasy concerning the direction which society was taking. An important way of achieving this objective was to report incidents suggesting a decay in traditional moral values. Having created an underlying cause of concern, the media then focused attention on an action that epitomised the perversion of traditional social values. This entails focusing on an issue that was then amplified out of all proportion to its real importance through sensationalised treatment and the provision of selective information. The media associated the issue with a specific group of people (termed 'folk devils') who become scapegoated. The resulting moral panic was directed against this group and their anti-social activities that epitomised the more general malaise within society. This caused public opinion to demand that the state act to curb their activities. This objective could be accomplished by legislation giving the police additional powers or by the more vigorous use of existing ones.

The state's response could create what is termed a 'deviancy amplification spiral' in which actions directed against a particular stereotyped group resulted in an increased number of arrests and prosecutions of its members. This activity created hostility from the targeted group who viewed this intervention by the state as harassment. As a result, relationships between the targeted group and the police deteriorated, leading to confrontational situations which could then be cited as evidence of the existence of the original problem and also be used as a justification for further tougher action.

Moral panics thus facilitated social control in three key ways:

- *They enabled the definition of criminal and deviant behaviour to be constantly adjusted.* The ruling elite could respond to any threat posed to its interests by instigating a moral panic which would initiate coercive action to criminalise that threat. Industrialised society's tendency to direct moral panics at the actions of the working class indicated a fear that the key threat to dominant social values was presented from this segment of society. Latterly race and gender supplemented social class as the basis on which marginalisation was formulated.

- *They diverted attention away from the fundamental causes of social problems.* Marxists identified these to be associated with the workings of capitalism, particularly the unequal distribution of power and resources throughout society and the resulting levels of inequality and social injustice. The institutionalisation via a moral panic of discriminatory practices against a targeted group thus resulted in a 'divide and rule' situation, in which the symptoms of society's problems rather than their root causes became the main subject of popular concern. According to this analysis, groups of citizens were placed in conflict with each other, thus impeding the development of class consciousness based upon common perceptions of injustice arising from the unjust nature of capitalism.

- *They manufactured consent for the introduction of coercive methods of state control.* These were particularly important in times of recession when social harmony could not be achieved through the provision of socio-economic rewards.

However, arguments alleging that moral panics were based upon manufactured sentiments were not universally accepted. There is no evidence to sustain allegations of conspiracies to create moral panics (Williams, 2001: 452). Further, left realism asserted that the behaviour on which a moral panic was based constituted a genuine source of public concern and was not simply a product of the media (Young, 1986).

Crime and the media

The media exerts an important influence on popular perceptions of the nature and effect of crime. Since many people lack first-hand experience of crime, the media is an important source of information regarding criminal behaviour.

However, the media does not necessarily provide an accurate portrayal of these events. It will focus its attention on crimes that are 'newsworthy'. This ensures that crimes of a sexual or violent nature receive prominent coverage (often in a sensationalised fashion) whereas other crimes are relatively under-reported. This may thus convey a misleading picture to the public regarding the nature and extent of crime and those who are victims of it.

The media may also have a political axe to grind. This may reflect the views of its owners or of the political party that it supports. This means that stories favourable to this viewpoint receive high-profile coverage to the detriment of stories that fail to substantiate this political opinion. Thus a newspaper wishing to support a tough line with criminals is likely to highlight crime caused by offenders that they claim have been treated leniently and disregard stories evidencing the success of non-custodial responses to crime.

There is, however, debate as to whether the media seeks to manipulate public opinion in connection with its coverage of crime or whether it seeks to reflect the views of large numbers of members of the general public.

Conservative criminology

Support of the existing social order is a key concern of conservative criminology as well as conservative political thought. The social order may be imperilled by actions which include moral misbehaviour as well as the more traditional forms of criminal activity directed against persons or their property.

Unlike positivist approaches, this perspective sees no essential difference between a criminal and non-criminal as all human beings are perceived to possess the potential to act in an unsocial manner. However, most people do not do so as their powers of self-restraint are sufficient to overcome any temptation to surrender to their innate instincts. Those who yield to temptation are deemed responsible for their actions, which are allegedly based on free choice and driven by moral failings such as greed. Conservative criminology emphasises the importance of social structures and processes to educate or coerce individuals into overcoming their potential to commit actions that threaten the social fabric. This includes the family unit in addition to the institutions of the criminal justice system.

'Right realism'

The practical application of conservative criminology was associated with 'right realism' in the UK and America. This emerged out of the economic crisis of the 1970s in which governments responded to recession by cutting public spending (Walklate, 1998: 34) thereby needing to find mechanisms other than social welfare policies to regulate the behaviour of the poor and underprivileged members of society. The prevailing philosophy of individualism was compatible with the proposition that the responsibility for crime rested with the individual rather than deficiencies in the operations of society. It was expressed in 1993 by the then Home Secretary, Michael Howard, who stated that he would have 'no truck with trendy theories that try to explain crime away by blaming socio-economic factors'. He emphasised that 'criminals are responsible for crime, and they should be held to account for their actions'. He insisted that 'trying to pass the buck is wrong, counter-productive and dangerous' (Howard, 1993b).

'Right realism' additionally incorporated socio-biological explanations for crime. These asserted that biological factors exercised a considerable (though not a total) influence on criminal behaviour (Wilson and Hernnstein, 1985). Some American studies equated race and intelligence suggesting that the social circumstances of black and Latino Americans was caused not by discrimination but by the 'fact' that they were innately less intelligent (Hernnstein and Murray, 1994). It was also alleged that low IQ was a significant explanation for black violence and criminality (Hernnstein and Murray, 1994).

The following section discusses the approach adopted by Conservative governments in the UK after 1979 to crime.

> Compare and contrast left and right realist approaches to the study of crime.

'New right' criminology in the United Kingdom

New right criminology was underpinned by an ideology of law and order which was summarised as consisting of a 'complex ... set of attitudes, including the beliefs that human beings have free will, that they must be strictly disciplined by restrictive rules, and that they should be harshly punished if they break the laws or fail to respect authority': essentially it meant 'getting tough on criminals' (Cavadino and Dignan, 1992: 26 and 51) who would receive the 'just deserts' for their actions. It was assumed that this stance would receive widespread popular backing and formed the basis of what became referred to as 'penal populism'.

In the United Kingdom, new right criminology embraced the harsh approach to crime associated with post-1979 Conservative government whose response to problems affecting the global economy was the adoption of free market economic policies. These were accompanied by coercive measures to control the dissent that arose from those adversely affected by this approach that had particular implications for state welfare policies.

Although the two pillars of post-1979 Conservatism (neo-liberalism and the social authoritarianism of neo-conservatism) did not seem to be innately compatible, post-1979 Conservative politics made them inextricably connected:

> If the state is to stop meddling in the fine-tuning of the economy, in order to let 'social market values' rip, while containing the inevitable fall-out, in terms of social conflict and class polarization, then a strong, disciplinary regime is a necessary corollary. In 'social market doctrine', the state should interfere less in some areas, but more in others. Its preferred slogan is 'Free Economy: Strong State'. (Hall, 1980: 4)

In order to secure widespread legitimacy for putting forward a coercive response to those who failed to benefit from the new social order, it was necessary to depict their behaviour in a negative light that would secure widespread public disapproval. The aim was to ensure that prevalent social ills were widely blamed on the behaviour of marginal groups within society and were not attributed to the failings of the economic system. The plight of the excluded was not deserving of pity but arose 'as the outcome of misguided welfare programmes; as a result of amoral permissiveness and lax family discipline encouraged by liberal elites who were sheltered from the worst consequences; as the irresponsible behaviour of a dangerous and undeserving underclass' (Sparks, 2003: 156). The appropriate response was thus control rather than social reform.

The main features of new right criminology as it was applied in the United Kingdom were as follows:

- *Those who broke the law should be properly punished for their actions.* At the 1993 Conservative party conference, the then Home Secretary, Michael Howard, put forward a 'Back to Basics' approach to law and order particularly emphasising the importance of imprisonment as a key aspect of government policy. He later stated that in future he expected burglars to be prosecuted rather than cautioned, and he further stated that he expected it to be the norm that anyone who reoffended following a caution should be prosecuted. He asserted that 'nothing infuriates people more than to hear of offenders receiving cautions again and again, rather than being brought to trial' (Howard, 1993a).
- *Social misbehaviour should be regulated by legislative sanction.* This formed a major aspect of Conservative policy after 1979. The desire to deter anti-social behaviour was contained in a range of measures that included the 1985 Sports Events (Control of Alcohol) Act, the 1986 Public Order Act, the 1988 Licensing Act, the 1990 Entertainments (Increased Penalties) Act and the 1994 Criminal Justice and Public Order Act. These sought to

combat actions such as football hooliganism, disorderly conduct, under-age drinking, 'acid house' parties, raves and tresspassory assemblies through the provision of wider police powers or stiffer penalties for those who engaged in these pursuits. The behaviour of young people became a particular target of the Conservative party's law and order policies.

- *The remoralisation of society*. Conservatives placed strong emphasis on the importance of traditional moral values as a means for reducing crime. They looked beyond the criminal justice system to encourage people to make the correct moral choices and emphasised the importance of institutions such as schools and the family to instil into children the ability to discern right from wrong. In the early 1980s Margaret Thatcher chaired a Cabinet Committee on Family Policy. Little emerged from this initiative but support for the family was fervently articulated by Conservative politicians after 1993 when it was argued that factors such as the breakdown of family networks and single parents were key factors which accounted for delinquency in schools.

The approach adopted by new right criminology was based upon very little 'hard' evidence and could thus be criticised for being based on emotion and prejudice as opposed to scientific evidence.

Crime and moral values

The Conservative perception of a link between crime and the decline of traditional moral values was influenced by the American, Charles Murray. He contended that liberal social welfare policy was chiefly responsible for creating a criminal underclass (Murray, 1984). He later depicted illegitimacy as the key social evil: 'In a neighbourhood where few adult males are playing the traditional role of father, the most impressive man around is likely to teach all of the opposite lessons: sleep with as many women as you can, rip off all the money you need and to hell with the rules, waste anyone who gets in your face.' This problem, he believed, needed to be eradicated by measures that included abolishing welfare payments to single mothers (Murray, 1994).

These views were echoed in the opinions put forward by leading Conservative politicians in the 1992–97 government. In 1993 the Conservative party's 'Back to Basics' campaign scapegoated single mothers for the level of crime and delinquency in society. Speaking in the debate on social security at the 1993 Conservative party conference in Blackpool, Peter Lilley asserted that 'ideally children need two loving parents' (Lilley, 1993). Similarly, the then Education Secretary, John Patten, stated that 'in the family ... children learn the difference between right and wrong. It is the family that instils moral values and it is the family that gives a child a sense of purpose and belonging' (Patten, 1993). Such assertions, however, overlooked the possibility of conflict within families being at the root of offending behaviour.

Social exclusion and new right criminology

The economic and social policies pursued by Conservative governments that had resulted in social exclusion were reinforced by new right criminology. This ensured that those who reacted to their social exclusion by engaging in criminal or disorderly actions would be dealt with harshly. The compassion which might once have been extended to those whose misfortunes were not solely of their own making gave way to an aggressive form of denunciation, in order to build consent for coercive responses directed against those who threatened social harmony. The use of language and imagery which (as with racism) sought to deny humanity to these people constituted an important aspect of Conservative policy to secure legitimacy for punitive action against those who transgressed key social values. Car thieves, for example, were depicted as 'hyenas' in campaigns mounted by the Home Office and a persistent juvenile offender in North Eastern England was dubbed 'ratboy' by the local press (Muncie, 1999: 27).

Critics of this approach argued that 'increasing the scope and use of the criminal law, making the courts more repressive, the penal sanctions more severe ... will not strength society's capacity to deal with disorder'. It was asserted that these problems existed because society was heading towards excluding a large group of citizens from the benefits enjoyed by the majority: the crimes that caused most concern were usually committed by young men from certain areas who often had a low level of education and were not trained for a job. They viewed their chances of being accepted as valued members of society as negligible. It was argued that the best way to deal with them was to reintegrate them into society and turn their destructive tendencies into constructive directions (Stern, 1993).

The legacy of new right criminology – penal populism

Populism advocates the pursuance of policies supported by majority public opinion. Politicians 'talk tough' on crime in order to attract political support on the assumption that this is what the public want. This approach is not derived from any coherent set of political beliefs but puts forward simplistic solutions to complex problems resting on 'common-sense' assumptions. Penal populism assumes that the general public are in favour of tough solutions to crime and seeks to politically exploit these sentiments. The terms 'penal populism' or 'populist punitiveness' were used during the 1990s (Bottoms, 1995: 40) and the approach was especially directed at the rise of persistent young offenders (an issue which is discussed in Chapter 9). It denies the relevance of any social explanation for crime and emphasises the need to adopt a harsh approach towards those who carry out such actions. It is characterised by factors that include the use of 'hard' policing methods, longer sentences and the increased size of the prison population, and harsher prison conditions.

The emergence of penal populism has been attributed to factors that include disenchantment with the liberal democratic process, the dynamics of crime and insecurity in a period of considerable social change, the growth of victimisation groups and the emergence of a new kind of penal expertise (Pratt and Clark, 2004) in which the influence wielded by liberal elites was superseded by pressure exerted by the media and organisations such as victimisation groups. It has been argued that in order to counter these new sources of influence it is necessary for the old elites to 'get their hands dirty' and engage with the public in order to marshal support for progressive penal policies (Ryan, 2003).

Although tough approaches to combat crime were not pursued consistently by Conservative governments after 1979, they were an important aspect of the policies initially pursued by Margaret Thatcher's post-1979 government in order to minimise the discontent from those affected by its social and economic policies. This approach became latterly associated with Michael Howard when he became Home Secretary in 1993 and were subsequently adopted by post-1997 Labour governments (Sparks, 2003: 165).

The prominence accorded to penal populism by successive governments can be explained by factors which include the suggestion that in a world in which the power of the nation state has been eroded by globalisation (thus making it difficult for governments to present themselves as effective managers of the economy), law and order remains one area which remains significantly subject to national policy-making. The emphasis placed on punitive responses to lawlessness enables the state to propagate a powerful image: it maintains the pretence of its power to *govern* by displaying its power to *punish* (Garland, 2001; Lacey, 2003: 185).

A further explanation for the emphasis placed on crime after 1979 was that it is an area of public concern, although it is debated whether this concern is engineered from above (by the media or politicians who attach the latent fear of crime to specific issues in an attempt to preserve or further their broader political interests) (Sparks, 2003: 161) or whether the concerns of the general public regarding what is perceived to be a worsening crime problem percolate upwards to influence the actions of the media and politicians (an approach which has been described as 'democracy-at-work' (Beckett, 1997) or 'bottom-up populism').

Administrative (or mainstream) criminology

The administrative criminology that emerged within the Home Office (or from research which it commissioned) in the 1980s was concerned with putting the study of crime and deviance to official practical use, with the aim of ensuring that those who controlled the criminal justice system were more effectively able to translate their intentions into practice.

Administrative criminology possesses many of the characteristics of classicist criminology that has been discussed earlier in this chapter. Additionally, administrative criminology was underpinned by rational choice theory and (especially in connection with research into victimisation) routine activity theory. The latter suggested that certain crimes conformed to a systematic pattern, the understanding of which could be used to prevent the individual suffering further offences. Neither of these theories addressed the reasons why individuals commit crime, but focused on ways of more effectively managing the problem.

Two key aspects of administrative criminology were as follows:

- *To focus on offences rather than offenders.* It abandoned attempts (based on positivism) to discover why offenders committed crime and instead sought to predict future patterns of criminal behaviour from a detailed analysis of crimes committed in the past. It utilised developments such as crime pattern analysis at a local or national level to identify where certain types of offences took place, to facilitate a targeted police response.
- *To further crime prevention schemes.* A major concern of administrative criminology was crime prevention, particularly situational methods (an approach which is discussed more fully in Chapter 2) involving alterations to the environment in order to limit opportunities for criminal activities to be committed. It included innovations such as CCTV, neighbourhood watch and multi-agency approaches. Administrative criminology has also been associated with studies of victimisation, especially repeat victimisation.

Administrative criminology was compatible with the new right political thrust of the new Conservative governments by emphasising individual enterprise and self-reliance as the basis on which criminal behaviour could be restrained.

Feminist criminologies

The study of female crime was traditionally a neglected area of criminology. Various reasons were offered for this omission which included the relatively low number of female offenders, the nature of the crimes they committed (female crime being especially identified with property crime such as shoplifting rather than the more 'spectacular' crime which was of most interest to males who dominated the discipline of criminology) and the tendency for female criminals not to reoffend. Accordingly explanations of female crime remained rooted in theories derived from late nineteenth-century biological positivism initially put forward by Lombroso and amplified, with specific regard to female offending, by Lombroso and Ferrero (1895). Thus female crime was primarily attributed to 'impulsive or irrational behaviour caused by a reaction to factors which included hormonal changes occasioned by biological processes of menstruation, pregnancy and childbirth'. This view insisted that women could not be held responsible for their criminal actions that additionally were virtually devoid of meaning for those who carried them out (Smart, 1995: 25).

A key development associated with feminist criminology was the publication of *Women, Crime and Criminology* (Smart, 1977). However, it has been argued that feminist criminology does not constitute a true paradigm, and is concerned more with establishing the gender biases of the criminal justice system and the general oppression of females than it is with explaining the causes of crime per se or in formulating general explanations of criminality (Fattah, 1997: 271). There is no coherent set of beliefs guiding feminist analysis, and the terms 'feminist criminologies' or 'feminist perspectives within criminology' (Gelsthorpe and Morris, 1990: 227) have alternatively been employed to describe this approach.

These diverse approaches are based on four strands within feminism (liberal, radical, socialist and postmodernist) (Walklate, 1998: 73–8 and 2004: 40–7) that have underpinned the varied agendas addressed within feminist criminologies. Some of these key themes are discussed below.

Female criminality

One aspect of feminist criminologies (underpinned by liberal feminism) is concerned to rectify the perceived deficiencies of mainstream (or 'malestream') criminology. This approach broadly accepted the underlying ethos and methodology of conventional criminology, but suggested that it could be enhanced by more female researchers and the inclusion of greater numbers of females in survey samples.

This has resulted in investigations of female offending behaviour, analysing the trends, patterns and causes of female crime both as a discrete subject and also in comparison with male criminality. The 'discovery' of girl gangs was one aspect of this approach (for example, Campbell, 1981; 1984) which has also suggested that women's crime was committed in different circumstances to that of men, being the crimes of the powerless (Carlen, 1992: 52). It has been further argued that much female crime is underpinned by rational considerations: a high proportion of female offenders steal 'in order to put food on the table for their children' (Walklate, 1995: 7).

Women as perpetrators of crime

Liberal feminism has also provided the underpinning for studies that examined the discriminatory practices of the criminal justice system towards women who had committed crime. Earlier criminologists had argued that victims were less willing to report female offenders and the criminal justice system was accused of operating in a manner which was overly protective towards women offenders who allegedly benefited from the application of what was termed 'male chivalry' (Pollak, 1950; Mannheim, 1965). Although evidence of favourable bias was discerned in later studies concerning the treatment of shoplifters (Farrington and Burrows, 1993: 63) and relating to sentencing policy (Allen, 1987), it was not conclusive. A key difficulty was the virtual impossibility of finding a set of male and female offenders in identical circumstances (in areas such such as previous convictions, family responsibilities and income). It is thus possible to argue that the apparent leniency towards women offenders stemmed from the nature of their crimes and their previous criminal record (Farrington and Morris, 1983).

Conversely, the criminal justice system has been accused of discriminating against women by the application of what is termed 'double deviance'. This suggested that women offenders were more badly treated by agencies operating within the criminal justice system because they were judged in accordance to the severity of the offence they had committed and also by the extent to which they have deviated from conformity to stereotypical female roles. The combination of rule breaking and role breaking resulted in harsher treatment (Carlen, 1983; Heidensohn, 1985).

According to this perspective, women offenders were more likely to be denied bail and be remanded in custody for medical or psychiatric reports, and were more likely to be placed on probation or be sent to prison for trivial offences. Unmarried women would be treated more harshly than married women. Those whose crimes constituted a rejection of the mothering characteristics of 'nurture' and 'protection' (such as Myra Hindley and Rosemary West) would be treated severely (Kennedy, 1993: 23), especially when they used violence. However, as with arguments related to male chivalry, the evidence supporting double deviance is not conclusive, and it has been argued that 'there is no clear and reliable evidence showing that female offenders are treated more harshly than men' (Hough, 1995: 22).

However, a reluctance to use one form of penalty against a woman offender does not necessarily benefit her: one study concluded that 'sentencers exhibit a greater reluctance to fine women. This can result in greater leniency (a discharge) or severity (a community penalty) – the results concerning the use of custody are less clear-cut' (Hedderman and Dowds, 1997: 1).

Women as victims of crime

The focus of radical feminism on female oppression derived from their sexual relationship with men has inspired many studies of women as victims of crime such as rape, domestic violence and female child abuse. The enhanced level of criminal victimisation experienced by women has also affected women's fear of crime that is connected to their public and private experience of men (Walklate, 2004: 100). The violence displayed by men towards women could be explained as 'a conscious and systematic attempt by men to maintain women's social subordination' (Eardley, 1995: 137), an aspect of 'a patriarchal culture' (Kennedy, 2005). However, the presumption that sexual abuse was based upon masculinity has been criticised for ignoring female sexual abusers (Smart, 1995).

The oppression experienced by women is reinforced by the gendered administration of the law and the operations of the criminal justice process. This may be illustrated by the way in which the courts have responded to female victims of crime, especially in cases of sexual misconduct by a male towards a female. These women often receive inappropriate treatment in the courts since the socially acceptable 'attribute' of masculinity may be utilised as an implicit or explicit defence of male actions or be accepted as a mitigating factor for their behaviour. This issue is discussed in fuller detail in Chapter 5.

Crime as a product of gender

Some aspects of feminist criminology seek to explain how socially constructed gender roles influence the levels of both male and female criminality. The concern of Marxist and socialist feminism with the status of women in society (whereby the source of gender inequality was located in capitalist social relations), and the focus of radical feminism on female oppression, were relevant to arguments which suggested that the low level of female offending could be attributed to pressures on women to conform to the role of housewife and mother. The biological differences between male and females gave rise to differential social roles, in which the female was the mother and housewife while the male was the household's provider. The family unit played a key role in developing and reproducing these differential social roles (Hagan, 1987). This suggested that female criminality is constrained, not by biological factors per se, but for reasons that included the values and attitudes that were learned by (or enforced on) girls as part of the socialisation process, or because of the limited opportunities available to them to commit crime.

The argument that differential socialisation might explain low levels of female criminality can be applied to provide an understanding of high levels of male rule breaking. Whereas the importance of traits that include passivity, domesticity, caring and nurturing are imposed on girls, boys are encouraged to be 'aggressive, ambitious and outward-going' (Smart, 1977: 66). Factors which include competitiveness, the demonstration of physical strength, aggressiveness and the importance of achieving (in particular in connection with supporting the family) are key aspects developed during the process of male socialisation which may also serve to underpin criminal behaviour (Oakley, 1982).

The concept of differential socialisation presented an alternative approach to the study of crime whereby a focus on the low level of female crime was substituted for attempts to explain the relatively high level of male offending. Sex role theories (such as those of Parsons, 1937, and Sutherland, 1947) emphasised the importance of the process of socialisation in cultivating differential attitudes between boys and girls. Boys learned attitudes such as toughness and aggression, which exposed them to situations in which antisocial behaviour and criminality was more likely to arise. Indeed, crime (or at least certain aspects of it) could be regarded as a normal (and thus acceptable) display of masculinity: part of the process of 'growing up'.

Girls, on the other hand, were subject to a greater degree of control within families than boys (Hagan et al., 1979). This control (or perhaps, over-control) developed attitudes that were not conducive to crime and also limited the opportunities to commit it. Girls were pressurised by the educational system and the media to conform to their social role and were also subjected to a range of informal sanctions to stop them acting improperly, including the stigma attached to such behaviour which was frequently couched in moral terms (Lees, 1989). This placed the male in a socially constructed position of dominance, providing a possible explanation for the low level of female crime.

Male and female crime in post-industrial society

The social role of the male as provider for the family may afford further understanding of the cause of crime among young males when this role cannot be fulfilled. The impact of recession in a number of Western countries in the 1980s had an adverse impact on the male identity by denying to them the status and material rewards traditionally derived from employment. This may have led males to seek out alternative ways to both fulfil their traditional role as family provider and also to enhance their self-esteem, including various forms of offending behaviour designed to provide either material gains or emotional satisfaction.

This situation affects the argument related to young people 'growing out' of crime. While this may be so for young women from socially deprived backgrounds (since motherhood and the subsequent responsibility to care for children may constrain their desire or ability to carry out offending acts), young males may find it more difficult to escape these pressures, especially when these are exerted by their peers.

The view that female criminality was constrained by the limited opportunities available to women to commit it was developed by the 'liberation of crime' thesis associated with some aspects of liberal feminism. This suggested that the extent and variety of women's criminal involvements would increase as they became more equal. However, there was disagreement concerning the nature of the crime that would emerge as women were liberated from their traditional roles (Adler, 1975; Simon, 1975), in addition to whether it was inevitable that a modern woman would wish to ape the behaviour of a male (Morrison, 1995).

A move away from positivist methodologies

Some feminist criminologies have employed different methodologies than those associated with traditional, especially positivist, criminology. This has entailed a move away from quantitative methodologies to ethnographic methods utilising qualitative approaches. What has been termed the 'epistomological and methodological project' (Gelsthorpe, 1997: 511) has sought to place 'women's experiences, viewpoints and struggles' at the centre of projects with the objective of trying 'to understand the world from the perspective of the subjugated' (Gelsthorpe, 1997: 522). One consequence of this has been a number of small-scale ethnographic accounts which seek to provide offending women with a voice.

Identify the contribution made by feminist criminologies to the study of crime.

Conclusion

This chapter has attempted to illustrate the very wide range of divergent ideas concerning the commission of crime and deviance. It has discussed the contribution made by classicist criminology to an understanding of the causes and solutions to crime, and has considered biological, psychological and sociological explanations for criminal behaviour. The approaches associated with ideas drawn from the left and right wings of the political spectrum have been contrasted and the chapter also examined the contribution made by feminist criminologies to the study of crime. A chapter of this length can only sketch the main ideas associated with the different schools of thought that are discussed and it is intended that this outline will provide a useful background for a more detailed examination of this key area of criminological study.

Some of the ideas contained in this chapter are developed in the following chapter. Many of the theories considered in this chapter explicitly or implicitly locate crime as a working-class phenomenon. However, crime is carried out by persons higher up the social ladder and the nature of this crime is considered in Chapter 2. This chapter also builds upon the material in Chapter 1 concerned with the causes of crime by seeking to explain how crime can be prevented and considers the contemporary application of crime prevention to the concept of community safety. First, however, Chapter 2 will examine the extent of crime in society and consider the different ways whereby this can be measured.

Further reading

There are many specialist texts that will provide an in-depth examination of the issues that have been discussed in this chapter. These include:

Burke, R. (2005) *An Introduction to Criminological Theory*, 2nd edn. Cullompton: Willan Publishing.

Croall, H. (1998) *Crime and Society in Britain*. Harlow: Longman.

Fattah, E. (1997) *Criminology: Past, Present and Future: A Critical Overview*. Basingstoke, Macmillan.

Muncie, J., McLaughlin, E. and Langan M. (2003) *Criminological Perspectives: A Reader*. 2nd edn. London: Sage.

Vold, G., Bernard, T. and Snipes J. (1998) *Theoretical Criminology*, 4th edn. Oxford: Oxford University Press.

Walklate, S. (2003) *Understanding Criminology: Current Theoretical Debates*, 2nd edn. Buckingham: Open University Press.

Williams, K. (2004) *Textbook on Criminology*, 5th edn, Oxford: Oxford University Press.

Key events

- **1764** Publication by Cesare Beccaria of *Dei deliti e delle pene* (*On Crimes and Punishments*): this provided an agenda for classicist criminology.
- **1876** Publication by Cesare Lombroso of *L'Uomo Delinquente* (*The Criminal Man*): Lombroso revised his ideas concerning the causes of crime in subsequent editions of this work, the fifth and final edition of which was published in 1897.
- **1893** Publication by Emile Durkheim of *De la division du travail social* (*On the Division of Labour in Society*) in which he put forward the concept of anomie. This was subsequently developed in a later work, *Le suicide* (*Suicide*) published in 1897.
- **1923** Publication by Sigmund Freud of *The Ego and the Id*, which was translated into English in 1927. This work revised his earlier discussion of psychoanalysis which had been pubished in 1920 (*A General Introduction to Psychoanalysis*) and asserted the importance for human behaviour of inner turmoil occurring within the subconscious mind of the individual.
- **1938** Publication by Robert Merton of his article on 'Social Structure and Anomie' in which he developed Durkheim's concept of anomie and put forward his ideas of social strain theory. His ideas were subsequently developed in his work *Social Theory and Social Structure* which was initially published in 1949 and rewritten and revised in 1957.
- **1942** Publication by Clifford Shaw and Henry McKay of *Juvenile Delinquency and Urban Areas* (a revised edition of which was published in 1969). Drawing on earlier work of the Chicago School (especially by Robert Park and Ernest Burgess), this asserted the importance of environment on criminal behaviour making for the existence of perennial high crime areas in what was termed the 'zone of transition' within cities. This is a particularly important discussion of the concept of social disorganisation that was advanced by the Chicago School.
- **1963** Publication by Howard Becker of his work *Outsiders: Studies in the Sociology of Deviance.* This developed the concept of labelling theory that had been initially associated with Edwin Lemert in his work *Social Pathology*, published in 1951.
- **1972** Publication of *Folk Devils and Moral Panics* by Stanley Cohen. This work focused on society's reaction to clashes between 'mods' and 'rockers' on South Coast holiday resorts in the 1960s and constitutes an important study of the concept of moral panics.
- **1973** Publication of *The New Criminology* by Ian Taylor, Paul Walton and Jock Young in 1973. This provided an important statement of radical criminology in the United Kingdom, the ideas of which were developed in a second work by the same authors published in 1975 entitled *Critical Criminology*.

- **1977** Publication in the United Kingdom by Carol Smart of *Women, Crime and Criminology*. This was an important text in the development of feminist criminologies which challenged a number of established arguments concerning women and crime.
- **1993** Michael Howard became Home Secretary in John Major's Conservative government. His tenure at the Home Office (until 1997) initiated the introduction of penal populist principles into criminal justice policy that have heavily influenced the subsequent agenda in areas such as the concern towards anti-social behaviour.

References

Adler, S. (1975) *Sisters in Crime*. New York: McGraw-Hill.

Agnew, R. (1985) 'A Revised Strain Theory of Delinquency', *Social Forces*, 64 (1): 151–65.

Aichorn, A. (1963) *Wayward Youth*. New York: Viking.

Ainsworth, P. (2000) *Psychology and Crime: Myths and Realities*. Harlow: Longman.

Akers, A. (1990) 'Rational Choice, Deterrence and Social Learning Theory in Criminology: The Path Not Taken', *Journal of Criminal Law and Criminology*, 81 (3): 653–76.

Allen, H. (1987) *Justice Unbalanced: Gender, Psychiatry, and Judicial Decisions*. Buckingham: Open University Press.

Baldwin, J. and Bottoms, A. (1976) *The Urban Criminal*. London: Tavistock.

Bandura, A. (1977) *Social Learning Theory*. Englewood Cliffs, NJ: Prentice Hall.

Beccaria, C. (1764) *Dei deliti e delle pene* (On Crimes and Punishments), trans. H. Paolucci (1963). Indianapolis, IN: Bobbs-Merrill.

Becker, H. (1963) *Outsiders: Studies in the Sociology of Deviance*. New York: Free Press.

Beckett, K. (1997) *Making Crime Pay: Law and Order in Contemporary American Politics*. New York: Oxford University Press.

Bonger, W. (1916) *Criminality and Economic Condition*. Boston: Little, Brown.

Bottoms, A. (1995) 'The Philosophy and Politics of Punishment and Sentencing', in C. Clarkson and R. Morgan (eds), *The Politics of Sentencing Reform*. Oxford: Clarendon Press.

Bottoms, A. and Wiles, P. (1994) 'Environmental Criminology', in M. Maguire, R. Morgan and R. Reiner (eds), *The Oxford Handbook of Criminology*, 1st edn. Oxford: Oxford University Press.

Bottoms, A., Claytor, A. and Wiles, P. (1992) 'Housing Markets and Residential Crime Careers: A Case Study from Sheffield', in D. Evans, N. Fyfe and D. Herbert (eds), *Crime, Policing and Place: Essays in Environmental Criminology*. London: Routledge.

Bowlby, J. (1946) *Forty-Four Juvenile Thieves*. London: Ballière, Tindall & Cox.

Bowlby, J. (1953) *Child Care and the Growth of Love*, based by permission of the World Health Organisation on the report *Maternal Care and Mental Health*. Harmondsworth: Penguin.

Box, S. (1987) *Recession, Crime and Punishment*. London: Macmillan.

Brantingham, P. J. and Brantingham, P. L. (1981) *Environmental Criminology*. Beverly Hills, CA: Sage.

Brantingham, P. J. and Brantingham, P. L. (1984) *Patterns in Crime*. New York: Macmillan.

Brunner, H. (1995) *MAOA Deficiency and Abnormal Behaviour: Perspectives on an Association*. Paper delivered at the Symposium on Genetics of Criminal and Anti-Social Behaviour, Ciba Foundation, London, 14–16 February.

Brunner, H., Nelen, M., Breakefield, X., Ropers, H. and van Oost, B. (1993) 'Abnormal Behaviour Associated with a Point Mutation in the Structural Gene for Monoamine Oxidase A', *Science*, 262: 578–80.

Burgess, E. (1925) 'The Growth of the City', in R. Park, E. Burgess and R. McKenzie (eds), *The City*. Chicago: University of Chicago Press.

Bursik, P. (1986) 'Ecological Stability and the Dynamics of Delinquency', in A. Reiss and M. Tonry (eds), *Communities and Crime*. Chicago: University of Chicago Press.

Bynum, J. and Thompson, W. (1996) *Juvenile Delinquency: A Sociological Approach*, 3rd edn. Boston: Allyn & Bacon.

Campbell, B. (1981) *Girl Delinquents*. Oxford: Blackwell.

Campbell, B. (1984) *Girls in the Gang: A Report from New York City*. Lexington, MA: Raytheon Company.

Carlen, P. (1983) *Women's Imprisonment*. London: Routledge & Kegan Paul.

Carlen, P. (1992) 'Criminal Women and Criminal Justice: The Limits to, and Potential of, Feminist and Left Realist Perspectives', in R. Matthews and J. Young (eds), *Issues in Realist Criminology*. London: Sage.

Cavadino, M. and Dignan, J. (1992) *The Penal System: An Introduction*. London: Sage.

Chambliss, W. (1975) 'Towards a Political Economy of Crime', *Theory and Society*, 2: 149–70.

Cicourel, I. (1968) *The Social Organisation of Juvenile Justice*. New York: John Wiley.

Cloward, R. and Ohlin, L. (1960) *Delinquency and Opportunity*. New York: Free Press.

Cohen, A. (1955) *Delinquent Boys: The Culture of the Gang*. Chicago: Chicago Free Press.

Cohen, S. (1980) *Folk Devils and Moral Panics*, 2nd edn. Oxford: Martin Robertson; first published in 1972.

Cohen, S. (1988) *Against Criminology*. Oxford: Transaction Books.

Coleman, C. and Moynihan, J. (1996) *Understanding Crime Data, Haunted by the Dark Figure*. Buckingham: Open University Press.

Conrad, P. and Schneider, J. (1992) *Deviance and Medicalization: From Badness to Sickness*. Philadelphia: Temple University Press.

Cooley, C. (1902) *Human Nature and the Social Order*. New York: Schoken Books.

Dugdale, R. (1877) *The Jukes: A Study in Crime, Pauperism, Disease and Heredity*. New York: Putnam.

Durkheim, E. (1893) *De la division du travail social (On the Division of Labour in Society)*. Paris: Alcan.

Durkheim, E. (1897) *Le suicide (Suicide)*. Paris: Alcan.

Eardley, T. (1995) 'Violence and Sexuality', in S. Caffrey and G. Mundy (eds), *The Sociology of Crime and Deviance: Selected Issues*. Dartford: Greenwich University Press.

Erikson, K. (1966) *Wayward Puritans*. New York: John Wiley & Sons.

Eysenck, H. (1960) *The Structure of Human Personality*. London: Methuen.

Eysenck, H. (1970) *The Structure of Human Personality*, revised edn. London: Methuen.

Farrington, D. (1994) 'Introduction', in D. Farrington (ed.), *Psychological Explanations of Crime*. Aldershot: Dartmouth.

Farrington, D. and Burrows, J. (1993) 'Did Shoplifting Really Decrease?', *British Journal of Criminology*, 33 (1): 57–69.

Farrington, D., Loeber, R. and Van Kammen, W. (1990) 'Long-Term Criminal Outcomes of Hyperactivity-Impulsivity-Attention Deficit and Conduct Probems in Childhood', in L. Robins and M. Rutter (eds), *Straight and Devious Pathways from Childhood to Adulthood*. Cambridge: Cambridge University Press.

Farrington, D. and Morris, A. (1983) 'Sex, Sentencing and Reconviction', *British Journal of Criminology*, 2 (2): 85–102.

Fattah, E. (1997) *Criminology Past, Present and Future: A Critical Overview*. London: Macmillan.

Ferri, E. (1917) *Criminal Sociology*. Boston: Little, Brown.

Foucault, M. (1977) *Discipline and Punish: The Birth of the Prison*. New York: Vintage.

Freud, S. (1920) *A General Introduction to Psychoanalysis*. New York: Boni & Liveright.

Freud, S. (1923) *The Ego and the Id*. Frankfurt: Fischer; trans. in 1927.

Freud, S. (1930) *Civilisation and Its Discontents*. New York: Cape & Smith.

Garland, D. (2001) *The Culture of Control*. Chicago: University of Chicago Press.

Gelsthorpe, L. (1997) 'Feminism and Criminology', in M. Maguire, R. Morgan and R. Reiner (eds), *The Oxford Handbook of Criminology*, 2nd edn. Oxford: Oxford University Press, pp. 511–33.

Gelsthorpe, L. and Morris, A. (1990) *Feminist Perspectives in Criminology*. Buckingham: Open University Press.

Glaser, D. (1956) 'Criminality Theories and Behavioural Images', *American Journal of Sociology*, 61: 433–44.

Gottfredson, M. and Hirschi, T. (1990) *A General Theory of Crime*. Stanford, CA: Stanford University Press.

Greenberg, D. (1977) 'Delinquency and the Age Structure of Society', *Contemporary Crises*, 1 (2): 189–224.

Hagan, J. (1987) *Modern Criminology: Crime, Criminal Behavior and its Control*. Toronto: McGraw-Hill.

Hagan, J., Simpson, J. and Gillis, A. (1979) 'The Sexual Stratification of Social Control', *British Journal of Sociology*, 30: 25–38.

Hall, S. (1980) *Drifting into a Law and Order Society*. London: Cobden Trust.

Hall, S., Critcher, C., Jefferson, T. and Roberts, B. (1978) *Policing the Crisis: Mugging, the State and Law and Order*. London: Macmillan.

Hedderman, C. and Dowds, L. (1997) *The Sentencing of Women: A Section 95 Publication*, Research Findings No. 58. London: Home Office Research and Statistics Directorate.

Heidensohn, F. (1985) *Women and Crime*. London: Macmillan.

Hernnstein, R. and Murray, R. (1994) *The Bell Curve: Intelligence and Class Structure in American Life*. New York: Free Press.

Hirschi, T. (1969) *Causes of Delinquency*. Berkeley, CA: University of California Press.

Hirschi, T. and Hindlelang, M. (1977) 'Intelligence and Delinquency: A Revisionist Review', *American Sociological Review*, 42: 571–87.

Holdaway, S. (1996) *The Racialisation of British Policing*. London: Macmillan.

Hough, M. (1995) 'Scotching a Fallacy, Sentencing Women', *Criminal Justice Matters*, 19: 22–3.

Howard, M. (1993a) Speech at Wokingham, 15 October, quoted in *Guardian*, 16 October.

Howard, M. (1993b) Speech at Basingstoke, 10 November, quoted in *Guardian*, 11 November.

Huesmann, L. and Podolski, C. (2003) 'Punishment: A Psychological Perspective', in S. McConville (ed.), *The Use of Punishment*. Cullompton: Willan Publishing.

Hutchings, B. and Mednick, S. (1977) 'Criminality in Adoptees and Their Adoptive and Biological Parents: A Pilot Study', in S. Mednick and K. Christensen (eds), *Biosocial Bases of Criminal Behaviour*. New York: Gardner Press.

Jacobs, P., Brunton, M. and Melville, M. (1965) 'Aggressive Behaviour, Mental Subnormality and the XYY Male', *Nature*, 25 December: 1351–2.

Jensen, A. (1969) 'How Much Can We Boost IQ and Scholastic Achievement?', *Harvard Educational Review*, 39: 1–123.

Jonassen, C. (1949) 'Re-Evaluation and Critique of the Logic and Some Methods of Shaw and McKay', *American Sociological Review*, 10: 792–8.

Kelly, G. (1955) *The Psychology of Personal Constructs*. New York: Norton.

Kennedy, H. (1993) *Eve Was Framed*. London: Vintage.

Kennedy, H. (2005) 'Why Is the Criminal Justice System Still Skewed Against Women?', *Guardian*, 10 March.

Kornhauser, R. (1978) *Social Sources of Delinquency*. Chicago: University of Chicago Press.

Lacey, N. (2003) 'Penal Theory and Penal Practice: A Communitarian Approach', in S. McConville (ed.), *The Use of Punishment*. Cullompton: Willan Publishing.

Lange, J. (1931) *Crime as Destiny*. London: Allen & Unwin.

Lees, S. (1989) 'Learning to Love', in M. Cain (ed.), *Growing Up Good*. London: Sage.

Lemert, E. (1951) *Social Pathology*. New York: McGraw-Hill.

Lemert, E. (1967) *Human Deviance, Social Problems, and Social Control*. Englewood Cliffs, NJ: Prentice Hall.

Lilly, J., Cullen, F. and Ball, R. (1989) *Criminological Theory: Context and Consequences*. London: Sage.

Lilley, P. (1993) Speech at the Conservative party Conference, Blackpool, 6 October, quoted in *Guardian*, 7 October.

Lombroso, C. (1876) *L'Uomo Delinquente*. Milan: Hoepl.

Lombroso, C. and Ferraro, W. (1895) *The Female Offender*. London: Fisher Unwin.

Mannheim, H. (1965) *Comparative Criminology*. London: Routledge & Kegan Paul.

Marsh, P., Rosser, E. and Harré, R. (1978) *The Rules of Disorder*. London: Routledge & Kegan Paul.

Matsueda, R. (1988) 'The Current State of Social Differentiation Theory', *Crime and Delinquency*, 34 (3): 277–306.

Matza, D. (1964) *Delinquency and Drift*. New York: John Wiley.

Matza, D. and Sykes, G. (1957) 'Techniques of Neutralization: A Theory of Delinquency', *American Sociological Review*, 22: 664–70.

Matza, D. and Sykes, G. (1961) 'Juvenile Delinquency and Subterranean Values', *American Sociological Review*, 26: 713–19.

Mawby, R., McCulloch, J. and Batta, I. (1979) 'Crime Amongst Asian Juveniles in Bradford', *International Journal of the Sociology of Law*, 7.

Mayhew, H. (1862) *London Labour and the London Poor*, Vol. 4, *Those That Will Not Work*. London: Griffin Bohn.

Mead, G. H. (1938) *Mind, Self and Society*. Chicago: University of Chicago Press.

Merton, R. (1938) 'Social Structure and Anomie', *American Sociological Review*, 3: 672–82.

Merton, R. (1957) *Social Theory and Social Structure*, 2nd edn. New York: Free Press; first published in 1949.

Miller, W. (1958) 'Lower Class Culture as a Generating Milieu of Gang Delinquency', *Journal of Social Issues*, 14: 5–19.

Mooney, J. (2003) 'It's the Family, Stupid: Continuities and Reinterpretation of the Dysfunctional Family as the Cause of Crime in Three Political Periods', in R. Matthews and J. Young (eds), *The New Politics of Crime and Punishment*. Cullompton: Willan Publishing.

Morris, T. (1957) *The Criminal Area: A Study in Social Ecology*. London: Routledge & Kegan Paul.

Morrison, W. (1995) *Theoretical Criminology: From Modernity to Post-modernism*. London: Cavendish.

Muncie, J. (1999) *Youth and Crime: A Critical Introduction*. London: Sage.

Murray, C. (1984) *Losing Ground*. New York: Basic Books.

Murray, C. (1994) quoted in G. Beddell, 'An Underclass Warrior', *Independent on Sunday*, 9 January.

Newburn, T. (1997) 'Youth, Crime and Justice', in M. Maguire, R. Morgan and R. Reiner (eds), *The Oxford Handbook of Criminology*, 2nd edn. Oxford: Oxford University Press.

Oakley, A. (1982) 'Conventional Families', in R. Rapoport, R. N. Rapoport and R. Fogart (eds), *Families in Britain*. London: Routledge & Kegan Paul.

Pakes, F. and Winstone, J. (2005) 'Community Justice: The Smell of Fresh Bread', in J. Winstone and F. Pakes (eds), *Community Justice: Issues for Probation and Criminal Justice*. Cullompton: Willan Publishing.

Park, R. (1925) 'The City: Suggestions for the Investigation of Human Behaviour in an Urban Environment', in R. Park, E. Burgess and R. McKenzie (eds), *The City*. Chicago: University of Chicago Press.

Park, R. (1928) 'Human Migration and the Marginal Man', *American Journal of Sociology*, 33: 881–93.

Parsons, T. (1937) *The Structure of Social Action*. New York: McGraw-Hill.

Patten, J. (1993) Speech to the Conservative Party Conference, Blackpool, 6 October, quoted in *Guardian*, 7 October.

Pavlov, I. (1927) *Conditioned Reflexes*. Oxford: Oxford University Press.

Pearson, G. (1983) *Hooligan: A History of Respectable Fears*. London: Macmillan.

Pitts, J. (1988) *The Politics of Juvenile Crime*. London: Sage.

Pollak, O. (1950) *The Criminality of Women*. New York: A. S. Barnes/Perpetua.

Pratt, J. and Clark, M. (2004) 'Penal Populism in New Zealand', *Punishment and Society*, 7 (3): 303–22.

Quinney, R. (1980) *Class, State and Crime*, 2nd edn. New York: Longman.

Raynor, P. and Vanstone, M. (2002) *Understanding Community Penalties: Probation, Policy and Social Change*. Buckingham: Open University Press.

Reckless, W. (1967) *The Crime Problem*, 4th edn. New York: Appleton-Century-Croft.

Reckless, W. (1973) *The Crime Problem*, 5th edn. New York: Appleton-Century-Croft.

Reiss, A. (1951) 'Delinquency as the Failure of Personal and Social Controls', *American Sociological Review*, 16: 196–207.

Rutter, M. and Smith, D. (1995) *Psychosocial Disorders in Young People*. New York: John Wiley.

Ryan, M. (2003) *Penal Policy and Political Cultures in England and Wales*. Winchester: Waterside Press.

Scott, D. (1975) 'The National Front in Local Politics: Some Interpretations', in I. Crewe, (ed.), *British Political Sociology Year Book*. London: Croom Helm, Vol. 2, pp. 214–38.

Sellin, T. (1938) *Culture, Conflict and Crime*. New York: Social Science Research Council.

Shaw, C. (1930) *The Jackroller*. Chicago: University of Chicago Press.

Shaw, C. (1938) *Brothers in Crime*. Chicago: University of Chicago Press.

Shaw, C. and McKay, H. (1942) *Juvenile Delinquency and Urban Areas*. Chicago: University of Chicago Press.

Sheldon, W. (1949) *Varieties of Delinquent Youth*. New York: Harper.

Simon, R. (1975) *Women and Crime*. Lexington, MA: DC Heath.

Smart, C. (1977) *Women, Crime and Criminology: A Feminist Critique*. Boston: Routledge & Kegan Paul.

Smart, C. (1995) *Law, Crime and Sexuality*. London: Sage.

Sparks, R. (2003) 'States of Insecurity: Punishment, Populism and Contemporary Political Culture', in S. McConville (ed.), *The Use of Punishment*. Cullompton: Willan Publishing.

Stern, V. (1993) *NACRO, Annual Report 1992/3*. London: NACRO.

Sutherland, E. (1939) *The Professional Thief*. Chicago: University of Chicago Press.

Sutherland, E. (1947) *Principles of Criminology*. Philadelphia: Lippincott.

Sutherland, E. (1973) *On Analyzing Crime*. Chicago: University of Chicago Press.

Sutherland, E. and Cressey, D. (1955) *Principles of Criminology*. Chicago: J. B. Lippincott.

Sykes, G. and Matza, D. (1957) 'Techniques of Neutralisation: A Theory of Delinquency', *American Sociological Review*, 22: 664–70.

Tannenbaum, F. (1938) *Crime and Community*. Boston: Ginn & Co.

Tarde, G. (1876) *La Criminalité Comparée*. Paris: Alcan.

Taylor, I., Walton, P. and Young, J. (1973) *The New Criminology*. London: Routledge.

Taylor, I., Walton, P. and Young, J. (eds) (1975) *Critical Criminology*. London: Routledge.

Thomas, D. (2003) 'Judicial Discretion in Sentencing', in L. Gelsthorpe and N. Padfield (eds), *Exercising Discretion: Decision-Making in the Criminal Justice System and Beyond*. Cullompton: Willan Publishing.

Tittle, C. (1995) *Control Balance: Towards A General Theory of Deviance*. Boulder, CO: Westview Press.

Tittle, C. (2000) 'Control Balance', in R. Paternoster and R. Bachman (eds), *Explaining Criminals and Crime: Essays in Contemporary Theory*. Los Angeles: Roxbury.

Vold, G., Bernard, T. and Snipes, J. (1998) *Theoretical Criminology*, 4th edn. Oxford: Oxford University Press.

Walklate, S. (1995) *Gender and Crime*. Hemel Hempstead: Harvester Wheatsheaf.

Walklate, S. (1998) *Understanding Criminology: Current Theoretical Debates*. Buckingham: Open University Press.

Walklate, S. (2004) *Gender, Crime and Criminal Justice*, 2nd edn. Cullompton: Willan Publishing.

White, R. and Haines, F. (2004) *Crime and Criminology: An Introduction*, 3rd edn. Oxford: Oxford University Press.

Williams, K. (2001) *Textbook on Criminology*, 4th edn. Oxford: Oxford University Press.

Wilson, J. Q. and Hernnstein, R. (1985) *Crime and Human Nature*. New York: Simon & Schuster.

Women's Unit (2000) *Living Without Fear: An Integrated Approach to Tackling Violence Against Women*. London: Cabinet Office.

Young, J. (1986) 'The Failure of Criminology: the Need for a Radical Realism', in R. Matthews and J. Young (eds), *Confronting Crime*. London: Sage.

Zola, I. (1972) 'Medicine as an Institution of Social Control', *Sociological Review*, 20: 487–504.

2 Crime and crime prevention

This chapter examines the manner in which society is informed about crime and the approaches that can be used to prevent it. It devotes particular attention to white-collar crime that has not been addressed by the theories examined in the previous chapter and also discusses the contemporary importance attached to community safety.

Specifically this chapter:

- examines the various methodologies used to ascertain how much crime exists within society and in particular draws attention to the weaknesses of official crime statistics as a provider of this assessment;
- discusses crime committed by persons not drawn from the working class, namely white-collar, middle-class and corporate crime. The chapter considers the nature of this activity and the way in which the state responds to it;
- furthers the discussion in Chapter 1 concerning the causes of crime by considering how crime might best be prevented. Considerable attention is drawn to the contemporary importance of crime prevention policy, in particular situational methods and the onus placed on potential victims to prevent crime. This approach is contrasted to social methods of crime prevention;
- analyses recent developments associated with crime prevention initiatives conducted at a local level under the approach of 'community safety'.

The measurement of crime

As has been argued in Chapter 1, crime is an issue of major political importance. A government that reduces crime will expect public recognition for this achievement. Conversely political support is likely to suffer if the level of crime increases. An important source of evidence on which claims of success or accusations of failure are based are crime statistics. These consist of figures collected by individual police forces and forwarded to the Home Office, enabling information concerning the national trend to be provided. However, the information does not reveal accurate information concerning the level of crime at any given period.

> Using an up-to-date set of crime statistics, outline what information these provide concerning the nature and extent of contemporary crime.

Official crime statistics

Official crime statistics document only a limited range of criminal activity. The gap between the volume of crime which is actually committed and that which enters into official crime statistics is referred to as the 'dark figure' of crime. This discrepancy may be explained by the nature of the process of crime reporting which is discussed below.

The process of crime reporting

There are a number of stages involved in translating a criminal act into an official statistic.

Discovery

It is necessary for a crime to be discovered if it is to become a statistic. Certain types of crime in which there is no individual victim (such as fraud or tax evasion) may not be easily identified as having taken place. Other crimes may not be perceived as such by the victim, who may attribute matters such as missing money or other forms of property to personal carelessness as opposed to another's criminal actions.

Reporting the crime to the police

If a crime is discovered the next stage is to report the matter to the police. Individual victims, however, may not wish to do this. The victim may believe the crime to be too trivial to warrant police intervention or that the police would be unable to do much about the incident were it reported. Alternatively, the victim may fail to report a crime as they fear that they will suffer reprisals if they do so. One study suggested that on high crime housing estates, 13 per cent of crimes reported by victims and 9 per cent reported by witnesses were the subject of intimidation, and that a further 6 per cent of crime not reported by victims and 22 per cent not reported by witnesses failed to be reported because of the fear of intimidation (Maynard, 1994: 5).

Victims may also not report crimes because they believe the criminal justice system will not handle the complaint justly. The law courts' poor treatment of women who are victims of serious sexual attacks and the consequent reluctance of women to report such crimes is one reason why official statistics have traditionally underestimated the number of crime of this nature. Embarrassment may also be a reason why crimes such as thefts from their clients by prostitutes or their accomplices are not reported.

Recording of an incident by the police

The final stage of the process whereby crime is entered into official statistics is the recording of the offence. The gap between offences reported to the police and what they record is called the 'grey area' of crime (Bottomley and Pease, 1986). Decisions concerning whether to record a reported crime are dependent on factors that are discussed below, and include the individual discretion of a police officer, police organisational culture and official procedures laid down by the Home Office. These especially affect the manner in which attempted crimes which are not fully committed are documented.

- *Too minor to record.* A police officer to whom a crime has been reported may decide that the offence is a minor one which can be dealt with informally, perhaps by warning a person who has behaved incorrectly. Decisions of this nature may be based upon individual bias or prejudice as to the seriousness of the matter, or upon a view derived from organisational culture. The latter means that minor offences may be disregarded by a popular view within the police service that their trivial nature makes official intervention inappropriate: an officer who disregarded such peer group pressure may find him/herself the subject of derision.

- *'Cuffing'.* The practice of 'cuffing' entails either not recording a crime which has been reported or downgrading a reported crime to an incident which can be excluded from official statistics. The decision to do this was initially motivated by a desire to avoid the time-consuming practice of filling out a crime report for minor incidents, although this problem was ameliorated by the increased utilisation of computerised crime recording systems. However, the introduction of performance indicators for the police service in 1992 intensified pressures on the police to avoid recording all offences notified to them. Crime statistics were a key source of evidence of police performance, so increased levels of reported crimes could imply inefficiency. Such political factors (Bottomley and Coleman, 1981) may reinforce the inclination of individual officers not to report crime in the first instance or of crime managers to discount it later.

- *Willingness of victim to give evidence in court.* The decision to declare an action 'no crime' may be influenced by a police manager's assessment of whether the victim will be prepared to give evidence in court. The perception that victims of domestic violence will ultimately drop such charges is one explanation for the traditional police reluctance to become involved in these matters.

- *Home Office directions.* The reporting of a crime by the police is also influenced by directions from the Home Office. The police are required to pass to the Home Office only details of 'notifiable offences'. Since 1999 these have included all crimes which are triable on indictment in a crown court, many which are triable 'either way' (that is either on indictment or summarily, before a magistrates' court) and some summary offences. Thus many crimes (including the great majority of motoring offences) are not notifiable and are therefore excluded from crime statistics. This may place pressure on individual police officers not to report a crime they have observed or which may be drawn to their attention. Additionally, what are termed 'Home Office Counting Rules' give guidance concerning how issues such as discounting recorded crimes (by classing them as 'no crimes') and recording multiple offences should be handled. Rules introduced in 1979 required the police to record certain types of offences (for example, theft from several cars in a car park) as one crime. These rules were altered in 1998 so that one offence was recorded for each victim in these circumstances (Home Office, 1998b). A final factor governing the recording of offences is that some crimes are investigated by agencies such as Customs and Excise or the DSS and not the police. For this reason crimes including fraud do not enter into official crime statistics, even if these matters were initially referred to the police service.

Changes to the procedures for crime reporting

As is discussed more fully in Chapter 3, the use of crime statistics as a measure of police performance (in particular in connection with the publication of league tables which compared one force with another) generated pressure on forces to manipulate both the level of crime that had been reported and also the detection rates. It was observed that the 'increasingly aggressive performance culture has emerged as a major factor affecting integrity, not least because for some years there has been an apparent tendency for some forces to trawl the margins for detections and generally to use every means to portray their performance in a good light' (HMIC, 1999: 19).

In 1999, this issue became public knowledge when the Channel 4 programme *Dispatches* alleged that in one force which they investigated (Nottinghamshire), officers induced criminals to confess to crimes regardless of whether or not they had committed them so that they could be listed as detected. The aim of this subterfuge (which the programme alleged was carried out in conjunction with 'cuffing' reported crimes) was to enhance the apparent efficiency of the force.

In 2000, a report by the police inspectorate (HMIC) referred to wide variations in the way police forces recorded crimes. It was alleged that offences were sometimes wrongly classified as less serious crimes, that there was inappropriate 'no-criming' of offences after they had been recorded and there was a failure to record the correct number of crimes (HMIC, 2000). A discussion paper subsequently made 66 recommendations concerning crime statistics, including a requirement that the police should ensure that every incident relating to crime and all allegations of crime and disorders which were brought to their attention should be recorded as an incident or a call for service (Simmons, 2000).

In 2002 ACPO, with the support of the Home Office, sought to address criticisms of this nature by introducing the National Crime Recording

Standard (NCRS). This sought to promote 'greater reliability and consistency in collecting and recording crime data. It requires police services to take an approach that focuses on the victims' perspective and requires all forces to record crimes according to a clear set of principles' (Audit Commission, 2004: 2) in order to 'produce more robust data on police performance for the dual purpose of measuring performance and informing local decision-making' (Audit Commission, 2004: 4).

However, progress towards achieving uniformity in this area was slow. In 2003 and 2004 the Audit Commission tested the compliance of police forces with the NCRS and Home Office Counting Rules against a selection of crime categories and examined the management arrangements that were in place to secure compliance. In 2004 only 17 police forces met the standards required to secure a 'green rating' which meant that '60 per cent of forces have still to achieve the overall Home Office standard'. Four received a red rating. One of these was the Metropolitan Police Service whose area accounted for 18 per cent of all recorded crime (Audit Commission, 2004: 2–3). It was concluded that although there was evidence of 'clear corporate commitment to national standards, with strong leadership and sound policies in place in the majority of forces', there 'remain variations in the quality of crime data between forces. Improvements have not been achieved consistently across the country... In some forces the drive to implement victim-focused crime recording that was evident two years ago has lost some of its impetus' (Audit Commission, 2004: 3).

The social construction of crime statistics

An institutionalist perspective on crime statistics argues that they are socially constructed, the 'outcomes of social and institutional processes' (Coleman and Moynihan, 1996: 16).

The public's willingness to report crime varies considerably according to the nature of the offence that has been committed: thus whereas thefts of vehicles are almost always reported (95 per cent in 2003/4), attempted vehicle theft, vandalism and common assault are much less likely to be drawn to the attention of the police (34 per cent, 31 per cent and 30 per cent respectively in 2003/4) (Dodd et al., 2004: 3). This means that official crime statistics contain not a true account of crime that has been committed, but a selective record of those crimes that the public chose to report. In this sense they reflect the public reporting preferences.

A further aspect of social construction affects the way in which offences are defined and categorised. These decisions are determined by the police service and the courts, whose actions are influenced by organisational considerations (Moore, 1996: 210). As is argued in Chapter 1, the media plays an important role in the construction of moral panics, whereby certain activities typically committed by marginalised social groups are singled out and given excessive attention, one consequence of which is that police resources become targeted on these groups. The content of crime statistics may be influenced in a number of ways by activities of this nature. Targeted groups will become over-represented in police arrests, and what will be perceived as harassment and discrimination by those on the receiving end of these activities may create further crime through processes which include self-fulfilling prophecies and deviancy amplification spirals.

Long-term crime trends

Problems of this nature affect the validity of using official crime statistics as indicators of long-term crime trends. The Departmental Report into Crime Statistics chaired by Wilfred Perks in 1967 warned against the use of any single figure, and especially the total number of recorded offences, as a general measure of the trend of crime. Several issues affect the reliability of such a comparison:

- *Changing definitions of criminality*. The labelling of an action as 'criminal' is subject to variation across historical periods. Thus an act that constituted an offence in one decade may not be similarly construed in the following one. The introduction of legislation to legalise homosexual acts between males and abortion in the 1960s thus decriminalised actions which had formally constituted offences.

- *Alterations in recording procedures*. A Home Office decision to remove a particular category of offence from those which have to be officially notified may create a misleading impression that the overall level of crime has reduced. Similarly, an extension of the scale of notifiable offences may create an illusory perception that offending behaviour has increased. Crime figures are further influenced by procedural changes. For example, changes in recording practices introduced in 1998 created a statistical rise in crime of around 600,000 offences that was not an accurate reflection of the true situation. The introduction of the NCRS in 2002 was also expected to result in an increase in the volume of reported crime, in particular in connection with less serious violent offences (Simmons and Dodd, 2003).

- *Variations in people's ability or incentive to report crime*. Developments such as the increased use of the telephone and the insurance companies' insistence on a police record of an incident have all contributed to the increased reporting of crime. An increase of crime recorded in official statistics may therefore be due to increased reporting rather than any actual rise in the volume of criminal activity. In recent years the increased willingness to report violent crime has been put forward as one explanation for the increase in this type of crime: it was concluded that in 2002/3, around one-third of the increase in violent crime could be explained by the increased reporting of incidents (Smith and Allen, 2004).

- *Police actions*. Police targeting of particular crimes may have consequences which imply an increase in their volume. It is impossible to know, however, whether these crimes have actually increased in number or whether the police have become more diligent in detecting existing criminal activities.

Clear-up rates

Official figures also include information concerning the extent to which recorded crimes subsequently result in the apprehension of an offender. This 'clear-up' or detection rate is a major means for assessing the efficiency of the police service. However, as with the level of crime, statistics governing clear-up rates also provide a distorted picture of the operations of the criminal justice system

The circumstances under which a crime is deemed to be solved (or 'cleared up') are laid down by the Home Office (Home Office, 1991). These relate to those found guilty of the offence but also include those acquitted by a court. Additionally, offences are classified as cleared up when:

- there are practical hindrances to a prosecution including the absence of witnesses willing to give evidence;
- the offender or key witness has died;
- the offender, having admitted an offence, is under the age of criminal responsibility;
- the police or CPS consider no useful purpose would be served by proceeding with a charge;
- the nature of the crime does not warrant a prosecution, but can be responded to through other ways (for example, a caution).

In these cases, however, there should be sufficient evidence justifying the police charging a person with the offence in order for it to be classed as 'detected by other means'.

A person convicted of an offence may also ask for the court to take similar crimes into consideration. What are termed 'secondary detections' enabled crimes to be recorded as 'cleared up' even though there may be no evidence to associate them with the person who admits to having carried them out. Those who ask for offences to be 'taken into consideration' do so for reasons that include the hope this will secure a lighter sentence.

The usefulness of crime statistics

The above discussion might suggest that official crime statistics have little value to those wishing to study crime and deviance. This impression would not, however, be totally accurate, since these figures do convey useful information both to those who work within the criminal justice system and those wishing to study its operations from outside. The information can be employed in two ways:

- *Crime pattern analysis.* Crime reports form the basis of crime pattern analysis, which seeks to establish trends in criminal activity in order both to prevent future occurrences and aid detection. Such analysis may be conducted locally or nationally. The National Criminal Intelligence Service conducts crime pattern analysis on a national basis to cover crimes that occur in different police force areas. Criminals may be identified by their peculiar trade marks (or modus operandi).

- *Omisions are revealing.* Useful information may be gleaned from omissions in crime statistics. The under-reporting of certain types of crime such as sexual violence may provide valid information concerning victims' perception of the operations of agencies within the criminal justice system. Conversely, changes in the rates at which certain crimes are reported may mirror improvements to the working practices of key bodies that operate within the system. It has been concluded that statistical products of this kind may reveal more about changing attitudes and decision-making of those involved in the process than about changes in offending behaviour itself (Bottomley and Pease, 1986). The tendency for such figures to be dominated by working-class crimes may also reveal a traditional desire to control the working class through the process of criminalisation. Middle-class, corporate and white-collar crimes, which typically pose no threat to society's fundamental values or interests, may be relatively ignored by the police.

> Why do crime statistics fail to provide an accurate assessment of the extent of crime in society?

Alternative studies of criminal activity

Victimisation surveys

Victimisation surveys have been used in official studies such as the British Crime Survey which have been published biannually since 1992 and annually since 2001/2. Each survey involved interviewing a randomly selected representative sample of the public (currently around 40,000 persons aged 16 and above) to ascertain information relating to their experience of victimisation during the previous year (although some categories of crime are omitted from the statistics). This sample was initially based upon the electoral register but since 1992 has utilised the postcode address file.

Since surveys of this nature are unaffected by changes to reporting and recording practices which affect official crime statistics, they are of greater use than the official figures in providing a measurement of national crime trends. Additionally, the existence of data derived from this source makes it possible to contrast comparable categories of crime used by both the police and the British Crime Survey, and in particular to obtain information on crimes which are either not reported or not recorded by the police. In 1992 it was estimated that incomplete reporting and recording resulted in only about 30 per cent of crimes being officially recorded (Home Office, 1992). It was later suggested that 16.4 million crimes had been committed in 1997, whereas the official statistics stated that, in the twelve months that ended in March 1998, only 4.5 million crimes had been committed (Home Office, 1998a). In 2003/4, the BCS estimated that approximately 11.7 million crimes had been committed against adults living in private households compared to the 5.9 million crimes recorded by the police (Dodd et al., 2004: 8–9).

One explanation for this has been the way official statistics counted incidents as opposed to victims. As has been noted above, until changes were introduced in 1998, official statistics classified an episode with several victims as one incident, whereas victimisation surveys would record it as several thus suggesting a higher level of crime. Additionally, victims of crimes such as racial violence may be more willing to reveal details of such incidents to those conducting victimisation surveys than to the police – possibly as they lack confidence that the criminal justice system will deal with their complaint justly.

A number of other problems affect the reliability of victimisation studies. They exclude 'victimless crimes' such as drug-dealing and serious crimes such as murder where there is no victim who can be interviewed (Dodd et al., 2004: 33). They are further distorted by the impossibility of obtaining a representative sample of victims of different categories of crime, and are influenced by what is termed 'forward and backward telescoping' (Coleman and Moynihan, 1996: 77–9). These terms refer to the reporting of an incident that occurred outside the period that is being surveyed, or a failure to remember minor incidents that took place during that time. Such studies also rely on the accuracy of a person's perception that a particular problem qualified as a crime.

It has thus been concluded that such studies provide only selective information on crime. They generate data on certain crimes, particularly of the type which enter into official statistics (Box, 1981: 164), but offences such as domestic violence or sexual assault which are often not reported to the police are also under-reported in victimisation surveys (Walklate, 1989), and for this reason are excluded from British Crime Survey estimates (Dodd et al., 2004: 33).

These surveys also fail to include crimes that were unobserved or apparently victimless. This latter problem may be addressed by self-report studies that present a further alternative to official statistics for the collection of crime data.

Self-report studies

Self-report studies ask individuals to record their own criminal activities. They typically consist of a series of questions addressed to selected groups asking them about their personal involvement in criminal or rule-breaking behaviour. These studies are not intended to address a representative sample of the population, and they rely on the honesty of persons responding to the survey who may choose to exaggerate or downplay their involvement in such activities. Yet despite these reservations they can still prove valuable.

They have elicited important information particularly connected with youth culture that suggests certain activities such as shoplifting or drug taking are relatively widespread (Farrington, 1989; Mott and Mirrlees-Black, 1993). They have also provided information on victimless crimes and offences conducted within the privacy of a home, such as child abuse. However, they often secure information on trivial offences that constitute minor infractions of the law not regarded as crimes by those who perpetrate them – such as using a work telephone to make a private call.

A recent study using self-reporting methods was the Crime and Justice Survey that was introduced in 2003. This was based upon interviews with around 12,000 people aged between 10 and 65 in England and Wales. Its findings suggested that there were around 3.8 million active offenders (defined as persons who committed at least one offence in the previous year). Those defined as 'serious or prolific offenders' (those who committed six or more offences in the previous year) were said to comprise about 2 per cent of the population but accounted for around 82 per cent of all crime (Budd and Sharp, 2005).

> Using examples of your own, compare and contrast the ways in which victim surveys and self-report studies seek to ascertain the extent of crime in society. What are the strengths and weaknesses of these two methodologies?

Participant observation

Another methodology used to elicit information concerning crime is that of direct or participant observation. This may be conducted by teams of case workers observing and keeping records on the activities of a selected group of persons, or by researchers closely involving themselves with an organisation such as a juvenile gang, perhaps by infiltrating it and acting as 'flies on the wall'.

Gathering information in this manner is time consuming and costly. Its reliability is influenced by the subjective interpretation placed upon any event by an observer and the researcher's need to retain a relationship with the subjects of the study. Ethical dilemmas may also arise from this situation, since a person who observes a crime being committed but fails to report it effectively becomes an accessory to that act.

White-collar, middle-class and corporate crime

Official crime statistics suggest that crime is predominantly associated with the lower classes. The theories concerned with crime that have been discussed in Chapter 1 therefore concentrate on providing explanations for crimes committed by such people. Such a preoccupation with lower-class crime implies that different forms of crime committed by the more 'respectable' members of society do not constitute a significant form of criminal activity. This view was, however, challenged by critical criminology that asserted that 'different social groups are treated differently for behaviour which is objectively identical' (Fattah, 1997: 177). For example, benefit fraud and tax evasion both entail a loss of revenue for the state but the former (which is identified with poorer persons at the lower end of the social scale) is proceeded against more vigorously.

Definition of white-collar, middle-class and corporate crime

The traditional neglect of crime other than that committed by the working class was challenged in the 1940s by Edwin Sutherland. He pioneered the concept of white-collar crime that he defined as 'a crime committed by a person of respectability and high social status in the course of his occupation' (Sutherland, 1949: 9).

This definition covered a broad range of activities some of which were local and others that were transacted on a global scale. It advanced the agenda of criminology into areas that were not traditionally its concern (such as financial regulation, health and safety and consumer affairs) (Croall, 2001: 2), some of which were regulated by civil rather than criminal law (Tappan, 1977). This definition also raised numerous problems which included the definition which should be given to terms used by Sutherland such as 'respectability' and 'high social status', and led to alternative classifications being provided for crimes of this nature which included 'occupational crime' (Quinney, 1977) or the abuse of trust inherent in an occupational role (Schapiro, 1990).

A useful categorisation of crime of this nature is as follows:

- *White-collar crime*. The term 'occupational crime' may also be used to describe activities which seek to advantage the perpetrator – who may be of any social status, thereby including 'blue-collar' occupational crime – at the expense of the employer or the employer's customers.
- *Corporate crime*. Sometimes referred to as 'organisational crime', this typically involves a form of collective rule breaking which is designed to advance organisational goals (Clinard, 1983). The term embraces a number of wrongdoings which include administrative, environmental,

financial, labour and manufacturing violations and unfair trade practices (Clinard and Yeager, 1980: 113–16).

- *Middle-class crime*. This refers to crime committed by persons of respectability and status but not within the workplace (Muncie and McLaughlin, 1996: 241): examples of this include insurance fraud (Clarke, 1989) and tax evasion (Croall, 1992), although some aspects of the latter practice are associated with the working environment of the self-employed and small business sector.

Economic crime

The diverse activities associated with white-collar, corporate and middle-class crime have been classified as 'economic crime'.

This term embraces a wide range of activities – asset misappropriation, bribery, cheque and credit card fraud, corruption, cybercrime, identity theft, insurance theft, money laundering, procurement fraud, product counterfeiting, revenue and VAT fraud (Robson Rhodes, 2004).

White-collar crime disadvantages a commercial enterprise by reducing its profits through theft, whereas corporate crime may be viewed as an indispensable activity enabling commerce and business to thrive. For example, big business may sometimes resort to bribing politicians or political parties in order to secure lucrative contracts abroad or to further their interests at home; manufacturers may market products containing potentially lethal faults since to correct them would be very costly for the company which would, rather, take its chance in a successful defence of any claim against it pursued through the courts. It follows, therefore, that the direct victim of white-collar and corporate crime is likely to be different. While the corporation suffers from white-collar crime, weaker and underprivileged groups – and ultimately society as a whole – may suffer as the result of corporate crime that may thus be viewed as the criminal activity of the powerful victimising the powerless.

However, the extent to which different motives underpin the actions of individuals who commit white-collar and corporate crime has been questioned. The desire for personal advancement may explain the latter as well as the former activity. It has been suggested that the inducement to commit corporate crime does not derive from a collective mentality but, rather, from the attitudes of a minority of employees who may see such rule-breaking as the means to personal gain such as promotion (Croall, 1992: 49).

The scale of white-collar, corporate and middle-class crime

White-collar and corporate crimes traditionally have a low visibility in official crime statistics but some criminologists have asserted both the large scale of these activities and the problems that they pose for society. Sutherland drew attention to the financial cost of white-collar crime (Sutherland, 1949: 12). In America it was estimated that in 1977 the economic losses from various forms of corporate crime were around $40 billion compared to $3–4 billion from 'ordinary' crimes (Conklin, 1977: 4). More recent estimates suggested that the annual cost of white-collar crime in America was $415 billion compared to $13 billion as the annual estimated cost of street crime (Barkan, 1997), and that activities including embezzlement, fraud, money laundering and corruption cost British businesses around £32 billion in 2003 and an additional £8 billion trying to combat these problems (Robson Rhodes, 2004). It has therefore been concluded that 'white-collar crimes exact a heavy aggregate toll, one that dwarfs comparable losses to street criminals' (Shover, 1998: 140).

Loss of life may also be occasioned by activities that are typically associated with business corporations. 'Corporate crime kills' (Box, 1983). At Bhopal, India, in 1984 the release of methyl isocyanate into the atmosphere resulted in several thousand deaths and many more injuries. Violations of safety regulations are a regular cause of accidents and fatalities at work. Consumers may also suffer from business practices which place profits before health and safety concerns.

White-collar and corporate crime in the twentieth century

The extent of white-collar and corporate crime has been influenced by various developments affecting the operations of postwar capitalism, including the following:

- *The divorce of ownership and control.* In most commercial concerns there is no single entrepreneur in total charge of all aspects of a company's affairs, and this has facilitated employees throughout the hierarchy exploiting their enhanced autonomy to undertake illicit actions. Additionally, owing to the spread of responsibility in large and complex business organisations, senior executives are often unaware of criminal undertakings being undertaken within the organisation. However, the diffusion of responsibility may abet corporate crime since the absence of a single person responsible for taking decisions may make it impossible to pinpoint the blame for corporate wrongdoings.

- *Market forces.* The emphasis on market forces in post-industrial capitalist societies has induced some firms to seek a competitive edge over their rivals by various criminal practices. These include industrial espionage, law or rule violation to the detriment of employers, consumers or society as a whole, fraud and entering into corrupt relationships with politicians in order to secure privileges such as government contracts.

- *Deregulation.* This entails government removing regulations affecting the conduct of business in order to encourage efficiency through increased competitiveness. In the United Kingdom, the 1986 Financial Services Act was responsible for deregulating the retail financial services sector. This measure (coupled with other Conservative policies affecting pension entitlements) encouraged pension providers to expand their operations. Public-sector workers who were members of pension schemes were especially targeted by aggressive sales techniques, seeking to secure their transfer to private schemes about which false and misleading information was provided. In 1998 the new Regulatory Body, the Financial Services Authority estimated that the cost of offences committed by pension providers amounted to £11 billion (quoted in Slapper and Tombs, 1999: 63). Other aspects of this policy (for example, the deregulation of the money markets) have also increased the scope for illicit activities.

- *Information and communications technology.* Developments in electronic communications have made companies more prone to abuses. These may be committed by their employees, ranging from illicit 'surfing the net' to more complex forms of theft and vandalism such as introducing viruses into computer systems, and also by outsiders who may 'hack' into a computer system and tamper with electronic records. The growth of technology and international finance has also led to big increases in white-collar crime such as stock market fraud.

- *Organised crime.* Organised crime traverses national boundaries and in particular takes advantage of countries with lax laws to counter money laundering. One estimate suggested that between £25 and £40 billion pounds of dirty money is laundered in the UK each year (Moore, 2004). Although money laundering rules have been introduced in the UK to cover financial institutions, a particular problem relates to those who provide specified services (such as acting as a director, nominee shareholder, secretary or trustee) to trusts and unlisted companies who are not subject to an effective supervisory regime. The lack of effective regulation of these service providers rather than the companies or trusts themselves through which money may be laundered was deemed to be important since they are in a position to ensure that those for whom they provide services act lawfully (Transparency International (UK), 2004).

Cybercrime

The growth of information technology has affected the scope and nature of crime. It has given rise to cybercrime, which broadly refers to crime involving the use of computers (Furnell, 2002: 21). There are two main forms of computer-related crime – computer-assisted crime (in which computers are utilised to carry out crimes which pre-dated their existence, such as fraud and theft) and computer-focused crime (in which computer technology has resulted in the emergence of new crimes, such as hacking and viruses) (Furnell, 2002: 22).

Although cybercrime can be carried out by any individual it is an activity which was initially identified with white-collar criminals since much of it occurred within the setting of the organisation which was directly affected by it: one estimate suggested that around 85 per cent of reported incidents were carried out by internal perpetrators and 15 per cent by external ones (Audit Commission, 1994). Affected companies suffered from several problems that included financial loss, disruption of their services, loss of data and damage to their reputation (Furnell, 2002: 28). Subsequently, however, the gap was reported to have narrowed, to a figure of 61 per cent and 39 per cent respectively (Audit Commission, 1998).

There are a number of activities associated with cybercrime. It includes attempts to obtain a person's bank or credit card details. One way to achieve this involves cash machine (ATM) fraud. This has become increasingly sophisticated through the use of devices such as computerised 'card readers' ('skimmers') which can siphon thousands of pounds from individual bank accounts by reading the data stored on the magnetic strip of cash cards and placing them on cloned cards of their own. Although individual account holders are the initial victims of this crime, the banks are required to return the cash to customers unless they can prove the individual has been negligent. In 2003 ATM fraud cost the banks £40 million, compared to £6 million in 1997 (Collinson, 2004).

On-line shopping and banking have opened further avenues to criminals, who often operate as organised gangs. Their activities include phishing whereby customers of a bank get a bogus e-mail purporting to come from the bank in response to which they give an array of personal information including card details, PIN numbers and passwords that criminals use to their own advantages. A further example is 'wi-fi' technology, whereby people using laptops or mobiles to access websites are diverted to bogus base stations (termed 'evil twins') that can obtain and transmit bank details and other personal information which can be put to criminal use. Keylogging may also be employed to extract personal information. This entails a virus being planted on a computer that is transmitted through an e-mail. This virus then spies on that computer and extracts an array of personal information about the user that can be used for illicit purposes. Computers attacked in this way can also be networked as a bot net and used to bombard a company's website causing it to crash. Bot netting is a global phenomenon and the aim is usually to extort money from the company to get the attacks to cease in order to avoid bankruptcy.

The regulation of white-collar, corporate and middle-class crime

It is widely assumed that there is an official reluctance to prosecute white-collar, corporate and middle-class offenders, and that the penalties meted out are inadequate when they are proceeded against. This situation has a number of social disadvantages. In particular, the existence of crime of this nature may legitimise other forms of criminal activity. Knowledge of corporate crime, for example, may encourage employees to pursue white-collar crime to their own advantage or it may make 'ordinary' criminal activity by other members of society seem justifiable. The spectre of apparently respectable entrepreneurs, financiers, business people and politicians acting improperly may destroy popular trust in finance, commerce and government, and encourage an attitude of 'what's good for them is also good for me'. In this sense it has been concluded that 'as long as legislators and administrators of criminal justice fail to take appropriate measures against white-collar crime, it is nonsensical to expect the penal system to be successful in its fight against the ordinary thief and burglar and small fry' (Mannheim, 1946: 119).

The reality of corporate crime

'Death and injury in the workplace are serious problems. It has been esti-mated that in the last ten years, 3,759 people have been killed in sudden deaths and over 205,000 have suffered major injuries at the workplace. Each year, 20,000 also die from industrial diseases, including 3–12,000 from occupational cancer' (information derived from miscellaneous sources, quoted in Bergman, 2000: 31).

Consumers are also at risk from corporate activities. 'Each year, over 1,100 people are killed and 1,390,000 injured as the result of home-based consumer products such as furniture, cooking appliances or toys. In addi-tion, it is estimated that, annually, almost 400 people are killed and 36,000 injured from the use of medicines' (information derived from miscellaneous sources, quoted in Bergman, 2000: 31).

It has also been estimated that 'in the last six years, 92 passengers, 50 railway staff and 74 others have been killed on the railways', that between 1992 and 1997, '144 crew members working on merchant ships or fishing vessels were killed', and that between 1993 and 1997 '2,424 crew members and 486 members of the public were injured' on merchant ships and three members of the public died. Although there are no figures relating to the numbers killed or injured as the result of the public being exposed to toxic chemicals emitted through corporate activities, it was likely that 'thousands' were affected (information derived from miscellaneous sources, quoted in Bergman, 2000: 33).

However, very few incidents resulting from corporate harm are made the subject of any criminal investigation. This includes around 88 per cent of major workplace injuries, virtually all deaths and injuries resulting from the use of dangerous products or medicines and all occupational and environ-mental diseases (Bergman, 2000: 11). Although the formal role of the police in investigating deaths at work was developed in 1998, below 2 per cent of these deaths are referred to the CPS (Bergman, 2000: 31).

The following section considers the reasons for the apparent indifference of the state towards white-collar, corporate and middle-class crime.

Is it criminal ?

White-collar, corporate and middle-class crime covers an extremely broad range of activities, many of which are not perceived as criminal by those who undertake them. For example, the actions of an employee who uses a telephone to make a personal call at work may be balanced by him or her using their home telephone to transact work-related business. Further, although the criminal law caters for some serious white-collar offences (such as fraud), many activities associated with white-collar and corporate crime are covered by regulatory rather than criminal law which classes offences as technical violations rather than transgressions which are essentially criminal (Croall, 2001: 105).

The application of the criminal law to corporate activities poses further problems, as follows:

- *Corporate activities are sometimes immoral rather than blatantly illegal.* This includes activities such as paying low wages to workers employed in developing nations, or charging excessive and unjustifiable prices for goods or services.

- *Corporate crime often exploits loopholes or grey areas in the law.* Companies may find ways to evade the spirit or strict letter of the law or undertake activities which are not illegal but are not sanctioned by the law either. An example of the former concerns the activities of UK arms manufacturers who have been able to evade post-Cold War arms embargoes through practices that include arms brokering or licensed production. Neither requires export licenses and thus enable arms manufacturers to evade embargoes (Oxfam, 1999).

Not socially threatening

Unlike 'ordinary crime' (which threatens the work ethic) white-collar, corporate and middle-class crime poses no fundamental threat to capitalist society or its underlying cultural values which 'support the aggressive, individualistic pursuit of monetary success' (Croall, 2001: 79) and the importance of maximising profits. Corporate crime in particular must be seen within the political context of the wider political economy (Slapper and Tombs, 1999: 160). This may result in police resources not being sufficiently focused on detecting such activities.

Not condemned by the general public

Many serious criminal activities (especially those involving violence) are viewed as wrong by most members of society who thus approve punitive measures against the perpetrators. Many forms of white-collar and middle-class crime, however, fail to excite such prejudices and the public may be tolerant towards some who carry out such activities, and even be envious of them. Additionally, the media tends to focus on sensational crimes involving violence and in general is less interested in white-collar, corporate and middle-class crime. This may influence the public's perception of the relative importance of crimes of this nature.

Difficult to detect, investigate and prosecute

White-collar, middle-class and corporate crimes are often difficult to discover. White-collar and corporate crime may involve numerous transactions carried out by a small number of senior company executives over a protracted period. This makes transgressions both complex and costly to investigate and may make it hard to prove them. Additionally, the detection of middle-class crime is often impeded by it being 'victimless' in the sense that it lacks a tangible victim. However, this is not always the case: fraud, for example, has a profound effect on those who are subject to it (Levi, 1999: 6–7). A further difficulty affecting prosecution is that it may not always be clear whether a wrongdoing committed by a corporation or its executives was based on criminality or arose from incompetence or hard luck.

These factors may mean that there is often an absence of knowledge that any offence has been committed, even though it may become apparent later. In the UK, threats of libel actions may discourage investigations into corporate activities by researchers or investigative journalists, and the intricate nature of some forms of corporate activity may make it very hard for an outsider to investigate and draw up evidence that could form of the basis of a trial and subsequent conviction.

Inadequate police resources

The investigation of white-collar, corporate and middle-class crime is carried out by a large number of agencies that include the police service, Inland Revenue and Customs and Excise. Regulatory control is exercised by a wide range of inspectorates

Fraud is dealt with by the fraud squads of individual police forces. The perception that local fraud offices were understaffed led to the Partners in Crime Scheme that was introduced in March 2002. This sought to bring police and private investigators together to fight fraud that was estimated to total £12 billion a year.

Additionally, a national unit, the Serious Fraud Office, was established (on the recommendation of the 1983 Roskill Committee) by the 1987 Criminal Justice Act to investigate large frauds that amounted to more than £1 million (a level which was subsequently raised to £5 million and latterly to £6 million). Its image has been undermined by failures affecting a number of high-profile cases which it was responsible for bringing to crown court. One of these concerned the Brent Walker case in which George Walker was charged with orchestrating a £19 million fraud at his company. 'The case took three years to bring to court, lasted four and a half months and probably cost the taxpayer £40 million'. In 1994, after seven days deliberation, the jury cleared Walker of any wrongdoing, although the company's former finance director was found guilty on one charge of false accounting involving £2.5 million (Widlake, 1995: xi–xii).

Reluctance to report

A certain degree of white-collar crime may be regarded as acceptable by a company (possibly viewed as 'perks' in the interests of good labour relations), which seeks to make good its losses from other sources, particularly consumers. A company that benefits from corporate crime will lack incentives to report or seek official action against activities of this nature unless they become public knowledge. In this case there is likely to be an attempt to blame what might be common practice within that organisation to the errant activity of a single employee.

Regulatory supervision

The actions of corporations may be subject to regulatory supervision or to the criminal law.

Problems that have been referred to above concerning the traditional reluctance of the state to intervene regarding corporate crime have resulted in the activities of companies being subjected to regulatory rather than criminal law. Although sanctions may still be applied to companies in breach of requirements laid down by regulatory law, transgressions of this nature are not regarded as criminal offences. Regulation may be imposed by self-regulation or it may be discharged by outside bodies.

Self-regulation

The activities of corporations are sometimes controlled by self-regulation rather than by legislation. Insider trading, for example, was historically dealt with in this manner in the UK until the passage of the 1994 Criminal Justice Act. There are several advantages of this approach that may be voluntary or enforced. Self-regulation avoids the 'delay, red tape and stultification of innovation associated with external regulation' (Ayres and Braithwaite, 1992: 106). 'Insiders' may possess a better grasp of corporate practices than those not intimately involved with a commercial undertaking and are thus best placed to spot wrongdoings. They may also be better placed to conduct more frequent and detailed investigations than external regulators (Braithwaite and Fisse, 1987: 222–4).

External regulation

A number of statutes or other forms of regulations impose regulatory controls over the conduct of commercial activities in order to protect consumers or workers employed in the industry. These include the 1974 Health and Safety at Work Act, the 1994 General Product Safety Regulations, the 1988 Merchant Shipping Act, the 1989 Air Navigation Order, the 1990 Environmental Protection Act and the 1991 Water Resources Act (Bergman, 2000: 55). These are enforced by a wide range of bodies, examples of which include the Health and Safety Executive, the Environment Agency, the Office of Fair Trading, and local authority trading standards departments and environmental health departments. There are, however, several weaknesses associated with this form of external control over corporate activities. These include the following:

- *Reluctance to prosecute.* Regulatory bodies often seek to secure compliance with laws and regulations through ways other than prosecution, which is frequently used only as a last resort when other courses of action have failed (Croall, 2001: 104–5).

- *Regulatory bodies possess insufficient powers.* Limits on the personnel employed and powers possessed by external regulatory bodies may prevent effective action against corporate abuses. Criticism has been directed against the record of the Health and Safety Executive in investigating deaths and injuries on building construction sites and prosecuting those responsible (Rayner, 2000). In August 2000 the House of Commons Public Accounts Committee referred to the view of the Office of Fair Trading that although unroadworthy vehicles had caused over 300 deaths in 1999, it lacked sufficient powers to deal with rogue car traders (Public Accounts Committee, 2000). Attempts have, however, been made to improve upon the regulation of corporations. The 2003 Water Act established the Water Services Regulatory Authority that (when operating in 2006) will be empowered to fine water or sewerage companies up to 10 per cent of their turnover if they failed to meet their standards of performance.

Inadequate penalties

The penalties associated with corporate crime are frequently small and fail to provide an effective deterrent to the commission of actions of this nature. Businesses whose actions have caused injury or death to their customers may be punished by a fine, the level of which often fails to mirror the seriousness of the wrongdoing and which may, in any case, be recouped by levying higher charges on clients or consumers.

For example, the penalties associated with causing pollution are woefully inadequate, since criminal law is predicated on the existence of a direct victim who can be seen to have suffered as the result of a criminal action, as opposed to less perceptible damage to society as a whole. An additional problem is the reluctance of magistrates to make full use of their powers when dealing with issues affecting the environment such as river pollution.

Additionally, a range of factors may aid corporation executives who are brought before a criminal court. These include resources to pay for good lawyers and the ability of the judge to take the defendant's 'respectable' character and reputation into account when passing sentence.

The issue of penalties is inevitably associated with the aims of punishment. As Chapter 7 argues, punishment can be associated with several objectives, including exacting retribution on wrongdoers, deterrence, incapacitation or rehabilitation. The diverse nature of these aims can be illustrated in connection with corporate wrongdoings.

The external regulation of corporate activity is frequently associated with punitive aims, whereas self-regulation is primarily motivated to deter (Slapper and Tombs, 1999: 184). Incapacitation, when applied to corporations, may range from placing restrictions on the charter of a company to placing it in public ownership or in the hands of a receiver (Braithwaite and

Geis, 1982: 307). It has been argued that rehabilitation is an especially effective response to corporate crime since 'criminogenic organizational structures are more malleable than are criminogenic human personalities' (Braithwaite and Geis, 1982: 310). Rehabilitation may be secured through means that include reintegrative shaming. An example of this approach was pursued by the UK Environment Agency that adopted a 'name and shame' approach in 1999 by publishing a pollution directory containing the names and locations of factories that caused pollution. This was designed to make industrial concerns adopt more socially responsible practices.

The criminal law

When persons are injured or killed by corporate activities it may be possible for the state to initiate a criminal prosecution. The most serious charge would be that of manslaughter. However, a criminal prosecution for corporate manslaughter will only succeed if it can be proved that the action undertaken by the organisation was deliberately fashioned to cause such a result, and, additionally, that a senior executive within a company could be pinpointed as having been responsible for the incident. This frequently leads to occurrences of this nature being the subject of a lesser charge (such as breaching health and safety regulations) or being dismissed as unfortunate 'accidents'. There have thus been only three successful prosecutions for corporate manslaughter (Wintour, 2004).

Public unease about episodes which included the sinking of the ferry the *Herald of Free Enterprise* (in which 192 died) and the King's Cross underground fire (which killed 31 people) in 1987, the fire on the Piper Alpha oil rig and the Clapham rail crash in 1988 (in which 167 and 37 persons died), and the *Marchioness* river boat sinking in 1989 (in which 51 people perished when the ship collided with the dredger, the *Bowbelle*) prompted a review of the existing law by the Law Commission. This put forward a proposal to replace the existing offence of corporate manslaughter with a new offence of corporate killing in which a jury would be asked to decide whether there had been a management failure, whether this was one of the causes of the person's death and whether this management failure 'fell far below what could reasonably be expected of the corporation in the circumstances' (Law Commission, 1996).

The government published a response to this (Home Office, 2000) and although no action was immediately forthcoming, further tragedies such as the 1999 Paddington rail disaster (in which 32 people died) and the 2000 Hatfield rail disaster (where an unrepaired broken rail caused the deaths of four people) reignited the debate. In the latter case, charges against the former chief executive of Railtrack and two other managers were dropped before the main trial when a High Court judge ruled there was insufficient evidence that this accident was due to profit having been put before safety. In 2004 the Prime Minister promised to bring forward legislation to provide for the offence of corporate manslaughter whereby company directors would be responsible for deaths due to management failure.

An additional reform was provided by the 2003 Criminal Justice Act. This measure permitted the removal of juries in fraud trials in some cases. This is discussed in Chapter 5.

Is white-collar crime trivial?

Much white-collar crime is perceived to be of a trivial nature, such as using a firm's telephone for a private call or taking home some office stationery. This calls into question whether such actions can be classed as criminal. However, the cumulative effect of behaviour of this kind can be quite costly. In 1999 it was estimated that if every British worker stole the following the annual cost to business would be:

● Bic ballpoint	£5.75 million
● HB pencil	£4.3 million
● Diskette	£5.4 million
● Envelope	£822,000
● Postage on 1 gas bill	£7.1 million
● Small Pritt stick	£27.1 million
● One minute on the Internet	£822,000
● 10 minutes on the phone at peak time	£21.6 million

Figures taken from *The Guardian*, 1 September 1999.

'White-collar, corporate and middle-class crime is a serious problem in contemporary society but is not taken seriously by the state.' To what extent do you agree with this statement, and how do you account for this perception?

Explanations of white-collar, corporate and middle-class crime

Interest in white-collar and corporate crime derive from nineteenth-century concerns regarding the crimes of the privileged and powerful and, in America, became associated with the populist tradition (Slapper and Tombs, 1999: 2). However, the study of white-collar and corporate crime has been neglected in traditional criminology that is most concerned to provide an understanding of the causes of male working-class crime. Some research linked white-collar and corporate crime with the individual pathology of those who committed it (Clinard, 1946), viewing psychological traits or aspects of personality such as greed, ruthlessness, lack of moral scruples and willingness to gamble as explanations for this behaviour. This approach may be criticised for individualising the causes of white-collar and corporate crime, whereas as others have stressed the importance of institutionalised practices within an organisation in connection with both white-collar (Sutherland, 1939) and corporate crime (Punch, 1996).

In addition, some of the theories discussed in Chapter 1 may be capable of adaptation to explain the causes of white-collar, corporate and middle-class crime.

Differential association

Sutherland's theory of differential association was based on social learning theory and argued that criminal behaviour was learned in a social setting. As was noted in Chapter 1, although this thesis can be applied to all crime, it was designed to explain white-collar crime (Sutherland, 1939), viewing the workplace as the social setting in which new employees were directly educated into criminal activity by other employees (if this was endemic to the organisation). Alternatively, new employees might determine the scope for these activities within the culture of the organisation and then indulge in them themselves.

Social control theories

Control balance theory asserts a link between crime and the power that an individual possesses in his or her relationships with others. A surplus of control may induce the powerful to extend the scope of their domination in situations in which there exists a trigger for their behaviour, the opportunity to commit an illicit act and the absence of constraints on this behaviour (Tittle, 1995; 2000). This may serve as an explanation for white-collar, corporate and middle-class crime, in which greed is an important underpinning to this behaviour. One solution to this situation is the redistribution of power to create a more egalitarian society in which surpluses (and also deficits) of power are eliminated (Braithwaite, 1997).

Marxist and critical criminologies

Marxist criminology proposes that white-collar, corporate and middle-class crime does not pose a fundamental threat to the capitalist economic system and, in particular, corporate crime may be driven by the worthy capitalist objective of maximising profits. This may explain why the process of criminalisation has not been traditionally directed at those who carry out such activities. Critical criminology particularly links crime committed by all social classes to the values identified with the post-industrial market society (Currie, 1997: 163). It is argued that this has bred a 'dog eat dog' attitude in which individuals seek wealth or profits regardless of the effect which their activities have upon others.

Anomie theory

Although Durkheim linked crime to structural inequalities, it might be argued that the successes which some enjoy during the boom period of capitalism will generate ambitions to profit to an even greater extent, which results in illegal conduct – 'wealth, exalting the individual, may always arouse the spirit of rebellion which is the very source of immorality' (Durkheim, 1897/1979: 254, quoted in Slapper and Tombs, 1999: 133). Additionally, it might be argued that corporate crime emerged in a period of normlessness during the first half of the twentieth century when the practices of emerging large-scale commercial concerns were not subject to established laws and regulations (Slapper and Tombs, 1999: 113).

Merton's theory of anomie may also be relevant to explaining white-collar and corporate crime, which emphasises the importance of innovation to attain success goals. Although he associated this approach with the actions of those at the lower end of the social ladder, it could also be adapted to account for attempts by those higher up the social scale to maintain or improve their social status. It has thus been argued to be of relevance in explaining corporate crime (Passas, 1990). Corporate crime may be seen as a deviant response to the strain experienced by an individual to succeed in a corporate setting (by pursuing actions directed at maximising the profits of the organisation) when confronted with obstacles that prevented the attainment of such goals. Although these criminal actions may be to the advantage of the organisation rather than to the individual, the latter may also directly benefit from rewards such as bonuses or promotion.

Individual choice

Conservative criminology suggests that innate impulses such as greed can be held responsible for white-collar, corporate and middle-class crime. This perspective also views crime as a rational activity that could be applied in order to advance the interests of an individual, a company, or both. Control theory also stresses the innate nature of crime that is viewed as being underpinned by rational choice seeking to promote self-interest. It attaches the presence or absence of formal controls over an individual's behaviour as a key element dictating his or her decision to comply with the law or commit crime (Hirschi, 1969). Factors that include the degree of autonomy possessed by employees and the importance attached by a company's management to abiding by the law (Braithwaite, 1985) might thus influence the level of crime. This approach has, however, been criticised for ignoring the impact of external social and economic forces on an individual's decision to commit crime (Croall, 1998).

Neutralisation

The techniques of neutralisation (Sykes and Matza, 1957) may serve both to justify and rationalise criminal activity. The collective nature of decision-making in large organisations may make it possible for individuals to deny their personal responsibility and guilt for criminal activity, particularly when those who suffer from it are thousands of miles away.

- *Subcultural theory*. Companies may develop their own ethical standards of behaviour. This implies that white-collar and corporate crime is viewed as a normal and legitimate activity within the organisational setting in which it occurs. These are condoned by senior management thus giving rise to a subculture of law-breaking.

- *Left realism.* The concept of relative deprivation was influential in left realist criminology (Lea and Young, 1993). The self-comparison with others in the same or a different social category in terms of pay, position or status could provide an explanation for crime committed by members drawn from any social class. This view is, however, less readily adaptable to crime designed to further corporate interests.

Political crime

Crime committed by persons of respectability also embraces political crime. This form of activity may involve a wide range of actions, some aspects of which are briefly discussed below.

Illicit activity conducted by national governments

Illicit activity carried out by national government is typically carried out by state agents (such as ministers, civil servants, members of security services, police officers or the military) or by third parties who are recruited to act on its behalf and may be underpinned by the motive of seeking to advance the national interest. Actions of this nature may include the deliberate breach of national or international agreements by politicians, their aides or officials (as was the case, for example, with the Iran-Contra policy conducted by members of President Reagan's staff during the 1980s).

The climate of official secrecy in the UK may abet attempts by governments to carry out clandestine actions of this nature. One high-profile example of this was the connivance by a government department, the Department of Trade and Industry, to allow a manufacturing firm, Matrix-Churchill, to export materials to Iraq that could be used in the manufacture of arms. The difficulty with this action was that the government had imposed an arms embargo on both protagonists in the Iran–Iraq war during the 1980s. When the firm was prosecuted in 1992, five ministers signed Public Interest Immunity Certificates in an attempt to ensure that documents showing that the government was acting in contravention of its own embargo would not be available to the defence. The government's conduct in this matter was described as 'akin to a criminal conspiracy' (Harris, 2003: 101–2).

Governments may also carry out acts of violence to further their own political purposes. Violence of this nature is differentiated from the legitimate use of coercive powers possessed by a state to enforce its laws and protect its citizens, and also from its accepted right under international law to utilise violence against external threats (in which case the violence is theoretically performed in accordance with international agreements, the 'laws of war'). Although states are frequently the target of campaigns involving the use of violence to further a political cause, occasionally, states or governments may resort to illegitimate forms of violence to further their own ends. This may be directed against their internal or external opponents and take forms which include murder/assassination, genocide/ethnic cleansing, torture and 'proxy terrorism'.

Actions intended to further a politician's individual interests

Typically, illicit political activities pursued by individual politicians involve abuse of power and corruption. Although personal advantage in the sense of material gain, sexual gratification or career advancement is frequently the prime aim of actions of this nature, they may also be designed to further the interests of a political party or political interest with which the errant politician is associated.

Actions of this nature at the level of national government have been relatively infrequent in the United Kingdom since politicians will usually seek to advance their own interests and ambitions through conventional means such as the party system. However, there have been accusations of wrongdoing in the House of Commons that have been responded to internally by introducing improved mechanisms of internal regulation rather than by the use of the criminal law.

Accusations that a Labour MP, Gordon Bagier, had been hired by a public relations firm to improve the profile of the ruling Greek military junta prompted the establishment of the Select Committee of Members' Interests in 1969. In 1975 a Register of Members' Interests was introduced (which was 'beefed up' in 1994). Further accusations of what became known as 'sleaze' were directed at a small number of MPs whose actions were alleged to include taking money in return for asking Parliamentary questions. These actions resulted in the appointment of Lord Nolan to chair a committee whose report, *Standards in Public Life* (1995), subsequently resulted in the appointment of a Parliamentary Commissioner in 1999 to maintain a register of Members' interests.

Additional reforms have also been introduced in an attempt to prevent illegal activities such as bribery affecting the actions of political parties. Following a report, *The Funding of Political Parties in the United Kingdom* (1998) by Sir Patrick Neill, legislation was introduced in the form of the 2000 Parties, Elections and Referenda Act. This established an Independent Election Committee to oversee the management of specific elections and referendum campaigns and imposed restrictions on both donations and campaign expenditure.

Political crime on a global scale

Political crime conducted at the global level frequently involves politicians or public officials being bribed in order to secure an environment in which illicit activities can flourish. These are often designed to promote the operations of business interests or those of organised crime.

It has been observed that 'the limited and partial nature of international law and law enforcement' makes the international 'society' vulnerable to a wide range of ineffectively policed illegalities (Harris, 2003: 10). Attempts at regulation include the Convention on Combating Bribery of Foreign Public Officials, which was initiated by the Organisation for Economic Cooperation and Development in 1999. This sought to impose and enforce common rules against companies and individuals seeking to bribe foreign public officials for business purposes.

Crime prevention

Crime prevention assumed greater significance after 1980. Its importance increased on the back of the 'nothing works' pessimism of the 1970s (Martinson, 1974) and perceptions during the 1980s that the crime problem was escalating out of control, evidenced by rising crime rates and falling detection rates (Heal, 1987) which questioned the effectiveness of 'conventional' solutions to crime (such as increasing the resources made available to the police service and incarcerating increasing numbers of offenders). Much of the subsequent crime prevention policy was focused on public space, seeking to render it safer and create 'a public sense of well-being' (Walklate, 2002: 62), although some also targeted crimes such as domestic violence that was carried out in private space (Walklate, 2002: 63). The official importance attached to crime prevention gave rise to developments that included the formation of the Crime Prevention Unit in the Home Office in 1983 (latterly retitled the Crime Prevention Agency and the Crime Reduction Unit).

There is a close relationship between the theories that attempt to explain why crime occurs and the suggested methods of preventing it. Brantingham and Faust (1976) identified three broad approaches to crime prevention:

- *Primary prevention*. This focuses on the environment within which crime occurs. It suggests that crime can be prevented by reducing the opportunities conducive to its commission.
- *Secondary prevention*. This method targets those deemed to be most likely to embark on criminal activities and is the basis of programmes seeking to divert those perceived to be most at risk of offending. These include day visits to adult prison by young offenders where they attend presentations given by inmates on the realities of prison life. These visits are designed to educate or discourage these juveniles from committing acts that may result in a custodial sentence. Secondary methods of crime prevention also embrace what is termed 'developmental crime prevention'. This involves 'the organised provision of resources to individuals, families, schools or communities to forestall the later development of crime or other problems' (Homel, 2005: 71). This approach embraces activities such as early childhood intervention in the lives of those deemed most at risk of committing crime, and involves the identification of risk factors that can be used to predict future criminality (Farrington, 2002).
- *Tertiary prevention*. This approach is directed at known offenders and seeks to prevent crime by stopping them from reoffending.

Traditionally these varied approaches were associated with different agencies: the police service was historically associated with primary prevention methods and the Probation Service and penal institutions with tertiary prevention. However, the increased use of the multi-agency approach has tended to blur the borderline between these approaches and those who participate in them.

The police and crime prevention

Historically, from the origins of the 'new' police in the early decades of the nineteenth century until the middle decades of the twentieth century, crime prevention was an activity that was primarily carried out by the police service whose role was performed in three main ways:

- *The attachment of police officers to patrol specific geographic areas.* Initially police forces operated the home beat method of policing (which is discussed in Chapter 3) in the belief that the physical presence of a police officer was sufficient to prevent crime. Latterly, under the description of 'community policing', this style of policing was delivered through initiatives that included community constables, directed patrolling, focused patrolling and neighbourhood policing (Newburn, 2002: 105).

- *Physical methods of crime prevention.* Since the publication of the Cornish Committee in 1965 (Home Office, 1965), the main burden of physical security work fell upon specialist crime prevention officers, whose work was coordinated by the Home Office Standing Committee on Crime Prevention. In practice the role of these officers was mainly concerned with providing advice concerning how to protect persons and their property more adequately, although the extent to which their recommendations were followed was largely unknown.

- *Social methods of crime prevention.* This was largely concerned with creating a general feeling in a neighbourhood which opposed crime and criminals. This work was usually conducted by specialist officers drawn from community liaison departments (whose role often included visits to schools) and by area constables who were encouraged to cooperate with community initiatives or the work of other public and voluntary agencies.

However, the importance attached to crime prevention work within the service became devalued by the glamour attached to other areas of activity (especially crime detection). Accordingly, crime prevention work became a specialisation that involved relatively few officers.

The situational approach

Situational crime prevention primarily concerns ' "designing out" crime and opportunity reduction, such as the installation of preventive technologies in both private and public spaces' (Hughes and Edwards, 2005: 17). This approach typically entails a pre-emptive approach which is pursued by '(1) measures directed at highly specific forms of crime; (2) that involve the measurement, design or manipulation of the immediate environment in as systematic and permanent a way as possible; (3) so as to increase the effort and risks of crime and reduce the rewards as perceived by a wide range of offenders' (Clarke, 1992: 4). This approach emphasises that preventive measures have to be related to prior analysis of information. It has been argued that 'an examination of the situation in which particular types of offence take place can reveal the conditions necessary for, or conducive to, its commission and can suggest preventive measures which relate directly to these conditions' (Home Office, 1976, quoted in Weatheritt, 1986: 60).

The situational approach is heavily reliant on primary prevention methods. It is underpinned by the concept of 'opportunity', which suggests that in order for crime to occur there must exist both the material conditions which are conducive to it and the ability to elicit gains at minimal risk (Clarke, 1995). This approach did not seek to provide a universal explanation as to why crime was committed nor did it seek 'to affect *offenders'* propensities or motives'. Instead, 'it introduced specific changes to influence the offender's *decision* or ability to commit these crimes at *particular* places and times. Thus it sought to make criminal actions less attractive to offenders rather than relying on detection, sanctions or reducing criminality through ... improvements in society or its institutions' (Ekblom, 1998: 23). The main concern of situational crime prevention 'is with the spatial and temporal aspects of crime'. In contrast to the positivist agenda that focuses on the treatment of individual offenders, this approach is 'offence-based' (Hughes, 1998: 63).

Situational crime prevention draws from a wide range of theoretical criminological perspectives. It is especially associated with the theory of rational choice that echoed some of the tenets of classicist criminology. This sought to explain 'the way in which offenders make decisions about offending in particular situations and in relation to particular types of crime' (Coleman and Moynihan, 1996: 139) and viewed the criminal as an economic actor who weighed the potential gains of a criminal act against its possible losses. This theory (which was put forward, for example, by Clarke and Mayhew, 1980, and Clarke and Cornish, 1983) was augmented by Hirshi's control theory and routine activity theory (Cohen and Felson, 1979; Felson, 1998). These theories provided the key theoretical underpinnings for situational crime prevention (Hughes, 1998: 65).

As is discussed in Chapter 1, control theory held that crime was caused by the weakened social bonds of urban society (Hirschi, 1969). Routine activities theory suggested that the probability that certain types of crime (namely 'direct contact predatory violations', Cohen and Felson, 1979: 589) would occur at any specific time and place was the result of the convergence of likely offenders, suitable targets and the absence of capable guardians (Cohen and Felson, 1979: 589). This convergence was occasioned by the pattern of routine activities ('recurrent and prevalent activities which provide for basic population and individual needs', Cohen and Felson, 1979: 593) such as work, education and leisure. It was argued that changes to the structure of these activities, characterised by their 'dispersion ... away from the family and household' (Cohen and Felson, 1979: 600) resulted in the absence of capable guardians. The latter facilitated an increase in predatory crime rates including repeat victimisation. Although the analysis of the Kirkholt Burglary Prevention Project in Rochdale in 1986 indicated the relevance of this approach to household burglary, it is relevant to a wide range of crimes (Farrell, 2005: 144–5).

Situational crime prevention has also applied ideas derived from environmental criminology that asserts a link between crime and environmental factors (an issue which is discussed more fully in Chapter 1) and developed them into practical measures. The situational approach has drawn upon crime pattern theory that focuses on identifying the linkage between the commission of crime and the movement of people within specific areas.

The development of the situational approach to crime prevention

Situational crime prevention originated in America (Jacobs, 1961). An important early development focused on ways whereby communities could more effectively protect themselves against crime. In the United Kingdom, situational crime prevention was vigorously developed by administrative criminologists working in the Home Office in the late 1970s. The affinity of this approach with economic rationalist, neo-conservative and new right programmes helped to popularise it after 1979 (O'Malley, 1992: 263).

Situational crime prevention entails a number of activities, some of which are discussed below.

Action directed at the target(s) of crime

Crime may be prevented by actions designed to influence the behaviour of those who commit (or who may be tempted to commit) it. This may involve activities that seek to make the target(s) of crime less attractive:

- *Target removal.* Here objects which may be the focus of criminal activity are removed from the environment to which criminals may have access. Examples include firms paying their employees' wages directly into bank accounts thus eliminating the possibility of a payroll robbery.
- *Target hardening.* Here the objective is to undertake activities which are designed to make it more difficult for crime to be committed. It includes a wide range of physical security measures such as burglar alarms, car steering locks and property marking. Although these methods are not totally foolproof, they may make the commission of crime a more complex or lengthy operation, and/or increase the possibility of being caught.
- *Target devaluation.* Here the aim is to prevent crime through actions which ensure that goods are of use only to their authorised owners.

Actions designed to enhance surveillance

Situational crime prevention methods may entail activities undertaken within communities to enhance surveillance. It is believed that potential offenders will be deterred by the threat of being seen. The use of closed-circuit television (CCTV) (a development discussed more fully below) is an important contemporary example of a form of physical intervention designed to facilitate an improved degree of surveillance.

Redesigning the physical environment

The concept of defensible space (Newman, 1972), highlighted the relationship between the physical environment and crime. This suggested that urban crime could be partly explained by the breakdown of social mechanisms that once kept crime in check arising from the virtual disappearance of small-town environments that framed and enforced moral codes. This made it virtually impossible for communities to come together in joint action. Newman put forward a solution that centred on reconstructing residential environments to foster territoriality, to facilitate natural surveillance and to re-establish access control. This approach is frequently referred to as 'designing out crime'. In the United Kingdom, Coleman (1985) emphasised the importance of redesigning public-sector housing estates to eliminate the design factors which led to crime – anonymity, lack of surveillance and ease of escape – and this approach was endorsed by central government (Department of the Environment, 1994) whose approach was compatible with the role performed by architectural liaison officers who had been appointed by some police forces in the late 1980s.

Closed-circuit television

CCTV is an important aspect of situational crime prevention. It may be used by individuals, commercial organisations or public authorities in order to protect persons and property.

Although CCTV has been in existence since the 1970s, its use (for example, in city centres) became widespread in the 1990s in connection with situational crime prevention. When used in public spaces, it involves banks of CCTV cameras being placed in fixed locations and remotely controlled with operators able to 'zoom in' on those acting in a criminal or disorderly manner. On 30 August 1999, *The Guardian* reported that 70 CCTV cameras were deployed at the 1999 Notting Hill Carnival in an attempt to cut crime, and it was suggested that 'Britain now has around a million CCTV cameras. It is estimated that the average person in a major city could be filmed up to 300 times a day by CCTV cameras in shops, banks, places of work and, increasingly, the street itself' (Bright, 1999). In 1995 the Home Office launched the 'CCTV Challenge Competition' that funded bids to provide CCTV cameras in public places as a crime prevention measure (Home Office, 1995b).

There are a number of factors on which the assumption that CCTV reduces crime is based. The potential offender may be deterred from committing crime (since there is an increased likelihood of apprehension if caught on film) and, whether real or imagined, 'the threat of potential surveillance ... acts to produce a self-discipline in which individuals police their own behaviour' (Armitage, 2002: 2). Victims may be reminded of the risk of crime and alter their behaviour accordingly, and cameras also provide a 'capable guardian' thus reducing the likelihood of crime. CCTV cameras also enable those monitoring them to call upon police resources when necessary (Armitage, 2002: 2).

There are, however, a number of difficulties associated with the use of CCTV. Its effectiveness is variable – 'it has least effect upon public order offences and most effect when used in car parks' (Armitage, 2002: 7). The quality of the images sometimes produced (and public knowledge of this) may reduce the effectiveness of CCTV as a means of crime prevention. Civil liberties issues arise from the activities of 'eyes in the sky' that keep observations on those going about their everyday lives in a perfectly law-abiding manner (although the 1998 Data Protection Act and the Human Rights Act offer increased protection to the individual). An additional problem is the criteria used by operators when deciding to 'zoom in' on a particular subject. It has been suggested that social categories such as teenagers and members of minority ethnic groups were prone to being the subjects of such surveillance in which 'suspicion was predicated on stereotypical assumptions as to the distribution of criminality' (Norris and Armstrong, 1998: 10; Armitage, 2002: 4). As with accusations of police harassment of similar groups, this situation accounts for the relatively low level of arrests of those subject to this form of surveillance and may deprive the CCTV system of legitimacy. It may also lead to vandalism of the camera installations.

The effectiveness of situational forms of crime prevention

Situational crime prevention measures have a number of strengths. These are discussed below.

Evaluation

Situational methods of crime prevention typically lend themselves to evaluation so that the key issue of whether they work or not can be assessed. One example of this was the installation of CCTV cameras in four of the 19 most victimised London Underground stations in 1975. It was possible to judge the effectiveness of this initiative by both comparing crime levels before and after cameras had been installed in those stations where they were located, and also assessing crime levels in the four high crime stations with CCTV and the 15 without (discussed in Clarke, 1995; and Hughes, 1998: 66–7).

Some crime is prevented

Evidence obtained from a small number of studies has suggested that this approach 'can be an economically efficient strategy for the reduction of crime' (Welsh and Farrington, 1999: 366). If it is accepted that the criminal is heavily influenced by opportunity, the denial of scope for criminal action by situational methods may result in no crime being committed. Home Office research has concluded that situational crime prevention 'can contribute significantly' to crime control, although the localised nature of the schemes that have been introduced made it difficult to generalise concerning the wider application of such methods (Ekblom, 1998: 30 and 36).

The weaknesses of situational crime prevention

Situational crime prevention has been criticised for a number of reasons. Some of the main issues are considered below.

A managerial solution to crime

It has been argued that situational crime prevention divorces rationality from the social context (Rock, 1989: 6). Chapter 1 has asserted that there are a large number of views concerning why criminals commit crime, some of which may override free will and rationality. It has thus been argued that:

> Situational and opportunity factors might help to determine when and where crime occurs, but they do not play a role in whether crime occurs ... The only effective way to prevent crime is to deal with its root causes through psychological, social or political interventions ... Generating this theoretical understanding is the core focus of criminology.
> (Clarke, 2005: 40–1)

Situational crime prevention is thus accused of being 'a fundamentally conservative approach to crime, content to manage the problem and keep it from overwhelming the forces of law and order' (Clarke, 2005: 57).

Displacement

Situational crime prevention may not prevent crime but instead may result in merely altering the pattern of offending behaviour. This is referred to as displacement which may take four forms – temporal (in which the crime is committed at a different time than had been intended), spatial (in which the crime is committed in a different place to that originally intended), tactical (in which the methods used to commit a crime are adjusted to take account of initiatives such as target hardening) or target/functional (in which a different crime from that originally intended is carried out) (Barr and Pease, 1992; Pease, 1997: 977).

One aspect of target displacement is downward displacement. Barr and Pease (1990) suggested that situational methods could force a criminal to commit a lesser offence than that originally intended, thereby reducing its scale and danger to the public. Situational methods to improve bank security might, for example, forced an armed robber to commit car crime instead. There is, however, the danger that situational crime prevention methods may have the opposite effect, for example encouraging a thwarted house burglar to diversify upwards or to encourage more serious crimes such as kidnapping to overcome the impediments to crime caused by target hardening measures.

However, rational choice theorists do not see displacement as a major problem since they assert that much crime is committed on the spur of the moment and is thus not behaviour which is readily adjusted to suit changed circumstances caused by situational crime prevention methods.

Additionally, it has been asserted that spatial displacement was influenced by the intensity of programme. When measures designed to prevent burglary action were of a moderate or high intensity, the benefits diffused into surrounding areas thus reducing the overall level of crime, whereas when a programme was of low intensity displacement of crime to neighbouring areas was more likely (Ekblom, 1998: 31).

Fragments society

One aspect of situational methods of crime prevention is the creation of communal structures designed to identify strangers whose presence in a neighbourhood is deemed undesirable by those who live there and to take pre-emptive action against them. The creation of 'gated communities' in which 'access is restricted to residents in the hope of keeping out offenders who cruise neighbourhoods looking for crime opportunities' (Clarke, 2005: 59) is one aspect of this approach. Although this approach may help to gel community feeling and reinforce social controls within protected areas, it may heighten the sense of social exclusion of those who are targeted by initiatives of this nature.

Blames the victim

Situational crime prevention has been accused of victim-blaming (Walklate, 1996: 300). Individuals and communities that have failed to adequately protect themselves against crime might be held partly to blame for its occurrence, and the manufacturers of business products and other providers of goods and services to the public have also been enjoined to consider crime prevention in the design of their products (Ekblom, 2005: 203–44). One danger with this approach is that it shifts blame away from the perpetrator, although it may also help to protect the potential victim through the provision of information as to how to avoid crime risks.

Does not focus on all crimes

The scope of crime addressed by situational prevention methods is limited, and it ignores many illegal activities. Robbery, burglary and street crimes are particularly targeted by situational methods, whereas corporate crime and domestic violence are ignored.

Diminution of civil liberties

The emphasis which situational crime prevention methods place on intrusive surveillance is likened to a 'Big Brother' society in which personal freedoms are subjected to intrusions. The tradition of seeking to restrict the 'snooping' capacity of the state is a lengthy one in the United Kingdom, and is currently evident in the heated debate about the introduction of identity cards. However, it has been asserted that 'people are willing to surrender some freedoms or endure inconvenience in specific contexts if they gain protection from crime', and that much of the new surveillance methods are introduced by businesses rather than governments (Clarke, 2005: 61).

Not a once-and-for-all cure

Situational methods of crime prevention need to be sustained even when it appears the problem that they targeted has been solved. If these initiatives are not continued, there arises the danger of the problem resurfacing. Those whose activities are targeted by situational methods may adapt them to take into account the situational crime prevention initiatives that thus need to be adjusted in order to keep one step ahead of those whose activities they seek to curtail.

> Using examples of situational methods of crime prevention, assess the strengths and weaknesses of this method of crime prevention.

The social approach to crime prevention

Social crime prevention is based upon the belief that social conditions have a key bearing on crime. The concern of social crime prevention 'is focused chiefly on changing targeted social environments and the motivations of offenders, and "community" development initiatives in order to deter potential or actual offenders from future offending' (Hughes and Edwards, 2005: 17–18).

Social crime prevention rejected both classicist and positivist explanations of crime (which focused on the operations of the criminal justice system and the 'defects' of the offender respectively) and instead suggested a comprehensive strategy to tackle crime. This approach sought to reduce risk factors and strengthen protective ones and was directed at neighbourhoods rather than individuals (Bright, 1997: 40). It embraced measures that aimed to improve social conditions, strengthen community institutions and enhance recreational, educational and employment opportunities. Unlike situational methods of crime prevention (which tend to focus on opportunity reduction), social approaches seek to tackle crime 'at its roots'.

The arguments put forward by the Chicago School (which suggested that recreation could divert potential delinquents from criminal behaviour and also provide a means whereby behaviour could be examined and problems identified) were important aspects of this strategy. It was also compatible with the approach associated with left realism, which emphasised that factors such as labelling by the state, inadequate defence against crime by its victims and the functioning of society need to be considered alongside the study of offenders (Young, 1988: 28).

Social crime prevention has been pursued through a number of initiatives that are often delivered through locally orientated multi-agency approaches. The use of social methods of crime prevention which have been employed since 1997 in connection with juvenile offending are discussed in Chapter 8.

The approach does, however, suffer from a number of deficiencies. In particular, critics have asked the following:

- *Does it work?* One difficulty associated with social crime prevention is that evaluation (a key feature of situational approaches which are often funded and evaluated by central government) has not always been rigorously conducted. This tends to mean, therefore, that perceptions of youth clubs helping to divert young persons from crime are based upon faith rather than empirical evidence.
- *If it does work, why?* Social crime prevention typically embraces a range of actions which are pursued simultaneously. It is thus difficult to analyse the effectiveness of individual measures within the overall programme.

Community safety

The application of the term 'community' in relation to criminal justice activities has assumed increased importance after the 1970s. This term has been applied to wide-ranging developments that include community policing, crime prevention and 'community safety', community mediation schemes and community sentencing. There is, however, no consensus concerning the definition of this term. It has been argued that 'community' acts 'as a genial host which is accompanied by layered ideological assumptions and presuppositions all seeking to serve ulterior political aims, strategies and interests' (Crawford, 1999: 198). It has further been observed that the terms 'multi-agency' and 'community' are often used interchangeably in relation to crime prevention (Hughes, 1998: 75), although the latter theoretically entails the involvement of local people in the initiatives that are developed.

This section focuses on community-oriented crime prevention activities. Crime prevention schemes of this nature may be delivered in a number of ways, often utilising both situational and social approaches thereby blurring the distinction between these two approaches to crime prevention that have been described above. Community crime prevention was based upon the work of the Chicago School which sought to tackle aspects of social disorganisation which resulted in crime and delinquency and thereby to revitalise community life. An early initiative to achieve this was the Chicago Area Project (which commenced in 1932) that embraced features such as the development of leisure and recreational opportunities for young people, the improvement of the environment of the neighbourhood and youth contact work directed at delinquents and gang members. Later applications of crime prevention policy have been directed at disadvantaged rather than disorganised communities (Walklate, 1996: 306).

Community-oriented crime prevention initiatives: developments before 1997

Community-based crime prevention initiatives involving both situational and social methods of crime prevention have a long pedigree. This section briefly refers to some of the relevant developments that were in operation before the election of the Labour government in 1997 that heralded a new approach to activities of this nature.

Neighbourhood watch

Community historically played an important role in crime-related issues and has been traced back to the tything system of the Anglo-Saxon period (Critchley, 1978: 2). However, the development of 'new' policing in the nineteenth century and changes affecting the administration of justice served to locate these functions as responsibilities performed by the central state (Crawford, 1999: 23).

However, in the late 1960s the Home Office began to emphasise that effective crime prevention needed to involve the local community as well as the police (Home Office, 1968). Initially this gave rise to an enhanced role to be performed by crime prevention panels. These were mainly composed of representatives of local business and commercial interests, voluntary agencies and professional organisations. Their role was to examine proposals put forward by the police, members of the public and panel members, and disseminate information on crime prevention. They had no formal status and their establishment was left to the discretion of individual forces.

A more wide-ranging initiative (in the sense of involving greater numbers of people) was provided through neighbourhood watch. This approach was pioneered in America, being introduced by the City of Seattle's police department in 1974, although some police forces in Britain had developed similar 'good neighbour schemes'. The essence of neighbourhood watch

> is that groups of neighbours band together to act as their own and each other's 'eyes and ears'. They take note of anything suspicious and pass it onto the local police and they keep an eye on one another's houses or other property. Neighbourwatch schemes ... encourage people to take a greater interest in crime prevention ... The idea behind neighbourhood watch is to heighten people's awareness of the possibility of crime occurring and to improve the scope for reducing crime by removing opportunities and increasing surveillance. (Weatheritt, 1986: 82)

Neighbourhood watch schemes originate from initiatives put forward either by the police or the community itself. Typically, a meeting is organised and local coordinators are chosen who maintain a key role in the administration of the scheme and the recruitment of new members. They provide a point of contact between the community and the police and may initiate local crime prevention initiatives (which are often situational, such as property marking). There is no organisational blueprint for these schemes, whose structure and activities are thus subject to wide variation.

Neighbourhood watch has proved popular in many areas. Its operations have, however, been subject to criticism. These concern the following:

- *Effectiveness.* The extent to which neighbourhood watch prevents crime is unknown. Crime may be displaced to areas without such schemes. Further, the strategy is based upon the belief that crime is committed by non-local people. However, this is not invariably the case, especially on urban housing estates.

- *Level of interest by police and public.* The extent to which residents join local schemes and the police commitment to them (particularly in terms of institutionalised back-up to the crime prevention function) varies. In general, neighbourhood watch schemes tend to predominate in middle-class areas rather than on working-class housing estates.

- *Reduced levels of policing.* Neighbourhoods which demonstrate the ability to take increased responsibilities for their own protection against crime may receive a reduced level of formal policing (especially routine foot and car patrols).

- *Impact on civil liberties.* It has been alleged that neighbourhood watch is a police-driven initiative which is part of an overall strategy for increased surveillance of the population and intelligence gathering which, in turn, is facilitated by the police use of computers. It has also been argued that these schemes are designed to divide local populations, thereby making it easier for the police to control them (Donnison, et al., 1986).

In addition to neighbourhood watch, other community initiatives to combat crime have been developed. These included street watch that entailed groups of local people patrolling their neighbourhoods. This was launched in 1995 but objections by the police service to the use of the word 'patrol' forced the then Home Secretary, Michael Howard, to describe the scheme as citizens 'walking with a purpose'.

The Safe Neighbourhood Unit

This was designed as an alternative to the allegedly police-driven neighbourhood watch. The scheme was put forward in 1980 by the National Association for the Care and Resettlement of Offenders (NACRO), and was pioneered on a number of housing estates in London. It sought to bring together all interested parties (including residents, local councillors and the police) into a steering committee that would put forward a comprehensive improvement plan for the estate that utilised both situational and social crime prevention measures which were delivered by a range of statutory and voluntary agencies.

The Safe Neighbourhood Unit placed considerable emphasis on tackling the fear and actuality of victimisation. The policies that were put forward to combat crime encompassed a wide range of issues involving the quality of life (such as repairs to property and facilities for all categories of residents). The scheme encountered problems though, including the ability of local authorities to adequately fund the improvements which were suggested, and the disinclination of the police to deliver the kind of policing which residents deemed appropriate for their locality. Nonetheless, aspects of the approach taken up by the Safe Neighbourhood Unit were taken up by other initiatives that included the Home Office's Safer Cities (initially launched in 1988).

Multi-agency initiatives

Many community-oriented crime prevention initiatives undertaken before 1997 were based on multi-agency cooperation.

The multi-agency approach entailed joint action by a number of different organisations (which may be public, private or voluntary sector bodies) that were designed to prevent crime within specific localities. If the gelling of working practices took place within the confines of a partnership organisational structure, the term 'inter-agency' rather than 'multi-agency' was often applied (Crawford, 1998).

The multi-agency approach was based on a belief that crime could be most effectively prevented by various bodies working together rather than leaving the entire burden of crime-fighting in the hands of the police (Moore and Brown, 1981: 52). Street crime, for example, might be deterred by more adequate street lighting, the improved layout of housing estates or alterations to public transport timing. But it could not be taken for granted that individual agencies appreciated this situation, and even if they did it was likely that tunnel-vision parochialism would serve as an impediment to locally orientated inter-agency operation.

There were, however, a number of problems associated with this approach before 1997. These are discussed below.

Lack of community involvement

It has been argued that multi-agency crime prevention initiatives were typically driven by the central state with little local participation or ownership. However, local concerns did not need to be totally excluded from the crime prevention agenda. It was argued that multi-agency crime prevention programmes displayed local diversity and absence of uniformity (Liddle and Gelsthorpe, 1994: 27) and an evaluation of phase I of the Safer Cities programme similarly pointed to variations in activities despite the influence exerted over the scheme by administrative criminologists working within and outside the Home Office and the constraints which were imposed on it by the Conservative administration (Tilley, 1994: 42). It has thus been concluded that multi-agency crime prevention initiatives in the United Kingdom have at times displayed the ability to 'draw on, and create, agendas and projects which are beyond the control of the centre' (Hughes, 1998: 102).

Did it work?

It was difficult to accurately assess whether multi-agency crime prevention initiatives (which frequently utilise both situational and social methods) were successful. For example, crime reduction might occur because of factors not related to the crime prevention programme, especially when it operated over a relatively long period of time. It has been argued that 'it is vital to recognize the complex mixture of demographic, cultural and technological factors ... in any explanation of the shifts in the sense of security or insecurity and in the material reality of crime and disorder' (Hughes, 1998: 100). However, initiatives of this nature might help to reduce the fear of crime (Ekblom and Pease, 1995: 598), even if their actual success in reducing it is debateable.

Increased social control

It was alleged that the formation of large numbers of multi-agency organisations engaged in crime prevention work resulted in 'net-widening' whereby the social control apparatus of the state was extended so that increased numbers of deviants become ensnared in its net (McMahon, 1990). Multi-agency crime prevention initiatives were thus accused of 'rolling out' rather than 'rolling back' state power resulting in the 'dispersed state' (Clarke, 1996: 15): 'we are witnessing not a diminution of particular forms of the state's role but rather an extension of particular forms of state power, albeit through new and unfamiliar means' (Hughes, 1998: 78). There was thus a danger that the new forms of state-sponsored activity might increase the exclusion of marginalised groups, and those on the receiving end of the new initiatives might perceive a lack of justice in the way they were treated.

> Assess the strengths and weaknesses of seeking to prevent crime through the use of multi-agency initiatives.

Community-oriented crime prevention initiatives: developments after 1997 – the role of local government

In 1971 the Bains Committee recommended incorporating the police service into their proposals to modernise the management of local government. It effectively proposed transforming policing into an arm of local government thereby giving a chief constable the status of a local government officer who would become part of the chief executive's management team (Oliver, 1987). This proposal implied a radical departure from the tradition of constabulary independence, but was watered down by the HMIC so that it became an expression of hope that local authorities and chief constables would cooperate as and when required to do so.

The role of local government in crime-related issues was particularly directed at crime prevention, and this became a major concern for central government with the establishment of the Home Office Crime Prevention Unit in 1983. Although the hostility of the Conservative party towards local government prevented it from endorsing a more dominant role for this tier of government, much support for multi-agency work was subsequently forthcoming. This approach had been previously recommended in connection with juvenile offending (Home Office, 1978), and Government Circular 8/84 (issued by the Home Office and four other Departments) recognised that the police alone could not tackle crime and disorder and thus encouraged multi-agency work (Home Office, 1984). This approach also featured in the Five Towns initiative in 1986 and the Safer Cities Programme, phase I of which commenced in 1988 (phase II being taken over by the Department of the Environment and launched in 1992). The latter comprised initiatives that utilised both situational and social crime prevention measures which were managed by organisations such as NACRO and Crime Concern rather than local government. Other incentives that promoted inter-agency cooperation included the report into child abuse in Cleveland in 1987 (Butler-Sloss, 1988). In 1990, a Home Office Blue Paper stated that well-planned and well-executed inter-agency schemes were to be found throughout the country (Home Office, 1990a: 1). Subsequently central government encouragement to adopt multi-agency solutions to crime prevention was given in 1990 (Home Office, 1990b) and 1994 (Department of the Environment, 1994). The 1990 circular was endorsed by ten government departments and the latter circular served to popularise the role of police architectural liaison officers who had been appointed in some police forces in the late 1980s.

A major catalyst to increase the involvement of local government in crime prevention work was the publication of a report prepared by the Home Office Standing Conference on Crime Prevention, which was chaired by James Morgan, in 1991 and was subsequently known as the Morgan Report. This was set up to monitor 'the progress made in the local delivery of crime prevention through the multi-agency approach in the light of the guidance contained in the booklet accompanying 44/90' (Home Office Standing Conference on Crime Prevention, 1991: 10). The report stated that 'the local authority is a natural focus for coordinating, in collaboration with the police, the broad range of activities directed at improving community safety, (Home Office Standing Conference on Crime Prevention, 1991: 19) and argued that 'the lack of a clear statutory responsibility for local government to play its part fully in crime prevention has clearly inhibited progress' (Home Office Standing Conference on Crime Prevention, 1991: 20).

The Morgan Report further introduced the concept of 'community safety' as opposed to crime prevention, arguing that the latter term suggested that crime prevention was solely the responsibility of the police. Partnership was thus seen as the appropriate direction on which future policy of this nature should be based. The new designation asserted the important role that communities should play in crime prevention strategies and sought to stimulate greater participation from all members of the general public in the fight against crime. It would also enable fuller weight to be given to activities that went beyond the traditional police concentration on 'opportunity reduction' methods of crime prevention, and would encourage greater attention to be paid to social issues (Home Office, 1991: 13 and 20–1).

Political support for local government playing a lead role in coordinating multi-agency crime prevention partnerships was, however, unlikely to be given in the early 1990s. The negative views held by Conservative governments towards local government made it unlikely that they would seek to increase its role in this area of work. Therefore there was no central funding made available to implement any of the proposals contained in the Morgan Report (a situation which was clearly stated in the 1993 Home Office publication, *A Practical Guide to Crime Prevention for Local Partnerships*). Progress in involving local government in multi-agency work was also impeded by the attempt to discern between the core and ancillary tasks of policing which led a number of forces to disband their headquarters community affairs departments that had a history of close cooperation with other agencies, including local government.

Local government and community safety – the progress of an idea

Although many of the ideas contained in the Morgan Report were ignored by the Conservative government, local authorities began to implement them in what has been described as the 'discretionary phase' (Hawksworth, 1998: 11). A survey of local authorities in June 1996 found that:

- 53 per cent of respondent authorities had published a policy statement on community safety;
- 51 per cent had a separately identified budget for community safety;
- 37 per cent had community safety coordinators (although almost one-third were part time);
- 35 per cent had conducted a crime audit to monitor the success of local initiatives (Audit Commission, 1999: para. 38, p. 20)

The types of community-focused prevention programmes were also subject to great variation across the country (Hope, 1998a: 56–7), many resembling 'comprehensive community initiatives' consisting of a variety of measures and implementation strategies (Hope, 1998a: 57).

One difficulty with the uneven application of community-oriented crime prevention initiatives was that this made possible the spatial displacement of law and order problems. The universal introduction of community safety initiatives driven by CDRPs (which are discussed below) might help to alleviate this problem.

Community-oriented crime prevention initiatives: developments since 1997

Developments initiated by post-1997 Labour governments sought to provide an enhanced degree of community influence over police affairs. This has in part been achieved by the enhanced level of involvement of local government in crime prevention. The 1998 Crime and Disorder Act gave local government a major role in this area of work through the establishment of Crime and Disorder Reduction Partnerships. This role was reinforced by section 17 of the legislation which imposed a statutory duty on agencies which included local government and police authorities to 'do all that it reasonably can do to prevent crime and disorder in its area' in relationship to the performance of its other responsibilities.

The 1998 Act thus transformed local government into a major player in the area of fighting crime and a resource on which the police could call upon which meant that crime prevention would thus increasingly be waged through the use of multi-agency initiatives, some of which have been managed by charities such as NACRO and Crime Concern.

Crime and disorder reduction partnerships

The 1998 Crime and Disorder Act placed crime prevention at the heart of the Labour government's response crime strategy, thus making this activity an essential aspect of contemporary public policy. A key aspect of their approach was to place the multi-agency approach (or what became known as the 'partnership approach') on a statutory basis. Although this legislation failed to give local government as dominant a role in multi-agency crime prevention activity as had been urged in the Morgan Report, its role in crime prevention was officially acknowledged.

The 1998 Act placed a statutory duty on police forces and local authorities (termed 'responsible authorities') to act in cooperation with police authorities, health authorities and probation committees in multi-agency bodies which became known as crime and disorder reduction partnerships (CDRPs), although this designation did not appear in the legislation. In Wales CDRPs are termed community safety partnerships. The role of these partnerships was to develop and implement a strategy for reducing crime and disorder in each district and unitary local authority in England and Wales. They act as the engine of community safety initiatives.

The starting point of the process to reduce crime and disorder in each locality was the preparation of a local crime audit (conducted by the local authority) that would form the basis of the local crime reduction strategy. This required all local service providers to record crime through which local 'hot spots' could be identified. To do this, local authorities developed tools such as geographic information systems (GIS) (Loveday, 2005: 74).

The audit also had to take into account the views of the public who lived and worked in the local authority area concerning crime and disorder. This required a detailed process of popular consultation, in particular with groups deemed 'hard to reach'. One intention of this was to give ordinary members of the general public the opportunity to influence the policy-making agenda. Following this, the CDRP would formulate priorities and a strategy would be published containing the objectives required to be implemented and targets related to them. Progress in attaining these objectives would be monitored so that adjustments could be made as required. This cycle was of three years' duration.

CDRPs also provide a mechanism for the pooling of information collected by the participants to the process and for conducting community safety projects.

The funding for these is scarce, with most initiatives being fixed-term projects conducted at neighbourhood level that are funded from sources which include the Home Office crime reduction programme or regeneration programmes. This has led in some areas to a succession of short-term projects engendering community mistrust for 'here today, gone tomorrow' initiatives (NACRO, 2003: 2).

Most CDRPs established multi-agency community safety units (CSUs) whose main role is to link the local authority and the crime and disorder reduction partnership and to ensure that the work carried out by other relevant agencies (such as youth offending teams and drug action teams) was coordinated with this partnership. CSUs frequently provide the lead role in implementing section 17 of the 1998 legislation. CSUs also act as the first port of call for local people who have concerns regarding crime and disorder (who may prefer to report the matter in this way rather than having to contact the police), and may deliver initiatives designed to prevent crime, including tackling anti-social behaviour.

The work of CDRPs is superintended by the nine Government Offices for the Regions. These were established in 1994 to coordinate the activities of a number of government departments operating at regional level which both fund and staff the regional bodies. They are headed by a Regional Director and now report to the Office of the Deputy Prime Minister. Each has a Home Office Crime Reduction Team that is responsible for liaising with CDRPs operating in the region. Its work includes that of providing guidance, support and training to these partnerships, monitoring the performance of projects which have been funded by the Home Office, and ensuring that an appreciation of crime reduction issues is reflected in the work performed by all government offices which operate in the region. It has been proposed to extend the feedback role of Home Office Regional Directors whereby they would provide regular information to CDRPs on their performance relative to neighbouring CDRPs (National Audit Office, 2004: 7).

The Home Office has a Crime Reduction Team based within the machinery of the Welsh Assembly whose work is to provide support to that country's community safety partnerships (in particular to ensure that they meet performance targets set by the Welsh Assembly and the Home Office). Additionally it ensures that community safety issues are adequately addressed in other aspects of the Assembly's work. The task to reduce crime and disorder in Wales is superintended by the Welsh Assembly, whose Minister for Social Justice and Regeneration has control over a Crime Fighting Fund to provide for programmes of community safety.

Community safety is not a statutory function performed by local authorities in either Scotland or Northern Ireland. However, work of this nature is undertaken by Scottish councils and voluntary and statutory bodies in Northern Ireland.

Crime and disorder reduction partnerships in operation

Crime and disorder reduction partnerships were the machinery developed to combat crime and disorder through the use of 'joined-up government'. The coordination of the efforts of individual agencies was justified by the belief that crime and other forms of anti-social behaviour were caused by factors such as drug and alcohol abuse and social exclusion. However, although partnerships were responsible for setting goals, the implementation of specific programmes to achieve them frequently remained in the hands of the existing agencies and could thus be jeopardised by an agency's need to devote priority to their mainstream tasks which were measured by performance indicators. In some cases (as with school exclusions) the need to attain agency targets could work against the objectives of crime and disorder reduction partnerships.

Although the Home Office provided guidelines concerning the structure, organisation and operating practices of crime and disorder reduction partnerships, their operation was subject to local definition, and the structures and terms of reference were subject to wide variation (Home Office, 1999). For example, in some local authorities (such as Brighton and Hove) a single steering group was set up to coordinate the activities of crime and disorder reduction partnerships and youth offending teams.

The 2002 Police Reform Act amended the 1998 legislation. Police and fire authorities became responsible authorities as defined by the 1998 legislation in April 2003, and in the following year were joined by primary care trusts in England (and health authorities in Wales). Crime and disorder reduction partnerships were required to work closely with drug action teams in areas with a two-tier structure of local government and to integrate their work with drug action teams in areas which had a unitary structure of local government by April 2004. This latter requirement did not specify a merger of the two bodies, but required them to undertake appropriate arrangements to secure integration.

The 2002 Act also enabled CDRPs to merge where this course of action seemed appropriate to issues traversing a number of related local authority areas. An example of this would be crime committed in one CDRP where the perpetrators lived in a neighbouring CDRP area. Preventive measures could thus be coordinated across local authority boundaries.

The powers of CDRPs in connection with drug misuse and anti-social behaviour were amended by the 2002 Police Reform Act and the 2003 Anti-social Behaviour Act.

Problems affecting crime and disorder reduction partnerships

There were a number of perceived deficiencies in the operations of CDRPs that are discussed below.

Crime audits

Although crime audits were viewed as an important mechanism through which community involvement in police affairs would be secured, previous experience indicated that these tended to rely heavily on police data, 'which is likely to be narrowly focused on reported crime' (Audit Commission, 1999: 33). Although audits conducted under the 1998 Act have not solely relied on information derived from police sources, a further problem was the analysis of data. Many partnerships lacked the skills required to evaluate local crime trends (Phillips, 2002: 179), and many audits failed to analyse data in such a way as to enable them to provide a guide for action, for example by identifying 'hot spots' (Audit Commission, 1999: 34).

A final difficulty is whether all of those who suffered from crime would be equally able to voice their concerns through the consultation procedures that were adopted. These traditionally empower members of the middle class more readily than the working class, and some crimes (such as domestic violence) may disproportionately evade the crime audit if victims move out of the CDRP area to escape further attacks.

The perception that crime audits fail to provide a full account of local crime and disorder problems has been developed into a critique that the concept of community safety is too limited in scope. 'Rather than start with crime per se we believe it would be more useful to start with the broader issue of hazard and hazard management, of which crime and disorder are then sub-sets' (Byrne and Pease, 2003: 287–8). The Home Office, it is argued, has approached the problem by viewing community safety as a subset of crime and disorder (Hughes and Edwards, 2005: 21).

Locally developed crime prevention strategies may not enhance a sense of community

Although it has been observed that 'community development and empowerment is central to the work of many regeneration and community safety projects' (NACRO, 2003: 6), this is often hard to realise in practice. Community safety projects often rely on existing groups and organisations to provide community imput, but this may mean that 'hard to reach' groups and those who are frequently ignored in community development (such as young people) may be sidelined in community safety work (NACRO, 2003: 5–6). For reasons such as this, community safety projects may divide communities rather than unite them.

The absence of a consensus regarding how best to provide for community safety or how social problems should be addressed also affects other aspects of the work designed to reduce crime and disorder. For example, some of the solutions that may be put forward in response to issues raised in crime audits (such as the use of CCTV or the deployment of sanctions such as curfews) may be directed at socially unpopular groups (such as disorderly youths) thus increasing their sense of social exclusion. Public opinion is frequently ill-informed on the subject of law and order, and there are thus difficulties in using their views as the basis of a strategy to prevent crime and disorder.

In extreme cases, the involvement of local people may legitimise vigilante action or other forms of coercive measures that some local people may take against others, and may contribute to the downfall rather than the upholding of law and order. Examples of this include the violence meted out to suspected paedophiles in the wake of the campaign by the *News of the World* newspaper to 'out' them in 2000.

Police authority – CDRP relationships

The local policing plans prepared annually by police authorities are required to take account of local opinion expressed through consultative arrangements. This procedure was initially governed by section 106 of the 1984 Police and Criminal Evidence Act and latterly by section 96 of the 1996 Police Act. Local government is further required by the 1998 Crime and Disorder Act to consult in relation to the preparation of a crime audit. There thus arises the possibility of 'consultation overload' affecting both the police service and those groups or community representatives who are 'repeatedly bombarded with requests to participate in consultation exercises' (Newburn, 2002: 112). Additionally, time and money might be saved by rationalising the activities that are currently performed by diverse bodies.

One development that is compatible with improving the relationship between police autorities and CDRPs was contained in the 2002 Police Reform Act. This sought to align the period covered by CDRP and police authority three-year strategy plans to ensure that these local plans effectively supported each other when setting targets for crime reduction (Home Office, 2002: 19).

Administrative Problems

Section 5(1) of the 1998 Act designated county councils as well as district councils as 'responsible authorities' that would formulate and implement strategies to reduce crime and disorder in their areas. This required the two tiers of local government to cooperate where these existed (which is mainly in rural areas). Combined effort may, however, be difficult to secure if the political control and management structures of these two tiers of authorities are different (Pierpoint and Gilling, 1998: 25–6). Similarly, in urban areas police authorities operate across the geographic boundaries of a number of district councils. Again, the issues of political control and diverse management structures may make the task of cooperation complex. Although the divisional boundaries used by urban police forces (termed 'basic command units') often correspond to those of district councils, the officer in charge (typically a chief superintendent) may feel constrained to refer major issues upwards through the force hierarchy of command – which complicates decision-making.

Various attempts have been made to solve administrative problems of this nature. The 2002 Police Reform Act amended section 97 of the 1998 Crime and Disorder Act to permit the responsible authorities for different CDRP areas to work together as a single partnership through a formal merger into a combined area. This reform may help alleviate some of the problems facing partnerships operating in areas served by two-tier councils.

Inter-agency working arrangements

Problems may arise when a number of agencies are required to work together. One of these is leadership that in a multi-agency setting might be difficult to achieve, perhaps resulting in one partner taking the lead. This may create resentment by other partners who effectively disengage themselves from the partnership process. Further difficulties may arise between the various agencies involved in the partnerships derived from the different perspectives of these bodies, the differential power relationships between them and whether they succeed in gelling together behind common aims and objectives. A study that was conducted into inter-agency work involving the police and probation services before the 1998 Act concluded that there were 'very real differences ... between police and probation officers' understandings of the causes of crime and "appropriate" preventative interventions' (Crawford, 1999: 144). This may prevent the easy formulation of crime prevention initiatives.

A subsequent study of CDRPs argued that success in reducing crime depended on generating a 'synergy' among those in partnership and a commitment to tackle crime that was most likely to arise when issues of genuine local concern were targeted. However, divisional police commanders and chairs of CDRPs typically rated their local probation service and local health service as less active than other key statutory partners due to resource constraints and competing priorities (National Audit Office, 2004: 3).

Various reforms have been put forward in an attempt to improve inter-agency working relationships. The concept of joined-up government at the local level may help to facilitate cooperation by CDRP partners. One example of this has been the alignment of the boundaries of local authorities and police Basic Command Units.

There has also been the growth of entirely new locally oriented bureaucracies to manage inter-agency cooperation. The increased importance attached to crime prevention by central government (which is evidenced by the issuance of performance indicators by central bodies such as the Audit Commission and Home Office and the appointment of regional crime directors to each of the nine regional government offices in 2000 to improve the effectiveness of crime prevention throughout the area) may enhance the importance attached to these new administrative structures. These are not, however, subject to formal mechanisms of local accountability.

Local strategic partnerships

One problem associated with attempts to create new administrative structures to advance multi-agency initiatives is that this development may be to the detriment of the autonomy and accountability of established organisations such as local government. One solution to this problem has been the establishment of local strategic partnerships (LSPs).

An LSP is a non-statutory, multi-agency non-executive body whose boundaries are coterminous with those of a local authority (either a district or county council or a unitary authority). Their role is to bring together the public, private, voluntary and community sectors in order to tackle problems such as crime that require a response from a range of different bodies acting in partnership. They perform a key role in delivering the government's neighbourhood renewal strategy, and although they are not directly funded, the 88 LSPs in the most deprived areas benefit from additional resources provided out of the Neighbourhood Renewal Fund.

The 2000 Local Government Act imposed a statutory duty on local authorities to prepare community strategies. LSPs were subsequently developed to drive it forward. Typically, the LSP develops themes to advance the local authority's community strategy. The delivery mechanisms of these themes are multi-agency bodies such as CDRPs and the role of the LSP is to rationalise the existing range of separate partnerships.

LSPs are established by local authorities and thus provide the potential for local government to assert its pre-eminent role in multi-agency crime prevention initiatives. However, once set up other agencies may play the lead role in LSPs.

Resourcing

Initially no additional funding was made available to CDRPs as it was assumed that their activities could be financed from the budgets of the participating agencies. However, the Home Office established a Partnership Development Fund to provide both money and support for activities that included the implementation of partnerships' strategies and the promotion of good and innovative practice. This was latterly amalgamated with the Community Action Drugs Programme and the Safer Communities Initiative Fund to form the Building Safer Communities Fund (Home Office, 2003). The new fund financed a number of initiatives performed by crime and disorder reduction partnerships (or by new administrative arrangements which combined crime and disorder reduction partnerships with drug action teams) which sought to tackle crime and drug-related problems. However, central funding of CDRP initiatives came at a cost, in particular in connection with the 'burden of bureaucracy' that was placed on CDRPs (National Audit Office, 2004: 5).

The government proposed further rationalisation whereby a number of separate streams of Home Office funding for CDRPs would be merged with funding streams available from the Office of the Deputy Prime Minister into a single Safer and Stronger Communities Fund which would be initiated in England in 2005–6. Additionally, 21 local area agreement pilot schemes would be launched incorporating funding streams currently available from the Home Office, the Office of the Deputy Prime Minister, the Department of Education and Skills and the Department of Health into spending directed into three areas – Children and Young People, Safer and Stronger Communities and Healthier Communities and Older People (National Audit Office, 2004: 2).

Localism versus centralism

The 1998 Crime and Disorder Act considerably advanced existing provisions for police–public liaison that had been initially laid down in section 106 of the 1984 Police and Criminal Evidence Act. However, this had largely failed to secure a major role for the public in police affairs.

Research into the role of consultative committees suggested that their ability to represent local opinion was adversely influenced by the frequent absence of community unanimity on matters affecting policing and from their lack of any form of mandate on which to base requests for changes in police policy. These bodies have been viewed as mechanisms to increase surveillance over local communities or to provide legitimacy for operational policing decisions by providing the police with a forum through which they could manipulate public opinion to endorse the course of action they wished to pursue. This legitimation was facilitated by the composition of consultative committees. These were typically socially unrepresentative, dominated by middle-aged and middle-class persons with little or no prior experience of police work and who were generally prone to be supportive of police actions (Morgan and Maggs, 1985: 91).

The approach embodied by the 1998 legislation involved decentralising the responsibility for crime and disorder prevention away from the central state (Hope, 1998b: 6). It could be seen as a development to encourage popular participation in this area of activity, in particular through the process of crime audits that permitted local people to be involved in defining problems and in suggesting solutions. In this sense, the Act encouraged 'a stronger and more participatory civil society' (Crawford, 1998: 4) and a 'radical empowerment of local people in the fight against crime and disorder' (Blackmore, 1998: 21). The 1998 legislation should be seen in the context of the Labour government's 'broader agenda for local democratic change' whose key proposals were contained in the 1998 White Paper *Modern Local Government: In Touch with the People* (Blackmore, 1998: 21) and the subsequent 1999 and 2000 Local Government Acts. The 1998 document made it clear that best-value principles (of which a key feature was effective consultative mechanisms) applied to all agencies involved in the objective of community safety, and the related auditing process would impact on the operations of CDRPs.

This 'bottom-up' system of objective setting contained in the 1998 Act was, however, threatened by the increased involvement of the Home Office in the operations and performance of CDRPs. This resulted in targets being set for CDRPs in connection with vehicle crime, domestic burglary and robbery and the introduction of performance indicators for CDRPs that inevitably shifted the local crime prevention agenda onto outputs that were capable of measurement. The emphasis exerted by the Home Office also tended to direct the work of CDRPs towards crime control activities to the detriment of longer-term measures concerned with addressing the causes of crime. The performance of CDRPs was monitored by the Home Office and, commencing in 2003/4, CDRPs were required to complete an annual report on the implementation of their crime and disorder reduction strategy. As has been noted above, additional control over CDRPs was also exerted after 2000 by the appointment of regional crime directors to each of the nine regional government offices in 2000 whose role was to improve the overall effectiveness of crime prevention.

These actions indicated a move towards centralisation whereby 'CDRPs are increasingly subject to pressures to conform to national police agendas' (Loveday, 2005: 81). This is at variance with the spirit of the 1998 Act and provides the potential for clashes when local concerns and central directions make conflicting demands on the use to which finite resources should be expended.

Lack of local accountability

One difficulty with CDRPs concerns the extent to which the activities performed by these bodies is subject to adequate mechanisms of local accountability. One solution to this problem has been to enhance the extent to which their operations are linked to local government that is democratically accountable to local people. LSPs (whose work is described above) and local area agreements (which are considered in the conclusion) have been put forward as ways to achieve this objective.

Proposals for police reform contained in the 2004 White Paper (which are discussed in Chapter 4) whose aim is to secure an enhanced role for councillors in crime-related issues are also compatible with the desire to make the work of bodies such as CDRPs more accountable and visible to local communities. Additionally, the government's *Together We Can* proposals that seek to empower citizens in eight key public policy areas spread across twelve government departments include (under the heading of 'building safer communities') the desire to improve CDRP–community engagement (Home Office, 2005).

Implications of the 1998 Act for policing

The 1998 Act posed considerable implications for policing. The service ceased to have an exclusive claim to prevent crime and disorder but was compelled to enter into 'joint working and collective responsibility' arrangements with the community and other agencies to identify and respond to crime and disorder issues (Newburn, 2002: 107). The legislation made the police service unambiguously part of a problem-solving team. This may have an adverse impact on the autonomy of the police service and impacts on matters such as the style of policing which is required to embrace problem-solving approaches (Newburn, 2002: 112). This issue is explored in more detail in Chapter 3 in connection with problem-oriented policing.

The emergence of local government as a key player in police work complicates the existing system of police control and accountability. It has been argued that this development provided the potential for the development of the tripartite system of police control and accountability into a quadripartite structure (Houghton, 2000). It could also have a detrimental effect on the role of both police authorities and chief constables in the long term. It may become difficult for a police authority to hold a chief constable accountable for his or her performance when key elements of crime and disorder policies are delivered by a partnership arrangement involving other agencies. It has thus been concluded that fragmented responsibility makes for blurred accountability (Newburn, 2002: 109).

> With reference to the area where you live, critically evaluate the work performed by CDRPs.

Assessment of the principle and practice of community safety

It has been argued above that the theme of community safety plays an important role in contemporary crime prevention work. This section briefly evaluates some of the problems that this concept might raise.

Empowerment or manipulation?

Attempts to involve members of the general public in the functioning of the criminal justice system can be viewed as beneficial to the operations of a liberal democratic political system. Initiatives pursued after 1997 (including the process of crime audit in association with the work of crime and disorder reduction partnerships set up by the 1998 Crime and Disorder Act and the establishment of Youth Offender Panels (YOPs) by the 1999 Youth Justice and Criminal Evidence Act) seem compatible with the goal of civic involvement in criminal justice affairs. It may, however, be debated as to whether community initiatives have empowerment or manipulation as their goal.

Empowerment entails an adjustment of the power relationship between the central state and the citizen to the benefit of the latter who become collectively able to take decisions affecting their everyday lives. The rolling back of the boundaries of the central state can be viewed as a prerequisite to a participatory, as opposed to representative, democracy in which local people become key stakeholders in defining the public interest and the 'interests and needs of diverse communities can be recognised and addressed' (Hirst, 2000).

However, an alternative view of community initiatives sees them as an attempt to manipulate localities into pursuing law and order goals. The net result of pursuing this 'responsibilization strategy' which encourages widespread popular involvement in combating crime (Garland, 1996: 445; Hughes, 1998: 128) through the incorporation of new elements (or what has been referred to as 'the intermediate institutions which lie between the state and the individual', Leadbeater, 1996: 34) is the erosion of modes of government which were characteristic of the welfare state (Edwards and Hughes, 2002: 4). This may result in the creation of a self-policing society, albeit it one comprised of communities with diverse resources and abilities to provide this function for themselves.

Partnership arrangements such as those provided for in the 1998 Crime and Disorder Act provided an important new mechanism for coopting a wide range of agencies and local groups into the criminal justice process (Crawford, 1999: 72). It is, however, subject to debate as to whether this approach is designed to roll back the frontiers of the state or to increase its scope by providing its objectives with enhanced legitimacy derived from popular participation. It has alternatively been suggested that partnership arrangements that provide for the dispersal of disciplinary forms of control herald the advent of the disciplinary society with neighbourhoods rather than the central state as the locus of power (Cohen, 1979).

Effectiveness

The increased use of community-orientated crime prevention initiatives might be justified on grounds of efficiency. One aspect of this argument is the perception that the central state has become overloaded and cannot effectively discharge the ever-increasing responsibilities thrust upon it. There are various rationales for seeking to reduce the role of the central state (including cost, dependency, over-bureaucratisation and depoliticisation derived from the shift of responsibility for success or failure away from the central state) but it could be argued that community initiatives will provide for a more effective form of crime prevention.

Diversity

One further problem relating to community crime prevention initiatives is that they cannot be 'taken off the shelf and applied to all communities'. Instead it is necessary 'to develop quite a sophisticated understanding of how particular localities are structured: who is powerful and why; what kind of intervention might solicit support and why. This ... may result in quite different crime reduction agendas in different localities' (Walklate, 2002: 73). Although in theory crime audits conducted under the 1998 Crime and Disorder Act might provide for diversity of this nature, pressures from central government in connection with the activities and evaluation of CDRPs may result in making their activities standardised.

Conclusion

This chapter has developed the discussion provided in Chapter 1 concerning the causes of crime by discussing a further range of general issues related to the study of criminal behaviour. It has considered the ways in which the level of crime in society can be measured and has focused on the deficiencies of official crime statistics in providing information of this nature and how alternative methodologies might provide a truer estimate of the extent of crime. The chapter then examined the concept of white-collar crime, differentiating between white-collar, corporate and middle-class crime. It sought to explain the manner in which the state responds to activities of this nature and to account for the attitude that it has adopted. The account also attempted to adapt some of the ideas discussed in Chapter 1 as explanations for criminal behaviour of this nature.

This chapter sought to provide an insight into the way in which crime can be prevented. It contrasted situational and social methods to prevent crime and assessed the strength and weaknesses of each of these approaches. Considerable attention was devoted to the contemporary application of crime prevention to the concept of community safety. The origins of this idea was explained and the application of this approach by post-1997 Labour governments was described and evaluated.

The aim of Chapters 1 and 2 has been to provide a general discussion of a wide range of issues concerned with criminal behaviour. This was designed to provide a background to the operation of the agencies in the criminal justice process that are charged with responding to criminal behaviour. The following chapter commences this discussion by considering the impact of crime on the methods, structure and organisation of policing.

Further reading

There are many specialist texts that will provide an in-depth examination of the issues discussed in this chapter. These include the following:

Coleman, C. and Moynihan J., (1996) *Understanding Crime Data: Haunted by the Dark Figure*. Buckingham: Open University Press.

Crawford, A. (1999) *The Local Governance of Crime: Appeals to Community and Partnership*. Oxford: Clarendon.

Croall, H. (2001) *Understanding White Collar Crime*. Buckingham: Open University Press.

Crowe, T. (2000) *Crime Prevention Through Environmental Design*, 2nd edn. Boston: Butterworth-Heinemann.

Hughes, G., McLaughlin, E. and Muncie, J. (eds) (2002) *Crime Prevention and Community Safety: New Directions*. London: Sage.

Slapper, G. and Tombs, S. (1999) *Corporate Crime*. Harlow: Longman.

Tilley, N. (ed.) (2005) *Handbook of Crime Prevention and Community Safety*. Cullompton: Willan Publishing.

Key events

- **1932** Initiation of the Chicago Area Project. This was an important example of community-oriented crime prevention activity. It sought to tackle aspects of social disorganisation that led to crime and delinquency, thus revitalising community life.
- **1972** Publication by Oscar Newman of *Defensible Space: Crime Prevention Through Urban Design*. This helped to popularise the objective of 'designing out crime' as a key aspect of situational crime prevention methods.
- **1974** Publication of an article by Robert Martinson entitled 'What Works? Questions and Answers About Prison Reform', suggesting that 'nothing works'. This helped to popularise crime prevention policy as a response to crime.
- **1979** Publication by Lawrence Cohen and Marcus Felson of an article entitled 'Social Change and Crime Rate Trends: A Routine Activity Approach' which suggested that the probability that certain types of crime would occur at any specific time and place was the result of the convergence of likely offenders, suitable targets and the absence of capable guardians. This theory of routine activities subsequently exerted an important influence on situational methods of crime prevention.
- **1983** Establishment of the Home Office Crime Prevention Unit, indicating the commitment of central government to this area of activity.
- **1984** Issuance by the Home Office of Circular 8/84 entitled *Crime Prevention*. This was an influential development advocating the use of multi-agency work in the area of crime prevention policy.
- **1986** Initiation of the Kirkholt Burglary Prevention Project. The findings of this report had significant repercussions for crime prevention policy, especially that directed at repeat victims of crime.
- **1991** Publication of the report of the Home Office Standing Conference on Crime Prevention, chaired by James Morgan. This developed the concept of community safety and advocated that local government should play a major role in activities of this nature.
- **1998** The enactment of the Crime and Disorder Act. This legislation exerted a considerable influence on the subsequent role of local government in crime prevention work and the development of community safety initiatives carried out through multi-agency bodies, especially crime and disorder reduction partnerships.
- **2002** The introduction by ACPO of the National Crime Recording Standard that sought to promote a greater degree of consistency in the way in which police forces collect and record crime data.

References

Armitage, R. (2002) *To CCTV or Not to CCTV? A Review of Current Research into the Effectiveness of CCTV Systems in Reducing Crime*, Community Safety Practice Briefing. London: NACRO.

Audit Commission (1994) *Opportunity Makes a Thief*. London: HMSO.

Audit Commission (1998) *Ghost in the Machine – An Analysis of IT Fraud and Abuse*. London: HMSO.

Audit Commission (1999) *Safety in Numbers: Promoting Community Safety*. Abingdon: Audit Commission Publications.

Audit Commission (2004) *Crime Recording: Improving the Quality of Crime Records in Police Authorities and Forces in England and Wales*. London: Audit Commission.

Ayres, I. and Braithwaite, J. (1992) *Responsive Regulation. Transcending the Deregulation Debate*. Oxford: Oxford University Press.

Barkan, S. (1997) *Criminology – A Sociological Understanding*. Upper Saddle River, NJ: Prentice Hall.

Barr, R. and Pease, K. (1990) 'Crime Placement, Displacement and Deflection', in N. Norris and M. Tonry (eds), *Crime and Justice: A Review of Research*, Vol. 12. Chicago: University of Chicago Press.

Barr, R. and Pease, K. (1992) 'The Problem of Displacement', in D. Evans, N. Fyfe and D. Herbert (eds), *Crime, Policing and Place: Essays in Environmental Criminology*. London: Routledge & Kegan Paul.

Bergman, D. (2000) *The Case for Corporate Responsibility: Corporate Violence and the Criminal Justice System*. London: Disaster Action.

Blackmore, J. (1998) 'Government's Agenda for Local Democracy', *Criminal Justice Matters*, 33: 21–3.

Bottomley, K. and Coleman, C. (1981) *Understanding Crime Rates*. Farnborough: Gower.

Bottomley, K. and Pease, K. (1986) *Crime and Punishment: Interpreting the Data*. Buckingham: Open University Press.

Box, S. (1981) *Deviance, Reality and Society*, 2nd edn. London: Holt, Rinehart & Winston.

Box, S. (1983) *Power, Crime and Mystification*. London: Tavistock.

Braithwaite, J. (1985) 'White Collar Crime', *American Journal of Sociology*, 11: 1–25.

Braithwaite, J. (1997) 'Charles Tittle's Control Balance and Criminal Theory', *Theoretical Criminology*, 1: 77–97.

Braithwaite, J. and Fisse, B. (1987) 'Self Regulation and the Control of Corporate Crime', in C. Shearing and P. Stenning (eds), *Private Policing*. Beverley Hills, CA: Sage.

Braithwaite, J. and Geis, G. (1982) 'On Theory and Action for Corporate Crime Control', *Crime and Delinquency*, April: 292–314.

Brantingham, P. and Faust, F. (1976) 'A Conceptual Model of Crime Prevention', *Crime and Delinquency*, 22: 130–46.

Bright, J. (1997) *Turning the Tide: Crime, Community and Prevention*. London: Demos.

Bright, J. (1999) 'They're Watching You', *Guardian*, 29 August.

Budd, T. and Sharp, C. (2005) *Offending in England and Wales: First Results from the 2003 Crime and Justice Survey*. London: Home Office, Home Office Research, Development and Statistics Directorate, Findings 244.

Butler-Sloss, E. (1988) *Report of the Inquiry into Child Abuse in Cleveland*. London: HMSO.

Byrne, S. and Pease, K. (2003) 'Crime Reduction and Community Safety', in T. Newburn (ed.), *Handbook of Policing*. Cullompton: Willan Publishing.

Clarke, J. (1996) 'The Problem of the State After the Welfare State', in M. May, E. Brunsdon and C. Craig (eds), *Social Policy Review 8*. London: Social Policy Association.

Clarke, M. (1989) 'Insurance Fraud', *British Journal of Criminology*, 29 (1): 1–21.

Clarke, R. (1992) *Situational Crime Prevention: Successful Case Studies*. New York: Harrow & Heston.

Clarke, R. (1995) 'Situational Crime Prevention', in M. Tonry and D. Farrington (eds), *Building A Safer Society: Strategic Approaches to Crime*. Chicago: University of Chicago Press.

Clarke, R. (2005) 'Seven Misconceptions of Situational Crime Prevention', in N. Tilley (ed.), *Handbook of Crime Prevention and Community Safety*. Cullompton: Willan Publishing.

Clarke, R. and Cornish, D. (1983) *Crime Control in Britain: A Review of Policy Research*. Albany, NY: State University of New York Press.

Clarke, R. and Mayhew, P. (eds) (1980) *Designing Out Crime*. London: HMSO.

Clinard, M. (1946) 'Criminological Theories of Violations of Wartime Regulations', *American Sociological Review*, 11: 258–70.

Clinard, M. (1983) *Corporate Ethics and Crime: The Role of Middle Management*. Beverly Hills, CA: Sage.

Clinard, M. and Yeager, P. (1980) *Corporate Crime*. New York: Free Press.

Cohen, L. and Felson, M. (1979) 'Social Change and Crime Rate Trends: A Routine Activity Approach', *American Sociological Review*, 44 (4): 588–608.

Cohen, S. (1979) 'The Punitive City: Notes on the Dispersal of Social Control', *Contemporary Crises*, 3: 339–63.

Coleman, A. (1985) *Utopia on Trial*. London: Hilary Shipman.

Coleman, C. and Moynihan, J. (1996) *Understanding Crime Data: Haunted by the Dark Figure*. Buckingham: Open University Press.

Collinson, P. (2004) 'Fraudsters Go Underground', *Guardian*, 30 October.

Conklin, J. (1977) *Illegal But Not Criminal*. Englewood Cliffs, NJ: Prentice-Hall.

Crawford, A. (1998) 'Community Safety Partnerships', *Criminal Justice Matters*, 33: 4–5.

Crawford, A. (1999) *The Local Governance of Crime: Appeals to Community Partnerships*. Oxford: Oxford University Press.

Critchley, T. (1978) *A History of Police in England and Wales*. London: Constable.

Croall, H. (1992) *White Collar Crime*. Buckingham: Open University Press.

Croall, H. (1998) *Crime and Society in Britain*. Harlow: Longman.

Croall, H. (2001) *Understanding White Collar Crime*. Buckingham: Open University Press.

Currie, E. (1997) 'Market, Crime and Community: Towards a Mid-Range Theory of Post-Industrial Violence', *Theoretical Criminology*, 1 (2): 147–72.

Department of the Environment (1994) *Planning Out Crime*, Circular 5/94. London: Department of the Environment.

Dodd, T., Nicholas, S., Povey, D. and Walker, A. (2004) *Crime in England and Wales, 2003/2004*, Home Office Statistical Bulletin 10/04. London: Home Office.

Donnison, H., Scola, J. and Thomas, P. (1986) *Neighbourhood Watch: Policing the People*. London: Libertarian Research and Education Trust.

Durkheim, E. (1979) *Suicide: A Study in Sociology*. London: Routledge & Kegan Paul; originally published in 1897.

Edwards, A. and Hughes, D. (2002) 'Introduction: The Community Governance of Crime Control', in G. Hughes and A. Edwards (eds), *Crime Control and Community: The New Politics of Public Safety*. Cullompton: Willan Publishing.

Ekblom, P. (1998) 'Situational Crime Prevention: Effectiveness and Local Initiatives', in P. Goldblatt and C. Lewis (eds), *Reducing Offending: An Assessment of Research Evidence on Ways of Dealing with Offending Behaviour*, Home Office Research Study 187. London: Home Office.

Ekblom, P. (2005) 'Designing Products Against Crime', in N. Tilley (ed.), *Handbook of Crime Prevention and Community Safety*. Cullompton: Willan Publishing.

Ekblom, P. and Pease, K. (1995) 'Evaluating Crime Prevention', in M. Tonry and D. Farrington (eds), *Building A Safer Society: Strategic Approaches to Crime*. Chicago: University of Chicago Press.

Farrell, G. (2005) 'Progress and Prospects in the Prevention of Repeat Victimisation', in N. Tilley (ed.), *Handbook of Crime Prevention and Community Safety*. Cullompton: Willan Publishing.

Farrington, D. (1989) 'Self-Reporting and Official Attending from Adolescence to Adulthood', in M. Klein (ed.), *Cross National Research in Self-Reported Crime and Delinquency*. Dordrecht: Kluwer.

Farrington, D. (2002) 'Developmental Criminology and Risk-Focused Prevention', in M. Maguire et al. (eds), *The Oxford Handbook of Criminology*. Oxford: Oxford University Press.

Fattah, E. (1997) *Criminology, Past, Present and Future: A Critical Overview*. Basingstoke: Macmillan.

Felson, M. (1998) *Crime and Everyday Life: Insights and Implications for Society*. Thousand Oaks, CA: Pine Forge Press.

Furnell, S. (2002) *Cybercrime: Vandalizing the Information Society*. Edinburgh: Pearson Education.

Garland, D. (1996) 'The Limits of the Sovereign State', *British Journal of Criminology*, 36 (4): 445–71.

Gillan, A. (2004) 'Late Arrivals and No-shows – But New Court's Friendly Judge Keeps Smiling', *Guardian*, 10 December.

Harris, R. (2003) *Political Corruption: In and Beyond the Nation State*. London: Routledge.

Hawksworth, L. (1998) 'Meeting the Challenge', *Criminal Justice Matters*, 33: 11–12.

Heal, K. (1987) *Crime Prevention in the United Kingdom: From Start to Go*, Home Office Research and Planning Bulletin 34. London: Home Office.

Her Majesty's Inspectorate of Constabulary (1999) *Police Integrity: Securing and Maintaining Public Confidence*. London: HMIC Press.

Her Majesty's Inspectorate of Constabulary (2000) *On the Record*. London: HMIC Press.

Hirschi, T. (1969) *Causes of Delinquency*. Berkeley, CA: University of California Press.

Hirst, P. (2000) 'Statism Pluralism and Social Control', in D. Garland and R. Sparks (eds), *Criminology and Social Theory*. Oxford: Oxford University Press.

Home Office (1965) *Report of the Committee on the Prevention and Detection of Crime*. London: HMSO.

Home Office (1968) *Crime Prevention: The Home Office Standing Committee on Crime Prevention*, 17 May.

Home Office (1976) 'Report of the Working Group on Crime Prevention', unpublished, quoted in M. Weatheritt (1986) *Innovations in Policing*. London: Croom Helm.

Home Office (1978) *Juveniles: Cooperation between the Police and Other Agencies*, Home Office Circular 211/78. London: Home Office.

Home Office (1984) *Crime Prevention*, Home Office Circular 8/84. London: Home Office.

Home Office (1990a) *Partnership in Crime Prevention*. London: Home Office.

Home Office (1990b) *Crime Prevention: The Success of the Partnership Approach*, Home Office Circular 44/90. London: Home Office.

Home Office (1991) *Criminal Statistics, Volume IV, Annual & Miscellaneous Returns*. London: Home Office.

Home Office (1992) *British Crime Survey*. London: HMSO.

Home Office (1993) *A Practical Guide to Crime Prevention for Local Partnerships*. London: HMSO.

Home Office (1995a) *Criminal Statistics: England and Wales*, 1994. London: HMSO.

Home Office (1995b) *Closed Circuit Television Challenge Competition 1996/97*. London: Home Office.

Home Office (1998a) *British Crime Survey*. London: HMSO.

Home Office (1998b) *Counting Rules for Recorded Crime Instructions for Police Forces*. London: Home Office Research and Statistical Directorate.

Home Office (1999) *Crime and Disorder Act, 1998, Statutory Partnerships: Pathfinder Sites Report*. London: Home Office Communication Directorate.

Home Office (2000) *Reforming the Law on Involuntary Manslaughter: The Government's Proposals*. London: Home Office.

Home Office (2002) *The National Policing Plan 2003–2006*. London: Home Office Communication Directorate.

Home Office (2003) *The Building Safer Communities Fund (BSC), 2003–4*, Home Office Circular 34/2003. London: Home Office.

Home Office (2005) *Together We Can*. London: Civil Renewal Unit, Home Office Communities Group.

Home Office, Lord Chancellor's Department and the Attorney General (2002) *Justice for All*, Cm 5563. London: TSO.

Home Office Standing Conference on Crime Prevention (1991) *Safer Communities: The Local Delivery of Crime Prevention Through the Partnership Approach* (the Morgan Report). London: Home Office.

Homel, R. (2005) 'Developmental Crime Prevention', in N. Tilley (ed.), *Handbook of Crime Prevention and Community Safety*. Cullompton: Willan Publishing.

Hope, T. (1998a) 'Community Crime Prevention', in P. Goldblatt and C. Lewis (eds), *Reducing Offending: An Assessment of Evidence on Ways of Dealing with Offending Behaviour*, Research Study 187. London: Home Office.

Hope, T. (1998b) 'Are We Letting Social Policy Off the Hook?', *Criminal Justice Matters*, 33: 6–7.

Houghton, J. (2000) 'The Wheel Turns for Local Government and Policing', *Local Government Studies*, 26 (2): 117–30.

Hughes, G. (1998) *Understanding Crime Prevention: Social Control, Risk and Late Modernity*. Buckingham: Open University Press.

Hughes, G. and Edwards, A. (2005) 'Crime Prevention in Context', in N. Tilley (ed.), *Handbook of Crime Prevention and Community Safety*. Cullompton: Willan Publishing.

Jacobs, J. (1961) *The Life and Death of Great American Cities*. New York: Vintage Books.

Law Commission (1996) *Legislating the Criminal Code: Involuntary Manslaughter*, Law Commission Paper 237. London: HMSO.

Lea, J. and Young, J. (1993) *What Is To Be Done About Law and Order?*, 2nd edn. London: Pluto Press.

Leadbeater, C. (1996) *The Self-Policing Society*. London: DEMOS.

Levi, M. (1999) 'The Impact of Fraud', *Criminal Justice Matters*, 36: 5–7.

Liddle, M. and Gelsthorpe, L. (1994) *Inter-Agency Crime Prevention: Organising Local Delivery*, CPU Paper 53. London: HMSO.

Loveday, B. (2005) 'Police and Community Justice in Partnership', in J. Winstone and F. Pakes (eds), *Community Justice: Issues for Probation and Criminal Justice*. Cullompton: Willan Publishing.

Mannheim, H. (1946) *Criminal Justice and Social Reconstruction*. London: Routledge & Kegan Paul.

Martinson, R. (1974) 'What Works? Questions and Answers About Prison Reform', *Public Interest*, 34: 217–27.

Maynard, W. (1994) *Witness Intimidation: Strategies of Prevention*, Crime Detection and Prevention Series, Paper 55. London: Home Office, Police Policy Directorate.

McMahon, M. (1990) 'New-Widening: Vagaries in the Use of a Concept', *British Journal of Criminology*, 30 (2): 121–49.

Moore, C. (2004) 'Britain Is Haven for Money Laundering, Says Report', *Guardian*, 30 October.

Moore, C. and Brown, J. (1981) *Community Versus Crime*. London: Bedford Square Press.

Moore, S. (1996) *Investigating Crime and Deviance*. London: Collins Educational.

Morgan, R. and Maggs, C. (1985) *Setting the PACE: Police–Community Consultation Arrangements in England and Wales*, Bath Social Policy Paper No. 4. Bath: University of Bath.

Mott, J. and Mirrlees-Black, C. (1993) *Self-Reported Drug Misuse in England and Wales: Main Findings from the 1992 British Crime Survey*, Research Findings No. 7. London: HMSO, Home Office Research and Statistics Department.

Muncie, J. and McLaughlin, E. (1996) *The Problem of Crime*. London: Sage.

NACRO (2003) *Setting Up Neighbourhood Community Safety Projects*, Research Briefing No. 5. London: NACRO.

National Audit Office (2004) *Reducing Crime: The Home Office Working with Crime and Disorder Reduction Partnerships*. London: National Audit Office, Value for Money Reports.

Newburn, T. (2002) 'Community Safety and Policing: Some Implications of the Crime and Disorder Act', in G. Hughes, E. McLaughlin and J. Muncie (eds), *Crime Prevention and Community Safety*. London: Sage.

Newman, O. (1972) *Defensible Space: Crime Prevention Through Urban Design*. London: Architectural Press.

Norris, C. and Armstrong, G. (1998) 'The Suspicious Eye', *Criminal Justice Matters*, 33: 10–11.

O'Malley, P. (1992) 'Risk, Power and Crime Prevention', *Economy and Society*, 21 (3): 251–68.

Oliver, I. (1987) *Police, Government and Accountability*. London: Macmillan.

Oxfam (1999) *Out of Control*. London: Oxfam.

Passas, N. (1990) 'Anomie and Corporate Deviance', *Contemporary Crises*, 14: 157–78.

Pease, K. (1997) 'Crime Prevention', in M. Maguire, R. Morgan and R. Reiner (eds), *Oxford Handbook of Criminology*, 2nd edn. Oxford: Clarendon Press.

Perks, W. (1967) *Report of the Home Office Committee on Criminal Statistics*. London: HMSO.

Phillips, C. (2002) 'From Voluntary to Statutory Status: Reflecting on the Experience of Three Partnerships under the Crime and Disorder Act 1998', in G. Hughes, E. McLaughlin and J Muncie (eds), *Crime Prevention and Community Safety*. London: Sage.

Pierpoint, H. and Gilling, D. (1998) 'Crime Prevention in Rural Areas', *Criminal Justice Matters*, 33: 25–6.

Public Accounts Committee (2000) *The Office of Fair Trading: Protecting the Consumer from Unfair Trading Practices*, Session 1999/2000, Thirty-Seventh Report, House of Commons Paper 501.

Punch, M. (1996) *Dirty Business: Exploring Corporate Misconduct*. London: Sage.

Quinney, R. (1977) 'The Study of White Collar Crime: Towards a Re-orientation in Theory and Practice', in R. Geis and R. Maier (eds), *White Collar Crime: Offences in Business, Politics and the Professions – Classic and Contemporary Views*. New York: Collier and Macmillan.

Rayner, J. (2000) 'Corporate Victims', *Observer*, 28 May.

Robson Rhodes LLP (2004) *Economic Crime Survey*. London: Robson Rhodes.

Rock, P. (1989) 'New Directions in Criminological Theory', *Social Studies Review*, 5 (1): 2–6.

Schapiro, S. (1990) 'Collaring the Crime, Not the Criminal', *American Sociological Review*, 55: 346–65.

Shover, N. (1998) 'White-Collar Crime', in M. Tonry (ed.), *The Handbook of Crime and Punishment*. Oxford: Oxford University Press.

Simmons, J. (2000) *The Review of Crime Statistics, A Discussion Document*. London: Home Office.

Simmons, J. and Dodd, T. (2003) *Crime in England and Wales, 2002/2003*, Home Office Statistical Bulletin 07/03. London: Home Office.

Slapper, G. and Tombs, S. (1999) *Corporate Crime*. Harlow: Longman.

Smith, C. and Allen, J. (2004) *Violent Crime in England and Wales*, on-line report 18/04. London: Home Office.

Sutherland, E. (1939) *Principles of Criminology*, 3rd edn. Philadelphia: Lippincott.

Sutherland, E. (1949) *White Collar Crime*. New York: Dryden.

Tappan, P. (1977) 'Who Is the Criminal?', in R. Geis and R. Maier (eds), *White Collar Crime: Offences in Business, Politics and the Professions – Classic and Contemporary Views*. New York: Collier and Macmillan.

Tilley, N. (1994) 'Crime Prevention and the Safer Cities Story', *Howard Journal*, 32 (1): 40–57.

Tittle, C. (1995) *Control Balance: Towards A General Theory of Deviance*. Boulder, CO: Westview Press.

Tittle, C. (2000) 'Control Balance', in R. Paternoster and R. Bachman (eds), *Explaining Criminals and Crime: Essays in Contemporary Theory*. Los Angeles: Roxbury.

Transparency International (UK) (2004) *Corruption and Money Laundering in the UK, 'One Problem Two Standards': Report on the Regulation of Trust and Company Service Providers*, Policy Research Paper 003. London: Transparency International (UK).

Walklate, S. (1989) *Victimology: The Victim and the Criminal Justice Process*. London: Unwin Hyman.

Walklate, S. (1996) 'Community and Crime Prevention', in E. McLaughlin and J. Muncie (eds), *Controlling Crime*. London: Sage.

Walklate, S. (2002) 'Gendering Crime Prevention', in H. Hughes, E. McLaughlin and J. Muncie (eds), *Crime Prevention and Community Safety: New Directions*. London: Sage.

Weatheritt, M. (1986) *Innovations in Policing*. London: Croom Helm.

Welsh, B. and Farrington, D. (1999) 'A Review of the Costs and Benefits of Situational Crime Prevention', *British Journal of Criminology*, 39 (3): 345–68.

Widlake, P. (1995) *Serious Fraud Office*. London: Little, Brown.

Wintour, P. (2004) 'Straw Tries to Block Law on Death at Work', *Guardian*, 22 October.

Young, J. (1988) 'Risk of Crime and the Fear of Crime: A Realist Critique of Survey Based Assumptions', in M. Maguire and J. Ponting (eds), *Victims of Crime: A New Deal?* Buckingham: Open University Press.

3 Policing: methods, structure and organisation

This chapter examines the manner in which policing is delivered in England and Wales. In particular it seeks to identify alterations to the methods, structure and organisation of policing resulting from changes to police work, in particular in connection with the response to crime and public order. These issues are considered in the context of policing by consent and the chapter seeks to assess whether the changes on which it focuses have eroded this historic principle of policing and given rise to a less consensual style of policing which is paramilitary in nature.

Specifically this chapter:

- considers the development of the principle of policing by consent in the formative years of 'new' policing in the twentieth century and the extent to which this objective was achieved by the early decades of the twentieth century;

- identifies the methods used to police local communities from 1829 onwards and evaluates the strengths and weaknesses of these methods;

- discusses the contemporary importance of random patrol work as a method whereby local communities are policed and appraises contemporary developments by bodies other than the police service to provide policing of this nature;

- examines the changing nature of crime and how this influenced a departure from the traditional localised structure and organisation of policing;

- considers how the need to respond to public disorder after 1970 influenced a more centralised and standardised structure of policing and helped to develop a paramilitary style of operating;

- evaluates whether changes to policing brought about by changing patterns of crime and the need to handle public order have eroded the principle of policing by consent;

- discusses developments since 1945 that have led to police functions being carried out by private sector organisations.

Policing by consent

Reforms to policing that were carried out in the nineteenth century sought to establish the principle of policing by consent. This emphasised the importance of this service operating with the support and consent of those they policed. A number of key developments (that are discussed by Reiner, 2000: 50–9) were pursued in order to achieve this objective.

Developments in policing by consent

Local organisation and control

Outside London (where the Home Secretary served as the police authority between 1829 until 1999), policing was organised locally and controlled by local people. Initially watch committees in the towns and magistrates in rural areas exercised considerable authority over policing in order to dispel the impression that the reformed system would act in the manner of the 'Bourbon' police in France and be the agent of the government, trampling roughshod over the rights of the people.

The style of policing

The initial aim of policing was to prevent crime and this was performed by the home beat method whereby police officers patrolled small geographic areas on foot. Their task was essentially passive based on the belief that their physical presence would deter the commission of crime. They were not encouraged to pursue a more active role within the community since actions regarded as an unnecessary intrusion in people's lives would have had an adverse impact on popular support for the reformed system of policing.

Limited powers

The spectre of police officers equipped with an array of special powers that might be used in an arbitrary manner was thought to be inconsistent with the citizens' exercise of civil and political liberties. Accordingly, the police were initially given common law powers to emphasise their image as 'citizens in uniform' (Royal Commission on Police Powers and Procedure, 1929).

Minimum force

The desire to dispel the image of the reformed police service as arbitrary and overbearing extended beyond the powers given to police officers and affected the weaponry with which they were provided. Officers were not routinely armed and merely carried a truncheon that was designed for their protection. The absence of weaponry that could be used in an offensive posture was designed to ensure that when the police were required to intervene to uphold law and order they would utilise the least possible degree of force. This concern was also evident in the choice of colour for police uniforms that were frequently blue or brown but never red, the colour associated with the military.

The service role of policing

Although a reformed policing system that more effectively protected life and property would appeal to all law-abiding persons, the latter role was clearly of most benefit to the wealthy. Thus in order to 'sell' policing to a wider audience (and in particular to the working classes), it was necessary that the task of policing extended beyond law enforcement. This was the origin of the 'social service function of the police' (Fielding, 1991: 126) in which a diverse range of activities (some of which were designed to tackle the social causes of crime and others which were not crime-related) were pursued by officers seeking to befriend the community. Several studies (Cummings et al., 1965 and Punch and Naylor, 1973) attest the extent to which police activities were devoted to this area in work in postwar Britain.

Recruitment

Initially police forces deliberately recruited their personnel from the working class (save for the most senior ranks of the service who in the formative years of the reformed system were frequently ex-army officers). This policy of recruiting 'fools dressed in blue' (Steedman, 1984: 7) was partly pursued for economic reasons (since members of the working classes could be paid less than members of higher social groups) but was also designed to help cultivate good relationships between the police and working classes since police officers who were drawn from the lower end of the social scale might be expected to deal more sympathetically with fellow members of the working class with whom they came into contact while performing their duties. Initially the personnel of police forces was heavily drawn from the ranks of 'labourers' and other unskilled occupations (Joyce, 1991: 142), which also meant that policing had the status of a job, the performance of which required little training.

The attainment of policing by consent

The extent to which the developments cited above succeeded in securing the consent of all members of society is the subject of much academic debate. The view of orthodox police historians was that after some initial opposition in the 1830s, the success of the police in combating crime and disorder enabled them to overcome any serious resistance to their presence on the streets and secure the consent of most sections of society (Reith, 1943: 3; Critchley, 1978: 55–6). However, the extent to which consent was obtained has been challenged.

Revisionist police historians suggest that the prime role of policing was to regulate the habits of the working classes in order to serve the interests of industrial capitalism which entailed police officers acting as 'domestic missionaries' to alter the behaviour and moral habits of the lower social orders (Storch, 1976). Accordingly, these historians alleged that consent from the working classes was not readily accorded to the police. Storch drew attention to widespread opposition to the police in the middle decades of the nineteenth century within industrious working-class communities, who saw them as 'unproductive parasites' (in the sense of men who did not work in a productive sense for a living) and viewed their presence as 'a plague of blue locusts' (Storch, 1975, quoted in Fitzgerald et al., 1981: 93). Brogden argued that the extent of consent was heavily determined by a person's position in the social ladder. He argued that the level of consent was greatest from property-owners whereas those at the lower end of the social hierarchy, the 'participants in the street economy' (Brogden, 1982: 232), granted tolerance to the police which was, at best, 'passive acquiescence', broken by frequent outbreaks of conflict throughout the nineteenth century (Brogden, 1982: 202–28). Similarly, Reiner asserted that policing was borne most heavily by 'the economically marginal elements in society' (Reiner, 2000: 78).

However, although the police service failed to secure universal consent, its relationship with the general public did show signs of improvement during the twentieth century. Legitimacy (that is, an acceptance of the right of the police to function in civil society) became widespread even though specific interventions might be less acceptable, especially by those on the receiving end of them. One local study suggested that the generally improved relationship between police and public can be mainly explained by changes which occurred after the First World War affecting 'the conditions and composition of the ... working class ... the position of youth within the generational division of labour, and ... the changing function of the police force in the developing structure of the capitalist state'. These resulted in changing the relations between the police and working class 'from outright confrontation to an unwritten system of tacit negotiation' (Cohen, 1979, quoted in Fitzgerald et al., 1981: 119). Subsequent developments included the greater level of working-class affluence after the Second World War that created a more socially integrated society. These changes underpinned what has been described as 'the golden age of policing' that was 'marked by popular respect and obedience for authority' (Fielding, 1991: 36). This was epitomised in the television programme, *Dixon of Dock Green*, in which an avuncular police constable, George Dixon, enjoyed the respect of the majority of members of the working-class area of London's docklands in which he both lived and worked.

The following discussion focuses on changes affecting the way in which crime was carried out and seeks to assess whether changes affecting the policing of local communities, alterations in the pattern of crime and the policing of public order have eroded the foundations of the historical principle of policing by consent.

Analyse the measures that were pursued in the nineteenth century to ensure that police forces operated with the consent of the general public. To what extent do these measures still operate today?

The policing of local communities

This section analyses the various methods through which policing has been delivered to local communities since the early part of the nineteenth century.

Preventive policing

The emphasis of nineteenth-century police work was upon the prevention of crime. This was implemented by 'home beat' policing, whereby a police officer was allocated a small geographic area that he would patrol on foot and thus become acquainted with its inhabitants. It was believed that the physical presence of a police officer in uniform was sufficient to reduce the level of crime within an area, so that the crime prevention role of the police being an essentially passive task.

By the early decades of the twentieth century the bulk of police work was performed by officers who worked (and often lived) in the one area. This was believed to have a beneficial impact on the relationship between police and public that was exemplified by the postwar BBC television programme, *Dixon of Dock Green*. However, the effectiveness of preventive policing conducted by the traditional home beat method was increasingly questioned in postwar Britain. This was so for the following reasons:

- *It was costly in terms of personnel.* As late as the 1960s urban patrol work followed what was termed 'the fixed point system' whereby officers patrolled between a series of contact points (such as police boxes) at pre-set times (Chatterton, 1979). The bulk of a force's officers were therefore engaged on foot patrol which was an expensive use of personnel, especially in a period when many urban police forces found it difficult to recruit to their establishment figure.
- *The nature of the work.* The work was undemanding and monotonous and lacked the glamour associated with other aspects of police work, particularly that performed by the CID.
- *It was out of date.* Home beat policing did not facilitate the use of technology (including motor vehicles) which was needed to combat the increased sophistication and mobility of criminal activity. It was also detrimental to the specialisation of functions within police forces – a specialisation that was increasingly required to respond to changing patterns of crime and disorder.
- *It was hard to gauge efficiency.* The extent to which crimes were actually prevented by this method of policing was incapable of any objective assessment, so that it was impossible to ascertain whether this was an effective use of personnel.

These problems inspired the development of an alternative method through which policing could be delivered to the general public, especially in urban areas.

Reactive policing

During the 1960s preventive policing began to be replaced by reactive policing. This was dubbed 'fire brigade policing' by Sir Robert Mark, then Commissioner of Police in London. It involved redirecting police work to respond to events after they had occurred rather than seeking to forestall them.

Reactive policing was implemented by the 'unit beat' method which was intimately associated with the use of panda cars and two-way radios. Foot patrol increasingly assumed a low status and priority within police forces, the bulk of whose work was performed by officers driving from one incident to another. Reactive policing was especially associated with the establishment of units whose officers were not tied to any particular division within a police force. One of their major roles was to mount operations designed to combat a particular type of crime when such had reached a level deemed unacceptably high by police commanders. An early example of such a unit was the Metropolitan Police's Special Patrol Group.

The main benefit of this system was that it provided tangible measurements whereby efficiency could be judged (such as response times and arrest figures). However, benefits were obtained at the expense of the police's relationship with the general public, especially in urban areas. A number of specific criticisms were levelled against reactive policing and the methods used to perform it. These included:

- *The lack of intimate knowledge of local communities*. Officers who performed most of their work patrolling in cars saw no need (and, indeed, would have found it difficult) to establish relationships with the 'ordinary' people they policed. Their inability to communicate with people resulted in accusations of insensitive policing (Weatheritt, 1983: 133). This loss of contact between the police and urban communities was a particular problem aggravated by increased facilities (especially those afforded by higher pay) enabling police officers to live outside such areas.

- *Stereotyping*. With no intimate knowledge by the police of neighbourhoods, the police had a tendency to stereotype them and the people who lived in them. This sometimes resulted in the use of police powers in a random fashion. There was considerable criticism of the way in which stop and search powers were used against black youths, implying a perception by the police that all members of this social group posed a problem for society.

- *'Hard' policing*. Concern was also expressed over the operation of units such as the Special Patrol Group in London. The support and cooperation of the public was not of prime importance for the officers of these units, and it was alleged that they sometimes acted aggressively and substituted 'hard policing' methods for those traditionally associated with policing by consent (Bunyan, 1977: 96). Accusations of this nature tended to alienate the public, reducing their level of cooperation with the police and eroding the legitimacy of the police function within the affected communities.

- *It down-valued the role of the general public in police work*. Policing by reactive methods was almost entirely delivered by the police themselves, who saw no need to involve the public in their operations This meant there was less need to consult with the public or seek to construct good relationships with them.

Some of the problems that emerged were not unforeseen when unit beat policing was introduced and resulted from the tactics used to implement reactive policing rather than from the method itself. It had not been envisaged that foot patrol would be entirely abandoned: it was also assumed that the 'collator system' (which involved an officer usually of sergeant rank recording snippets of intelligence gathered by officers while performing their duties in particular areas) would provide the police with an acceptable level of knowledge of local communities. Other difficulties that emerged arose not because of the weaknesses of policing methods but because of factors such as a large increase in the demand made by the general public for police assistance. However, the criticisms levelled against reactive policing had major implications for police accountability since the switch to such methods originated from experiments conducted by the police service. The public had participated in these decisions and the absence of their involvement fuelled the demand for enhanced police accountability to local people.

Community policing

The police service responded to criticisms of reactive policing by introducing proactive policing. This was implemented through a diverse range of methods that were individually or collectively referred to as 'community policing'. A particular objective of these varied initiatives was to shift the ethos of policing away from law enforcement (and the control function which underpinned this) and towards the service function of policing which was founded on the general duty to befriend the community. Community policing was thus advanced as the means through which police–community relationships would be improved in those places where friction between police and community had occurred.

Proactive policing emphasised the need for the police to prevent crime rather than merely react to it, and like preventive policing it was directed at limiting the opportunities for crime to occur rather than focusing on those who committed it. But unlike old-style preventive policing, the proactive style required the police to assume an active role and undertake a range of measures designed to prevent crime from occurring.

This proactive philosophy was particularly associated with John Alderson, Chief Constable of Devon and Cornwall from 1973 until 1982. His approach was based upon the belief that the fight against crime was most likely to succeed through the involvement of local people and other agencies in the public and voluntary sectors. A particular aim was to mobilise the perceived common interests shared by members of communities and direct these to combat crime. Alderson presented his community policing proposals as a coordinated package of measures (which are discussed in detail in Moore and Brown, 1981).

During the 1980s, most chief constables adopted similar methods under the general heading of 'community policing', even if these were combined with reactive strategies. This allowed officers on foot patrol to be backed up by mobile response units. Community policing initiatives included the following:

- *An increased commitment to foot patrol.* The revival of foot patrols was intended to bring the police into a more regular contact with 'normal' people. Those who performed this work were given new titles such as 'neighbourhood' or 'area' constable or 'community beat officers'.
- *The deployment of community liaison or contact departments.* These sought to formalise police relationships with specific groups of local inhabitants. Their work included regular meetings with minority ethnic groups and school liaison programmes.
- *Constructing a sense of community.* John Alderson's version of community policing extended beyond attempts to build contacts with local individuals and groups. He perceived the police to be at their most effective when they reinforced community values or standards of behaviour. If the views of the community and the police were in accord concerning the undesirability of a particular activity, the support of the former for the intervention of the latter was assured.

However, the fragmentation of communities or the absence of community values was often a feature of postwar urban living. An attempt to remedy this problem was thus a key feature of Alderson's community policing initiatives that were undertaken in Exeter that thus extended the police task beyond a focus on the offender. It led the police to take a lead in establishing local bodies such as tenants' and residents' associations to bond citizens together and help develop a community spirit that could be directed towards the maintenance of social harmony. During the 1980s neighbourhood watch schemes were encouraged on a national basis to develop such a sense of community. These were viewed as 'an exercise on social engineering by the police to produce a "village community" ' (Fletcher, 2005: 63).

Multi-agency policing

This was also associated with community policing. It was underpinned by a belief that the police could not wage an effective war against crime single-handedly, but required the active cooperation of other public and voluntary sector bodies to produce a coordinated approach to combat crime. For example, factors such as the layout and design of housing estates or the effectiveness of street lighting were viewed as relevant factors in a crime prevention policy. This justified diverse agencies meeting together and tailoring their respective concerns to the objective of crime prevention.

The Home Office enthusiastically endorsed many of the multi-agency schemes introduced by the police. The importance of community-based objectives and priorities for policing was emphasised in 1983 (Home Office, 1983) and the following year impetus was given to the involvement of agencies other than the police in a crime prevention role (Home Office, 1984).

Critique of community policing

A key rationale of community policing was to reconstruct consent and the underlying requirement of legitimacy, thereby reducing the intensity of the demand for increased accountability of the police to the public that had been made in places such as Merseyside and Greater Manchester. In this sense, consent was described as a surrogate form of accountability (Brogden, 1982: 197). For this reason, those on the left of the political spectrum seeking enhanced police accountability were often sceptical of the initiatives introduced by the police. Such criticisms included the following:

- *The police exercised too dominant a position in local affairs.* It was asserted that multi-agency ventures and police involvement in community development were designed to enable decisions related to resource allocation to be taken by the police instead of local government (Short, 1982: 80).
- *It enhanced surveillance.* It was alleged that neighbourhood watch was designed to enhance the degree of surveillance exerted over working-class communities, thus enabling the police to act as a more effective agency of social control (Donnison et al., 1986: 51–2).
- *It involved social engineering.* It was argued that the construction of communities involved the police in social engineering which was beyond their capabilities (Weatheritt, 1987: 18).

Nonetheless, the increased level of involvement of local people in the policing of their areas provided the potential for a much wider degree of popular participation in police affairs, especially in the area of crime prevention.

> Why were reactive methods of policing introduced during the 1960s? What problems became identified with this approach and how did community policing seek to redress them?

The policing of fragmented communities

It has been argued that the economic and social changes that were evident during the 1960s resulted in social disintegration (Alderson, 1979, 46–7). These were most noticeable in urban areas where the consequent absence of a sense of community had knock-on effects for police–public relationships by increasing the level of police intervention to regulate anti-social behaviour.

This section of the chapter addresses the way in which the styles of policing discussed above have been adopted in order to address the demands of policing contemporary local communities. A particular focus of the concern of these methods of policing has been to address the problems posed by fragmented communities, suggesting that the police service has a crucial role to play in securing social cohesion. This view was forcibly articulated by the Metropolitan Police Commissioner when he delivered the Richard Dimbleby lecture in 2005 when he stated that the agencies of social cohesion such as churches, trade unions and voluntary clubs had declined in influence and the agents of social enforcement such as park keepers, caretakers and bus conductors had disappeared: 'this has left many people looking – in the absence of anyone else – to the police service for answers to the neighbours from hell, the smashed bus stop, the lift shaft littered with needles and condoms, the open drugs market, the angry, the aggressive and the obviously disturbed' (Blair, 2005). Thus contemporary styles of policing emphasise the importance of working with communities in order to create a sense of cohesion and restore an element of neighbourhood self-policing (an issue which is explored in Chapter 2).

Basic command units

Local policing is delivered through basic command units (BCUs), which replaced the position formerly occupied in the police organisational hierarchy by Divisions (although some forces, such as the Greater Manchester Police, have reverted to the former designation). Their role in community policing has been much enhanced since 1997 through developments that include the establishment of CDRPs to drive multi-agency crime prevention initiatives, and the development of styles of policing such as problem-oriented policing that emphasise the role of the police as managers of local crime concerns. It has been argued that the focus of crime reduction activities has moved from force to BCU level, and that these have become the most important level 'at which there is engagement between the police and local communities' (HMIC, 2001: 15).

The vital role performed by BCUs in local policing has been acknowledged by the commencement in April 2001 of HMIC inspections of this tier of policing. Further reforms affecting funding (including the provision of some Home Office money directly to BCUs) will serve to enhance the autonomy of these units of police organisation. Changes affecting BCUs have considerably enhanced the power and status of BCU commanders. In 2001 HMIC recognised the importance of this post when it argued that BCU commands were an 'especially challenging post at the cutting edge of service delivery. Officers should be selected for these against detailed competencies' (HMIC, 2001: 68). The 2006 Police and Justice legislation proposes to place BCU's on a statutory footing and requires them to be coterminous with local authority boundaries.

Problem-oriented policing

Problem-oriented policing (POP) was developed in America (where it is commonly referred to as problem-*orientated* policing) by Herman Goldstein (Goldstein, 1979; 1990) as a rejection of the professional model of policing which entailed 'tight central control, standard operating procedures and increasing use of cars, computers and modern communications technologies' (Bullock and Tilley, 2003: 2). It has been argued that 'the concept of POP' is about examining patterns of incident clusters to identify and tackle underlying problems within the community. The development of POP was based on the perception that demands placed upon the police service meant that key issues of community to the community were often neglected (Tilley, 2003: 318), 'thus the active involvement of the community and external agencies is often vital to the identification of problems and the development of strategies to solve them' (Leigh, Reid and Tilley, 1996: 5). The basic premise of POP 'is that the core of policing should be to deal effectively with underlying police-recurrent problems rather than simply to react to incidents calling for attention one by one as they occur' (Bullock and Tilley, 2003: 1). This approach places the application of scientific methods at the heart of policing (Ekblom, 2002; Bullock and Tilley, 2003: 5–6; John and Maguire, 2003: 38) and involves:

- identifying and analysing recurrent problems;
- interrogating their underlying sources;
- finding some points of intervention that will block causes and risk factors. This intervention need not be concerned with the law enforcement aspects of policing, for example repeat victims of crime could be given financial aid to improve levels of security;
- implementing the initiatives that have been devised;
- evaluating the success of initiatives put forward to respond to identified problems.

The main features of POP emphasise targeting specific problems. These may be addressed by law enforcement activities or through multifaceted initiatives carried out by a range of participants working as a coordinated partnership or a combination of both. POP serves to enhance the role of neighbourhood police, especially when the response to crime involves activities being performed by other agencies since this entails them coordinating the response to crime problems in addition to evaluating the effectiveness of approaches adopted to solve them. The reorientation of the role performed by local police officers is defined by the use of terms such as 'Community Beat *Manager*' that is employed by the Lancashire Constabulary. POP has a number of advantages over more traditional methods of delivering policing that have been discussed above. These benefits include the following:

- *Decentralisation.* POP attempts to move the focus of police decision-making away from managers and towards front-line officers who are in a better position to understand the causes and possible solutions for problems (John and Maguire, 2003: 65). It has been argued that 'officers must know the underlying issues locally, be in contact with the community, have information to help understand the nature of the underlying problems that generate clusters of incidents, be supported by senior officers in attempting to solve problems imaginatively and tailor problem-solving to emerging local issues' (Jordan, 1998: 73). This should enable police resources to become more directly related to community needs.

- *Enhances the status of neighbourhood officers.* POP envisages a significant role for local police officers whose status in the police service is likely to rise. It has been suggested that some beat officers should also possess enhanced powers (such as time-limited, summary powers to impose driving disqualifications or anti-social behaviour orders) (Blair, 2005).

- *A shift away from law enforcement.* POP involves activities to solve crime-related issues which are undertaken by agencies other than the police and by local communities. One example of this was a burglary reduction initiative on a large housing estate in Stockport, Greater Manchester that was one of 30 pilot schemes to secure Home Office funding in the first phase of the government's £50 million anti-burglary campaign. This involved firm police action to target offenders in the specified areas combined with civil action (which embraced improvements to the physical environment of the estate) and community action (which sought to create a sense of community and included the involvement of local people in projects directed at young people (Bratby, 1999: 28–9).

- *Emphasises the importance of intelligence to police work.* POP places considerable emphasis on the gathering and analysis of intelligence as the basis of society's response to crime. The emphasis is on eliminating problems in the future as opposed to reacting to past incidents.

POP was hesitantly introduced into police forces in England and Wales during the 1980s, and was applied with slightly more vigour towards the end of the 1990s (Leigh et al., 1996; 1998). However, progress in applying a problem-oriented approach to policing was patchy (HMIC, 1998) and many forces were identified as being a long way off from implementing it fully (HMIC, 2000). There are several reasons which might explain the relatively slow progress of this approach to police work:

- *The need to respond to incidents.* Much police work is demand-led, having to respond to calls for help made by members of the general public in relation to specific incidents. It is always necessary, therefore, that police personnel are constantly available to deal with these issues as and when they occur.

- *Performance indicators.* The use of performance indicators to measure police performance inevitably means that police resources are directed into activities which are relevant to these measurements.

- *Complexity.* Considerable social science skills are required in connection with problem identification, the analysis of their causes and the evaluation of strategies to respond to these issues. However, these skills are not necessarily to be readily found within the police service. Further, these activities are time-consuming and to be performed may require sacrifices to be made to other aspects of police service provision (Goldstein, 2003; Matassa and Newburn, 2003: 213).

- *Does it work?* It has been argued that 'POP is interpreted and implemented in too many ways to permit any firm conclusion' to be made to this question (Stockdale and Whitehead, 2003: 244). It has further been argued that the assessment of outcomes in monetary terms is insufficiently developed to be able to assess whether POP is cost-effective (Stockdale and Whitehead, 2003: 249).
- *Involvement of outside agencies.* POP entails a partnership approach to solve problems. However, there may be a reluctance to fully involve these (HMIC, 2000).

As an incentive to induce police forces to adopt this approach, following the 1997 Comprehensive Spending Review around £30 million over three years was earmarked for the Targeted Policing Initiative that funded schemes to help the service develop and implement a problem-orientated approach to its work.

The law enforcement aspects of POP may make use of other forms of policing (including zero tolerance approaches). Some of these other methods of policing are discussed below.

Intelligence-led policing

Intelligence-led policing derived from a perception that the police service was failing to address 'the systemic sources of crime and crime patterns' (Tilley, 2003: 313). It thus seeks to improve the standard of police performance in particular by raising the level of detected crimes. Intelligence-led policing requires the collection of vast stores of information (using devices which include the use of informants, varied forms of surveillance and technological and academic applications such as offender profiling) which enables specific groups of offenders (especially prolific offenders) or particular patterns of behaviour to be targeted and then eliminated. These developments indicate a move towards establishing the management of risk as a police role (Neyroud, 1999).

Although POP makes considerable use of intelligence as the basis of intervention, it is not the same as intelligence-led policing. POP typically adopts a more systematic analysis of intelligence than does intelligence-led policing and the latter focuses law enforcement as a response to crime.

Intelligence-led policing does not necessarily require the involvement of outside agencies (Bullock and Tilley, 2003: 8) although it may serve to orientate the enforcement role to community safety (Tilley, 2003: 321).

The National Intelligence Model

The National Intelligence Model (NIM) was developed within the National Criminal Intelligence Service and was adopted by ACPO that viewed it as a mechanism that would blend existing methods of policing (including community policing, intelligence-led policing and POP) to ultimately provide a vehicle 'through which all major police business is channelled and delivered' (John and Maguire, 2003: 38). In particular it was viewed as the major vehicle through which intelligence-led policing would be delivered (Tilley, 2003: 321).

NIM identified three levels of crime: Level 1 concerned local criminality that could be handled within a BCU, Level 2 related to crime and major incidents affecting more than one BCU, and Level 3 concerned crime operating at the national or international level. NIM set a framework for tackling crimes at all these levels on the basis of a clear threat assessment. It provided a standard template for the 43 police forces in England and Wales regarding the collection, management and dissemination of intelligence (Home Office, 2004b: 29). It was essentially a business model – 'a means of organising knowledge and information in such a way that the best possible decisions can be made about how to deploy resources, that actions can be co-ordinated within and between different levels of policing, and that lessons are continually learnt and fed back into the system' (John and Maguire, 203: 38–9). The 2003 National Policing Plan required all forces to adopt NIM and it was intended that it should be implemented by all forces to commonly accepted minimum standards by April 2004.

Zero tolerance policing

Zero tolerance policing has an aim akin to that of a moral crusade – regaining control of the streets in order to re-establish the informal controls whose absence characterised socially disorganised neighbourhoods. This entailed pursuing measures that were designed to alter the nature of the environment to make it less conducive to the commission of crime and to reduce the public's fear of crime. Zero tolerance policing concentrated on 'ordinary' crime which troubled large sections of the public rather than serious crime, and it targeted local concerns. It was adopted in American cities such as New York where it seemed to have a major impact on the level of crime and has been associated with a diverse range of tactics that are discussed below.

Zero tolerance policing was launched on the back of the 'broken windows' thesis that was put forward in the 1980s (Wilson and Kelling, 1982). It entailed strenuously addressing petty offending (such as broken windows, graffiti or abandoned cars) which gave the impression that nobody cared about the area. This uncaring attitude encouraged an area to slide into crime since it 'creates fear on the part of citizens in a neighbourhood' who respond by withdrawing physically from public places, 'and when they do so, they withdraw those kinds of normal social controls that tend to operate. Once that social control has gone ... what you have then is an invitation to perpetrators of serious crime' (Kelling and Coles, 1998: 8). However, those associated with the development of the 'broken windows' approach denied such a linkage and were, additionally, sceptical of the concept of zero tolerance policing' (Kelling and Coles, 1998: 9). Although zero tolerance shared with the broken windows thesis the need to control minor transgressions of the law, it placed considerable emphasis on the law enforcement aspects of policing that was delivered in what was termed a 'hard-edged' or 'confident' manner (Dennis and Mallon, 1997). It concentrated on specific geographic areas, and took strict action within them with the aim of regaining the control of the streets on behalf of law-abiding people and seeking to overcome the 'culture of fear' that existed within them (Furedi, 1997). Specifically:

- It *emphasised law enforcement*. Zero tolerance policing is based upon law enforcement and thus makes little attempt to tackle the underlying causes of crime or develop approaches designed to divert persons from criminal activity.

- *All forms of crime became the subject of police activity*. It was assumed that police intervention against even the most minor of crimes could prevent the perpetrators moving on to more serious forms of criminal activity. The aim, therefore, was to nip criminal activity in the bud to stop it developing into more serious types of misbehaviour. This approach also sent out the message to all offenders that crime would not be tolerated, and made life more difficult for major criminals whose activities were screened by those of petty offenders.

- *The police assumed a tough response to criminal activity*. In Middlesbrough, Cleveland, zero tolerance policing (which was particularly associated with Superintendent Ray Mallon) involved activities such as high-profile raids on the homes of suspected criminals and the use of road blocks and stop-and-search operations. Tough action was associated with paramilitary policing methods (which are discussed below) and included the willingness to use weaponry such as CS spray. On 29 September 1998, *The Guardian* reported that CS spray was used 600 times in one year in Cleveland, the highest in any constabulary area.

The main objective of zero tolerance policing was to reduce crime, especially burglary, as evidenced in crime statistics. Unlike preventive policing, however, it pursued its aim by using law enforcement activities. It achieved results, but was also associated with a number of problems:

- *Public acceptability*. The emphasis on law enforcement downplayed other crucial aspects of police work such as its service role, which are important in creating good relationships between police and public. The public also reacted adversely to tough policing methods if these were deemed to constitute an overreaction on the part of the police. Errors of judgement were likely to arise when officers are 'psyched up' to be tough on the streets, resulting in the friction between police and public that has been a significant factor in urban disorders since 1980.

- *It could lead to the harassment of unpopular minority groups*. Concentration on, for example, disorderly youths could be associated with abuses of power by police officers.

- *Police work became result driven*. Zero tolerance policing sought to demonstrate success in the war against crime. This might lead to the use of improper practices in the belief that the end justified the means. Thus in October 1997, two Middlesbrough officers were suspended after allegations that prisoners in police cells were given heroin in return for confessions. As a result several crown court cases collapsed because police evidence was deemed to be unsafe, and a major inquiry was initiated by the Police Complaints Authority into corruption and malpractice in the Cleveland force and the alleged supply of drugs for confessions. On 30 November 1998, it was reported in *The Guardian* that 46 officers were under investigation and that 300 separate complaints had been made.

- *It reduced the patrol work performed by the 'bobby on the beat'.* Zero tolerance and related developments entailed the use of police resources on a directed basis, at the expense of random patrols mainly designed to provide a uniformed presence on the streets.

- *Its effectiveness was uncertain.* Evidence suggested that zero tolerance policing could reduce crime in selected areas in the short term, but that this may merely displace it to others. The success of methods such as the broken windows approach in New York might have been due to the large increase in police officers rather than the tactic itself. Additionally, the zero tolerance approach relied on the 'short sharp shock' working over a brief period of time and may not be sustainable as a longer-term police method.

The 1997 Labour government and 'order maintenance'

Provisions of the 1998 Crime and Disorder Act, such as anti-social behaviour orders and curfew notices, were compatible with zero tolerance policing. However, the concern with the symptoms rather than the causes of crime and the reactive nature of zero tolerance policing did not fit easily alongside the preventive aspects of this legislation and other initiatives pursued by the Labour government to tackle the social causes of crime. These considerations, together with other problems associated with zero tolerance policing which have been discussed above (which were raised in a 1998 Home Office research study, *Reducing Offending*), resulted in the announcement of refinements to this approach being announced by the Prime Minister at the 1998 Labour party conference.

Blair announced the introduction of what was termed 'order maintenance' into 25 crime 'hot spot' areas throughout Britain that were identified through the use of methods such as crime pattern analysis. This proposed a more targeted use of police patrols, and blended the reactive aspects of zero tolerance with crime prevention based upon the use of problem-orientated and 'intelligence-led' policing.

However, there were problems with such methods. These included the criteria used to identify activities which justified intervention from the police, the negative impact on communities which were officially labelled crime hot spots, and the possible creation of a false sense of security in areas which were not singled out for such attention.

Neighbourhood policing

It has been noted that a central aspect of Labour's Third Way agenda is to develop a sense of responsibility and citizenship by treating citizens as key stakeholders in the services they use (Giddens, 1998). This has led to a further development affecting police methods that seeks more closely to orientate the delivery of policing according to local needs. It is termed neighbourhood policing and goes beyond placing enhanced numbers of uniformed personnel (including police officers and police community support officers) on the streets in localities (a development which is discussed in this chapter), and extends to creating structures whereby policing can become more closely oriented to local needs. This issue was initially discussed in a consultative paper (Home Office, 2003) that put forward proposals designed to move 'away from a notion of policing simply by consent, to policing carried out with the active cooperation of the public' (Blunkett, 2003: 1). This led to firm suggestions being made in a subsequent White Paper (Home Office, 2004a), a key intention of which was 'to deliver community policing for today's world' (Blunkett, 2004: 5). This entailed 'the spread of neighbourhood policing ... to every community', and 'the greater involvement of communities and citizens in determining how their communities are policed' (Home Office, 2004a: 6–7).

The government announced its intention to extend neighbourhood policing by reducing bureaucracy and improving scientific and technological support so that by 2008 the equivalent of 12,000 officers will be freed for front-line duties. By the same date, it was intended that every community 'would benefit from the level and style of neighbourhood policing that they need' (Home Office, 2004a: 7), the essence of which would be neighbourhood policing teams composed of fully trained officers working alongside police community support officers who would take 'an intelligence-led, proactive, problem-solving approach to enable them to focus on and tackle specific local issues' (Home Office, 2004a: 7). Neighbourhood policing teams would correspond to local authority ward boundaries. The minister responsible for the police stated that it was intended that officers would give a long-term commitment to the communities in which they worked, so that local people 'should know their names, their mobile phone numbers, their emails, how to contact them, who they are and that there is continuity' (Blears, 2005). Local communities would be engaged in establishing and negotiating priorities for action and identifying and implementing solutions. The delivery of services (at neighbourhood, BCU and force levels) would be subject to guaranteed standards of customer service to the public, and a local contract would be agreed between the community and the police to deliver these. Performance measurement of the police would include a level of public satisfaction (Home Office, 2004a: 7–8).

The White Paper also argued that the police service should become much more closely engaged with local people. This would be achieved by improved dissemination of information on issues such as the mechanics of their involvement in keeping their communities safe and setting local priorities, and by enhancing the current role of councillors and local authority community safety officers 'to give them an explicit remit to provide a focal point for the local community in terms of dealing with those agencies responsible for community safety. They would ensure effective representation for people's concerns and empower people to work with the police and others to find better solutions to their problems' (Home Office, 2004a: 10). The police would be accountable to the community for their actions (or non-actions) through mechanisms which included public meetings at which they (or other relevant agencies) would discuss issues of concern that the community did not feel were being effectively addressed and explain what action they intended to take. Research that suggested that most members of the general public had not heard of police authorities and that those who had were generally unaware of their role (Myhill et al., 2003) was responded to with the proposals that police authorities should oversee the process of local consultation and the local government cabinet member responsible for community safety should sit on the police authority to strengthen democratic accountability. These reforms were designed to make police authorities 'more closely connected to and visible to their local community' (Home Office, 2004a: 11).

In order to implement these suggestions, the National Centre for Police Excellence subsequently developed Ten Principles of Neighbourhood Policing that were based on neighbourhood policing teams who engaged with the public to identify the problems that were of most concern to them. The National Reassurance Policing Programme was also initiated, a key feature of which was its focus on signal crimes and disorders. This also emphasised the importance of involvement with the public in selecting problems and designing remedies to them. Particular attention was to be devoted to tackling what were termed 'signal crimes and disorders'. These were activities (that included anti-social behaviour) that had an adverse impact on people's sense of security and caused them to alter their beliefs or behaviour. Success in tackling these would thus have a disproportionate impact on neighbourhoods, especially in alleviating their fear of crime, and serve to strengthen community cohesion.

A key difficulty with this approach is that it seems to be at variance with the increased volume of central control over police affairs. However, this is not necessarily the case if the role of police officers operating at neighbourhood level is reorientated so that they become managers of the response to crime. Their main role is that of analysing local crime problems, coordinating responses to them (which are delivered by a wide range of agencies utilising multi-agency approaches rather than by the police acting in isolation and relying on enforcement methods alone), and evaluating the success (or otherwise) of the responses that have been adopted. Thus the drain which neighbourhood-oriented policing places on police resources may not be substantial.

Reassurance policing

The reassurance agenda was particularly directed at tackling the fear of crime. Reassurance policing is based upon the provision of a uniformed presence within communities. Historically it was the task of the police service to perform this function. It was carried out by random patrol work. This section assesses the reasons why this style of policing fell out of fashion in the police service and discusses a number of initiatives that have been put forward to achieve the objectives of random patrol work through other mechanisms.

What is termed 'random patrol work' entails police officers walking a beat. This historic method of policing is popular with the public since it symbolises the presence of lawful authority within a community. It is thus an important source of reassurance for the public and appreciation for this style of policing is evidenced in national and local surveys (Skogan, 1990). Politicians seeking to court public approval for their law and order policies frequently advocate the return of 'more bobbies on the beat'. However, the patrol function of policing performed in this manner came under increasing critical scrutiny in the latter part of the twentieth century. As a result, politicians and the public have been enjoined to understand that such a method of policing is 'not a panacea for all policing problems' (Audit Commission, 1996: 6). This is so for the following reasons:

- *It is viewed as a lowly task within the service.* One of the consequences of the unit beat method of policing was that random foot patrol was devalued within the service. It is often viewed as a form of apprenticeship which probationer constables are required to undertake at the outset of their careers, before moving on to more 'glamorous' or 'worthwhile' activities.
- *Police forces lack the necessary personnel.* Factors such as specialisation of tasks within the police service and the reactive nature of much police work have meant that there are insufficient resources to sustain a commitment to random police patrol work.
- *Patrol work is of questionable efficiency.* One difficulty with random patrol work is that it is widely viewed as having a negligible impact on crime levels (an opinion upheld by Jordan, 1998: 67) and that the benefits with which it might be associated (especially securing good relationships between police and public) are not easily quantifiable. A particular difficulty with random patrol work is that its objectives are not clearly defined for those undertaking the task; this led one study to suggest the introduction of 'directed patrolling' to address this issue (Burrows and Lewis, 1988).
- *The relevance of patrol work is influenced by debates concerning the main tasks of policing.* Disputes exist in areas which include whether the prime task of policing is to fight crime or to maintain the Queen's peace, the extent to which local concerns have become subordinated to central direction (in the wake of the 1994 Police and Magistrates Courts Act), and the attempt to distinguish between core and ancillary functions.

Reforms directed at patrol work

A uniformed presence in neighbourhoods is popular with the public and is an essential feature of modern methods of policing including zero tolerance and neighbourhood policing. There are a number of ways in which this can be delivered which are discussed below.

The police service should resume major responsibilities for this work

There are various ways whereby this could be achieved. One way would be for the police service to re-prioritise this activity. However, a study in 1996 estimated that although around 55 per cent of a police force's strength was theoretically classed as operational patrol, the nature of policing meant that an average sized force of around 2,500 officers serving a population of 1 million citizens had only 125 officers (or 5 per cent of its strength) to conduct patrol work and that most of this was carried out in cars rather than on foot (Audit Commission, 1996: 10–11). Although reforms have been subsequently proposed to increase the presence of police officers in communities (for example by implementing suggestions made in Sir David O'Dowd's Policing Bureaucracy Taskforce Report which sought to reduce the administrative burdens placed on front-line officers), there would need to be an enormous, and costly, recruitment of additional police officers to make any significant improvement in this area of activity.

An alternative development would be the introduction of a second tier to the police service, consisting of designated patrol officers whose role would emphasise this aspect of police work and provide a physical presence in communities.

The 2002 Police Reform Act enabled chief constables to designate suitably skilled and trained civilians to exercise powers and undertake duties to carry out specific functions which could be in one of four categories – investigating officer, detention officer, escort officer and community support officer.

Police community support officers (PCSOs) are funded by the Home Office. Around 4,000 were employed by the end of 2004, but the government intended to recruit a further 20,000 paid for out of a neighbourhood policing fund. These would work alongside fully trained officers in dedicated neighbourhood policing teams operating across the country (Home Office, 2004a: 7) and their prime purpose was to act as the eyes and ears for these officers. PCSOs receive less training, and are paid less, than members of regular police forces nor are they equipped in the same manner. Their effectiveness to deal with potentially confrontational situations was adversely affected by their lack of powers. Accordingly, it was intended to increase these, including the power to detain (Home Office, 2004a: 9), and in December 2004 the power of PCSOs to detain suspects who refused to give their names and addresses for up to 30 minutes was extended from six pilot areas to the whole of England and Wales. They may also use reasonable force to detain suspects. The 2006 Police and Justice legislation proposed to standardise the powers of PCSOs across England and Wales.

One difficulty with this reform, however, is whether PCSOs can operate effectively as enforcement officers. Officers on the beat never know what issue they might suddenly confront, perhaps requiring PCSOs to receive thorough training and a full range of powers. There is also the problem that the routine work performed by PCSOs is boring which may make it difficult to recruit and retain staff. An alternative solution is to place increased emphasis on the Special Constabulary to carry out routine patrol functions.

The Special Constabulary

The Special Constabulary was formed in 1831 under the provisions of the Special Constables Act, and consists of members of the general public who volunteer their services to perform a limited number of hours of police work in their spare time. Special Constables are unpaid, although they receive out-of-pocket expenses. They are given a limited amount of training delivered (since a recommendation made by a Police Advisory Board for England and

Wales report in 1981) at weekend residential training courses. They exercise full police powers for the areas in which they are appointed.

The Special Constabulary was initially designed to 'beef up' policing in times of crisis (such as during the two world wars and at the time of the General Strike in 1926). Accordingly, the state has adopted a more sceptical view of its importance in 'normal' times and to a large extent the organisation suffered from benign neglect after 1945. This may be evidenced by the contracting size of the organisation: in 1938 the Special Constabulary numbered in excess of 118,000 volunteers, but by 1989 this figure had shrunk to around 16,000 (Fielding, 1991: 87).

However, in the 1990s the Special Constabulary was reinvigorated to undertake routine patrol tasks. In 1993 the Home Secretary announced the establishment of the Parish Constable scheme in rural areas. This involved deploying Special Constables to provide a foot patrol presence and address nuisance and minor crime, and parish wardens (who were not members of police forces) to channel information and advice between the police and community. This scheme was subsequently extended throughout the country as part of the Neighbourhood Constable initiative.

There are a number of problems with the extended use of the Special Constabulary. Traditionally, the Police Federation has not viewed them sympathetically, seeing the Specials as a device to undermine a professional police service with persons who are poorly trained to undertake police work. The turnover of volunteers is also rapid, although one explanation for this is the transfer of its younger members to the regular police service, using their time in the Specials to obtain practical experience (Fielding, 1991: 87). In 2000 a £700,000 recruiting scheme was launched to boost recruitment to the Special Constabulary and the 2006 Police and Justice legislation proposed that Special Constables could exercise their powers anywhere in England and Wales.

Plural policing initiatives

Plural policing entails an enhanced role for organisations other than the police service in performing random patrol work. These effectively constitute a second tier of police service providers and the organisations supplying work of this nature may be located in either the public or private sectors (or embrace aspects of both in areas such as funding and the status of those performing the work – giving rise to what has been referred to as 'hybrid' policing bodies (Johnston, 1993). These developments have resulted in what has been described as 'a pluralized, fragmented and differentiated framework of policing' (Crawford, 2003: 136), a key concern of which is to tackle the fear of crime and fill the gap caused by the removal of a number of 'secondary social control occupations' (Jones and Newburn, 2002) such as park keepers and guards on public transport. Plural policing provides an important example of the implementation of a strategy of responsibilisation (Garland, 2001) whereby the responsibility for crime prevention has been 'hived off' from the central state and has become intimately associated with the objective of community safety.

One aspect of the 1998 crime and disorder legislation was the introduction of crime audits, enabling local people to articulate their concerns regarding crime and disorder. This has tended to formalise pressure for more police patrols to respond to problems such as hooliganism, stray dogs and litter at a time when restraints on police budgets made it impossible for police forces to devote increased resources into any activity of doubtful effectiveness.

However, if routine patrol work is not perceived as a core element of policing this activity might be carried out by private bodies or local authorities. A number of local authorities have funded law enforcement initiatives and routine patrols in areas such as housing estates. These included the Sedgefield Community Force that was established in 1992 as an aspect of a community safety initiative entailing a 24-hour patrol operated by the local authority. Those who perform these activities are local authority employees and the main advantage of local government performing work of this nature is that they are subject to local accountability. On 17 July 1998, *The Independent* stated that in 1998, local authorities in 18 of the 43 police force areas in England and Wales operated their own security patrols, and private firms operated on housing estates in a further seven police force areas.

In 1999 the Metropolitan police announced the launch of a pilot scheme in four areas of the capital whereby routine patrol work would be shifted from the police service to other agencies including uniformed council staff and other private bodies. Two of these schemes would be licensed by the police, constituting what the chief constable of Surrey, Ian Blair, described at the annual conference of the Association of Chief Police Officers (ACPO) at Birmingham in 1998 as the 'third way' of policing; the other two were controlled by local government.

In March 2000 proposals for paid neighbourhood wardens to patrol housing estates and inner-city streets were announced. This led to the development of a system of neighbourhood wardens (to whom alternative descriptions such as neighbourhood safety patrols are sometimes applied) throughout England and Wales whose purpose was to offer a semi-official presence in communities which suffered from disorderly and anti-social behaviour committed by young people, thereby providing assurance to the areas in which they operate and reducing the fear of crime. Further developments based on wardens were subsequently developed. The Street Wardens programme (which was initiated in 2001) extended the concept of neighbourhood wardens beyond residential areas, and in 2002 Street Crime Wardens were introduced as an aspect of the government's Street Crime Initiative in the ten police forces with the highest level of street crime.

Wardens do not possess police powers. Their main role is to relieve the police service from low-level tasks (especially patrol work) but they may perform additional functions including acting as professional witnesses (for interventions such as anti-social behaviour orders) and providing the police with intelligence. Their working arrangements with the police are governed by guidelines prepared by ACPO in 2000 and protocols entered into by local police forces and the wardens' organisers. Typically neighbourhood wardens are operated by private companies that obtain funding from a range of central sources (including, initially, money provided from the Office of the Deputy Prime Minister) with which to employ the wardens. The employer provides wardens with basic training (for example in the area of drug awareness).

Problems with this initiative include the relatively low wages paid to wardens, the uncertain long-term status of the funding, and the possibility that the presence of wardens in one area will merely transfer anti-social activities and crime to neighbouring areas without them.

The developments referred to in this section were divorced from the police service. This posed the problem of accountability and led to suggestions that mechanisms should be developed to provide for the overall supervision of all agencies and bodies engaged in the delivery of policing policy (Loader, 2000). Some attempts have been made to enhance the coordination of the diverse bodies associated with various aspects of police work. However, the 2002 Police Reform Act enabled chief constables to establish closer cooperation with these developments through the establishment of a Community Safety Accreditation Scheme. This would enable police forces to work in closer cooperation with local authorities, housing associations and private security companies. Additionally, the 2002 legislation enabled chief constables to designate wardens, security guards and others as Accredited Community Safety Officers who would have powers to deal with anti-social behaviour (although these would be more limited in scope than those possessed by PCSOs).

Question

'The public want a uniformed presence in their communities but the police service alone cannot provide this service.' Critically assess how this dilemma has been addressed in recent years.

Serious crime, police structure and organisation

This section examines developments that have contributed towards transforming Britain's essentially decentralised system of policing into a more centralised organisation, the activities of which have increasingly become standardised throughout the country. These innovations (many of which were initiated by the police service) need to be viewed in conjunction with changes to the control and accountability of policing that are discussed in Chapter 4.

The changing nature of crime

The evolution of crime has significantly contributed towards the changing structure and organisational nature of policing. A decentralised organisation was appropriate when crime was a predominantly local affair, often carried out by individual criminals for some of whom crime was a full-time job

(Sutherland, 1937: 197) that was characterised by craft-based forms of crime such as 'safe cracking'.

The Second World War and its immediate aftermath witnessed the continuation of this pattern of crime. During the war a considerable number of offences were based on breaches of the Defence Regulations (which were concerned with a number of matters relevant to the conduct of the war) and crime committed by juveniles such as looting (Taylor, 1981: 46). Following the war fraud and corruption in and around the black market (which entailed the provision of foodstuffs and goods whose supply was restricted by government control and rationing) boosted the crime level. Crime in the later years of the war and in the immediate postwar period was attributed to the activities of those termed 'spivs' and 'drones', terms which were 'applied to sharp practitioners, con men and other skilled operators on the margins of legitimate and illegitimate business practices' (Taylor, 1981: 59). Much of the crime with which they were associated was property crime coupled with some acts of violence. Nonetheless, the character of crime remained essentially local.

However, significant changes began to occur to the nature of crime after 1945. The enterprise of individual criminals gave way to more collective forms of activity frequently involving armed robbery. Although the teams that carried out these crimes were sometimes recruited on an ad hoc basis (Morton, 2003: 229–30), the shift from craft-based forms of crime to project-based enterprises was sometimes characterised by careful planning and organisation (McIntosh, 1971). The latter were organised by professional criminal masterminds who recruited teams specifically for a particular criminal enterprise (often an armed robbery) and were willing to use violence to achieve their aims. This resulted in spectacular crimes involving vast sums of money, the first successful major postwar example of which was the 'Great Mail-bag Robbery' on 21 May 1952 in which £287,000 in cash was stolen (Morton, 2003: 235). Other examples included the 'Great Train Robbery' on 8 August 1963 when an estimated £2.5 million was stolen, which at that time was the biggest theft the world had ever known (Morton, 2003: 242). Activities of this nature were continued into the 1970s when cash in transit became a particular target.

A related (although separate) development was the rise of criminal gangs wielding control within specific geographic areas and whose focus was particularly directed at controlling existing criminal activities. Gangs of this nature were not a new development and had existed in the latter years of the nineteenth century in a number of cities. In many ways the activities of the Sabinis in London in the interwar years (which embraced protection rackets centred on gambling and drinking pursuits) provided a model for the development of subsequent criminal gangs which were characterised by being centred on families for whom crime was important both for profit and also for the power and prestige it bestowed on gang leaders. This form of criminal enterprise was epitomised by the activities of the Krays in East London and the Richardsons in South London during the 1950s and 1960s and provided the roots of modern professional, organised crime (Carrabine et al., 2004: 188).

The scope of criminal enterprise extended after the 1960s, fuelled by factors such as increased affluence, consumerism, changes in moral attitudes and technological developments. This gave rise to activities that included pornography, the counterfeiting of goods, VAT fraud and (especially during the 1980s) drugs. It has been argued that the promotion of materialist values during the Thatcher era helped to fuel criminal enterprise (Carrabine et al., 2004: 190). Gun-related crime became particularly prevalent in the early years of the twenty-first century, with offences involving firearms increasing 40 per cent between 2000 and 2002 (Muir, 2005).

These modern forms of criminal enterprise required new forms of management and are referred to as 'organised crime' which embraced activities conducted at national and international levels, characterised by an enhanced degree of organisation than had previously existed. Organised criminals have been defined as 'those involved, normally working with others, in continuing serious criminal activities for substantial profit, whether based in the UK or elsewhere' (NCIS definition, quoted in Home Office, 2004a: 7). This definition highlighted that many organised crime groups 'were, at root, businesses and often sophisticated ones' (Home Office, 2004a: 7), whose scale of operations was vast and included drug trafficking, excise fraud, VAT fraud and organised immigration crime (Home Office, 2004a: 8). Globalisation and technology helped to fuel the growth of organised crime – 'globalisation ... has made it increasingly easy for foreign organised criminals to set up base in major European cities such as London ... New technologies provide new and more effective means to commit crime ... as well as more secure ways of communicating with criminal groups' (Home Office, 2004a: 11).

One aspect of these new patterns of criminal enterprise has included crime based on diverse ethnic communities, although it has been argued that 'the extent to which ties into ethnic communities translate into international criminal operations or conspiracies' (such as the Yardies or Triads) is 'complex and debatable' (Carrabine et al., 2004: 192). However, the existence of organised criminal gangs whose members derived from London's minority ethnic communities prompted the Metropolitan Police to set up a specialist unit to combat their activities in 2005. These were said to include activities such as running protection rackets, importing fake electrical games and trafficking women to use as prostitutes (Cowan and Hyder, 2005).

The changed patterns of crime after 1945 were matched by police reorganisation that initially (during the 1960s) took the form of regional crime squads operating across police force boundaries. Developments connected with the national and international organisation of crime resulted in changes to policing which tended to promote national responses that were at the expense of traditional organisational structures. These are discussed more fully below.

Technology and policing

Technology is an important crime-fighting weapon that has also contributed towards the centralisation of policing. The ability of police officers anywhere in the country to access certain basic information such as lists of known criminals, wanted or missing persons, stolen firearms and registered vehicles from anywhere in the country was enhanced by the introduction of the Police National Computer (PNC) into police work in 1974 (the latest version of which entered service in 1991). The PNC has subsequently been developed by Phoenix which provides the police with instant access to records of arrests, convictions and cautions; this enables those provisions of the 1993 Criminal Justice Act to be acted upon which permit a previous criminal record to be taken into account as an aggravating factor.

The requirement that all police forces should report information in a standardised fashion has also been developed by the Crime and Incident Reporting application of the National Strategy for Police Information Systems that was launched in 1994. This application enables all forces to record crime data in a standard format. The ability of the police to respond to major incidents involving criminal activity in several parts of the country – and thus necessitating cooperation by different police forces – was enhanced by the Home Office Large Major Enquiry System. HOLMES 2 will enable incidents in different forces to be linked by cross-matching details of a person, vehicle, address or telephone in one investigation's database with details held in another.

Related developments involving the use of computer technology include the establishment in 1995 of the DNA database for the police that is managed by the Forensic Science Service. By 2000 there were 775,000 DNA samples in the database (Barnett, 2000). That year the government announced that it intended to include the genetic fingerprints of all arrested persons in this database which could then be matched against evidence gathered from crimes which had been unsolved. The National Automated Fingerprint Identification System (NAFIS) further provides the police service with a national fingerprint database.

The use of computers has been supplemented by other forms of technology to fight crime. These include the use of closed-circuit television (CCTV) to monitor the activity of the general public in the hope of deterring or identifying those responsible for urban crime and disorder. A significant development of this was the introduction of a face recognition surveillance system at Newham, London in 1998. This employed CCTV cameras that could match images of faces of passers-by in the streets with known criminals. When a match was made, the police would be alerted. A drawback with this scheme was that the matching-up system was not perfect and errors could be made.

All vehicles entering or leaving the City of London or British seaports are watched by robot automatic number plate scanners that are linked to the PNC at Hendon. This enables vehicles 'of interest' to the police to be speedily identified. Individual forces also experimented with other forms of technology, such as the helmet-mounted video cameras introduced by Cleveland Constabulary in 1997. These were used to record images that could be used later as evidence in court.

The main objection to such developments has come from those concerned with their potentially damaging impact on personal rights and freedoms. Particular adverse attention has been directed against the use by the police of computers that facilitate the gathering of information on individuals: 'information gathering, daily on the increase, does not prevent crime ... but it does attack the liberty of the individual' (Manwaring-White, 1983: 219).

National police organisation

This section discusses the formation of the National Criminal Intelligence Service (NCIS) and the National Crime Squad (NCS), and examines the involvement of the Security Service (MI5) in crime-related tasks.

The formation of NCIS and the NCS

During the 1970s a number of national squads were formed to gather intelligence on activities that included the drugs trade, illegal immigration and football hooliganism. These units were brought together in 1992 under the organisational umbrella of the National Criminal Intelligence Service (NCIS) to perform 'a supply and support role in relation to agencies which … have enforcement and investigative functions' (Walker, 2000: 202). It was controlled by the Home Office and additional functions (such as the formation, in 1995, of a special unit to focus on groups involved in the theft of vehicles and mobile building equipment) were subsequently added to its responsibilities. This body had no executive arm, although its regional organisation matched that of the regional crime squads that were themselves subject to a loose form of national coordination based in London. A further related development occurred in 1995 with the establishment of the National Crime Facility within the Police Staff College at Bramshill to provide police forces with information and expertise to help them solve serious crimes.

In 1995, the Home Affairs Committee advocated the establishment of a national crime squad to tackle organised crime. In a speech delivered to an ACPO conference at Manchester in July 1996, the Home Secretary announced his intention to form a new national crime unit to tackle drug traffickers and other organised crime. It would be composed of two sections. One would be concerned with intelligence gathering, based on the existing NCIS supplemented by some MI5 officers. The other unit, with which it would closely cooperate, was the National Crime Squad (NCS). This would be an operational unit, consisting of the regional crime squads amalgamated into a national unit. According to information published in *The Independent* on 3 July 1996 and *The Guardian* on 13 March 1998, this would consist of 1,450 detectives seconded from their own forces and in excess of 200 support staff, based in 44 locations in England and Wales. The functions of the NCS would be serious crime that was of relevance to more than one police force in England and Wales, and it was anticipated that drugs would form an important aspect of its work. It was proposed that the Home Office would relinquish its control of the NCIS and two 'service authorities' would be set up, one for the NCIS and the other for the NCS. These would reflect the tripartite composition of police authorities, being composed in total of 17 members. These would comprise independent members appointed by the Home Secretary, representatives of ACPO, nine members selected by the Association of Police Authorities and one Home Office representative.

These reforms were subsequently incorporated into the 1997 Police Act. This measure also placed the NCIS on a statutory footing and established a Criminal Records Agency to facilitate criminal background checking on around an estimated 8 million job applicants each year. The purpose of this reform was to enable employers to demand a criminal conviction certificate. This legislation established other central bodies concerned with police work, including the Police Information Technology Organisation. This was established to conduct activities related to information technology equipment for the use of police forces and police authorities.

Developments in European integration involving the removal of barriers to permit the free movement of goods and capital have created new opportunities for criminal activity on an international scale. Organised crime takes advantage of countries such as the UK that have lax laws to regulate money-laundering. On 22 August 1999, for example, *The Observer* reported the case of a Russian alleged to be a senior figure in the country's biggest crime gang who was said 'to be involved in the traffic of nuclear materials, drugs, precious gems and stolen art as well as contract killings'. He was linked to an investigation by officers of the NCIS at the London office of the Bank of New York, 'after it emerged that between $4.2 billion and $10 billion of dirty money had been laundered through a single account'.

Technology and international crime

The existence and sophisticated nature of much national and international crime is one justification for the UK having a national policing organisation. The annual report of NCIS in 1999 pointed out that organised crime was Britain's third largest industry, worth around £50 billion a year. Many of these activities involve communications technology and the Internet.

On 12 September 1999, for example, *The Observer* reported that the boom in Internet shopping was fuelling a massive rise in credit card fraud. In turn this has required an appropriate response by the law enforcement agencies. In 1996 NCIS launched Project Trawler to study the extent of criminal use of the Internet, and the following year urged laws to enable the police to intercept and monitor e-mails. Following this, ACPO launched a series of seminars with Internet service providers designed to promote informal agreements for police access to e-mail and Internet information.

In 1999 the formation of a specialist code-cracking unit was announced to counter the growing use of encrypted e-mail messages by drug runners and paedophile rings. This unit drew staff from the Government Communications Headquarters (GCHQ) and the NCIS and was designed to give the police and Customs and Excise information such as details of drugs deals. Its work was underpinned by the 2000 Regulation of Investigatory Powers Act. This legislation required all UK Internet service providers to install black boxes to monitor all data traffic (including websites visited and e-mails sent and received) passing through its computers. These were linked to a special centre at MI5 headquarters. Enforcement agencies were empowered to demand the surrender of keys to encrypted data as a weapon that could be used against paedophiles. The 2000 budget further allocated money to the Home Office to establish a centre to eavesdrop on e-mail messages and other types of electronic communication.

The new role of the Security Service (MI5)

M15 was formed in 1909 to thwart the spying activities conducted in Britain by the nation's enemies. It was primarily an intelligence-gathering body. The end of the Cold War resulted in MI5 straying from its initial brief, and in 1992 it was assigned the lead role in countering terrorism on mainland Britain. The bulk of MI5's resources were then devoted to this function which provided the main reason for the agency's continued existence and approximately one half of its resources were devoted to Northern Irish terrorism (Rimington, 1994).

The IRA ceasefire necessitated the development of new areas of responsibility, and the 1996 Security Services Act allocated MI5 the responsibility for dealing with 'serious crime' in addition to its existing functions. This theoretically gave MI5 a broad remit since 'serious crime' was defined as an offence that carried a sentence of three years or more on first conviction, or any offence involving conduct by a large number of persons in pursuit of a common purpose. Theoretically, therefore, 'mugging' or obstruction of the highway by protesters could become the concerns of MI5. This raised the possibility of demarcation disputes (or 'turf wars') arising between the police and MI5, although the relatively small size of MI5 (which has below 2,000 staff) made it unlikely that this agency would usurp mainstream policing roles.

The role given to MI5 by the 1996 Security Services Act was contentious. Civil libertarians expressed concerns that the term 'serious crime' was a broad one and that the Act:

- provided no definition of the categories of persons liable to surveillance;
- failed to place limits on the activities which were subject to this form of scrutiny;
- lacked adequate mechanisms of accountability.

In connection with the last point, a former chief constable, John Alderson, argued that it was fatal to involve MI5 with ordinary crime because of its lack of accountability. He stated that this organisation worked by infiltrating organisations, jobs and lives, operating 'almost like a cancer ... destroying trust and security between people', and accused the Home Secretary of seeking to turn Britain into a police state, with MI5 becoming an East German-style Stasi force with half the population spying on the other half (Alderson, 1996).

The police service was also concerned about this development. The 1989 Security Service Act gave MI5 statutory recognition, and unlike ACPO or individual chief constables, the Director General of MI5 had direct access to ministers who might give operational directions to this agency. The police service was therefore concerned that MI5 would become the lead agency in dealing with matters such as drugs and organised crime and become a de facto national police organisation, the British equivalent of the American FBI. This led ACPO to view favourably the formation of a national police squad to deal with serious crime, which would act as the operational arm of the NCIS. Fears concerning MI5 dominance in dealing with serious crime also arose as only this agency had specific legal power to enter a person's premises and plant a bugging device to effect surveillance. Accordingly, ACPO and the NCIS urged police powers in connection with bugging to be placed on the same legal footing as those of MI5.

This innovation was introduced in the 1997 Police Act. It provided the police with powers to 'bug and burgle', using methods such as hidden cameras and listening devices to prevent or detect serious crime. The legislation defined this as offences involving the use of violence which resulted in substantial financial gain likely to result in a prison sentence of at least three years, or which involved conduct by large numbers of persons in pursuit of a common purpose. To protect civil liberties, a code of practice was drawn up to govern surveillance operations, and the office of Surveillance Commissioner was created to consider complaints and make an annual report to Parliament.

MI5's new role posed additional problems regarding the manner in which the agency had traditionally gathered intelligence. It would now be required to gather evidence that was capable of standing up in court under cross-examination. The solution offered by the 1997 Police Act was to give NCIS primacy to coordinate and disseminate criminal intelligence in relation to serious crime.

A related development was announced in *The Observer* on 5 September 1999. Special Branch (whose main work had traditionally been concerned with terrorism and political crime) would join forces with mainstream CIDs and investigate crimes such as drug smuggling and protection rackets.

The Serious Organised Crime Agency

The Labour government's concern with the extent of organised crime was evidenced by the formation in September 2003 of a Cabinet Subcommittee on Organised Crime which was tasked with advancing a national and international strategy to combat organised crime and whose initial role was to set the priorities towards which the relevant law enforcement agencies should work (Home Office, 2004b: 3).

In order to pursue the campaign against organised crime, on 9 February 2004 the Home Secretary, David Blunkett, announced his intention to bring forward legislation to establish a Serious Organised Crime Agency (SOCA). This was accomplished in the 2005 Serious Organised Crime and Police Act. The new agency brought together under one roof a number of existing bodies – the National Criminal Intelligence Service, the National Crime Squad, the investigative and intelligence work performed by HM Customs and Excise in relation to serious drug trafficking and the recovery of criminal assets and the responsibilities exercised by the Home Office for organised immigration crime. The Agency would also employ specialist financial investigators who would work closely with the Serious Fraud Office and forces' fraud squads to combat organised crime. SOCA would be headed by a Director General. Its work is guided by a small board and the organisation is accountable to the Home Secretary who is responsible to Parliament for its performance. Specialist prosecutors answerable to the Attorney General would work closely with officers from this agency 'to provide comprehensive, practical and specialist advice to help shape investigations and to develop strong and well-presented cases for prosecution. These officials were provided with similar powers to those given to the Serious Fraud Office in the 1987 Criminal Justice Act whereby individuals would be compelled to cooperate with investigations by answering questions or producing documents. The agency also cooperates closely with police forces, border agencies and other law enforcement agencies at home and overseas (Home Office, 2004b: 3–4).

The government also advocated the need for new powers to combat organised crime. These included extending the powers of the Serious Fraud Office to compel witnesses to produce documents and answer questions, and reviewing the law on conspiracy since it was believed that the existing conspiracy legislation did not always reach the real 'godfather' figures, failed to provide a practical means of addressing more peripheral involvement in serious crime and did not allow sentencing courts to assess the real seriousness of individual offences by taking into account the wider pattern of the accused's criminal activities (Home Office, 2004b: 6 and 40). Other new powers included placing on a statutory footing Queen's Evidence provisions to encourage defendants to testify against co-defendants, developing new arrangements for plea bargaining to inspire defendants to plead guilty, reviewing the case for a National Witness Protection Programme, examining whether the existing sentencing regime was producing sentences which matched the seriousness of the underlying offences and creating new licence conditions to ensure that serious and acquisitive criminals' finances were kept under much closer scrutiny after release. These proposals were coupled with the ongoing review of the case for permitting the evidential use of intercept material in court proceedings (Home Office, 2004b: 6).

The main advantage of SOCA was that it brought together under one organisational roof a number of bodies that were currently concerned with combating serious crime. This was designed to remedy existing defects that included overlapping responsibilities (for example both the NCS and HM Customs and Excise had responsibilities to combat drug trafficking) (Home Office, 2004b: 22). It was concluded that this new body would 'lead to a greater consistency of approach', and provide 'a critical mass in key skill areas, address current problems of duplication and coordination, limit bureaucracy, provide opportunities for economies of scale, and represent a "one-stop shop" for our international partners. High-quality intelligence was argued to be of utmost importance in the fight against organised crime, and SOCA was designed to address some of the key weaknesses in the generation, dissemination and use of intelligence material' (Home Office, 2004b: 22 and 29).

There were, however, difficulties associated with the government's proposals. Concern was expressed regarding the introduction of a raft of new legislation to give SOCA enhanced powers with which to combat organised crime since these, in conjunction with reforms to the criminal justice system enacted in the previous decade, might serve to complicate the system of criminal law and make it less accessible to the public (Justice, 2004: 4). Additionally, there was the further danger that powers which are introduced to deal with a specific issue (in this case organised crime) might ultimately percolate into other areas of the criminal justice process and produce a system which was, overall, more arbitrary. Particular concern was voiced concerning the proposal that specialist prosecutors should be empowered to compel individuals to answer questions on the grounds that it represented a fundamental change in the relationship between the state and its citizens who had historically enjoyed the right that they were not compelled to cooperate with the authorities, and that this power was subject to insufficient safeguards as to who could authorise these procedures, in what circumstances they should be used and to whom they should apply (Justice, 2004: 4–5). Reforms to plea bargaining raised the issue of the extent to which pressure on a defendant to plead guilty eroded the historic presumption that a person was presumed innocent until proved guilty and could potentially result in miscarriages of justice when innocent people felt compelled (for reasons which included racial bias in the operations of the criminal justice process) to plead guilty (Justice, 2004: 8–9).

It was suggested that measures not concerned with criminal justice procedures should be brought forward to tackle the causes of organised crime which included the difference in rates of excise and tax duties between the UK and her near neighbours in the EU, the poverty and political corruption that existed in many of the major illegal drug-producing countries and impediments to the legal 'economic' migration of people into the UK (Justice, 2004: 2).

Other related developments to combat serious crime included the creation of Special Branch Regional Intelligence Cells (RICs) to coordinate Special Branch activity on a regional basis and the appointment of a new national coordinator of Special Branch in October 2003, one of whose key roles was to develop the RICs 'to act as clearing houses for intelligence in their regions' (Home Office, 2004b: 5). Regional Tasking and Coordination Groups were also established.

Police force reorganisation

The changed nature and increased complexity of contemporary crime has also prompted consideration to be given to the way in which police forces are organised. Reform of this nature threatens to erode the local basis around which policing has historically been organised.

In 1993 a White Paper suggested that the present structure of police forces in England and Wales did not make the most effective use of resources available for policing, and section 14 of the 1994 Police and Magistrates' Courts Act provided the Home Secretary with the ability to amalgamate forces. No progress was made with this reform, but it was resurrected in the government's 2003 Green Paper which queried whether the present 43-force structure was the right one and floated the idea of the creation of larger 'strategic' forces at regional level and of 'lead' forces which might develop particular specialisms (Home Office, 2003: paras 6.6 and 6.10). This issue was subsequently taken up by the HMIC in a report published in 2005.

Structural reform might be justified for several reasons. These include the need to locate the work performed by BCUs within a broader corporate framework and to provide them with an appropriate level of specialist staff from headquarters (HMIC, 2001: 16). The main problem subsequently identified concerned the delivery of what were termed the 'protective services' that embraced new forms of serious and organised crime (HMIC, 2005).

These were activities grouped under seven headings:

- counter-terrorism and extremism;
- serious organised (including that committed by criminal gangs) and cross-border crime;
- civil contingencies and emergency planning;
- critical incident handling;
- major crime investigations and homicide;
- public order;
- strategic roads policing.

These tasks (which are designated as Level 2 Services by the National Intelligence Model) were performed at force, rather than BCU, level since they affected more than one BCU. But it was argued that they were not performed to a consistently high standard across the board. It was pointed out, for example, that not all forces had Major Investigation Teams whose role was to counter major crimes (HMIC, 2005: 7). Further, only 13 of the 43 forces had fully resourced specialist murder units that allowed for the better use of skilled specialist teams for serious crime and which minimised the disruption to the everyday aspects of BCU work (HMIC, 2005: 11). Intelligence was viewed as essential in combating serious crime and was singled out as an area of work that required particular improvement.

The thrust of the report was that 'size mattered' when it came to making improvements in police performance in order to enable all forces to deliver the 'protective services' to an acceptable standard (HMIC, 2005: 7). The aim of the reform was to create organisations 'that are large enough to provide a full suite of sustainable services, yet small enough to be able to relate to local communities' (HMIC, 2005: 13). It was argued that the minimum size of a force should be 4,000 officers (HMIC, 2005: 14).

There were various ways whereby this reform could be achieved but the report backed the strategic force proposal 'with forces being re-grouped against a framework of design considerations, such as: exceeding critical mass; criminality; and geography' (HMIC, 2005: 15–16). The HMIC report argued that this proposal was the best option for improving the level of protective services and providing enhanced value for money. However, the report also argued against a mere structural change and, alternatively, called for a different configuration, the key elements of which were structure, processes and relationships (HMIC, 2005: 14–15).

A key problem with structural reform is remoteness. The HMIC report argued that the aim of this reform was to provide 'a more efficient, integrated operating platform above BCU level' (HMIC, 2005: 6), and emphasised that local policing arrangements conducted at BCU, and below that at neighbourhood, level would remain unchanged. BCUs were described as 'the critical building blocks of both the current structure and a possible new arrangement' (HMIC, 2005: 13) and it was suggested that the absence of change below force level might help to overcome public resistance to structural reform (HMIC, 2005: 11). However, larger police forces in most places will result in police authorities that are remote from the general public and, at the very least, may require the initiation of reforms to the composition of these bodies to enable them to reflect the views and opinions of the enlarged communities that are the consequence of organisational reform.

If this reform is acted upon it will provide England and Wales with a three-tier policing system based upon the differentiation of tasks performed by each level of the organisation. When fully operational, neighbourhood policing teams will provide a fourth tier to this policing structure.

Outline the factors that led to the creation of the Serious Organised Crime Agency in 2005. What are the strengths and weaknesses associated with this agency?

The European dimension to policing

Britain's membership of the European Community – and in particular the passage of the Single European Act which was signed by members of the European Council in 1986 (envisaging an economic area without internal frontiers) and the 1991 Maastricht Treaty on European Union – had implications for the workings of the criminal justice system and the organisation of British domestic and international policing requirements. The end of the Cold War and the opening of the previously sealed borders of central and Eastern Europe aggravated existing crime problems. It also created new ones, especially in connection with refugees fleeing the war in the former Yugoslavia. It was argued that a national British force was inevitable due to developments worldwide, especially in Europe (Condon, 1994), which enhanced the possibilities for cross-border crime.

These developments might also justify enhanced levels of international police cooperation in Europe. There are two important terms that describe changes of this nature to national police forces. One of these is 'international police cooperation' (in which the police forces of individual nation states owe their authority and allegiance first and foremost to their own state) and the other is 'transnational policing' (which is characterised by networks that are relatively autonomous of individual nation states or which owe their authority and allegiance to other non-state polities or political communities, such as the European Union) (Walker, 2003: 111).

A number of initiatives have been pursued to advance both of the concepts referred to above. A particular incentive has been the recent need to combat crimes such as terrorism, drug trafficking, commercial fraud and illegal immigration. The initiatives pursued have included the construction of arrangements between EU countries on law and order issues which include extradition and immigration issues, and granting members of police forces powers to operate outside their own country under certain specified circumstances. Secondments and formalised communication and consultative arrangements have also been concluded between police forces in different countries, including cooperation between the Kent Constabulary and the French police in connection with the policing of the Channel Tunnel. There are also several forms of police organisation that operate across national boundaries, which are discussed below.

The International Criminal Police Organisation (Interpol)

Interpol was established in 1923 to further assistance between police forces to combat international crime. It is not an operational organisation and fulfils its responsibilities primarily by collecting and circulating information about individuals. Its General Secretariat is housed in Lyon and liaises with the National Central Bureaus of each member country, of which there are now in excess of 150. Its broadening membership has moved it away from its original European orientation to that of a worldwide body.

The Schengen Acquis

The Schengen Agreement (1985) and Convention (1990) sought to further the objective of a single market by facilitating the freedom of movement of people, goods and transport. Schengen (and the Trevi Group which is discussed below) operate outside the framework of the Maastricht Treaty but although they are outside the formal EU structure they have nonetheless been a source of pressure for the creation of a coordinated EU criminal justice process.

There are a number of aspects to the arrangements which have been concluded under Schengen which include:

- the establishment of a database (initially known as the Schengen Information System (SIS)) with descriptions of people and objects wanted or missing in each Schengen country. The UK opted into this system in 2000 and, as subsequently developed, the SIS is viewed as an important tool with which to combat organised crime;

- cooperation over drugs-related crime (especially designed to limit drug smuggling);
- cooperation between police forces and legal authorities across national frontiers (which in countries which included Holland resulted in police organisational reform);
- the development of standardised policies in connection with illegal immigration and visas;
- simpler extradition rules between member countries.

A further aspect of the Schengen Agreement was the abolition of frontier controls, coupled with stringent immigration controls along the EU's borders. The United Kingdom was, however, sceptical of this development, believing that while open EU frontiers were of benefit to law-abiding citizens, other groups including criminals, terrorists and illegal refugees could take advantage of this situation. For this reason, therefore, Britain remains outside of Schengen, a course of action affirmed by Tony Blair at the Amsterdam summit in 1997.

The Trevi Group

In 1974 the Trevi Group of the European Council of Ministers was formed. As with the Schengen Acquis, Trevi also operates outside the formal structures of the EU. Trevi provided for regular meetings of ministers responsible for internal affairs and senior European police officers. Its main purpose was to provide a forum for the exchange of information. It was initially conceived to combat terrorism but its work subsequently developed into different areas that included serious crime and drug trafficking. Much of the day-to-day work of this body was performed by working groups composed of police officers, civil servants and others with relevant expertise, which in addition to terrorism considered issues such as police training and technology, serious crime and public order and disaster prevention (Morgan and Newburn, 1997: 67). As is discussed below, the work performed by Trevi became the responsibility of the Coordinating (or K4) Committee established under the 1991 Maastricht Treaty.

Europol

The 1991 Maastricht Treaty provided for the possibility of an enhanced degree of police cooperation within the formal EU structure. This objective would be developed under the auspices of the Treaty's 'third pillar' of justice and home affairs that was concerned with policing, immigration, asylum and legal cooperation. One aspect of these new arrangements was the creation of Europol, which was conceived as a central organisation to supply national policing units with criminal intelligence and analysis and receive information from them on transnational criminal activities (Walker, 2003: 119). In 1993 an embryo Europol, the Europol Drugs Unit, was created, but progress in establishing the fully-fledged organisation was slow and it was not fully operational until 1999.

Traditionally, the progress of cross-border cooperation in police and judicial affairs was impeded by the absence of a Directorate of Justice and Home Affairs within the European Commission (Tupman and Tupman, 1999: 94). However, in 1993 the Council of Ministers of Justice and Home Affairs established a Coordinating (or K4) Committee and a Directorate General. This was a significant development in securing EU-wide direction for the processes of harmonisation. The Coordinating Committee appointed three steering groups concerned with policing and customs and excise, immigration and asylum, and judicial cooperation. These steering groups in turn appointed a wide range of working groups. The Coordinating Committee reports to meetings of the European Council of Ministers of Justice and Home Affairs whose work will be made available to both the European Commission and European Parliament.

In 1995 Conventions under Maastricht's 'third pillar' were drawn up which provided Europol with a role in covering serious organised international crime which included terrorism, drug trafficking, illegal immigration and trafficking in people for sexual exploitation. These tasks envisaged the coordination of investigations, which was facilitated by the secondment of liaison officers drawn from police forces in member countries to Europol Headquarters. The progress of Europol was further advanced by the 1997 Treaty of Amsterdam that promoted the objective of 'an Area of Freedom and Justice'. Further EU-wide police and criminal justice cooperation within the framework of this objective took place at the 1999 meeting of the European Council at Tempere, Finland. This meeting resulted in the establishment of a European Police College and a European Police Chiefs Operational Task Force (whose remit to coordinate anti-terrorist and public order planning took it beyond the organisational confines of Europol). The Tempere meeting also proposed the establishment of a judicial cooperation unit, Eurojust, which was designed to enhance the effectiveness of the procedures adopted by member states to investigate and prosecute serious cross-border and organised crime. This was set up in 2002, consisting of senior lawyers, magistrates, prosecutors and judges.

The European Union and organised crime

The concern of the EU to provide structural arrangements to combat organised crime was initially voiced at the 1996 Stockholm Conference in connection with activities arising from European economic integration and social exclusion. The 1997 Treaty of Amsterdam referred to the need to prevent crime in EU policies that sought to promote freedom, security and justice. However, the main development concerned with organised crime occurred in April 1997 when the European Council adopted an *Action Plan to Combat Organised Crime*. It put forward a number of recommendations that were designed to prevent organised crime by focusing on the circumstances that facilitated its development rather than on those who carried out such activities. The recommendations included the development of an anti-corruption policy within government apparatus, banning persons convicted of offences related to organised crime from tendering procedures, devoting financial resources to prevent larger cities in the EU from becoming breeding grounds for organised crime, and developing closer cooperation between EU member states and the European Commission on combating fraud where the financial interests of the EU were concerned. The *Action Plan* also reiterated the desirability of promoting effective cooperation between the judicial and police services across national boundaries.

Subsequent positive action to foster knowledge on preventing organised crime and improving the exchange of information among member states have included the Falcone and Hippocrates programmes, which have been carried out under the auspices of the European Council within the Programme for Police and Judicial Cooperation in Criminal Matters (AGIS). In May 2000 the European Council published a new plan to combat organised crime. This followed the direction of the 1997 *Action Plan*, but embraced some new ideas that included proposals to improve the sharing of information between member states and the European Commission. Since the 11 September 2001 attacks in America, tackling organised crime has been increasingly viewed within the EU as an aspect of combating terrorism (van de Bunt and van der Schoot, 2003: 18–20). The 2003 Crime (International Cooperation) Act provided for an enhanced level of police and judicial cooperation directed at terrorist activities.

Impact on UK policing arrangements

Currently, although UK police forces make considerable use of Europol (Home Office, 2004b: 18), it has exerted limited influence over British policing arrangements. However, it is anticipated that the establishment of a European Police Chiefs Task Force and a European Police Training College will provide for further enhanced cooperation between all police forces across Europe.

The 'europeanisation' of British policing has been advanced by developments other than Europol. The work of the National Crime Squad has entailed cooperation with police forces across Europe. Its Director General, Barry Penrose, announced in *The Guardian* on 13 March 1998 that he anticipated around half of the investigations launched by this unit would involve European connections, a particular target being the multinational career criminal. The application of computer technology to policing may also enhance the level of coordination between law enforcement agencies in countries that are members of the European Union. A computer system, Eucaris (European Car and Driving Licence Information System), makes it possible for police forces in EU countries to have instant access to the UK's driving licence records in order to enforce traffic penalties across the EU.

Bilateral forms of cooperation have also taken place such as that between the British and French police in connection with policing arrangements conducted for the 1998 World Cup tournament. The Football Intelligence unit of

NCIS passed information on known English football hooligans to their French counterparts, and French officers visited Blackburn and Nottingham in 1998 to view the way in which football matches were policed.

EU-wide cooperation in criminal justice matters has also occurred in areas other than policing. The 2003 Crime (International Cooperation) Act implemented EU arrangements that were designed to simplify the procedures for Mutual Legal Assistance. The introduction of the European Arrest Warrant (which became operational in the UK on 1 January 2004) was designed to combat criminal activity across Europe. A further European-wide organisation, Eurojust, is responsible for coordinating prosecutions. Other developments designed to combat organised crime outside of the EU include the Financial Action Task Force on money laundering and initiatives pursued by the G8 group of countries in areas that include the tracing, freezing and confiscation of assets and the use of DNA evidence (Home Office, 2004b: 19). A major problem with all of the organisations and arrangements that have been discussed in this section is the absence of adequate mechanisms of accountability.

The policing of public order

The policing of public order has exerted a major impact on the organisation and style of policing. The postwar period witnessed the police being required to intervene in a wide variety of circumstances that included industrial disputes, riots and various forms of protest including demonstrations, civil disobedience and direct action. What has been referred to as 'the politics of contention' (Waddington, 2003: 415) has been significantly influenced by the growth of social movements.

The main developments affecting the response of the police to these activities are discussed below.

Mutual aid

Mutual aid entails one chief constable calling on another for assistance. Requests of this nature are usually made in connection with public order events. Mutual aid was initially organised on an ad hoc basis until the 1890 Police Act formalised the practice, enabling police forces voluntarily to enter into standing arrangements to supply officers to each other in the event of major disorder. The arrangements governing mutual aid were not significantly altered until 1964, when section 14(2) of the 1964 Police Act effectively made it obligatory for forces to come to the aid of another to provide an effective response to public disorder.

The decision to apply for mutual aid and from where to seek it was initially in the hands of a chief constable faced with disorder. However, following the success of the National Union of Miners in forcing the closure of Saltley Coke Depot during the 1972 miners' dispute, these matters have been determined centrally. In that year ACPO established a mechanism that was initially known as the National Reporting Centre (NRC) but now termed the Mutual Aid Coordination Centre or MACC. This body operated from New Scotland Yard, was operationally under the control of ACPO's president and became activated when an event arose with major implications for public order. Its role was to coordinate the deployment of police officers from across the country to the area affected by disorder. This arrangement was utilised in the 1984/5 miners' dispute where it was viewed as a key aspect of a centralised system of policing. It was alleged, for example, that the NRC issued operational directions to police units on the ground during the miners' dispute (Bunyan, 1985: 298–9).

Specialist public order units

Since the 1960s a number of police forces have developed units which are not tied to a specific division or concerned with implementing routine police functions but which operate anywhere within a force's boundaries. An early example of this was the Metropolitan Police's Special Patrol Group. This was initially established as the Special Patrol Group Unit in 1961 and renamed the Special Patrol Group in 1965. It was augmented in the 1970s by the creation of a number of District Support Units. Both were replaced in 1986 by Territorial Support Groups located within each of the Metropolitan Police districts. Other forces, however, have retained a centralised specialist unit such as the Tactical Aid Unit of the Greater Manchester Police. The main role of these units has been concerned with crime but they have also been extensively utilised in public order situations.

Police support units

Specialist public order units have been augmented by police support units (PSUs). These consist of uniformed police officers whose main role is to perform routine police duties but who receive a limited degree of public order training on a regular basis. Police support units are organised at divisional level and their organisation became standardised in 1989 whereby each was to consist of one inspector, two sergeants and 20 constables (Home Office, 1989). They train together as a unit and are available for deployment in public order situations when the need arises.

Public order tactics, weaponry and training

Initially police forces were ill-equipped to handle the public order problems that surfaced during the 1970s and 1980s. In many public order situations officers under attack were required to improvise their own defence from materials that included dustbin lids (Thackrah, 1985: 6). A number of significant developments subsequently occurred in connection with the policing of public disorder. A key development was the publication in 1983 of ACPO's *Public Order Manual of Tactical Operations and Related Matters*. Each force was issued with a binder that contained 'a detailed analysis of the stages of a riot and the police responses appropriate to them'. A total of 238 tactics and manoeuvres were set out in its 30 sections 'arranged in order of escalating force, from normal policing up to plastic bullets, CS gas and live firearms' (Northam, 1989: 42). This was designed to ensure that the response by the police in public order situations would become standardised.

The publication of the *Public Order Manual* in 1983 was accompanied by the formation of an ACPO body, the Public Order Forward Planning Group, to review all new developments and emerging tactics. Other centralised developments followed this ACPO initiative, including the formation of a Central Intelligence Unit during the miners' dispute 1984–5 to analyse intelligence gathered by officers on the ground.

The deployment of officers from across the country in specific crowd situations generated further pressures for further standardisation of both equipment and training. All forces were subsequently required to train a number of PSUs according to common standards, one advantage being that an officer from one force could command PSUs drawn from different forces. Central government supported these centralising ACPO initiatives that were especially detrimental to the role exerted by police authorities over policing. It became possible, for example, for the Home Office to override the refusal of a police authority to supply riot equipment to a local force, provided that the chief constable's request for this material was supported by the HMIC (Home Office, 1986).

Increased use of technology

Technology such as closed circuit television has been increasingly used to police public order events. This has facilitated a greater level of managerial control to be exerted over these situations and has given rise to the introduction of gold, silver and bronze commanders (a procedure which was introduced following the 1985 Broadwater Farm Estate riot). Improved organisation underpinned by technology has greatly improved the ability of the police to control crowd situations and may have benefited protest since the police have confidence in their ability to control events that previously they might have banned.

Political control of policing

One danger with the increased level of coordination and standardisation of policing discussed above was that it enhanced the ability of central government to influence police actions. The NRC/MACC, for example, provided senior ministers with one police body with which they could liaise and to which they could indicate government concerns in connection with specific events (Kettle, 1985: 30–1). The main problem associated with this close relationship between the police and a political party concerns the legitimacy of the police within the wider community. The perception that the police were used in industrial disputes during the 1980s as 'Maggie's Boot Boys' (Smith, 1994b: 101) had an adverse effect on the image of the police in working-class communities and on the legitimacy they were accorded there.

The policing of public disorder – key events

The police response to public disorder has been shaped by a number of events.

- *Saltley* (1972). This episode occurred during the miners' dispute, when flying pickets were able, by weight of numbers, to secure the closing of the gates of Saltley Gas Works, Birmingham. In order to avoid future embarrassments of this nature, the government established a National Security Committee (later renamed the Civil Contingencies Unit) to conduct advance planning. One immediate development was the establishment of the National Reporting Centre (later renamed the Mutual Aid Coordination Centre), controlled by ACPO and housed in New Scotland Yard. Its main purpose was to coordinate mutual aid arrangements in the event of anticipated or actual public disorder. A related body, the National Information Centre (NIC), may be used to coordinate and disseminate information between police forces in connection with events that pose the potential for public disorder but where it is thought the widespread use of mutual aid is not required. An example of the use of the NIC was in connection with the Pope's visit to Britain in 1982.
- *The Notting Hill Carnival* (1976). This event witnessed widespread public disorder arising from police action to deal with street crime which many carnival participants deemed to be overly aggressive. The spectre of police officers having to fend for themselves in the face of extreme violence resulted in the provision of improved weaponry and protective clothing. The first fruit of this was the utilisation of riot shields, which first took place in the policing of a National Front march at Lewisham in 1977.
- *The 1981 riots*. Although police officers who responded to these disorders were relatively well provided for in terms of weaponry and protective clothing, the tactics used by different forces in an attempt to quell disorder were varied. This resulted in the production of the ACPO training manual in 1983 which was designed to standardise public order tactics.
- *The miners' dispute* (1984/5). Although the policing of this industrial dispute made full use of earlier developments (in particular the NRC), it highlighted other deficiencies in connection with mutual aid, in particular the different training which individual police forces provided to their PSUs. This led to new developments whereby each force was required to train a number of its PSUs according to minimum standards which would enable, for example, an officer from one force to command PSUs from others. Developments in connection with police communications systems were also initiated in response to events in 1981 and 1984/5.
- *Broadwater Farm* (1985). The confused management of police resources in this riot contributed to one police officer being murdered and several others being seriously injured. Subsequently a defined hierarchy of command (the gold/silver/bronze control system) was established in an attempt to improve the way in which police deployments in public order situations were organised.

The decline of policing by consent – towards paramilitary policing?

'Data from the three British Crime Surveys conducted in the 1980s ... showed that the proportion of the public who gave the police the highest possible rating dropped from just over one third in 1982 to under a quarter in 1988' (Morgan and Newburn, 1997: 3). Although factors that included the increase of crime and reduction in clear-up rates during the 1980s were important explanations for the fall in public satisfaction with the police service, there were other significant changes that occurred after the 1960s which have influenced the concept of policing by consent.

The decline of policing by consent?

A number of factors discussed above have exerted a negative impact on policing by consent. These are discussed below.

Local organisation and control

Key changes to the organisation of policing have been discussed above. These have placed (or threaten to place) a number of key policing functions in the hands of bodies whose scope is far greater than that of nineteenth-century police forces. Similar developments have also affected the control of policing.

As will be discussed in more detail in Chapter 4, the local control which (outside of London) initially characterised policing was replaced by a tripartite system in which local government, the Home Secretary and chief constables jointly exercised responsibility for the conduct of police affairs across large geographic areas. Changes affecting the control of policing emerged during the course of the nineteenth century, although these were not formalised until the enactment of the 1964 Police Act. The ability of the government to influence police actions through informal mechanisms was subsequently supplemented by the increased power of the Home Secretary (who was empowered by the 1994 Police and Magistrates' Courts Act to set national objectives which every force was required to implement) which was particularly contentious as it gave rise to accusations of politicisation, that is that the police service's prime role was to advance the political interests of the government rather than to serve the needs of local communities. This eroded the non-partisanship that was asserted to have played an important part in constructing consent for the police in the formative years of the nineteenth century (Reiner, 2000: 54). Although subsequent legislation (in particular the 1998 Crime and Disorder Act) provided local government with an important role in crime prevention in addition to the functions carried out by local police authorities, central government exercises a considerable influence over the conduct of contemporary policing.

Style of policing

As has been argued earlier in this chapter, preventive policing gave way in the 1960s to reactive policing which was blamed for creating a distance between police and public. The tendency to use powers (particularly stop and search) in what was perceived as a random manner resulted in creating poor relationships between the police service and public, especially in multi-ethnic inner-city areas. Local studies made reference to 'an intimidatory style of policing, deeply stained with racial prejudice' (Moss Side Defence Committee, 1981: 3) and the 'catastrophically bad relationships' between police and public were cited as the main cause of the 1981 inner-city disturbances (Kettle and Hodges, 1982: 247). Although changes were subsequently made to the style of policing they did not totally succeed in securing the consent of disaffected communities. The lack of understanding between the police service and minority ethnic communities continued to be cited as a cause of urban disturbances in places which included Bradford in 1995 (Allen and Barratt, 1996: 155) and Oldham in 2001 (Oldham Independent Review, 2001: 41) and has given rise to allegations of perennial aggressive police action and insensitivity towards those they view as 'police property' (Cray, 1972; Reiner, 1985: 97), that is 'the powerless groups at the bottom of the social hierarchy' who were policed *against* (Reiner, 1985: 50).

Limited powers

The powers that the police possess have steadily increased since the nineteenth century and far exceed those that ordinary citizens can utilise if they choose to do so. The 1984 Police and Criminal Evidence Act set out a clear distinction between the powers of police officers and those of the general public. The existence of a large armoury of police powers provides for the possibility of overbearing actions being pursued towards those whom the police target.

Minimum force

The weaponry used by the police has considerably altered since the early decades of the nineteenth century. Key developments have included the use of batons rather than traditional truncheons, the introduction of pepper and CS sprays and the increased use of firearms by the police. Firearms training is given to a relatively small number of officers who work in specialist units such as the Metropolitan Police's SO19 firearms unit which was formed in 1966. Much of the work of armed officers is performed by patrolling in armed response vehicles (ARVs) that were introduced into the Metropolitan Police in 1991. However, in 2000 the Nottinghamshire Constabulary became the first force to routinely arm some of its foot patrols.

CS sprays

CS sprays were routinely issued to police forces in England and Wales for the protection of police officers. In September 1998, following health concerns over their use, new scientific tests on the safety of CS gas sprays were conducted by the Department of Health. A key issue was the hazard posed by the solvent methyl isobutyl ketone, which is used to dissolve the solid CS irritant in the canister, and the high concentration of CS in the canister.

In the year up to March 1999 the PCA received 425 complaints about CS sprays compared to 254 the previous year (Wright and Evans, 1999). Allegations were made that the chemical was used inappropriately, perhaps to make an 'easy' arrest. In the summer of 1998 Judge Daniel Rodwell strongly criticised a Bedfordshire police officer who had 'single-handedly managed to convert a drunken incident into a riot by not inquiring what was going on, using physical force and the totally inappropriate use of CS spray'. Quoted in *The Guardian* on 25 September 1998, the judge argued the spray should be used only for self-defence in an attack and was not a device of containment.

A key difficulty with the improved weaponry capabilities of the police service is that these may be used inappropriately, in particular in an offensive rather than defensive posture. In December 1998 the report of an investigation by the PCA into 450 official complaints arising from the use of batons warned the police not to use these weapons to hit suspects on the kneecaps or shins since this could result in long-term injuries, and recommended that forces should abandon the more confrontational use of this weaponry as was recommended in American training manuals. The report also pointed out that while batons and CS gas spray had reduced the number of minor assaults against officers, serious assaults had increased. This implies that the level of consent may suffer, especially when the public perceive there are no adequate remedies against what is perceived as police overreaction.

Between 1990 and June 2000, 22 people were shot dead by police officers with charges being preferred only in two cases. One of these cases included the shooting of Harry Stanley in 1999 by armed police officers who mistook the chair leg he was carrying for a shotgun. Five years later an inquest jury ruled that these officers had unlawfully killed him. The suspension of two officers in the wake of this verdict in 2004 resulted in around one quarter of the Metropolitan Police's SO19 unit temporarily withdrawing themselves from firearms duty in protest against this decision. A key concern of these officers was that they should be offered a greater degree of legal protection when using lethal force in the course of their duties.

The service role of policing

As will be argued in the following chapter, the emphasis which was placed after 1983 on the need for the police service to demonstrate that it provided the public with good value for money was increasingly directed towards what were deemed to be key functions which were capable of measurement, in particular related to the service's law enforcement role. This meant that the service side of policing became increasingly neglected since the tasks with which it was associated were not regarded as core ones nor was it possible to scientifically measure the impact that they had on police–public relationships.

Recruitment

Since the nineteenth century, policing became transformed from a job into a trade (which required those who performed the task of policing to be trained) and thence to a profession (Joyce, 1994: 117–18). This had an impact on recruitment into the service, since career advancement became dependent on passing professional examinations. The implementation of the Edmund Davies pay award soon after the Conservative party's 1979 election victory, coupled with economic recession, meant that the service became increasingly attractive to graduates and the ideal of a police service which represented the social make-up of the population which it policed (Scarman, 1981: 76) was increasingly lost. Police officers were politically (Reiner, 1978) and socially unrepresentative, and the latter posed a particular problem in multi-ethnic, inner-city areas. Although (as will be argued in more detail in Chapter 10) strenuous attempts have been made to broaden the recruitment base of police forces, accusations remain that the service discriminates against minority ethnic groups, in particular with regard to the use of stop and search powers. This has had a detrimental impact on the level of consent given to the police service in such areas and to the legitimacy accorded to the function of policing.

Paramilitary policing?

Paramilitary policing was initially associated with the response to public order situations and industrial unrest, and was characterised by new forms of weaponry, equipment and training utilised by a police service that became increasingly standardised and centralised in its operations. It was also characterised by a reduced level of personal accountability of individual officers, whose personal responsibility became subsumed into a group identity. The more coercive stance adopted by the police in public order situations also exerted an influence on police tactics in routine matters. In addition to the use of new weaponry, the emphasis placed on public order in police training programmes since the 1980s threatened to exert a detrimental effect on the performance of 'regular' police work since it was difficult for officers to adjust readily from the attitude required for policing public disorder to an attitude compatible with the routine tasks of community policing. This problem was aggravated when specialist public order units were deployed to combat crime (Rollo, 1980: 153–202).

Critics of this approach argue that it entails 'policing by consent' giving way to a more aggressive style of policing which is incompatible with fundamental freedoms traditionally associated with liberal democratic political systems and more appropriate to the treatment of subjugated populations under colonial regimes (Northam, 1999; Jefferson, 1990). This may have a detrimental effect on the legitimacy accorded to the police by the public. If police officers are perceived as aggressive and overbearing in their dealings with sections of the general public (whether this is concerned with law enforcement related to public order or 'ordinary' crime), this will have an adverse effect on the level of support (or consent) which they receive from the affected groups. It may even result in police officers being denied the right to operate in the places where these people live.

However, the appropriateness of applying the term 'paramilitary policing' to the policing of crowd situations has been challenged (for example by King and Brearley, 1996, and Reiner, 1998). An important consideration in relation both to public order and crime is whether the developments associated with paramilitary policing were designed to create a more highly regulated society in which civil and political liberties were sacrificed in the name of law and order, or whether the changes which occurred were mainly reactive in the sense of responding to changes in the behaviour of some members of the general public. It has also been argued that the police will frequently police crowd situations through the use of negotiation rather than coercive tactics (Waddington, 2003: 409).

The violence meted out by law-breakers also justifies some of the developments that have been outlined above. The need for the police service to use improved weaponry may be justified by the requirement for police officers to defend themselves when encountering violent crime, or violent behaviour by criminals. A Parliamentary inquiry stated that there had been 13,671 recorded armed offences in 1999 and that there were three million firearms illegally in circulation. Some episodes have been characterised by extreme violence using firearms. These included the murder of a female police officer and the shooting of her partner in Bradford in 2005 and gang-related crime wars such as those between Jamaican Yardie gangs in London. According to *The Observer* on 18 July 1999, the Yardie gangs' fight for control of the crack cocaine trade had resulted in 13 murders in London and more than 30 shootings in North West London in the first seven months of 1999. On 4 July 1998, *The Guardian* also stated that there are around 19,000 cases of assault on police officers each year.

> To what extent and for what reasons has the principle of policing by consent been eroded in recent years?

The privatisation of policing

The performance of police-related functions by bodies other than regular police forces is not a new development. Private security organisations figured prominently in the late eighteenth century, when deficiencies in the old policing system resulted in widespread criminal activity such as theft and highway robbery. This led to ventures that were initially privately financed, including the Bow Street Runners and the Marine Police Establishment. In the 1840s and 1850s railway companies funded their own police organisations to protect towns from navvies who were engaged in railway construction. More recently, state agencies have established their own police forces, including the Atomic Energy Authority and the Ministry of Defence. The boundary between these private bodies and the regular police is difficult to draw precisely, and in some cases (most notably concerning the British Transport Police) has effectively been eliminated.

The work performed by specialist policing organisations has been supplemented by commercial organisations. These carry out a very wide range of functions broadly concerned with the operations of the criminal justice system but are unlike other plural policing bodies discussed earlier in this chapter which operate in the public sector and are funded by central or local government. The organisations discussed here function in the private sector (hence the use of the term 'private policing' in this section), they exist to make a profit from the work that they carry out, and their operations are conducted within the framework of a contract between the company and its clients. Some aspects of the work performed by the commercial sector have been encompassed within plural policing, a development that is referred to earlier in this chapter.

Nature of the work performed by private policing bodies

The role performed by commercial policing organisations can be broadly divided into security work and detective work. Security work includes activities such as guarding premises, the manufacture, installation and provision of security devices, retail security and guard duty. Detective work is typically carried out by private investigators and includes activities such as monitoring personal relationships, work on behalf of solicitors in connection with civil and criminal matters (such as insurance fraud and tracing missing persons), and examining allegations of white-collar crime such as theft by employees. Some aspects of detective work (such as industrial espionage and functions concerned with defending the state against subversion) are controversial.

The growth of the private policing sector

The precise size of the private sector is unknown but it considerably dwarfs the numbers employed as regular police officers. In 1977, one estimate referred to 700 firms employing 250,00 uniformed personnel and owning 10,000 vehicles (Bunyan, 1977: 230). Subsequently, a Home Office discussion paper (quoting figures obtained from the 1971 census), argued that 80,000 persons in England and Wales were employed as 'security guards, patrolmen, watchmen, nightwatchmen, gate keepers and other relevant types of guards and related workers' (Home Office, 1979: 3). A more recent study published in 1998 suggested that the private sector employed around one-third of a million workers (Jones and Newburn, 2002).

The total market size of the private sector in security work rose from £807 million in 1987 to £2.1 billion by 1992 (Smith, 1994a) and was estimated by *The Guardian* on 26 April 2000 to be worth around £3 billion. The sizeable growth of commercial policing is a postwar phenomenon, and has occurred in two 'waves'.

The first 'wave' of private policing bodies

The first period of growth of private policing bodies occurred in the 1950s and, especially, in the 1960s. This was due to the following factors:

- *The boom in consumerism.* Prime Minister Macmillan's announcement in 1957 that 'you've never had it so good' related to a period of increased working-class affluence which was coupled with (and to some extent fuelled by) improved facilities for obtaining credit. This resulted in a growth of private property ownership and required both owners and sellers to devote attention to measures providing for the physical protection of their goods, premises and money.
- *The British workers' dislike of bank accounts.* This meant that large sums of money for the wages of employees had constantly to be collected from banks and taken to firms and factories.
- *The preference of insurance companies.* These began to insist upon regular security arrangements for the protection of large premises. By the 1990s it became quite common for insurance companies to offer lower premiums to householders who could demonstrate that measures had been taken to protect their property from burglary.

The second 'wave' of private policing bodies

By the late 1970s it was possible to describe private policing as 'a second-string police force in this country' (Draper, 1978: 168). A further growth phase occurred during the 1980s. It arose in response to a number of developments that are discussed below.

The increased emphasis on crime prevention

The increased emphasis that was given to crime prevention after 1980 encouraged the growth of private policing organisations to perform activities of this nature. This work embraces a wide range of activities such as various forms of patrol work and the installation of physical methods of crime prevention. The involvement of the private sector in crime prevention activities is an aspect of the assertion that security has become commodified, that is 'distributed by market forces rather than according to need' (Garland, 1996: 463).

Changes in police methods

As is referred to earlier in this chapter, changes affecting police work after 1979 tended to be at the expense of routine patrol work which was deemed to be an inefficient use of police resources. However, the public tended to obtain reassurance from this form of police activity; this factor, coupled with the increased fear of crime in this period, resulted in the public demand for specific types of police work outstripping the capacity of the police service to deliver it. This created a vacuum which private bodies were able to exploit alongside other public (or quasi-public) ventures associated with plural policing.

The growth of mass private property

The phrase 'mass private property' refers to property in private ownership but which is open to the public (Shearing and Stenning, 1981) such as shopping malls and night clubs. Although crime might occur at such venues, property of this nature was outside the domain of public policing and therefore had to be policed by private bodies. Examples of this included the use of private security companies to patrol large shopping centres and the deployment of doormen ('bouncers') to regulate entry into nightclubs. The expansion of the night-time economy, fuelled by alcohol-based leisure industries, has provided a major boost to the employment of security personnel such as club doormen (Crawford, 2003: 154).

The privatisation policies of the Conservative governments, 1979–97

The Conservative governments of 1979–97 sought to subject the police service to the discipline of the market. One feature of their approach sought to provide effective forms of competition. This was achieved by 'load shedding' whereby services were ceded to commercial or voluntary providers (Johnston, 1992: 12). This aspect of new public management emerged as the product of 'globalisation', one feature of which was 'hollowing out', which involved the state shedding its peripheral activities that were subsequently discharged by other agencies (Leishman et al., 1996: 10–11).

The extent to which privatisation eroded traditional policing functions to the benefit of the commercial sector has, however, been disputed. Although some functions (such as prisoner escort duties) were relinquished, it has been argued that 'privatisation of policing has been relatively limited and ... not extensive enough to explain the large growth in private security over the longer period' (Newburn and Jones, 1998: 31).

Factors restricting the growth of the private sector

The extent to which the commercial sector can be expected to grow, especially at the expense of 'regular' policing, is subject to a number of considerations.

- *Reduced demand for some areas associated with private policing activity.* This particularly applies to work performed in connection with industrial unrest and subversion. Changes in the law reducing the power of trade unions, the reduced willingness of workers to take strike action and the collapse of the Soviet Union and Eastern bloc are likely to reduce the demand for the services of the commercial sector in these areas of activity.

- *Changes in police activity and powers.* The new role of MI5 in connection with serious crime, and the legalisation of practices such as 'bugging and burglary' both for MI5 and the regular police, are likely to reduce the need for the state to employ private policing organisations to obtain information by activities such as covert surveillance and infiltration.

- *The civil orientation of much private policing activity.* Much of the work performed by private policing agencies (especially of a detective nature) is concerned with issues or disputes affecting private parties, underpinned totally or significantly by civil law. This suggests that the growth of the commercial policing sector has not necessarily occurred at the expense of the functions of the regular police, since many of the issues handled by the former are not, and never have been, the responsibilities handled by the latter.

Problems associated with private policing

There are a number of problems associated with the role performed by private policing organisations.

Coordination

The increase in the number of police functions carried out by the private sector has resulted in 'a world of fragmented, plural policing' (Loader, 2000). This justifies attempts to coordinate the activities of bodies which perform police tasks at the local level, perhaps by establishing local police commissions as were advocated by the Patten Commission on Northern Ireland which reported in 1999.

Standards

The backgrounds of those who work in the private policing sector have not traditionally been subject to the same rigorous checking as that employed by regular police forces. In 1999, it was suggested that 40,000 of the 80,000 people who applied for work in private security companies each year would possess some sort of criminal record, and in 24,000 the crimes involved ranked above minor offences (Home Office, 1999: 25). This problem is partly explained by the poor pay rates in some sectors of the industry.

The training and methods used by private companies have also been subjected to criticism. Regular police officers undergo a two-year period of probationer training. They operate in accordance with procedures laid down by the 1984 Police and Criminal Evidence Act and its related Codes of Practice, and their conduct is further constrained by the Police Code of

Conduct and the Police Complaints Procedure. The personnel employed by commercial bodies are not regulated in the same rigorous manner, and the use in some areas of activity (such as debt collection) of the system of 'payment by results' may induce members of private bodies to resort to methods that would not be tolerated by regular police forces. Training has not traditionally received a high priority in the industry, although the establishment in 1990 of the Security Industry Training Organisation (SITO) sought to remedy this deficiency.

Accountability

There are a number of trade associations that organisations in the private sector may join. These include the National Approval Council for Security Systems, the British Security Industry Association, the Association of British Investigators, the Association of Professional Investigators and the International Professional Security Association. These trade associations may seek to set standards for the industry (concerning matters such as recruitment, qualifications, training and fees charged). Some of these regulatory bodies have the theoretical ability to expel members who contravene acceptable standards of behaviour. However, since membership is purely voluntary, their ability to meaningfully control the private sector is significantly limited. In recent years inspectorates (such as the Inspectorate of the Security Industry, established in 1992) have been set up to supplement existing machinery to supervise the operations of the industry. Some local authorities have also introduced registration schemes for specific activities (especially in connection with door staff in clubs) that usually entailed vetting procedures and training courses.

Privatisation may not benefit the public

Although privatisation might be put forward as beneficial to the consumer (in that competition depresses charges) it may also have adverse effects on them. They may be required to pay for services at the point of delivery that were previously financed from taxation, resulting in the danger that the ability to pay will determine the standard or level of services consumers receive. It has been observed that 'one of the central paradoxes of crime prevention and security provision is that there is often an inverse relationship between activity and need' (Crawford, 2003: 161). If the level of security reflects a person (or community's) ability to pay, the notion of common good that underpins regular policing is eroded (Newburn and Jones, 1998: 32). This may result in crime being displaced to neighbourhoods unable or unwilling to pay for their own security and may thus contribute to other people's feelings of insecurity.

Finally, the myriad of bodies which deliver privatised police services are likely to provide an uneven quality of service unless subject to regulation – something which governments have traditionally been reluctant to impose upon the private policing sector.

The relationship between the private and public policing sectors

The relationship between private sector policing organisations and the regular police service has become close in the postwar period. The private sector may perform services for the legal system including delivering court orders and serving summonses. This link poses two problems, as follows.

The demarcation of boundaries between the private and public sectors

The activities performed by private policing organisations may encroach on areas of work performed by the regular police. There is no precise definition as to which activities should remain in the public domain and which could be located elsewhere. However, it has been argued that while there has been a significant blurring of the boundaries between the two sectors, public policing performs a broad range of activities whereas the scope of private bodies is far more limited. It was 'the wide-ranging nature of the public police mandate on each of these dimensions' which was its defining characteristic (Newburn and Jones, 1998: 32).

The definition of appropriate tasks to be delivered by the public and private sectors

An independent committee of inquiry set up under the joint auspices of the Police Foundation and Policy Studies Institute sought to establish the relationship between the regular police and private bodies. Its report concluded that only sworn PCs should be able to arrest, detain and search citizens, and search and seize property under statutory powers; that only they should be able to bear arms and exercise force for the purpose of policing; and that they should have the exclusive right of access to criminal records and criminal intelligence for the purposes of operational policing. It was proposed that other groups and agencies not having these powers could engage in a number of policing activities 'to complement and supplement what sworn constables do' (Cassels, 1994: 19). This proposal created the basis for a two-tier system of police service provision that has been realised in the growth of plural policing as has been described earlier in this chapter.

Reforms to private policing

The most important reform to private policing has been stricter regulation by the state. The control that it has exerted since 1945 was initially directed at the practices utilised by some commercial concerns (such as the 1970 Administration of Justice Act, the 1973 Guard Dogs Act and the 1974 Consumer Credit Act). Compulsory registration and licensing (which can be used to exert control over standards) has long been a requirement in most American states and European countries but successive governments shied away from instituting this. This reform was suggested by the 1972 Younger Committee on Privacy in connection with private detective work but was not subsequently acted upon. However, the 1987 Emergency Provisions Act (which applied only to Northern Ireland) did introduce a licensing system for security firms in that country.

In 1999 the Labour government announced its intention to establish a self-financing Private Security Industry Authority (PSIA). This would vet the background of individuals wishing to form companies or seek employment in a wide range of activities concerned with private security (including club 'bouncers') and would grant licences only to those judged to be 'fit persons'. It was also proposed to establish a Voluntary Inspected Companies Scheme under the PSIA to cover matters such as training, equipment and standards. Penalties would be imposed on those who either worked in private security without a licence or who ran a company without a licence (Home Office, 1999).

Reform was implemented in 2001 when the Private Security Industry Act established the Security Industry Authority (SIA). Its role was to issue licences to people working in different designated sectors of the security industry. In order to obtain a licence from this body, the applicant was required to have undergone a criminal records check and to demonstrate that he or she had the appropriate skills required for the type of work to be carried out. Applicants could be required to carry out a course of SIA-approved training in order to obtain a licence. The aim of these innovations was to raise levels of professional skills in the industry. SIA inspectors became empowered to enter certain types of premises to ensure that security staff held valid licences and persons operating in the industry without a licence were liable, on conviction at a magistrates' court, to a penalty of six months' imprisonment, a £5,000 fine, or both. The SIA would also create a public register of approved security firms. The main aim of this reform was to prevent undesirable persons (including those with a criminal record) from working as doormen. One weakness of this reform, however, was that it was restricted to personnel employed by security organisations. 'In-house' security staff employed directly by the organisation in which they operated were exempt from regulation (Crawford, 2003: 151).

> Why has the private sector been increasingly involved in performing police duties since 1945? Is this a good or a bad development?

Conclusion

This chapter has considered the styles of policing that have been used to deliver this service since the inception of 'new' policing in 1829. It has discussed preventive, reactive and proactive approaches to policing and the ways in which these have been implemented and has assessed more contemporary methods of policing associated with developments such as problem-oriented and zero tolerance policing. The discussion of methods of policing has also embraced the contemporary role of the police service to secure the cohesion of fragmented communities. The chapter has also examined the structure of policing and has assessed issues affecting this associated with contemporary forms of crime and the need to police public disorder. It has been argued that these developments have implications both for the organisational basis around which policing is organised and the manner in which policing is delivered.

The chapter has argued that the demands placed upon the police to provide a uniformed presence in communities has given rise to a system of plural policing in which agencies other than the police service respond to this demand. The role of organisations operating in the private sector has been discussed in this context and also in connection with the other functions that they perform in the delivery of contemporary policing. It has been argued that one of the problems associated with the performance of policing functions by organisations that are not part of the regular police service is the extent to which they are accountable for their actions. The following chapter focuses on this issue and examines the mechanisms of control and accountability that apply to the police service.

Further reading

There are many specialist texts that will provide an in-depth examination of the issues discussed in this chapter. These include the following:

Bullock, K. and Tilley, N. *Crime Reduction and Problem-oriented Policing*. Cullompton: Willan Publishing.

Jefferson, T. (1990), *The Case Against Paramilitary Policing*. Buckingham: Open University Press.

Johnston, L. (1992) *The Rebirth of Private Policing*. London: Routledge.

Newburn, T. (ed.) (2003) *Handbook of Policing*. Cullompton: Willan Publishing.

Reiner, R. (2000) *The Politics of the Police*. Brighton: Harvester Wheatsheaf, 3rd edition.

Walker, N. (2000) *Policing in a Changing Constitutional Order*. London: Sweet and Maxwell.

Key events

- **1831** Formation of the Special Constabulary. The 'Specials' enable members of the general public to perform police duties on a voluntary basis.
- **1923** The establishment of Interpol to facilitate international police cooperation against serious crime.
- **1955** Screening of the first episode of the television programme *Dixon of Dock Green*. George Dixon (played by the actor Jack Warner) epitomised the image of the friendly neighbourhood bobby who lived in the community in which he worked and was respected by all members of it. The last (367th) episode of the programme was shown on television in 1976.
- **1961** Formation of the Special Patrol Group Unit within the Metropolitan Police, renamed the Special Patrol Group in 1965. It consisted of police officers with specialist training who operated throughout the area covered by the Metropolitan Police Service to combat crime and public order situations which local divisions could not cope with. The unit was viewed as being at the cutting edge of 'hard policing' and concerns about the behaviour of some of its officers at events such as the Anti-Nazi League demonstration at Southall in 1979 led to its replacement in 1986 by Territorial Support Units.
- **1963** The 'Great Train Robbery' took place on 8 August when an estimated £2.5 million was stolen, which was the biggest theft the world had then known. This crime was an important landmark affecting the development of organised crime in Britain.
- **1969** The Kray twins, Ronnie and Reggie, were found guilty of the murder of Jack McVitie in 1967 and given life sentences. This ended their influence on gang-related crime in London.
- **1972** The victory secured during the miners' strike by flying pickets that succeeded in closing Saltley Gas Works led to the government setting up the National Security Committee (later renamed the Civil Contingencies Unit). One immediate development was the establishment of the National Reporting Centre (later renamed the Mutual Aid Coordination Centre), whose role was to coordinate the use of mutual aid between police forces in the event of major public order situations. The NRC (which played an important role during the 1984/5 miners' dispute) has been viewed as a major aspect of centralised police organisation.
- **1973** John Alderson became Chief Constable of the Devon and Cornwall Constabulary (a post he held until 1982). He played a crucial role in the development of community policing which was popularised following the 1981 riots. His forward-thinking ideas regarding multi-agency policing were latterly adopted in the 1998 Crime and Disorder Act.
- **1974** The introduction of the Police National Computer, the project having been approved in 1969. This enabled police officers anywhere in the country to access certain basic information such as lists of known criminals, wanted or missing persons, stolen firearms and registered vehicles from anywhere in the country and was an important step in the introduction of technology into police work. The latest version of the PNC, PNC 2, entered service in 1991.

- **1981** Riots occurred in a number of urban areas of England. A report to the Home Secretary (prepared under the 1964 Police Act and written by Lord Scarman) drew attention to poor police relationships with minority ethnic communities. This problem was particularly attributed to the use of stop and search powers by the police that those on the receiving end viewed as being used in a random and racially discriminatory manner. These events, and Lord Scarman's report, served to popularise community policing to the detriment of reactive policing which had become the dominant style of policing in the areas affected by disorder.
- **1992** The formation of the National Criminal Intelligence Service (NCIS). This brought together a number of existing nationally oriented police intelligence-gathering units.
- **1996** Enactment of the Security Services Act that gave MI5 a role in combating serious crime.
- **1997** The enactment of the Police Act. This established the National Crime Squad (NCS) that amalgamated the existing regional crime squads and placed the NCIS on a statutory footing. This Act marked an important development in the formation of a national tier of policing in England and Wales.
- **2001** Enactment of the Private Security Industry Act that established the Security Industry Authority (SIA). This constituted an important step affecting the state regulation of the private policing sector. Its role was to issue licences to people working in different designated sectors of the security industry.
- **2002** The enactment of the Police Reform Act. This introduced police community support officers to provide a uniformed presence in communities in addition to that provided by the regular police service.
- **2005** The enactment of the Serious Organised Crime and Police Act. This established a new body, the Serious Organised Crime Agency, to combat organised crime

References

Alderson, J. (1979) *Policing Freedom*. Plymouth: Macdonald & Evans.

Alderson, J. (1996) 'A Fair Cop', *Red Pepper*, Number 24 1 May.

Allen, S. and Barratt, J. (1996) *The Bradford Commission Report: Report of an Inquiry into the Wider Implications of Public Disorders which Occurred on 9, 10 and 11 June 1995*. London: HMSO.

Audit Commission (1996) *Streetwise: Effective Police Patrol*. London: HMSO.

Barnett, A. (2000) 'Fury at Police DNA Database', *Observer*, 11 June.

Blair, Sir I. (2005) *The Richard Dimbleby Lecture*, 16 November.

Blears, H. (2005) Quoted in *Guardian*, 9 November 2004.

Blunkett, D. (2003) 'Home Secretary's Foreword', in Home Office, *Policing: Building Safer Communities Together*. London: Home Office, Police reform – Performance Delivery Unit.

Blunkett, D. (2004) 'Home Secretary Foreword', in Home Office, *Building Communities, Beating Crime: A Better Police Service for the 21st Century*, Cm 6360. London: Home Office.

Bratby, L. (1999) 'Home Help', *Police Review*, 23 April, pp. 28–9.

Brogden, M. (1982) *The Police: Autonomy and Consent*. London: Academic Press.

Bullock, K. and Tilley, N. (2003) 'Introduction', in K. Bullock and N. Tilley, *Crime Reduction and Problem-oriented Policing*. Cullompton: Willan Publishing.

Bunyan, T. (1977) *The History and Practice of the Political Police in Britain*. London: Quartet Books.

Bunyan, T. (1985) 'From Saltley to Orgreave via Brixton', *Journal of Law and Society*, 12 (3): 293–303.

Burrows, J. and Lewis, H. (1988) *Directing Patrol Work: A Study of Uniformed Policing*, Home Office Research Study 99. London: HMSO.

Carrabine, E., Iganski, P., Lee, M., Plummer, K. and South, N. (2004) *Criminology: A Sociological Introduction*. London: Routledge.

Cassels, Sir J. (1994) *Independent Committee of Inquiry into the Role and Responsibilities of the Police*. London: Police Foundation and Policy Studies Institute.

Chatterton, M. (1979) 'The Supervision of Patrol Work under the Fixed Points System', in S. Holdaway (ed.), *The British Police*. London: Edward Arnold.

Cohen, P. (1979) *Capitalism and the Rule of Law, in* National Deviancy Conference/Conference of Socialist Economists. London: Hutchinson, quoted in M. Fitzgerald, G. McLennan and J. Pawson (1981) *Crime and Society: Readings in History and Theory*. London: Routledge.

Condon, Sir P. (1994) 'Britain's Top Cop Sees National Police Force as Inevitable Step', *Guardian*, 12 January.

Cowan, R. and Hyder, K. (2005) 'Met Targets Gangs' Grip on Minorities', *Guardian*, 25 March.

Crawford, A. (2003) 'The Pattern of Policing in the UK: Policing Beyond the Police', in T. Newburn (ed.), *Handbook of Policing*. Cullompton: Willan Publishing.

Cray, E. (1972) *The Enemy in the Streets*. New York: Anchor.

Critchley, T. (1978) *A History of Police in England and Wales*. London: Constable.

Cummings, E. et al. (1965) 'Police as Philospher, Friend and Guide', *Social Problems*, 22: 3.

Dennis, N. and Mallon, R. (1997) 'Confident Policing in Hartlepool', in N. Dennis (ed.), *Zero Tolerance Policing in a Free Society*. London: Institute of Economic Affairs.

Donnison, H., Scola, J. and Thomas, P. (1986) *Neighbourhood Watch: Policing the People*. London: Libertarian Research and Education Trust.

Draper, H. (1978) *Private Police*. Harmondsworth: Penguin.

Ekblom, P. (2002) *Towards A European Knowledge Base*. Paper presented at EU Crime Prevention Network Conference, Aalborg, October, quoted in K. Bullock and N. Tilley, 'Introduction', in K. Bullock and N. Tilley, *Crime Reduction and Problem-orientated Policing*. Cullompton: Willan Publishing.

Fielding, N. (1991) *The Police and Social Conflict: Rhetoric and Reality*. London: Athlone Press.

Fletcher, R. (2005) 'The Police Service: From Enforcement to Management', in J. Winstone and F. Pakes (eds), *Community Justice: Issues for Probation and Criminal Justice*. Cullompton: Willan Publishing.

Furedi, F. (1997) *Culture of Fear*. London: Cassell.

Garland, D. (1996) 'The Limits of the Sovereign State: Strategies of Crime Control in Contemporary Societies', *British Journal of Criminology*, 35 (4): 445–71.

Garland, D. (2001) *The Culture of Control*. Oxford: Oxford University Press.

Giddens, A. (1998) *The Third Way*. Oxford: Polity Press.

Goldstein, H. (1990) *Problem-orientated Policing*. New York: McGraw-Hill.

Goldstein, H. (1979) 'Improving Policing: A Problem-orientated Approach', in *Crime and Delinquency*, 25 (2): 234–58.

Goldstein, H. (2003) 'On Further Developing Problem-orientated Policing: The Most Critical Need, the Major Impediments and a Proposal', in J. Knutsson (ed.), *Problem-Orientated Policing: From Innovation to Mainstream*. Cullompton: Willan Publishing.

Her Majesty's Inspectorate of Constabulary (1998) *Beating Crime: HMIC Thematic Inspection Report*. London: Home Office.

Her Majesty's Inspectorate of Constabulary (2000) *Calling Time on Crime: A Thematic Inspection on Crime and Disorder*. London: Home Office.

Her Majesty's Inspectorate of Constabulary (2001) *Report of Her Majesty's Chief Inspector of Constabulary for the Year 2000–2001*. London: TSO.

Her Majesty's Inspectorate of Constabulary (2005) *Closing the Gap – A Review of 'Fitness for Purpose' of the Current Structure of Policing in England and Wales*. London: Home Office.

Home Office (1979) *The Private Security Industry: A Discussion Paper*. London: HMSO.

Home Office (1983) *Manpower, Effectiveness and Efficiency in the Police Service*, Circular 114/83. London: Home Office.

Home Office (1984) *Crime Prevention*, Circular 8/84. London: Home Office.

Home Office (1986) *Plastic Baton Rounds/CS: Central Facilities*, Circular 10/86. London: Home Office.

Home Office (1989) *The Mutual Aid Coordinating Centre: Mutual Aid and Police Support Units*, Circular 36/89. London: Home Office.

Home Office (1995) *Review of the Police Core and Ancillary Tasks*. London: HMSO.

Home Office (1999) *The Government's Proposals for Regulation of the Private Security Industry in England and Wales*, Cm 4254. London: TSO.

Home Office (2003) *Policing: Building Safer Communities Together*. London: Home Office, Police Reform – Performance Delivery Unit.

Home Office (2004a) *Building Communities, Beating Crime: A Better Police Service for the 21st Century*, Cm 6360. London: TSO.

Home Office (2004b) *One Step Ahead: A 21st Century Strategy to Defeat Organised Crime*, Cm 6167. London: TSO.

Jefferson, T. (1990) *The Case Against Paramilitary Policing*. Buckingham: Open University Press.

John, T. and Maguire, M. (2003) 'Rolling Out the National Intelligence Model: Key Challenges', in K. Bullock and N. Tilley (eds), *Crime Reduction and Problem-oriented Policing*. Cullompton: Willan Publishing.

Johnston, L. (1992) *The Rebirth of Private Policing*. London: Routledge.

Johnston, L. (1993) 'Privatisation and Protection: Spatial and Sectoral Ideologies in British Policing and Crime Prevention', *Modern Law Review*, 56 (6): 771–92.

Jones, T. and Newburn, T. (2002) 'The Transformation of Policing', *British Journal of Criminology*, 42: 129–46.

Jordan, P. (1998) 'Effective Policing Strategies for Reducing Crime', in P. Goldblatt and C. Lewis (eds), *Reducing Offending: An Assessment of Evidence on Ways of Dealing with Offending Behaviour*, Home Office Research Study 187. London: Home Office.

Joyce, P. (1991) 'Recruitment Patterns and Conditions of Work in a Nineteenth Century Urban Police Force: A Case Study of Manchester 1842–1900', *Police Journal*, LXIV (2): 140–50.

Joyce, P. (1994) 'Local Government and Policing: The End of an Historic Relationship?', *Police Journal*, Volume LXVII (2): 117–24.

Justice (2004) *Response to White Paper 'One Step Ahead – A 21st Century Strategy to Defeat Organised Crime'*. London: Justice.

Kelling, G. and Coles, C. (1998) 'Policing Disorder', *Criminal Justice Matters*, 33: 8–9.

Kettle, M. (1985) 'The National Reporting Centre and the 1984 Miners' Strike', in B. Fine, M. King and N. Brearley, (1996) *Public Order Policing: Contemporary Perspectives on Strategy and Tactics*. Leicester: Perpetuity Press, Crime and Security Shorter Study Series, Number 2.

Kettle, M. and Hodges, L. (1982) *Uprising! The Police, the People and the Riots in Britain's Cities*. London: Pan Books.

King, M. and Brearley, N. (1996) *Public Order Policing*, Crime and Security Shorter Study Series, No. 2. Leicester: Perpetuity Press.

Leadbeater, C. (1996) *The Self-Policing Society: Brit Pop*. London: Demos.

Leigh, A., Reid, T. and Tilley, N. (1996) *Problem-orientated Policing*, Home Office Crime Prevention and Detection Series Paper 75. London: Home Office.

Leigh, A., Reid, T. and Tilley, N. (1996) *Problem-orientated Policing: Brit Pop*, Crime Detection and Prevention Series Paper 75. London: Home Office Police Policy Directorate.

Leigh, A., Reid, T. and Tilley, N. (1998) *Brit. Pop II: Problem-orientated Policing in Practice*, Police Research Series Paper 93. London: Home Office.

Leishman, F., Cope, S. and Starie, P. (1996) 'Reinventing and Restructuring: Towards a "New Policing Order"', in F. Leishman, B. Loveday and S. Savage (eds), *Core Issues in Policing*. Harlow: Longman.

Loader, I. (2000) 'Plural Policing and Democratic Governance', *Social and Legal Studies*, 9 (3): 323–45.

Manwaring-White, S. (1983) *The Policing Revolution: Police Technology, Democracy and Liberty in Britain*. Brighton: Harvester Press.

Matassa, M. and Newburn, T. (2003) 'Problem-orientated Evaluation? Evaluating Problem-orientated Policing Initiatives', in K. Bullock and N. Tilley (eds), *Crime Reduction and Problem-orientated Policing*. Cullompton: Willan Publishing.

McIntosh, M. (1971) 'Changes in the Organisation of Thieving', in S. Cohen (ed.), *Images of Deviance*. Harmondsworth: Penguin.

Moore, C. and Brown, J. (1981) *Community Versus Crime*. London: Bedford Square Press.

Morgan, R. and Newburn, T. (1997) *The Future of Policing*. Oxford: Clarendon Press.

Morton, J. (2003) *Gangland*, omnibus edn. London: Time Warner.

Moss Side Defence Committee (1981) *The Hytner Myths*. Manchester: Moss Side Defence Committee.

Muir, H. (2005) 'Lives Blighted by Adversity and Governed by the Gun', *Guardian*, 4 March.

Myhill, A., Yarrow, S., Dalgleish, D. and Docking, M. (2003) *The Role of Police Authorities in Public Engagement*, Online Report 37/03. London: Home Office.

Newburn, T. and Jones, T. (1998) 'Security Measures', *Policing Today*, 4 (1): 30–2.

Neyroud, P. (1999) 'Danger Signals', *Policing Today*, 5 (2).

Northam, G. (1989) *Shooting in the Dark: Riot Police in Britain*, paperback edn. London: Faber & Faber.

Oldham Independent Review (2001) *One Oldham: One Future*. Manchester: Government Office for the North West.

Punch, M. and Naylor, T. (1973) 'The Police: A Social Service', *New Society*, 17 May.

Reiner, R. (1978) *The Blue-Coated Worker*. Cambridge: Cambridge University Press.

Reiner, R. (1985) *The Politics of the Police*, 1st edn. Brighton: Harvester Wheatsheaf.

Reiner, R. (1998) 'Policing Protest and Disorder in Britain', in D. della Porta and H. Reiter (eds), *The Control of Mass Demonstrations in Western Democracies*. Minnesota: University of Minnesota Press.

Reiner, R. (2000) *The Politics of the Police*, 3rd edn. Oxford: Oxford University Press.

Reith, C. (1943) *British Police and the Democratic Ideal*. Oxford: Oxford University Press.

Rimington, S. (1994) 'Security and Democracy – Is There a Conflict?', *The Richard Dimbleby Lecture*, BBC Television, 12 June.

Rollo, J. (1980) 'The Special Patrol Group', in P. Hain (ed.), *Policing the Police*, Vol. 1. London: John Calder.

Royal Commission on Police Powers and Procedure (1929) *Report of the Royal Commission on Police Powers and Procedure*, Cmd 3297. London: HMSO.

Scarman, Lord (1981) *The Brixton Disorders 10–12 April 1981: Report of an Inquiry by the Rt Hon the Lord Scarman, OBE*. London: HMSO.

Shearing, C. and Stenning, P. (1981) 'Modern Private Security: Its Growth and Implications', in M. Tonry and N. Norris (eds), *Crime and Justice: An Annual Review of Research*, Vol. 3. Chicago: University of Chicago Press.

Short, C. (1982) 'Community Policing – Beyond Slogans', in T. Bennett (ed.), *The Future of Policing: Papers Delivered to the Fifteenth Cropwood Round-Table Conference, December 1982*. Cambridge: Cambridge Institute of Criminology, Cropwood Conference Series 15.

Skogan, W. (1990) *The Police and Public in England and Wales: A British Crime Survey Report*, Home Office Research Study Number 117. London: Home Office Research and Planning Unit.

Smith, Sir J. (1994a) Speech to a Fabian Society Conference, Ruskin College, Oxford, 9 January, quoted in *Guardian*, 10 January.

Smith, Sir J. (1994b) 'Police Reforms', *Police Journal*, LXVII (2): 104.

Steedman, C. (1984) *Policing the Victorian Community: The Formation of English Provincial Forces, 1856–1880*. London: Routledge & Kegan Paul.

Stephens, M. and Becker, S. (1994) 'Introduction: Force Is Part of the Service', in M. Stephens and S. Becker (eds), *Police Force, Police Service: Care and Control in Britain*. Basingstoke: Macmillan.

Stockdale, J. and Whitehead, C. (2003) 'Assessing Cost Effectiveness', in K. Bullock and N. Tilley (eds), *Crime Reduction and Problem-Oriented Policing*. Cullompton: Willan Publishing.

Storch, R. (1975) 'The Plague of Blue Locusts: Police Reform and Popular Resistance in Northern England 1840–1857', *International Review of Social History*, 20: 61–90, quoted in M. Fitzgerald, G. McLennan and J. Pawson (1981) *Crime and Society: Readings in History and Theory*. London: Routledge.

Storch, R. (1976) 'The Policeman as Domestic Missionary', *Journal of Social History*, IX (4): 481–509.

Sutherland, E. (1937) *The Professional Thief*. Chicago: University of Chicago Press.

Taylor, I. (1981) *Law and Order – Arguments for Socialism*. Basingstoke: Macmillan.

Thackrah, J. (ed.) (1985) *Contemporary Policing: An Examination of Society in the 1980s*. London: Sphere Books.

Tilley, N. (2003) 'Community Policing, Problem-oriented Policing and Intelligence-led Policing', in T. Newburn (ed.), *Handbook of Policing*. Cullompton: Willan Publishing.

Tupman, B. and Tupman, A. (1999) *Policing in Europe: Uniform in Diversity*. Exeter: Intellect.

van de Bunt, H. and van der Schoot, C. (2003) 'Introduction', in H. van de Bunt and C. van der Schoot, *Prevention of Organised Crime: A Situational Approach*. Amsterdam: Boom Juridische Uitgevers, distributed by Willan Publishing.

Waddington, P. (2003) 'Policing Pubic Order and Political Contention', in T. Newburn (ed.), *Handbook of Policing*. Cullompton: Willan Publishing.

Walker, N. (2000) *Policing in a Changing Constitutional Order*. London: Sweet & Maxwell.

Walker, N. (2003) 'The Pattern of Transnational Policing', in T. Newburn (ed.), *Handbook of Policing*. Cullompton: Willan Publishing.

Weatheritt, M. (1983) 'Community Policing: Does it Work and How do We Know?', in T. Bennett (ed.), *The Future of Policing*. Cambridge: Cambridge Institute of Criminology.

Weatheritt, M. (1987) 'Community Policing Now', in P. Willmott (ed.), *Policing and the Community*, Discussion Paper 16. London: Policy Studies Institute.

Wilson, J. and Kelling, G. (1982) 'Broken Windows', *Atlantic Monthly*, March: 29–38.

Wright, S. and Evans, R. (1999) 'British Police Face a CS Gas Attack', *Guardian*, 8 July.

Policing: control and accountability

This chapter examines the control and accountability of the police service in England and Wales. It addresses changes that have been made to the control and accountability of the service since 1964, and evaluates the reasons for, and the significance of, these reforms. In particular the chapter:

- considers the tripartite division of responsibilities for police work in England and Wales which was established by the 1964 Police Act;
- discusses problems associated with the tripartite division of responsibilities for police affairs and how these were resolved during the 1980s;
- examines how the imposition on the police service of policies derived from new public management resulted in a greater degree of central government control over police affairs, culminating in the 1994 Police and Magistrates' Courts Act;
- evaluates reforms introduced by post-1997 Labour governments derived from new managerialist principles;
- discusses the accountability of police officers for their actions in the context of the development of the police complaints machinery.

The 1964 Police Act

By the middle of the twentieth century, responsibility for policing was shared by local government, central government and chief constables. However, the separation of responsibilities was unclear and justified the need to determine a more precise division between the three bodies. The 1964 Police Act sought to achieve this objective and its main provisions are outlined below.

Separation of responsibilities under the Act

Local government

The 1964 Police Act ended the direct control previously exercised by local government over policing outside of London. Local responsibilities for policing would henceforth be discharged by a police committee (later termed a police authority); although attached to the structure of local government, this did not derive its powers by delegation from the local council (which had been the position previously) but directly from the Act itself. The role of the local council was confined to approving the police force budget that was prepared by the police authority.

Two-thirds of the members of the police committee were councillors and the remaining one-third were magistrates who served in the area covered by the police force. The role of the police committee was to 'secure the mainte- nance of an adequate and efficient [re-defined as 'efficient and adequate' in the 1996 Police Act] police force for their area', and to keep themselves informed regarding how complaints by members of the public against police officers were dealt with by the chief constable. Police authorities were given a number of powers in order to fulfil these responsibilities, which included the appoint- ment and dismissal of senior officers of the force and the provision and maintenance of premises, vehicles, clothing and other equipment. Additionally, police committees acted as disciplinary authorities for the chief constable and deputy and assistant chief constables, and could require the chief constable to submit a report in writing related to the policing of the area.

The policing of London

Different arrangements applied in London where the Home Secretary was the police authority. This situation persisted until the enactment of the 1999 Greater London Authority Act which established the Greater London Assembly and an independent Metropolitan Police Authority (MPA) to over- see policing in London. This consists of 23 people – twelve assembly members appointed by the Mayor of London (an office that was also created by the 1999 legislation), seven independents (one of which is appointed by the Home Secretary) and four magistrates. The role of the MPA is similar to that performed by police authorities elsewhere in England and Wales, incor- porating changes to their functions which occurred after 1964 (which are discussed below). It was charged with maintaining an efficient and effective police force, with securing best value in the delivery of police services, with publishing an annual police plan and with setting policy targets and moni- toring the performance of the police against them. It was given a role in appointing, disciplining and removing senior officers and approves the police budget that is set by the Mayor of London (subject to reserve powers possessed by the Home Secretary to set a minimum budget). The Greater London Assembly performs a limited role in policing, its main power being the ability to summon members of the MPA to answer questions.

The chief constable

The 1964 Police Act placed each force under the operational 'direction and control' of its chief officer, whose prime responsibility was to enforce the law and maintain the Queen's peace. The legislation gave the chief constable a number of day-to-day functions in relation to the administration of the force, which included the appointment and dismissal of officers up to the rank of chief superintendent and the specific requirement to investigate all complaints made by the public against any junior officers.

Central government

The Home Secretary exercised a prerogative power to maintain law and order. The 1964 Police Act gave this minister a range of strategic and tactical responsibilities designed to promote the overall efficiency of the police service. These included powers to:

- pay or withhold the government grant to particular police authorities;
- require police authorities to insist upon the retirement of their chief officer;
- make regulations connected with the 'government, administration and conditions of service of police forces';
- appoint Inspectors of Constabulary and instruct them to carry out duties designed to further police efficiency;
- exercise control over the standard of equipment used by police forces;
- supply and maintain a number of services available to the police service generally;
- require a chief constable to submit a report on the policing of an area and to order a local inquiry on any police matter;
- direct a chief constable to provide officers to another force under the mutual aid procedure;
- exercise control over the amalgamation of forces;
- act as the appeal body for officers found guilty of disciplinary offences.

Home Office circulars and the enhanced role of the Inspectorate (HMIC) tended to increase central control over the police service that was to the detriment of control exercised by police authorities.

An assessment of the 1964 Police Act

The 1964 Police Act gave rise to a number of subsequent problems.

Control of police responsibilities

The division of responsibilities provided for in the 1964 legislation was put forward in vague language. This created grey areas that could become a battleground as to who had the right to determine a particular activity. This was the background of notable disputes between chief constables and their police committees in Greater Manchester and Merseyside (episodes which are discussed in more detail below).

The tripartite system of control and accountability

For much of the nineteenth century the mechanism of police accountability had been straightforward. Outside London, policing was controlled by local government to whom the police were accountable for their actions. The subsequent involvement of central government and chief constables in police affairs complicated this historic form of accountability and in many ways the 1964 Police Act formalised what had become a three-way (or 'tripartite') division of responsibilities. However, this division of control made for an unwieldy system of accountability whereby the actions undertaken by the Home Office, chief constables or police committees were subject to scrutiny by one or both of the other bodies involved in policing.

One difficulty with the tripartite system of control was that it marginalised some bodies that had a legitimate interest in police affairs. Police committees were remote bodies, no longer directly accountable to either a local authority or to local voters, although the 1972 Local Government Act made it possible for a local authority to conduct an enquiry into police affairs (a provision utilised by Bedfordshire County Council in 1994 to examine the police action in connection with 'rave' organisers). Although the Home Office was not completely unaccountable to Parliament for the exercise of its functions related to policing (Oliver, 1987: 36), the system was also imperfect. This inadequacy was only partially remedied with the introduction of a new Select Committee on Home Affairs in 1979 that has periodically conducted investigations into aspects of police work. Finally, the 1964 Police Act failed to provide Londoners with a voice in police affairs, a deficiency which remained until the enactment of the 1999 Greater London Authority Act.

In addition to these difficulties, there were two further weaknesses to the mechanisms of control and accountability that were established in the 1964 Police Act.

Ineffective sanctions

The 1964 Police Act failed to provide for meaningful sanctions whereby one party to the tripartite system could exert influence over the actions of another. For example, the Home Office could withhold the government's grant if it deemed a police force to be operating inefficiently. But the practical impossibility of bankrupting a police force meant this penalty could never be applied even in a situation where it might have been justified. The HMIC inspections of Derbyshire illustrated this problem when the force was denied a certificate of efficiency in 1992 and 1993, a penalty which merely had implications for the force's public image.

Absence of precise demarcation of responsibilities

Under this system, accountability was a complex system of checks and balances. For example:

- A police committee was empowered to require a chief constable to produce a report on police activities. However, the chief constable could appeal to the Home Office to countermand this request.
- A police committee could appoint and dismiss its chief constable. However, the Home Office could override its decisions on such matters.

In 1993, a White Paper concluded that such an 'entanglement' of responsibilities resulted in uncertain lines of accountability which made it 'hard to find sufficient basis for calling any of the parties to account' (Home Office, 1993a: 7).

The debate concerning police accountability in the 1980s

The 1980s were a period when considerable debate arose both within and outside the police service regarding accountability. The reasons for this and the main aspects of this debate are considered below.

The demand for police accountability to local communities

The 1980s witnessed several disputes in some areas between police committees and chief constables. The key issue was an attempt by the former to make chief constables more accountable for their actions to local opinion, especially when formulating priorities concerning police activities. These disputes were most intense in Greater Manchester and Merseyside where personality clashes between the chief constables and the chairs of their police committees intensified these clashes. The demand for enhanced police accountability to the local public was based upon a number of factors that are discussed below.

Public involvement in policy-making

The official promotion of public participation in local government policy-making which was evident in the Town and Country Planning Act of 1968 (and the subsequent Skeffington Report, *People and Planning* (Ministry of Housing and Local Government, 1969)) influenced a wide range of local government services during the 1970s (Boaden et al., 1982). Policing was inevitably affected by this climate as it was organisationally attached to local government.

The politicisation of policing

Perceptions of the politicisation of policing arose after 1979. Those on the left of the political spectrum viewed the police as a coercive instrument, used to advance Conservative economic policies by countering the dissent that arose in opposition to them from those who became unemployed and unemployable. This resulted in police actions directed against industrial disputes, protests and inner-city disturbances. The changed climate in which law and public order was enforced, together with the methods that were used to undertake such functions, resulted in policing becoming 'more controversial than it has been for half a century' (Morgan and Swift, 1987: 263).

The miners' dispute of 1984–5 had particular significance for the demand for enhanced local accountability since local police committees were powerless to prevent their officers being sent to preserve the peace in areas where coal mines remained working during the national strike.

The urban left of the Labour party

The political environment altered in some areas following Labour's defeat at the 1979 general election. A temporary loss of influence by Labour's social democrats and the ascendancy of the left of the party occurred. One aspect of the left's ideology was the democratisation of the key institutions of the state so that they could not impede the future progress of socialism as, it was alleged, had been the case in the past. A number of Labour-controlled local authorities fell under the political domination of what was termed the 'urban left' who sought 'an effective system of accountability whereby those to whom power is delegated account for the way they have used it' (Simey, 1985: 3).

Chief constables who were faced with such demands responded in two ways. The first was to allege that political accountability was unnecessary since the police were adequately accountable in law for their actions. Chief constables could be instructed by the courts to implement the law if this was not being done or could order them to desist from pursuing actions that were contrary to it. However, although the courts have intervened to scrutinise the actions undertaken by chief constables (in connection with actions that occurred at Luxylan in 1981 and Shoreham in 1995) these are rare occurrences and fail to provide any routine examination of police policies. Additionally, legal accountability is secured through individual officers being subject to disciplinary or legal proceedings if they act improperly.

A second response made by chief constables embattled with their police committees was to turn to the Home Office for support. The Home Secretary's functions concerning the operations of the entire police service enabled this minister to override police committees when they had clashed with their chief officer over matters such as the provision of equipment. For example, a chief constable was enabled to proceed with the purchase of CS gas and plastic bullets for riot control training when the police authority refused to approve the purchase of these items (Home Office, 1986). This procedure initially strengthened chief constables in their dealings with police committees but in the long term this reliance on central government tended to establish the Home Office as the pre-eminent power driving police affairs. The content of major aspects of police policy became determined centrally (Reiner, 1994) and was subject to minimal local influence. Home Office circulars, drawn up by civil servants in consultation with ACPO and enforced by the Inspectorate, became the key source of influence on police policy-making (Jones and Newburn, 1997: 6).

Corruption and abuse of power

Allegations of abuse of power and corruption provided a further explanation for demands for improved mechanisms of police accountability to the general public. Sir Henry Fisher's report in 1977 into the Confait murder investigation revealed abuse of the rights of suspects, which in this case had resulted in three boys being convicted of murder on the basis of false confessions. The death of Jimmy Kelly in Merseyside police custody and the conduct of the West Midlands Serious Crime Squad during the 1980s added to perceptions that abuse of power sometimes occurred because of the lack of effective supervision over the actions of police officers.

Allegations of abuse of power were aggravated by accusations of corrupt behaviour. Problems of this nature had arisen in the Metropolitan Police in the mid-1970s in connection with alleged systematic malpractice performed by the Drugs Squad and Obscene Publications Squad. The appointment of Robert Mark as Commissioner of Police was viewed as indicating that a battle would be waged against corruption in that force (Reiner, 2000: 63). Between 1978 and 1982, Operation Countryman investigated alleged corruption by members of the Metropolitan Police Force. Forty-one officers were reported to the Director of Public Prosecutions and four were subsequently prosecuted. These problems had a disadvantageous effect on the image of the police service and helped to legitimise demands for improved mechanisms of accountability.

A particular problem concerned the activity undertaken by police officers on the streets. Searches of persons and vehicles by the police became an emotive issue in inner-city areas in the late 1970s and early 1980s. Police powers to undertake such activities were derived either from local legislation or the 'sus' provisions of the 1824 Vagrancy Act (which was repealed in 1981 and replaced by the Criminal Attempts Act). It was alleged that the switch to reactive policing methods (an issue which is discussed in Chapter 3) resulted in the police losing contact with local communities, a problem which in inner-city areas was compounded by inadequate police contact with, and understanding of, minority ethnic groups. This led some officers to use powers of this nature in a random fashion, based not upon the likelihood of a person being engaged in an illegal activity but upon criteria which included colour of skin, style of dress or simply being in what was regarded as a 'high crime' neighbourhood. Accusations of racism, insensitivity or a desire to exert coercive control over certain groups who were perceived as causing a problem for society justified demands for improved methods of external control over police actions. Concern was further expressed about the aggressive way in which policing was often delivered. Units such as the Metropolitan Police's Special Patrol Group were singled out for particular criticism (Rollo, 1980: 173–8).

The major public disturbances that took place in a number of urban areas in 1981 ensured that there would have to be an official response to the demands made for improved mechanisms of police accountability to local populations. This was initially delivered through Lord Scarman's inquiry (which is discussed in Chapter 10), many of whose recommendations were subsequently embodied in the 1984 Police and Criminal Evidence Act.

Why did the 1964 Police Act fail to provide a final settlement for the exercise of responsibility over police affairs?

Main provisions of the 1984 Police and Criminal Evidence Act

The 1984 Police and Criminal Evidence Act (PACE) was particularly motivated by the desire to 'head off' demands for improved formal mechanisms of police accountability. Accordingly, it introduced reforms that were designed to enhance the extent to which the police operated with the consent of the general public. It was anticipated that these reforms would result in higher standards of police behaviour and improved relationships between police and public, especially in urban areas. This would render any fundamental changes to the formal structure of police accountability unnecessary. Reforms to policing methods (especially community policing) were also 'kick-started' by Scarman's report.

The main provisions of the 1984 Act are discussed below.

Safeguards to the exercise of police powers

One solution to the problems arising from the use of stop and search powers would have been to remove them entirely from the armoury of police resources. Lord Scarman accepted, however, that these were essential to the effective discharge of police duties (Scarman, 1981: 113). Thus the government's response in the 1984 legislation was to retain them, but to govern their use by the introduction of safeguards that replaced the constraints previously imposed by 'Judges' Rules'.

The main problem with safeguards was that they were embodied in a Code of Practice. The breach, by an officer, of any aspect of these Codes was not a criminal offence, although it might be the subject of a disciplinary charge. This meant that the influence that they exerted over the actions of police officers 'on the streets' was partially dependent on the officers' willingness to abide by them, reinforced by the stance which judges adopted towards breaches in cases which subsequently came to court.

Safeguards

The use by the police of stop and search powers became governed by safeguards that were contained in Codes of Practice provided for in the 1984 Police and Criminal Evidence Act. Henceforth:

- stop and search could only be conducted on the grounds that an officer had reasonable suspicion that it would produce evidence of criminal activity;
- the officer making the search was required to give the suspect his or her name, the location of the police station to which he or she was attached, the purpose of the search and the grounds for undertaking it;
- a person who had been stopped and searched and subsequently arrested was entitled to a copy of the record of the search.

The introduction of safeguards governing stop and search procedures was designed to ameliorate a particularly abrasive issue that had considerably soured police–public relationships in urban areas.

Other safeguards were also introduced to cover the detention, treatment and questioning of a person by the police, identification procedures and, latterly, the tape recording of interviews. The Act imposed new restraints on police actions that included stipulating the length of time a suspect could be detained at a police station and providing for supervision of a suspect by the new post of 'custody officer'. All Codes were revised in 1991 when a suspects' right to legal advice was emphasised. The latest versions were implemented in 2005.

The Police Complaints Procedure

The 1984 Act altered the method used to investigate complaints against the police. This reform is discussed in more detail later in this chapter.

Liaison machinery

The belief that poor police–public relationships in inner-city areas were a significant cause of the 1981 disorders legitimised demands for new mechanisms to make the police more accountable to the public for their actions. Scarman's inquiry addressed this issue and suggested a compromise, designed to reconcile the claims of the police for professional autonomy with a desire by many members of the public for greater involvement in police work. The principles of 'independence and accountability' (Scarman, 1981: 63–4) were reconciled with a proposal that machinery should be developed to enable the police and public to consult. The active involvement of the community in policing was promoted by the Home Office (Home Office, 1982) and was latterly incorporated into the 1984 Police and Criminal Evidence Act. Section 106 of this measure required police authorities outside London to make arrangements to secure the views of the public on the policing of their area by establishing consultative committees, the role of which was further elaborated upon by the Home Office (Home Office 1985). Consultative arrangements were subsequently catered for in section 96 of the 1996 Police Act.

Measures to combat racism in the police service

Lord Scarman's report also triggered a number of reforms designed to enable the police service to police multiracial societies more adequately. The most important developments affected recruitment and training that were designed to ensure that police forces more accurately reflected the composition of the public they policed, and that racist attitudes held by police officers were effectively combated. Additionally, he suggested that a specific disciplinary offence should be added to the Police Disciplinary Code, so that officers who displayed or articulated racist conduct should be disciplined with the normal punishment of dismissal.

The aftermath of the PACE

Two key developments reduced the intensity of the demand for enhanced mechanisms of police accountability.

The abolition of the metropolitan counties

Following the implementation of the 1985 Local Government Act, the role previously performed by police committees in metropolitan counties became discharged by joint boards, composed of magistrates and representatives from the constituent district councils. This development reduced the demand to improve mechanisms of local police accountability since the new police authorities in metropolitan areas were no longer associated with any single local authority and could not thus claim any form of mandate for their demands which might previously have been derived from county council elections. Section 85 of the 1985 Local Government Act made joint boards subject to a much greater degree of central control in key areas of work for the first three years of their existence, and the councillors who were appointed to serve on them lacked experience and were more willing to accept the chief constable's definition of their responsibilities (Loveday, 1987: 14–15). The establishment of unitary local authorities following the 1992 Local Government Act further extended the number of localities where no direct link existed between a police authority and local government.

Changes to the balance of power within the Labour party

The influence of the left (who had been most associated with demands to improve the mechanisms of police accountability) diminished following the 1983 general election. This tended to tone down the party's official criticisms, both of police performance and the power of chief constables to control operations and determine policy. In 1990 Roy Hattersley addressed the Police Federation conference and used this occasion to seek an improvement in the relationship between the police and the Labour party. Although the party continued to advocate a greater role for police authorities in police affairs during the 1992 general election campaign, the rationale that was presented for this reform was principally directed at the growing influence exerted by the Home Office over police affairs rather than the power of chief constables. This theme formed one of Labour's criticisms of the 1994 Police and Magistrates' Courts Act, suggesting it involved 'more control exerted by the Home Office and less input from local people' (Labour Party, 1995: 3).

Central control of the police service

After 1979, Conservative governments sought to increase the hold which central government was able to exert over the operations of the police service. These reforms broadly fell under two headings: changes to the working practices of the police services and alterations to the control and accountability of the service.

Changes to the working practices of the police service

The police service and Conservative government enjoyed a cordial relationship during the early part of the 1980s. The close nature of this relationship was reflected in improvements to police pay through the implementation of the Edmund Davies award soon after the Conservatives won the 1979 general election. The police service did not suffer initially from the scale of public spending cuts inflicted on other public services after 1979 that were designed to reduce the level of public spending.

However, the perception that increased spending on the police service was not succeeding in reducing the levels of crime and disorder prompted a change of direction by the government. A number of reforms directed at its working practices (and in particular its performance culture) were introduced. These innovations denote 'the drive to improve cost efficiency and performance effectiveness via the imposition of market disciplines on the police service' (Jones, 2003: 615). The main developments associated with this process of 'marketisation' are discussed below.

The police service: good value for money?

A key reason for increased central government involvement in police affairs in the early 1980s was a perception that the service was failing to provide good value for money. For example:

- the number of police officers and civilians employed by police forces rose from 79,000 in 1960 to 155,000 in 1983;
- the number of recorded crimes rose from 0.75 million in 1960 to 3.25 million in 1982;
- clear-up rates fell from 47 per cent in 1973 to 37 per cent in 1982 (Sinclair and Miller, 1984).

However, suggestions that police inefficiency was responsible for the problems highlighted in these statistics must be balanced against arguments that suggest crime is influenced by factors over which they have no control. These include demography and especially the number of males aged 14–25 in the population (Nuttall, 1999), the growth of a consumer society (resulting in the greater availability of goods to steal), the level of male unemployment and the extent of wage inequality among male manual workers. It has, however, been suggested that increases in the size of police forces may influence the extent of property crime (Witt et al., 1999).

The Financial Management Initiative and policing by objectives

The principles of value for money and effective use of resources which were embodied in the 1982 Financial Management Initiative were applied to the police service by Home Office Circular 114/83 entitled *Manpower, Effectiveness and Efficiency in the Police Service* (Home Office, 1983). This marked the beginning of imposing the principles associated with new public management on the police service (a concept that is discussed more fully below) and coupled earlier experiments with output budgeting (involving attempts to relate expenditure to objectives) with the introduction of performance measurement to assess the extent to which the stated objectives had been accomplished – thereby focusing public attention on the delivery of services by the police. The role of the HMIC was developed to ensure that forces adopted 'the language of objectives and demonstrable achievement' (Weatheritt, 1986). Subsequent circulars furthered the ideas incorporated into the 1983 circular, especially in connection with producing quantifiable evidence on which to base claims of effectiveness (Home Office, 1988b, 1988c and 1989).

Policing by objectives

This was instigated by Home Office Circular 114/83 and sought to ensure that police resources were used more efficiently and that the junior ranks of the service became involved in the determination of force policy. It involved a number of stages (Weatheritt, 1986):

- preparing a force mission statement which indicated the overall objectives to which its activities were directed;
- producing a goal statement to specify the mission statement;
- specifying the objectives which were derived from the goals;
- devising action plans to indicate how the mission statement would be implemented;
- initiating impact assessment to monitor the extent to which action plans had succeeded in achieving their objectives, enabling alterations to be made in the light of actual achievement.

The adoption of policing by objectives was left to individual chief constables. Most forces adopted aspects of it by the end of the 1980s (Ackroyd and Helliwell, 1991), although only the Metropolitan Police and the Northamptonshire Constabulary implemented it thoroughly. The 1983 circular was viewed as a major step towards centralisation by increasing pressure on individual forces to produce results comparable to those of other forces (Burrows, 1989: 24). However, a number of deficiencies were initially perceived with this system. These included the following:

- Mission statements frequently consisted of generalised statements of police activity which were handed down from the chief constable's office without necessarily securing any commitment from those whose activities were designed to implement them.
- The performance measurements which were utilised tended to be poorly focused and uncoordinated (Audit Commission, 1990a).
- An activity as diverse and demand-led as policing was not readily amenable to clarification or classification in terms of separate objectives (Walker, 1994: 57).

Civilianisation

The employment of civilians within the police service proceeded slowly after 1945. The main impetus for the progress of this development was the desire of Conservative governments after 1979 to prune public spending. In 1983 a Department of the Environment Audit Inspectorate report, *Police Service: Civilianisation and Related Matters*, estimated that the cost of employing a civilian was half that of employing a police officer and that there was scope for further civilianisation within the service.

Accordingly Home Office Circular 114/83 stipulated that one of the criteria to be fulfilled before increases in police establishments were approved by the Home Office would be evidence that the force was using its existing resources to its best advantage, and especially that civilian personnel were effectively freeing police officers for operational duties. Civilianisation was pursued in subsequent circulars (Home Office, 1988b, and Home Office, 1988c). Initially, the bulk of civilian posts consisted of manual and clerical appointments which had previously been performed by police officers drawn from the lower ranks of the service, but subsequently some civilians were brought in at a much higher level. Between 1960 and 1986 the total number of civilians increased from 8,933 to 43,675 and totalled 53,011 in 1997 compared to 127,158 police officers (HMIC, 1998: 48). In 1995/6 expenditure on civilian salaries amounted to £1.02 billion compared with £3.95 billion for police salaries (HMIC, 1998: 40).

One difficulty with the progress of the policy of civilianisation was the grant system used in England until 1994. Whereas increases in the establishment for police forces (if approved by the Home Office) were paid for by grants received from the Home Office Police Grant and the Department of the Environment Revenue Support Grant, increases in the number of civilians employed by police forces did not attract central government financial aid. This increased the burden on local community charge payers, and provided an incentive for police authorities to seek increases in the number of police officers employed for which they would not have to pay. It was concluded that 'pressure to civilianise would clearly be stronger if the aims of HMIC and the incentives delivered by the grant mechanism reinforced one another, rather than pulling in different directions' (Audit Commission, 1990b: 8).

New public management

The key characteristics of new public management were the assertion of the supremacy of the market over the state, the introduction of greater competition between the public and private sectors to promote efficiency (an objective which was also pursued within the public sector, making use of the mechanism of league tables), the centralisation of strategic policy-making, the decentralisation of the provision of public policy onto a variety of agencies (including private contractors) and the fragmentation of government (Leishman et al., 1996: 11–12). New public management has been described as 'a way of reorganising public sector bodies to bring their management and reporting closer to a particular conception of business methods' (Dunleavy and Hood, 1994: 9). Thus the use of management techniques traditionally associated with the private sector (such as performance indicators, business plans and the costing and market testing of all activities) were vigorously developed to redress perceived organisational inefficiencies and promote enhanced value for money.

As has been observed above, Home Office Circular 114/83 marked the beginning of the attempt to introduce new public management ideals into the police service, thereby focusing attention on its performance culture which was a particular concern of new public management (Savage and Charman, 1996: 45). Although initial reforms had a limited impact on the working practices of the police service, a more vigorous attempt to pursue new public management was subsequently attempted during the 1990s. The key developments derived from new public management that attempted to change the performance culture of the police service are discussed below.

Objectives and performance indicators

The application of the principle of value for money to the police service might, in the long term, involve the introduction of an internal market in which a police authority (as a free-standing corporate body acting as the purchaser of services) could seek value for money through competition between service providers in both public and private sectors. In the short term, however, the absence of competition in most areas of police work has resulted in the development of numerous initiatives which sought to enhance police performance and productivity by promoting and testing efficiency in the delivery of services.

An important development to achieve this was the devising of a range of centrally determined performance indicators, which related only to those areas of police work for which quantifiable data could most easily be compiled. These particularly related to the goal of controlling crime (Martin, 2003: 161). The performance indicators that were used were in the nature of output controls and were initially devised by a variety of bodies (including the Home Office, Audit Commission, HMIC and ACPO), but, following the enactment of the 1992 Local Government Act, became the responsibility of the Audit Commission. The emphasis placed on quantifiable data meant that crime statistics generated by individual police forces became an important measure of police efficiency. A Home Office circular put forward a set of core statistics to be included in the chief constables' annual reports (Home Office, 1995b) and since 1995, the Audit Commission has published 'league tables' containing comparative information on issues such as the level of crime, the detection rates per police officer and clear-up rates for all crimes in each of England and Wales's 43 police forces. In this way politicians and the public were able to assess police performance and ascertain whether good value for money was being provided for money expended on the police service, which in 1997/8 amounted to £115 per head of population (Audit Commission, 1999).

Core and ancillary functions

The desire to improve police performance was underwritten by an attempt to define the main tasks of policing. The responsibilities discharged by British police forces had not developed in a systematic manner but frequently arose from the fact that police stations were open 24 hours a day and thus attracted calls for assistance from members of the public and also other agencies which resulted in the police providing 'a host of friendly supportive services to people in need' (Reiner, 1994: 13).

In 1962 the Royal Commission on Policing discerned eight major police functions, of which the last was the vague duty of befriending those in need. The Royal Commission saw the police as 'a general factotum of community administration' (Oliver, 1987: 13) which suggested that the police service was more than a mere law enforcement agency. The demand for these 'service functions' outweighed the law enforcement role of policing (Punch and Naylor, 1973) and were important in securing widespread legitimacy for the police function within society.

However, the emphasis placed on promoting efficiency by measurable activities was inevitably at the expense of service roles since it was not generally possible to quantifiably measure them. This problem was accentuated when attempts were made to differentiate between core and auxiliary functions to ensure that police resources were devoted to the former – most of which were related to law enforcement activities.

In 1993 the attempt to determine what activities could be relinquished (or 'hived off') by the police was handed to a Home Office review team, which was charged with distinguishing between core and peripheral (or ancillary) functions. Its role was to examine the services provided by the police, to make recommendations about the most cost-effective way of delivering core police services and to assess the scope for relinquishing ancillary tasks. Twenty-six areas were identified in which time and money could be saved if the police effort was streamlined or reduced and it was recommended that these activities could either be offloaded onto commercial or voluntary-sector providers or be made subject to the process of compulsory competitive tendering which had been introduced in the 1988 Local Government Act. The report also endorsed the increased use of charging by the police for the services they provided, and emphasised the relevance of private sector management styles to police work (Home Office, 1995a).

Consumerism

Attempts to reform the performance culture of the police service became associated with consumerism. This approach was enhanced by developments based upon the *Citizens' Charter* which was launched in 1991 which sought to improve the choice, quality, value for money and accountability of public services by seeking to ascertain what the public expected of the police and ensure that services were delivered effectively. Particular emphasis was placed on consumerism, seeking to enhance the rights and responsibilities of ordinary citizens through the avenue of market choice (Brake and Hale, 1992: 37) rather than through political structures of accountability. This approach entailed transforming the general public from citizens into consumers who thereby became better informed concerning police affairs and more able to insist upon high standards of efficiency, directed at areas of activity which they deemed to be of importance. Police authorities (which were revamped by the provisions of the 1994 Police and Magistrates' Courts Act) came to play a key role in this process by acting as the 'champions of the consumers' (Weatheritt, 1994: 35).

The Sheehy Inquiry

The reform of police management was designed to improve the overall performance of the police service and was underpinned by new public management. In 1992, the Home Secretary, Kenneth Clarke, appointed a team headed by Sir Patrick Sheehy to conduct an independent inquiry into the 'rank structure, remuneration and conditions of service of the police service'. The report suggested that the rank structure should be simplified and that the roles of the remaining ranks should be reassessed and in a number of cases expanded. It was proposed that the police pay structure should be reformed with the introduction of locally determined starting pay and allowances, and that performance and achievement of objectives should influence the remuneration of all ranks. Officers whose performance was regarded as unsatisfactory should receive no annual pay increase and not benefit from automatic incremental progression.

Sheehy proposed that police pay levels should cease to be index-linked and instead be determined in relationship to private sector non-manual pay. The report recommended that existing police regulations concerning conditions of service should to be replaced by a National Code of Standards supplemented by local arrangements determined by the chief constable in consultation with officers and their representatives.

Sheehy suggested that fixed-term appointments should be introduced for all ranks, so that all officers newly joining the police service would be appointed for an initial ten-year period. This could then be renewed for further periods of five years. A review would take place before the end of a fixed-term appointment at which police managers could decide whether to grant a further fixed term if the officer applied for it. Their decision would be based upon structural considerations and the performance and conduct of the applicant. A particular problem with this approach concerned the measurement of an individual's efficiency and the likely need to utilise indicators that stressed quantity rather than quality.

The full pension would normally be available after 40 years' service or at age 60 for new recruits and officers whose employment was made subject to fixed-term appointments (Home Office, 1993b).

Police reaction was hostile to the majority of these proposals. Over 20,000 officers attended a rally at Wembley to protest against them. Accordingly, the government did not introduce Sheehy's full recommendations concerning the rank structure or performance-related pay and fixed-term contracts were ultimately confined to the most senior posts. However, other reforms (including the abolition of the housing allowance) were acted upon.

Quality of service

Quality of service was an important aspect of reforms designed to improve police performance. The objective of improving quality of service became the concern of a number of initiatives put forward by the police service such as quality awareness programmes, performance indicators, questionnaire surveys directed at the public, and procedures such as activity analysis which were designed to enable an officer's time on duty to be used to maximum effectiveness. These have sought to ensure public satisfaction with the manner in which policing was delivered and were derived from methods employed by business, particularly from the Japanese adoption of Total Quality Management, which emphasised the importance of a commitment to quality from all levels of industry. In Britain this is assessed by procedures associated with achieving BS5750 accreditation. Although compatible with the new emphasis on consumerism, these developments were also compatible with the traditional public service ethic of the service, resulting in a possible tension between quality judged from a professional and consumerist perspective (Waters, 1996: 215).

As has been noted above, reforms which were imposed on the police service in connection with efficiency and value for money tended to be at the expense of service roles and served to promote activities which could be quantified. Additionally, certain functions became subject to competition from private agencies. However, the impact of these changes on police officers as well as the general public was unknown. The perception that public approval for police activities was declining (Home Office, 1988a: 76) prompted ACPO to initiate the *Operational Policing Review*, which was conducted under the supervision of the Joint Consultative Committee (consisting of officers from ACPO, the Superintendents' Association and the Police Federation). It was designed to assess the impact of reforms which had been initiated within the service on both police officers and the general public, and in particular to assess public expectations of policing and how these could be addressed.

The findings of this survey resulted in the publication of a strategic document that sought to create a corporate image for the police service through the adoption of its statement of common purpose and values. This emphasised the need for the police to be 'compassionate, courteous and patient', to act without fear, favour or prejudice with regard to the rights of others and to be 'professional, calm and restrained' in the face of violence, applying only such force as was necessary to accomplish their duties. The police were charged with the responsibility for reducing the fears of the public and to reflect such priorities as far as they could in the actions that they took. The service was urged to respond to well-founded criticism with a willingness to change.

The ACPO document made a number of further recommendations related to the behaviour of individual police officers. These included suggestions that each chief constable should draw up a policy statement on quality of service, in which responsibilities for its implementation were allocated throughout the police management hierarchy. This would emphasise the central responsibility of all officers to provide a fair, courteous and non-discriminatory service. It was proposed that customer satisfaction could be veri-fied by the use of consultative and communicative procedures including the use of questionnaires. The chief constable would have the responsibility to monitor the service provided by the police in conjunction with comments made by members of the general public (ACPO, 1990).

Statement of Common Purpose and Values for the Police Service

This statement (ACPO, 1990) defined the role of the police being to:

● Uphold the law
● Prevent crime
● Bring law-breakers to justice
● Keep the Queen's peace
● Protect, help and reassure the community
● Fulfil all such roles with integrity, common sense and sound judgement.

It was argued that, through this approach, ACPO was attempting to shift the policing paradigm away from 'a narrow conception of police enforcement to a broader conception of police service' (Bennett, 1994: 107). The importance ascribed to quality of service required a renewed emphasis on community policing methods, particularly upon multi-agency (or 'partnership policing') approaches.

Police forces responded to the ACPO document with their own measures. These included the production of policy statements based on the working party's report, and the establishment of departments charged with producing quality initiatives throughout the force. Some, such as the Kent Constabulary, employed firms of outside consultants to determine public opinion and its expectations of the police service. The Greater Manchester Police adopted a 'systems approach', emphasising that quality was under-pinned by organisational factors.

The response of the Metropolitan Police was prompted by an earlier inde-pendent report (Wolff Ohlins, 1988) as well as the ACPO working party document. The former was based upon an audit of external and internal atti-tudes towards the Metropolitan Police that had made a number of adverse comments on the public image of that force, particularly the inappropriate attitude which some officers displayed towards members of the public. The then Commissioner, Sir Peter Imbert, responded by the preparation of an action plan, *Plus*, in 1992 which sought to address areas of concern by initia-tives which included attitude training courses, the realignment of the activities of the police with the needs of the public (who became viewed as 'consumers'), and the pursuance of measures designed to improve the image of the force which became renamed the 'service'. The impact made by these measures was assessed through a series of performance indicators.

A major problem with quality of service initiatives has been the extent to which the actions of individual police officers are positively affected. The initiatives need to be effectively communicated within the organisation, explaining their rationale and how individual officers can contribute to their attainment. Without this, cultural resistance and bureaucratic or individual inertia may prevent the accomplishment of quality-enhancing objectives. An additional problem concerns the extent to which pressure of work (derived from increased demands made by the public on the police, especially in connection with the service role of policing) is compatible with officers delivering a quality service to members of the public. Factors such as stress and tiredness may result in officers conducting their work in a manner that the public deems to be unacceptable.

> Evaluate the success of initiatives pursued by Conservative governments between 1983 and 1997 to secure enhanced value for money from the police service.

The 1994 Police and Magistrates' Courts Act

Many of the developments discussed above served to increase the role of central government in police affairs. The implementation of the 1983 circular, for example, provided the HMIC with a key role, namely to report on police efficiency, and to identify and disseminate good practice. The Audit Commission also increased the extent of central direction over police affairs, especially when it was authorised to conduct inspections of police forces in 1986. Many of its reports exerted a major influence on the management of police forces and the manner in which police activities were performed.

In addition to developments directly linked to public management, changes also had to be made to the control of policing to ensure that the service would implement the changes demanded by the government in order to reform its performance culture. One of these concerned the determination of police priorities. Policies to reform the structure of police control and accountability were put forward in a White Paper (Home Office, 1993a) and subsequently incorporated into the Police and Magistrates' Courts Bill which was introduced into the House of Lords in 1993 and became law in 1994. This measure was viewed as the crystallisation of Conservative new public management policy that rested on the pillars of value for money, setting priorities, self-help, consumerism and transparent stewardship (Morgan, 1989). The main proposals and consequences of this legislation are discussed below.

The main proposals of the Act

The 1994 Police and Magistrates' Courts Act introduced the following innovations to the control and accountability of the police service:

- *National objectives*. The Home Secretary would set national objectives (later termed 'ministerial priorities') for the police service, accompanied by performance indicators to assess their attainment. The practical impact of this was that henceforth ministers and not chief constables would determine police priorities. This reform arose in part from attempts that had been made in the 1990s to differentiate between the core and ancillary tasks of policing. The inability to secure consensus within the service on this issue prompted the government to intervene and take steps whereby it could enforce its own priorities on the police.

- *Cash limits*. It had been observed that, prior to the Act, the revenue grant paid by central government to police forces 'was not distributed ... according to a visibly objective assessment of need'. Nor, unlike most other areas of public expenditure, was the grant cash limited – 'the Home Office will meet 51% of forces' net expenditure, whatever it is' (Audit Commission, 1990b: 2). The Act introduced cash-limited budgets, thereby giving the government total control over expenditure. Henceforth its contribution towards the budget for each force was based on a Standard Spending Assessment that was derived from the 'crime index' based upon five key policing activities. The Home Secretary was given reserve powers to order a police authority to spend more than it intended in the interests of efficiency.

- *Amalgamation of police forces*. Simplified procedures were introduced for amalgamating forces. This was justified by the argument that the existence of 43 separate forces in England and Wales did not make the most effective use of resources available for policing (Home Office, 1993a: 41–2).

Home Office control was to be underpinned by political innovations. It was originally proposed that police authorities (the key role of which was to draw up an annual costed local policing plan containing a statement of national and local objectives, performance indicators and finances available) would consist of 16 persons; five of these would be directly appointed by the Home Secretary, who would additionally choose the chair of each authority. However, these reforms raised a spectre of political control that was too alarming for majority opinion in the House of Lords. Opposition, including that of former Conservative Home Secretaries Viscount Whitelaw and Lord Carr, forced the government to back down and permit each authority to select its own chair; it was also forced to abandon the proposal that some members should be directly appointed by the Home Office.

Under the new arrangements provided in the 1994 Act (which were confirmed in the 1996 Police Act), a police authority consists of 17 members: nine are councillors, three are magistrates and the remaining five are independent members appointed by the police authority from a list of names drawn up by selection panels in each police area (Butler, 1996: 223). The new police authorities were free-standing bodies, divorced from the structure of local government, and to whom the Home Office directly paid central government's financial allocation for local police work.

The changing role of HMIC

The changes initiated by the 1994 legislation were supplemented by other reforms which potentially increased the extent to which central government could influence police work. These included an enhanced role for the HMIC whose work became extended into the area of effectiveness as well as its traditional concern for efficiency. To expedite these changes, the HMIC's role was subsequently (in 1994) separated into three functions – primary inspection, performance review inspection and thematic inspection (O'Dowd, 1998: 7).

Performance review inspection further increased the emphasis on the production and assessment of performance data using a database termed the HMIC Matrix of Indicators. The latter (which is concerned with the assessment of a single function across a number of forces) typically involves areas of activity delivered by a multi-agency approach, and the inspections of which may use experts from bodies such as the Commission for Racial Equality (CRE) and the Crown Prosecution Service (CPS). The adoption of best value further affected the role of the HMIC, requiring it to move into 'a prospective role of certification when historically the task has been ex post facto review' (O'Dowd, 1998: 7). In 2004 HMIC published its new baseline assessments that set baselines for particular activities against which forces should be performing to enable HMIC to focus on areas within a force that required improvement (Home Office, 2004: 155).

Impact of the 1994 Police and Magistrates' Courts Act on the police service

There are three contrary views regarding the impact of the 1994 Act on the subsequent development of the police service.

Increased central control and politicisation

One view is that while the 1994 Act retained the tripartite system of police governance that had been developed in the 1964 Police Act, the balance between these three partners was substantially altered. This opinion asserts that chief officers were reduced in status and subjected to increased central control whereby the service could be directed into areas stipulated in the Home Secretary's national objectives, assessed by the newly created Police Performance Unit at the Home Office which monitored performance indicators, and relegated to providing services determined by police authorities in their local policing plan. It is further alleged that the latter were themselves subject to increased central direction exercised by the Home Office, effectively transforming them into an intermediary of central government and a direct agent of the Home Office (Loveday, 1994: 232). The Act was condemned as an attempt to achieve a national police force without such an objective being openly declared (Alderson, 1994) and for its effect in transforming the police from a local service to a state police (Loveday, 1995: 156).

The main objection to enhanced central control was that it would politicise the police service, transforming it into an agency whose purpose was to advance the government's political objectives. However, the existence of national objectives can be alternatively justified by the need to focus the minds of chief constables and police authorities on significant problems faced by minorities (such as racial violence) that might otherwise be ignored locally. Additionally, while there is the potential in the Act to define political tasks (or at least activities which are politically appealing to the party in government) as national objectives, the latter have not been used in this way. National objectives have been largely uncontentious and, additionally, have been framed following a process of consultation involving key bodies such as ACPO (Jones and Newburn, 1997: 36). Similarly, performance indicators, although the responsibility of the Audit Commission, subsequently included suggestions made by the Inspectorate. Nor has increased central control been used to its full potential, initial findings suggesting that 'there is no clear evidence ... that national considerations dominate local ones' (Jones and Newburn, 1997: 47).

Increased managerial responsibilities for senior police officers

An alternative assessment challenges the view that the 1994 legislation effectively transformed police forces into a police service controlled in all its main aspects by central government. New public management was associated with the twin goals of centralisation and decentralisation. The new controls could be viewed as strategic in nature and within their confines offered enhanced autonomy for both police authorities and chief constables by replacing existing Home Office controls over personnel and financial matters. The 1994 Act gave chief officers full management responsibility for all police personnel, and operational control to direct local policing in accordance with a business plan drawn up within the context of the local policing plan and the Home Office's cash limited budget.

One example of this was that chief constables, rather than the Home Office, would henceforth determine the number of police officers employed. Also, the chief constable inevitably plays an important role in drawing up the local policing plan for the local police authority. The increased tendency for local commanders to be given control of their own budgets (as recommended by the Audit Commission, 1994) within the framework of the local policing plan through the process of devolved budgeting also serves to increase the power of these officers.

Enhanced role for police authorities

Police authorities continued to exercise their traditional functions that included disciplinary matters (demonstrated, for example, in connection with the suspension of the chief constables of Gwent in 1997 and Sussex in 1999) and their key role of budgetary control. These were supplemented with several additional new powers which included the determination of police priorities (following consultation with the local community), the publication of an annual costed policing plan and reporting back to the community at the end of the year concerning the extent to which the policing plan had been met.

The existence of published objectives (which local policing plans generally linked to targets attached to performance indicators) increased the ability of police authorities to hold chief constables to account for the way in which policing was delivered locally, and was achieved by the publication of an annual report which compared objectives against performance. It has been observed that, although at the outset many police authorities were content to play a minor role in determining objectives and targets and setting policing plans, they subsequently adopted 'a more active role in the policing plan process ... recognising the critical importance of their role in monitoring performance and making sure that the chief constable delivers' (Henig, 1998: 8).

It has also been argued that the independent members of police authorities have played a considerable role in making these bodies more assertive than their predecessors; this could result in local issues becoming a prominent aspect of local policing plans (Savage, 1998: 4). Finally, the formation of the Association of Police Authorities in 1997 (representing police authorities in England, Wales and Scotland) was designed to strengthen the collective voice of these bodies in police affairs and also to guard against the isolation of individual authorities.

> Assess the significance of innovations introduced by the 1994 Police and Magistrates' Courts Act in relation to the control of policing.

Labour's reforms of policing

Many of the reforms that were put forward by Conservative administrations affecting the performance culture of the police service were retained by post-1997 Labour governments. However, the previous underpinning which new public management provided to these reforms gave way to a new agenda. This was frequently referred to as 'new managerialism', although it is alleged that the government's proposals went beyond managerialism to embrace the objective of modernisation that devoted attention to the impact of crime on society and sought to address its underlying causes through measures that included the involvement of local people and communities (Martin, 2003: 166–7).

The modernisation agenda of post-1997 Labour governments entailed a number of developments (discussed, for example, by Newman, 2000) based on new managerialism. These included initiatives that are discussed below.

Police performance

Post-1997 Labour governments have pursued a number of initiatives designed to improve police efficiency. These are discussed below.

Efficiency and best value

Government concern with the efficiency and performance of the police service was justified by the large amount of public money expended on the service, which totalled £9,117 million in 2002–3 (Home Office, 2002: 23). Although this expenditure could be linked to desirable outcomes (in particular a fall in the overall levels of crime) other problems remained, in particular a decline in detection and conviction rates and police performance that was variable across the country (Home Affairs Committee, 2005: 1).

In order to obtain further improvements, best value became a statutory obligation imposed on police authorities by the 1999 Local Government Act and was latterly described as 'the central plank in the drive to improve police performance' (Spottiswoode, 2000: 4) by enabling efficiency to be measured. It replaced previous attempts to achieve efficiency and cost-effectiveness in the delivery of services through the introduction of internal markets by the process of compulsory competitive tendering and was not underpinned by any suggestion that services should be passed either permanently or temporarily to the private sector. The new approach also emphasised the importance of quality of service in addition to efficiency and effectiveness. Best value provided public bodies with enhanced freedom as to how they achieved goals, and they were encouraged to pursue innovative ways to do this. Local service providers were required to demonstrate that they were providing best value to a process of independent audit (which in the case of the police service is the Audit Commission and HMIC), and were also required to consult to ensure that service delivery matched local needs.

The mechanics of best value entailed the development of universal aims and objectives for the police service to which performance indicators (termed 'Best Value Performance Indicators' – BVPIs) to measure progress in attaining these objectives were established under the provisions of the 1999 Local Government Act.

The aim of best value was to provide 'a rigorous system for delivering high quality, responsive services based on locally determined objectives' (Cabinet Office, 1999). It has been argued that best value was 'a way to achieve efficiency, effectiveness and quality in public service provision, but in the process local authorities, and police and fire authorities, have been given the opportunity to decide how they review and deliver services' (Martin, 2003: 166). Best value considerably enhanced the role of police authorities in the delivery of police services. From 1 April 2000, they were required to develop a five-year programme of service reviews, summarise the findings and produce action plans within their annual performance plans that showed past and projected performance (Spottiswoode, 2000: 9) with the aim of ensuring continuous improvements in service delivery. To do this, their review took into account the

> four C's – challenge (questioning how and why a service was provided), compare (judging their performance in comparison with other service providers, with a view to improving the services for which they were responsible), compete (ensuring that the service they provided was efficient) and consult (seeking the views of local tax payers, service users and the business community). (Martin, 2003: 168)

Best value was designed to measure comparative efficiency so that the relative performance of all police forces could be compared. However, this goal was undermined by the government setting 'uniform, across-the-board efficiency targets which failed to take into account the 'starting position of each authority and force' (Spottiswoode, 2000: 4–5). To remedy this it was proposed that comparative efficiency measures, based on the joint use of Stochastic Frontier Analysis and Data Envelopment Analysis, should be integrated with the existing Best Value outcome performance information to enable police authority and police performance in meeting police objectives to be matched with the differential resources of each authority and force, thereby providing an assessment of their relative efficiency and enabling forces to be grouped into relative 'efficiency' bands (or league tables). This would enable across-the-board efficiency targets to be abolished in favour of differentiated performance targets which would provide a more realistic measurement of police efficiency and enable comparative performance to be more accurately evaluated (Spottiswoode, 2000: 4–5).

Criticisms of this nature prompted changes to be made in the manner in which comparative information on police force performance was disseminated. When the Home Office published comparative performance data about police forces in England and Wales for the first time in 2003, an attempt was made to avoid comparing the performance of any given police force against a national average for a given performance measure and instead to use specific comparison groups for each force, enabling the performance of 'most similar forces' to be compared. This approach was adopted as 'force areas vary in their socio-economic, demographic and geographic makeup and we know that … crime rates are dependent on some of these underlying characteristics' (Home Office, 2003a: 5). A later development (an information system known as *i*Quanta which was launched in 2003 under the auspices of the Police Standards Unit whose work is discussed below) provided police forces, police authorities and CDRPs with comparative information on the performance of all forces, BCUs and CDRPs in connection with the 'interim' performance indicators laid out in the 2003–6 National Policing Plan (Police Standards Unit, 2005: 2). Its focus on outputs enables a force to see its position relative to other comparable forces and BCUs within them and facilitates the Police Standards to take an overview by comparing forces across the country and highlighting both good and unsatisfactory performance (Home Office, 2004: 154).

Subsequently a new Policing Performance Assesssment Framework (PPAF) was put forward by the Unit (PSU) to assess police performance (including cost) across the full range of policing responsibilities for all forces in England

and Wales (Martin, 2003: 173). To do this, PPAF divided policing responsibilities into six outcome areas (or domains) that consisted of citizen focus, promoting safety and security, resource usage, investigating crime, reducing crime and helping the public. A seventh area, measuring force performance against local priorities, was also included in the PPAF. The attainment of these would be measured by a number of key performance indicators, and commencing in 2004–5, the BVPIs were incorporated into the PPAF. Although the full assessment schedule was intended to be in place by April 2005, measures compatible with its approach were introduced earlier. In April 2003 activity based costing was introduced in all forces, and the first PPAF performance measures were introduced in April 2004. Comparison between police forces was made on the basis of 'most similar force' comparison groups (Home Office, 2002: 51; Home Office, 2003: 102–5). One difficulty with the approach adopted by PPAF was that it did not take into account the resourcing available to a force, which made comparisons between them difficult. Nonetheless, it was useful in that it could help to evaluate the year-by-year performances of individual forces (Fox, 2005).

Action by ACPO

In addition to policy directed by central government, it has been observed that ACPO was a key centralising influence on the police service (Jones, 2003: 615). In conjunction with reforms that have been discussed above, at the behest of ACPO, activity based costing was introduced in all forces to improve the understanding of the cost of services and to guide more effective decision-making at force level. ACPO further piloted business process analysis to provide for an understanding of the differences in processes, costs and effectiveness between forces (Spottiswoode, 2000: 10).

Reforms to police management

Post-1997 Labour governments sought to improve police performance by introducing managerial reforms. Examples of this included the introduction of Comprehensive Spending Reviews that operated over a three-year cycle. This was initiated in 1997/8 and highlighted the need for savings to be made in areas such as sickness, ill-health retirements and asset management and procurement. This resulted in police authorities and forces from April 1999 being required to include in their annual policing plan an efficiency plan to demonstrate continuous improvement equivalent to 2 per cent of their annual budget year on year (Spottiswoode, 2000: 10).

The 2001 White Paper highlighted the need to reform police employment regulations (Home Office, 2001: para. 6.3). Subsequently a number of reforms were introduced. In 2002 a package was agreed by the Police Negotiating Board in 2002 which introduced new elements into police pay. These included payments (termed Special Priority Payments) for the most experienced officers who could demonstrate a high level of professional competence and extra rewards for officers in the most difficult and demanding posts. The Police Negotiating Board also agreed to a service-wide target of a

15 per cent reduction in overtime expenditure over the three years from 2003/4 and accepted changes to Police Pension Regulations to reduce the level of ill-health retirement. The government further set a target for the police service to reduce sickness absence in all forces (Home Office, 2002: 25–7).

The 2004 White Paper set out further reforms to secure the goal of work-force modernisation, including arrangements for more flexible working, the introduction of multiple points of entry to the service and removing the requirement that officers could not be promoted until they had served specific periods in the junior ranks (Home Office, 2004: 135–40).

Inter-agency collaboration

Labour's approach to the delivery of public services emphasised a collaborative (or partnership) approach whereby government and public bodies were induced to work with each other and with other bodies in the private and voluntary sectors. The 1998 Crime and Disorder Act was responsible for developing the process of collaboration by the role which it accorded to local government in section 17, and through mechanisms which included crime and disorder reduction partnerships and youth offending teams. The enhanced efficiency in the delivery of services related to criminal justice was also sought by developments affecting joined-up government, one aspect of which was the setting of targets across the criminal justice system (Cabinet Office, 1999).

A particular deficiency in police performance related to detection rates. The government sought to tackle this by setting a local justice gap target for every local criminal justice board. The police and other local criminal justice services, working through the criminal justice boards were required to develop a local inter-agency 'narrowing the justice gap' plan that identified a number of priorities designed to improve the number of offences brought to justice, one of which had to be the Persistent Offender Scheme (Home Office, 2002: 16).

Central control over police affairs

Although best value emphasised the importance of tailoring the delivery of the services provided by police forces to local needs, other policies pursued by post-1997 Labour governments entailed a considerable degree of enhanced central control. The main ways through which this objective was achieved are discussed below.

The 2002 Police Reform Act

This was based upon a White Paper (Home Office, 2001) that was concerned to tackle police inefficiency (in particular the low detection rates for crime) and to tackle problems of sick leave and ill-health retirement. The Act contained a number of important provisions that related to the performance culture of the service and constituted what has been described as the first phase of the 2001–5 government's reform agenda (Home Affairs Committee, 2005: 1). The main provisions of this Act were as follows:

- *National Policing Plans*. These set out the strategic priorities for the police service over a three-year period and the indicators against which the performance of the service would be judged. Following consultation with key stakeholders represented on the National Policing Forum (including ACPO and the Association of Police Authorities), the first of these was published for the period 2003–6. The Plan was designed to influence the annual policing plans prepared by chief officers and police authorities and also to underpin their local three-year strategy plans (a development which was introduced by the 2002 legislation). This meant that the content of local policing plans became increasingly directed by central government, the first National Policing Plan listing 51 actions that chief officers and police authorities should take account of in their local policing plans, which included the requirement that these plans were required to include three-year targets for reducing vehicle crime, burglary and robbery (Home Office, 2002: 44–8).

National Policing Plans

The first National Policing Plan established four key national priorities (tackling anti-social behaviour, reducing volume, street, drug-related, violent and gun crime, combating serious and organised crime operating across force boundaries and increasing the number of offences brought to justice) that were linked to the Home Office Public Service Agreements (Home Office, 2002: 3 and 6). It 'sets out a clear national framework for raising the performance of all forces and publishes the indicators against which performance will be judged'. Police authorities would set local targets against these indicators, and in this way the National Plan 'will form the basis for local plans drawn up by Chief Officers and police authorities to improve standards and ensure forces are responsive to the needs and priorities of their communities' (Blunkett, 2002: 2).

- *The Police Standards Unit (PSU)*. In conjunction with the HMIC the Police Standards Unit was designed to promote improved operational performance by embedding a performance culture within the police service (Home Affairs Committee, 2005: 2). In particular it focused on specific areas where variations had been identified and provided support to BCUs and forces where this was required. It was established within the Home Office in July 2001 and its work included the preparation of a Police Standards Unit Management Guide which set out a number of hallmarks (which included clarity about the roles and responsibilities of the police authority, chief constable and managers at all levels for performance and the development of a framework linking performance to corporate planning, budgeting and resource management) which underpinned good organisation and the ability to drive and sustain high standards of performance (Home Office, 2004: 155). A key aspect of the role of the PSU has been to supervise the development of new methodologies in order to assess police performance with a view to reducing the performance gap between the best and the worst forces. These methodologies include *i*Quanta and the PPAF, which have been discussed above.

● *National Centre for Police Excellence*. This was established in 2003 to work with ACPO, HMIC, the PSU and the Association of Police Authorities in identifying, developing and spreading good practice in operational policing throughout the service. It was operated by the Central Police Training and Development Authority (Centrex). It would also provide operational support to forces in the investigation of major and high-profile cases. The Police Reform Act enabled good practice that had been identified to be enshrined in codes of practice, which initially covered the use of firearms and less lethal weapons and the management of health and safety within the service (Home Office, 2002: 13).

● *Reserve powers*. The Home Secretary was provided with new powers to intervene if any force was failing to achieve an adequate level of performance and a new power to direct a police authority, in conjunction with its chief officer, to produce an action plan to address poor performance highlighted by HMIC.

Further reforms related to the performance culture of the police service were subsequently put forward (Home Office, 2004). Considerable emphasis was placed on modernising the service. For individual officers this objective would be based upon national occupational standards and an effective Performance and Development Review system. A new national mechanism to superintend aspects of police work was also put forward.

One difficulty with the reforms associated with phase 1 of the 2001–5 Labour government's police reform agenda was that a variety of bodies were given responsibility to oversee various aspects of policing, resulting in some overlapping of responsibilities. To remedy this the government proposed in the 2006 Police and Justice legislation to establish a National Policing Improvement Agency (NPIA) that would provide for the continuous reform of the operations of the service. The NPIA would focus on three key areas – the development of good policing practice, the implementation of the support function and operational policing support. It would further be responsible for driving the delivery of a small number of 'mission critical priorities' that would be established in the National Policing Plan (Home Office, 2004: 112). This new agency would sit alongside the Police Standards Unit and the Home Office with a consequent diminution of the role of other national bodies such as Centrex, the National Centre for Police Excellence and the Police Information Technology Organisation. The 2004 White Paper further proposed that a single overall grade for each force in England and Wales would be published, and those graded excellent would be rewarded with an enhanced degree of autonomy in the form of freedoms on targets, a break from general inspections and increased funding.

Chief constables and the Home Office

The new powers given in the Act to the Home Secretary in the 2002 Police Reform Act were used in connection with the chief constable of Humberside, David Westwood, in 2004. Following a damning report by Sir Michael Bichard following the murder by Ian Huntley of two schoolgirls in Soham, Cambridgeshire in 2002 (which stated that the chief constable should take personal responsibility for his force's 'systematic' failings over the gathering and keeping of intelligence on potential offenders such as Huntley), the Home Secretary instructed the Humberside Police Authority to suspend their chief constable. They initially refused to do this, and the Home Secretary required a High Court injunction to secure their compliance to suspend him. This action was the preliminary step to a further decision by the Home Secretary as to whether the chief constable should be dismissed (which he would take after an independent inquiry had been held). In this case the chief constable was allowed to return to work but required to retire one year early, in March 2005.

A further example concerned the Chief Constable of Nottingham, Steve Green, who complained in 2005 that government budgets imposed recruiting restrictions on his force that had an adverse impact on its ability to cope with the sharp rise in gun crime. In response, the Home Secretary ordered an HMIC inspection, and the adverse conclusions contained in its report relating to the deployment of police resources led to the Home Office sending an outside specialist to Nottingham in an attempt to remedy the force's alleged managerial deficiencies.

The 2004 White Paper

Further police reform was envisaged in the publication of a White Paper in 2004 (Home Office, 2004). This constituted the second phase of the police reform agenda put forward by the 2001–5 Labour government and placed considerable emphasis on the concept of localism. It placed three key aims at the centre of the reform agenda – the spread of neighbourhood policing to every community through the mechanism of neighbourhood policing teams (a reform which is discussed in Chapter 3), the modernisation of the workforce and the greater involvement of communities and citizens in determining how their communities should be policed. Enhanced local involvement would not, however, be secured through enhanced methods of accountability but instead would be provided by 'a strong customer service culture' whereby forces, basic command units and neighbourhood teams would deliver services with the needs of their customers firmly in mind (Home Office, 2004: 8). Consumerism was thus viewed as the driving force behind police reform.

Using material additional to that contained in this chapter, conduct your own study of the work performed by a police authority. How has the role of these bodies changed since their creation in the 1964 Police Act?

The accountability of individual police officers

Police accountability operates at two levels. The first (which has been discussed earlier in this chapter) concerns the ways whereby those responsible for setting force policy must account for their actions to persons and bodies that are external to the police service. The second level of accountability (which is the concern of this chapter) concerns the mechanisms whereby individual police officers may be required to answer for the actions they have undertaken. These structures are particularly important in dealing with accusations of abuse of power and allegations of corrupt behaviour.

There are several ways whereby police officers may be held accountable by others both outside and within the service for actions that they have taken. These include the following:

- *The law*. Police officers are not above the law. Those whose actions constitute a transgression of it will be the subject of a criminal investigation and a criminal or civil trial, and if found guilty will receive the same punishment as would any other citizen who committed the same offence.

- *Hierarchy*. The police service is a hierarchical organisation and the actions undertaken by officers are subject to scrutiny by their superiors.

- *The police Code of Conduct*. This Code sets out the professional standards of behaviour required of a police officer. If these requirements are not met, the officer becomes the subject of a disciplinary hearing and, for serious offences against the Code, may be dismissed from the service. Offences included within the Code are neglect of duty, indulging in corrupt practices, abuse of authority and incivility to members of the general public.

- *Organisational culture*. This is an informal sanction but one which may nonetheless exert considerable influence over the behaviour of individual officers whose peers will expect them to adhere to standards which are commonly regarded as acceptable norms of behaviour.

In addition to these mechanisms of accountability, formal machinery has been developed to investigate claims that officers have committed offences either against the law or against the Code of Conduct. The following section discusses the development of this mechanism, which is referred to as 'the police complaints machinery'.

The police complaints machinery

For many years, complaints by the public against police officers were handled internally, a procedure that commenced when the first two police commissioners in London (Charles Rowan and Richard Mayne) invited aggrieved members of the public to refer complaints directly to them (Lewis: 1999: 2). Perceptions that this was an ineffective way to combat police misbehaviour resulted in the development of formal machinery to handle complaints made against individual police officers. There have been three main developments to achieve this – the establishment of the Police Complaints Board (PCB) in the 1976 Police Act, its replacement by the Police Complaints Authority (PCA) in the 1984 Police and Criminal Evidence Act and the formation of the Independent Police Complaints Commission (IPCC) in the 2002 Police Reform Act.

The Police Complaints Board

The 1964 Police Act placed police forces under the control of chief constables, thereby making these officers vicariously liable for torts committed by officers under their command. It also introduced a common system for handling complaints by members of the general public against police officers. The 1976 Police Act considerably developed this procedure by establishing a Police Complaints Board, the role of which was to consider complaints alleging that an officer had breached Police Disciplinary Regulations. Under the provisions of the 1976 Act, all complaints against police officers made by members of the general public became monitored by the force's deputy chief constable. The complaint was then investigated either by officers from that force's Complaints and Discipline Department or by those drawn from another force. If this led the deputy chief constable to believe that a criminal offence may have been committed, a file was sent to the Director of Public Prosecutions who would then decide whether or not to prosecute that officer. Following the establishment of the Crown Prosecution Service, this body decided whether to prosecute officers although it is still performed in the name of the DPP.

However, if the deputy chief constable felt that the investigation had revealed no evidence of a criminal offence, or if the Director of Public Prosecutions decided not to initiate a prosecution, the deputy chief constable was empowered to prefer a disciplinary charge against the officer who had been complained against. It was at this stage that the PCB became involved. It was sent a copy of the investigating officer's report, accompanied by a memorandum from the deputy chief constable indicating if it was intended to institute disciplinary proceedings or, if not, why this was not deemed to be an appropriate course of action. In the latter circumstance, the PCB was able to recommend that disciplinary charges should be brought and ultimately could insist on it. Alternatively, it could call for further investigations into the matter.

The introduction of the PCB as a lay element in the system of investigating complaints against police officers was criticised both within and outside the police service. It resulted in the resignation of the Metropolitan Police Commissioner, who objected to the dilution of the authority of chief officers whom he deemed more likely to arrive at the truth and take effective action in connection with such issues (Mark, 1978: 207–9). A number of other criticisms were made against the operations of the 1976 Act (which are discussed in Hewitt, 1982: 12–25). These included the following.

Reluctance to prosecute officers

It was alleged that the Director of Public Prosecutions was insufficiently zealous in prosecuting officers who had acted improperly by insisting on the operation of the '50 per cent rule', whereby a prosecution would be sanctioned only if there was a reasonable chance that a jury would convict. This calculation was influenced by the presumed reluctance of juries to convict police officers.

Double jeopardy

Critics objected to the way in which, for many years, the PCB applied the 'double jeopardy' rule intended to prevent a person being tried twice for the same offence. The PCB effectively took the position that the sending of a file to the Director of Public Prosecutions constituted a trial and thus would not recommend disciplinary proceedings that relied on the same evidence. This was a major factor in why the Board infrequently disagreed with the deputy chief constable's decision not to institute disciplinary proceedings and why it was extremely rare for this body to insist that such proceedings should take place. This perverse interpretation of double jeopardy was, however, revised following criticism from the courts in the case of *R. v. Police Complaints Board, ex parte Madden* in 1983.

Public perceptions of inadequacy

The public had a negative perception of a procedure whereby complaints against the police were investigated by the police themselves. Although this practice is normal in professions, this procedure failed to 'command the confidence of the public' (Scarman, 1981: 115). Aggrieved citizens were loath to make an official complaint, one consequence of which was the increased tendency for those alleging police wrongdoing to resort to the civil courts for a remedy. The burden of proof in civil cases is less than that required in criminal proceedings (the 'balance of probabilities' rather than 'beyond all reasonable doubt') and on occasions the civil courts have made large damage awards.

The Police Complaints Authority

The 1984 Police and Criminal Evidence Act sought to respond to some of the criticisms of the police complaints machinery. Its main features were as follows:

- *The introduction of conciliation.* This process applied to minor complaints when the complainant wanted an explanation or an apology for a police officer's actions. Conciliation (which did not involve the PCA) was conducted in a less adversarial climate to that which had previously governed the handling of complaints against the police.

- *The abolition of the Police Complaints Board.* The PCB was replaced by a Police Complaints Authority. This consisted of a chair, deputy chair and 11 members drawn from a wide variety of backgrounds. The budget of the PCA was around £3 million in 2000 (Home Office, 2000).

- *An enhanced role.* The remit of the PCA was extended to cover criminal as well as disciplinary complaints involving police officers. All serious complaints made against or involving police officers (including death, serious injury, actual bodily harm, corruption and serious arrestable offences) were automatically notified to this body that was empowered to *supervise* their investigation. It could also supervise the investigation of complaints submitted to it by chief constables or police authorities of the force concerned. Supervision included approving the appointment of an investigating officer and imposing requirements on the conduct of an investigation. When investigations are supervised by the PCA, the report from the investigating officer is presented directly to this body that transmits it to the chief constable or police authority.

- *Overruling powers.* The PCA had the power to overrule a chief constable and instruct this officer to send a copy of a report to the DPP for action in the courts, or to recommend (and ultimately insist) that disciplinary charges should be brought.

Continued weakness of arrangements for handling complaints against the police

The amendments introduced in 1984 provided a half-way house situation between independent and internal investigation of complaints and were intended to render unnecessary any fundamental changes to the structure of police accountability. It was anticipated that these reforms would result in improved standards of police behaviour and would secure better relationships between the police and public, especially in urban areas. However, in spite of the reforms that were enacted in 1984, it was alleged that officers who were accused of committing serious offences were still dealt with inadequately. Key problems included the following.

No link with civil actions against the police

The situation whereby those alleging police misconduct towards them resort to a civil case rather than using the disciplinary system resulted in absurdities that were often inconceivable to the general public. All too frequently the police settled these claims out of court (often for large sums of money, although the Court of Appeal issued guidelines in 1997 which stated that a ceiling of £50,000 was appropriate for complaints alleging assaults) yet usually refused to accept any liability. In 1998 Scotland Yard paid out around £3 million to settle or compensate claims made against them, and the Greater Manchester Police paid in excess of £2 million (Smith, 1999), although this later figure embraced the costs of all civil actions including those from its own staff that arose from health and safety legislation and employment tribunals. Details of these awards and the circumstances that prompted payment were not always made public, and officers who were involved in such actions frequently escaped any sanction since no official complaint had been made against them.

Most disciplinary complaints against the police were thrown out

The reasons why complaints were thrown out included the absence of adequate evidence to support them, the ability of officers against whom complaints have been made to exercise the right to silence and the very high standard of proof ('beyond all reasonable doubt') required to substantiate them. Thus during the year ending 31 March 1998, the PCA dealt with 9,608 complaint cases which involved 18,354 individual complaints. However, only 1,130 disciplinary outcomes resulted (PCA, 1998: 11–13).

Officers guilty of disciplinary offences may escape sanction

There are a number of ways whereby officers who had committed disciplinary offences could avoid action being taken against them. They might retire (thereby keeping full pension rights), take extended sick leave, resign or agree to an 'admonishment' (that is a reprimand). Around 80 per cent of complaints made between 1987 and 1999 were dealt with by the latter course of action (Smith, 1999).

Lack of independence

The main weakness with the method used to investigate complaints was that members of the police service remained responsible for conducting investigations. Outside involvement in these matters was limited, the PCA's supervisory role extending to only around one-third of them. This situation provoked a perception, whether founded or not, that police officers investigating their colleagues did not always pursue a complaint with the vigour which they would deploy in other criminal matters. Additionally, members of the PCA were appointed and dismissed by the Home Secretary, who could in some cases give guidance to them.

Lack of transparency

A key problem affecting public faith in the work performed by the PCA was that investigations into complaints which were submitted as a report to the PCA were subject to Public Interest Immunity Certificates and thus the public had no access to them. Further, the reason behind a decision by the DPP/PCA (whose work is discussed below) not to prosecute an officer was not disclosed to the public.

Role of the Crown Prosecution Service

Decisions by the CPS not to prosecute officers who were alleged to have committed criminal offences were sometimes contentious, and led to accusations that it was too protective of abuses of power by the police. In 1999, for example, the CPS determined that no police officers should face prosecution over the case of a Yardie gangster who entered Britain illegally but was allowed to stay on as a police informer and then went onto rape and murder a mother of two in 1995.

The role of the CPS was especially delicate when decisions were required concerning whether to prosecute officers in cases involving deaths in custody or arising from the use of lethal force by firearms officers. In 1997 an inquiry was initiated under the chairmanship of Judge Gerald Butler that reported in 1999. This report suggested that in two of the cases reviewed by the judge the CPS had taken too pessimistic a view of the prospects of securing a conviction. One of these cases concerned the death of the Nigerian asylum seeker 'Shiji' Lapite in London in 1994, in which an inquest jury had recorded a verdict of unlawful killing. The judge advised that the CPS should prosecute officers when there was a case to answer and be more willing to seek counsel's advice than it had in the past (Butler, 1999).

In 2005, an article in *The Independent* newspaper stated that since 1993, 30 members of the public had been shot dead by police marksmen, not one of whom had been convicted of any crime (Verkaik and Bennetto, 2005). One explanation for this was that the level of evidence required by the CPS to mount a prosecution had been set too high. It was alleged that a claim by the police of self-defence was likely to block a prosecution (Verkaik, 2005).

Reforms introduced by the 1997 Labour government

The Home Affairs Select Committee investigated the police discipline and complaints system (Home Affairs Committee, 1998). Its ineffectiveness led to criticisms from the European Commission of Human Rights in 1998 in connection with a complaint by Michael Govell, whose home had been illegally bugged by the police. The Commission found that his right to privacy had been violated and the complaints system had denied him redress. Following the Macpherson Report (which is discussed in Chapter 10), the Labour Home Secretary Jack Straw introduced reforms in 1999 which entailed replacing the police disciplinary code with a code of conduct, breach of which made an officer liable for disciplinary proceedings, and new regulations which covered police conduct and efficiency. These reforms included lowering the burden of proof that was required to substantiate complaints (reducing this test to the civil one of 'the balance of probabilities'), removing their 'right of silence' and introducing a six-week 'fast-track' system to deal with serious allegations. The Home Office also commissioned a study to examine whether an independent system was needed and could be afforded. This had been introduced for the Royal Ulster Constabulary by the 1998 Police (Northern Ireland) Act, whereby an independent ombudsman was given responsibility for investigating complaints against officers.

The Independent Police Complaints Commission

The 2002 Police Reform Act introduced a new method of handling complaints made against police officers (and also civilian support staff) in England and Wales. This replaced the Police Complaints Authority that had formerly dealt with these matters.

Under the new system, which commenced on 1 April 2004, complaints against the police can be investigated in one of four ways:

- Independently, using investigators employed by the IPCC. Initially 72 of these were employed whose role was to investigate the most serious cases such as police shootings.
- Managed by the IPCC, but using police officers to carry out the task of investigation.
- Supervised by the IPCC, with the investigation conducted by police officers. This procedure is similar to the way in which the PCA formerly carried out supervised investigations.
- Local resolution involving a complaint investigated by the local police force's Professional Standards Department with no IPCC involvement. The complainant is required to agree to this course of action, which has become extended to deal with complaints against senior officers. It is envisaged that most complaints will be dealt with in this manner which is similar to the previous practice of informal resolution.

The new system provides additional rights for complainants which include the ability to appeal to the IPCC against the non-recording by the police of a complaint (although these do not have to be made at a police station), the manner in which a complaint is investigated, the outcome of an investigation or a decision by the police to stop an investigation against the wishes of the complainant. Complaints could also be taken from persons not directly involved in a dispute such as witnesses to an event of others who were 'adversely affected' by it. Unlike the former PCA, the IPCC may also scrutinise actions (using the 'call-in' procedure) that have not been made the subject of an official complaint. The Act also removed the anomaly whereby civil actions against the police were not tied in with the complaints procedure. The Act requires chief officers and police authorities to examine civil proceedings brought by the public against the police to ascertain if the claim contains a 'conduct matter' (which is defined in the Act as an action undertaken by a person serving in the police service which may constitute either a criminal offence or warrant disciplinary proceedings). If it is decided that a civil case involves a conduct matter it is recorded as such by the force. Some categories of conduct matter must be referred to the IPCC to determine how the issue will be investigated. Those not referable to the IPCC may be dealt with by the force. The IPCC is empowered to compel police forces to hold disciplinary hearings and may, under certain circumstances, present evidence at these hearings.

The new system is superintended by a team of commissioners (initially numbering 18). Their role is to set, monitor and enforce standards across

England and Wales relating to the investigation of complaints. They are provided with powers to inspect any part of the complaints procedure, carry out force inspections and seize documentation relevant to a complaint. Police authorities are provided with specific responsibilities. Under the new system they are required to communicate with complainants and other interested parties on the progress of an investigation, its provisional findings, any disciplinary actions which are proposed in the investigating officer's report and the outcome of these actions (Wadham, 2004: 21). Providing copies of an investigating officer's report to the complainant is an innovation introduced by the new system.

Although it is likely that the new system will prove to be more effective than its predecessors, there are, nonetheless, some problems that will need to be overcome in order for the system to command the confidence of the general public. It is important that the IPCC is adequately funded to ensure that investigating officers are not overburdened with excessive caseloads. Starving oversight bodies of funds is an extremely effective way for governments to neuter their impact (Lewis, 1999: 94).

There is also the danger of lack of cooperation by the police service. Police culture may hinder investigations. This refers to the 'exceptionally strong unwritten code that police must stick together at all times' which may help to cover up police wrongdoing (Lewis, 1999: 23). Although investigators from within the service may be well placed to overcome restrictions of this nature, particular problems affect examination by those not from the police service who may face what has been referred to as the 'blue wall of silence' (Kappeler et al., 1998) in their attempts to investigate complaints of police misconduct.

Additionally, senior officers may seek to hinder an independent investigation of a complaint. This problem emerged following the shooting by officers of the Metropolitan Police of an innocent young Brazilian who had been mistaken for a suicide bomber. Following this incident, the Metropolitan Police Commissioner contacted the Home Office arguing that this error should be internally investigated as an external investigation might have an adverse impact on national security and intelligence and would also undermine the morale of his force's firearms section. The Home Office overruled the Commissioner, but IPCC investigators were kept away from the scene of the shooting for several days (Cowan et al., 2005) allegedly on the direct orders of the Commissioner, Ian Blair (Dodd, 2005).

Outline the changes made to the investigation of complaints against the police since 1976. Why have these changes been made?

Police corruption

Since 1945 there have been a number of high-profile allegations of police corruption. These include six that are discussed below.

The first was initiated by Sir Robert Mark when Commissioner of the Metropolitan Police; this led to the departure of 478 police officers, although only 80 were dealt with through the courts or disciplinary proceedings (Campbell, 1998) and 13 were jailed. The second was Operation Countryman, mounted in 1978 to investigate the City of London and Metropolitan Police forces. Here, allegations of corrupt association between the police and criminals were the central concern, but the investigation resulted in only four officers being prosecuted. In 1989 the West Midlands Serious Crimes Squad was disbanded and an investigation was initiated into its activities. Although this led to a number of convicted criminals being freed by the Court of Appeal, no officer was convicted of an offence. In the early 1990s an investigation, known as 'Operation Jackpot', was mounted into allegations of corruption at Stoke Newington police station in Hackney, London. Alleged police malpractice at this station resulted in the Metropolitan Police paying £1 million in damages and costs and one officer was jailed for drug dealing.

The fifth case of alleged police corruption became public knowledge when Sir Paul Condon informed the House of Commons Home Affairs Select Committee in 1997 that there were between 100 and 250 corrupt officers (which amounted to 0.5–1.0 per cent of the strength of the force) in his force. Although he stated that this figure was 'numerically lower than in the 1970s', he conceded that 'however tiny that is in percentage terms, the damage they can do to the reputation and morale of the overwhelming majority of officers is enormous' (Home Affairs Committee, 1998). It was subsequently reported in *The Guardian* on 3 March 2000 that between 110 and 120 officers were allegedly guilty of serious misconduct. By that date, 75 persons had been charged with corruption, including 26 serving police officers and 11 former officers. Six serving Metropolitan Police officers were suspended because of continuing corruption-related investigations.

The final case involved the South Wales Police where accusations of wrongful imprisonment based on fake police interview notes, false or missing evidence, bribes or intimidation were made over two decades. This prompted the Welsh Assembly in October 2000 to ask the Home Secretary to launch a public inquiry.

Police corruption

Corrupt behaviour by police officers has historically taken a number of forms:

- *Collaboration with criminals*. This involves officers participating in criminal activities, which may come about through involvement with informants.
- *Theft*. This arises in connection with money (or property such as drugs) which comes into the hands of the police as the result of apprehending a criminal.
- *Intimidation*. This involves officers putting mental or physical pressure on a suspect to confess to having committed a crime or on vulnerable witnesses to give false evidence.
- *Suppression of evidence*. This entails failing to disclose to the defence material gathered during the course of an investigation which might undermine the prosecution's case or aid that of the defence.
- *Fabrication of evidence*. This entails the police manufacturing (or 'planting') evidence in order to secure a conviction.
- *Abuse of the office*. This is done to obtain perks and privileges for personal gain (and involves behaviour such as accepting a bribe in return for turning a blind eye to criminal activity).

Corruption investigations are handled by police forces, which may deploy specialist units to investigate such matters. These include the Complaints Investigation Bureau of the Metropolitan Police. The techniques used to root out corruption have become increasingly sophisticated, involving the use of supergrasses and surveillance techniques. In 1999, it was reported that nearly half of England and Wales's 43 police forces had officers facing dishonesty or corruption charges, and that 19 of these had 100 or more officers suspended or charged over allegations which included the misuse of police information, drug offences or perversion of the course of justice. More than 90 criminal charges and suspensions had been instigated in connection with a purge against corrupt officers in the Metropolitan Police (Campbell, 1999).

The introduction of tape recording for police interviews by the 1984 Police and Criminal Evidence Act, the establishment of the CPS in 1985 and the CCRC in 1995 and the enactment of the 1996 Criminal Procedure and Investigation Act were designed to tackle corrupt behaviour of the sort referred to above.

Perceptions of corruption by some police officers prompted the Metropolitan Police to introduce 'integrity tests' in 1998. This involved leaving marked banknotes in police stations where questions had arisen previously regarding the proceeds of robberies. This approach would mainly be targeted at suspected police officers, although some would be applied randomly. This innovation was prompted when criminals claimed they were charged with stealing less than was in their possession when taken to a police station. The issue of corruption was subsequently addressed in an HMIC report into the broader area of integrity; this made a number of recommendations which included the need for proper guidelines covering gifts and gratuities and for the introduction of more effective supervision of officers handling informants (HMIC, 1999).

Freemasonry

In April 1999, the connection between freemasonry and corrupt behaviour was raised at a police corruption trial, in which a former officer was jailed for attempting to abuse his masonic connections within the Metropolitan Police. In 1999 the Home Affairs Select Committee stated, in connection with their investigations into the influence of freemasonry, that this factor could not be ruled out as a significant issue in both the Stalker affair and the miscarriage of justice involving the West Midlands Serious Crime Squad in the 1980s (Home Affairs Committee, 1999). This resulted in all new recruits to the police service being obliged to declare their membership of the masons.

> To what extent have reforms undertaken since the 1980s succeeded in eliminating police corruption and abuse of power?

Conclusion

This chapter has examined the development of the machinery to provide for the control and accountability of the police service. It has examined the tri-partite division of responsibilities for police affairs that was provided for in the 1964 Police Act and discussed attempts to change the balance of power between these three parties that were subsequently put forward.

A particular theme of this chapter has been the increased role played by central government in police affairs. This approach was initiated during the 1980s under the guise of seeking to secure enhanced value for money and efficiency in the service. This resulted in the introduction of a range of policies associated with new public management and the enactment of the 1994 Police and Magistrates' Courts Act in 1994 that enabled the Home Secretary to set objectives that each of the 43 police forces in England and Wales were required to implement. The chapter also discussed how post-1997 Labour governments have attempted to secure improvements to the manner in which policing is delivered through policies such as best value that are underlaid by new managerialist principles.

The chapter also considered the way in which individual police officers are accountable for their actions and has charted the development of the police complaints system. A particular theme of this account has been the movement towards the independent investigation of serious complaints against police officers that was finally provided for in the 2002 Police Reform Act that established the Independent Police Complaints Commission.

This and the previous chapter have considered a wide range of issues specifically concerned with the police service. The following chapter examines the role performed by the police in conjunction with a range of other agencies that are involved in the prosecution of offenders.

Further reading

There are many specialist texts that will provide an in-depth examination of the issues discussed in this chapter. These include the following:

Jones, T. and Newburn, T. (1997) *Policing After the Act: Police Governance after the Police and Magistrates' Courts Act 1994*. London: Policy Studies Institute.
Leishman, F., Loveday, B. and Savage, S. (2000) *Core Issues in Policing*. 2nd edn. Harlow: Pearson Education.
Newburn, T. (2003) *Handbook of Policing*. Cullompton: Willan Publishing.
Morgan, R. and Newburn, T. (1997) *The Future of Policing*. Oxford: Clarendon.
Rawlings, P. (2002) *Policing: A Short History*. Cullompton: Willan Publishing.

Key events

- **1964** Enactment of the Police Act which sought to establish a tripartite division of responsibility for police affairs, shared between the Home Secretary, chief constables and the newly created police committees (latterly termed police authorities).
- **1976** Enactment of the Police Act. This set up the Police Complaints Board whose remit was to consider whether disciplinary proceedings should be levelled against officers who were the subject of complaints by members of the general public.
- **1983** Issuance of Home Office Circular 114/83, *Manpower, Effectiveness and Efficiency in the Police Service*, which imposed the principles of the Financial Management Initiative on the police service. It set in motion a range of proposals designed to ensure that the service provided enhanced value for money.
- **1984** Enactment of the Police and Criminal Evidence Act. Key provisions of this legislation (such as the Codes of Practice governing the use of stop and search powers, the introduction of consultation with communities and the establishment of the Police Complaints Authority) sought to improve the relationships between the police and public (especially with minority ethnic communities), thereby reducing the intensity of the demand to increase the power of police authorities at the expense of the autonomy enjoyed by chief constables.
- **1991** Launching of the *Citizens' Charter* that sought to improve the choice, quality, value for money and accountability of all public services (including the police service) by seeking to ascertain what the public expected of them and to ensure that they were delivered effectively.

- **1993** Publication of the report by Patrick Sheehy that suggested a number of reforms to the management structure of the police service. Opposition to these reforms by police officers prevented most of them from being introduced.
- **1994** Enactment of the Police and Magistrates' Courts Act. This measure provided the Home Secretary with considerable powers over policing by giving the minister the ability to set national objectives for the service with which each force was required to comply.
- **1995** Publication of the Posen Report which was set up to examine the services provided by the police, to make recommendations about the most cost-effective way of delivering core police services and to assess the scope for relinquishing ancillary tasks.
- **1999** Enactment of the Greater London Authority Act that established the Greater London Assembly and an independent Metropolitan Police Authority to oversee policing in London. This replaced the position that had persisted since 1829 whereby the Home Secretary was the police authority for London.
- **1999** Enactment of the Local Government Act that introduced the principles of Best Value into the police service. This entailed the development of universal aims and objectives for the police service to which performance indicators (termed 'Best Value Performance Indicators' – BVPIs) to measure progress in attaining these objectives were attached. The aim of best value was to provide a system that delivered high-quality, responsive services based on locally determined objectives.
- **2002** Enactment of the Police Reform Act. This replaced the Police Complaints Authority with the Independent Police Complaints Commission that was empowered to undertake the investigation of serious complaints thereby providing an independent element in the investigation of these matters. This legislation also established the Police Standards Unit and the National Centre for Police Excellence and introduced National Policing Plans.

References

Ackroyd, S. and Helliwell, C. (1991) 'What Happened to Objectives?', *Policing*, 7: 132–43.

Alderson, J. (1994) 'Hark, the Minister of Police Approaches', *Independent*, 19 January.

Association of Chief Police Officers (1990) *Strategic Policy Document: Setting the Standards for Policing: Meeting Community Expectations*. London: ACPO.

Audit Commission (1990a) *Effective Policing: Performance Review in Police Forces*. London: Audit Commission.

Audit Commission (1990b) *Footing the Bill: Financing Provincial Police Forces*, Police Paper No. 6. London: Audit Commission.

Audit Commission (1994) *Cheques and Balances: A Framework for Improving Police Accountability*. London: HMSO.

Audit Commission (1999) *Local Authority Performance Indicators: Police and Fire Services. 1997/8*. London: Audit Commission.

Bennett, T. (1994) 'Recent Developments in Community Policing', in M. Stephens and S. Becker (eds), *Police Force, Police Service*. Basingstoke: Macmillan.

Blunkett, D. (2002) 'Home Secretary's Foreword', in Home Office, *The National Policing Plan, 2003–2006*. London: Home Office Communications Directorate.

Boaden, N., Goldsmith, M., Hampton, W. and Stringer, P. (1982) *Public Participation in Local Services*. Harlow: Longman.

Brake, M. and Hale, C. (1992) *Public Order and Private Lives – The Politics of Law and Order*. London: Routledge.

Burrows, J. (1989) 'Achieving 'Value for Money' from Police Expenditure: The Contribution of Research', in M. Weatheritt (ed.), *Police Research: Some Future Prospects*. Aldershot: Avebury.

Butler, A. (1996) 'Managing the Future: A Chief Constable's View', in F. Leishman, B. Loveday and S. Savage (eds), *Core Issues in Policing*, 1st edn. London: Longman.

Butler, G. (1999) *Inquiry into Crown Prosecution Service Decision-Making in Relation to Deaths in Custody and Related Matters*. London: TSO.

Cabinet Office (1999) *Modernising Government*, Cm 4310. London: HMSO.

Campbell, D. (1998) 'Operation Bent', *Guardian*, 29 January.

Campbell, D. (1999), 'Police in New Scandal', *Guardian*, 27 February.

Cowan, R., Dodd, V. and Norton-Taylor, R. (2005) 'Met Chief Tried to Stop Shooting Inquiry', *Guardian*, 18 August.

Dodd, V. (2005) 'Met Chief Tried to Block Shooting Inquiry', *Guardian*, 1 October.

Dunleavy, P. and Hood, C. (1994) 'From Old Public Administration to New Public Management', *Public Money and Management*, 14 (3): 9–16.

Fox, C. (2005) *Press statement*, 27 October.

Henig, R. (1998) 'Strengthening the Voice in Local Policing', *Criminal Justice Matters*, 32, Summer: 8–9.

Her Majesty's Inspectorate of Constabulary (1998) *What Price Policing? A Study of Efficiency and Value for Money in the Police Service*. London: HMIC.

Her Majesty's Inspectorate of Constabulary (1999) *Police Integrity: Securing and Maintaining Public Confidence*. London: HMIC.

Hewitt, P. (1982) A *Fair Cop: Reforming the Police Complaints Procedure*. London: National Council for Civil Liberties.

Home Affairs Committee (1998) *Police Disciplinary and Complaints Procedure*, First Report, Session 1997/8, House of Commons Paper 258-1.

Home Affairs Committee (1999) *Freemasonry in Public Life*, Second Report, Session 1998/9, House of Commons Paper 467.

Home Affairs Committee (2005) *Police Reform*, Fourth Report, Session 2004/5, House of Commons Paper 370.

Home Office (1982) *Local Consultation Arrangements between the Community and the Police*, Home Office Circular 54/82. London: Home Office.

Home Office (1983) *Manpower, Effectiveness and Efficiency in the Police Service*, Home Office Circular 114/83. London: Home Office.

Home Office (1985) *Arrangements for Local Consultation between the Community and the Police Outside London*, Home Office Circular 2/85. London: Home Office.

Home Office (1986) *Plastic Baton Rounds and CS: Central Facilities*, Home Office Circular 40/86. London: Home Office.

Home Office (1988a) *The British Crime Survey*, 1988. London: Home Office.

Home Office (1988b) *Civilian Staff in the Police Service*, Home Office Circular 105/88. London: Home Office.

Home Office (1988c) *Applications for Increases in Police Establishments*, Circular 106/88. London: Home Office.

Home Office (1989) *Police Buildings and Other Capital Expenditure*, Home Office Circular 35/89. London: Home Office.

Home Office (1993a) *Police Reform: A Police Service for the Twenty-First Century*, Cm 2281. London: HMSO.

Home Office (1993b) *Inquiry into Police Responsibilities and Rewards* [The Sheehy Report], Cm. 2280. London: HMSO.

Home Office (1995a) *Review of the Police Core and Ancillary Tasks: Final Report* [The Posen Report]. London: HMSO.

Home Office (1995b) *Performance Indicators for the Police and Core Statistics for Chief Officers' Annual Reports*, Home Office Circular 8/95. London: Home Office.

Home Office (2000) *Complaints Against the Police: A Consultative Paper*. London: Home Office Operational Policy Unit.

Home Office (2001) *Policing a New Century: A Blueprint for Reform*, Cm 5326. London: Home Office.

Home Office (2002) *The National Policing Plan 2003–2006*. London: Home Office Communications Directorate.

Home Office (2003) *Police Performance Monitoring, 2002/03*. London: Home Office Communications Directorate on behalf of the Police Standards Unit.

Home Office (2004) *Building Communities, Beating Crime: A Better Police Service for the 21st Century*, Cm 6360. London: Home Office.

Jones, T. (2003) 'The Governance and Accountability of Policing', in T. Newburn (ed.), *Handbook of Policing*. Cullompton: Willan Publishing.

Jones, T. and Newburn, T. (1997) *Policing After the Act: Police Governance After the Police and Magistrates' Courts Act 1994*. London: Policy Studies Institute.

Kappeler, V., Sluder, R. and Alpert, G. (1998) *Forces of Deviance: Understanding the Dark Side of Policing*, 2nd edn. Prospect Heights, IL: Waveland Press.

Labour Party (1995) *Safer Communites, Safer Britain: Labour's Proposals for Tough Action on Crime*. London: Labour Party.

Leishman, F., Cope, S. and Starie, P. (1996) 'Reinventing and Restructuring: Towards a 'New Police Order'', in F. Leishman, B. Loveday and S. Savage (eds), *Core Issues in Policing*, 1st edn. Harlow: Longman.

Lewis, C. (1999) *Complaints Against the Police: The Politics of Reform*. Annandale, New South Wales: Hawkins Press.

Loveday, B. (1987) *Joint Boards for Police: The Impact of Structural Change on Police Governance in the Metropolitan Areas*, Occasional Paper New Series No. 20. Birmingham: Department of Government and Economics, City of Birmingham Polytechnic.

Loveday, B. (1994) 'The Police and Magistrates' Courts Act', *Policing*, 10 (4): 221–33.

Loveday, B. (1995) 'Reforming the Police: From Local Service to State Police?', *Political Quarterly*, 66 (2): 141–56.

Mark, Sir R. (1978) *In the Office of Constable*. London: Fontana.

Martin, D. (2003) 'The Politics of Policing: Managerialism, Modernisation and Performance', in R. Matthews and J. Young (eds), *The New Politics of Crime and Punishment*. Cullompton: Willan Publishing.

Ministry of Housing and Local Government (1969) *Report of the Committee on Public Participation in Planning: People and Planning* [The Skeffington Report]. London: HMSO.

Morgan, R. (1989) 'Police Accountability: Current Developments and Future Prospects', in M. Weatheritt (ed.), *Police Research: Some Future Prospects*. Aldershot: Avebury.

Morgan, R. and Swift, P. (1987) 'The Future of Police Authorities: Members' Views', *Public Administration*, 65: 259–76.

Newman, J. (2000) 'Beyond the New Public Management? Modernising Public Services?', in J. Clarke, S. Gewirtz and E.McLaughlin (eds), *New Managerialism: New Welfare*. London: Sage.

Nuttall, C. (1999) 'Rising Optimism', *Guardian*, 13 October.

O'Dowd, D. (1998) 'Inspecting Constabularies', *Criminal Justice Matters*, 32, Summer: 6–7.

Oliver, I. (1987) *Police, Government and Accountability*. Basingstoke: Macmillan.

Police Complaints Authority (1998) *The 1997/8 Annual Report of the Police Complaints Authority*, House of Commons Paper 805. London: TSO.

Police Standards Unit (2005) iQuanta (available at: www.policereform.gov.uk/psu/quanta.html).

Punch, M. and Naylor, T. (1973) 'The Police: A Social Service', *New Society*, 24 (554): 358–61.

Reiner, R. (1994) 'The Dialectics of Dixon: The Changing Image of the TV Cop', in M. Stephens and S. Becker (eds), *Police Force, Police Service*. Basingstoke: Macmillan.

Reiner, R. (2000) *The Politics of the Police*, 3rd edn. Oxford: Oxford University Press.

Rollo, J. (1980) 'The Special Patrol Group', in P. Hain (ed.), *Policing the Police*, Vol. 1. London: John Calder.

Savage, S. (1998) 'The Shape of the Future', *Criminal Justice Matters*, 32, Summer: 4–6.

Savage, S. and Charman, S. (1996) 'Managing Change', in F. Leishman, B. Loveday and S. Savage (eds), *Core Issues in Policing*, 1st edn. Harlow: Longman.

Scarman, Lord (1981) *The Brixton Disorders, 10–12 April 1981: Report of an Inquiry by the Rt. Hon. The Lord Scarman, OBE*, Cmnd 8427. London: HMSO.

Simey, M. (1985) *Government by Consent: The Principle and Practice of Accountability in Local Government*. London: Bedford Square Press.

Sinclair, I. and Miller, C. (1984) *Measures of Police Effectiveness and Efficiency*, Research and Planning Unit Paper 25. London: Home Office.

Smith, G. (1999) Quoted in M. Honigsbaum, 'Doreen Lawrence Speaks', *Observer*, 14 February.

Spottiswoode, C. (2000) *Improving Police Performance: A New Approach to Measuring Police Efficiency*. London: Public Services Productivity Panel.

Verkaik, R. (2005) 'Level of Evidence Has Been Set Too High, Say Lawyers', *Independent*, 21 October.

Verkaik, R. and Bennetto, J. (2005) 'Shot Dead by Police 30: Officers Convicted 0', *Independent*, 21 October.

Wadham, J. (2004) 'A New Course for Complaints', *Policing Today*, 10 (1): 21.

Walker, N. (1994) 'Care and Control in the Police Organisation', in M. Stephens and S. Becker (eds), *Police Force, Police Service*. Basingstoke: Macmillan.

Waters, I. (1996) 'Quality of Service: Politics or Paradigm Shift?', in F. Leishman, B. Loveday and S. Savage (eds), *Core Issues in Policing*, 1st edn. Harlow: Longman.

Weatheritt, M. (1986) *Innovations in Policing*. London: Croom Helm.

Weatheritt, M. (1994) 'Measuring Police Performance: Accounting or Accountability?', in R. Reiner and S. Spencer (eds), *Accountable Policing – Effectiveness, Empowerment and Equity*. London: Institute for Public Policy Research.

Witt, R., Clarke, A. and Fielding, N. (1999) 'Crime and Economic Activity: A Panel Data Approach', *British Journal of Criminology*, 39 (3): 391–400.

Wolff Ohlins (1988) *A Force For Change: Report on the Corporate Identity of the Metropolitan Police*. London: Metropolitan Police.

5 The prosecution process

This chapter examines the procedures that are used to deal with those accused of having committed a crime from their arrest to sentencing. Specifically this chapter:

- describes the procedures used in connection with those accused of crime, from arrest to trial;
- evaluates the role of the Crown Prosecution Service;
- describes the structure of the legal profession and the criminal and civil courts in England and Wales and evaluates reform proposals;
- analyses the rationale, strengths and weaknesses of the system of trial by jury and discusses reforms made or proposed to be made to this system;
- evaluates why miscarriages of justice occur and analyses the impact of reforms designed to reduce the likelihood of such occurrences;
- considers the use of discretion in the prosecution process and evaluates reforms designed to reduce its usage by key professionals in the criminal justice process;
- evaluates the nature of gender discrimination in the prosecution process and reforms that have been put forward to tackle it;
- discusses the procedures within the prosecution process that cater for victims of crime.

Arrest

The legal process commences when a person breaks the law, thereby committing an offence. The offence may have been observed by a police officer or be based on allegations made to the police by a member (or members) of the general public. On other occasions the analysis of forensic or other forms of evidence may form the basis of suspicion that a person has committed a crime.

A person who is suspected of having committed an offence for which arrest is sanctioned under the 1984 Police and Criminal Evidence Act will be taken to a police station where he or she will be asked questions relating to that offence. Suspects will be advised as to why they are being arrested and be given a caution that advises them of their right not to say anything but (since the enactment of the 1994 Criminal Justice and Public Order Act which eroded the historic right of silence) also warns them that it could harm their defence if they do not mention anything during questioning which they later rely on in court. If there are insufficient grounds to warrant an arrest, persons may be invited to voluntarily attend a police station in order to assist the police with their inquiries by answering questions.

The procedures governing the treatment of a suspect in a police station are laid down in Codes of Practice under the provisions of the 1984 Police and Criminal Evidence Act, the latest versions of which were implemented in 2003. The Codes of Practice stipulate how long a person can be held for questioning, the rights of that person to legal representation, what steps the police need to take in order to extend the initial period of questioning and the arrangements governing tape and visual recording of interviews with suspects. While in a police station, a suspect is under the charge of a custody officer. This post was created in the 1984 Act and was designed to guard against mistreatment by providing a person with specific legal responsibility for all those detained in this manner. It was generally held by an officer of the rank of sergeant, but there is now debate as to whether the post should be civilianised.

When questioning has ceased, under the provisions of the 2003 Criminal Justice Act the police have the option either to release the suspect, to charge him or her with an offence or to release the suspect on police bail but without charge to enable further inquiries to be made or in order to seek advice from the Crown Prosecution Service. If a charge is preferred, the suspect may be detained in custody pending an appearance before a magistrates' court or the police may decide to release him or her until a court hearing can be arranged. If the latter course of action is adopted, the person may be released on police bail. This procedure was provided for in the 1976 Bail Act, and enables conditions to be placed on a freed suspect's movements if this course of action is thought necessary. The 2003 Criminal Justice Act introduced a change to the system of police bail whereby an officer could grant bail to an arrested person without having to convey him or her to a police station. The rationale for this reform (sometimes referred to as 'street bail') was to enable officers to remain on patrol for longer periods.

The prosecution of offences

Those who are formally charged with having committed a criminal offence are prosecuted on behalf of the state to emphasise that society as a whole has been the victim of his or her actions.

With the exception of prosecutions mounted by private individuals (which are few in number), decisions relating to the prosecution of criminal offences are made by the Crown Prosecution Service (CPS). This body was established under the 1985 Prosecution of Offences Act and began work in 1986. It is headed by the Director of Public Prosecutions (DPP) and the Attorney General is accountable to Parliament for its operations. Its role is as follows.

- *To review cases presented by the police and decide whether to proceed with them or discontinue them.* In arriving at decisions of this nature CPS lawyers are guided by the Code for Crown Prosecutors which gives guidance concerning the general principles to be followed when making decisions concerning whether or not to prosecute. These emphasise the need for there to be a realistic prospect of securing a conviction (the evidential test) and whether the public interest is served by pursuing a prosecution. The Code is prepared by the DPP, the most recent edition of which was issued in 2004.
- *To decide what the precise charge against a person who is being proceeded against should be.* The Code for Crown Prosecutors puts forward guidelines to aid decisions of this nature.
- *To conduct the prosecution.* CPS lawyers commonly present cases themselves in magistrates' courts and liaise with barristers who conduct the prosecution in a crown court. As an aid to prosecutors, the CPS prepares Legal Guidance in relation to a large number of criminal offences and procedural issues.

The prosecution of offenders was formerly carried out by the police and the rationale for divorcing the investigation of crime from its prosecution was to eliminate bias. It was argued the close involvement of the police (who gathered the evidence) with the prosecution of the offence gave them a vested interest in the successful conclusion of a case. This could be a factor that induced some police officers to apply undue pressure on a suspect to admit guilt, resulting in an eventual miscarriage of justice. Accordingly, the new system enabled lawyers (who had no previous involvement with a case) to take an objective and dispassionate view of the evidence gathered by the police.

However, this body has been subject to a number of criticisms since its inception. The problems that have been identified are as follows.

Remoteness

It is alleged that the CPS is insufficiently accountable for the decisions that it takes, particularly with regard not to prosecute. This issue received prominent attention with the murder of Stephen Lawrence in 1993. Conversely, some of its decisions to prosecute have also received adverse comment such as the decision in 1993 to charge Colin Stagg in connection with the murder of Rachel Nickell. He protested his innocence and the case was thrown out after it was revealed that the police had sought to use a policewoman to trap him into confessing the crime.

Inadequate organisational integration with police forces

The desire to ensure that the investigation and prosecution processes were separate resulted in police forces and the CPS being structurally detached from each other. Initially the CPS was divided into 31 areas, although this number was reduced to 13 in 1993 (with central casework constituting a 14th). This impeded cooperation that was desirable, for example, in connection with the charging of offenders and resulted in the publication of charging standards in 1994 to enhance the level of cooperation between the two agencies in this area of activity. However, a report in 1998 stated that the CPS had become 'too centralised and bureaucratic', and in particular was too isolated from the police forces that send cases to it (Glidewell, 1998). Reorganisation designed to secure a joined-up approach within the criminal justice process resulted in reorganisation in April 1999 so that CPS and police force boundaries coincided.

Further reform sought to more fully integrate the operations of the CPS lawyers and police forces. A number of pilot schemes were initiated in England in which the practice in Scotland was followed. This involved the CPS giving early advice to the police and, in most cases, taking over the responsibility for charging defendants. It was reported (Home Office, 2004a: 32) that these pilot schemes saw conviction rates improving by 15 per cent, guilty pleas at the first hearing rising by 30 per cent, discontinuance rates falling by 69 per cent and a reduction in the rate of ineffective trials of 10 per cent (Home Office, 2004a: 32). This resulted in the 2003 Criminal Justice Act creating the necessary legal framework to transfer the responsibility for charging from the police to the CPS.

Work dominated by financial restraints

It has been argued that the pursuit of justice is hindered by financial considerations that govern the operations of the CPS. This has led to it being under-resourced and understaffed since its establishment in 1986. The imposition of cash limits aggravated these difficulties.

The economics of prosecution

Like other agencies in the Criminal Justice System, the CPS functions in a political environment, so financial constraints imposed by governments have a significant impact on its work. This may mean that the pursuit of justice for those who have been the victims of crime becomes of secondary importance to economic considerations. Financial pressures led to the following accusations regarding the operations of the CPS in the late 1990s:

- It is understaffed, which is likely to mean that solicitors are forced to handle too many cases at once resulting in poor preparation. Financial restraints forced CPS lawyers to prosecute cases themselves rather than 'buy in' solicitors to do the work as was the initial practice of this organisation.

- The discontinuance rate (that is, the decision not to proceed with a pros-ecution) is high. Approximately 12 per cent of cases are not pursued (Comptroller and Auditor General, 1997). This may be explained both by the high test applied by the CPS regarding the likely success of the case, financial considerations, the CPS approval system which regards good practice as dropping a case at the outset rather than having a judge throwing it out of court at the beginning or end of a trial and technical reasons (such as a 'missing legal element').
- Offences may be downgraded in order to get them heard by magistrates rather than by a crown court. The former are both quicker and cheaper. Thus actual bodily harm cases are often downgraded to charges of common assault. Charge reduction (and discontinuance) have been fre-quently employed in cases of domestic violence (Gregory and Lees, 1999: 76–8).

The Labour government latterly accepted that 'in 1997 the Crown Prosecution Service was operating on a shoestring budget and struggling to improve the prosecution process as it was set up to do. Front-line staff in the CPS had no computers at all.' It was argued that reforms introduced after 1997 had revitalised the CPS and resulted in it 'prosecuting more cases, and prosecuting more successfully' (Office for Criminal Justice Reform, 2004: 14).

Plea bargaining

As practised in the United Kingdom, plea bargaining entails a defendant entering a plea of guilty to secure a reduction in sentence. Although histori-cally judges have been constrained not to indicate the likely sentence in the event of a guilty plea being entered (on the grounds that this would place undue pressure on the defendant), it has been suggested that judicial sen-tencing guidelines should be introduced to provide for 'a system of sentencing discounts graduated so that the earlier the tender of plea of guilty the higher the discount for it' (Auld, 2001: 443). The government subse-quently endorsed this reform, announcing their intention to introduce a clearer tariff of sentence discount, backed up by arrangements whereby defendants could seek advance indication of the sentence they would get if they pleaded guilty. This 'should help more defendants who are guilty to plead guilty earlier' (Home Secretary, Lord Chancellor and Attorney General, 2002: 77). Although such a reform could be introduced into crown courts without legislation, the 2003 Criminal Justice Act allowed a magistrate to give an advanced indication as to whether a sentence would be custodial or non-custodial after it had been decided that an either-way offence was within their jurisdiction and before the defendant elected to go to the crown court for trial.

There are, however, problems with this procedure. In 2000 the Court of Appeal criticised the way in which plea bargaining had been used in connection with a former head teacher who had sexually abused pupils between 1969 and 1977. This led the Attorney General to issue guidelines to the CPS to restrict its use to exceptional cases such as where the defendant was seriously ill or where witnesses were unlikely to come forward. In addition to the objection that this procedure can result in serious crimes being dealt with too leniently, it might be argued that increasing the pressure on defendants to plead guilty undermines the presumption of innocence (Justice, 1993a) and may result in miscarriages of justice whereby innocent people feel constrained to plead guilty to avoid a harsher sentence which may be inflicted upon them if they fear that their plea of not guilty will be rejected by the court (Justice, 2004: 8–9).

Lighter sentences may also be given to defendants who plead guilty and cooperate with the prosecution, typically aiding the successful prosecution of their accomplices. This process of Queen's Evidence is currently used relatively infrequently. The problems with it include the perceived juries' suspicion of the character of the cooperating defendant and the incentives to him or her not being seen as sufficiently clear or substantial (Home Office, 2004a: 48).

> Does the Crown Prosecution Service consistently deliver justice to victims of crime? What reasons might be given to explain deficiencies in this aspect of its service?

The judicial process

If the CPS decides to prosecute a person for a criminal offence, he or she will be required to defend themselves in a court. This may be a magistrates' court or a crown court (which are discussed in the following chapter). Here they will seek either to show that they did not commit the crime of which they are accused by pleading 'not guilty', or pleading 'guilty' but seek to excuse the action by presenting mitigating circumstances to explain it. Although a person may defend him or herself (which often happens in magistrates' courts) it is quite common, particularly for a serious charge, to seek the aid of professional experts. These are barristers and solicitors, whose work is discussed in more detail in the following chapter.

Trial procedure in England and Wales

A person charged with a criminal offence (termed the 'defendant') will be asked to plead 'guilty' or 'not guilty' to the charge. If the latter plea is entered it will necessary for those bringing the charge on behalf of the state (the 'prosecution') to prove their case 'beyond all reasonable doubt'. The 2003 Criminal Justice Act introduced a number of important changes into trial procedure. The prosecution was enabled to bring forward evidence of a defendant's previous bad character and to appeal against rulings made by judges that would prejudice the prosecution. Additionally, the double jeopardy rule (which prevented a defendant, having been acquitted, to be retried for the same offence) was amended whereby a defendant in a serious case could be subsequently retried if compelling new evidence became available. The background to this latter reform is discussed in Chapter 10.

British courts utilise the adversarial system of justice in which the defendant and prosecution each seek to assert the validity of their own case by destroying the arguments put forward by their opponents. Many European countries use the inquisitorial system, in which the judge supervises the gathering of evidence and the trial is used as a forum to resolve issues uncovered in this earlier investigation.

Two alternative systems may be used in civil cases in England and Wales. One is mediation, whereby (if both parties agree) a lawyer trained in mediation seeks to get both parties to agree to a settlement. Another is arbitration, in which an arbitrator determines the outcome of a case. New civil court rules that came into force in April 1999 enabled judges to adjourn a case to try mediation, but although judges may recommend either arbitration or mediation, they cannot enforce either of these alternatives to trial in the courts.

Although members of the public can attend trials and newspapers may report proceedings (unless a judge determines otherwise), cameras were not allowed inside courtrooms. However, in November 2004, as part of a consultation process launched by the Department for Constitutional Affairs, the proceedings of a court in Lincoln were filmed and shown to a group of senior judges and politicians who would determine whether the law should be amended to permit the routine televising of court proceedings in England and Wales.

The system of legal aid

An important aspect of equality before the law is equality of access to it. The 1949 Legal Aid and Advice Act gave defendants facing a serious criminal charge the right to proper legal representation in court. Additionally, aid was available to enable citizens to defend or to enforce their rights in civil litigation. The 1949 legislation was amended on a number of occasions and was subject to significant reform in the 1988 Legal Aid Act that repealed all previous legislation in this area.

The 1999 Access to Justice Act replaced the Legal Aid Board (which was established by the 1988 legislation) with a Legal Services Commission (LSC) for England and Wales. The Legal Services Commission was given responsibility for operating two schemes – the Community Legal Service and the Criminal Defence Service.

The role of the Community Legal Service is to offer advice, help and legal representation in civil and family cases. The level of this aid is based upon the applicant's income and, in some cases, capital. Henceforth, the state's support for civil actions was restricted through the imposition of cash limits on legal aid for civil actions. Since April 2001, only legal firms with a contract with the LSC could provide advice or representation in civil cases funded by the LSC and were required to meet quality standards. A small number of specialist firms were funded with regard to family cases and specialist areas such as immigration and clinical negligence. State funding also became more difficult to obtain, being subject to a stringent funding code which involved calculating the chances of success against the likely award of damages and costs. Alternatives to litigation (such as mediation in divorce disputes) were encouraged. The manner in which this reform was implemented involved the introduction of a single cash-limited block grant (the Community Legal Service Fund) to cover both criminal and legal aid. There was no intention to restrict criminal civil aid (since such might place the government in breach of the Human Rights Act), so that civil legal aid was, effectively, funded with money left over when the cost of criminal legal aid had been met.

The rationale for this reform was the spiralling cost of civil legal aid – from £544 million in 1994 to £671 million in 1997 (Goodhart, 1999) – despite reforms that had reduced the categories of persons eligible for it. This situation was attributed to a number of factors that included the state funding of weak and hopeless cases, the funding of cases in which the costs far exceeded any possible benefit which the litigant might secure and the absence of any meaningful controls over the quality of work delivered by lawyers who undertook legal aid work. However, it has been argued that if criminal legal aid continued to rise as it had during the 1990s, the new procedure would effectively result in civil legal aid being 'steadily squeezed out of existence', funded by 'scraps from the table of criminal legal aid' (Goodhart, 1999). The perception that this problem had arisen (since between 1997 and 2004/5 the legal aid budget had risen from £1.5 billion to £2.1 billion a year but spending on civil legal aid had fallen in real terms by 24 per cent in that period whereas spending on criminal legal aid had risen by 37 per cent in the same period) (Department for Constitutional Affairs, 2005a: 11) prompted the Lord Chancellor to propose reforms to place time limits on criminal trials to prevent them consuming large sums of money in criminal legal aid. This reform would be achieved by methods such as making improvements to the way in which cases were managed by judges and introducing alterations to the payments system through methods such as competitive bidding between lawyers for legal aid cases (Department for Constitutional Affairs, 2005a).

Further problems, which included low fees and the bureaucratic demands of the LCS, contributed to what was latterly described as a crisis in legal aid funding that particularly affected the vulnerable and socially excluded (Nightingale, 2005). It had been intended that some deficiencies in civil legal aid funding would in part be bridged by an extension of lawyers accepting cases on a 'no-win, no-fee' basis. Personal injury cases, for example, are invariably funded in this way following the Lord Chancellor's decision in 2000 to end legal aid for actions of this nature, although partial (or 'support') funding may be available in some circumstances.

Criminal legal aid was also subjected to reforms in the 1999 Access to Justice legislation. This Act set up the Criminal Defence Service that is managed by the Legal Services Commission to provide advice and legal representation for persons facing criminal charges. The defendant's right to choose his or her own lawyer was ended, and henceforth state-funded defence work (including free advice and assistance to a person held for questioning at a police station) would be handled by firms which had secured a contract with the Legal Services Commission or by a salaried defender who was directly employed by this body. The use of salaried defenders employed by the Legal Services Commission was a development that was compatible with the introduction of American-style public defenders and was piloted in six areas in 2001. The government believed, however, that initially a mixed system of lawyers in both private practice and in public employment was the best approach since salaried lawyers would provide a benchmark against which the Criminal Defence Service could assess the reasonableness of prices charged by lawyers in the private sector (Lord Chancellor's Department, 2000).

The object of this reform was to reduce the costs of criminal legal aid, which had been bloated by the high fees paid to some 'fat cat' lawyers, so that 1 per cent of cases heard in crown courts consumed around 40 per cent of legal aid funding in these courts. Figures from the Lord Chancellor's Department that were published in *The Guardian* on 3 August 1999 estimated that in 1996/7, 35 barristers earned gross fees between £270,000 and £575,000 in legal aid payments for criminal work. As has been observed above, expenditure of this nature depletes the money available for civil legal aid. However, fees of this nature were not typical: figures quoted in *The Guardian* on 25 April 1999, however, showed that the average income for a legal aid solicitor was £25,000 per year, and junior barristers have adversely suffered from the freezing of legal aid rates since 1997 for work on trials lasting between one and ten days.

One danger with attempts to place restrictions on criminal legal aid work is that it might intensify the distinction between work funded by legal aid (much of which is transacted by high-street firms of solicitors) and corporate work (which is performed by City law firms). The large fees attracted by corporate work may induce young lawyers to specialise in this area to the detriment of work funded by the state, much of which is socially valuable (since it covers areas such as crime, immigration and mental health). In 1999 the Law Society mounted a provocative campaign against the government's reforms to legal aid, arguing that these would act against the interests of vulnerable groups who would no longer be able to go to court to protect themselves against such matters as domestic violence, bad housing or industrial injury.

Trial by jury

Juries are designed to provide a trial by one's peers and are composed of ordinary people selected at random from the electoral register. They are used in crown court trials and in some civil cases (although their use in civil matters has been greatly reduced since the implementation of the 1933 Administration of Justice Act). Their main role is to listen to the evidence which is presented by the defence and prosecution in a trial and to determine on the guilt or innocence of the defendant based upon an objective consideration of the facts which emerge during the proceedings. In doing this they follow instructions given to them by the trial judge, who further sums up proceedings for them. However, although the judge may indicate to the jury that a guilty verdict is the only reasonable decision, he or she cannot instruct them to convict an accused person and there is no appeal against an acquittal. Juries consist of 12 persons (eight in civil cases), although this number may occasionally be reduced if, during the course of a trial, a juror is discharged by the judge because of illness or some other form of emergency.

Initially the universal agreement of all 12 members was required to reach a verdict but the 1967 Criminal Justice Act permitted the outcome of a trial to be determined by a majority verdict of 10 : 2. Under libel law, judges can permit a smaller majority than 10 : 2 provided both parties to the action agree with this. However, a judge will prefer a unanimous verdict and may initially ask for this, only settling for a majority verdict when it becomes apparent that unanimity is impossible. One of the reasons for introducing majority verdicts was tampering with the jury ('jury nobbling') and the 2003 Criminal Justice Act introduced a further reform to respond to this situation in which a trial could take place before a judge alone in cases where there was a substantial risk of jury tampering or where this had occurred resulting in the jury being discharged.

Between 1825 and 1972 there were a number of qualifications governing jury service, the chief of which was a property requirement: a juror had to be a householder. This qualification was abolished by the 1972 Criminal Justice Act that provided that all persons aged 18–65 were eligible to serve provided their names had been included on the electoral register compiled by local authorities for local and Parliamentary elections. The 1974 Juries Act amended the upper age limit to 70. This legislation was designed to broaden the social composition of juries, since the former qualification tended to prevent membership drawn from particular key groups in society, especially women. There were, however, certain categories of persons who were not qualified for, or were excused from, jury service (Department for Constitutional Affairs, 2003: 4–5). These were as follows:

- *Those who were ineligible.* This includes members of the judiciary, the clergy and mentally disordered persons.
- *Those who were excused as of right.* This includes MPs, members of the armed forces and those from medical or similar professions who, if summoned, could elect or decline to serve.
- *Those who were disqualified.* This includes those who had served or who were serving prison sentences or community orders and – following the enactment of the 1994 Criminal Justice and Public Order Act – those on bail in criminal proceedings.

Additionally, those who are summonsed may seek to have their service excused or deferred to a more convenient date. The 2003 Criminal Justice Act radically altered the eligibility for jury service by removing most of the categories of individuals who were disqualified, ineligible or entitled as of right to be excused from service.

The defence formerly had the right of peremptory challenge whereby they could challenge up to three jurors without giving reasons. The maximum number of peremptory challenges was reduced from seven to three by the 1977 Criminal Law Act and was abolished by the 1988 Criminal Justice Act.

Around 480,000 persons are summoned to sit as jurors each year, normally in criminal cases (Falconer, 2003: 3), of which less than half actually serve. Jury selection is the responsibility of the Lord Chancellor and the process which is followed is set out in the 1974 Juries Act. Juries are randomly selected by computer from the electoral register. This was formerly the responsibility of the jury summoning officer of the crown court until 1999 when a national Jury Central Summoning Bureau was established for all of England and Wales. The 1974 legislation stipulated that persons who serve as jurors are exempt from a further period of service for two years.

Advantages to the system of trial by jury

The main advantages of trial by jury are discussed below.

Juries enable popular conceptions of right and wrong to influence the system

Juries are able to go beyond the dispassionate application of the law and pay regard to considerations such as a person's motives for breaking the law or his or her personal circumstances. Juries may also acquit someone who is technically guilty of an offence which public opinion feels is trivial or founded on an unjust law. Although it has been argued that 'there is little evidence that jurors depart from the fact-finding task to follow the dictates of conscience or to apply their sense of fair play when deciding criminal trial verdicts', it was argued that 'there are conditions where jurors' ultimate verdicts are guided by considerations of fairness, equity, and justice that conflict with the "official" legal definition of their task' (Hastie, 1994: 29). There are both advantages and problems associated with such a course of action. One advantage is that the law may be kept in line with the prevailing public con-sensus. Thus if public opinion feels that the law itself or the penalties proscribed in it are unreasonable their ability to pronounce 'not guilty' may influence legislators to bring about change.

However, the ability to pronounce a verdict of 'not guilty' in the face of ovewhelming evidence to the contrary may result in injustices which bring the legal system into disrepute. In America a jury's acquittal of Los Angeles police officers who had severely attacked the black American Rodney King in 1992 resulted in riots against the obvious manifestation of racial bias behind this verdict.

A jury acts as a neutral arbiter between the state and its citizens

Trial by jury provides a safeguard against oppressive behaviour by the state towards an individual. In 1985, for example, a jury rejected the assertion by the trial judge that the interests of the government and the state were identi-cal, and acquitted the civil servant Clive Ponting who had been charged with breaching the Official Secrets Act by leaking a document concerning the sinking of the Argentinian cruiser, the *General Belgrano*, during the 1982 Falklands War to a Labour MP, Mr Tam Dalyell. The jury accepted his defence that he believed the government has misled Parliament, and hence the coun-try, on this issue, and that his duty to the nation as a public servant outweighed his loyalty to the government.

This particular benefit can, however, be subverted by the process of 'jury vetting'. This process goes beyond an examination to ensure that those sum-monsed are not in a category of persons unable to serve through disqualification (which may be speedily ascertained by searching crime records), and involves a more detailed scrutiny into the background of jurors (including an examination of records held by Special Branch) which is used in cases which include terrorism and the Official Secrets Act. The vetting process is controlled by guidelines issued to the police by the Attorney General, and to invoke the procedure it is necessary for the DPP to agree and for the Attorney General to be informed. This procedure may be abused in cases involving state interests by being used to eliminate potential jurors whose politics make them unlikely to be sympathetic to the state (or, alterna-tively, this procedure may be used to ensure the inclusion of those who are likely to be supportive of these interests).

The practice of jury vetting became public knowledge in the ABC trials in 1978 which involved two journalists (Crispin Aubrey and Duncan Campbell) and a former corporal in Signals Intelligence (John Berry) who had been concerned with analysing intercepted radio signals; they were charged under section 1 of the 1911 Official Secrets Act for what amounted to spying. The jury was vetted, and in the first trial its foreman was a former member of the SAS (Aubrey, 1981: 172). The revelation of this fact in a Saturday night television programme forced this trial to be halted and the proceedings had to be recommenced.

Civic participation

Juries facilitate popular involvement in the operations of the criminal justice process. In particular they take decisions that not only affect individual defendants but also affect the communities in which they live: 'few decisions made by members of the public have such an impact upon society as a jury's verdict' (Falconer, 2003: 3).

Problems associated with juries

There are a number of problems associated with trial by jury, the most obvious of which is that they do not always arrive at the right verdict – on occasions the guilty walk free (thus denying justice to the victim of a crime) and the innocent are convicted. This section examines why problems of this nature may arise.

Social representativeness

The system of trial by jury is designed to ensure that a representative cross section of society give their verdict on an issue that comes before the courts. Juries that are socially representative ensure that the attitudes of one section of society will not dominate judicial decision-making.

One major difficulty with this is that the composition of juries often fails to mirror that of society as a whole. The perception that jurors tended to be male, middle aged and middle class (Devlin, 1956) has not been totally redressed by the reform introduced in 1972. Women and members of minority ethnic communities remain under-represented (Baldwin and McConville, 1979) and it has been concluded that outside urban areas black defendants are likely to face an all-white jury (CRE, 1991), thus undermining the legitimacy accorded this system by minority communities.

There are a number of reasons that explain why juries are not socially representative. These include non-registration for voting, for although registration is a legal requirement it has historically tended to be lower for young people and members of minority ethnic groups. This led to a suggestion that potential jurors should be identified from a number of public registers and lists rather than the electoral register alone, and also that provision should be made to enable minority ethnic representation on juries where race was likely to be relevant to an important issue in the case (Auld, 2001: 156–9). Persons summoned for jury service are also able to indicate whether they are available for short or long periods and this may result in juries used to try lengthy, complex cases being composed of 'the elderly, the unemployed, the housewife' who constitute 'a rather skewed cross-section of the community' (Bingham, 1998). Additionally, those who are summonsed may seek to have their service excused or deferred. Between April 2002 and March 2003, 25 per cent of the 480,000 persons who were summonsed were excused (Department for Constitutional Affairs, 2003: 6–7). There is a tendency for certain categories of persons to seek exemption when summoned for jury service. Professional and self-employed people are least prepared to give up their time or money to serve as jurors and are thus relatively under-represented. The exclusion of these latter groups may result in juries being deprived of the views of the educated and self-reliant members of society.

Decision-making by juries

It has been argued that no single scientific approach adequately provides an account of juror decision-making and that a juror's decision

> is the product of a complex set of factors including ... the juror's personal history, character and social background; attitudes, ideologies and values; limits and proclivities of his or her cognitive processes; the nature of the evidence presented at trial; and legal rules that are supposed to govern the ways in which the evidence is interpreted, weighted, and applied to a decision. (Casper and Benedict, 1994: 65)

It is especially difficult to make an accurate assessment of how juries reach decisions in Britain. Following attempts by the *New Statesman* to scrutinise the operations of the jury which deliberated in the trial of Jeremy Thorpe for conspiracy to murder in 1979, the 1981 Contempt of Court Act safeguarded the confidentiality of jury deliberations and thus prevented further investigation by journalists or academic researchers into their workings. Information on this subject has thus been based on alternative methods, including experiments involving 'mock juries' or through examinations of the jury system in other countries, especially America. The key problems that have been identified in the operations of juries include the following:

- *Jury deliberations may be dominated by a minority of members*. This offsets the perceived benefits of collective decision-making. In particular, a juror's socio-economic background may exert a considerable influence over his or her level of participation in a jury's deliberations.
- *Polarisation*. It is possible that decisions may become influenced by the process of group dynamics, resulting in verdicts reflecting the jurors' views of each other rather than their opinions of the evidence.
- *Jurors' personal prejudices may influence decisions*. Jurors may be swayed by factors other than the evidence presented in a trial, such as race, gender, accent, dress, occupation, level of articulation, body language, the performance of lawyers retained by the defence and prosecution, or irrational considerations in which a juror's emotions form the basis of a decision. This may result in the proceedings of a jury trial verging on the theatrical.
- *Jurors lack knowledge of the law and court proceedings*. Thus they may be unable to grasp the law, understand the evidence or comprehend the judge's summing up.
- *Jurors may lose track of the evidence*. Jurors' abilities to retain oral evidence may be deficient, especially if the trial is a lengthy one. Collective memory, however, may help to offset the shortcomings of individual memory, and the judge provides a summary of the evidence before a jury considers its verdict.

Jurors concerned with the conduct of the jury may raise their worries with the trial judge before sentence is passed. Although in 2004 (in the case of *R v. Connor and Mirza*) the Law Lords reaffirmed that the courts were not entitled to examine what had taken place in a jury room, the following year they ruled that jurors could act after the trial by contacting the clerk of the court or the jury bailiff or by sending a sealed letter to the court through an outside agency such as the Citizens' Advice Bureau.

Trial by jury in England and Wales

In 1997, 104,350 cases were tried before a judge and jury. Many of the offences concerned were not serious in terms of the nature of the offence or the resulting penalty. They included, for example, minor theft. However, persons accused of relatively small offences may opt for jury trial because they wish to clear their name of the slur cast upon it and feel there is a better chance of doing so if the verdict is delivered by ordinary citizens rather than officials paid by the state (Mortimer, 1999).

Twenty-one per cent of jury trials in 1997 (21,783) arose from a defendant opting for this method of trial. In 1987 this figure had been 53 per cent. This reduction may in part be attributable to the 1996 Criminal Procedure and Investigation Act, which required a defendant to enter a plea before a decision was taken concerning which court would hear the case. Having pleaded guilty, an accused person may wish to avoid the case being heard by a crown court whose powers regarding sentence are greater than those enjoyed by magistrates.

In 1997, 40 per cent of those pleading not guilty in a crown court were acquitted, compared with 25 per cent in a magistrates' court. This has given rise to the perception that magistrates' courts are overly likely to convict, and helps to explain why persons accused of crimes may opt for trial by jury. Black defendants are especially sceptical of magistrates' courts and prefer trial by jury.

It is estimated that, in 1997, the average cost of a contested jury trial was £13,500 compared to £2,500 for a case heard in a magistrates' court.

Information taken from Home Office (1998) and *The Guardian*, 29 July 1998.

Reform to the system of trial by jury

Factors that have been identified above, in particular the time and cost of jury trials, coupled with the belief that guilty people are sometimes acquitted because of the problems identified above with jury decision-making, have prompted suggestions that the system of trial by jury should be reformed. There are a number of directions that such reform may take.

Permit research into jury deliberations

The 2001 Labour government suggested the possibility of lifting the ban on *all* research in jury deliberations. Research might be allowed if permitted by the Lord Chancellor and undertaken in accordance with conditions laid down by the Lord Chief Justice. It was argued that such research would help to improve the support provided to jurors in discharging their duty and would also address allegations of improper behaviour in the jury room which might undermine a fair trial (Department for Constitutional Affairs, 2005b: 2). Although it argued that the circumstances in which allegations of juror impropriety might be investigated should, as at present, be dealt with by the courts on a case-by-case basis, it suggested that improved guidance could be provided to jurors on what constituted jury impropriety, their duty to report such behaviour and the options available to them for doing so (Department for Constitutional Affairs, 2005b: 5).

Reduce the offences eligible for trial by jury

This reform would be accomplished by increasing the number of offences which could be tried summarily in a magistrates' court thus confining trial by jury to the more serious cases. A succession of legal reviews (including the James Committee, 1975, the Runciman Royal Commission on Criminal Justice, 1993, and Narey, 1997) have suggested removing the defendant's right to ask for trial by jury in cases which were triable 'either way' (including theft, grievous bodily harm and some drugs offences) – a right which had existed in its modern form since 1855. This would have the effect of bringing the legal system in England and Wales in line with the situation in Scotland where the prosecution has historically decided where a case should be prosecuted.

This proposal was endorsed by the then Home Secretary, Michael Howard, in 1996. There were a number of reasons for proposing it which included considerations of costs and the perception that defendants were using this right to manipulate the legal system (in the hope that they would 'buy time', perhaps resulting in plea bargaining for a lesser charge or acquittal if witnesses failed to turn up).

This reform was not acted upon at the time, but was subsequently resurrected by the succeeding government in 1998. It was argued that although only a small proportion of those able to elect for trial by jury actually did so, these constituted around 20 per cent (or 22,000) of the work of crown courts in England and Wales in 1997 (Home Office, 1998). Two Bills to reform the system of trial by jury were rejected by the House of Lords in January and September 2000.

The government failed to invoke the 1949 Parliament Act to secure the introduction of this reform, perhaps because it awaited the report by Lord Justice Auld into the organisation of the criminal courts which was finally published in September 2001. As has been observed above, this report recommended a unified criminal court to replace the separate system of crown and magistrates' courts. Most offences would be heard by a district judge and two lay magistrates, with juries being retained for only the most serious cases. The government failed to act on this report and in 2003 Home Secretary

David Blunkett revisited proposals to reduce the offences which could be tried by a jury. However, resistance to these proposals by the House of Lords forced him to accept a much watered-down version of his reforms. The 2003 Criminal Justice Act enabled the prosecution to apply for certain fraud cases to be heard without a jury (as had been urged by Lord Justice Auld who endorsed the findings of Lord Roskill's Fraud Trials Commission in 1986) (Auld, 2001: 200–14), and (as is referred to above) also allowed the prosecution to apply for a trial to be heard without a jury if there was 'a real and present danger' of jury tampering.

A subsequent piece of legislation, the 2004 Domestic Violence, Crime and Victims Act, further permitted the trial of some, but not all, counts included on an indictment to be conducted without a jury.

Introduce changes to the procedure of jury trials

Changes have been proposed which would enhance the ability of jurors to make objective judgements based on the evidence presented to them. They include permitting jurors to question witnesses and providing them with facilities to see video tapes of the trial to clarify confusing or forgotten issues. Technology may facilitate further reforms to aid trial by jury, including the use of virtual reality technology to replace the jury's task of sifting through large numbers of crime scene photographs. The Review of the Criminal Courts in England and Wales proposed that while the law should not be amended to permit more intrusive research than was currently permissible into the workings of juries, the Court of Appeal should be entitled to examine alleged improprieties in the jury room and that the law should be declared that juries had no right to acquit defendants in defiance of the law or in disregard of the evidence (Auld, 2001: 164–76).

Streamline the jury system

This would secure a trial by a reduced number of persons. Six are used in many American states and seven was used in Britain during the Second World War. The problems with this reform include whether this reduced number of persons is sufficient to provide either an adequate social mix or to permit sufficient robust conversation.

The replacement of the system of trial by jury

Problems associated with trial by jury have led to suggestions that the system could be replaced, at least in connection with certain types of offences.

In Northern Ireland, trial by jury for what were termed 'scheduled offences' associated with politically motivated violence was abolished in 1973, and trials henceforth took place before one judge. A major rationale for this reform was the inability to guarantee the impartiality of jurors. However, popular trust in the fairness of this system was eroded by the accusation of 'case hardening' – that is the view that the relatively low number of acquittals in contested cases could be attributed to the judge having an inbuilt disposition to declare a defendant to be guilty (Harvey, 1980: 31–2).

In 1986 the Roskill Fraud Trials Committee proposed that fraud cases (that are frequently complex and lengthy) should be heard by a tribunal of judges and laypersons with expertise in these matters. The rationale for this reform may have been enhanced following the lack of success experienced by the Serious Fraud Office in a number of high-profile trials in the 1990s. One of these (involving the Maxwell brothers) stretched over 131 days, cost the taxpayer an estimated £25 million – and at the end of it the defendants were acquitted. As has been noted above, a reform along these lines was introduced in the 2003 Criminal Justice Act. However, the controversial nature of this reform forced ministers to agree to a compromise whereby it would not be implemented until there had been an affirmative resolution of both Houses of Parliament.

> Evaluate the strengths and weaknesses of the system of trial by jury. Why have recent governments sought to impose limitations on the ability of citizens to exercise this right?

Miscarriages of justice

In liberal democratic states that adhere to the rule of law it is important that citizens should be treated fairly and impartially by the courts, and that adequate mechanisms should exist to ensure that, if mistakes are made, they can be speedily rectified. The appeals procedure plays a vital role in this process, but it does not necessarily offer an effective safeguard against all miscarriages of justice, and the experiences of the 'Birmingham Six', the 'Guildford Four' and the 'Cardiff Three' indicated the weaknesses of the appeals procedure. The former consisted of six persons who were jailed for life in 1975 in connection with IRA bombings during the 1970s. In 1991 they were freed when before the Court of Appeal accepted that the convictions were unsafe. It was alleged that police officers who had investigated the case fabricated evidence and that prosecution lawyers withheld evidence that was vital to the defence. The 'Guildford Four' were four persons who were given life sentences in 1975 in connection with bombings carried out in Woolwich and Guildford. They were freed by the Court of Appeal in 1989 because improper methods were used by the police to obtain their confessions. The 'Cardiff Three' were wrongly jailed in 1990 for the murder of a Cardiff prostitute. Fifteen years later the police arrested the person who had been responsible for this crime. It was alleged that the original conviction was obtained by the police manipulation of vulnerable witnesses to give false evidence.

This section examines the manner in which miscarriages of justice resulting in wrongful conviction are dealt with in the UK.

Reasons for miscarriages of justice

A miscarriage of justice is defined as a wrongful conviction whereby a person is punished for a crime they did not commit. They have traditionally arisen in Britain for one or other of five main reasons that are discussed below.

Inadequate work by defence lawyers

A person may be unfairly convicted because the lawyers defending him or her failed to perform their job effectively. One report estimated that around half of the victims of alleged miscarriages of justice believed that their lawyers made key errors (Justice, 1993a). However, the Court of Appeal has traditionally been reluctant to recognise mistakes by defence lawyers as grounds for appeal.

Improper pressure was placed on a defendant by the police to confess to a crime

Police pressure, which may include the use or threat of violence, may result in a person confessing to a crime he or she did not commit or result in witnesses giving false evidence. The former was a particular problem in Northern Ireland when the process of interrogation was utilised to extract confessions related to terrorist crimes. The unique judicial climate in Northern Ireland (provided by the Emergency Provisions Act and the Diplock Courts) underpinned this process, although accusations of unreasonable treatment were sometimes made in connection with police activity in England and Wales. The introduction of the practice of tape recording interviews in police stations provided for in the 1984 Police and Criminal Evidence Act subsequently deterred treatment of this nature. However, the 1994 Criminal Justice and Public Order Act potentially aggravated this problem, both by eroding the right to silence and by failing to require corroborating evidence to support confessions.

The fabrication of evidence

This activity is usually referred to as 'planting' evidence and is undertaken to ensure that a watertight case exists against a person or persons suspected by the police of having committed a crime. The practice arose because the police firmly believed that a suspect was guilty of an offence but did not have convincing evidence to persuade a jury of that person's guilt. It may be linked to other forms of police malpractice, including failing to follow up vital leads in an inquiry when these are unhelpful to the case the police are making against a suspect.

Failure by the prosecution to disclose information relevant to the defence

The task of investigating criminal offences is performed by the police. In theory all material relevant to the prosecution's case should be disclosed to the defence who lack the resources to carry out a detailed investigation of their own. The failure to do this may severely prejudice the ability of defence lawyers to defend their client(s), especially if the police suppress evidence that is potentially damaging to the prosecution's case.

The non-disclosure of evidence by the police has been the basis of some high-profile miscarriages of justice – including those of Gerry Conlon (who was accused of the Guildford bombings which took place in 1974 but whose conviction was ruled unsafe and quashed in 1989) and Stefan Kiszko who was imprisoned for the murder of a schoolgirl in 1975. After spending 16 years in prison, Kiszko was cleared by the Appeal Court in 1992 after medical evidence proved that it was impossible for him to have committed the crime for which he had been sentenced.

The existing position regarding the disclosure of evidence was improved by the 1996 Criminal Procedure and Investigation Act (and the subsequent 2003 Criminal Justice Act). The legislation required a prosecutor to disclose to the defence any prosecution material that had not been previously disclosed and which might, in the prosecution's opinion, undermine the prosecution's case. This is termed 'primary disclosure'. The Act further required the prosecution to disclose material not previously disclosed which might aid the defence case. This is termed 'secondary disclosure', whose divulgence was dependent on the defence having served the prosecution with a defence statement within 14 days of the primary disclosure. Decisions regarding what material to disclose are made by a disclosure officer. This is a police officer whose responsibility is to draw up schedules of material that are then vetted by a prosecutor.

Uncorroborated evidence

The courts are generally sceptical concerning the weight which should be put on uncorroborated evidence, and this is one of the many reasons why the conviction rate for the offence of rape is low: the prosecution case may solely rest on the victim's testimony. However, on occasions, the opinion expressed by expert witnesses has formed the basis of the prosecution's case and resulted in a person's conviction.

The potential weaknesses of this situation were revealed in 2004 in connection with several cases related to cot deaths in which mothers were convicted of killing their children on the testimony of a paediatrician, Sir Roy Meadows, who held that more than one death in a family was unlikely to be a natural event. This view was subsequently challenged by research that suggested that deaths of this nature could occur more than once in the same family (Boseley, 2004). A disciplinary hearing into Professor Meadow's conduct in the trial of Sally Clark (whose conviction for killing two of her children was overturned by the Court of Appeal in 2003) heard that he had stated that the chance of two babies dying from cot death within a family were 'one in 73 million' whereas the actual figure was 'one in 77' (Meikle, 2005). Professor Meadows was subsequently struck off the medical register for gross professional misconduct in connection with the statistical evidence he put forward in this case. He was later reinstated on appeal. The conviction of Angela Cannings for murdering two of her children (which was also based on the testimony of Professor Meadows) was overturned by the Court of Appeal in 2003 and in the same year Trupti Patel was cleared at her trial of murdering three of her children when the jury declined to accept the views of expert witnesses.

Problems connected with the use of expert witnesses led the chair of the Criminal Cases Review Commission, Professor Graham Zellick, to call for an overhaul of the rules governing expert testimony whereby 'areas of expertise would be clearly defined and experts registered, judges should be able to throw out expert evidence they considered unreliable, it should be made clear to juries to what degree such testimony is a matter of opinion rather than undisputed fact, and different views should be offered where appropriate' (Zellick, 2004).

The Criminal Cases Review Commission

Allegations of miscarriages of justice were traditionally handled by the Home Office (or in Northern Ireland by the Northern Ireland Office) that was empowered to refer cases back to the Court of Appeal. However, the procedures adopted were slow, secretive and lacked independence, and decisions tended to support the status quo. Suggestions were made that a body independent of the Home Secretary should be appointed to consider issues of this nature (Devlin, 1976; Home Affairs Committee, 1982) but this reform was not immediately acted upon. However, the experiences of the 'Guildford Four' and the 'Birmingham Six' indicated the weakness of the established appeals process and the need for stronger safeguards for defendants. This led to the establishment of a new independent body, the Criminal Cases Review Commission (CCRC), which was proposed by the Royal Commission on Criminal Justice chaired by Lord Runciman (Runciman, 1993). This body was established under the provisions of the 1995 Criminal Appeals Act and commenced work in April 1997.

The Commission consisted of 13 members and was initially chaired by Sir Frederick Crawford. Its jurisdiction was somewhat wider than had previously been the case when complaints alleging miscarriages of justice were handled by the Home Office. The remit of the new body extended to Northern Ireland, and a similar body was established for Scotland under the provisions of the 1997 Crime and Punishment (Scotland) Act. A particular aim of this body was to restore public confidence in the operations of the criminal justice system.

The role and powers of the CCRC

The CCRC is a back-up to other procedures designed to remedy wrongful convictions. Crown courts regularly overrule convictions dispensed by magistrates' courts and the Court of Appeal also quashes convictions from lower tier courts.

The CCRC can receive complaints directly from individuals or their representatives (such as solicitors) if they believe a person has either been wrongfully found guilty of a criminal offence or has been wrongly sentenced. The ability of the Criminal Cases Review Commission to re-examine a case after receiving a complaint alleging a miscarriage of justice is governed by the following criteria:

- The CCRC will normally only consider a case which has been through the appeals process (and the appeal failed or leave to appeal was refused).
- With regard to conviction, there must be new evidence that was either not available or not disclosed at the original trial (or at any subsequent appeal).
- With regard to sentence, there must be new information not raised during the original trial or at any subsequent appeal.

An initial assessment by CCRC staff will determine whether these conditions are met and the case is thus eligible for consideration by the CCRC. In this case a CCRC caseworker and a Commission member will carry out a more detailed examination of the case that may involve questioning applicants and potential witnesses in order to evaluate doubtful issues. At the end of this process, a view is formulated as to whether the case should be referred back to the Court of Appeal and a decision whether to do so or not is made by a panel of three Commission members. In a small minority of cases, the CCRC may appoint professional experts (for example, forensic scientists) to investigate a case.

The investigative powers of the CCRC are limited; it cannot, for example, search premises, use police computers or make arrests. This means that should a reinvestigation be ordered, it is carried out by those who have these powers (usually the police or, if a police reinvestigation was deemed 'unsuitable', by non-police personnel such as Customs Officers, former police officers, lawyers or private investigators). Once a case is investigated, a committee of at least three CCRC members will then decide whether to refer a case back to the Court of Appeal which has the power to uphold or quash the sentence. If the CCRC decides not to refer a case to the Court of Appeal, it may be re-approached if new evidence subsequently emerges.

Advantages of the Commission

The CCRC possesses a number of advantages over the previous system used to investigate allegations of a miscarriage of justice. These include the following:

- *Transparency*. The operations of the CCRC are far more open than had been the case when these matters were dealt with by Department C3 of the Home Office. A particular feature of its working practices is its willingness to communicate with clients.

- *Speed*. The Commission tends to work more quickly than the Home Office. The first annual report pointed out that, in its first year of operation, 1,700 applications alleging wrongful conviction had been referred to the CCRC. Reviews of 422 had been completed (around 25 per cent). Seventeen cases (including that of Derek Bentley, executed in 1953) had been referred back to the Court of Appeal, and a further 281 cases were under active consideration. Subsequently, in 1999, the Commission referred the case of James Hanratty (who had been executed in 1962 for the murder of Michael Gregsten) back to the Court of Appeal.

- *Focus*. The CCRC can focus single-mindedly on miscarriages of justice. It was impossible for the Home Office or Northern Ireland Office to do this since their responsibilities were far wider.

- *Independence*. The CCRC is not attached to any government department, thus eliminating possibilities of ministerial involvement in the review process.

Problems faced by the Commission

Despite its advantages, the CCRC faced a number of difficulties at the outset. Some practitioners in the criminal justice system queried the legitimacy of applying current standards to old situations when practices (for example concerning the disclosure of evidence) were different. There is also a limit to the extent to which a body of this nature can effectively repair the emotional or psychological damage inflicted upon a person who has been wrongly convicted and perhaps spent several years in prison as a consequence of this (Grounds, 2004: 165). Other difficulties included the following:

- *Volume of work*. When the establishment of such a body was initially proposed in 1994, it was estimated that it would handle around 1,000 cases each year. In the first year, however, it received 1,700 applications. This inevitably resulted in the review of sentences being subjected to undue delay, and prompted the House of Commons Home Affairs Committee to urge additional funding to deal with the delay in processing cases (Home Affairs Committee, 1999).

- *Funding*. At the outset of its operations, the Commission comprised 13 commissioners, 25 case workers and a total staff of 65. Its budget was £4.8 million. In December 1998 the CCRC informed the House of Commons Home Affairs Committee that its caseload had exceeded the resources originally established and allocated for its operations.

Why do miscarriages of justice occur? Analyse the effectiveness of reforms introduced since 1984 designed to prevent this problem occurring.

Discretion in the prosecution process

Although the prosecution process is governed by formal rules and procedures, these are tempered by the exercise of discretion by those professionals who are engaged in all aspects of this work. The term 'discretion' conjures up a variety of images. These include 'rule-bending', the application of 'tact', 'sympathy', 'understanding' and 'common sense', or the exercise of independent judgement by professionals on a situation with which they are faced. It has been argued that discretion 'refers to the freedom, power, authority, decision or leeway of an official, organisation or individual to decide, discern or determine to make a judgement, choice or decision, about alternative courses of action or inaction' (Gelsthorpe and Padfield, 2003: 1). It is frequently exercised in the context of an encounter between an individual and criminal justice practitioner in which the latter applies his or her independent judgement to provide what the professional believes to be a just outcome. It does not necessarily follow, however, that a professional's view of a 'just outcome' will be shared by those on the receiving end of the decision.

Practitioners in the criminal justice system possess a considerable degree of discretion (or what has been termed 'mandated flexibility') (Gelsthorpe and Padfield, 2003: 1) but they do not possess complete freedom as to how they exercise it. 'Judgements or choices are in practice much constrained, not only by formal (and sometimes legal) rules but also by the many social, economic and political constraints that act upon the exercise of choice' (Gelsthorpe and Padfield, 2003: 3). There are several factors that influence the exercise of discretion. These include 'process' (whereby practitioners have been provided with the ability to screen out or divert cases from the criminal justice system based on legal or practical considerations), 'environment' (which suggests that actions undertaken by practitioners will be influenced by community views concerning appropriate courses of action) and 'context' (in which a practitioner's decisions are influenced by 'internal' organisational and occupational factors). What are termed 'illicit considerations' (whereby factors such as class, race and gender underpin a professional's actions) may also influence the manner in which discretion is utilised (Gelsthorpe and Padfield, 2003: 6–9).

Discretion can be used in both negative and positive ways. It provides practitioners with 'the space to engage in discriminatory activities and to subvert policies that they do not agree with' (Gelsthorpe and Padfield, 2003: 2) and, as has been discussed in Chapter 1, classicist criminology opposed the use of discretion in the legal process (since this made for inconsistency so that it was impossible for persons to make a rational choice regarding the commission of crime). It has been concluded that discretion 'is a force for ill when it leads to unjustifiable decisions (negative discrimination) and inconsistency (disparity), but it can be a good thing in that it provides a mechanism to show mercy which, even if defying precise definition, many would recognise as being necessary to the conception and delivery of justice' (Gelsthorpe and Padfield, 2003: 6).

Discretion is widely practised at all stages of the prosecution process. The justice model (whose characteristics are defined in Chapter 8) sought to limit the discretion exercised by professionals. The following discussion considers the way in which discretion is used by key officials in the criminal justice process and the way in which contemporary governments have sought to limit its usage.

The police service and discretion

Discretion operates at two levels in the police service: it is exercised by chief constables and senior police mangers but is also a feature of the work of junior officers. These issues are discussed below.

Chief constables

The principle of constabulary independence that had developed during the course of the nineteenth century with regard to enforcing the law was affirmed in the case of *Fisher* v. *Oldham Corporation* [1930]. This meant that no outside body could dictate to a chief constable how the law should be enforced. The 1964 Police Act placed police forces under the 'direction and control' of their chief officers which gave them the ability to determine the law enforcement priorities for their forces (a task with which Watch Committees in some towns had previously attempted to become involved). One reason for the need to exercise discretion of this nature was that it was impossible to enforce every law and thus a choice had to be made as to what was the most important for a particular force.

Although the exercise of discretion by a police force's senior management was beneficial (in that the specific needs of particular communities could be reflected in police actions), a key problem was that it could be based on the personal views or prejudices of the most senior officers. Although the judiciary (and, ultimately, the European Court of Human Rights) might intervene, especially when it appeared that a police force was deliberately not enforcing the law (an issue that arose in 1968 and 1973 when Raymond Blackburn brought cases against the Metropolitan Police Commissioner in connection with legislation concerned with illegal gambling and the distribution of obscene material), interventions of this nature have been, at best, sporadic. Further, judges have usually declined to interfere with what they regard as police operational decisions even when (as was the case in *R.* v. *Chief Constable of Devon and Cornwall*, ex parte *Central Electricity Generating Board* [1981]) they perceived that the police action was based on incorrect assumptions. However, as is argued in Chapter 4, the ability of chief officers to determine priorities for their force was considerably constrained by the 1994 Police and Magistrates' Courts Act which enabled the Home Secretary to set key priorities for the entire police service in England and Wales.

Junior officers

Junior officers are required to exercise their discretion in a number of key aspects of their work, and in particular it underpins their conduct 'on the streets' where they may be required to exercise their judgement as to whether the law is being broken and, if so, what action to take concerning this. Often discretion at this level of police work is a decision taken on the spur of the moment. If an officer uses his or her discretion to arrest a person, other discretionary actions follow (for example, what crime to charge the suspect with, whether to release on bail or remand in custody). The origins of discretion are legal, based upon the fact that a constable's authority 'is original and not delegated, and is exercised at his own discretion by virtue of his office, and on no responsibility but his own' (*Enever* v. *The King* [1906]). A further, practical, justification for the existence of discretion at this level stems from the impossibility of police managers being able to effectively supervise every action taken by an officer, and it also reflects the impossibility of enforcing all laws.

Although a junior officer's conduct has never been totally free of constraints (since constraints which include the law, the Police Disciplinary Code and organisational culture exercise some control as to how discretion is exercised), it was perceived that officers had too free a rein in enforcing the law which could become influenced by their personal or collective biases. Accordingly legislation such as the 1984 Police and Criminal Evidence Act and the 2000 Race Relations (Amendment) Act sought to impose controls on how some of the more contentious displays of discretion (in particular the use of stop and search powers) were exercised. Additionally, the enhanced use of technology in police work may also serve to rein in some of the autonomy exercised by individual police officers (Chan, 2003: 661).

The Crown Prosecution Service

As is argued above, crown prosecutors exercise discretion concerning whether to charge a person and, if so, with what offence. Although their conduct is governed by the Code for Crown Prosecutors, they nonetheless possess considerable autonomy in relation to the charging process. This may be abused in connection with decisions to charge or not to charge a person and (especially when plea bargaining occurs) the charge that is preferred.

Judicial sentencing

As is discussed more fully in Chapter 6, judges possess considerable discretion in connection with the conduct of trials. This is exercised in connection with key decisions that include:

- the interpretation of the law (since the law may be unclear);
- the admissibility of evidence;
- summing up;
- sentencing (one rationale for which is that to ensure that justice is done it may be necessary to take an offender's mitigating circumstances into account).

The discretion possessed by judges in sentencing is an important issue. The origins of judicial latitude in this matter date from the Consolidation Acts of 1861 in which the courts were given discretion to fix the length of a sentence, subject to a maximum laid down by Parliament. New forms of sentencing available to judges in the early decades of the twentieth century (such as the introduction of the Probation Service and borstals for young offenders) increased judicial discretion in this aspect of their work, and the basis of modern sentencing law was laid down in the 1948 Criminal Justice Act (Thomas, 2003: 53–4).

However, a number of problems arise from the use of discretion by the judiciary. Judges are not formally accountable for their decisions (although they may be informally accountable by means such as the media scrutinising their actions), and they may be unduly influenced by individual or corporate biases (Griffith, 1991: 275). Governments may also feel the need to impose greater control over the sentencing process in order to secure the attainment of their own objectives which excessive judicial independence may undermine. This has been an important rationale for reforms that seek to influence judicial sentencing policies.

The 1961 Criminal Justice Act attempted to promote the use of borstals rather than imprisonment for young offenders, and the 1967 Criminal Justice Act introduced suspended sentences (which, until repealed by the 1972 Criminal Justice Act, required the courts to suspend any custodial sentence which did not exceed six months in duration). It further introduced discretionary parole (whereby a judge relinquished the ability to determine the length of a prison sentence by the introduction of provisions whereby a prisoner would be released after serving one-third of the sentence imposed or 12 months (which the 1982 Criminal Justice Act permitted the Home Secretary to reduce to six months), whichever was the longer (Thomas, 2003: 55–8). The 1976 Bail Act imposed strict limitations of the ability of the courts to refuse bail. This development mainly affected magistrates' courts, but later innovations were directed against the sentencing practices of crown courts. The 1982 Criminal Justice Act restricted the use of custodial sentences on young offenders, and the 1991 Criminal Justice Act applied these restrictions to adults. The 1991 Act sought to reserve custodial sentences for the most serious offences by setting out the criteria for imposing custodial sentences and for determining their length. Henceforth judges were supposed to impose the latter only when the offence was 'so serious that only a custodial sentence was justified'. However, the Act failed to define 'serious' and judges tended to make wide use of custodial sentences (Thomas, 2003: 62–3). The 1991 Criminal Justice Act additionally introduced the system of unit fines that restricted the sentencing powers of magistrates until this reform was abandoned in 1993.

The Conservative government and sentencing reform

Sentencing

Judges have traditionally possessed a wide degree of freedom in determining the sentences of those convicted in their courts. As has been noted above, in some matters (such as the mandatory sentence of life imprisonment for murder) they have no room for manoeuvre, but in others they may exercise considerable choice. The degree of discretion available to the courts has been viewed as a key component for the establishment of a cooperative working relationship between the executive and judicial branches of government (Walker and Padfield, 1996: 378). Ministerial interventions were largely confined to exhortations (for example to adopt alternative forms of punishment to custodial sentences during the 1980s). It has been argued that the discretion accorded to the judiciary created a number of problems that included the following:

- *Inconsistent sentencing*. Those found guilty of similar offences could receive widely different punishments depending, it appeared, on the whim of the judge. This undermined the principle of equality of treatment under the law.
- *Excessive leniency*. The perception that the criminal justice system, and especially judges, were treating offenders too leniently prompted a reform introduced in the 1988 Criminal Justice Act which gave the Attorney General the power to appeal against an excessively lenient sentence. In the 1996 British Crime Survey, four out of five respondents asserted (albeit on the basis of grossly inaccurate perceptions) that judges were too lenient in their sentencing policies.

In 1996 the Conservative government proposed more wide-reaching interventions in sentencing policy (Home Office, 1996) which have been viewed as part of a long-term programme to make the operations of the criminal justice system more rational, in the sense of being governed more closely by rules and precedents and less influenced by individual circumstances and cases (Hudson, 1996: 89–91). A particular aim was to ensure that the actions of the judiciary mirrored the penal populist stance of the Conservative government which sought to 'get tough' with criminals. It was perceived that sentencers were being excessively lenient in the sentences they handed out.

Reforms to sentencing policy

Reforms to sentencing policy were proposed in a 1996 White Paper (Home Office, 1996: 46–53). The main innovations put forward were as follows:

- Offenders convicted for a second time of a violent or sex offence would receive automatic life sentences unless there were 'genuinely exceptional circumstances' which the court would be required to justify. Judicial discretion concerning life sentences was limited to determining whether such sentences were appropriate for offences that included arson, kidnapping and false imprisonment. This was referred to as the 'two strikes and you're out' rule.
- Offenders aged 18 or over who were convicted of drug trafficking offences involving class A drugs with two or more previous convictions for similar offences would receive a mandatory sentence of seven years.
- Offenders aged 18 or over who were convicted of domestic burglary and who had two or more previous convictions for similar offences would receive a mandatory sentence of three years. This approach was popularly referred to as 'three strikes and you're out'.

Reactions to government policy concerning sentencing

The 1996 White Paper was subjected to a number of criticisms.

Constitutional objections

Accusations of ministerial interference in the operations of the judiciary were made in connection with proposed changes to sentencing policy. Lord Donaldson, a senior judge, argued that the transfer of sentencing powers from the judiciary to the executive branch of government posed a threat to the freedom of the individual citizen, while Lord Hailsham, a former Lord Chancellor, declared that mandatory sentences imposed upon the independence of the judiciary.

Injustice

The White Paper was based on the principle of deterrence through punishment and harsh sentences. However, this approach went beyond any concept of 'just deserts' since the punishment took into account an offender's previous criminal record and repeat offenders might receive a harsher sentence than that warranted by the specific crime they had committed. It was alleged that injustice could result from this approach.

Injustice might also derive from other problems connected with mandatory sentences. Judges dispense justice rather than exact revenge for criminal behaviour. In assessing a just sentence, a judge needs to take into account all circumstances that have been revealed during the trial. This would no longer be possible when sentences were predetermined. Additionally, these proposals might result in minor offenders receiving unduly severe sentences. This would increase the costs of a trial since it was likely that defendants, knowing the sentence in advance, would be more likely to plead not guilty. The objectives of deterrence through punishment and harsh sentences that underpinned the White Paper were also specifically rejected by those who believed that the likelihood of detection was more likely to deter crime (Taylor, 1996).

Encourage violent crime

It was also feared that the Home Secretary's proposals might increase the murder rate since, as the mandatory sentence for rape and murder would be the same, a rapist would have no incentive not to kill his victim.

The 1997 Crime (Sentences) Act

The government's White Paper received a hostile reception in a debate in the House of Lords on 23 May 1996. In response to such criticisms, some amendments were incorporated into the subsequent 1996 Crime (Sentences) Bill which became law in 1997. These included a 20 per cent discount on the new mandatory minimum sentences for a timely plea of guilty. Changes were also proposed in the formulae to enable judges to exercise an additional degree of discretion in sentencing.

However, the implementation of this Act was itself subject to the exercise of judicial interpretation. In November 2000 the Court of Appeal effectively quashed the 'two strikes and you're out' rule when – in connection with appeals made by five prisoners – they interpreted 'exceptional circumstances' to mean that the courts were permitted to pass a lesser sentence if they felt that the offender posed no substantial risk to the public.

The 2000 Powers of the Criminal Courts (Sentencing) Act subsequently revised the 1997 Act, providing for a mandatory sentence of life for a second serious offence such as rape or grievous bodily harm (unless there were exceptional circumstances), and establishing automatic minimum sentences of seven years imprisonment for the third offence of trafficking class A drugs and three years for the third offence of domestic burglary (unless such a sentence resulted in injustice).

The 1997 Labour government, sentencing and judicial discretion

The Labour government staggered the introduction of the mandatory sentence provisions of the 1997 Crime (Sentences) Act. In June 1998 an armed robber with previous convictions for rape became the first offender to be given a life sentence under the 'two strikes and you're out' policy of the 1997 Act. The trial judge informed him that before the new law was implemented he would have received a sentence of seven years. The policy of 'three strikes and you're out' was initiated in December 1999, the Home Secretary deciding that convictions previous to the enactment of the legislation would not count in the application of this rule.

Post-1997 Labour governments added to the raft of mandatory sentences by the 1998 Crime and Disorder Act (which included the mandatory requirement that racial aggravation should be treated as an aggravating factor) and the 1999 Youth Justice and Criminal Evidence Act (which introduced the mandatory penalty of a referral order and subsequent appearance before a Youth Offender Panel for first-time offenders below the age of 18 who pleaded guilty and whose offence did not require a custodial sentence). Subsequently the 2000 Criminal Justice and Court Services Act provided for the imposition of mandatory disqualification orders which prevented those who were convicted of an offence against children from working with them (whether they intended to do so or not) (Thomas, 2003: 62–4).

Sentencing guidelines

Judicial discretion in sentencing was traditionally influenced by the senior judiciary. The introduction in 1908 of what was initially referred to as the Court of Criminal Appeal (renamed the Court of Appeal in 1966) enabled defendants to appeal against sentences. The decisions reached by this Court tended to influence the actions taken by judges in similar cases, and the role of the Court of Appeal was extended during the 1970s by its issuance of 'guidelines judgement' that provided judges with generalised guidance as to how certain types of crime should be dealt with. The ability of the Attorney General to refer what are perceived as unduly lenient sentences to the Court of Appeal provided a further rationale for it to influence the sentencing actions of judges (Thomas, 2003: 64–70). It has been concluded that 'there can be no doubt that the Court of Appeal provides a powerful influence on sentencing in the Crown Court, discourages maverick sentencers from going to the extremes of severity or leniency, and has established a substantial body of guidance on sentencing issues which is available to judges in the Crown Court' (Thomas, 2003: 70).

At the 1992 general election, the Labour party had proposed the establishment of a Sentencing Council whose role would be to produce guidelines on a range of cases, thereby ensuring a greater level of consistency between the courts on sentencing policy. Although the appeal court issued guidelines on specific offences when it was asked to determine sentencing appeals, its coverage was not comprehensive, being directed at the more serious offences that were heard in crown courts. Accordingly, the appeal court had not formulated such guidelines for a large number of offences and the sentencing policies of magistrates' courts and non-custodial sentences tended to be ignored by this process of peer review. The 1998 Crime and Disorder Act sought to enhance the role of the Court of Appeal in sentencing matters by setting up the Sentencing Advisory Panel. Its role was to stimulate the development of sentencing guidelines by this Court by suggesting areas where these needed to be drawn up. Its role was advisory only, but the Court of Appeal was required to consult it when preparing guidelines (Thomas, 2003: 70).

Further reform was provided by the 2003 Criminal Justice Act. This legislation adopted a recommendation made by a review of the sentencing framework (Halliday, 2001) and established the Sentencing Guidelines

Council (SGC). The existing Sentencing Advisory Panel continued to function, providing advice to the new body. Its remit was also extended to enable it to comment on any issue affecting sentencing rather than being confined to the consideration of specific offences. The SGC was chaired by the Lord Chief Justice but contained representatives from both the judiciary (who were appointed by the Lord Chancellor) and from criminal justice practitioners (who were appointed by the Home Secretary). Parliament exercises a scrutinising role through the Home Affairs Select Committee in connection with the Council's draft guidelines (Criminal Justice Portal, 2004).

The rationale for the SGC was 'to develop a coherent approach to sentencing across the board' (Home Office, 2004b: 10). It was argued that although judges and magistrates would continue to make independent decisions on sentences in individual cases, 'the wide range of sentencing outcomes across the country was inexplicable and unsustainable' (Home Office, 2004b: 10) and was a cause of public concern. The role of the SGC was to improve the consistency of sentencing by providing sentencers with 'comprehensive, clear and practical guidance' to cover all offences which would enable judges and magistrates to know what was needed in terms of punishment and, aided by advice provided by offender managers, what was most likely to work with individuals in reducing their chances of reoffending (Home Office, 2004b: 10). One difficulty with this approach was that the circumstances related to criminal behaviour assumed lesser importance and might account for developments such as the increased incarceration of women (Hudson, 2003: 181–2).

The guidelines prepared by the SGC were required to take account of cost and effectiveness. A key objective of this reform was to reduce the size of the prison population, which (in conjunction with the added workload placed upon the Probation Service derived from the increased use of community sentences) was attributed to increased severity of sentence, which was frequently directed at offenders with no previous convictions (Carter, 2003: 10–11 and 18). In order to counter this trend, the 2003 Act introduced the 'persistence principle' (which was designed to ensure that sentencers treated persistent offenders more harshly) and made it clear that 'a court must only pass a custodial sentence if it is of the opinion that the offence or offences are so serious that neither a fine nor a community sentence can be justified'. (Home Office, 2004b: 13).

In what ways do police officers and judges exercise discretion within the criminal justice process? To what extent, and why, has their discretion been restricted in recent years?

Gender discrimination in the prosecution process

It has been discussed in Chapter 1 that some aspects of feminist criminologies have argued that the criminal justice process fails to treat women equally. This section seeks to examine arguments that allege the prosecution process operates in a discriminatory way towards women and to analyse some of the reforms that have been put forward to address this problem.

The police service

The police service performs a crucial role in the prosecution process by determining how those who break the law should be dealt with. In order for the service to be regarded as adopting a non-discriminatory attitude towards women who become involved with the prosecution process either as perpetrators or as victims of crime, it is necessary for it to be perceived as an organisation which is free of gender biases. It has been argued that 'genuine and long-standing improvements in service delivery' first require the service to put its own house in order (Gregory and Lees, 1999: 200–1). This section examines the extent to which the police service can claim to be non-discriminatory by examining its stance towards the recruitment of women officers, the treatment accorded to them within the service and the manner in which crimes of violence against women have been dealt with.

Recruitment

The police service was historically an occupation for males. In the nineteenth century some forces employed women to superintend female prisoners while in police custody but the employment of women as police officers did not occur until the First World War. After 1914 a number of independent organisations (such as the Women's Auxiliary Service) were set up, performing functions such as protecting girls from the 'brutal and licentious soldiery' (Ascoli, 1975: 207). At the end of the war women police patrols were set up by the Metropolitan Police Commissioner, although the women were not sworn in as constables. An attempt to regularise the employment of women was subsequently made when a Select Committee argued that women should be fully attested and trained and become an integral element of police forces in England and Wales (Baird, 1920). However, opposition to the implementation of these proposals meant that only a few women were sworn in as constables and even this limited progress was undermined in 1922 when the Home Secretary met the Joint Central Committee of the Police Federation and agreed to remove all female officers.

Further pressures to secure the employment of women officers included the Bridgeman Committee (1924) (which asserted that police efficiency had been strengthened by the employment of police women but argued that their appointment should not be seen as a substitute for the employment of men) (Bridgman, 1924) and the Royal Commission on Police Powers and Procedure (1929). In 1930 the Home Secretary standardised the pay and conditions of service for women officers and specified that their main purpose was to perform police functions concerned with children and women. The 1933 Children and Young Persons Act gave legal recognition to the status of female officers by requiring that such officers should be available to deal with juveniles. However, the number of female officers remained low: by 1971 only 3,884 were employed throughout England and Wales. They were organised in their own departments, had their own rank and promotion structures and their actions were supervised by their own inspectorate. Their pay was only nine-tenths of that of their male counterparts.

The recruitment and conditions of work of female police officers was improved by the 1970 Equal Pay Act and the 1975 Sex Discrimination Act. These measures (and other related reforms undertaken by individual forces) were designed to boost the recruitment of female officers and secure their full integration into police forces. Separate women's police departments were abolished and female officers received the same pay as their male counterparts. However, although the number of women police officers increased, most were in the lower ranks. The progress of these officers was impeded by the entrenched nature of 'cop culture' that made the service resistant to any changes that conflicted with long-established practices and attitudes (Gregory and Lees, 1999: 199). An important aspect of this culture was the 'macho' belief that policing was 'man's work', especially in the sense that the physical and violent nature of some aspects of it (such as general patrol work and public order situations) required police work to be performed by males. This gave rise to suggestions within the service that 'women as police officers are physically and emotionally inferior to men, police work is not women's work and is unfeminine, and that they do not stay in the job for any length of time' (Jones, 1986: 11).

The problem in changing entrenched core attitudes and values in police culture led to the conclusion that:

> Although integration has occurred theoretically in the police service, the role of policewomen is ambiguous in that they are not fully accepted as equals by their male colleagues, and, furthermore, they no longer have the recognition of being specialists in their 'traditional' policewomen's work which in some sense might compensate for the lack of general equality with their male counterparts. At the heart of all these issues is the question of what kind of impact the Sex Discrimination Act has had on the career prospects of women in an organisation which is characterised by its predominantly male-oriented culture in which physical strength and prowess are prized attributes. (Jones, 1986: 21–2)

The treatment of female officers

The manner in which the police service treats female officers is an important indicator to the public of the manner in which females who commit crime or who are the victims of it will be treated. It has been argued that policing is dominated by men and male values (Heidensohn, 1992) and that the police occupational culture is characterised by 'an almost pure form of hegemonic masculinity' which emphasises 'aggressive physical action, competitiveness, preoccupation with the imagery of conflict, exaggerated heterosexual orientation and the operation of patriarchal misogynistic attitudes' (Fielding, 1994: 47). A sexist culture which directly or indirectly promotes discriminatory attitudes towards female police officers may lead to similar stances being displayed towards civilians who have dealings with the police service.

In 1987 the British Association for Women in Policing was set up. This was open to all ranks and aimed to enhance the role and understanding of the specific needs of women employed in the police service. Although police forces were enjoined to demonstrate their opposition to discrimination within the service and in their dealings with the general public (Home Office, 1989), the 'serious problem' of sexual harassment within the police service was officially recognised in 1993 (HMIC, 1993: 16). A subsequent report welcomed the enhanced employment of female officers (who constituted 14 per cent of all police officers by the end of 1994) but pointed to the less spectacular progress up the promotion ladder or into departments or specialisms by female officers. By the end of 1994 only five female officers were of ACPO rank. This situation was blamed on 'entrenched attitudes' in the service that frustrated or diluted the best efforts of reformers. Evidence was also found of 'high levels of sexist ... banter' (HMIC, 1995: 10).

During the 1990s, there were several well-publicised cases of female officers suffering sexual discrimination. These included Alison Halford who in 1992 took the Merseyside Police Authority to an industrial tribunal alleging that sexual discrimination accounted for her failure to secure promotion to the rank of deputy chief constable. She settled the dispute for a large payment and secured a further £10,000 in 1997 for the breach of her right to privacy arising from her office telephone being tapped when she communicated with her lawyers over the sexual discrimination case. Other female officers who took legal action in response to sexual discrimination included Libby Ashhurst (who received an out-of-court settlement of £600,000 in 1996 for allegations of routine sexual harassment and intimidatory behaviour by male officers at Harrogate police station in North Yorkshire) and Dee Mazurkiewicz (whose allegations of sexual harassment in the Thames Valley Police Force were accepted by an industrial tribunal in 1998, following which she agreed a settlement of £150,000).

It was argued that the service had to encourage a greater understanding of equal opportunities in order to counter problems of this nature. It was urged that equality of opportunity should be promoted through a service-wide strategy that reflected local achievement (HMIC, 1995: 13–14). In terms of practical policies it was recommended that part-time working and job sharing should be available for all ranks and grades in order to make employment practices consistent with the requirements of family life (HMIC, 1995: 14). However, although reforms of this nature might address some aspects of discrimination suffered by females employed in the police service, they did not offer the prospect of effectively eliminating sexual harassment. This problem existed in the most senior ranks of the service as was evidenced in 2005 when the chief constable of Cambridgeshire resigned following allegations that he had sexually harassed a woman at a police conference.

The treatment of female victims of crime

Discriminatory behaviour towards female police officers by their male colleagues may create a perception of injustice towards female members of the public, especially when these are victims of crime. This section examines the manner in which violence against women has been responded to by the police service.

One of the unintended consequences of the abolition of separate women's police departments was the loss of an orientation that was favourable towards female victims of crime. Serious crimes such as rape were routinely investigated by male officers who sometimes lacked the empathy with victims that female officers might have more readily displayed. Evidence for this assertion included the number of instances of domestic violence and sexual assault that were either 'no-crimed' by the police (Gregory and Lees, 1999: 60–6) or, if accepted as a crime, not transmitted to the CPS (Gregory and Lees, 1999: 68–71). In 1982 a television fly-on-the-wall documentary, *Police*, made public this problem by publicising the insensitive and inappropriate manner in which officers from the Thames Valley force responded to a complaint of rape. This resulted in guidance being provided to chief constables concerning handling offences of rape and the treatment of victims (Home Office, 1983), one practical consequence being the establishment of rape suites. Guidance on this subject was developed in a subsequent Home Office circular. This suggested that chief officers might wish to consider whether their forces should provide special suites for the examination of victims of rape, and emphasised the importance of medical advice and contact with them.

The need for effective training to foster a greater level of understanding of the needs of victims and to develop the skills and sensitivities necessary to encourage the confidence and cooperation of crimes of this nature was also emphasised. In connection with domestic violence, officers were reminded of their power of arrest under sections 24 and 25 of the 1984 Police and Criminal Evidence Act (Home Office, 1986). Individual forces also introduced reforms to the way in which rape investigations were undertaken, including the establishment in 2001 of specialist rape centres (called Sapphire units) in each of London's 32 boroughs by the Metropolitan Police. These were designed to ensure that any person making an allegation of rape was sympathetically treated. The 2002 Rape Action Plan required all forces to review their facilities for examining victims and specialist training was developed for officers. Additionally, Sexual Assault Referral Centres were set up across England and Wales by the police and health services.

Further guidance was latterly given in respect of domestic violence. This term embraced a wide area of abuse ranging from threatening behaviour and minor assault to serious injury and death and it was stated that such incidents were rarely isolated occurrences. The Home Office argued that 'domestic violence … is a crime and it is important that the police should play an effective and positive role in protecting the victim' (Home Office, 1990: 2). Police officers arriving at the scene of a domestic violence incident were advised not to attempt to 'smooth over the dispute and reconcile the partners' (Home Office, 1990: 5) and it was suggested that female officers should attend incidents of this nature where possible. Reference was also made to the utilisation of section 39 of the 1988 Criminal Justice Act in connection with incidents of this nature (Home Office, 1990: 7). Chief constables were also advised to liaise with other agencies and voluntary bodies to set up arrangements to refer victims of such attacks to long-term support (Home Office, 1990: 9).

Domestic Violence Units became an important aspect of the police's response to crime of this nature. The first of these had been set up by the Metropolitan Police in Tottenham in 1987. The 1990 circular urged chief officers to consider establishing dedicated domestic violence units (Home Office, 1990: 9) and by the end of 1992 62 of the Metropolitan Police's 69 divisions had set up such units which were also found in 20 of the remaining 42 police forces (Home Affairs Committee, 1993: para. 23). Officers from these units were responsible for cooperating with other agencies such as Women's Aid and reflected the need for the police service to become victim-orientated in the sense of accepting women's experiences and understandings of domestic violence (Morley and Mullender, 1994: 26). One difficulty with this approach, however, was that what amounted to hiving off the responsibility for tackling domestic violence onto specialist units had the effect of marginalising the work and the officers who performed it from mainstream policing (Home Affairs Committee, 1993: para. 27).

Pressure on the police service to act robustly with regard to domestic violence was exerted by government programmes such as the 1998 Crime Reduction Programme. This included the Reducing Violence Against Women Initiative. This focused on domestic violence, rape and sexual assault by perpetrators known to their victims. Research into the scale of the problem and the effectiveness of police policies to counter domestic violence also contributed to further changes. In 1995 it was estimated that there had been 3.29 million incidents of domestic violence against women, 1.86 million of which resulted in physical injury. Additionally, women were estimated to have received over five million frightening threats in that year. Although it was estimated that men had been the subject of a similar number of assaults (3.25 million), they received far fewer frightening threats (1.98 million) than women (Mirrlees-Black, 1999: 22). A further report noted that there were wide variations in the scope and content of force policies on domestic violence, the definition of domestic violence was subject to wide variation and standards of performance monitoring were generally poor. A range of organisational models for dealing with domestic violence was found, and it was argued that the line management of domestic violence officers was blurred and that some of these officers felt themselves to be isolated from force structures. Other difficulties that were identified included the frequent lack of accessibility of the records of domestic violence officers (thus undermining their general intelligence potential) and the need to improve the training given to both junior and senior officers on domestic violence (Plotnikoff and Woolfson, 1998: 5–7). It was recommended that the role of domestic violence officers should be more clearly integrated into force structures and that HMIC inspections should continue to assess the quality of the force's arrangements for dealing with this crime (Plotnikoff and Woolfson, 1998: 58).

Findings of this nature prompted the Home Office to revise its 1990 circular on the subject of domestic violence. The new guidance stated that a woman was killed every three days in a domestic violence incident. It stated that domestic violence was 'a serious crime which is not acceptable, and should be treated as seriously as any other such crime' (Home Office, 2000: 1). Accordingly, it was stated that the duty of officers attending a domestic incident was to protect the victims and (if applicable) any children present from further acts of violence and it was anticipated that the perpetrator would normally be arrested. The Home Office further required a force policy on domestic violence to be drawn up to give guidance to officers regarding how the force prioritised the issue, what standards of investigation were expected and the procedures that should be followed. The police service was also urged to maintain regular contact with victims and keep them informed of developments regarding the case (Home Office, 2000). Further changes occurred in 2002 when all forces were required to review their facilities for examining victims.

The effectiveness of changes

The above account has argued that during the 1990s the police service made several important changes to the manner in which they responded to female victims of violence and sexual assault. These reforms were supported by appropriate sanctions against errant officers in some cases: in 1998, for example, an officer was forced to resign from the South Wales police and another was fined £1,000 in connection with a complaint of domestic violence by a wife against her husband who was subsequently jailed for four years. The inclusion of domestic violence in the annual plans of local Crime and Disorder Reduction Partnerships might also go a considerable way to tackling this problem by providing enhanced police accountability to local communities and contribute to offsetting the present imbalance of power which is alleged to be prejudiced against women and children (Gregory and Lees, 1999: 216). But problems, nonetheless, remain.

One important omission has been the failure to appreciate that meaningful changes in the orientation of policing towards viewing issues such as domestic violence and rape as key concerns first require the deep-rooted gender assumptions on which policing is based to be addressed (Silvestri, 2003: 184) in order to provide 'a redefined conception of what policing is about' (Walklate, 2004: 171). The failure to embark upon this examination is likely to mean that crimes such as rape and domestic violence remain on the margins of the police agenda. One example of this was a report by *The Observer* newspaper in 2005 that trainee detectives were being left in charge of complex rape investigations in the Sapphire units of the Metropolitan

Police because of lack of funding and a shortage of qualified officers. It was suggested that this was one factor that might account for convictions for this offence falling to an all-time low (Hill, 2005), an issue that is discussed more fully below.

The judiciary

It has been argued above that the extent to which the prosecution process operates in a manner which is fair towards women perpetrators or victims of crime is considerably influenced by the extent to which the police service is free from sexist attitudes or biases. This section examines whether accusations of sexual discrimination can be made against the judicial system.

The legal profession

As with the police service, accusations have been made that sexism is an aspect of the culture of the legal profession. This will exert an adverse impact on the work performed by professionals whether in private practice or working in the public sector such as for the Crown Prosecution Service or as members of the judiciary.

The refusal of the Law Society to admit women as solicitors was upheld by the Court of Appeal in the case of *Bebb* v. *Law Society* in 1913 that ruled that women were not 'persons' as defined in the 1843 Solicitors Act. This ruling was set aside in the 1919 Sex Disqualification (Removal) Act which made it illegal to exclude women from a wide range of occupations on grounds of sex. The first two women in the United Kingdom to qualify as barristers did so in Dublin in 1921. The following year Ivy Williams became the first woman in England to qualify as a barrister, and the first woman solicitor was also admitted. Subsequently, however, there were several accusations of discrimination against female solicitors. Problems that were identified included the low number of women solicitors, the high wastage rate among qualified female solicitors and the low rate of progression by female solicitors to partners (Law Society, Working Party, 1988). This resulted in a number of recommendations being made to benefit women solicitors, including easing the procedure for reapplying for a practising certificate following a career break (Law Society, Working Party, 1988). Further reforms included the introduction by the Law Society of a practice rule to outlaw discrimination on grounds of race, sex, disability or sexual orientation in 1995.

Subsequently, progress was reported in the admission of women as solicitors. Women were in the majority of those admitted to the profession between 1992/3 and 1997/8, and the number of women holding practising certificates rose by 152.8 per cent between 1988 and 1998 (Law Society, 1998: 74). However, it was argued that the large increase in the number of female solicitors masked other inequalities within the profession. A relatively low proportion of female solicitors were partners (around 22 per cent) and a greater proportion of women were in part-time work and received lower rates of remuneration than their male colleagues. Additionally, there was evidence of horizontal segregation in the profession. Women solicitors tended to be concentrated in certain areas of the law, particularly family work and employment and personal injury law, making these 'female specialisms' (Bolton and Muzio, 2005: 2–3 and 11).

Allegations of sexual discrimination have also been made in connection with barristers. In the early 1990s a Bar Council survey found evidence of unequal treatment between the sexes at many levels of the profession. It was argued that women were treated disadvantageously in connection with pupillage and tenancy applications and the allocation of work, pay and advancement (Bar Council and Lord Chancellor's Department, 1992). Separate research surveyed 822 Bar students on the 1989/90 Bar Finals course, through pupillage and into practice and stated that 40 per cent of the women surveyed had experienced sexual harassment, 10 per cent of which was of an extremely serious nature (Shapland and Sorsby, 1995). A further report detailed a large number of incidents of sexual harassment experienced by females undertaking pupillage. It was stated that that some barristers indulged in 'disgraceful' behaviour towards pupils whom they were responsible for training (Bar Council Working Party, 1995). This led one commentator to assert that 'sexual harassment is still unacceptably prevalent in our profession' (Hewson, 1995: 626).

Findings of sexual harassment and discrimination against female barristers prompted reforms by the Bar Council. It established a Sex, Sexual Orientation and Age Committee in 1992 and adopted an Equality Code of Practice in 1993. In 1995 other reforms to tackle harassment were introduced which included setting up an advice hotline, providing advice to chambers on how complaints of this nature should be handled, and appointing a panel of barristers to advise complainants and to mediate. In 1995 a new Equality Code for the Bar gave detailed guidance on the implementation of good equal opportunity practice. A subsequent Equality and Diversity Code for the Bar (a revised version of which was adopted by the Bar Council in 2004) covered areas that included pupillage and tenant recruitment policy, fair access to work in chambers, and the right to maternity, paternity and parental leave, and detailed the recommendations of the Bar Council concerning flexible and part-time working and career breaks. The Code also defined harassment and outlined the procedure for bringing forward complaints of this nature.

However, complaints by victims concerning sexist abuse are rare since complainants may feel that action of this nature might prejudice their future careers. Thus despite the reforms referred to above, conduct of this nature went largely unpunished, although there were examples of sanctions being applied to those guilty of actions of this nature. In 1995 a QC and Recorder was suspended for three months after being found guilty of harassing a solicitor's clerk and a woman client, and in 1998 a barrister and part-time Recorder was found guilty of sexually harassing a female pupil and fined £500. Additionally, it was latterly reported that reforms initiated by the Bar Council had some impact on reducing the level of sexual discrimination and harassment of women in the profession (Shapland and Sorsby, 2003).

The display of sexist attitudes by members of the judiciary might also be explained by the relatively low number of female judges. The issue of the historic social unrepresentitiveness of the judiciary and the policies that have been put forward to tackle the problem will be explored in more detail in the following chapter. It might be argued, however, that the low number of female judges has an adverse bearing on women who come before the courts either as perpetrators or as victims of crime.

The courts' treatment of women as victims of crime

One aspect of feminist criminologies that was discussed in Chapter 1 highlighted the manner in which the gendered administration of the law and the criminal justice process abetted the oppression of women. As has been argued above in connection with the Crown Prosecution Service, crimes that include domestic and sexual violence have often been adversely affected by decisions to downgrade or discontinue cases. It has also been alleged that the quality of prosecution of offences of this nature by prosecuting barristers has sometimes been deficient (Gregory and Lees, 1999: 78–9). These practices may be heavily influenced by the sexist culture of the legal profession that has been referred to above.

Arguments relating to the gendered administration of law may be further illustrated by the way in which the courts have responded to female victims of crime, especially in cases of sexual misconduct by a male towards a female. Female victims of crime of this nature often receive inappropriate treatment in the courts since the socially acceptable 'attribute' of masculinity has been put forward as an implicit or explicit defence of male actions or has been advanced as a mitigating factor for their behaviour.

The outcome of rape trials has often been determined by the credibility of the witnesses, and the defence case frequently relied on denigrating the character of the complainant. Defence lawyers might, for example, adopt the practice of quizzing a woman about details of her lifestyle and her sexual life, in particular the length of time between her last act of sexual intercourse and the rape, in order to excuse male actions. Her answers could be used to support the defence case either way: 'a long time before implies sexual frustration, a reason for seeking out intercourse with anyone' whereas revelations of an active sexual life 'implies a voracious, indiscriminate appetite. There is no winning' (Kennedy, 1993: 22).

Courts have sometimes downgraded the severity of rape on the grounds that a woman's style of dress or actions indicated that she was a willing sexual partner thereby arousing a male's *natural* masculine sexual urges. In 1982 Lord Hailsham repudiated a comment of a judge who stated that a rape victim who was hitch hiking was guilty of contributory negligence. This line of defence was graphically illustrated in 1996 in the case of a dental nurse who was the victim of stalking by a convicted rapist. Although she endured over 200 incidents of harassment over an eight-month period, the defendant's barrister, David Stanton, accused the victim of provoking the situation by the way in which she dressed. He urged the jury to consider whether it was fair 'that a young lady who dresses to attract, the queen bee attracting the drones, the queen bee that dresses to kill ... cries foul because somebody finds her attractive?' The jury, however, found his client guilty and the trial judge, Gerald Butler, took the opportunity to 'publicly and entirely disassociate myself from your comments' that, he asserted, 'ought never to have been made'.

A number of changes designed to improve the manner in which the courts have dealt with female victims of male violence have been initiated. The 1996 Family Law Act attempted to give greater protection to those suffering from domestic violence by reforms which included streamlining the process of applying for civil injunctions. The 1997 Protection from Harassment sought to provide a defence against stalking and from September 2002 defendants without legal representation were banned from personally cross-examining rape victims.

A key reform was the 2003 Sexual Offences Act which strengthened and brought up to date the existing law surrounding sexual offending and offenders. It redefined the offence of rape to include penetration of the mouth as well as the vagina or anus by the penis, and created new offences of sexual assault by penetration and non-penetrative sexual assaults. This measure further sought to provide a clearer definition of what constituted consent whereby a person consented if he or she 'agrees by *choice* and has the freedom and capacity to make that choice'. Persons would be considered unlikely to have consented to sex if they were unconscious, drugged, abducted, subjected to threats or the fear of serious harm, or if they were unable to give consent due to a learning disability or mental disorder. The former requirement for a defendant to have an 'honest belief that consent had been given' was replaced by a new requirement that his or her belief that consent had been given' was reasonable. The 2003 Act also updated the law to take into account technological innovations by introducing a new offence of Internet grooming which was designed to protect young people from predatory paedophiles. In order to protect the public in general, the police and courts were provided with increased powers to monitor those convicted of a sexual offence (Office for Criminal Justice Reform, 2004: 18). It was stated that this legislation 'puts the victims first. It ... set out clear boundaries about what is, and what is not, acceptable' (Home Office 2004c). Additionally, a ruling by the House of Lords in 2000, which permitted the prosecution to bring forward evidence related to previous acquittals of a defendant who was again being tried for rape, was followed by the 2003 Criminal Justice Act which abolished common law rules governing the admissibility of bad character as evidence of, or indicating a disposition towards, misconduct under certain circumstances.

The 2004 Domestic Violence, Crime and Victims Act included measures to make breach of a non-molestation order punishable by up to five years' imprisonment. The powers of the court were increased to impose restraining orders which could be made on conviction or acquittal for any offence in order to protect the victim from harassment, and established multi-agency domestic homicide reviews in order to learn the lessons from deaths resulting from violence, abuse or neglect inflicted by someone to whom the victim was related, who was a member of the same household or with whom the victim had an intimate personal relationship (Office for Criminal Justice Reform, 2004: 19). Improved mechanisms to respond to crimes of violence against women have been initiated which have included the piloting of domestic violence courts and the development of special units by the Crown Prosecution Service to deal with rape cases (Kennedy, 2005).

However, it has been argued that these developments have not significantly improved the position of female victims of male violence since they have failed to tackle a root problem affecting women's experiences within the criminal justice process which derive from 'the gendered nature of certain crimes and their victims and the gendered nature of so much law, because it is largely created and administered by men' (Kennedy, 2005). Thus the number of cases of rape reported to the police is low, and a large number of these fail to reach the court. A study which examined nearly 500 incidents initially recorded as rape by the police in 1996 found that only 6 per cent of the cases originally recorded by the police as rape resulted in convictions for this offence. The conviction rate nationally has dropped from 24 per cent in 1985 to 9 per cent in 1997 (Harris and Grace, 1999: ix–x), and to 6 per cent in 1999 (Sarler, 2000). A later study based on cases in 2002 reported similar findings whereby 11,766 allegations of rape resulted in 655 convictions (5.6 per cent). The researchers argued that rape was unique in that the victim was subjected to intense scrutiny in court and the defendant was likely to argue that the victim had consented to the attack (Kelly et al., 2005). The procedure adopted in rape trials has been criticised for 'the privileging of a male-centred view of both female and male sexuality' (Walklate, 2004: 183) and it has been argued that the development of 'courtroom advocacy that does justice to the complainant's account' should be embraced (Kelly et al., 2005).

> With reference to material contained in this chapter and in Chapter 1 (in connection with feminist criminologies) assess the extent to which the prosecution process discriminates against women defendants and victims of crime. How do you account for this situation?

Victims of crime

The above account has discussed legal reforms that were designed to help the victims of domestic and sexual violence. This section examines the manner in which the prosecution process treats all victims of crime and in particular assesses those reforms that have been introduced in an attempt to ensure that this process produces fair outcomes to those who have suffered from criminal activities.

Background to the study of victims

Traditionally, criminological theory was concerned with those who committed crime. Since the Second World War, however, increased academic attention has been focussed on those who are victims of this activity. An early study (von Hentig, 1948) suggested that victims made some form of contribution to the offences to which they had been subjected, and this led to research into areas which included the role which victims played in precipitating crime and the extent to which certain categories of persons seemed prone to being on the receiving end of criminal behaviour. Much of the initial research was founded on the presumptions of positivism that suggested that victims possessed particular characteristics that made it possible to identify them from non-victims. These differences could be uncovered by social scientific investigation into the circumstances surrounding those who were victims of crime. These crime victimisation surveys could then be put to practical use in developing responses to these situations that were designed to prevent future occurrences of victimisation. As is argued Chapter 2, one important consequence of making victims the focus of research has been the attention directed at the lifestyles and routines of victims of crime (especially repeat victims).

In addition to accounts of victimisation founded on positivist principles, there are other approaches that have extended to focus on victimology. The liberal strand within victimology has extended research underpinned by positivist perspectives to embrace white-collar, middle-class and corporate abuses. Further accounts have been based on radical and critical perspectives. The radical-critical strand within victimology 'extends to all forms of human suffering and is based on the recognition that poverty, malnutrition, inadequate health care and unemployment are all just as socially harmful as, if not more harmful than, most of the behaviours and incidents that currently make up the official "crime problem"' (Carrabine et al., 2004: 118). This perspective has also embraced structural explanations of victimisation which seek to locate the study of victims within a broader economic, social and political context (Mawby and Walklate, 1994).

As with criminological theory, the criminal justice system in England and Wales also traditionally focused on the offender, leaving the victim as 'the forgotten party in the criminal justice process' (Newburn, 1995: 146). However, the criminal justice system has displayed an increasing concern for the victims of crime. A number of practical steps have been developed to aid those who have suffered from crime, and in particular to ensure that the prosecution process takes their concerns fully into account. The key developments affecting the prosecution process are briefly discussed below.

The Victims' Charter: a statement of the rights of victims of crime

This was initially published in 1990 (and redrafted in 1996). It sought to make all agencies within the criminal justice system more responsive to the needs of victims by setting out more than 50 standards concerning how victims should be treated and what information they should be provided with at every stage of the criminal justice process. It emphasised the need to keep victims informed about the progress of their case, and pay regard to their interests when deciding, for example, whether to charge an alleged offender or whether to proceed with, or discontinue, a prosecution.

Compliance with these standards is monitored by a Victims Steering Group, which includes representatives of the main criminal justice agencies and Victim Support. Other pronouncements (such as the CPS's *Statement on the Treatment of Victims and Witnesses*) have reinforced the objectives of the Charter. It was concluded that the measures undertaken by the government 'will ensure that victims get better information about the progress of their case; that their views are obtained and considered before decisions are taken; and that witnesses receive proper facilities and assistance in court' (Home Office, 1996: 32). Additionally, since 1995 the Probation Service has been required to take account of victim impact when preparing pre-sentence reports.

The victim support movement

The National Victims Association was established in 1972 to provide services to victims and to encourage experiments in conciliation between victims and offenders. This organisation was, however, eclipsed by the Bristol Victims Support Scheme (a key feature of which was to provide outreach work to victims of crime). In 1979 this developed into a national movement known as the National Association of Victims Support Scheme, and by the mid-1990s covered the whole of England and Wales. It is now organised by the charity Victim Support, and provides emotional support and practical help to those who are victims of crime. Home Office support commenced in a small way in 1979 but its contribution significantly increased in 1986 and amounted to nearly £11 million in 1995/6 (Home Office, 1996: 32).

The Crown Court Witness Service

A new offence of witness intimidation was created by the 1994 Criminal Justice and Public Order Act. An additional measure to aid witnesses, the Crown Court Witness Service, was initially established as a pilot scheme in 1990 and was later extended to all crown courts by the end of 1995/6. Funded by the government, it provides a full range of services to victims of crime and other witnesses, including advice and information to help them through the stress of a court appearance.

The victim personal statement scheme

This was introduced in England and Wales in 2001, and provided relatives of murder victims the opportunity to put on record the anguish caused to them by the crime and to state how it affected them physically, emotionally, psychologically and financially. These statements are collected by the police when they take witness statements and are made available to the courts. In a compatible move, the Code for Crown Prosecutors was amended in October 2000 in the wake of the Macpherson Report (which is discussed in Chapter 9) requiring prosecutors to take the views of victims (or the victim's families in cases of murder) into account when deciding whether to prosecute.

The Criminal Injuries Compensation Scheme

Initiated in 1964 and subsequently amended in 1969 and 1979, this provides compensation from public funds to the innocent victims of violent crime. In 1994/5, £175 million was paid out to around 40,000 victims (Home Office, 1996: 33). The scheme was placed on a statutory footing by the 1995 Criminal Injuries Compensation Act.

Reparation

Compensation orders may be imposed upon convicted offenders by the criminal courts, ordering them to pay compensation to their victims for personal injury, loss or damage arising from the offence. The courts have further powers (including that of imprisonment) to enforce payment. The obligation of reparation imposed on the offender dates back to the nineteenth century, but the circumstances under which the courts could adopt this course of action were extended by the 1972 Criminal Justice Act. The 1982 Criminal Justice Act enabled a compensation order to be used either as an ancillary order or as a penalty in its own right for offences committed by children and young persons, and the scope of these orders was extended by the 1988 Criminal Justice Act. As is argued in Chapter 7, the 1998 Crime and Disorder Act and the 1999 Youth Justice and Criminal Evidence Act contain reparative provisions.

Reforms carried out since 1997

The government's objectives of reducing the level of crime and bringing more offenders to justice was designed to 'rebalance the criminal justice system in favour of the victim' (Home Office, 2002: 15). Additionally, a wide range of schemes and processes to specifically aid victims of crime were in place before Labour's victory in the 1997 general election but their disparate nature led to accusations that Britain 'lacks a coherent victims policy' (Newburn, 1995: 169). The effectiveness of the policies that were in place was also questioned since 'over 30,000 cases were abandoned in 2001 because witnesses and victims refused to give evidence in court or failed to turn up'. Reasons for this situation were said to include witnesses' fear of intimidation or the experience of cross-examination in court, the manner in which victims and witnesses were sometimes 'left feeling ill-informed and badly treated', and the waste of people's time because of hearings failing to take place or because defendants changed their plea at the last minute (Home

Secretary et al., 2002: 36). A further explanation for this situation was that witness orders (which compelled a person to attend court and give evidence) had been abandoned in 1996.

Thus in addition to initiatives under the broad umbrella of 'restorative justice' (which are discussed in Chapter 7), further reforms which sought to improve the effectiveness of the prosecution process for victims of crime were introduced. These included extending the Witness Service into magistrates' courts in April 2002. Measures were also undertaken to protect vulnerable or intimidated witnesses which included providing video technology and satellite centres with television link facilities to enable the most vulnerable witnesses to give their evidence from outside the court room.

Further measures were also proposed to 'ensure that victims and witnesses are at the heart of the system' (Home Secretary et al., 2002: 38). These included appointing an independent commissioner for victims and witnesses and producing (under powers provided in the 2004 Domestic Violence, Crime and Victims Act) a Victims' Code of Practice to set out what protection, practical support and information every victim of crime had a right to expect from the criminal justice agencies. In order to hold these agencies to account, it was proposed that victims and witnesses who felt that this Code had not been followed would have the right of appeal to a Parliamentary Ombudsman.

The principle of joined-up government was also advanced to improve the level of service to victims and witnesses. All criminal justice agencies were required to work towards achieving a joint Public Service Agreement target to meet the needs of victims and witnesses (Home Secretary et al., 2002: 48–9). In 2003 the Criminal Case Management Programme was launched. This consisted of three elements – statutory charging, effective trial management and the no witness, no justice project – and was designed to ensure that the police, CPS and courts cooperated more effectively with each other and with other key stakeholders in the prosecution process. One important aspect of the no witness, no justice project was the provision of information to victims and witnesses on the progress of cases through the nationwide introduction of Witness Care Units, operated jointly by the police and CPS, for all cases where someone was charged with an offence. These would provide information, advice and support to both victims and witnesses.

Additionally, the 2000 Criminal Justice and Court Services Act imposed a statutory duty on the Probation Service to keep victims informed about the custodial process for offenders who received a custodial sentence of 12 months or more for a sexual or violent crime. All crown court and most magistrates' courts buildings were to have separate waiting facilities for victims and witnesses by 2008 and new witness protection legislation would be introduced to offer victims and witnesses who feared for their safety a greater degree of protection. A Victims' Fund was also introduced to pay for better support services for victims, and the 2004 Domestic Violence, Crime and Victims Act (which increased the protection, support and rights of victims and witnesses) included provisions to place a surcharge on all criminals who were convicted to boost the total value of this fund (Office for Criminal Justice Reform, 2004: 9 and 26–8).

The shape of things to come?

An innovative way to encourage witnesses to give evidence was utilised in the trial of five men accused or murdering two teenage girls in a drive-by shooting in Birmingham in January 2003. The victims were innocent bystanders in a gang-related feud.

The conviction of four of the defendants at a trial at Leicester Crown Court in 2004/5 was secured by providing a key witness (who was himself a convicted criminal) with an unprecedented degree of anonymity and protection. He testified he had seen some of the convicted men in the car used to carry out the murders. In court he was allowed to use a pseudonym and give evidence from behind a screen. His identity was not revealed to either the defendants or their legal representatives. Anonymity had previously been allowed only for witnesses about whom there was no concern that they would lie about the defendants. His voice was electronically distorted and subject to a 15-second time delay to enable his testimony to be broken off if he said anything that might have revealed his identity.

Defence lawyers protested at these arrangements that they believed prevented them from cross-examining the anonymous witness and intended to appeal. It was anticipated, however, that these measures could be repeated in connection with similar serious crimes involving gangsters or terrorists (Morris, 2005).

To what extent does the prosecution process adequately cater for victims of crime?

Conclusion

This chapter has considered a number of issues affecting the operations of the prosecution process and has discussed reforms to this procedure. It has focused on the role and operations of key agencies in this process, most notably the Crown Prosecution Service, and has considered the strengths and weaknesses of the system of trial by jury and the rationale of proposals to reform the operations of this system. It has also discussed the reasons why miscarriages of justice occur (in the sense of an innocent person being wrongly convicted or inappropriately sentenced) and has evaluated reforms that have sought to prevent these problems from occurring.

The chapter has also considered a number of general issues affecting the manner in which the prosecution system operates. It has evaluated the concept of discretion by those who take key decisions in the prosecution process and has considered the rationale and content of reforms that have sought to reduce the amount of discretion exercised by these professionals. The chapter has also evaluated the extent to which women as either defendants or perpetrators of crime are treated fairly within the prosecution process and has analysed reforms that have been put forward to counter gender discrimination in this process. It has also considered reforms to the operations of the prosecution process that have sought to improve the position of victims and witnesses of crime.

The chapter has discussed the role performed by the judiciary in the prosecution service alongside the role of other key agencies. This is a key agency within the criminal justice process, and the following chapter specifically discusses its operations and the relations between the judiciary and the state.

Further reading

There are many specialist texts that will provide an in-depth examination of the issues discussed in this chapter. These include:

Gelsthorpe, L. and Padfield, N. (eds) (2003) *Exercising Discretion: Decision-Making in the Criminal Justice System and Beyond.* Cullompton: Willan Publishing.

Mawby, R. and Walklate, S. (1994) *Critical Victimology.* London: Sage.

Silvestri, M. (2003) *Women in Charge: Policing, Gender and Leadership.* Cullompton: Willan Publishing.

Walklate, S. (2004) *Gender, Crime and Criminal Justice*, 2nd edn. Cullompton: Willan Publishing.

Key events

- **1919** Enactment of the Sex Disqualification (Removal) Act. This Act set aside a previous ruling by the Court of Appeal that had upheld the right of the Law Society not to admit female solicitors. The first woman solicitor was admitted in 1922.
- **1967** Enactment of the Criminal Justice Act. One aspect of this legislation enabled juries to return majority verdicts of 10 : 2.
- **1972** Enactment of the Criminal Justice Act. This affected the composition of juries by enabling all persons aged 16–65 who were on the electoral register to be summoned for jury service. An upper age limit of 70 was introduced by the 1974 Juries Act.
- **1984** Enactment of the Police and Criminal Evidence Act. This measure provided for Codes of Practice governing the procedures affecting persons arrested by the police and detained within police stations.
- **1985** Enactment of the Prosecution of Offences Act. This legislation removed the task of prosecuting criminals from the police and allocated it to a new body, the Crown Prosecution Service, headed by the Director of Public Prosecutions.

- **1987** Establishment of the first Domestic Violence Unit at Tottenham, London. This development subsequently became more widespread throughout the police service.
- **1994** Enactment of the Police and Magistrates' Courts Act. This measure permitted the Home Secretary to set national objectives for the police service and constituted an important restriction on the power of chief constables who had previously determined the priorities for their forces.
- **1994** Enactment of the Criminal Justice and Public Order Act. This measure eroded a suspect's right to silence.
- **1995** Enactment of the Criminal Appeals Act. This established the Criminal Cases Review Commission to investigate allegations of miscarriages of justice, a role previously performed by the Home Office. This new body could refer cases to the Court of Appeal when they believed a mistake had occurred in terms of either conviction or sentencing.
- **1996** Enactment of the Criminal Procedure and Investigation Act. This legislation made improvements to the existing procedure regarding the disclosure of evidence.
- **1997** Enactment of the Crime (Sentences) Act. This measure restricted the sentencing discretion of magistrates and judges by introducing a new range of mandatory sentences for crimes including violence, drug trafficking and household burglary. It was subsequently revised by the 2000 Powers of the Criminal Courts (Sentencing) Act.
- **1999** Enactment of the Access to Justice Act. This measure abolished the Legal Aid Board and set up the Legal Services Commission for England and Wales. This new body administered the Community Legal Service and the Criminal Defence Service which were concerned with civil and criminal cases respectively.
- **2001** Publication of the Rt Hon Lord Justice Auld's *Review of the Criminal Courts of England and Wales*. Subsequent legislation based on this report included the 2003 Courts Act which provided for the unified administration of the courts by Her Majesty's Courts Service.
- **2003** Enactment of the Criminal Justice Act. This introduced a wide range of reforms to the prosecution process, including the possibility that criminal trials could be heard by a judge without a jury (when there was a serious risk of jury 'nobbling'). The measure also permitted evidence of a defendant's previous bad character to be brought forward where relevant to the present case, and enabled the double jeopardy rule to be set-aside in exceptional circumstances. A Sentencing Guidelines Council was also established to develop a coherent approach to sentencing, thereby undermining the discretion of sentencers in this aspect of their work.
- **2003** Enactment of the Sexual Offences Act. This measure strengthened and brought up to date the existing law surrounding sexual offending and offenders.

References

Ascoli, D. (1975) *The Queen's Peace*. London: Hamish Hamilton.

Aubrey, C. (1981) *Who's Watching You? Britain's Security Services and the Official Secrets Act*. Harmondsworth: Penguin.

Auld, Rt Hon. Lord Justice (2001) *Review of the Criminal Courts of England and Wales*. London: TSO.

Baird, L. (1920) *Report of the Committee on the Employment of Women in Police Duties*, Cm 877. London: HMSO.

Baldwin, J. and McConville, M. (1979) *Jury Trials*. Oxford: Martin Robertson.

Bar Council and Lord Chancellor's Department (1992) *Without Prejudice? Sex Equality at the Bar and in the Judiciary*. London: Bar Council of England and the Lord Chancellor's Department.

Bar Council Working Party (1995) 'Soliciting Equality'. London: Bar Council, unpublished.

Bingham, Lord (1998) Press conference, 7 October, quoted in *Guardian*, 8 October.

Bolton, S. and Muzio, D. (2005) *Can't Live with 'em; Can't Live Without 'em: Gendered Segmentation in the Legal Profession*, Working Paper 2005/39. Lancaster: Lancaster University Management School.

Boseley, S. (2004) 'Cot Deaths Can Strike Repeatedly, Study Confirms', *Guardian*, 31 December.

Bridgeman, W. (1924) *Report of the Departmental Committee on the Employment of Police Women*, Cm 2224. London: HMSO.

Carrabine, E., Iganski, P., Lee, M., Plummer, K. and South, N. (2004) *Criminology: A Sociological Introduction*. London: Routledge.

Carter, P. (2003) *Managing Offenders, Reducing Crime*. London: Home Office Strategy Unit.

Casper, D. and Benedict, K. (1994) 'The Influence of Outcome Information and Attitudes on Juror Decision Making in Search and Seizure Cases', in R. Hastie (ed.), *Inside the Juror: The Psychology of Juror Decision Making*. Cambridge: Cambridge University Press.

Chan, J. (2003) 'Police and the New Technologies', in T. Newburn (ed.), *Handbook of Policing*. Cullompton: Willan Publishing.

Commission for Racial Equality (1991) *Evidence to the Royal Commission on Criminal Justice*. London: Commission for Racial Equality.

Comptroller and Auditor General (1997) *The Crown Prosecution Service*. London: National Audit Office, Session 1997/98, House of Commons Paper 400.

Criminal Cases Review Commission (1998) *Annual Report*. Birmingham: Criminal Cases Review Commission.

Criminal Justice Portal (2004) *New Body to Improve Sentencing Practice*. London: Criminal Justice Portal, press release (available at: www.cjp.org.uk/servlet/PageServer?page =PressReleaseHome &UserAction=9&).

Department for Constitutional Affairs (2003) *Jury Summoning Guidance, Consultation Paper*. London: Department for Constitutional Affairs, December.

Department for Constitutional Affairs (2005a) *A Fairer Deal for Legal Aid*, Cm 6591. London: Department for Constitutional Affairs.

Department for Constitutional Affairs (2005b) *Jury Research and Impropriety: A Consultation Paper to Assess Options for Allowing Research into Jury Deliberations and to Consider Investigations into Alleged Juror Impropriety*, Consultation Paper 04/05. London: Department for Constitutional Affairs.

Devlin, Lord (1956) *Trial by Jury*. London: Stevens & Sons.

Devlin, Lord (1976) *Report of the Departmental Committee on Evidence of Identification in Criminal Trials*. London: House of Commons, Session 1975–6, Paper 338.

Falconer, Lord (2003) 'Foreword by the Secretary of State', in *Jury Summoning Guidance, Consultation Paper*. London: Department for Constitutional Affairs.

Fielding, N. (1994) 'Cop Canteen Culture', in T. Newburn and E. Stanko (eds), *Just Boys Doing Business: Masculinity and Crime*. London: Routledge.

Gelsthorpe, L. and Padfield, N. (2003) 'Introduction', in L. Gelsthorpe and N. Padfield (eds), *Exercising Discretion: Decision-Making in the Criminal Justice System and Beyond*. Cullompton: Willan Publishing.

Glidewell, Sir I. (1998) *Review of the Crown Prosecution Service: A Report*, Cm 3960. London: TSO.

Goodhart, Lord William (1999) 'Legal Aid', *Guardian*, 3 March.

Gregory, J. and Lees, S. (1999) *Policing Sexual Assault*. London: Routledge.

Griffith, J. (1991) *The Politics of the Judiciary*, 4th edn. London: Fontana.

Grounds, A. (2004) 'Psychological Consequences of Wrongful Conviction and Imprisonment', *Canadian Journal of Crime and Criminal Justice*, 46 (2): 165–82.

Halliday, J. (2001) *Making Punishments Work: Report of a Review of the Sentencing Framework for England and Wales*. London: TSO.

Harris, J. and Grace, S. (1999) A Question of Evidence? *Investigating and Prosecuting Rape in the 1990s*, Home Office Research Study 196. London: Home Office.

Harvey, R. (1980) *Diplock and the Assault on Civil Liberties*. London: Haldane Society.

Hastie, R. (1994) 'Introduction', in R. Hastie (ed.), *Inside the Juror: The Psychology of Juror Decision Making*. Cambridge: Cambridge University Press.

Heidensohn, F. (1992) *Women in Control? The Role of Women in Law Enforcement*. Oxford: Clarendon.

Her Majesty's Inspectorate of Constabulary (1993) *Equal Opportunities in the Police Service*. London: Home Office.

Her Majesty's Inspectorate of Constabulary (1995) *Developing Diversity of the Police Service: Equal Opportunities, Thematic Report*. London: Home Office.

Hewson, B. (1995) 'A Recent Problem?', *New Law Journal*, 145 (6694): 626–7.

Hill, A. (2005) 'Untrained Detectives Left to Solve Complex Rape Cases', *Observer*, 1 May.

Home Affairs Committee (1982) *Miscarriages of Justice*. London: House of Commons, Session 1981-2, Sixth Report, House of Commons Paper 421.

Home Affairs Committee (1993) *Domestic Violence*. London: House of Commons, Session 1992-3, Third Report, House of Commons Paper 245).

Home Affairs Committee (1999) *The Work of the Criminal Cases Review Commission*. London: House of Commons, Session 1998/9, First Report, House of Commons Paper 106.

Home Office (1983) *Investigation of Offences of Rape*, Circular 25/83. London: Home Office.

Home Office (1986) *Violence Against Women: Treatment of Victims of Rape and Domestic Violence*, Circular 69/86. London: Home Office.

Home Office (1989) *Equal Opportunities Policies in the Police Service*, Circular 87/89. London: Home Office.

Home Office (1990) *Domestic Violence*, Circular 60/90. London: Home Office.

Home Office (1996) *Protecting the Public: The Government's Strategy on Crime in England and Wales*, Cm 3190. London: HMSO.

Home Office (1998) *Determining Mode of Trial in Either-Way Cases: A Consultation Paper*. London: TSO.

Home Office (2000) *Domestic Violence*, Circular 19/2000. London: Home Office.

Home Office (2002) *The National Policing Plan 2003–2006*. London: Home Office Communication Directorate.

Home Office (2004a) *One Step Ahead: A 21st Century Strategy to Defeat Organised Crime*, Cm 6167. London: TSO.

Home Office (2004b) *Reducing Crime – Changing Lives: The Government's Plans for Transforming the Management of Offenders*. London: Home Office.

Home Office (2004c) *Working Within the Sexual Offences Act 2003*. London: Home Office, Home Office Communications Directorate.

Home Secretary, Lord Chancellor and Attorney General (2002) *Justice For All*, Cm 5563. London: TSO.

Hudson, B. (1996) *Understanding Justice*, 1st edn. Buckingham, Open University Press.

Hudson, B. (2003) *Understanding Justice: An Introduction to Ideas, Perspectives and Controversies in Modern Penal Theory*. Buckingham: Open University Press.

James, L. (1975) *Report of the Interdepartmental Commitee on the Distribution of Criminal Business between the Crown Court and Magistrates' Courts*, Cm 6323. London: HMSO.

Jones, S. (1986) *Policewomen and Equality, Formal Policy versus Informal Practice*. Basingstoke: Macmillan.

Justice (1993a) *Negotiated Justice – A Closer Look at the Implications of Plea Bargains*. London: Justice.

Justice (1993b) *Miscarriages of Justice: A Defendant's Eye View*. London: Justice.

Justice (2004) *Response to White Paper One Step Ahead – A 21st Century Strategy to Defeat Organised Crime*. London: Justice.

Kelly, L., Lovett, J. and Regan, L. (2005) *A Gap or a Chasm? Attrition in Reported Rape Cases, Home Office Research Study*. London: Home Office.

Kennedy, H. (1993) *Eve Was Framed*. London: Vintage.

Kennedy, H. (2005) 'Why Is the Criminal Justice System Still Skewed Against Women?', *Guardian*, 10 March.

Law Society (1998) *Annual Statistical Report: Trends in the Solicitors' Profession*. London: Law Society Research and Planning Unit.

Law Society Working Party on Women's Careers (1988) *Equal in the Law: Report of the Working Party on Women's Careers*. London: Law Society.

Lord Chancellor's Department (2000) *Criminal Defence Service: Establishing a Salaried Defence Service and Draft Code of Conduct for Salaried Defenders Employed by the Legal Services Commission*, Consultation Paper 9/00. London: Lord Chancellor's Department.

Mawby, R. and Walklate, S. (1994) *Critical Victimology*. London: Sage.

Meikle, J. (2005) 'Professor's Evidence Misleading, Rules GMC', *Guardian*, 14 July.

Mirrlees-Black, C. (1999) *Domestic Violence*, Home Office Research Study 191. London: Home Office, Research, Development and Statistics Directorate Report.

Morley, R. and Mullender, A. (1994) *Preventing Domestic Violence*, Crime Prevention Unit Series Paper 48. London: Home Office, Police Research Group.

Morris, S. (2005) 'Witness Scheme to Trap Gangsters', *Guardian*, 19 March.

Mortimer, J. (1999) 'Taking a Liberty', *Guardian*, 20 May.

Narey, M. (1997) *Home Office Review of Delay in the Criminal Justice System*. London: HMSO.

Newburn, T. (1995) *Crime and Criminal Justice Policy*. Harlow: Longman.

Nightingale, B. (2005) Quoted in C. Dyer and D. Taylor, 'A Safety Net in Tatters', *Guardian*, 15 February.

Office for Criminal Justice Reform (2004) *A Strategic Plan for Criminal Justice 2004–08*. London: TSO.

Office for Criminal Justice Reform (2004) *Cutting Crime, Delivering Justice: A Strategic Plan for Criminal Justice 2004–08*, Cm 6288. London: TSO.

Plotnikoff, J. and Woolfson, R. (1998) *Policing Domestic Violence: Effective Organisational Structures*. London: Home Office, Research, Development and Statistics Directorate, Policing and Reducing Crime Unit.

Royal Commission on Police Powers and Procedure (1929) *Report of the Royal Commission on Police Powers and Procedure*, Cmnd 3297. London: HMSO.

Runciman, Lord (1993) *Royal Commission on Criminal Justice Report*, Cm 2263. London: HMSO.

Sarler, C. (2000) 'All Rapes Are Not the Same', *Observer*, 9 April.

Shapland, J. and Sorsby, A. (1995) *Starting Practice: Work and Training at the Junior Bar*. Sheffield University: Institute for the Study of the Legal Profession.

Silvestri, M. (2003) *Women in Charge: Policing, Gender and Leadership*. Cullompton: Willan Publishing.

Taylor, Lord (1996) Speech at King's College, London, quoted in *Guardian*, 6 March.

Thomas, D. (2003) 'Judicial Discretion in Sentencing', in L. Gelsthorpe and N. Padfield (eds), *Exercising Discretion: Decision-Making in the Criminal Justice System and Beyond*. Cullompton: Willan Publishing.

von Hentig, H. (1948) *The Criminal and His Victim*. New Haven, CT: Yale University Press.

Walker, N. and Padfield, N. (1996) *Sentencing: Theory, Law and Practice*, 2nd edn. London: Butterworths.

Walklate, S. (2004) *Gender, Crime and Criminal Justice*, 2nd edn. Cullompton: Willan Publishing.

Zellick, G. (2004) Quoted in R. Cowan, 'Call for Overhaul of Expert Testimony', *Guardian*, 30 November.

6 The judiciary

This chapter examines the structure of the courts in England and Wales. It evaluates the operations of the judiciary and in particular assesses the relationship between the judiciary, the state and the government. Specifically this chapter:

- describes the structure of the courts in England and Wales;
- discusses the composition of the legal profession;
- considers the way in which judges are appointed and analyses the rationale and content of reforms proposed to this system;
- distinguishes the relationship between judges and the state and judges and the government and assesses whether judges display bias in these relationships;
- discusses the role of judges, in particular their ability to make law;
- evaluates changes to the role of the judiciary introduced by the 1998 Human Rights Act.

Organisation of the courts in England and Wales

The civil and criminal courts in England and Wales are organised in a hierarchy, with the Court of Appeal and, ultimately, the House of Lords dealing with cases referred from lower-tier civil and criminal courts see (Figure 6.1).

Criminal courts in England and Wales

There are two levels of criminal courts: the magistrates' courts and the crown courts.

Magistrates' courts

A person who has been formally charged with an offence will appear at a magistrates' court as soon as is practicable. The least serious criminal charges (those which are termed 'summary offences') will be tried in this court. These were those offences that merited a short term of imprisonment and/or a fine (which was generally a maximum of six months/£5,000). The 2003 Criminal

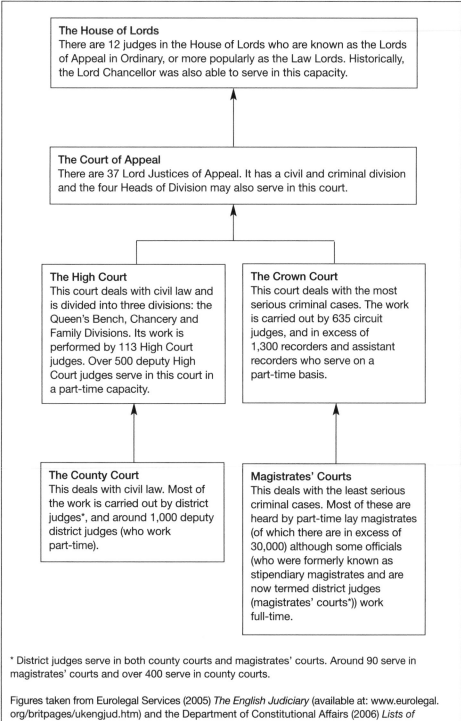

The House of Lords
There are 12 judges in the House of Lords who are known as the Lords of Appeal in Ordinary, or more popularly as the Law Lords. Historically, the Lord Chancellor was also able to serve in this capacity.

The Court of Appeal
There are 37 Lord Justices of Appeal. It has a civil and criminal division and the four Heads of Division may also serve in this court.

The High Court
This court deals with civil law and is divided into three divisions: the Queen's Bench, Chancery and Family Divisions. Its work is performed by 113 High Court judges. Over 500 deputy High Court judges serve in this court in a part-time capacity.

The Crown Court
This court deals with the most serious criminal cases. The work is carried out by 635 circuit judges, and in excess of 1,300 recorders and assistant recorders who serve on a part-time basis.

The County Court
This deals with civil law. Most of the work is carried out by district judges*, and around 1,000 deputy district judges (who work part-time).

Magistrates' Courts
This deals with the least serious criminal cases. Most of these are heard by part-time lay magistrates (of which there are in excess of 30,000) although some officials (who were formerly known as stipendiary magistrates and are now termed district judges (magistrates' courts*)) work full-time.

* District judges serve in both county courts and magistrates' courts. Around 90 serve in magistrates' courts and over 400 serve in county courts.

Figures taken from Eurolegal Services (2005) *The English Judiciary* (available at: www.eurolegal.org/britpages/ukengjud.htm) and the Department of Constitutional Affairs (2006) *Lists of Judges, Senior Judiciary List* (available at: www.dca.gov.uk/judicial/senjudfr.htm).

Figure 6.1 The structure of the courts in England and Wales.

Justice Act enabled magistrates' courts to impose prison sentences of 12 months and placed severe restrictions on their ability to mete out prison sentences of less than this period. However, the imposition of imprisonment by magistrates is relatively infrequent and the conditional discharge is often used as a preferred option in these courts.

Additionally a defendant may opt for a trial in a magistrates' court if charged with an offence which is 'triable either way' (that is, one which may be heard in either a magistrates' court or a crown court). Theft and burglary are examples of offences that can be tried in either court. Typically a defendant in a case of this nature will plead guilty and hope that he or she will benefit from the reduced sentencing powers of the magistrates, although they have the right to try the case and then submit it to a crown court for sentencing if they feel their powers are inadequate to deal with the seriousness of the matter.

Persons charged with the more serious criminal charges (those which are triable on indictment, in a crown court) also initially appear at a magistrates' court. The defence may ask for the prosecution's case to be outlined at this initial stage (a process which is termed *voire dire*) in an attempt to undermine prosecution evidence and seek to have it rendered inadmissible. This procedure was used, for example, in connection with the charges made against the former leader of the Liberal party, Jeremy Thorpe, in 1979. Although this practice is not regularly invoked, the magistrates' court must routinely decide how a defendant who is awaiting a crown court trial should be treated. The choices at the magistrates' disposal are to remand in custody or to free on bail (to which conditions may be attached). The granting of bail became a politically contentious issue during the 1990s when arguments were made (for example by the Home Secretary in his speech to the Conservative party conference in October 1993) that those freed on bail went on to commit further serious offences. The 1994 Criminal Justice and Public Order Act removed the right to bail from a person charged with a further indictable offence while on bail. The 2003 Criminal Justice Act amended provisions related to bail, reversing the presumption that it would be granted in some cases, and extending the prosecution's right to appeal against a decision to grant bail.

Those who staff magistrates' courts are mainly laypersons serving in a part-time capacity. In 2003 there were around 30,000 of these officials who tried more than 95 per cent of all criminal cases (Department for Constitutional Affairs, 2003b: 20). Local political nomination is an important source of recruitment for the lay magistracy. Responsibility for appointing magistrates was historically shared between the Lord Chancellor's Department and (in connection with the County Palatine of Lancaster) the Duchy of Lancaster, although the 2003 Courts Act terminated this arrangement. This legislation provided lay magistrates with jurisdiction covering England and Wales, and established one Commission of the Peace for England and Wales, divided into local justice areas. However, existing arrangements providing for local input into their appointment by the local Advisory Committees was retained. The Judicial Appointments Commission (which is discussed later in this chapter) could, however, be given a role in the appointment process (Department for Constitutional Affairs, 2003b: 21).

Some magistrates serve in a full-time capacity and have training either as barristers or solicitors. The latter were formerly termed stipendiary magistrates until the 1999 Access to Justice Act retitled them as 'District Judges (magistrates' courts)' and expanded their jurisdiction to enable them to sit in every Justice of the Peace Commission area in England and Wales. The volume of work they perform has significantly increased in recent years, mainly in the larger cities (Sanders, 2001). In February 1998 there were around 30,000 unpaid magistrates, 91 stipendiary, and 83 acting stipendiary magistrates. Between them they try around 95 per cent of all criminal cases in England and Wales (Sanders, 2001). They are appointed by the monarch.

Trials in lay magistrates' courts are before a 'bench' of magistrates (which normally numbers three) but only one official presides over trials that take place before district judges (magistrates' courts). Juries are not used in magistrates' courts.

Crown courts

These were established by the 1971 Courts Act to try the more serious forms of criminal activity (that is, crime which is dealt with on indictment). They are presided over by judges (see below) and use juries (whose work is considered in more detail in the previous chapter).

> With reference to material contained in this and the previous chapter, distinguish between the work performed by magistrates' courts and crown courts. What are the strengths and weaknesses of this two-tier legal system?

The civil courts in England and Wales

Civil courts hear disputes between two private parties. The state is not directly involved with the presentation of a case, and the aim is for one party to assert wrongdoing by another and seek redress. This may involve the party bringing the case (the 'claimant') seeking damages against the defendant.

Any person bringing a civil case is required to satisfy the judge or judges that 'on the balance of probabilities' the defendant was responsible for alleged wrongdoing. This test is far easier to prove than that used in criminal courts, and this is one reason why those alleging wrongdoing by the police often resort to civil courts to secure either damages or out-of-court settlements. In April 1999, new Civil Procedure Rules were applied to the High Court and county court to tackle the problems of cost and delay.

As with criminal courts, civil courts are also graded. There are three levels: the small claims courts, the county courts and the High Court.

Small claims courts

The small claims system was established in county courts in 1974, and deals with minor disputes in which the maximum sum demanded as damages does not exceed £5,000 (save in the case of personal injury where the limit was £1,000).

County courts

These courts deal with a wider range of civil disputes that include actions in contract and tort, debt and land recovery, and family matters.

The High Court

This court tries the more serious civil cases, such as personal injury actions where there was a possibility that the plaintiff could secure in excess of £25,000 in damages. Its work is performed by three Divisional Courts: the Queen's Bench Division, the Family Division and the Chancery Division.

The Appeal Courts

Appeals from the lower-tier criminal or civil courts are heard by the Court of Appeal and may be referred to the House of Lords. The Judicial Committee of the Privy Council also exercises a limited range of appeal functions.

Court of Appeal

The Court of Criminal Appeal was established in 1908 and was renamed the Court of Appeal in 1966. This court hears criminal appeals from the crown courts, and also hears civil appeals from county courts and the High Court. It is a forum in which mistakes committed by junior judges can be rectified by their senior colleagues. Defendants who believe that they have been excessively punished possess the right to appeal to this court for a review of their sentence and in 1988 the Criminal Justice Act gave the Attorney General the ability to refer sentences related to serious crimes to this court when these sentences were felt to be too lenient.

House of Lords

The Judicial Committee of the House of Lords constitutes the final court of appeal for both criminal and civil cases which derive from decisions initially made by the Court of Appeal in England and Wales, and the Court of Appeal in Northern Ireland; it also hears civil but not criminal appeals from Scotland. Cases are normally heard by a panel of five judges and the outcome of a case may be determined by a 3 : 2 majority vote. The small size of this panel gives individual judges considerable influence over particular decisions and contrasts with the practice of the European Court of Human Rights or the European Court of Justice, both of which use a larger panel of judges.

The Judicial Committee of the Privy Council

This was established by the 1833 Judicial Committee Act and is composed of a diverse group of people who include the Law Lords, retired Law Lords below the age of 75, privy councillors who are or were senior judges, past and present members of the Court of Appeal of England, Wales and Northern Ireland or of the Inner Court of Session in Scotland, and privy councillors who are judges of certain superior courts in countries of the Commonwealth (Department for Constitutional Affairs, 2003b: 18). This body hears appeals regarding both civil and criminal matters for 16 former British colonies, when its decisions are reached on the basis of the law of the countries from which each appeal comes; it also hears appeals from Guernsey, Jersey and the Isle of Man and exercises technical jurisdiction in areas which include appeals against pastoral schemes of the Church of England. It formerly heard appeals against decisions made by the disciplinary committee of the General Medical Council, but in April 2003 most of its jurisdiction regarding appeals from decisions made by various governing bodies concerned with health care was transferred to the High Court (or the Court of Session in Scotland).

One example of the exercise of its powers occurred in October 1998 when it sanctioned (by a vote of 3 : 2) the execution of a convicted murderer in the Bahamas and subsequently (by a unanimous vote of 5 : 0) rejected death row appeals by nine convicted murderers in Trinidad and Tobago. One problem with this situation is that cases heard in London may fail to appreciate local feelings regarding crimes and their appropriate punishment. Sentiments of this nature led the government of Trinidad and Tobago to suggest in 1998 that the Judicial Committee's role as a final court of appeal should be ended and replaced by a Caribbean Court of Justice.

The role of the Judicial Committee of the Privy Council was expanded by devolution legislation (consisting of the 1998 Scotland Act, the 1998 Northern Ireland Act and the 1998 Government of Wales Act) that made it responsible for adjudicating on constitutional matters derived from this legislation. The government proposed to transfer these powers to a newly created Supreme Court (Department of Constitutional Affairs, 2003b: 21) and this reform was accomplished in the 2005 Constitutional Reform Act.

Other courts in England and Wales: coroners' courts

In addition to the courts that have been referred to above, coroners' courts are also used in connection with some matters where criminal actions may have taken place. Coroners are appointed by local authorities, although the Lord Chancellor has the power to remove them in certain circumstances. Reform of the appointment system entailed the Department for Constitutional Affairs taking responsibility for this process (Luce, 2003), which might eventually be assumed by the Judicial Appointments Commission.

The function of coroners' courts is to hold inquests in cases where there was reasonable cause to suspect that the dead person suffered a violent or unnatural death, where a sudden death occurred and the cause is not known, or where a death occurs in prison or in police custody. Juries (of seven, nine or eleven persons) are used in cases dealing with deaths in prison or police custody and may be used in other cases at the discretion of the coroner. Witnesses cannot, however, be compelled to answer questions in coroners' courts, and a refusal to answer is not held against them as it would be in a normal criminal trial (under the provisions of the 1994 Criminal Justice and Public Order Act where the jury may draw inferences from a witness's silence).

The remit of coroner's courts is limited: they cannot, for example, examine the circumstances surrounding a death. Coroners are relatively unaccountable for their actions, and it is difficult to pursue a complaint against a coroner who may have made a mistake resulting in the wrong verdict being delivered. Until 1977, inquest juries were able to declare that one person had been murdered by another, which led to the accused person being automatically tried for murder. This power was last used in 1975 when Lord Lucan was declared to be the murderer of his children's nanny (although his subsequent disappearance prevented him from being tried for that offence). It was then abolished, for reasons that included the fairness of a future trial when such an emotive verdict had been delivered. Currently, the powers of an inquest jury are limited to declaring that a death arose from either 'unlawful killing', misadventure or accidental death.

International courts with jurisdiction in the UK

There are two European courts with the power to overrule decisions made by British courts of law. These are the European Court of Justice and the European Court of Human Rights.

The European Court of Justice

This court is staffed by judges and advocates drawn from member countries of the European Union (EU) who serve for six years. The main purpose of the court is to ensure that EU law is adhered to within member countries. Disputes between states, between the EU and member states, between individuals and the EU or between the institutions of the EU are all referred to this court. It has the power to declare unlawful any national law that contravenes EU law and also has the power to fine companies in breach of this legislation.

A number of national courts (including those of France and the UK) have upheld the view that European law has precedence over national law. One example of the power wielded by this court over UK domestic law occurred in 1995, when the European Court ruled that men in Britain should receive free medical prescriptions at the age of 60 (rather than 65), to bring them into a position of equality with women.

The European Court of Human Rights

In 1950 the Council of Europe (whose membership is wider than that of the EU with which it should not be confused) drew up the European Convention of Human Rights. This is enforced by the European Commission of Human

Rights based in Strasbourg. This body investigates complaints that may be made by states or individuals and its findings are then considered by the European Court of Human Rights which is also based in Strasbourg. Many European states have accepted its decisions as binding which has resulted in aggrieved citizens taking their cases to Strasbourg.

An important example of how the operations of the European Court of Human Rights can affect Britain occurred in 1998. This body ruled (in the case of *Osman* v. *The United Kingdom*) that when the police were aware of a physical threat to a person they were under a legal obligation to protect that person. This ruling effectively ended the police immunity from legal action in cases alleging negligence and could be applied to the issue of racial attacks.

Administrative tribunals

Tribunals provide a mechanism whereby the rights of the citizen can be safeguarded against actions undertaken by central or local government. They are typically concerned with adjudicating on the correctness of a decision reached by officials operating in these areas. They are also used to settle certain types of disputes between two private parties.

Tribunals are viewed as a more effective manner for handling intricate personal cases than civil courts because of the cost and delay which aggrieved members of the public would be likely to experience in the courts. Their operations are governed by the 1971 Tribunals and Inquiries Act (which was amended in 1992). Members of a tribunal were historically appointed by the minister concerned with its area of activity, but the 2001 Labour government proposed to establish a unified Tribunal Service, with all appointments becoming the responsibility of the Lord Chancellor. This activity might eventually be assumed by the Judicial Appointments Commission. There are several different types of administrative tribunals, including the following:

- *Industrial tribunals.* These deal with a very wide range of issues concerned with disputes between employers and employees. They adjudicate on complaints of unfair dismissal, complaints alleging sexual or racial discrimination and complaints arising from an employers' failure to comply with changes in employment law such as the Working Time Directive and the minimum wage. The maximum compensation an employee can expect from a tribunal was increased in October 1999 to £56,600.
- *Employment tribunals.* These deal with a wide range of matters connected with employment issues. These tribunals may order an employer to pay compensation to an employee who has been unfairly dismissed and can issue a reinstatement order restoring the employee to the post from which he or she was sacked.

The Scottish legal system

Scotland possesses its own, distinct, legal system consisting of District and Sheriff Courts, and the High Court of Justiciary. The latter constitutes the highest criminal court in Scotland and there is no appeal to the House of Lords against its decisions. The Lord Advocate has the ultimate responsibility for investigating crime in Scotland and prosecutions are conducted by him or his deputies or (at local level) by Procurators Fiscal. There are two forms of criminal procedure – summary (in which juries are not used, taking place in District and Sheriff Courts) and solemn (which entails a trial before a judge and jury and is used in the High Court of Justiciary and in Sheriff Courts). Scottish juries (which consist of 15 persons) have the option of three verdicts: 'guilty', 'not guilty' or 'not proven'.

A distinct system is used in connection with juvenile crime in Scotland. Here the age of criminal responsibility is 8, but offending by young people below the age of 16 is primarily treated as a welfare issue. The procedure is governed by the 1995 Children (Scotland) Act. Offenders aged 8–15 are referred by the police to the Children's Reporter Administration which determines whether to refer the matter to the Children's Hearings System. This forum can decide to take no further action or it may impose a Supervision Requirement to which a wide range of conditions can be attached. Offenders aged 16–17 are referred by the police to the Procurator Fiscal who decides whether to refer the matter to the criminal courts. The case may, however, alternatively be referred to the Children's Hearing which has the power to impose a range of penalties including fines, probation and custody (Utting and Vennard, 2000: 14–15).

The 1998 Scotland Act transferred the responsibilities previously exercised by the Scottish Office in connection with criminal justice matters. Control over policing was devolved to the Scottish Parliament and Executive.

Reforms of the Labour government

The Auld Report

One solution to the difficulties experienced by consecutive Home Secretaries in reforming the system of trial by jury (an issue which has been discussed in the previous chapter) was put forward in a review of the criminal courts of England and Wales. This review proposed to create a unified criminal court consisting of three divisions: the Crown Division (constituted as the present crown court) which would exercise jurisdiction over all indictable crimes and the more serious ones which were 'triable either-way'; the District Division (constituted by a judge – normally a district judge or recorder who would be solely responsible for sentencing decisions – and at least two magistrates) which would exercise jurisdiction over a mid-range of 'either-way' cases, the penalty for which was a maximum of two years imprisonment; and the Magistrates' Division (constituted by a district judge or magistrate as was currently the case with magistrates' courts) which would exercise jurisdiction over the less serious 'either-way' cases and over all summary cases. Juries would be used only in the Crown Division, although it was proposed that a defendant in a case heard before either the Crown or the District Division could opt for trial before a judge alone. The decision as to which court would hear 'either-way' cases would be taken away from the defendant and instead would be vested in the magistrates' Division courts (with the possibility of an appeal from the defendant which would be heard by a district judge) (Auld, 2001: 94–114, 177–99 and 270–81). It was proposed that the loss by the defendant of his or her right to opt for trial by jury in an 'either-way' case should be introduced even if the court structure was not reformed.

Although the government failed to implement the reforms that were proposed to the structure of the criminal courts, the 2003 Courts Act unified the administration of magistrates' courts (which had previously been conducted locally) with the administration of other courts through the creation in 2003 of a unified administration, Her Majesty's Courts Service. This would replace the existing management structure that consisted of Magistrates' Courts Committees and the Court Service. It was intended that the new management structure would be locally accountable and was designed 'to enable management decisions to be taken locally by community-focused local management boards, but within a strong national framework of standards and strategy direction' (Home Secretary et al., 2002: 148). The new Service would operate on the basis of 42 areas, in line with the organisational structure utilised by other agencies in the criminal justice process, and would be accountable to Parliament through the Lord Chancellor's Department.

The 2003 Criminal Justice Act also sought to introduce a number of changes to the system of trial by jury but opposition from the House of Lords prevented most of these from becoming law. One major recommendation from the review that was introduced concerned the ability of a trial judge to remove juries in complex fraud cases (Auld, 2001: 200–14).

Abolition of the office of Lord Chancellor

The 2001 Labour government intended to abolish the 1,400 year-old office of Lord Chancellor.

The rationale for this reform was that the Lord Chancellor was a member of all three branches of government. The enhanced role played by the judiciary in both human rights and the judicial review of decisions taken by public officials made it undesirable that a judge should also be a member of the legislature and executive branches of government. The Lord Chancellor's role as head of the judiciary might be more appropriately discharged by the Lord Chief Justice than by a politician, and the increased responsibilities (coupled with enhanced spending) of the Lord Chancellor's Department justified the minister in charge of this department being a member of the House of Commons where accountability could be more adequately enforced (Jowell, 2004).

On 12 June 2003 the Lord Chancellor's Department was replaced by the new Department for Constitutional Affairs, which was headed by Lord Falconer. Initially he took the title of 'Secretary of State for Constitutional Affairs and Lord Chancellor'.

However, the case in favour of the abolition of this office was not universally accepted. It might be argued that the Lord Chancellor was more able to champion the impartiality of the judicial system because of the office-holder had 'a foot in all three parts of the constitutional divide' (Garnier, 2004). The House of Lords' Committee that was considering the Constitutional Reform Bill refused to endorse the abolition of this office in 2004. This legislation did, however, introduce significant changes to the office whereby the Lord Chancellor would no longer sit as a judge or be head of the judiciary (a role which would henceforth be performed by the Lord Chief Justice) and whose role in appointing judges would be significantly reduced following the appointment of a Judicial Appointments Commission. The 2005 Constitutional Reform Act also specified that holders of this office would not henceforth be required to be lawyers or members of the House of Lords. Instead, office-holders would be required to meet the criterion of having experience that the Prime Minister considered to be relevant.

The creation of a Supreme Court

The 2001 Labour government proposed to create a Supreme Court to take over the judicial functions of the House of Lords. It would be a court of the United Kingdom as a whole and although its initial members would be the existing Law Lords, members would ultimately be nominated in ways other than by the Judicial Appointments Commission for England and Wales (a reform which is discussed in the following chapter). The consequence of this reform would be that those sitting on the Supreme Court would only exercise judicial functions and would no longer be members of the House of Lords.

The government was eager to argue that the new court would not be modelled on the American Supreme Court. Although it would assume the powers currently exercised by the Judicial Committee of the Privy Council in connection with devolution issues, it would not constitute a specific constitutional court and would not be given the power to overturn legislation. Nor would its main role be that of giving preliminary rulings on difficult points of law (Department of Constitutional Affairs, 2003b: 9).

This new body was created by the 2005 Constitutional Reform Act and it is anticipated that it will be sitting by October 2008.

The composition of the legal profession

In Britain the legal profession is divided into solicitors and barristers. The work which each perform is discussed below.

Solicitors

Solicitors deal with the general public who may require legal advice on a range of problems. The training of solicitors requires either a degree in law or a non-law degree plus a one year's conversion course, and a postgraduate

Legal Practice Course, followed by a one-year period of traineeship in a solicitor's office (which was formerly termed 'articles'). This equips them to deal with a very wide range of legal issues, although there is an increasing tendency to specialise, especially when employed by large practices. In 2005 there were 96,757 solicitors in England and Wales with a practising certificate, of whom 75,079 were in private practice (Department for Constitutional Affairs, 2005: 12).

Solicitors are regulated by the Law Society, whose Office for the Supervision of Solicitors (OSS) was established in 1996 to handle complaints from the public (replacing the Solicitors Complaints Bureau); the OSS is overseen by the legal services ombudsman (who also scrutinises the way in which the Bar (see below) handles complaints against barristers). Complainants who are dissatisfied with the way in which their complaints have been dealt with can refer the matter to the ombudsman for a ruling as to whether it was handled satisfactorily.

Concerns relating to the number of complaints made by members of the public against solicitors (including a growth in claims for negligence) and the length of time taken to resolve them (so that in 1999 the OSS had a backlog of 17,000 cases) resulted in a perception that self-regulation was proving ineffective. This situation led the government to provide itself with reserve powers in the 1997 Access to Justice Act that would be invoked if self-regulation failed to improve. This involved the creation of a legal services commissioner with the power to set targets to reduce the backlog of complaints and the processing of new ones, to require the complaints handling body to submit a plan and to impose financial penalties if it failed to keep to this plan. In 2004 the OSS was replaced by the Consumer Complaints Service. This was part of the Law Society, whose main role was to deal with complaints about poor service provided by solicitors.

The Lord Chancellor subsequently announced proposals to change the way in which both the Law Society and the Bar Council dealt with complaints against the conduct of their members. A new body, the Legal Services Board (LSB), would be established to oversee the actions taken by front-line regulators (which included the Law Society and Bar Council). Additionally, a new agency, the Office for Legal Complaints (OLC), would handle complaints by consumers concerning legal service providers who were members of bodies or organisations regulated by the LSB. The OLC would investigate complaints (thereby ending the powers of both the Law Society and Bar Council to investigate complaints against their members in England and Wales), and refer any issues relating to professional misconduct to the relevant front-line regulator, and would then monitor the decisions taken by the latter in connection with the complaint. The LSB would oversee the disciplinary arrangements of the Law Society and Bar Council (Department for Constitutional Affairs, 2005: 58).

Barristers

Barristers specialise in one area of the law. There are far fewer barristers than solicitors, numbering 14,364 in 2005 in England and Wales. The majority of these (numbering 11,564) were in private practice (Department for Constitutional Affairs, 2005: 12). Their training entails a degree in law followed by a one-year Bar Vocational course regulated by the General Council of the Bar that serves as the regulating body for this profession. Following successful completion of their professional training, barristers undertake a period of training (termed 'pupillage') with an established barrister. They receive their work from solicitors rather than a direct approach from the general public and become involved in a case either when a solicitor seeks the opinion of a specialist or when a case goes to court. In criminal cases, traditionally solicitors prepared the paperwork and barristers appeared in court as advocates to present the case, although this work distinction was less marked in civil law practices.

The Human Rights Act has had important consequences for the operation and discipline of barristers. Traditionally barristers enjoyed immunity from negligence actions over the way they conduct a case in court (as do solicitors when engaged in court work) although Article 6 of the European Convention on Human Rights (which guarantees the right to a fair hearing in civil claims) threatened to terminate this practice when the Human Rights Act became part of English law in 2001. Accordingly, in July 2000, the Law Lords pre-empted this situation by ending barristers' immunity in both civil and criminal cases.

In March 2005, an appeal panel (the Visitors to the Inns of Court) headed by a High Court judge ruled that the Bar's system for disciplining (which was performed by disciplinary panels and appeal panels) contravened both the Human Rights Act and the rules of natural justice by failing to provide an accused lawyer with an independent and impartial tribunal. The key issue was the role of lay members in the procedure who performed a dual role, that of determining whether disciplinary charges should be brought and then taking part in the adjudication of them. This meant that this category of persons (even if they did personally participate in both processes) had a conflict of interest.

Queen's Counsel

Senior members of the legal profession (around 10 per cent of the total number of barristers) may be appointed Queen's Counsel (QC). This process is known as 'taking silk', because of the silk gowns that QCs wear in court. QCs are appointed by the Lord Chancellor. Historically, only barristers could be QCs, but since 1997 solicitors have also been appointed. This is, however, a very small number: in 1999 only 700 solicitors out of a total of 80,000 were eligible for consideration as QCs (Peach, 1999: 27), and in 1999 there were four solicitor QCs. The QCs are viewed as the elite of the legal professions, and although the skills required for advocacy are not necessarily identical with those required of a judge, traditionally judges were selected from their ranks. This was affirmed by one Lord Chancellor, who stated that 'the appointment of Queen's Counsel helps me to identify the pool from which potential candidates for high judicial office are usually drawn' (Mackay, 1993). Thus biases affecting the appointment of QCs have exerted a significant influence on the composition of the judiciary.

The criteria for selection is dependent on 'soundings' taken of the views of judges, QCs and leading solicitors, which have traditionally remained secret. However, in 1999 the Lord Chancellor asked Sir Leonard Peach to examine how the system for appointing QCs and also judges could be made fairer, a key issue being that barristers in elite sets of chambers were favoured with appointment and that there was lack of access for some lawyers (particularly minority ethnic lawyers) to work of the quality which provided the platform and visibility for assessment of the requisite qualities for silk (Joint Working Party, 1999).

The place of QCs in the modern legal profession is, however, now being challenged. In 1998 a report published by the Adam Smith Institute urged that QCs should be abolished (Reeve, 1998), and in 1999 over 100 MPs signed a House of Commons motion to call on the Lord Chancellor to abolish this office. The primary reason for these calls primarily is that the QC system inflates costs. Historically, a QC could not appear in court unless accompanied by a junior barrister, and although this practice was theoretically abolished in 1977 it remained widely practised. Additionally, QCs command high fees when they appear in court, where their work is frequently financed out of public funds.

The merger of the legal professions?

The two-tier nature of the legal profession drives up the cost of legal proceedings. The rigid distinction between the work of solicitors and barristers was broken down in 1990 when the Courts and Legal Services Act enabled solicitors to appear as advocates in the higher courts. But solicitors were required to undergo a complex procedure to obtain permission to conduct such cases so that by 1998 only 634 were qualified to do so. In June 1998, the then Lord Chancellor, Lord Irvine, announced further measures to enable solicitors to appear in the higher courts. The ability of any one of the four senior judges (the Master of the Rolls, the Lord Chief Justice, the Vice-Chancellor and the President of the Family Division of the High Court) to block solicitors from appearing was ended.

> Why is the legal profession in England and Wales divided into barristers and solicitors? Evaluate arguments for and against the proposal to create a merged legal profession.

The judiciary and the state

The separation of powers

The neutrality of the judiciary is theoretically upheld in the doctrine of the separation of powers and is especially important in defending the citizen from arbitrary actions undertaken by the state. This doctrine is, however, undermined in a number of important ways, one of which is the involvement of politicians in judicial affairs.

Politicians are able to influence the environment and working practices of the judicial system. During the 1990s, the courts and Crown Prosecution Service, like the police service, became subject to new public management (the details of which are discussed in Chapter 4 in connection with the police service). The philosophy of the *Citizens' Charter* was specifically applied to the courts by the publication of the *Courts Charter* in 1992 that became effective in 1993. This document set out what citizens could expect when they came into contact with the courts and what could be done if something went wrong. In particular it set out standards of service and performance that those coming to a court as jurors, witnesses or defendants should receive. Consumerism was further aided by the publication of annual reports by the three departments most directly concerned with the courts (namely, the Lord Chancellor's Department, the Crown Prosecution Service and the Home Office).

Politicians may also intervene in sentencing issues. They may do this in a number of ways. Historically, the Home Secretary had the ability to determine the tariff (that is, the period of time to be served in prison) for those receiving a mandatory life sentence for murder (although this did not apply to life imprisonment for discretionary sentences of life imprisonment, when the term to be served was fixed by judges). The trial judge and the Lord Chief Justice proposed the tariff that should be served in prison, but the Home Secretary had the final say in this matter.

However, the involvement of the Home Secretary in sentencing decisions has been significantly eroded in recent years. Criticisms arose with the way in which the Home Secretaries used their power to intervene in sentencing decisions, a major concern being whether a politician's need to court public opinion undermined his or her objectivity in connection with the sentencing of offenders. In 1997, in connection with the imposition of a 15-year sentence for the two children who had abducted and murdered James Bulger in 1993, the House of Lords ruled that an inflexible minimum period of detention with no allowance for the prospect of rehabilitation was unlawful for those under 18. Further pressure to reform this situation arose in 1999 when the European Commission of Human Rights determined (in relationship to the trial and sentencing of these same two children) that the Home Secretary was not 'an independent and impartial tribunal'. In 2000 the tariff for James Bulger's murderers was set by the Lord Chief Justice, and the 1998 Human Rights Act is likely to eventually lead to the end of the involvement of politicians in any decisions related to sentencing. A further development occurred in 2002 in connection with the convicted murderer, Dennis Stafford. The European Court of Human Rights ruled that the ability of the Home Secretary to overrule the Parole Board in determining the release date of a life prisoner who had served their minimum tariff should be ended since it breached Article 5 of the Convention.

The appointment procedure

The way in which judges are appointed is fundamental to their standing as impartial arbiters of the law. The majority of judges in both civil and criminal courts are appointed from the ranks of barristers. On 1 December 1995 only one High Court judge, Mr Justice Sachs, was a solicitor. There has, however, been an attempt to broaden the recruitment base of judges, resulting in a greater number of judges operating in the lower-level civil and criminal courts being solicitors. On 1 December 1995 virtually all (321 out of 322) district judges (who sit full time in county courts to hear the less important civil and family cases) were solicitors, and 19 per cent of assistant recorders and 9 per cent of recorders (who sit part time in crown courts and county courts) were solicitors.

Judges are appointed by the Lord Chancellor's Department (which is now known as the Department for Constitutional Affairs). Judges in the Court of Appeal and above are appointed by the Queen on the recommendation of the Prime Minister who takes advice from the Lord Chancellor; other judges are appointed by the Queen on the advice of the Lord Chancellor.

In order to become a judge it is first necessary for a candidate to be eligible, as defined in the 1990 Courts and Legal Services Act. This legislation stipulated the number of years' right of audience required in the type of court over which the applicant would preside was required: to serve as a High Court judge, for example, it is necessary for a lawyer to have had rights to appear in that court for ten years. If eligibility is satisfied, selection is governed by three guiding principles (Memorandum from the Lord Chancellor's Department in evidence to Home Affairs Committee, 1996):

- *Merit*. Appointments were made on the basis of merit, regardless of ethnic origin, gender, marital status, sexual orientation, political affiliation, religion or disability. In certain judicial posts the criteria used to assess merit has been identified. Decisions on merit are based on an assessment of applicants against the specific criteria for appointment that include legal knowledge and experience, intellectual and analytical ability, sound judgement, decisiveness, communication and listening skills, and authority and case management skills (Department for Constitutional Affairs, 2003a: 7).

- *'Soundings'*. The appointments procedure places considerable weight on the views of serving members of the judiciary who have knowledge of the performance of a potential candidate. These views are gathered by a process of consultation initiated by the Department for Constitutional Affairs known as 'soundings'. Thus the names of candidates applying for judicial office (including that of Queen's Counsel) are sent to judges, heads of bar circuits and other senior practitioners. Their confidential comments are collated (or 'sifted') by a panel that puts together a shortlist of candidates to be interviewed (Dyer, 1999; Department for Constitutional Affairs, 2003a: 8). Applicants may also nominate other people whom they would like to be consulted. This system is defended by judges who argue that it 'permits the expression of the judgements and evaluations made by those most able to formulate these based on experience and awareness of the needs of the post, and of the environment and the knowledge of candidates' (Peach, 1999: 6).

● *Proof of competence and suitability*. This requires a candidate for full-time judicial office to first serve on a part-time basis 'for long enough to establish his or her competence and suitability' (Memorandum from the Lord Chancellor's Department in evidence to Home Affairs Committee, 1996: 13).

How judges are appointed

Job descriptions provide details of the content of the posts to be filled and the knowledge, skills and qualities needed by applicants (Peach, 1999: 3). Since September 1994 lower-level judicial appointments (which include circuit judges, district judges and assistant recorders) have been advertised, with the exception of recorders (since these are chosen from those serving as assistant recorders). On 24 February 1998 a further innovation in the judicial appointments system occurred with the first advertisement in *The Times* for the post of High Court judge, which had previously been by invitation only. The advertisement advised female and minority ethnic lawyers to 'give this opportunity serious thought'. Currently all but the most senior judicial appointments are advertised. However, the Lord Chancellor retained the ability to offer appointments as High Court judges to lawyers who did not apply to an advertisement.

'Soundings' are taken for candidates who formally apply for selection, following which a shortlisting panel (composed of a judge, a lay member and a senior civil servant from the Lord Chancellor's Legal and Judicial Services Group) draw up a shortlist. These candidates are interviewed (either by the same panel or by one similarly constituted) and assessed against the criteria for appointment. Those candidates chosen for appointment are recommended to the Lord Chancellor (Peach, 1999: 3–4). The monarch formally appoints to the offices of High Court judge, circuit judge, recorder and district judge (magistrates' courts) on the Lord Chancellor's recommendation. Other full- and part-time appointments are made directly by the Lord Chancellor.

The most senior appointments (that is, Lords of Appeal in Ordinary, the Heads of Division, the Lord Justices of Appeal and High Court judges, which in total comprise around 150, of which almost 100 are High Court judges) are handled differently, although (as has been noted above) vacancies for High Court judges are now advertised. These were traditionally filled as the result of a consultation process that was initiated by the Lord Chancellor involving senior members of the judiciary (which includes the Lord Chief Justice, other Heads of Division and the Senior Presiding Judge) who nominated candidates for consideration. This process is proactive, occurring in advance of vacancies arising so that potential appointees can be identified and their progress monitored. There are no interviews since the candidates are well known with proven track records. In these cases, the Lord Chancellor directly appoints on the basis of the consultations that have taken place (Peach, 1999: 4), although recommendations for the most senior judicial appointments (namely the Lords of Appeal in Ordinary, the Heads of Division of the Supreme Court and Lord Justices of Appeal) are forwarded to the Prime Minister who, acting on the advice of the Lord Chancellor, transmits the names of those to be appointed to the monarch.

Problems associated with the system of judicial appointments

There are a number of problems associated with the method of choosing judges, especially the most senior members of the judiciary. These are discussed below.

Political interference

One major difficulty with the appointments process is that it gives the executive branch of government a considerable influence over the composition of the judicial branch. Political affiliation is a crucial factor affecting the appointment of judges in America, and until the Second World War Lord Chancellors were perceived to have used their powers of appointment in a partisan way in Britain. Although the Home Affairs Committee argued in 1996 that they had received 'absolutely no evidence that the present Lord Chancellor has used his powers of patronage regarding judicial appointment to favour those who shared the ideology of the government', they were more sceptical of the role played by the Prime Minister's involvement in the appointment of the most senior judges (Home Affairs Committee, 1996: 38 and 39–40).

A key problem posed by political influence over the composition of the judiciary is that it performs the process of judicial review, involving adjudicating on the legality of actions undertaken by the executive branch of government.

In May 1999 a committee of the law reform group, Justice, argued that the ability of the Lord Chancellor to sit as a judge in the House of Lords was 'inherently flawed' and created an appearance of bias in the wide range of cases in which the executive branch of government was directly or indirectly interested. It further recommended that the Law Lords should no longer serve in a legislative capacity by participating in Parliamentary debates and called for the creation of a new supreme court (Justice, 1999). However, while the then Lord Chancellor, Lord Irvine, made it clear that he had no intention to relinquish his power to act as a judge (Irvine, 1999), further pressure to end this role was applied when the European Convention on Human Rights came into force in October 2000, since Article 6 of the Convention guaranteed the right to a fair and impartial hearing before an independent tribunal.

A similar problem arose in connection with the work to be performed by the Judicial Committee of the Privy Council (a body on which the Lord Chancellor may sit) in connection with devolution to Scotland, Wales and Northern Ireland. These arguments (in conjunction with the enhanced role of the judiciary in connection with the implementation of the 1998 Human Rights Act) could be used to justify the establishment of a separate Constitutional Court whose membership might include judges and laypersons with expertise in such issues.

These issues were tackled by the 2005 Constitutional Reform Act, whose provisions are discussed later in this chapter.

Not socially representative

The advice given by Lord Scarman that the police service should represent the make-up of the society it served (Home Office, 1981: 76) has not been a feature of the practices adopted within his own profession. Judges are not socially representative, and many in the profession feel this to be unnecessary. One recent Lord Chancellor asserted that it was 'not a function of the judiciary to be representative of the people as a whole' (Mackay, 1990), and serving judges have asserted that there is no place for affirmative action if this means selecting anyone other than the candidate most fitted for the office (Judges' Council, 1995). In 1997 the then Lord Chancellor, Lord Irvine, stated that while he was keen to increase the number of women judges, promotions would continue to be made on merit without the use of positive discrimination measures. It was subsequently observed that 'the risk of indirect discrimination in those cases where the candidate for judicial appointment may not have had much exposure in the consultation process, notably women, ethnic minorities and solicitors, is the most constantly raised and anxious concern of those who feel that the appointments system is unfair to them'. The Lord Chancellor was urged to 'vigorously pursue his declared policy of consulting as widely as possible in all cases' (Auld, 2001: 254–62).

The make-up of the judiciary is especially influenced by the 'soundings system', which, its critics informed Sir Leonard Peach, was a flawed procedure since 'it was unclear who was consulted, those who gave opinions were untrained in assessment, much was hearsay ... There was agreement that women, ethnic minorities and solicitors, because of lack of visibility, could be disadvantaged' (quoted in Peach, 1999: 6–7). The 'soundings system' enables those already occupying judicial office to secure the appointment of those from a similar background to themselves. This system provides the possibility of judges becoming a self-perpetuating elite. This explains the small number of solicitors who are appointed judges, and the tendency for the Law Lords to be selected from the ranks of commercial lawyers to the detriment of criminal lawyers. In 1999 the Lord Chancellor sought to head off demands to replace the secret 'soundings' system by asking Sir Leonard Peach to review the system of choosing judges and appointing Queen's Counsel in England

and Wales. In particular he was asked to advise on the extent to which candidates were assessed objectively against the criteria for appointment and the existence of safeguards in the procedures against discrimination on grounds of race or gender (Peach, 1999: 1).

The social composition of the judiciary

'Judges come from a remarkably similar background, male, white, public school and Oxbridge, which has changed little in the past 50 years' (Dyer, 1998).

- In 1995, one member of the Court of Appeal and seven out of 96 High Court judges were women, who comprised 14.69 per cent of assistant recorders and 10.25 per cent of district judges (Home Affairs Committee, 1996: 27).
- In 1994, 80 per cent of the senior judiciary had been educated at an independent school and 80 per cent of senior judges, 51 per cent of circuit judges and 12 per cent of district judges had obtained their first degree at Oxbridge (Home Affairs Committee, 1996: 35).
- In 1995, five out of 517 circuit court judges, 12 out of 891 recorders, nine out of 354 assistant recorders and two out of 322 district judges were of minority ethnic origin (Home Affairs Committee, 1996: 30).

In the 1998–9 judicial appointments round, 76.5 per cent of those appointed to judicial office were men and 23.5 per cent were women. The vast majority of the successful applicants (92.9 per cent) were white (Peach, 1999: 20).

Appointments made by the Labour government since 1997 were initially stated to have worsened rather than challenged this situation so that 'most of the 85 judges appointed since 1997 have been white men, just seven have been women ... Almost eight of ten (79 per cent) of those appointed or promoted since 1997 went to public school ... Likewise 73 per cent of those appointed in the last two years went to Oxbridge Universities' (Labour Research, June 1999: 13). By 2005, only 17 per cent of judges were women and below 4 per cent came from minority ethnic groups (Dyer, 2005).

However, although relatively few women and members of minority ethnic groups have been appointed to judicial office, some progressive changes have been implemented. In 1999 Elisabeth Butler-Sloss, the only female judge to reach the Court of Appeal, was appointed as President of the Family Division of the High Court and in 2004 the first female Law Lord, Brenda Hale, and the first black High Court judge, Linda Dobbs, were appointed. In 2000 Lawrence Collins became the first solicitor to be appointed to the High Court directly from private practice. However, in March 2003, 15 per cent of the total legal professional judiciary were women and 1.6 per cent were from minority ethnic backgrounds (Office for Criminal Justice Reform, 2004: 52).

Does judicial bias matter?

It has been observed above that judges are political appointees who are not socially representative. The nature of their training and the position they occupy in the machinery of the state may reinforce other aspects of their social exclusivity and has led to accusations of a corporate bias affecting the views of judges (Griffith, 1991: 275). These issues are important not simply for the negative image with which they imbue the judiciary, in particular to social groups that are poorly represented within their ranks, but also because judges are in a position to translate their biases into action. This may arise in a number of circumstances:

- *Interpretation of the law.* Judges do not merely enforce the law, but are often required to interpret its meaning and apply this interpretation to the case with which they are dealing. This situation (which is discussed more fully below) gives judges the potential to inject their views into legal proceedings.

- *Presiding over a trial.* Judges preside over trials and in this capacity make several important decisions. These include determining issues such as the admissibility of evidence, the aborting of a trial and whether material should be made available to the defence. This situation, which is covered by Public Interest Immunity Certificates, is very important with regard to trials held in connection with the Official Secrets Act. Judges also have the power to intervene during trials to question witnesses. These actions may be influenced by views founded upon bias.

- *Summing up.* Judges sum up the proceedings of a trial for the benefit of the jury. This role is a further occasion where bias may enable judges to influence the outcome of a trial.

- *Sentencing.* Until the passage of the 1997 Crime (Sentences) Act, only murder was subject to a mandatory sentence. Thus judges had a relatively wide degree of discretion in passing sentence, and this might be used in a discriminatory way, giving rise, for example, to accusations that black defendants, when convicted, were given harsher sentences than white persons for the same offence.

- *Inadequate accountability.* Problems related to the perception of judicial bias are compounded by the relative lack of accountability to which judges are subject. They may express opinions or make decisions which are highly contentious but which are subject to inadequate outside control. Although judges are not totally free from outside control over their actions (since some of their decisions may be the subject of appeal to a higher court, juries may disagree with the views expressed by them and the Lord Chancellor has the ability to discipline judges of the rank of circuit judge and below), they are not accountable for many of the decisions which they make. Additionally (as is discussed below) the more senior ranks of the judiciary enjoy considerably more autonomy than their junior counterparts.

'Judges should reflect the composition of the society whose laws they administer.' To what extent do you agree with this statement, and what problems arise if this ideal is not realised in practice?

Reforms to the appointment process

A number of reforms might be suggested to remedy the problems outlined above concerning the composition of the judiciary. These are discussed below.

Broaden the base of applicants

The composition of the judiciary could be broadened by reforms seeking to extend appointment to groups that are currently excluded. These might include changes to the arrangements for part-time sittings (for example that these should be concentrated in blocks of one or two days rather than being spread over several weeks) in order not to disqualify those unable to fit in with existing practices (and thus, by being unable to serve in a part-time capacity, be ineligible for full-time appointment). It has also been proposed that the ban on employed lawyers (those serving in the Crown Prosecution Service or the Government Legal Service) becoming judges should be lifted and that existing practical assistance (such as work-shadowing and mentoring arrangements) to currently under-represented groups should be extended in order to increase the number of women and minority ethnic judges (Joint Working Party, 1999).

Some of these recommendations were subsequently adopted. Restrictions previously imposed on CPS prosecutors in applying for circuit judge appointments were removed if they had experience of sitting part-time in another jurisdiction. In January 2005, the former Director of Public Prosecutions was appointed a High Court judge. There are, however, limits to reforms of this nature: it has been observed that there are 'no obvious solutions for barristers or solicitors of ethnic minority origin who have been poorly represented in the "best" chambers or firms and so cut off from the "best" and most visible work' to secure appointment to judicial office (Peach, 1999: 20). Other reforms that have been introduced by post-1997 Labour governments include removing the lower age limits for most appointments.

In 2004 the Lord Chancellor and Lord Chief Justice jointly launched a drive to recruit more women, minority ethnic and solicitor judges. Among the proposals to achieve this aim that were put forward were suggestions that judges in the more junior posts could be allowed to return to work as lawyers, that the period of time a lawyer must have been qualified to be eligible for a judicial post could be reduced and that persons not practising as lawyers (such as university law teachers) could be eligible for appointment. Intensive periods of sitting as part-time judges might also be introduced to replace the current procedure whereby candidates for full-time appointment are required to spend several years sitting as part-time judges while also practising law. It was thought that this procedure discriminated against solicitors (Department for Constitutional Affairs, 2004).

A further range of radical proposals to broaden the social composition of the judiciary were put forward by the Lord Chancellor in 2005. These included the possibility of enabling persons such as university law teachers and legal executives who had not qualified as barristers or solicitors to become judges in England and Wales, allowing judges to take career breaks to help them balance their working life with their commitments as parents, fast-tracking lawyers who sat as lay magistrates to the judiciary and reducing the period of eligibility ('rights of audience') that applicants for judicial posts were required to have (Falconer, 2005). These proposals were not, however, to the liking of the Lord Chief Justice who was concerned that they might 'undermine the high quality of the judiciary and the need for appointments to be made on the grounds of merit alone' (Woolf, 2005).

Improved selection procedures

Criticisms of the existing procedures for selecting judges (in particular the 'soundings system' and the interview) might be addressed by reforms that included the introduction of an assessment centre as a key element in the selection process for those seeking initial entry as part-time appointees, and the introduction of psychometric tests to evaluate judicial skills and qualities. The Peach report suggested that a pilot scheme for a one-day assessment centre should be produced and that psychometric and competences tests currently available should be tested for relevance, and, if necessary, others should be commissioned for use in judicial appointments (Peach, 1999: 13–14). In autumn 2004 assessment centres for appointments of recorders were introduced and it was intended that recorders and circuit judges would be assessed under a new competence framework.

Changes to the appointments system

Pressure to change the appointments system was provided by a report that audited the selection procedure used to appoint High Court judges in 2003. It was argued that there was a 'lack of transparency and accountability of significant parts of the selection process by which candidates are considered' which did not comply with the requirement that judicial appointments should be made on the basis of suitability to hold judicial office measured against the stated criteria for the post (Commission for Judicial Appointments, 2004: 25). Particular concern was expressed regarding the dual system of appointment, whereby some candidates applied to an advertisement but others were nominated by senior members of the judiciary. In 2003, of the 175 candidates, 92 responded to an advertisement and 83 were nominated (Commission for Judicial Appointments, 2004: 4). The report argued that these two methods of appointment were incompatible and recommended that in future appointment should only be on the basis of responding to an advertisement. One fundamental problem with the process of nomination was that nominees were not aware that their names had been put forward. In response to this report, the process for appointing High Court judges was changed in February 2005 with the introduction of a revised set of competence-based qualities and skills against which candidates would be assessed.

Other reforms (either suggested or implemented) to the appointments procedure are discussed below.

The hearings system

This procedure enables a candidate's views and opinions to be assessed to determine their suitability for the public office they wish to hold. It may be used in conjunction with an appointments commission and is used in a number of liberal democratic states, such as America, in connection with a wide range of appointments to senior government office. The hearings system has not commonly been used in Britain, although the House of Commons Treasury Select Committee did adopt such a process in 1997 in connection with appointments to the Bank of England's Monetary Policy Committee. It would compel potential judges to disclose their views and beliefs on a wide range of issues that were relevant to their work.

One justification for introducing this procedure to judicial appointments is that their role has been extended following the incorporation of the European Convention on Human Rights into British law in the 1998 Human Rights Act. This justifies an examination of the attitudes of judges in the area of human rights and civil liberties, since they exert considerable influence in matters which include privacy and the relationship between the state and the individual.

A Commission for Judicial Appointments

Although feedback to unsuccessful applicants for appointments as judges or Queen's Counsel had been available from the civil servant member of the appropriate panel, it was considered that the legitimacy of the appointments process might be enhanced through the appointment of a body, the Commission for Judicial Appointments, which would audit the processes and policies used for making and renewing judicial appointments, for handling grievances and appeals resulting from the application of these processes/ policies, and for recommending improvements and changes to the Lord Chancellor (Peach, 1999: 15).

This body was created in 2001 to oversee the appointment procedures for judges and Queen's Counsel, to investigate complaints, to receive comments from individuals and organisations regarding the appointments processes and to make recommendations to the Lord Chancellor for improvement to the process. This body also audits the way in which the Department for Constitutional Affairs selects judges, the first of which occurred in 2003 in connection with the appointment of High Court judges in the previous year's competition (Commission for Judicial Appointments, 2004). It was headed by a First Commissioner and contains seven Deputy Commissioners, one of whom also serves as Commissioner for Judicial Appointments in Northern Ireland (Department for Constitutional Affairs, 2003a: 9).

If the Commission found a complaint to be justified, it could make recommendations to the Lord Chancellor (for example, that a participant to the selection process should not take part in future selection procedures) or could unilaterally initiate action (for example, to restore the complainant, in the subsequent cycle of appointment that he or she was seeking, to the point in the competition at which he or she was disadvantaged and to amend or expunge any part of the judicial appointments records relating to any individual in order to eradicate any material which might disadvantage him or her in the future) (Commission for Judicial Appointments, 2002: 35). In 2002–3 this body received 13 complaints of which 12 were investigated during that year. Eight of these were fully or partly upheld and four were found not to be justified (Commission for Judicial Appointments, 2003).

A Judicial Appointments Commission

One solution to the problem of social unrepresentativeness is to transfer the appointment of judges from the executive branch of government to an independent Judicial Appointments Commission.

In 1972 the law reform group, Justice, called for the establishment of an appointments commission. This reform could be justified by legislation passed in the 1990s (affecting devolution and the Human Rights Act) that will require judges to adjudicate on a range of sensitive political issues – something that could induce governments to appoint judges for partisan reasons. This proposal was rejected by the Home Affairs Select Committee in 1996, partly because it would detract from the principle of ministerial accountability for decisions relating to appointment, but it was supported in 1999 by a senior judge, Lord Steyn.

In 2003 the government proposed to establish an independent Judicial Appointments Commission which would take the selection of judges out of the hands of the Lord Chancellor and his Department by recommending candidates for appointment as judges on a more transparent basis than at present. It argued that 'in a modern democratic society it is no longer acceptable for judicial appointments to be entirely in the hands of a Government Minister … the appointments system must be … independent of Government. It must be transparent. It must be accountable. And it must inspire public confidence' (Falconer, 2003: 2). In addition to the objection that the present system of appointment 'is a potential source of patronage over the judiciary and legal profession' (Department for Constitutional Affairs, 2003a: 11), it was further argued that the central role performed by the Lord Chancellor in the selection of judges was to the detriment of other work required of Lord Chancellors, in particular 'the core business of administering the justice system, and in particular running the courts' (Department for Constitutional Affairs, 2003a: 10). The aim of the new body was to 'bolster judicial independence' (Department for Constitutional Affairs, 2003a: 11) and to effect 'a major re-engineering of the processes for appointment', with a particular aim of 'examining the appointment process to see if new and better ways can help in attracting a wider range of people to the judiciary: more women, more minority members, and lawyers from a wider range of practice' (Falconer, 2003: 2). However, the desire to achieve 'diversity in appointments' would be conducted within the framework of ensuring that judges were appointed, as at present, on merit (Falconer, 2003: 3).

This reform was achieved in the 2005 Constitutional Reform Act that established a Judicial Appointments Commission for England and Wales

whose status would be that of a non-departmental public body. It was anticipated that it would be operational by spring 2006. It would consist of 15
members (drawn from the ranks of judges, lawyers and non-lawyers)
appointed following open competition by an appointing panel composed of
the permanent secretary, a senior judge, a senior figure not connected to the
legal system and an independent assessor. It was not envisaged that this body
would sift applicants for judicial office or routinely conduct interviews, but
would operate as a recommending commission, ratifying and approving decisions on whom to recommend or appoint, generally putting forward only
one name to the Lord Chancellor who would be empowered to reject that
name and require another to be put forward (Department for Constitutional
Affairs, 2003: 13 and 17). Its relatively limited role led to concerns that 'the
new commission might just be a shell in which traditional practices might
continue' (Campbell, 2004).

At the same time as this reform was implemented, it was proposed that the
role of the Commission for Judicial Appointments would be transferred to a
separate Judicial Appointments and Conduct Ombudsman who would
handle complaints from candidates who were dissatisfied with the manner in
which their application for judicial appointment had been handled.

Evaluate the significance of changes made since 2000 to the way in which
judges are appointed.

The judiciary and freemasonry

The objective of a hearings system – to require judges to defend their opinions prior to appointment, thus providing a defence against personal bias
and prejudice – was partially addressed by the Labour government after
1997 in connection with freemasonry.

In July 1998 the Lord Chancellor's Department sent a questionnaire to all
magistrates and judges on this matter, following the refusal of the United
Grand Lodge to divulge the names of judges who were masons. The Lord
Chancellor informed the House of Commons Home Affairs Committee on 10
November 1998 that 13.6 per cent of male magistrates who responded to
the questionnaire (females not being eligible to join) had disclosed their
membership of the masons, and a further 5.4 per cent had failed to reply to
this question. Of the full- and part-time judges, 4.9 per cent had disclosed
their membership and 64 of the respondents failed to answer the question.

Subsequently the Lord Chancellor announced his intention to publish a
register of all judges, which would record their membership of the masons
or whether they refused to answer such a question. Judges in particular
resented such interventions on the grounds that it breached their rights of
privacy and freedom of association.

The judiciary and state interests

Marxists assert that judges are a key component of a state which serves the interests of the economically powerful in society: they 'operate as an essential part of the democratic machinery of administration' (Griffith, 1991: 270) who are concerned 'to preserve and protect the existing order' (Griffith, 1991: 328). This implies that those whose actions pose fundamental challenges to the state or the values that underpin it cannot receive impartial treatment by judges. This assertion is allegedly borne out in the definition which judges accord to the term 'public interest'.

Griffith, a neo-Marxist, asserted that judges have acquired a 'strikingly homogeneous collection of attitudes, beliefs and principles' as to what comprises the public interest. This is based on their common experiences derived from education, training and pursuit of the profession as barristers (Griffith, 1991: 275). The perception that all judges adhered to the view that the public interest embraced 'the interests of the state (including its moral welfare) ... the preservation of law and order; and ... the promotion of certain political views normally associated with the Conservative party' (Griffith, 1991: 278) led to a conclusion that:

> It is demonstrable that on every major social issue which has gone before the courts during the last 30 years – concerning industrial relations, political protest, race relations, government secrecy, police powers, moral behaviour – the judges have supported the conventional, established and settled interests. (Griffith, 1991: 325)

An important example of a circumstance in which a definition of the term 'public interest' is required concerns cases when the public's 'right to know' is challenged by the state's requirement of 'official secrecy'. This issue was at the root of the trial of the civil servant, Clive Ponting, which is discussed in Chapter 5.

However, Griffith's neo-Marxist view (which was initially put forward in 1977) has been challenged by what is termed the 'pluralist' position. This disputes the Marxist perception that the actions of judges are characterised by 'a sense of uniformity of approach' (Roshier and Teff, 1980: 67). Clashes which have taken place between the Court of Appeal and the House of Lords suggest there is no single conception of public interest, and while most judges are conservative there are elements of 'independence and variety' to be found among them: although a 'conservative, formalist approach to interpretation is a distinctive feature of the judicial tradition, many judges display a bluff, no-nonsense pragmatism and a few are conscious social reformers' (Roshier and Teff, 1980: 70).

It has further been argued that Griffith's notion of a conservative judiciary is not necessarily applicable to the new generation of senior judges whose values have been influenced by the postwar social democratic consensus. In the 1990s some judges could be described as 'liberal' in that they acted to protect and preserve the principles on which the UK welfare state was based, viewing welfare provision as a fundamental human right (Woodhouse, 1998).

The absence of a consistent direction pursued by judicial decisions can be illustrated by two trials related to the sale of arms to Iraq by British companies. A common feature of these 'Iraqgate' trials was the attempt by the government to utilise Public Interest Immunity Certificates to withhold material from the defence, on the grounds that this would prejudice national security. The trial judge has the ability to agree with this suppression of evidence or can decide to overturn it. In the first case, involving the firm Ordtec in 1992, the trial judge endorsed the government's wishes to deny the defence access to documents that might have proved their argument that the export of a shell assembly line to Iraq was transacted with full knowledge of the security services. Following plea bargaining, two persons were given suspended sentences and one was fined, although one of those sentenced subsequently successfully appealed against conviction. In the second case, involving Matrix-Churchill, the judge overruled the government and the trial quickly collapsed in 1992. Whether the motive for the inconsistency of judicial decisions relating to two very similar trials illustrated the extent of judicial diversity or was designed to advance the myth of judicial impartiality (in order to secure legitimacy for an unfair social system) is ultimately dependent on a political interpretation of the nature of the state, the purpose of law and the function performed by the judiciary.

Two further cases in July 1999 may lend support to the pluralist case. In one, a judge upheld the notion of 'squatters' rights' and awarded a £200,000 house to a jobless squatter who had lived in the property since 1983 after ruling that the owner (the London Borough of Lambeth) had made no attempt to assert its right of ownership. In another case an Old Bailey judge dismissed an attempt by the City of London police force to force *The Guardian* newspaper to hand over photographs and notes made by journalists at the 'Carnival Against Capitalism' demonstration in June 1999, at which considerable public disorder and arson occurred. The grounds of the judge's decision were that the police had not followed the requirements of the 1984 Police and Criminal Evidence Act before making their demand.

> Write a critical account of the concept of corporate judicial bias as put forward in John Griffith's book, *The Politics of the Judiciary*.

Judges and government policy

The defence of state interests needs to be differentiated from the defence of government interests. While it is open to debate whether the judiciary display a relatively consistent line in connection with the former, their actions may be expected to be less consistent when a matter referred to them for adjudication has significance for the objectives of the government but not the interests of the state. This may be illustrated in connection with the task of judicial review, one aspect of which involves the courts conducting an examination of the actions of the executive to ensure that they are legal.

Traditionally the doctrine of Parliamentary sovereignty meant that the courts were restrictive in their approach to judicial review (Woodhouse, 1995: 401). In the 1940s a Law Lord, Lord Atkin, described some judges as 'more executive-minded than the executive'. However, this stance altered in the 1980s and especially in the 1990s when the courts regularly overturned decisions made by governments. Examples included the following:

- *1995* – the Appeal Court delayed the process of rail privatisation by a decision which hinged on the interpretation of 'minimum standards'.
- *1996* – the High Court set aside the decision of the then Home Secretary, Michael Howard, to expel the Saudi dissident, Professor Mohammed al-Mas'ari, to Dominica.
- *1996* – decisions (initially by the High Court and latterly by the Court of Appeal) overturned Michael Howard's attempt to fix a 15-year minimum custodial sentence for the child killers of James Bulger.
- *1998* – the Court of Appeal ruled that the Labour Home Secretary, Jack Straw, had acted illegally in refusing an asylum application by a Nigerian woman and ordering her deportation on the same day, thus denying her the ability to exercise her right of appeal.
- *1998* – the High Court ruled that the Secretary of State for the Environment, Transport and the Regions, John Prescott, had acted unlawfully when he agreed to a plan to construct 113 new homes on a greenfield site in Peacehaven, East Sussex. The judge ruled that the minister and a public planning inquiry inspector had failed properly to consider the concerns of the local authority.

The willingness to act independently of the executive branch of government in connection with the process of judicial review upheld the spirit of the separation of powers. However, these actions projected the judiciary forcefully into the political arena and could be viewed as an attack on the ability of an elected government to govern. This situation is likely to become more widespread as a consequence of the enactment of the 1998 Human Rights Act that gives the judiciary the ability to challenge (although not overturn) legislation that is incompatible with the European Convention on Human Rights.

The judiciary and law-making

The role of judges in the UK is commonly perceived to be concerned with adjudicating in civil and criminal trials. Their role, however, may extend beyond this to embrace functions associated with law-making.

Interpretation of statutes

What is termed 'judicial creativity' rests upon the judges' need to interpret the law in order to resolve the meaning of words and phrases contained in

Acts of Parliament. There are three basic rules governing this form of statutory interpretation (Zander, 1994: 108–10), as follows:

- *The 'literal rule'*. Here the courts rigorously apply the literal meaning of the words contained in a statute regardless of whether the outcome makes sense.
- *The 'golden rule'*. In this case the literal meaning of the words in an Act may be departed from in order to prevent an absurdity from arising, in which case the judge will look for alternative meanings conveyed by such words.
- *The 'mischief rule'*. This encourages the courts to depart from the precise language of the statute and instead to consider the context within which the Act was passed: this may include considering the 'mischief' which arose in common law which the statute was designed to remedy.

Although the literal rule is normally followed by a trial judge, judicial creativity is facilitated by the application of the golden rule and particularly the mischief rule.

Interpretation of common law

Statutes constitute only one source of English law. There is also common law which consists of judicial precedent created either by historic custom or by the earlier decisions of judges which become binding in later, related cases. Judges are able to exercise creativity in connection with common law that has been said to provide 'a general warrant for judicial law-making' (Devlin, 1976: 9). One example of this arose when Lord Simmonds proclaimed the existence of the common law offence of 'conspiracy to corrupt public morals' in the 'Ladies' Directory case (*Shaw* v. *DPP*) in 1962. More recently in 1998, senior judges, including Lord Chief Justice Bingham, indicated their willingness to develop the common law on breach of confidence into a fully fledged privacy law in advance of the enactment of the 1998 Human Rights Act.

Judicial creativity arises either because the common law is imprecise or because a judge decides to ignore precedent. Lord Denning was associated with the latter course of action and has been described as the 'living negation of the declaratory theory' (Roshier and Teff, 1980: 64). He held that the prime purpose of the law was to secure justice; thus he held that when trying a case a judge was entitled to apply his or her own judgement concerning what was the just outcome, regardless of precedent.

Judges and law-making

The ability of judges to interpret statute or common law makes them potential law-makers. Their capacity to act in this way is, however, governed by two factors:

- *judges are not proactive* – their ability to act in a law-making capacity depends on cases being brought to them;
- *inconsistency* – judges do not have a consistent view concerning the desirability to act as law-makers.

Judges as law-makers – three contrasting views

The extent to which judges believe it is correct to exercise judicial creativity varies.

Lord Reid (a Law Lord, 1948–74) expressed the minimalist position, or passive approach, to judicial law-making. This held that the courts strictly followed the law, whether it was established by Parliament or precedent, and should not be concerned to bring about changes to it (Reid, 1972).

Other judges have emphasised the desirability of judicial law-making through the process of interpretation. Lord Devlin (a Law Lord, 1961–4) emphasised the importance of the law being shaped according to the prevailing political consensus. Judges should interpret the law in accordance with what public opinion deems to be acceptable at the time when the decision is required. This view accepted that the political climate within which the judiciary functioned was indispensable in providing legitimacy to its decisions. This was termed 'judicial activism' and involved judges 'keeping pace with change in the consensus' (Devlin, 1979: 2).

A final view of judicial creativity extended the concept of judicial activism by arguing that it was acceptable for judges to use the process of judicial interpretation as a mechanism to bring about change. This 'dynamic' conception of judicial law-making was particularly associated with Lord Denning (who served as Master of the Rolls between 1962 and 1982). An extreme form of this view could be taken to mean that the law was what the judge wanted it to be rather than what it actually was. Although Lord Denning's judgements were frequently overturned by the House of Lords on appeal, his actions were designed to place pressure on Parliament to bring about a change in the law.

'The role of judges is limited to that of implementing the law.' To what extent is this a true assessment of the work performed by judges?

Human rights and the judiciary

The concept of human rights developed from the tradition of natural rights that sought to establish boundaries to protect an individual from unwarranted interference either by another individual or by the government.

Human rights were thus closely associated with the political ideology of liberalism that wished government to be limited in its scope and sought to impose restraints on the actions that others might undertake. The English political philosopher John Locke (1632–1704) defined human rights as embracing 'life, liberty and property', while the American Declaration of Independence referred to them in 1776 as including 'life, liberty and the pursuit of happiness'. These definitions viewed human rights as basic entitlements that all persons should be permitted to enjoy and which no government was entitled to take away.

In the contemporary period, human rights embrace a wider range of civil and political liberties. These are often provided for in a codified constitution (such as the first ten amendments to the American Constitution which were inserted in 1791 and are collectively referred to as the 'Bill of Rights'). In countries such as the United Kingdom that lack a codified constitution, the rights of the citizen are based on common law. Although civil and political rights are specific to individual countries, the designation of them as *human rights* implies that they should be universal in application and that governments that fail to adhere to these standards are rejecting the humanity of their citizens.

The most recent declarations of human rights are to be found in the United Nations Declaration of Human Rights (1948) and the European Convention for the Protection of Human Rights and Fundamental Freedoms (1950).

The Human Rights Act

The 1998 legislation identified 15 basic rights (all of which were derived from the European Convention on Human Rights). These were:

- the right to life (Article 2);
- the prohibition of torture (Article 3);
- the prohibition of slavery and forced labour (Article 4);
- the right to life and security (Article 5);
- the right to a fair trial (Article 6);
- the right not to be punished save in accordance with the law (Article 7);
- the right to respect for private and family life (Article 8);
- freedom of thought, conscience and religion (Article 9);
- freedom of expression (Article 10);
- freedom of assembly and association (Article 11);
- the right to marry (Article 12);
- the prohibition of discrimination (Article 14);
- the protection of property (Article 1 of Protocol 1);
- the right to education (Article 2 of Protocol 1);
- the right to free elections (Article 3 of Protocol 1).

However, these rights are not of equal standing under the Act. Article 3 is absolute and can never be contravened. Articles 2, 4, 5, 6 and 7 are fundamental but may be restricted for specific reasons identified in the

Convention. Articles 8, 9, 10 and 11 are qualified rights that may be limited in connection with certain circumstances or conditions that are laid down in the Convention, which require the interference to be justified and prescribed by law. The procedure of opting out of the Convention on Human Rights is known as 'derogation'. In the latter case the state may be required to prove that its action is proportionate to the threat posed to the general well-being of society.

In 1997 the Labour government published a Human Rights Bill which became law in 1998 and came into effect in October 2000, thus placing the rights of the subject on a statutory basis. The key consequence of the 1998 Act was that the European Convention on Human Rights was incorporated into British law. This reform sought to increase the defences available to a citizen against abuse of power by the agencies of the state (although the government might also benefit from domestic judges interpreting the Convention rather than judges working from Strasbourg). The consequence of this legislation was that henceforth allegations by aggrieved citizens that public authorities had acted in such a manner as to deny them any of these basic rights (either by interfering with them or by failing to take measures to ensure that citizens could exercise them) could be heard in British courts rather than complainants having to take their grievances to the European Commission for Human Rights and the Court of Human Rights. This latter process was both costly and lengthy: in 1997 it was estimated that the average cost of a case heard by the European Court of Human Rights was £30,000 and the average time taken for judgement to be pronounced by this body was five years.

The 1998 Human Rights Act had significant consequences both for the power of the judiciary and for the operations of the criminal justice system. These issues are briefly elaborated below.

Human rights and the power of the judiciary

The ability of the judiciary to overturn legislation passed by Parliament was significantly affected by the 1998 Human Rights Act since the judiciary was enabled to use this legislation as a yardstick with which to judge other Acts passed by Parliament. This judgement could be made retrospectively in connection with old legislation as well as with new Acts. However, in order to uphold the concept of the sovereignty of Parliament, judges could not directly overturn an Act of Parliament that they felt contravened the principles of the human rights legislation. Instead, they were empowered to issue a certificate that declared a law passed by Parliament to be 'incompatible with the convention'. Although it was assumed that such declarations by the courts would induce the government and Parliament to introduce corrective measures to bring such complained-of legislation into line with the

Convention on Human Rights, there was nothing to prevent either of these bodies ignoring these rulings. This might induce an aggrieved person to refer the matter to Strasbourg which (if it became commonplace) would mean that the Act had failed to substantially improve the pre-October 2000 position regarding the defence of human rights.

One objection to placing human rights on a statutory footing in the UK was the ability of the judiciary to interpret other legislation in relation to the 1998 enactment. Although there may be objections to the power exercised by modern executives, it is open to question whether the situation is improved by subjecting actions of the legislature or executive to the approval of socially unrepresentative, unelected and politically unaccountable judges. The manner in which the incorporation of the European Convention on Human Rights into British law would both defend civil liberties in Britain and, at the same time, enhance the power of the judiciary was demonstrated in 1999 in connection with the prevention of terrorism legislation.

The power of the judiciary was demonstrated in December 2004 when, by a majority of 8 : 1, the Law Lords passed negative judgement on the use being made of section 23 of the 2001 Anti-terrorism, Crime and Security Act legislation which provided for the indefinite detention without trial of foreign terror suspects. Detention was authorised by the Home Secretary and those subject to this process were not allowed to see the evidence on which this decision by a member of the executive branch of government was based. Those detained were able to challenge their detention before the Special Immigration Appeals Commission at which the detainees are represented by Special Advocates who receive security clearance. Much of the evidence is heard by a panel of judges sitting in secret.

This power had been used to detain a number of Muslims who had been certified as 'suspected international terrorists'. The Law Lords argued that Britain's opt out of Article 5 of the European Convention on Human Rights constituted interference with liberty and equality that was disproportionate to the threat posed by terrorists to the nation. As these powers applied only to foreign nationals, they were further branded as discriminatory. Thus the government's actions were in contravention of the European Convention on Human Rights since they denied to those detained the ancient liberty of freedom from arbitrary arrest and detention.

This did not lead to the automatic release of those detained. The 2001 legislation was due to lapse in March 2005 which presented ministers with the opportunity to introduce modifications to address the concerns raised by the Law Lords. Their response to this ruling was to introduce the 2005 Prevention of Terrorism Act which substituted indefinite detention with time-limited 'control orders' (which consisted of house arrest and could be applied to both British subjects and foreign nationals who were reasonably suspected of involvement in terrorism). These new orders required a derogation from the European Convention on Human Rights and would be obtained by the Home Secretary on application to a High Court judge. Lower-level control orders (entailing lesser restrictions on civil liberties such as electronic tagging and curfews) which did not require derogation could be imposed by the

Home Secretary, subject to confirmation by a High Court judge within a period of seven days. In making this decision, the Home Secretary, Charles Clarke, rejected measures (such as the use of intercept evidence in court) that would enable suspected terrorists to be brought to trial.

However, those subject to detention could apply to the European Court of Human Rights if they perceived the government was acting too slowly in announcing the steps they intended to take in this matter.

> Using examples of your own taken from newspapers and journals, consider the extent to which the 1998 Human Rights Act has enhanced the power of the judiciary.

The control and accountability of the judiciary

Although the relative weakness of formal mechanisms of accountability has, to some extent, been ameliorated by the role of the media that scrutinises the actions of judges and may exert influence over the way they act, judges have traditionally enjoyed considerable freedom of action. There have, however, been changes proposed to this situation that include the introduction of an Office for Judicial Complaints in April 2006 (to investigate complaints about judges' personal conduct).

This section assesses two important dimensions underpinning judicial independence – their security of tenure and their relative immunity from sanctions relating to poor standards of professional performance in office.

Judges and security of tenure

The ability of judges to exercise independent judgement and resist pressures that may be applied to them by the executive branch of government is underpinned by the security of tenure that they enjoy. Judges remain in office until they reach retirement age, which for the majority of them is 70 as stipulated by the 1993 Judicial Pensions and Retirement Act. The Lord Chancellor may, however, authorise a judge below the level of the High Court bench to remain in office for a period of up to one year more, which can be renewed until the judge reaches the age of 75.

Once judges are appointed it is very hard to remove them. The conduct of lower-level judicial appointees (including circuit judges, district judges and recorders) is subject to supervision by the Lord Chancellor who may reprimand, suspend or dismiss them. In practice, the removal of a judge is exercised jointly with the Lord Chief Justice and will follow an investigation conducted by a judge nominated by the Lord Chief Justice. However, since the passage of the Act of Settlement in 1701, the senior judiciary (consisting of High Court judges, the Lord Justices of Appeal and the Lords of Appeal in Ordinary) may only be removed by an Address to the Monarch, passed by both Houses of Parliament. This makes it virtually impossible for a senior member of the judiciary to be dismissed, although criticisms voiced by colleagues may induce resignation. This is a rare occurrence, and has taken place only twice since 1960. The most recent example occurred in 1998 when Justice Jeremiah LeRoy Harman resigned as a High Court judge following criticism of his conduct by the Court of Appeal.

Discipline

Although it is important in a liberal democracy that judges should exercise a considerable degree of independence (in particular from government), this situation poses problems, in particular regarding the treatment of errors committed by members of the judiciary. For example, judges may make mistakes during the conduct of a trial or pass a sentence that is overly lenient or unduly severe. Although it is almost inevitable that every judge will at some time or other in his or her career make decisions which others feel to be unjust, there is no formal mechanism to respond to the behaviour of the very small minority of judges who constantly make mistakes (in the sense that their decisions are frequently overturned on appeal). This issue was discussed by the reporter Mark Eaton in a Channel Four programme, *Judges in the Dock*, screened on 18 December 2003.

The existing procedure to deal with judicial errors is to refer the matter to the Court of Appeal. In some instances reference to the Court of Appeal may be invoked by the Attorney General (where the issue concerns a lenient sentence) and in other cases by the defending counsel involved in a particular case who feel that their client was treated unfairly. But this course of action (which is extremely costly in financial terms) is only possible if there is a good legal reason to justify it. This means that this court hears only those cases that constitute the worst judicial errors. The Court of Appeal possesses several powers including the ability to quash a verdict, order a new trial or increase a sentence. They may also order the immediate arrest and imprisonment of a person pending a new trial.

If an appeal is successful, the Appeal Court will communicate with the judge whose decision has been overturned or amended and inform him or her of the reasons for this. But there is no supervisory process whereby judicial errors are monitored with a view to advising or disciplining judges whose actions are frequently the subject of successful appeals. Those who have suffered as the result of judicial errors cannot sue the errant judge, and the absence of any effective monitoring process means that no judge has ever been sacked for incompetence. It is in this sense that it might be argued that judges wield power without responsibility.

One reform to address this situation is to establish a formal and transparent system of professional discipline for judges. It would have been possible to give the Judicial Appointments Commission the power to monitor the actions of judges and, as an ultimate sanction, to dismiss those who make frequent mistakes. But this role was not made part of this body's functions. Judges are fiercely opposed to any measure that would erode their freedom, believing that injustices would occur if their actions are subject to constant outside vetting procedures.

Conclusion

This chapter has examined a number of issues related to the judiciary and the judicial system. It has examined the structure of the courts and the work that they perform within the judicial process. It has discussed the structure of the legal profession and has considered the relationship between the judiciary and the state. It has particularly addressed the way in which judges are appointed, arguing that the traditional method (in which the opinions of existing judges carried considerable weight) was a key explanation for the socially unrepresentative nature of the judiciary and has examined proposals that have been suggested to remedy this deficiency. The chapter also examined the work carried out by judges in interpreting the law, arguing that on occasions this transforms judges into law-makers. The impact of the 1998 Human Rights Act on the operations and power of judges was evaluated and the chapter also considered the extent to which judges are adequately accountable for their actions, in particular when they make errors of judgement.

A major role of judges is to deliver the response of the state to those who have committed serious crime. The following chapter develops this theme by examining the diverse aims of punishment and discussing the rationale for changes that have been made to the nature of punishment.

Further reading

There are many specialist texts that will provide an in-depth examination of the issues discussed in this chapter. These include:

Griffith, J. (1991) *The Politics of the Judiciary*, 4th edn. London: Fontana.

Sanders, A. (2001) *Community Justice: Modernising the Magistracy in England and Wales*, London: Central Books.

Woodhouse, D. (1998) 'The Judiciary in the 1990s: Guardians of the Welfare State', *Policy and Politics*, Volume 48 (3): 457–470.

Zander, M. (1994), *The Law Making Process*, 4th edn. London: Butterworths.

Key events

- **1833** Enactment of the Judicial Committee Act. This legislation established the Judicial Committee of the Privy Council.
- **1907** Enactment of the Criminal Appeal Act. This Act established the Court of Criminal Appeal to hear appeals from lower level criminal and civil courts. It was renamed the Court of Appeal in 1966.
- **1971** Enactment of the Courts Act. This measure established crown courts to try serious criminal cases, replacing the jurisdiction previously exercised by crown courts in London, Manchester and Liverpool and by Assize and Quarter Sessions courts elsewhere.
- **1977** Publication of the first edition of *The Politics of the Judiciary*, written by John Griffith. This thought-provoking account of the workings of the judiciary is now in its fifth edition, the most recent being published in 1997.
- **1998** Enactment of the Human Rights Act. This measure incorporated the 1950 European Convention on Human Rights and Fundamental Freedoms into UK law, thus giving domestic courts jurisdiction over claims by UK citizens that their rights had been flouted. The measure did not come into force until October 2000.
- **2001** Establishment of the Commission for Judicial Appointments. This body was set up to oversee the appointment procedure for judges and Queen's Counsel and to investigate complaints regarding this process.
- **2003** Enactment of the Courts Act. This measure set up Her Majesty's Courts Service to provide for a unified administration of magistrates' and other courts.
- **2004** Appointment of the first female Law Lord, Brenda Hale.
- **2005** Enactment of the Constitutional Reform Act. This legislation made important changes to the office of Lord Chancellor (who would no longer sit as a judge or be head of the judiciary), set up a Supreme Court to replace the judicial functions of the House of Lords and created the Judicial Appointments Commission for England and Wales to remove the selection of judges from the Lord Chancellor, thereby making the appointments process more transparent.

References

Auld, Rt Hon. Lord Justice (2001) *Review of the Criminal Courts of England and Wales.* London: TSO.

Campbell, Sir C. (2004) Quoted in *Guardian*, 7 October.

Commission for Judicial Appointments (2002) *Annual Report, 2002.* London: Commission for Judicial Appointments.

Commission for Judicial Appointments (2003) *Annual Report, 2002–3.* London: Commission for Judicial Appointments.

Commission for Judicial Appointments (2004) *Her Majesty's Commissioners for Judicial Appointments: Report of the Commissioners' Review of the High Court 2003 Competition.* London: Commission for Judicial Appointments, Commissioners' Report to the Lord Chancellor.

Department for Constitutional Affairs (2003a) *Constitutional Reform: A New Way of Appointing Judges*, Consultation Paper. London: Department for Constitutional Affairs.

Department for Constitutional Affairs (2003b) *Constitutional Reform: A Supreme Court for the United Kingdom. A Consultation Paper Prepared by the Department for Constitutional Affairs*, Consultation Paper CP 11/03. London: Department for Constitutional Affairs.

Department for Constitutional Affairs (2004) *Diversity in the Judiciary*, Consultation Paper. London: Department for Constitutional Affairs.

Department for Constitutional Affairs (2005) *The Future of the Legal Services: Putting the Consumer First*, Cm 6679. London: Department for Constitutional Affairs.

Devlin, Lord (1976) 'Judges and Lawmakers', *Modern Law Review*, 39 (1): 1–16.

Devlin, Lord (1979) *The Judge*. Oxford: Oxford University Press.

Dyer, C. (1998) 'Analysis: Law Lords', *Guardian*, 5 August.

Dyer, C. (1999) 'Lord Chancellor Kills Hope of Judicial Jobs Reform', *Guardian*, 26 July.

Dyer, C. (2005) 'Top Judges Clash over Plan for More Diverse Judiciary', *Guardian*, 14 July.

Falconer, Lord of Thoroton (2003) 'Foreword', *Constitutional Reform: A New Way of Appointing Judges*, Consultation Paper. London: Department for Constitutional Affairs.

Falconer, Lord of Thoroton (2005) Speech to the Woman Lawyer Forum, London, 5 March, quoted in *Guardian*, 5 March.

Garnier, E. (2004) 'He Champions the Independence of the Entire Justice System', *Guardian*, 20 July.

Griffith, J. (1991) *The Politics of the Judiciary*, 4th edn. London: Fontana.

Home Affairs Committee (1996) *Judicial Appointments Procedures*, Third Report, Session 1995–1996, House of Commons Paper 52-1.

Home Office (1981) *The Brixton Disorders, 10–12 April 1981: Report of an Inquiry by the Rt. Hon. The Lord Scarman, OBE*, Cmnd 8427 [The Scarman Report]. London: HMSO.

Home Secretary, Lord Chancellor and Attorney General (2002) *Justice For All*, Cm 5563. London: TSO.

Irvine, Lord (1999) Speech at Edinburgh, 5 July.

Joint Working Party (1999) *Equal Opportunities in Judicial Appointments and Silk*. London: Joint Working Party, Report to the Lord Chancellor.

Jowell, J. (2004) 'It's A Beast of Many Heads', *Guardian*, 20 July.

Judges' Council (1995) 'Evidence to the Home Affairs Committee', quoted in *Guardian*, 26 January.

Justice (1999) *Evidence of a Working Party of Justice to the Royal Commission on the Reform of the House of Lords*. London: Justice.

Labour Research (1999) 'Judging Labour on the Judges', *Labour Research*, 88 (6): 13–14.

Lord Chancellor's Department (1996) Memorandum from the Lord Chancellor's Department to the Home Affairs Committee, cited in Home Affairs Committee (1996) *Judicial Appointments*, Third Report, Session 1995–1996. London: House of Commons Paper 52.

Luce, T. (2003) *Death Certification and Investigation in England, Wales and Northern Ireland – The Report of a Fundamental Review 2003*, Home Office Review Team Report. London: TSO.

Mackay, Lord of Clashfern (1990) Speech at the Inner Temple Hall, London, 6 November, quoted in *The Times*, 7 November.

Mackay, Lord (1993) Statement, October, quoted in Sir L. Peach (1999) *Judicial Appointments and Queen's Counsel Selection Report: Main Report*. London: TSO.

Office for Criminal Justice Reform (2004) *Cutting Crime, Delivering Justice: A Strategic Plan for Criminal Justice 2004–08*, Cm 6288. London: TSO.

Peach, Sir L. (1999) *An Independent Scrutiny of the Appointment Processes of Judges and Queen's Counsel in England and Wales*. London: Lord Chancellor's Department.

Reeve, P. (1998) *Silk Cut*. London: Adam Smith Institute.

Reid, Lord (1972) 'The Judge as Lawmaker', *Journal of the Society of Public Teachers of Law*, 12 (22): 22–9.

Roshier, B. and Teff, H. (1980) *Law and Society in England*. London: Tavistock Publications.

Sanders, A. (2001) *Community Justice: Modernising the Magistracy in England and Wales*. London: Central Books.

Utting, D. and Vennard, J. (2000) *What Works with Young Offenders in the Community?* London: Barnardo's.

Woodhouse, D. (1995) 'Politicians and the Judiciary: A Changing Relationship', *Parliamentary Affairs*, 48 (3): 401–17.

Woodhouse, D. (1998) 'The Judiciary in the 1990s: Guardians of the Welfare State', *Policy and Politics*, 48 (3): 457–70.

Woolf, Lord (205) Quoted in *Guardian*, 14 July.

Zander, M. (1994) *The Law Making Process,* 4th edn. London: Butterworths.

7 The aims and rationale of punishment

S ociety may respond to transgressions of the law in various ways. These are associated with diverse objectives, as was made clear in the 2003 Criminal Justice Act which stated that the purpose of sentencing by the courts was to punish offenders, reduce crime (including by deterrence), bringing about the reform and rehabilitation of offenders, protecting the public and providing for offenders to make reparations to those affected by their actions. This chapter examines the way in which the state responds to crime. Specifically the chapter:

- discusses the concept of punishment;
- examines diverse views concerning the purpose of punishment;
- analyses the strengths and weaknesses of restorative justice as a response to crime;
- considers sociological approaches to the study of punishment;
- discusses postwar sentencing trends.

Punishment

The term 'punishment' is capable of several definitions: it has been referred to as 'crime-handling' (Fatić, 1995) and is often used synonomously with 'sentencing' (Daly, 2000), although its meaning is often restricted to measures which are unpleasant and intended to inflict pain on an offender (Christie, 1982) in response to an offence that he or she has committed. In this latter context it has been defined as 'the deliberate use of public power to inflict pain on offenders' (Andrews, 2003: 128). It has further been suggested that the pain that is inflicted should be an essential part of what is intended rather than being an unintended consequence arising from the state's intervention (Benn and Peters, 1959). However, the infliction of pain is not universally accepted as a goal of punishment. Others prefer the use of the term 'sanction' 'as the general term for any measure which is imposed as a response to crime, with adjectives distinguishing the various kinds of sanction according to their primary purpose' – punitive sanctions, rehabilitative sanctions, punitive/rehabilitative sanctions (which are ambivalent about their aims), reparative sanctions and sanctions designed to protect the public through containment (Wright, 2003: 6–7).

The scientific study of punishment is known as penology which seeks to provide an understanding of the issues that underlie penal strategies. There are a number of perspectives from which punishment can be studied and these are briefly outlined in the following section of this chapter.

The aims of punishment

Strategies that are based upon what is termed the 'juridical perspective' (Hudson, 2003:15) are rooted in moral and political philosophy. They have a practical application in that they seek to link punishment with a desired outcome – what purpose does society wish to achieve through punishment? There are a number of approaches associated with this perspective.

Utilitarian theories of punishment: reductivism

What are termed 'utilitarian perspectives' derive from the approach towards crime that Chapter 1 identified with classicist criminology whose key proponents included Cesare Beccaria and Jeremy Bentham. Utilitarians viewed punishment as 'a prima facie evil that has to be justified by its compensating good effects in terms of human happiness or satisfaction' (Lacey, 2003: 176). A key concern of these political-moral philosophers was how to prevent criminal actions from occurring in society. They were reductivists in that their outlook was fixed on the future and not the past. Reductivism may be carried out by a wide range of strategies including deterrence and incapacitation (which entails depriving an offender of his or her liberty), or programmes that seek to secure the rehabilitation of offenders.

However, a particular problem with all reductivist strategies is whether behaviour can be altered through punishment, whatever form it takes. This is because while punishment may temporarily suppress anti-social behaviour, once the punishment is removed the previous behaviour may return (Huesmann and Podolski, 2003: 77). Accordingly, it is also necessary to identify and remove the factors which underpin that behaviour in order to prevent future offending: 'people must "internalise" mechanisms that regulate behaviour so that in the absence of the threat of punishment, they will choose not to act aggressively – not because of the threat of punishment, but because they agree with the behaviour which has been taught' (Huesmann and Podolski, 2003: 78). The problems inherent in seeking to change behaviour through punishment have led many who advocate restorative justice (an issue which is discussed more fully later in this chapter) to disassociate this response to crime with punishment.

Jeremy Bentham and the panopticon

As has been argued in Chapter 1, Jeremy Bentham was an important influence in the development of classicist criminology in Great Britain. One of his concerns was to use prisons to bring about the reform of inmates thus transforming them into useful members of society.

In 1791 he wrote a three-volume work, *The Panopticon*, in which he devised a blueprint for the design of prisons in order for them to be able to bring about the transformation of the behaviour of offenders. Central to his idea was the principle of surveillance whereby an observer was able to monitor prisoners without them being aware when they were being watched. This 'invisible omniscience' secured the constant conformity of inmates since they were unable to discern when their actions were not being observed. It induced in inmates 'a state of conscious and permanent visibility that assures the automatic functioning of power'. Surveillance was thus 'permanent in its effects, even if it is discontinuous in its action' (Foucault, 1977).

To achieve this function, Bentham proposed that prisons should be designed with a central tower which housed the observers from which rows of single cells arranged in tiers and separate blocks would radiate. These cells would be isolated from each other. He promoted this design in Millbank Penitentiary (whose construction he personally directed and which was opened in 1821). Pentonville Prison (opened in 1842) was also influenced by this concept.

As is argued later in this chapter, Michel Foucault was heavily influenced by Bentham's ideas, especially in connection with the way in which power and knowledge were intertwined: he argued that the disciplinary surveillance of the prison created knowledge of the convict's body thus creating a new kind of power (Foucault, 1977: 27).

Deterrence

Deterrence may be individual or general. Individual deterrence seeks to influence the future behaviour of a single convicted offender whereas general deterrence seeks to influence the future actions of the public at large. Deterrence views offenders as rational beings who calculate the costs and benefits of their behaviour and both approaches also assume that a consensus exists within society as to what constitutes punishment (Fleisher, 2003: 101). A major problem with this approach is that deterrence ignores the possibility that crime may be a spontaneous act, propelled by factors that override logical considerations.

Individual deterrence may be delivered in a variety of ways. These include indeterminate custodial sentences (whereby evidence of changed behaviour will be required before release is granted) or the imposition of severe custodial conditions on an offender which are designed to encourage him or her to refrain from future offending behaviour to avoid a further, and perhaps more severe and/or lengthier, repetition of these unpleasant circumstances.

General deterrence has a broader remit, that of influencing the behaviour of those who might be tempted to commit crime. The approach adopted may entail severe penalties (which in the United Kingdom historically included the death penalty) based on the assumption that it would be illogical for a person to commit an action attached to dire consequences. The logic of this approach is that tougher sentences will reduce the level of crime in society. One difficulty with this approach is that it assumes the behaviour of all members of the general public can be influenced by similar constraints and that it is possible to precisely identify what level of punishment will prevent a criminal act from being committed.

Incapacitation

Incapacitation places potential victims of crime at the forefront of its concern. It seeks to protect society from the actions of criminals by a range of strategies that include physically removing them from society (a goal that was historically implemented through transportation but which is now associated with imprisonment). Incapacitation may also involve various forms of pre-emptive action. This may be directed against those who have already offended with the aim of placing additional restrictions on the ability of the criminal to engage in further criminal actions (for example by increasing the length of sentences meted out to prolific offenders) or it may target those deemed likely to be offenders, even if this behaviour has not manifested itself when the intervention occurred. This latter approach has been associated with attempts to isolate factors that predispose individuals to commit crime and then to implement remedial action.

Reform and rehabilitation

Punishment may be inflicted on those convicted of crime with a view to changing their personal values and habits so that their future behaviour conforms to mainstream social standards. Penal reformers in the late eighteenth and early nineteenth centuries (whether driven by evangelical or utilitarian impulses) viewed prisons as an arena in which bad people could be transformed into good and useful members of society. Contemporary prisons remain charged with bringing about the reform and rehabilitation of inmates but, as Chapter 8 argues, there are several factors affecting the prison environment that serve to undermine this ideal. Reform and rehabilitation may also be attempted through programmes directed at tackling offending behaviour, which are often delivered in prison. A difficulty with this approach is the effectiveness of the programmes that are delivered. More coercive approaches entail interventions that are designed to make it impossible for convicted criminals to repeat their offending behaviour. This goal may be attained by interventions such as aversion therapy or drug treatment.

Retributivism

The various strategies associated with reductivism focus their concern on future behaviour. Punishment is justified because it may persuade a person or persons not to subsequently indulge in criminal actions. An alternative approach, retributivism, is backward-looking, in which punishment is justified in relation to offending behaviour which has already taken place.

Retributivism insists 'that punishment is justified solely by the offender's desert and blameworthiness in committing the offence' (Lacey, 2003: 176). Expressed simply, criminals are punished because they deserve it. This approach to punishment is akin to vengeance since pain is inflicted on transgressors for pain's sake rather than from a desire to bring about their rehabilitation (Lacey, 2003: 176): it enables society to 'get its own back' on those who commit criminal acts. A difficulty with this approach is that the deliberate infliction of violence by the state may legitimise the use of violence by its citizens, and there is also the problem of what has been termed 'collateral damage', whereby punitive sanctions of this nature have an adverse effect on the offender's family (Wright, 2003: 17).

In addition to exacting revenge, retributivists put forward other reasons to justify punishment. This approach is underpinned by arguments, based on classicist criminology which is discussed in Chapter 1, that crime will be deterred if the pain which is inflicted upon a transgressor will outweigh any possible reward which that person may secure by committing the offence. It may be alternatively argued that punitive responses to crime have a symbolic role, seeking to emphasise that society views crime as unacceptable. Punishment thus constitutes a public censure or denunciation of this form of behaviour (Duff, 1986), an aim of punishment that is considered in more detail below.

Punishment may further be used as a mechanism to take away from criminals the unfair advantages they have derived over other members of society as a consequence of their illicit activity. Punishment thus seeks to restore the 'balance of advantage and disadvantage disturbed by crime' (Hudson, 2003: 48), thereby restoring the principles of fairness and equality of treatment that underpin citizens' political obligation to the society in which they live (Rawls, 1972). Although this aim of punishment has been criticised for ignoring the extent to which society is characterised by inequalities, the objective of removing unfair advantages derived from crime has underpinned some legislation. For example, in the United Kingdom, the 2002 Proceeds of Crime Act established the Assets Recovery Agency to investigate and recover criminal assets and also provided for a civil recovery scheme to facilitate the recovery of proceeds of unlawful conduct if a criminal prosecution was not initiated. The perspective that punishment serves to uphold the core values which hold society together has been further developed into the view of punishment as an expression of the rational will of citizens who, by entering into a social contract, expect that those who violate the rules of society should be punished (Rawls, 1972).

New retributism

Many societies have based their response to crime on the principle of retributivism. The *lex talionis* was referred to in the Bible whereby the response to crime was of an equivalent nature to the crime itself ('an eye for an eye and a tooth for a tooth'). Other retributive penal systems were based upon a proportionate response to crime, in which the punishment reflected the seriousness of the crime (as this was perceived by either society or the victim). However, the association of retribution with vengeance made this response to crime an unpopular one for much of the twentieth century in Western societies. It became resurrected because problems were perceived in the sentencing policies associated with the reductivist goal of rehabilitation that were fashionable in a number of postwar Western societies. Left-wing critics of rehabilitation argued that the discretion accorded to sentencers (who could, for example, mete out indeterminate sentences) could be abused or used in a discriminatory fashion. Those on the right were concerned that the desire to achieve an offender's rehabilitation resulted in the use of non-custodial alternatives to imprisonment that they viewed as being too soft on crime (Hudson, 2003: 39–43). Accordingly, what has been termed a 'new retributivism' (Hudson, 2003: 40) emerged in America during the 1970s. The report of the Committee for the Study of Incarceration (Von Hirsch, 1976) was an important statement of the new penal philosophy.

The key features of new retribuvitism were:

- *Focus on the offence an offender had committed.* His or her circumstances were judged irrelevant to the sentence that was dispensed
- *The response to crime should be proportionate to the seriousness of the offence.* Since this could be regarded as subjective, 'seriousness' was often defined by devising guidelines which stipulated the appropriate response to specific types of crime. These guidelines further served to reduce the discretion possessed by sentencers
- *Punishment was the main aim of the penal system.* All disposals (whether custodial or community-based) were to reflect this objective.

Reductivism and retributivism may be united in what is referred to as a 'mixed' theory of punishment, one which argues that 'people should be punished because punishment has good social effects, but that only those who deserve it should be liable to punishment' (Lacey, 2003: 176).

> Distinguish between reductivist and retributivist approaches to punishment. Which do you regard as the most appropriate response to criminal behaviour?

Denunciation

Denunciation places the concerns of the community at the forefront of the state's response to crime. The punishment meted out to an offender reflects the seriousness with which the community views the offence and provides it with a mechanism through which it can express its sentiments thereby reinforcing the official disapproval of the act that has been committed with the community's social censure. In the words of Lord Denning, 'the ultimate justification of punishment is not that it is a deterrent, but that it is the emphatic denunciation by the community of a crime' (Lord Denning, quoted in Cavadino and Dignan, 1992: 41). This implies that punishment is justified not because it influences the behaviour of others not to commit similar acts but simply because it expresses society's abhorrence of crime, an approach that is termed 'expressive denunication' (Cavadino and Dignan, 1992: 42). This argument has been presented with specific reference to prisons where it has been contested that 'the separation of prisoners from the rest of society represents a clear statement that physical and social exclusion is the price of nonconformity' (Matthews, 1999: 26).

It is often the case, however, that public sentiments regarding how a particular crime should be dealt with are out of line with the views of officials, in particular with politicians (who make the law) and sentencers (who implement it). However, the ability of the public to air their concerns (for example on what they regard as an over-lenient sentence to a specific crime) may encourage public debate that helps to set the boundaries of society – 'we collectively define what sort of people we are by denouncing the type of people we are not' (Davies, 1993: 15).

Although the ability of citizens to air their views on any aspect of public policy might be seen as the hallmark of a liberal democratic political system, there are dangers that may arise if the official response to a crime fails to match the public's level of denunciation of it. This may fuel direct action in the form of vigilantism that at its worst may degenerate into mob rule and lawlessness. An example of this occurred in connection with the campaign by the *News of the World* newspaper directed against paedophiles in 2000 which resulted in acts of violence against those who were suspected (in some cases erroneously) of involvement in crimes of this nature.

Restorative justice

Restorative justice can be seen as a further practical measure which society might adopt as a response to crime, but it has the potential to develop into a penal strategy which might either replace or supplement existing penal objectives that have been described above (Hudson, 2003: 92). This new principle views the reintegration of offenders as the key rationale underpinning society's response to crime.

It has been argued (Hudson, 2003: 75–6) that restorative justice is underpinned by a number of impulses. These include the abolitionist tradition which sought to move away from an agenda driven by crime and punishment towards an approach that emphasised harm and redress, those who wished to ensure that the needs and sufferings of victims of crime were placed at the forefront of the response to crime, and minority (or 'first nation') groups who sought to retain their own values and traditions of criminal justice in the face of prosecution and sentencing processes which they felt acted in a discriminatory fashion towards them.

Restorative justice has been defined as consisting of 'values, aims and processes that have as their common factor attempts to repair the harm caused by criminal behaviour' (Young and Hoyle, 2003: 200). This approach entails a wide range of activities. Initially it was 'virtually synonomous with a specific model of practice called Victim–Offender Reconciliation Program (VORP) or Victim–Offender Mediation (VOM)' (Roberts, 2004: 241). VOM entailed a one-to-one mediation meeting facilitated by a neutral mediator and the term 'restorative justice' initially referred to the values and principles underpinning VOM (Roberts, 2004: 241).

Latterly, however, restorative justice has been identified with other models, including community mediation and conferencing. Conferencing was first developed in New Zealand under legislation enacted in 1989 and was subsequently developed in Australia, North America and Europe. It takes several forms – family group conferencing, community group conferencing and peace-making circles (McCold, 2003: 72–3). A particularly important role is performed by the facilitator, who should have no personal agenda in the questions they ask or who they invite to participate (Young and Hoyle, 2003: 211). The principle of restorative dialogue is at the heart of conferencing (Roberts, 2004: 245). This is an umbrella term that 'refers to a process that brings people together in dialogue to gain understanding and repair the harm caused by a crime or conflict' (Roberts, 2004: 251). A number of terms are associated with restorative justice, including 'positive justice', 'reintegrative justice', 'relational justice', 'reparative justice' and 'restitutive justice'. They are linked by the objective of seeking to 'build peace' rather than to 'fight crime' (Wright, 2003: 21).

Restorative justice was not entirely novel in Britain. It takes an approach that bears many similarities to the system of Children's Hearings utilised in Scotland that adopts a welfare-based stance focusing on future action rather than the determination of guilt of innocence (Muncie, 2002: 153). This approach also formed the basis of a number of community-based, dispute-orientated schemes. These included the four victim–offender mediation schemes that were piloted by the Home Office in 1985 but failed to produce changes in penal policy. Restorative cautioning was introduced by the Thames Valley Police Force in 1995, and victim–offender conferences for offenders aged 10–17 who pleaded guilty to an offence had been piloted in Lambeth and Hackney.

It is underpinned by a number of key principles which are discussed below.

Rejects retributive objectives

The main aim of punishment is to censure wrongful behaviour. As is argued in Chapter 6 the criminal justice process in the United Kingdom was traditionally founded on retributive principles. This meant that the sentencer deliberately intended to inflict pain on the offender. It has been argued that restorative justice is a 'more effective and more ethical way to censure behaviour' (Walgrave: 2004: 47). Although various aspects of the process of restorative justice may cause pain to the offender (such as meeting with the victim of crime and having to perform agreed tasks to make good the wrong done), this is not intentionally inflicted on him or her. Instead restorative justice emphasises why bad behaviour is being censured by focusing on the harm that a criminal act has inflicted on another member of the community (Walgrave, 2004: 55). It seeks to replace the values of vindictiveness and vengeance which underpin criminal justice interventions (values which may legitimise the use of violence by criminals) with those of healing and conciliation (Braithwaite and Strang, 2001: 1–2).

Takes the state out of sentencing

Restorative justice provides a mechanism whereby communities can sort out their own problems arising from the criminal behaviour of some of its members. Although the state may still have important roles to play in restorative justice by acting as an enabler (in the sense of providing a legal framework for the process), a resource provider, an implementer and a guarantor of quality practice (Jantzi, 2004: 190), the way in which offenders make amends for their actions is not determined by professional sentencers but is instead community-orientated to secure the interaction of victims, offenders and other participants to a conferencing process (Johnstone, 2004: 6). The purpose of intervention is to 'ensure that the community's adopted values are taken seriously by expressing and symbolising, unambiguously, those defining values' (Lacey, 2003: 187).

This approach views humans as fundamentally cooperative beings as opposed to individualistic beings in need of coercive forms of social control to suppress their innate warlike and competitive nature (Napoleon, 2004: 34). It places social cooperation at the heart of the definition of justice, regarding it as 'a system of social cooperation that supports and encourages peaceful coexistence' (Sharpe, 2004: 22). Social cooperation is achieved through social contracts – 'an implicit agreement about how we will treat each other and what we can expect from each other under certain circumstances' (Sharpe, 2004: 31). It is argued that those most affected by a violation of a social contract are the most appropriate persons to determine how to renegotiate them in order to restore justice between them (Sharpe, 2004: 24).

Although community-based interventions frequently form an aspect of the criminal justice process, activities such as mediation may operate outside of the formal criminal justice system, providing a mode of informal justice and thereby avoiding the danger of 'net widening and increasing state intrusion' (Marsh, 1988: 176).

Empowerment

It has been argued that traditional forms of justice have the effect of disempowering those who are most affected by an offence, transforming victims and offenders into 'idle bystanders in what, after all, is *their* conflict' (Barton, 2003: 26–7), whereas approaches associated with restorative justice such as family group conferencing seek to empower the primary stakeholders in a conflict – the victim, offender and their respective circles of social support, influence and care such as family, friends, peers and colleagues – so that they can 'address the causes and the consequences of the occasioning incident in ways that are meaningful and right for them' (Barton, 2003: viii and 15). This process also accords with republican theory (Braithwaite, 1995) that seeks to promote participatory democracy by fostering civil society's active participation in justice-related affairs (Strang and Braithwaite, 2001).

Victim involvement

Restorative justice intimately involves the victim of crime in the post-crime process, thereby elevating the victim to the position of being a stakeholder in the criminal justice process rather than being confined to the sidelines (Achilles, 2004: 65). In this way, the needs of the victim are placed at the very heart of the criminal justice process (Blunkett, 2003: 4). The involvement of the victim is designed to induce the offender to empathise with the victim (Wright, 2003: 9). It emphasises to the offender that crime is a violation of people and interpersonal relations (Achilles, 2004: 66) and does not permit him or her to neutralise their actions as infractions of an abstract ethical or legal code (Walgrave, 2004: 55). It is in this sense that restorative justice promotes a new understanding of crime as behaviour that causes tangible harm to real people and relationships (Johnstone, 2004: 8) rather than it being viewed as an impersonal infraction of the law.

Offender participation

Restorative justice does not marginalise the offender who is accepted as a key contributor to the decision-making process (Hudson et al., 1996). The role given to the offender is an active one – he or she has to make an active contribution to putting wrong to rights by accepting responsibility for their actions and agreeing to undertake measures to repair the negative consequences of the offence (Braithwaite and Roche, 2001). By contrast, retributive justice relegates the offender to the role of a passive recipient of a sentence handed out by a magistrate or judge.

Dialogue

It has been argued above that dialogue in the sense of 'a face-to-face encounter between the principal stakeholders' (Barton, 2003: 4) is a crucial underpinning of restorative justice. However, the adversarial system used in British courts does not promote dialogue between all parties to a crime, nor does it help offenders to repent for their actions (Walgrave, 2004: 50). It has been argued that the main weakness of the traditional criminal justice system is that it 'disempowers the primary stakeholders in the conflict' (Barton, 2003: 15) and that, by contrast, 'informal deliberative processes that include all parties with a stake in the aftermath of the crime' (Walgrave, 2004: 54) provides a more effective way to repair the harm caused by crime.

Effectiveness

The punitive response to crime fails to provide a greater level of security within society, does not provide relief for the victims of crime and fails to reintegrate offenders into society. By contrast, restorative justice 'appears to open ways of dealing with the aftermath of crime which is more satisfactory for victims, more constructive for communities, and more reintegrative for offenders' (Walgrave, 2003: ix). Arguments related to the effectiveness of restorative justice insist that punitive responses to crime give the victim only a short-lived sense of justice by inflicting pain on the offender. However, restorative justice has the potential for providing an enhanced sense of justice to the victim by ensuring that something positive is done by the offender to meet the needs of those who have been harmed by a crime (Johnstone, 2004: 9–10). Additionally, whereas the punitive response to crime is both costly and frequently fails to rehabilitate those who have broken the law (Wright, 2003: 4–5), the reintegrative aspects of restorative justice offer a better hope for reducing the level of recidivism since the approach is not socially destructive (Walgrave, 2004: 47).

There is evidence that approaches associated with restorative justice 'work'. The hurt experienced by victims may be ameliorated by their involvement in forums such as Youth Offender Panels (YOPs) (Crawford and Clear, 2003), and this approach may have a beneficial effect on rates of recidivism. An evaluation of YOPs in eleven pilot areas revealed that, overall, young people completed the contract successfully in 74 per cent of cases where a panel had met (Newburn et al., 2002: 30). Experiments conducted by the Thames Valley Police which commenced in 1994 with restorative (as opposed to traditional) cautioning initially pointed to a lower reoffending rate (Tendler, 1997), and it was later observed that around 25 per cent of offenders stated that they had either not reoffended or had reduced the scale of their offending behaviour (Hoyle et al., 2002). Findings of this nature induced the government to propose placing restorative cautioning on a statutory basis as an aspect of its restorative justice strategy (Home Office, 2003: 7). However, a subsequent study which compared the use of restorative cautioning by Thames Valley with two forces (Sussex and Warwickshire) which used the traditional caution and which also evaluated the use of different types of caution within Thames Valley concluded that 'there was no evidence to suggest that restorative cautioning had resulted in a statistically significant reduction in either the overall resanctioning rate (which consists of either a conviction or a police disposal such as a reprimand or final warning) or the frequency or seriousness of offending', although it was accepted that restorative cautioning had other benefits for both victims and offenders (Wilcox et al., 2004: ii and vi).

Research into family group conferencing in New Zealand also pointed to relatively high levels of reconviction. It was reported that 26 per cent of a sample of 14–16-year-olds who took part in Youth Justice Conferences were reconvicted within twelve months, 64 per cent were reconvicted after just over four years, and 24 per cent were persistently reconvicted over the same period (Maxwell and Morris, 1999). It was argued, however, that these 'disappointing' findings which 'fall short of legitimate expections' (Barton, 2003: 46–7) were mainly reflective of poorly organised conferences in which one or more of the main stakeholders felt 'silenced, marginalized or disempowered' (Barton, 2003: 30), and that family group conferences were effective in preventing reconviction provided that certain conditions (such as the offender feeling a sense of participation and not being stigmatically shamed or made to feel a bad person) were fulfilled (Maxwell and Morris, 1999). It has been further suggested that aspects of restorative justice such as family group conferences do not provide a similar experience for all young offenders and that factors which include the nature of the offence committed, how the young offender was treated in the family group conference, how young people interpreted and reacted to events in the conference and the history and backgrounds of the young offenders were all factors which affected the impact made by the conference on the offender's subsequent behaviour (Maxwell et al., 2003: 146–7).

Shaming

'Shame is the emotion a person feels when confronted with the fact that one's behaviour has been different to what one believes is morally required. Shame is moral self-reproach' (Crawford and Clear, 2003: 222). The importance of shaming to the process of restorative justice is contentious. Braithwaite (1989) emphasised the importance of reintegrative shaming to restorative justice. He asserted that countries such as Japan that shamed effectively had lower crime rates and drew attention to the manner whereby traditional conflict resolution in Maori communities in New Zealand placed great importance on ceremonies to communicate 'the shame of wrongdoing' (Braithwaite, 1993: 37). The process of shaming has been described as central to the reintegration of wrongdoers – 'reintegrative shaming means that expressions of community disapproval, which may range from a mild rebuke to degradation ceremonies (serious denunciations) are followed by gestures of reacceptance into the community of law-abiding citizens' (Braithwaite and Roche, 2001: 74). Shaming seeks to make those who have broken the law aware of the consequences of their crime, in particular to appreciate the denial of trust accorded to them by other members of their community (Fatic, 1995: 220). Offenders then become susceptible to undertaking measures designed to redress the harm their actions have caused.

However, others contend that shaming is not an essential aspect of restorative justice (Maxwell and Morris, 2004: 133). The problems posed by this approach are discussed in more detail below.

Repairing the harm

The aim of restorative justice is to enable those who have broken the law to be given the opportunity to make good the harm they have caused. Typically this will involve an agreement by the offender to make reparation to the victim or to the community.

Reintegration

The requirement of the offender to accept responsibility for his or her actions, apologise and make recompense to the victim is designed to help both parties put past events behind them, thereby facilitating the offender's reintegration into the community. The ethos of restorative justice is thus inclusionary, an alternative to the 'criminology of the other' in which offenders are viewed as a class distinct from the law-abiding and against whom the public needs to be protected (Young and Hoyle, 2003: 205).

A broad agenda

Restorative justice may require an approach which goes beyond events such as victim–offender mediation to embrace a wide range of measures to help repair the harm suffered by victims of crime (Bazemore and Walgrave, 1999: 48), and also to address social conditions which are conducive to crime.

Problems with restorative justice

There are, however, a number of difficulties with restorative justice. Some of the problems it poses are discussed below.

Public scepticism

There may be much popular support for punitive responses to crime, and restorative justice thus becomes viewed as a soft option, an alternative to punishment. However, there is also countervailing evidence which suggests that reparation to the victim or community are popular responses to crime (Wright, 2003: 12) and that, in the United Kingdom, 'a majority think that restorative sanctions ... make more sense than retributive ones' (Walker and Hough, 1988: 6). Additionally, some who advocate the merits of restorative justice suggest that this approach does not totally remove the use of punitive aspects of sentencing. Some argue that punitive responses to crime may be acceptable if restorative justice fails to work (Braithwaite, 1999) or provided that they constitute part of an overall sentencing package in which they are complemented 'with genuine caring, acceptance and reintegration of the person, as opposed to stigmatising, rejecting or crushing them' (Barton, 2003: 23). Others, however, disagree, and contend that retributive justice is 'fundamentally at odds with the defining values of restorative justice and cannot, therefore, be part of it' (Morris and Young, 1999).

The role of shaming

Shaming is often viewed as a key aspect of restorative justice. It has been observed, however, that cultural factors underpin the potential of shaming: it is easier to generate shame in group-orientated societies such as Japan rather than societies that are rooted in individualism, such as America (Benedict, 1946). Shaming has been described as a complex set of emotions (which include embarrassment, contempt, ridicule and humiliation) – there is no general theory of shame nor of the emotions which restorative justice seeks to invoke (Tomkins, 1987). Further, although shaming is designed to encourage a lawbreaker to avoid further offending behaviour, it does not necessarily have this consequence and may instead result in negative responses such as withdrawal or hostility. In this context, shaming has been described as the 'bedrock of much psychopathology' (Miller, 1996: 51). Although, in an attempt to avoid such negative reactions, those who advocate shaming as an aspect of reintegrative justice draw a distinction between stigmatic/disintegrative shaming (which arises when a person is stigmatised, demeaned and humiliated for what they have done) and reintegrative shaming (whereby a person's behaviour is condemned but their self-esteem and confidence is upheld) (Braithwaite, 1989: 4, 55 and 58), it cannot be guaranteed that those on the receiving end of the process will appreciate this distinction regarding the intention of their treatment and may instead view their experiences as punitive, in which pain is inflicted for pain's sake. To be effective, shame has to come from within an individual (Maxwell and Morris, 2004: 139). Some people do not accept that their behaviour has been wrong, and shame cannot be artificially induced by others.

Level of victim involvement

Although the involvement of victims is an important aspect of restorative justice, this is not consistently forthcoming. An evaluation of YOPs in eleven pilot sites revealed that the level of victim involvement was low, and 72 per cent of Community Panel Member (CPM) respondents reported that they had not sat on a panel with a victim present (Newburn et al., 2002: 78). Further, the feelings and needs of a victim of crime may take a long while to come to the surface (Achilles, 2004: 69) and there is the danger that decisions taken at a case conference close to the event will not, in the long run, prove adequate to those who have suffered from crime.

The nature of community involvement

Restorative justice developed as a community-based movement that was in direct opposition to the large-scale institutional way of conducting the affairs of the criminal justice process (Erbe, 2004: 289). It seeks to enable communities to take responsibility for responses to crime, but traditional communities (defined in terms of locality) are often absent in Westernised urban settings. Restorative justice could be used as a tactic to prevent crime by refashioning traditional communities (as did old-style community policing, an issue which is discussed in Chapter 3) but there arises the danger that what is (re)constructed is an oppressive social organisation in which the unequal division of power and resources results in displays of intolerance and prejudice (Crawford and Clear, 2003: 221), thus serving to promote the further exclusion of those who are already marginalised. This problem might be avoided if the reform agenda focused on the problems which contribute directly or indirectly towards crime (especially in high-crime communities) by seeking to improve the quality of community life, an approach which is associated with community justice (Crawford and Clear, 2003: 216) rather than restorative justice which 'cannot resolve deep structural injustices that cause problems' (Braithwaite, 1998: 329).

There is a further danger that the process can be detached from the community in particular by individuals who became involved in the process at an early stage and who became 'the de facto voice of their community efforts' (Erbe, 2004: 294). A key danger with this approach is that the involvement of these individuals may substitute for the active involvement of the community, thereby disengaging restorative justice from its local roots. It is important, therefore, that those who act on behalf of the community in this capacity are genuinely representative of it, but this is not a guaranteed outcome. An evaluation of the operations of YOPs in eleven pilot sites revealed that Community Panel Members were mainly white (91 per cent of the respondents), female (69 per cent), over 40 years of age (68 per cent) and employed in professional or managerial occupations (50 per cent). Nonetheless, 53 per cent of the respondents felt that CPMs represented the community 'reasonably well' (Newburn et al., 2002: 66 and 71).

The place of restorative justice in the criminal justice system

A key issue regarding restorative justice is whether this approach should be confined to the margins of the criminal justice system, being especially used in connection with juvenile offending, or whether it should become a mainstream response to crime (Johnstone, 2002: 15) in which the 'restoration of harm' becomes the core value of the criminal justice process (Willemsens, 2003: 25). In America restorative justice has been used in connection with serious crimes of violence and some experiments to apply restorative justice to more serious offences have also been conducted in England and Wales (Young and Hoyle, 2003: 210). Attempts have also been made to apply the principles of restorative justice more widely throughout the criminal justice system in England and Wales, thereby moving it from the margins towards the mainstream (Restorative Justice Consortium, 2000). The 2003 Criminal Justice Act introduced restorative justice as a component of the conditional caution (in which the offender agrees to the imposition of conditions on his or her behaviour), and pilots were initiated to test restorative justice as an alternative to prosecution for adults. It has also been suggested that this approach is successful in securing a more compliant approach to the law by companies (Young and Hoyle, 2003: 209).

> Evaluate the advantages and disadvantages of restorative justice as a response to crime.

The rationale of punishment – sociological perspectives

It has been argued above that approaches to punishment rooted in moral and legal philosophy focus on the practical aspects of punishment and seek to provide an understanding as to how various forms of state intervention seek to influence future behaviour. Sociological perspectives concentrate on the concept of punishment itself and seek to 'explore the relations between punishment and society, its purpose being to understand punishment as a social phenomenon and thus trace its role in social life' (Garland, 1990: 10). The focus of sociological perspectives is theoretical rather than practical, aiming to provide an understanding of the factors that underpin a coercive response to crime.

In attempting to provide an understanding of the role served by punishment, sociological perspectives analyse penal change and development (Hudson, 2003: 96), seeking to provide an understanding as to why the aims of punishment and the manner in which those aims are delivered is subject to wide variation both between countries and also within the same country through historical time. In Britain, for example, methods of punishment that included execution, transportation, various forms of corporal punishment and placing people in the stocks have passed out of favour and are no longer used. Sociological accounts of punishment seek to provide an understanding of the rationale of these changes by providing an understanding of what has been termed the 'penal temper of society' (Hudson, 2003: 96) that asserts the relationship between punishment and other aspects of social life and views changes to the forms of punishment as indicative of the changing nature of society. It is in this respect that it has been argued that styles and institutions of punishment should be studied as social constructions (Garland, 1990).

The following section briefly discusses a number of key developments affecting the sociology of punishment. It has been argued, however, that the sociology of punishment requires 'an analytical account of the cultural forces which influence punishment, and, in particular, an account of the patterns imposed upon punishment by the character of contemporary sensibilities' (Garland, 1990: 197). Leading social theories have been accused of providing a selective account of culture and it has been asserted that the historical development and present-day operation of penality require 'a pluralistic, multidimensional approach' that recognises punishment as a social institution conditioned by an array of social and historical forces (Garland, 1990: 280–3).

Durkheim and the sociology of punishment

Emile Durkheim (whose views on crime are briefly discussed in Chapter 1) played an important role in developing sociological approaches to the study of punishment. He focused on the key issue of how social order was maintained in societies, and asserted that it was based on consensual values and moralities. Crime was thus depicted as an act that was widely condemned throughout society because it conflicted with its core values. Punishment thus played a crucial role in securing social solidarity by providing a means whereby the conscience collective of that society (that is, 'the totality of beliefs and sentiments common to average members of society') (Cavadino and Dignan, 1992: 69–70) could be both expressed and regenerated (Garland, 1990: 23). The 'conscience collective' has been depicted as the 'foundation stone' of Durkheim's theory of punishment, being 'the ultimate source of the passionate reaction which motivates punishment' (Garland, 1990: 50). Crime was depicted as an attack on the 'conscious collective' of society that resulted in 'healthy consciences' uniting to reaffirm society's shared beliefs (Durkheim, 1893). Crime thus served to provoke 'a sense of outrage, anger, indignation, and a passionate desire for revenge' (Garland, 1990: 30). It has been argued that for Durkheim, 'punishment was primarily construed … as symbolic of group values and not as merely instrumental' (Valier, 2002: 29). However, he did not totally ignore the role which punishment might also play as a strategy to control crime.

Durkheim's view of punishment as the expression of moral outrage (Valier, 2002: 30) suggested that punishment reflected the nature of society's collective conscience at any one point in time. Changes to society's commonly held beliefs and values would be reflected in alterations to the mode of punishment. Durkheim held that punishment became less repressive in modern societies based on organic solidarity compared to traditional ones based on mechanical solidarity because the intensity of the conscience collective was based on consensual values that resulted in draconian measures being pursued against crime in primitive societies. However, it produced a more moderate reaction in advanced societies since its collective sentiments were characterised by moral diversity and the interdependence of cooperating individuals (Garland, 1990: 37). He argued that imprisonment became the main form of punishment in industrial societies, the leniency of which (compared to earlier reliance on capital or corporal punishment) reflected an increased degree of sympathy for the plight of the criminal (Durkheim, 1900).

Durkheim's views about punishment have been challenged on many fronts. His attempt to link forms of society to forms of punishment by arguing that punishments became more lenient as society developed from pre-industrial to industrial has been opposed by arguments that suggested advanced societies utilised more coercive forms as punishment as they had a greater capacity to adopt this course of action (Spitzer, 1979). It had further been argued that he tended to overstate the importance of repressive law in primitive societies and to understate its role in advanced ones (Garland, 1990: 48). His view that imprisonment became the main form of punishment in advanced capitalist societies has also been difficult to square with progressive leniency. Although his views on the existence of a collective conscience in society were not totally consistent, he ultimately argued that this constituted a crucial fact in any society that was conducive to maintaining social order (Durkheim, 1900). This view of punishment as a group phenomenon has been criticised for drawing heavily on primitive rather than advanced societies (Garland, 1990: 26), and has also been challenged for ignoring the power relationships within society whereby the law reflects the interests of the dominant group.

> Analyse the contribution made by Emile Durkheim to the evolution of the rationale of punishment.

Max Weber

Weber differentiated between the concepts of 'power' and 'authority' and concluded that these terms were distinguished by the notion of consent. An individual or organisation that possessed authority secured compliance to its demands because there was general agreement that those who put these ideas forward had the right to propose them – their exercise of leadership was widely viewed as legitimate. He further suggested that authority could be derived from one or other of three sources. These were traditional authority (whereby acceptance of the right to rule was based on custom), charismatic authority (in which the personal characteristics of a political leader determined the obedience of the public to his or her decisions) and legal-bureaucratic (or legal-rational authority). Weber believed that the latter was most appropriate to modern capitalist society characterised by the division of labour and the differentiation of tasks. In this case, public compliance to a leader's demands was accorded because of the office held by that individual (Weber, 1922) who governed according to formal rules and procedures.

Weber thus saw bureaucratic rationality as the key characteristic of an efficient, legitimately governed, modern state whereby 'judgements must be made according to rules; authority is vested in position-holders rather than in people themselves' (Hudson, 2003: 106). Bureaucracy was characterised by features that included 'impersonality, the inter-changeability of officials, routinization of procedure and a dependency on the existence of recorded information' (Cavadino and Dignan, 1992: 74). This was contrasted to the irrational means of social control that he contended were found in primitive societies. Rationality was thus seen as the hallmark of advanced societies and this characteristic was mirrored in its modes of punishment that were administered in a dispassionate, impartial and consistent manner by the professional functionaries of the central state. Aspects of the application of the principle of bureaucratic rationality in modern societies may be found in attempts to eliminate the discretion wielded by professionals in areas such as sentencing and in changes to the methods of punishment, which have been guided 'not so much by progress in humanitarianism as progress in bureaucratized rationalism, necessary to meet the social control needs and legitimacy conditions of modern society' (Hudson, 2003: 107). However, it has been argued that Weber overemphasised the extent to which rationalisation had succeeded in monopolising 'the realm of penality' (Garland, 1990: 189) and, like Durkheim, he has also been criticised for failing to devote attention to the manner in which power was wielded.

Marxist approaches to punishment

Marxist approaches to punishment are underpinned by their concept of the relations of production. This describes a social situation in which the means of production are owned by a few (the bourgeosie) and in which the many (the proletariat) sell their labour. This gives rise to a society that is fragmented into social classes whose interests are seen to inherently contradict, since in order to function capitalism requires that those who sell their labour should not be given its full value by those who own the means of production. Marxists contend that the unequal power relationships within society that derive from the relations of production are reflected in all its key institutions. These are not neutral but reflect the interests of the economically dominant class and exist to serve their key aim, that of self-preservation by maintaining the capitalist system of production. Penal policy is thus depicted as an aspect of a more general concern to regulate and control the activities of the poor.

Marxist penology places particular emphasis on the manner in which methods of punishment are fashioned by economic considerations. A key text in Marxist penology viewed punishment as determined by the mode of production whereby the way in which economic activity is organised and controlled shapes the rest of social life (Garland, 1990: 85). It was contended that changes affecting the mode of production and the consequential adjustments to the labour market were directly related to developments affecting the way in which society punished offenders resulting in punishment being a historically specific phenomenon. Rusche and Kirchheimer trace alterations to the methods of punishment from the Middle Ages to the rise of capitalism in the late sixteenth century and thence to the Industrial Revolution and argue that the labour market, rather than the role played by penal reformers, was the key factor that underpinned alterations to both the severity of punishment in society and the nature it assumed (Rusche and Kirchheimer, 1939).

This approach meant Durkheim's view of an ordered progression from severe to more lenient forms of punishment was replaced by an account that emphasised fluctuations in the way society responded to crime arising from changes affecting the labour market. A shortage of labour resulted in lenient punishments whereas an abundance of labour predicated a more severe response to crime. Accordingly, therefore, the rationale for punishment altered during the Industrial Revolution whereby the need to use prisons as mechanisms to reform inmates and thus provide a supply of labour gave way to an objective that these institutions should impose discipline and control over those whose criminal actions threatened to undermine the work ethic.

This approach has been criticised for failing to explain how the economic imperative is translated into penal practice (Cavadino and Dignan, 1992: 61) and for failing to explain how societies sharing similar economic conditions adopt a wide variation of penal practices (Garland, 1990: 107). Further, what has been criticised as a conspiratorial analysis of the rationale of punishment (Ignatieff, 1981) has also been criticised for oversimplifying the link between the labour market and the penal strategy adopted by a society since changes to the latter may be fashioned by factors additional to this explanation (Hudson, 2003: 117) such as ideology, political forces and the internal dynamics of penal administration (Garland, 1990: 108). However, it does emphasise that coercive responses to criminality (entailing strategies such as the increased use of imprisonment and enhancing the austerity of the prison environment) are not necessarily related solely to factors such as rising crime rates but may have other ulterior motives, namely as a method of social control to manage the reaction of those hardest hit by economic downturn.

Other accounts that accept the argument that the economic climate fashions the manner in which society punishes crime, devote attention to explaining the processes involved in bringing about transitions from leniency to severity (or vice versa). Periods of economic severity threaten to undermine the legitimacy normally accorded by large sections of society to capitalist values. However, the widespread use of repressive forms of punishment to uphold these values in times of economic difficulty is likely to create widespread social resistance. Accordingly it is necessary to change the underlying mood of the public to secure an acceptance of more coercive responses to crime. This is achieved through the use of what has been described as the ideological state apparatus (Althusser, 1971), whereby transitions in methods of punishment from leniency to severity are preceded by campaigns that seek to justify the new approach by highlighting anti-social activities associated with minority groups. This approach (which is compatible with the discussion of moral panics in Chapter 1) seeks to explain how the capitalist ruling class can secure widespread endorsement for the adoption of harsh penal strategies.

Foucault and the disciplined society

A further sociological account of the sociology of punishment was provided by Michel Foucault (1977) who developed the phenomenon of *penality* which has been described as 'a complex of theories, institutions, practices, laws and professional positions which have as their object the sanctioning of offenders'.

Foucault's key concern was the maintenance of social discipline. He discussed the manner in which fundamental economic and social changes in society had necessitated the development of new forms of social control. He graphically described the harsh mode of punishment associated with the *ancien régime* in France but argued that this display of what he termed 'sovereign power' became ineffective to maintain social order because it was only used intermittently. He believed that modern society required a system of social control, that of disciplinary power, whose hallmarks were 'uninterrupted, constant coercion' (Foucault, 1977: 137) implemented not by a central form of authority but through a myriad of mechanisms that were dissipated throughout society. Thus, for Foucault, punishment was viewed as a system of power through which domination over the individual was achieved in the modern world. It was based on the three interrelated concepts of 'power', 'knowledge' and 'the body' whose aim was to secure a self-controlled individual in the sense of a person whose obedience and conformity was based on internal constraints rather than external force (Garland, 1990: 137).

Foucault discussed the manner in which the prison system evolved as a mechanism of punishment to become an instrument of social control in response to the Industrial Revolution and the growth of towns. The infliction of pain associated with previous forms of punishment such as mutilation and execution was replaced by the deprivation of rights in the sense that inmates lost the ability to control their own time and space. Their main concern was thus to exercise power over the body. This new approach did not necessarily entail a movement towards a more lenient form of punishment but, rather, was designed to produce a system that operated more effectively (Foucault, 1977: 82).

Prisons were seen to serve numerous functions. These included the possibility of transforming inmates from criminals into useful and productive members of society by changing their moral habits and providing them with the skills to undertake a socially useful life in the future. However, as with Durkheim, Foucault also viewed prisons as institutions that served to affirm the values of society. They provided for the spatial separation of criminals from the remainder of society and in so doing transformed them into a separate and subordinate social category, delinquents. What was termed the 'disciplinary partitioning' of delinquents induced other members of society to accept that their punishment was legitimate thereby enhancing the overall level of social cohesion. It was in this sense that the impact of prisons permeated throughout society thereby serving to establish them as a mechanism of social control.

Like Jeremy Bentham (whose views are discussed in Chapter 1), Foucault focused on the disciplinary nature of prisons and he identified its key features as surveillance, categorisation, classification and regimentation. He viewed discipline as a method to master the body and make it obedient and useful (Foucault, 1977: 137) – 'the prison seizes the body of the inmate, exercising it, training it, organizing its time and movement in order to ultimately transform the soul' (Garland, 1990: 143). However, he discussed the way in which these methods of discipline that were developed within the prison system during the nineteenth century subsequently extended outwards to influence other aspects of social life. He contended that the techniques extended beyond the prison walls to penetrate the whole of society giving rise to what he referred to as the 'disciplinary society', the aim of which was to shape and train the body thereby upholding what he referred to as the power of the norm – 'there exists a kind of carceral continuum which covers the whole social body, linked by the pervasive concern to identify deviance, anomalies and departures from the relevant norms' (Garland, 1990: 151). Modern methods of surveillance made it possible for social conformity to be secured throughout society and it was in this sense that he referred to modern capitalist societies as 'confinement societies' (Foucault, 1977: 159). This view tended to blur the distinction between punitive and non-punitive institutions 'and presents a view of society that is a mesh of disciplinary relations' (Marsh, 2004: 53).

Foucault's main concern was the manner in which power was exercised within society in order to produce conformity, obedience and behavioural control (Garland, 1990: 171). He held that knowledge and power were both inseparable and interdependent (Foucault, 1977: 27) in the sense that the disciplinary procedures developed within prison provided knowledge of the convict's body that could be translated into a new kind of power over him or her (Cavadino and Dignan, 1992: 67). Although, as is argued in Chapter 8, aspects of his arguments related to the dispersal of discipline have been applied to critiques of community sentences, his views have been criticised for concentrating on the mechanics of power to the detriment of a detailed consideration of its sources, who wields it and the context in which it is deployed. Punishment may be underpinned by factors additional to the desire to exert control in order to enforce social conformity, and the fact that rebellions and riots occur within prisons (an issue that is discussed in Chapter 8) may also question the extent to which these institutions always succeed in promoting an effective form of discipline.

Alternative perspectives on punishment

It has been argued that 'jurisprudence and the philosophical tradition are concerned with the *ought* of punishment ... the sociological perspective is concerned with the *is* of punishment' (Hudson, 2003: 10). There are, however, other streams of penology that are briefly outlined below (Hudson, 2003: 10–13).

● *Technicist penology*. This approach to the study of punishment is concerned with efficiency and is an aspect of administrative criminology (that is discussed in Chapter 1). It seeks to assess the extent to which stated goals are being accomplished by the policies that have been adopted to implement them. This approach does not seek to provide an understanding of why certain goals have been put forward and what these are designed to achieve. Technicist penology accepts the agenda with which it is presented and focuses on its attainment.
● *Penology and oppression*. The link between penology and oppression stems from the Marxist view that punishment is designed to uphold capitalism and is thus directed against those whose views, values or attitudes imperil this economic system. The belief that punishment is a mechanism whereby the economically dominant can retain their power has been extended by some aspects of penology to embrace other forms of inequality, viewing punishment as a mechanism to secure gender or racial subordination.
● *Abolitionist penology*. This perspective is diverse. It encompasses approaches that suggest punishment is an inappropriate response to crime since this derives from social inequality. The state should thus focus on redressing this rather than punishing those whose actions stem from inferiority. Other approaches target specific forms of punishment that they wish to abolish (such as the use of the death penalty) or ameliorate (such as reducing the size of the prison population in the belief that this should not be used as a routine response to most forms of crime). A further aspect of abolitionist penology focuses on the victim rather than the offender and seeks to devise strategies to satisfy those adversely affected by crime. Restorative justice stems in part from this tradition.

Sentencing trends in England and Wales in the late twentieth century

The latter decades of the twentieth century witnessed the development of new approaches towards the punishment of offenders in which the welfare concerns of the treatment model that aimed to secure the rehabilitation of offenders gave way to more punitive sentiments that were associated with retribution. This change of direction was justified by arguments suggesting this approach was failing to address current levels of crime and lawlessness.

The new approach (which has been discussed above in connection with 'new retributivism') derived from the justice model that was augmented by a law and order ideology.

The justice model embraced what has been described as a minimalist approach that 'justified a neglect of offenders and their problems ... the state ... washed its hands of responsibility for anything other than punishing deviants, it ... absolved itself for the situation in which they find themselves' (Hudson, 1987: xi–xii). The compassion felt towards the less fortunate members of society was thereby eroded in favour of pursuing punitive action against criminals.

The justice model originated in America in the 1970s. Its key features have been listed (Hudson, 1987: 38) as:

- proportionality of punishment to crime;
- determinate sentences;
- an end to judicial and administrative discretion;
- an end to disparity in sentencing;
- protection of rights through due process.

This new approach sought to imbue punishment with a retributivist objective and was reinforced by a political goal to 'get tough with criminals'. The latter was a key aspect of law and order ideology embraced by Conservative governments between 1979 and 1997 (Cavadino and Dignan, 1992: 26–7) which resulted in significant departures from the justice model, in particular the 1997 Crime (Sentences) Act that provided for stiff sentences to certain categories of repeat offenders that took into account past offending behaviour in addition to the current offence.

As is argued in Chapter 8, the Conservative perception that the public required evidence that the government was pursuing a punitive approach towards those who committed crime served to place prisons at the forefront of their thinking.

The new trend in punishment has variously been depicted as marking the end of penal modernism and its replacement by a postmodern penality (Pratt, 2000) or as the penality of late modernity (Garland and Sparks, 2000: 199). These changes were pursued against the background of neo-liberalism (that sought to reduce the role of the central state) whereby punishment became one tactic of crime control directed at the most serious criminals that was pursued alongside a range of other methods located at the local and individual level operated by public bodies, private individuals and business concerns which were especially concerned with crime prevention and the creation of community safety (Hudson, 2003: 160). The role played by crime prevention and community safety in crime control are discussed in Chapter 2.

Bifurcation

Legislation that included the 1972, 1982 and especially the 1991 Criminal Justice Acts sought to introduce the principle of 'bifurcation' into sentencing policy. This approach sought to give criminals their 'just deserts' by matching punishment to the severity of a crime so that imprisonment was reserved for the most serious offenders and a range of non-custodial sentences were directed at less serious offending behaviour.

The 1991 Criminal Justice Act grouped offences under three headings – minor (which could be responded to by a fine or discharge), more serious (which merited a community sentence) and serious offences (which required a custodial sentence to be imposed). This legislation emphasised that the goal of non-custodial sentences was that of punishment. One difficulty with this approach was that the focus on the offence committed was seen as inadequate for prolific offenders. This resulted in the 1993 Criminal Justice Act allowing sentencers to take previous convictions into account when they dispensed a sentence. A further difficulty with this approach was the perception that offenders who escaped imprisonment had 'got off lightly'. There are various reasons for this belief, which included non-custodial sentences not being seen by the public or by sentencers as effective forms of punishment and that in a two-tier sentencing structure, those who received the lower-tier sentence were perceived as having been dealt with leniently. This situation tended to increase the use of custodial sentences, resulting in a prison population of unsustainable numbers.

The sentencing reform of Labour governments

When Labour assumed office in May 1997, the prison population in England and Wales stood at 60,131. On 3 January 2003 it had risen to 69,522, an important explanation for which was the rise in the number of long-term prisoners. England and Wales had the highest imprisonment rate in Western Europe at 134 per 100,000 population (Lyon, 2003). Ministerial perceptions that a prison population of this size was insupportable resulted in the 2001 Labour government embarking on its own review of sentencing policy. The key aspects of these reforms are discussed below.

The Halliday Report

In May 2000 the government initiated a review of the sentencing framework in England and Wales. Its aim was to ascertain whether change could be made to improve outcomes (especially in connection with reducing crime) at justifiable expense (Halliday, 2001: ii).

The key limitations affecting the present framework were stated to be 'the unclear and unpredictable approach to persistent offenders, who commit a disproportionate amount of crime, and the inability of short prison sentences (those of less than 12 months) to make any meaningful intervention in the criminal careers of many of those who receive them'. It was observed that short prison sentences were frequently inflicted on persistent offenders and were ineffective in that 66 per cent of those released were reconvicted within two years (Halliday, 2001: 22). Adverse comment was also made regarding the erosion of the principles contained in the 1991 Criminal Justice Act that sought to link punishment to the seriousness of the crime, which had resulted in 'muddle, complexity and lack of clear purpose or philosophy'. A new framework was proposed which 'should do more to support crime reduction and reparation, while meeting the needs of punishment' (Halliday, 2001: ii).

The reforms which were put forward included retaining the principle that punishment should be proportionate to the seriousness of the crime which had been committed, but modified to take recent and relevant previous convictions into 'clearer and more predictable account' – there should be 'a new presumption that severity of sentence will increase as a result of recent and relevant previous convictions that show a continuing course of criminal conduct' (Halliday, 2001: iii).

It was also argued that sentencing decisions should be structured so that if a prison sentence of 12 months or more was not necessary to meet the needs of punishment, sentencers should consider whether a non-custodial sentence would meet the assessed needs for crime reduction, punishment and reparation. This decision would be taken on the basis of an assessment related to the risk of their reoffending, the seriousness of the harm likely to result if they did reoffend and the measures most likely to reduce those risks. Imprisonment should be used when no other sentence would be adequate to meet the seriousness of the offence (or offences), having taken account of the offender's criminal history (Halliday, 2001: iii).

The review commented on the proliferation of community penalties in recent years, each containing its own content and enforcement, was complicated and had increased the risks of inconsistent sentencing. It was thus proposed that existing community sentences should be replaced by a new generic community punishment order, enforced by the court, which would be made up of elements designed to secure the objective of crime reduction. These elements might include accredited programmes to tackle offending behaviour, or provide treatment for substance abuse or mental illness, or embrace aspects such as compulsory work, curfew and exclusion orders, electronic monitoring and reparation to victims and communities. The punitive weight of this sentence should be proportionate to the current offence and any additional severity for previous convictions (Halliday, 2001: vi–vii).

The 2003 Criminal Justice Act

Following the Halliday Report, the government introduced the 2003 Criminal Justice Act that introduced significant reforms to sentencing policy. The legislation sought to combine the retributivist concern of delivering a tough response to crime (albeit through an approach that made placed less reliance on prisons) with the reductivist goal of lowering the overall level of crime. The measure emphasised that the aim of sentencing was to bring about the reform and rehabilitation of offenders, and sentencers were required to consider how the penalty (or penalties) that they meted out would achieve these goals. The Sentencing Guidelines Council (which was established by the legislation) further emphasised the need to limit the use of custodial sentences and its work has also attempted to bring about a reduction in the length of typical sentences.

The 2003 legislation made a clear distinction between dangerous and non-dangerous offenders. It introduced a new community order available to all offenders aged 16 and above that enabled sentencers to draw from a list of 'requirements' to enable them to produce a sentence that was specifically tailored to each offender in order to accomplish the dual aims of punishment and rehabilitation. These requirements were:

- the unpaid work requirement (this is a reparative, payback element involving community service);
- the activity requirement;
- the programme requirement;
- the prohibited activity requirement;
- the curfew requirement;
- the exclusion requirement;
- the residence requirement;
- the mental health treatment requirement;
- the drug rehabilitation requirement;
- the alcohol treatment requirement;
- the supervision requirement;
- the attendance centre requirement;
- the electronic monitoring requirement.

The community order is implemented by the Probation Service or the YOT and may not last for more than three years.

Following the passage of the 2003 Act, the government suspended the implementation of the community order for offenders below the age of 18. Existing sentencing options remained in force for those aged 16 and 17 until new legislation affecting youth justice could be introduced.

The 2003 Criminal Justice Act also introduced the new sentences of Custody Minus and Custody Plus. Custody Minus entailed an offender being given the chance to undertake a community-based punishment rather than serve a custodial sentence of between 28 and 51 weeks with the sanction of automatic imprisonment for any failure on his or her part. It replaced the disposal of a suspended sentence and although different from a community order utilised the same requirements as were contained in the latter penalty.

Custody Plus was designed to replace prison sentences of below one year. It involved a short term of imprisonment (of between two weeks and three months) followed by a longer period of at least nine months supervision in the community. This might entail a drug user being detoxed while in custody and then being given 'strict supervision, support and treatment in the community to help keep him off drugs and away from crime' (Home Office, 2004: 8). The aspect of the sentence that was served on licence in the community was similar to requirements imposed by community orders.

A further sentence also introduced by the 2003 legislation, that of inter-mittent custody, was designed to help offenders stay in employment while serving their sentence by combining a custodial sentence (served for part of the week, perhaps at weekends) with community punishment. Custody Plus and intermittent custody were designed to replace short terms of imprisonment which were regarded as 'ineffective' and associated with negative consequences such as 'loss of employment or accommodation and family break-up which are factors known to increase the risk of re-offending' (Home Office, 2004: 8).

The new direction of sentencing policy – towards trifurcation?

The sentencing policies of the Labour government amount to a system of trifurcation that is underpinned by the common objective of punishment. One benefit of trifurcation is that community-based sentences no longer constitute the bottom rung of the sentencing ladder, and may find favour with the public especially if their rationale and content is seen to be inflicting punishment on offenders. Additionally, community penalties that involve an element of supervision and imprisonment are closely intermeshed, emphasising the punitive aspects of the non-custodial responses to crime.

This three-tier sentencing structure consists of:

- *Fines and fixed-penalty notices.* These (and new disposals which include the conditional caution) are designed to punish for the least serious criminal offences such as anti-social behaviour and minor public order offences. One benefit of this approach is that this penalty places no demands on the Probation Service. As has been indicated in Chapter 3, the enforcement of the law relating to these low-level offences is increasingly discharged by officials such as police community support officers rather than members of the police service. As is discussed in more detail in the following chapter, attempts have been made (in particular by the 2003 Courts Act) to improve the collection rate of fines, thereby making this a more effective form of punishment.
- *Community penalties.* These embrace a range of non-custodial sentences which include supervisory and/or monitoring aspects, and are designed to punish for a wide range of offences which fall short of the most serious. Their rationale as forms of punishment is sometimes enhanced by being incorporated in a single sentence that combines both custodial and non-custodial dimensions.
- *Imprisonment.* This is reserved for the most serious offences. This approach was advocated in the Carter Report (Carter, 2003) and the 2003 Criminal Justice Act provided that the sentences for the most serious offenders could be indeterminate.

Parole and early release

The sentencing reforms contained in the 2003 Criminal Justice Act had a significant impact on parole.

The system of parole (whereby prisoners could be released before they had served the full sentence ordered by the court and be placed under the supervision of a probation officer until the original date for remission of sentence had been met) was introduced into the criminal justice system of England and Wales by the 1967 Criminal Justice Act. This legislation provided that a prisoner was eligible for release after serving one-third of the sentence imposed on him or her or 12 months, whichever was the longer. The 1982 Criminal Justice Act amended this to provide for eligibility for release after having served one-third of the sentence or six months, whichever was the greater. The decision as to whether early release should be granted was made by the Parole Board.

The 1990 White Paper, *Crime, Justice and Protecting the Public*, and the resultant 1991 Criminal Justice Act, introduced significant changes to the system of parole. Under the 1991 Criminal Justice Act, an adult offender serving a custodial sentence of at least 12 months and less than four years would be automatically released at the halfway point of the sentence and then be supervised under licence until the three-quarter point of the sentence had been reached. An offender serving a determinate sentence of four years or more would be eligible for release on parole from the halfway point of the sentence and would automatically be released at the two-thirds point. Following release the offender would be supervised under licence until the three-quarter point of the sentence had been reached.

These provisions sought to reduce the amount of discretion exercised by the prison authorities, so that the courts would be more able to determine the actual sentence served. However, a White Paper in 1996 acknowledged that the arrangements introduced in the 1991 legislation were 'complicated' and that 'the public, and sometimes even the courts, are frequently confused and increasingly cynical about what prison sentences actually mean' (Home Office, 1996: 43). New proposals were thus put forward in order to 'introduce greater honesty and clarity into the sentencing process, so that the sentence actually served will relate much more closely to the sentence passed by the court'. To achieve this, it was suggested that all offenders aged 16 and over who received a determinate custodial sentence should serve the full term ordered by the court and that automatic early release and parole would be ended. Instead, prisoners would be required to earn remission. It was argued that this philosophy of 'honesty in sentencing' would be coupled with greater transparency into the arrangements for calculating sentences so that 'all those involved – offenders, judges and the public – will know exactly where they stand' (Home Office, 1996: 45).

The incoming Labour government in 1997 decided not to implement the 'honesty in sentencing' provisions of the 1997 Crime (Sentences) Act. Its initial approach towards time served in prison entailed the introduction of a system whereby the magistrate or trial judge would provide full details concerning a sentence. This information would entail announcing the minimum time to be served with parole, the minimum time without parole, the maximum term possible and the earliest release date. The victim of the crime would be informed in writing of the sentence and the earliest possible release date. The 1998 Crime and Disorder Act introduced changes affecting the early release of short-term prisoners subject to a curfew condition, but a more comprehensive reform was put forward in the 2003 Criminal Justice Act.

The 2003 legislation limited the use of parole by introducing new arrangements for automatic release, whereby prisoners serving 12 months and over could be released at the half-way point of their sentence but be subject to licence requirements, which might include requirements such as curfews or undertaking rehabilitation programmes. Compliance with these requirements would be monitored by supervision in the community that would continue until the full sentence dispensed by the court had been served. Any breach of the conditions imposed by the licence could result in a return to custody. Separate provisions applied to prisoners who were deemed to pose a danger to the public, who would be released only when it was deemed safe to do so.

The release of prisoners serving discretionary life sentences is determined by the Parole Board's Discretionary Lifer Panel (DLP) that was established by the 1997 Crime (Sentences) Act. When a prisoner who is serving a discretionary life sentence has completed the tariff imposed by the trial judge (that is, the term of imprisonment which must be served to provide for 'punishment and deterrence'), the Home Secretary refers the prisoner's case to the DLP which then conducts an assessment of the risk which the prisoner will pose to the general public if released. The DLP uses this risk assessment to make recommendations to the Home Secretary as to whether the prisoner should remain in custody, be moved to an open prison or released. These Panels may also recall a paroled prisoner to prison. There are problems with this system and in particular with the process of risk assessment. It has been observed that 'there is an inherent difficulty in predicting and assessing a person's future behaviour at liberty whilst they are in captivity, (Padfield et al., 2003: 115).

Tackling recidivism by reintegrating offenders

It has been estimated that more than one million crimes – around 18 per cent of the total number of crimes committed each year – were carried out by released prisoners at an annual cost of around £11 billion per year (Ramsbotham, 2005: 69). Fifty-eight per cent of all adults, 78 per cent of all young offenders under the age of 21, and 88 per cent of all children aged 15–18 reoffend within two years of release (Ramsbotham, 2005: 70). Considerations of this nature prompted Labour governments to reassert the role of rehabilitation in their penal policies. This goal would be achieved by measures enabling offenders to be reintegrated into their communities.

The priority accorded to tackling recidivism was made clear by the Home Secretary in a speech to the Prison Reform Trust in September 2005 when he laid down the penal strategy of the third Labour government (Clarke, 2005). He made it clear that the prevention of reoffending had become the central focus to achieve the government's objective of reducing the overall level of crime. He accordingly put forward proposals to achieve the objective of 're-socialising offenders back into society'. The reintegration of offenders thus became a key aim of sentencing policy.

He argued that securing the reintegration of offenders into society required a thorough and systematic assessment of their needs and also their desire to reform that would be formalised in offender contracts. These required the offender to state his or her intention not to reoffend in return for which the state (in the form of the National Offender Management Service) would provide individualised help and/or treatment (delivered in prison or in the community or in a combination of both) to address the root cause of the offending behaviour. The Home Secretary stated that the key components of this individualised support package embraced the policy areas of health (including alcohol and substance abuse), education, employment, social and family links and housing and its effective delivery required a partnership between the state, private sector and voluntary agencies.

The government's policy thus sought to emphasise the rehabilitative function of prisons which Clarke now wished to be seen not as 'universities of crime' but as 'colleges of constructive citizenship'. Individualised treatment in prisons (or initiated in prisons and continued upon release in the community) was at the heart of the new thinking. However, this policy has a number of repercussions for the organisation and management of the prison estate to bring about individualised reform, in particular in connection with the provision of personal supervision to each prisoner and the acceptance of the importance of community prisons to achieving successful rehabilitation. Although in his speech the Home Secretary sought to move on from the debate about prison numbers and onto future statistics related to the reduction of reoffending, factors such as prison overcrowding (an issue which he acknowledged was considerably aggravated by the high numbers of persons remanded in custody) threatened to undermine his best intentions in this matter.

The key reforms to tackle recidivism are briefly discussed below.

The creation of the National Offender Management Service

The merger of the Prison and Probation Services into the National Offender Management Service (NOMS) (a reform that is discussed in greater detail in Chapter 8) provides a unified system of offender management. This means that each offender is provided with a single person (usually a probation officer) to oversee the implementation of their sentence plan as it is served both in prison and in the community. This approach emphasises the importance of continuity to secure the goal of resettlement. One difficulty with this approach is that the offender may become over-reliant on his or her case worker and may not be able to cope when this support is terminated once the full sentence has been served.

Resettlement

Resettlement entails the delivery of practical services to offenders to enable offenders to be reintegrated into communities. Traditionally resettlement programmes were delivered by the statutory and voluntary sectors whose work was guided by various models whereby some resettlement teams focused their work in prisons and others in the community. Mentoring was a key ingredient of resettlement practice. NOMS will integrate prison and community-based resettlement work and Regional Offender Managers will coordinate the work of various government departments in the region whose responsibilities for reducing reoffending were identified in the Social Exclusion Unit's 'seven pathways out of reoffending'. This report made it clear that resettlement was not an issue that criminal justice agencies alone could successfully promote (Social Exclusion Unit, 2002).

Actuarial justice

Contemporary penal policy emphasises the importance of risk. There are two main aspects associated with this development (Hudson, 2003: 161):

- the move from risk management to risk control, whereby attempts to reduce risk by interventions such as education and treatment programmes for offenders and post-release supervision give way to an approach whereby those who pose risks to society are physically removed from it. This approach ensures that the increased use of custodial sentences is a key aspect of contemporary penal trends;
- the reorientation of penal policy whereby the provision of security takes precedence over the imposition of discipline. This means that interventions targeted at individuals give way to approaches whereby communities define risks and develop strategies to respond to them.

The emphasis placed on the assessment of risk has given rise to what is termed 'actuarial justice' which forms the basis of what has been referred to as the 'new penology' (Feeley and Simon, 1992). It has been argued that this approach was underpinned by the cultural characteristics of late modernity embracing factors such as individualism and distrust of the role of the central state, the power of the media and the nature of contemporary forms of governance (Garland, 2000: 35). Changes of this nature were underpinned by the abandonment of attempts to secure a more equal distribution of wealth and resources and, instead, to manage the risks derived from these inequalities (Beck, 1992: 19).

Actuarial justice entails offenders being treated not as individuals but according to characteristics such as 'the type of offence, previous record, education and employment history, family size and income, residence, alcohol and addictions and relationship problems' (Hudson, 2003: 162). The aim of the new actuarial techniques of offender risk assessment 'is to place offenders into the categories of risk, and then isolate and exclude the high-risk, allowing only the low-risk to be punished by proportionate penalties' (Hudson, 2003: 163). This approach was embodied in the bifurcation principle governing sentencing in the late twentieth century.

> Evaluate the significance of changes to sentencing policy that were introduced by the 2003 Criminal Justice Act.

Conclusion

This chapter has considered a number of issues connected with the concept of punishment. It has examined the concept of punishment and differentiated between reductivist and retributionist approaches and has further discussed the aim of reintegrating the offender into society through the use of restorative justice. The strengths and weaknesses of this approach have been fully evaluated. The chapter contrasted these approaches to the study of punishment with sociological accounts that seek to explain why societies adopt different forms of punishment across historical periods. The contribution made by key thinkers (in particular Durkheim, Weber, Foucault and Marxist penologists) has been briefly examined. The chapter also sought to adapt the theoretical account of punishment by relating the themes that have been discussed to sentencing trends in England and Wales in the late twentieth century. It drew attention to the shift from the welfare model to the justice model and examined the aims and content of the sentencing policy pursued by post-1997 Labour governments.

The chapter has suggested that prisons play an important part in punishing those who commit criminal acts, especially in industrial and post-industrial society. The importance of this response to crime was emphasised by the law and order ideology initiated by the Conservative government in 1993 and continued by its Labour successors. The following chapter develops this argument by considering the development of prisons in England and Wales and assessing the role they are designed to fulfil. It also looks at the range of non-custodial disposals that are available to sentencers.

Further reading

There are many specialist texts that will provide an in-depth examination of the issues discussed in this chapter. These include:

Braithwaite, J. (1989) *Crime, Shame and Reintegration*. Cambridge: Cambridge University Press.

Foucault, M. (1977) *Discipline and Punish: The Birth of the Prison*. London: Allen Lane.

Garland, D. (1985) *Punishment and Welfare: A History of Penal Strategies*. Aldershot: Gower.

Garland, D. (1990) *Punishment and Modern Society*. Oxford: Clarendon.

Hudson, B. (2003) *Understanding Justice: An Introduction to Ideas, Perspectives and Controversies in Modern Penal Theory*, 2nd edn. Buckingham: Open University Press.

McConville, S. (ed) (2003) *The Use of Punishment*. Cullompton: Willan Publishing.

Tonry, M. (2004) *Punishment and Politics*. Cullompton: Willan Publishing.

Key events

- **1717** Enactment of the Transportation Act. This Act provided for the transportation of criminals to the American colonies. It was designed as a means of punishment and deterrence but also helped to redress the shortage of labour experienced in these colonies.
- **1820** The last beheadings took place in Great Britain when five members of the Cato Street Conspiracy led by Arthur Thistlewood suffered this fate. They had plotted to kill the cabinet and overthrow the government.
- **1821** Opening of Millbank Penitentiary. Its design was heavily influenced by Jeremy Bentham's panopticon blueprint and he personally supervised the construction of this institution.
- **1843** Abolition of gibbeting whereby executed corpses were displayed in public. The last person to be gibbeted was James Cook in 1832.
- **1868** The last transportations (to Fremantle in Western Australia) took place.
- **1868** Public executions were ended.
- **1900** Publication of *Deux Lois de L'évolution Penale* (*Two Laws of Penal Evolution*) by Emile Durkheim in which he put forward the view that there was an ordered progression from severe to more lenient forms of punishment as society progressed.
- **1955** Ruth Ellis was the last woman to be executed in Britain.
- **1964** The last executions (of Peter Allen and Owen Evans) took place in Britain.
- **1965** Enactment of the Murder (Abolition of the Death Penalty) Act that abolished the death penalty for murder in Great Britain. The measure provided for a temporary five-year ban, but in 1969 Parliament voted to make abolition permanent. In 1973 permanent abolition was extended to Northern Ireland. However, the United Kingdom only became truly abolitionist with the enactment of the 1998 Human Rights Act which removed the death penalty as a possible punishment for military offences committed under the Armed Forces Acts.
- **1972** Enactment of the Criminal Justice Act. This introduced the principle of bifurcation into sentencing policy that sought to punish serious offenders harshly but treat the perpetrators of less serious crime more leniently, typically by the imposition of non-custodial sentences. Subsequent Criminal Justice Acts enacted in 1982, 1991 and 2003 sought to enforce this principle of sentencing.
- **1997** Enactment of the Crime (Sentences) Act. This measure sought to curb the discretion of sentencers by introducing a range of mandatory sentences for crimes involving violence, drug trafficking and burglary. It was subsequently modified by the 2000 Powers of the Criminal Courts (Sentencing) Act.
- **1999** Enactment of the Youth Justice and Criminal Evidence Act. This measure introduced referral orders that considerably extended the principle of restorative justice into the youth justice system.
- **2003** Enactment of the Criminal Justice Act. This measure made important changes to sentencing policy, including the introduction of community orders, Custody Plus and Custody Minus, and put forward provisions to provide for the early release of prisoners.

References

Achilles, M. (2004) 'Can Restorative Justice Live Up to Its Promise to Victims?', in H. Zehr and B. Toews (eds), *Critical Issues in Restorative Justice*. New York: Criminal Justice Press.

Althusser, L. (1971) *Lenin and Philosophy and Other Essays*. New York: Monthly Review Press.

Andrews, M. (2003) 'Punishment, Markets and the American Model: An Essay on a New American Dilemma', in S. McConville (ed.), *The Use of Punishment*. Cullompton: Willan Publishing.

Barton, C. (2003) *Restorative Justice: The Empowerment Model*. Sydney: Hawkins Press.

Bazemore, G. and Walgrave, L. (1999) 'Restorative Juvenile Justice. In Search of Fundamentals and an Outline for Systematic Reform', in G. Bazemore and L. Walgrave (eds), *Restorative Juvenile Justice. Restoring the Harm of Youth Crime*. New York: Criminal Justice Press.

Beck, U. (1992) *Risk Society: Towards a New Modernity*. London: Sage.

Benedict, R. (1946) *The Chrysanthemum and the Sword: Patterns of Japanese Culture*. Boston: Houghton Mifflin.

Benn, S. and Peters, R. (1959) *Social Principles and the Democratic State*. London: Allen & Unwin.

Blunkett, D. (2003) 'Foreword from the Home Secretary', in Home Office, *Restorative Justice: The Government's Strategy: A Consultative Document on the Government's Strategy on Restorative Justice*. London: Home Office.

Braithwaite, J. (1989) *Crime, Shame and Reintegration*. Cambridge: Cambridge University Press.

Braithwaite, J. (1993) 'Shame and Modernity', *British Journal of Criminology*, 33: 1–18.

Braithwaite, J. (1995) 'Inequality and Republican Criminology', in J. Hagan and R. Peterson (eds), *Crime and Inequality*. Stanford, CA: Stanford University Press.

Braithwaite, J. (1998) 'Restorative Justice', in M. Tonry (ed.), *Handbook of Crime and Punishment*. Oxford: Oxford University Press.

Braithwaite, J. (1999) 'A Future Where Punishment is Marginalised: Realistic or Utopian?', *UCLA Law Review*, 46: 1727–50.

Braithwaite, J. and Roche, D. (2001) 'Responsibility and Restorative Justice', in G. Bazemore and M. Schiff (eds), *Restorative Community Justice: Repairing Harm and Transforming Communities*. Cincinatti, OH: Anderson Publishing.

Braithwaite, J. and Strang, H. (2001) 'Introduction: Restorative Justice and Civil Society', in H. Strang and J. Braithwaite (eds), *Restorative Justice and Civil Society*. Cambridge: Cambridge University Press.

Carter, P. (2003) Managing Offenders, *Reducing Crime: A New Approach*. London: Home Office Strategy Unit.

Cavadino, M. and Dignan, J. (1992) *The Penal System: An Introduction*, 1st edn. London: Sage.

Christie, N. (1982) *Limits to Pain*. Oxford: Martin Robertson.

Clarke, C. (2005) Speech to the Prison Reform Trust, London, 19 September.

Crawford, A. and Clear, T. (2003) 'Community Justice: Transforming Communities Through Restorative Justice?', in E. McLaughlin, R. Fergusson, G. Hughes and L. Westmarland (eds), *Restorative Justice Critical Issues*. London: Sage.

Daly, K. (2000) 'Revisiting the Relationship Between Retributive and Restorative Justice', in H. Strang and J. Braithwaite (eds), *Restorative Justice: Philosophy to Practice*. Aldershot: Ashgate.

Davies, M. (1993) *Punishing Criminals: Developing Community-based Intermediate Sanctions*. Westport, CT: Greenwood Press.

Duff, R. (1986) *Trials and Punishment*. Cambridge: Cambridge University Press.

Durkheim, E. (1893) *De la division du travail social (On the Division of Labour in Society)*. Paris: Alcan.

Durkheim, E. (1900) *Deux Lois de L'évolution Penale* (*Two Laws of Penal Evolution*), in *L'Année Sociologique*, IV: 65–95.

Erbe, C. (2004) 'What is the Role of Professionals in Restorative Justice?', in H. Zehr and B. Toews (eds), *Critical Issues in Restorative Justice*. New York: Criminal Justice Press.

Fatić, A. (1995) *Punishment and Restorative Crime-Handling: A Social Theory of Trust*. Aldershot: Avebury.

Feeley, M. and Simon, J. (1992) 'The New Penology: Notes on the Emerging Strategy of Corrections and Its Implications', *Criminology*, 30: 449–74.

Fleisher, M. (2003) 'Lost Youth and the Futility of Deterrence', in S. McConville (ed.), *The Use of Punishment*. Cullompton: Willan Publishing.

Foucault, M. (1977) *Discipline and Punish: The Birth of the Prison*. London: Allen Lane.

Garland, D. (1990) *Punishment and Modern Society*. Oxford: Clarendon.

Garland, D. (2000) 'The Culture of High Crime Societies: Strategies of Crime Control in Contemporary Societies', *British Journal of Criminology*, 40 (3): 347–75.

Garland, D. and Sparks, R. (2000) 'Criminology, Social Theory and the Challenge of our Times', *British Journal of Criminology*, 40 (2): 189–204.

Halliday, J. (2001) *Making Punishments Work: Report of a Review of the Sentencing Framework for England and Wales*. London: Home Office.

Home Office, (1996) *Protecting the Public: The Government's Strategy on Crime in England and Wales*, Cm 3190. London: Home Office.

Home Office (2003) *Restorative Justice: The Government's Strategy: A Consultative Document on the Government's Strategy on Restorative Justice*. London: Home Office.

Home Office (2004) *Reducing Crime – Changing Lives: The Government's Plans for Transforming the Management of Offenders*. London: Home Office.

Hoyle, C., Young, R. and Hill, R. (2002) *Proceed with Caution: An Evaluation of the Thames Valley Police Initiative in Restorative Cautioning*. York: Joseph Rowntree Foundation.

Hudson, B. (1987) *Justice Through Punishment: A Critique of the 'Justice' Model of Corrections*. Basingstoke: Macmillan.

Hudson, B. (2003) *Understanding Justice*, 2nd edn. Buckingham: Open University Press.

Hudson, J., Morris, A., Maxwell, G. and Galway, B. (1996) *Family Group Conferences*. Annandale, NSW: Federation Press.

Huesmann, L. and Podolski, C. (2003) 'Punishment: A Psychological Perspective', in S. McConville (ed.), *The Use of Punishment*. Cullompton: Willan Publishing.

Ignatieff, M. (1981) 'State, Civil Society and Total Institutions: A Critique of Recent Social Histories of Punishment', in M. Tonry and N. Morris (eds), *Crime and Justice*, Vol. 3. Chicago: University of Chicago Press.

Jantzi, V. (2004) What Is the Role of the State in Restorative Justice?', in H. Zehr and B. Toews (eds), *Critical Issues in Restorative Justice*. New York: Criminal Justice Press.

Johnstone, G. (2002) *Restorative Justice: Ideas, Values, Debates*. Cullompton: Willan Publishing.

Johnstone, G. (2004) 'How, and in What Terms, Should Restorative Justice Be Conceived?', in H. Zehr and B Toews (eds), *Critical Issues in Restorative Justice*. New York: Criminal Justice Press.

Lacey, N. (2003) 'Penal Theory and Penal Practice: A Communitarian Approach', in S. McConville (ed.), *The Use of Punishment*. Cullompton: Willan Publishing.

Lyon, J. (2003) *A Step in the Right Direction*, press release (avalable at: www.prison reformtrust.org.uk/news-prburglary.html).

Marsh, I. (2004) *Criminal Justice: An Introduction to Philosophies, Theories and Practice*. London: Routledge.

Marsh, T. (1988) 'Informal Justice: The British Experience', in R. Matthews, (ed.), *Informal Justice?* London: Sage.

Matthews, R. (1999) *Doing Time: An Introduction to the Sociology of Imprisonment*. Basingstoke: Macmillan.

Maxwell G. and Morris, A. (1999) *Understanding Reoffending: Final Report to the Social Policy Agency and the Ministry of Justice*. Wellington, New Zealand: Institute of Criminology, Victoria University of Wellington, quoted in G. Maxwell and A. Morris (2004) 'What Is the Place of Shame in Restorative Justice?', in H. Zehr and B. Toews (eds), *Critical Issues in Restorative Justice*. New York: Criminal Justice Press.

Maxwell, G. and Morris, A. (2004) 'What Is the Place of Shame in Restorative Justice?', in H. Zehr and B. Toews (eds), *Critical Issues in Restorative Justice*. New York: Criminal Justice Press.

Maxwell, G., Kingi, V., Morris, A., Robertson, J. and Anderson, T. (2003) 'Differences in How Girls and Boys Respond to Family Group Conferences: Preliminary Research Results', in L. Walgrave (ed.), *Repositioning Restorative Justice*. Cullompton: Willan Publishing.

McCold, P. (2003) 'A Survey of Assessment Research on Mediation and Conferencing', in L. Walgrave (ed.), *Repositioning Restorative Justice*. Cullompton: Willan Publishing.

Miller, S. (1996) *Shame in Context*. Hillsdale, NJ: Analytic Press.

Morris, A. and Young, W. (1999) *Reforming Criminal Justice: The Potential of Restorative Justice*. Paper presented to the Conference, 'Restorative Justice and Civil Society', Canberra, Australian National University, February, quoted in C. Barton (2003) *Restorative Justice: The Empowerment Model*. Sydney: Hawkins Press.

Muncie, J. (2002) 'A New Deal for Youth? Early Intervention and Correctionalism', in G. Hughes, E. McLaughlin and J. Muncie, *Crime Prevention and Community Safety: New Directions*. London: Sage.

Napoleon, V. (2004) 'By Whom, and by What Processes, Is Restorative Justice Defined?', in H. Zehr and B. Toews (eds), *Critical Issues in Restorative Justice*. New York: Criminal Justice Press.

Newburn, T. et al. (2002) *The Introduction of Referral Orders into the Youth Justice System: Final Report*, Home Office Research Study 242. London: Home Office Research, Development and Statistics Directorate.

Padfield, N., Liebling, A. and Arnold, H. (2003) 'Discretion and the Release of Life Sentence Prisoners', in L. Gelsthorpe and N. Padfield (eds), *Exercising Discretion: Decision-Making in the Criminal Justice System and Beyond*. Cullompton: Willan Publishing.

Pratt, J. (2000) 'The Return of Wheelbarrow Man: or the Arrival of Postmodern Penality', *British Journal of Criminology*, 40 (1): 127–45.

Ramsbotham, D. (2005) *Prisongate – The Shocking State of Britain's Prisons and the Need for Visionary Change*. London: Free Press.

Rawls, J. (1972) *A Theory of Justice*. Oxford: Oxford University Press.

Restorative Justice Consortium (2000) *Restorative Justice from Margins to Mainstream*. London: Restorative Justice Consortium.

Roberts, A. (2004) 'Is Restorative Justice Tied to Specific Models of Practice?', in H. Zehr and B. Toews (eds), *Critical Issues in Restorative Justice*. New York: Criminal Justice Press.

Rusche, G. and Kirchheimer, O. (1939) *Punishment and Social Structure*. New York: Russell & Russell.

Sharpe, S. (2004) 'How Large Should the Restorative Justice 'Tent' Be?', in H. Zehr and B. Toews (eds), *Critical Issues in Restorative Justice*. New York: Criminal Justice Press.

Social Exclusion Unit (2002) *Reducing Re-offending by Ex-Prisoners*. London: Cabinet Office.

Spitzer, S. (1979) 'Notes Towards a Theory of Punishment and Social Change', *Law and Sociology*, 2: 207–29.

Strang, H. and Braithwaite, J. (2001) *Restorative Justice and Civil Society*. Cambridge: Cambridge University Press.

Tendler, S. (1997) 'Criminals Made to Meet Victims "Are Far Less Likely to Re-offend"' *The Times*, 18 October.

Tomkins, S. (1987) 'Shame', in D. Nathanson (ed.), *The Many Faces of Shame*. New York: Guilford Press.

Valier, C. (2002) *Theories of Crime and Punishment*. Harlow: Pearson Education.

Von Hirsch, A. (1976) *Doing Justice: The Choice of Punishments*. New York: Hill & Wang.

Walgrave, L. (2003) 'Introduction', in L. Walgrave (ed.), *Repositioning Restorative Justice*. Cullompton: Willan Publishing.

Walgrave, L. (2004) 'Has Restorative Justice Appropriately Responded to Retribution Theory and Impulses?', in H. Zehr and B. Toews (eds), *Critical Issues in Restorative Justice*. New York: Criminal Justice Press.

Walker, N. and Hough, M. (1988) *Public Attitudes to Sentencing: Surveys from Five Countries*, Cambridge Studies in Criminology LIX, Aldershot: Gower.

Weber, M. (1922) *Wirtschaft and Gesellschaft (Economy and Society)*. Tübingen: J. C. B. Mohr.

Wilcox, A., Young, R. and Hoyle, C. (2004) *Two-Year Resanctioning Study: A Comparison of Restorative and Traditional Cautions*, Home Office Outline Report 57/04. London: Home Office.

Willemsens, J. (2003) 'Restorative Justice: A Discussion of Punishment', in L. Walgrave (ed.), *Repositioning Restorative Justice*. Cullompton: Willan Publishing.

Wright, M. (2003) 'Is It Time to Question the Concept of Punishment?', in L. Walgrave (ed.), *Repositioning Restorative Justice*. Cullompton: Willan Publishing.

Young, R. and Hoyle, C. (2003) 'Restorative Justice and Punishment', in S. McConville (ed.), *The Use of Punishment*. Cullompton: Willan Publishing.

8 Prison and its alternatives

This chapter discusses the manner in which crime has been responded to in England and Wales. It considers the development of the Prison Service, assesses the impact of the prison environment on the goal of reform and rehabilitation and evaluates non-custodial sentences as a response to crime. The chapter also analyses the rationale for the merger of the probation and prison services into the National Offender Management Service (NOMS). In particular, the chapter

- discusses the evolution of the English prison system from the late nineteenth century onwards, devoting particular emphasis to the period since *c*.1990;
- evaluates the nature of the prison environment, seeking to suggest why prisons have traditionally found it difficult to bring about the reform and rehabilitation of inmates;
- considers ways other than custodial sentences as responses to crime, and evaluates the strengths and weaknesses of these proposals;
- examines the development of the Probation Service, devoting particular emphasis to the changing role of this agency since the early 1990s;
- analyses the rationale for contemporary policy seeking to unify the work of the Prison and Probation Services.

The development of prisons in England and Wales

This section charts the historical development of prisons and the diverse aims with which they have been associated.

The prison population in England and Wales

There are 139 prisons in England and Wales employing approximately 44,000 staff. These are divided into high security prisons, local prisons, young offenders' institutions, remand centres, training prisons, open prisons and resettlement prisons. All prisoners commence their sentence in a local prison where they are assessed and given a security category.

The prison population has risen sharply since the beginning of the twentieth century. In 1901 the number of prisoners totalled 15,900 and this figures fell to between 10,000 and 11,000 in the interwar years. Between 1946 and 1986 the prison population rose at a rate of around 800 per year, but there were exceptions to this (most notably between 1951 and 1956, and 1986 and 1991). In 1992 the size of the prison population was 45,817 but the forceful advocacy of this response to crime by Michael Howard (who became Home Secretary in 1993) resulted in raising this figure to 55,281 in 1996.

When the Labour party assumed office in 1997, the size of the prison population was in excess of 60,000. Although the overall level of crime has fallen since then, the size of the prison population has continued to rise. It hit the figure of 75,000 for the first time in March 2004, and in December 2005 had further increased to 77,066. This compares to an operating capacity of 78,521 that would have been exceeded but for the Home Detention Curfew under which 3,205 prisoners were released.

Women constituted 16 per cent of the prison population in 1901, but the proportion of female prisoners has subsequently declined. They constituted around 3 per cent of the prison population in 1971, a figure that had grown to 5.9 per cent (4,529 prisoners) in December 2005. The great bulk of prisoners are males aged between 21 and 29, and in 2001 22 per cent of male prisoners were serving sentences for violence against the person.

Persons from minority ethnic communities are over-represented in the prison population. Minority ethnic groups comprise around 7 per cent of the total population but constitute 21 per cent of the male prison population and 26 per cent of the female prison population.

In 2002/3, the average annual cost of a prison place was £27,320. This figure should be seen in the context of the high level of recidivism: 59 per cent of persons discharged in 1998 were reconvicted of a standard list offence within two years of their release.

(*Sources*: Hick and Allen, 1999; Home Office 2003; National Offender Management Service, 2005.)

The Gladstone Report, 1895: prisons as rehabilitative institutions

Penal reformers in the late eighteenth and early years of the nineteenth century had identified the reforming potential of prisons in which opportunities would be presented to inmates to change their attitudes and behaviour. The 1779 Penitentiary Act indicated this change in the purpose of prisons. They had formerly existed as institutions to house those awaiting sentence or the implementation of it (either execution or transportation) or to hold debtors and those guilty of relatively minor crimes. Under the influence of evangelical reformers (such as Elizabeth Fry and John Howard) and utilitarian thinkers (such as Jeremy Bentham) prisons assumed a new purpose as institutions to deter crime and reform criminals. However, whether or not offenders availed themselves of the opportunities with which they were presented to reform themselves was primarily subject to their determination: reform was ultimately very much a personal decision.

Towards the end of the nineteenth century a new approach, that of rehabilitation, emerged as a key function of prisons. The difference between reform and rehabilitation was that the latter promoted a more positive role for the state to bring about changes to those offenders who were receptive to changing their ways. The Gladstone Report of 1895 was a key development in promoting the role of prisons as rehabilitative institutions (see Hudson, 1987: 3–11).

The report of Herbert Gladstone sought a move away from the harsh conditions that had existed in Britain's prisons since the middle of the nineteenth century. It identified the main fault of prisons being that 'it treats prisoners too much as irreclaimable criminals, rather than reclaimable men and women' (Gladstone, 1895: 16). The report was based upon the belief that prisoners were sent to these institutions *as* punishment rather than *for* punishment and resulted in changes to prison conditions, including the abandonment of the use of the crank and treadmill. Although the deterrent role of prisons was not abandoned, it was balanced by placing a similar emphasis on the objective of the reform of convicted offenders. The report argued that prison discipline and treatment should be designed to maintain, stimulate or awaken the higher susceptibilities of prisoners, to develop their moral instincts, to train them in orderly and industrial habits, and whenever possible to turn them out of prison better men and women, both physically and morally, than when they came in. Its key provisions were incorporated into the 1898 Prisons Act.

The emphasis placed on prisons as mechanisms to secure the rehabilitation of prisoners was underpinned by positivist assumptions (which are discussed in Chapter 1) that it was legitimate to focus remedial attention on the individual with a view to treating the causes of their offending behaviour. This approach gave rise to the 'treatment model' that was officially endorsed as the main aim of prisons. Government policy as late as the 1950s continued to assert that the constructive function of prisons was to prevent those committed to their care from offending again, and it endorsed the Gladstone Committee's belief that this objective would not be achieved solely through the use of a regime designed to deter through fear (Home Office, 1959). Nonetheless, the prison environment that operated as late as the 1960s was run on military lines. Staff frequently had a background in one of the three armed services and discipline was tight. Any infringement of the rules was harshly dealt with at internal hearings and punishments – which included the bread and water diet – were meted out for minor infractions of prison rules.

The decline of the treatment model

As is argued in Chapter 7, the individualism which Conservative governments promoted between 1979 and 1997 was reflected in its attitude towards those who broke the law. The existing emphasis on rehabilitation derived from the treatment model gave way to the justice model. This new approach sought to imbue punishment with a retributivist objective and was reinforced by a political goal to 'get tough with criminals'. The latter was a key aspect of law and order ideology that augmented the justice model and was embraced by Conservative governments between 1979 and 1997 (Cavadino and Dignan, 1992: 26–7). This resulted in significant departures from the justice model, in particular the 1997 Crime (Sentences) Act that provided for stiff sentences to certain categories of repeat offenders that took into account past offending behaviour in addition to the current offence.

The Conservative perception that the public required evidence that the government was pursuing a punitive approach towards those who committed crime served to place prisons to the forefront of their thinking. Consequently, 22 new prisons were constructed between 1979 and 1996. The incarceration of offenders provided tangible proof that criminals were being caught, and was the key feature of an approach summarised by the phrase 'prison works' (Howard, 1993a). This caused prison numbers to increase: the prison population rose above 50,000 in January 1994, reached 56,000 by the end of July 1996 and 60,000 on the eve of the May 1997 general election. This was due to a change in government policy concerning imprisonment rather than to any dramatic rise in crime. The increase in prison numbers had a direct impact on the prisoners' environment since it resulted in overcrowding.

Policy changes also affected conditions within prisons. The emphasis placed on the rehabilitation of individual prisoners by the treatment model was replaced by a harsher, 'decent but austere' environment that could be presented as additional proof that those who committed crime were being appropriately punished for their wrongdoings. Changes affecting prison conditions that were introduced by Conservative governments in the 1990s included:

- new and increased powers for prison governors;
- the removal of in-cell televisions for approximately 2,000 prisoners (although successive reports by Tumim (1990), Woolf (1991) and Learmont (1995) argued for wider availability of this facility on the grounds that it had a beneficial impact on prison life);
- the introduction of random mandatory drug tests (MDTs) throughout the Prison Service in 1996;
- the development of new rules governing home leave and temporary release provisions;
- the introduction of the Incentives and Earned Privileges Scheme (IEP) whereby prisoners were divided into three categories – basic, standard and enhanced. Prisoners started off in the standard category and could be downgraded for unsatisfactory behaviour (losing privileges such as evening association or visits and spending a greater proportion of their time in cells) or upgraded for good behaviour.

Additionally, financial stringency announced in January 1996 (which entailed a 15 per cent cut in the budget of the Prison Service over the following three years, involving the loss of 3,000 jobs) was followed by a later edict that costs per prisoner should be reduced by 10.2 per cent in 1998/9. This resulted in fewer staff working longer hours and superintending more inmates. Prisoners therefore spent more time in their cells and this reduction in contact between themselves and prison staff had a detrimental impact on the rehabilitation of offenders.

During the 1997 general election campaign the Conservative government asserted that treatment and rehabilitation were, and would be, adequately funded (Howard, 1997: 7), but it was subsequently pointed out that whereas the Prison Service spent £30 million a year on mandatory drugs testing, only £5 million was available for treatment programmes, with good ones being a rarity (Teers, 1997: 13).

Do prisons work?

Prisons 'work' if they successfully accomplish one or more of the objectives with which they are commonly associated.

- *Punishment*. This role is particularly designed to enable society to 'get its own back' on those who have offended. This retributive objective may be undermined if the public feel that prison regimes are too 'soft' on inmates.
- *Reform or rehabilitation*. These reductivist aims may be tested by the extent to which released inmates reoffend: a high rate of recidivism will suggest that prisons fail in achieving this purpose.
- *Incapacitation*. Although imprisonment prevents inmates from committing further crime while in prison, the extent to which it reduces the overall level of crime in society is dependent on the proportion of criminals who are locked up. This is revealed by statistics concerned with crime levels and detection and conviction rates.
- *Deterrence*. The extent to which the threat of prison sentences deter crime is affected by a number of factors. It assumes that offending behaviour derives from some form of logical thought process as opposed to opportunism. The extent to which prisons deter criminal behaviour is also heavily influenced by the effectiveness of the criminal justice system. If detection and conviction rates are low, prisons may be viewed more in the nature of an occupational hazard rather than a realistic sanction acting as a constraint on criminal activities.
- *Denunciation*. Prisons provide society with a mechanism with which it can condemn criminal actions. Those who commit them are removed from society, thus enabling prisons to be the tangible evidence of the triumph of good over evil.

Criticisms of Conservative prison policy

The prison policies pursued by Conservative governments between 1979 and 1997 were subject to widespread criticism. The belief that tougher sentences and more austere prison regimes had a deterrent effect on crime was challenged by the views that many crimes were committed on impulse (Prison Reform Trust, 1993: 3–4). The belief that prison might 'work' as a deterrent was also put into question by low detection and conviction rates, which meant that the fear of prison was a relatively minor factor in the decision to commit a crime; it was perhaps viewed as an occupational hazard rather than the inevitable consequence of criminal activity.

Conservative policy also argued that prison could 'work' by incapacitating offenders. This approach was based upon what has been described as the 'eliminative ideal' (Rutherford, 1997) that underpinned measures such as transportation. It was defended by the then Home Secretary asserting that between 3 and 13 crimes would be prevented if a burglar was sent to prison for a year rather then being given a community sentence order. (Howard, 1993b). However, the validity of this assertion (which was based on the re-offending rates of a sample of 197 convicted burglars given community sentence orders in 1987) was questioned. In 1993 a Home Office study suggested that, as few offenders were caught and only 1 in 12 of those arrested were jailed, it would require a disproportionate increase in the prison population to make a substantial impact on the annual crime rate. It was estimated that in order to decrease the level of crime by 1 per cent it would be necessary to expand the prison population by 25 per cent (Tarling, 1993). The expenditure required to build new prisons to accommodate this influx of prisoners was estimated at £1 billion (Prison Reform Trust, 1993: 6).

The policy of building more prisons and jailing more offenders was condemned by one author of the report into the Strangeways prison riot as 'short sighted and irresponsible' (Woolf, 1993). The Prison Governors' Association chairman warned that rising numbers coupled with financial cuts and an emphasis on security created a serious danger of prison riots (Scott, 1995). Many of those in prison (34 per cent) were on remand awaiting trial, and a significant number had been given custodial sentences for failing to pay fines (Prison Reform Trust, 1995: 3). This latter problem disproportionately affected women whose 'crimes of poverty' included non-payment of television licences and fines (O'Friel, 1995).

The belief that prison might 'work' by reforming criminals was also scrutinised. A Home Office study on recidivism was based on 65,624 offenders who had left prison in 1987. Criminal records were examined after two and four years to ascertain how many of these offenders were subsequently reconvicted. The figures showed a reconviction rate of 71 per cent for young male offenders, 49 per cent for adult male offenders and 40 per cent for female offenders within the two-year period. The respective reconviction rates for all males over a four-year period was 68 per cent, and 48 per cent for women (Home Office, 1994b: 133–8). Research by the Home Office suggested that one half of prisoners discharged from prison in 1994 were reconvicted of a standard list offence within two years of release (White, 1998).

The Labour government and prison policy

Many of the initial policies pursued by the 1997 Labour government were similar to those of their Conservative predecessors. The aim of the Prison

Service was redrafted in 1999, becoming the 'effective execution of the sentence of the court so as to reduce reoffending and protect the public'. The view that prisons should chiefly serve the needs of society by protecting it from those who acted anti-socially was most obviously reflected in the Home Secretary's announced intention in 1999 to lock away psychopaths and others with severe personality disorders – whether or not they had been convicted of a criminal offence – for indefinite, though reviewable, sentences.

Additionally, the Labour government failed to redress the reliance on custodial sentences that had been the hallmark of Michael Howard's tenure as Home Secretary so that the prison population stood at 66,000 in December 1998 (or approximately 125 per 100,000 of population). In February 1998 the Director General of the Prison Service warned that if the prison population continued to grow at its current rate it would reach a figure of between 82,000 and 93,000 in 2005. This would require the construction of 24 new prisons at a capital cost of £2 billion and annual running costs of £300 million (Prison Report 42, 1998a: 13). However, the emphasis on constructive prison regimes to reform and rehabilitate prisoners indicated an important change in the rationale for the use of custodial sentences after 1997.

The Labour government and constructive prison regimes

It has been argued that prisons 'work' if they do something useful with offenders (Matthews and Francis, 1996: 19). Jack Straw (Labour's Home Secretary in 1997) emphasised that prisons constituted 'one element in a radical and coherent strategy to protect the public by reducing crime', but he was especially concerned to ensure that prison regimes were constructive (Straw, 1998). He argued that constructive regimes were underpinned by prison communities that were

- *safe* – in the sense that bullying, drug dealing and violence had to be regarded as an anathema to what prison stood for;
- *fair* – so that the government's commitment to human rights became translated into fairness in the way in which prisoners were treated;
- *responsible* – which meant that prisoners should be encouraged to make choices and be given some responsibility for the conduct of their own affairs, and that trustworthiness should be rewarded.

He further announced that the prison budget would be increased by £660 million spread over three years, £200 million of which would be expended on the development of prison regimes.

To what extent, and in what ways, can it be argued that 'prison works'?

The rehabilitation of prisoners

A key issue concerning imprisonment is whether it is primarily designed to serve the interests of society or those of the prisoner. The former belief suggests that prisons may serve as 'warehouses that quarantine or incapacitate those men and women who either cannot be deterred by the threat of sanctions or those whose actions are so harmful to society that they are best kept away from the rest of us' (Andrews, 2003: 120). The latter view emphasises the role of prisons to bring about the reform and rehabilitation of those who have broken the law.

Throughout the twentieth century, emphasis has been placed upon the reductivist role of prisons. Although views have been expressed that the environment of prisons and the impact that this has on offenders makes it difficult for these institutions to secure the rehabilitation or cure of individuals (Goffman, 1968; Morris, 1974), reductivist aims were prominent concerns of the treatment model, the loss of faith in which was an important aspect of what has been referred to as the 'penal crisis' of the second half of the twentieth century (Raynor and Vanstone, 2002: 73). Nonetheless, rehabilitation was retained as a desirable objective by the 1979–97 Conservative governments and was especially addressed through individualist programmes designed to address offending behaviour. It should also be noted that traditionally most persons have been sent to prison for short terms, which usually provided insufficient time to re-educate or retrain them. One consequence of this situation was that sentences need to be longer, or even indeterminate, in order to achieve the rehabilitative ideal.

This section examines the nature of the prison environment on the capacity of these institutions to reform, rehabilitate or cure inmates. Other issues discussed in a later section concerned with the causes of prison riots are also relevant to this discussion.

Security

The emphasis placed on security within prisons may not be compatible with the reform and rehabilitation of prisoners. The escape of a number of top-security inmates including Charles Wilson (1964), Ronald Biggs (1965) and George Blake (1966) prompted the Home Office to commission a report into prison escapes and security, chaired by Earl Mountbatten. It reported in 1966 and made a number of recommendations, including the early categorisation of prisoners while held in local prisons. The resultant A, B, C, D categorisation related to a prisoner's security risk and was reviewed during the course of the sentence (Mountbatten, 1966). This indicated that the key rationale of prisons was to provide secure internment to protect society from dangerous criminals, thereby placing society's needs above those of the prisoner. This new thinking was embodied in a White Paper that subordinated treatment and training to the aim of holding those committed to custody in conditions that were acceptable to society (Home Office, 1969).

A subsequent report coupled security considerations with the treatment model's emphasis on rehabilitation by suggesting that Prison Rule 1 should be redrafted to state the purpose of detaining convicted prisoners was to keep them in custody that was both secure and positive. To this end it directed the behaviour of the authorities and staff to create an environment which could assist prisoners to respond and contribute to society as positively as possible, would preserve and promote their self-respect, would minimise the harmful effects of their removal from normal life, prepare them for discharge and help them re-enter society (Home Office, 1979).

Although some dismissed this philosophy as 'zookeeping' (Fitzgerald and Sim, 1980: 82), it found official support in the mission statement for the Prison Department published in 1988, the first sentence of which stated that 'HM Prison Service serves the public by keeping in custody those committed by the courts. Our duty is to look after them with humanity and help them lead law abiding and useful lives in custody and after release'. Although the paramount need for security was recognised in subsequent official pronouncements, it was later argued that the time had arrived for a more prominent focus on the rehabilitative functions of prison (Prison Service, 1997).

Consequences of the emphasis placed on security

The view that security considerations should dominate the operations of prisons implied that their prime role was that of incarceration. This required an environment that was not necessarily conducive to the rehabilitation of prisoners. The extent or availability of training or education was considerably influenced by a prisoner's security categorisation, and prison officers were primarily concerned with the security aspects of prison life rather than with its reforming role. Security needs could lead to prisoners remaining locked in their cells for long periods so that they were unable to improve themselves through training.

This situation was aggravated by the way that prisoners deemed to pose a high security risk were housed throughout the prison system. The Mountbatten Report had suggested that one ultra-high security prison should be built. This recommendation was not acted upon, and instead the dispersal policy proposed by the Radzinowicz Committee in 1968 was implemented. This resulted in dangerous prisoners being placed in several prisons, in the belief that mixing dangerous and non-dangerous criminals would make the former easier to handle. In practice, however, this policy resulted in enhanced security and surveillance throughout the entire system, to the detriment of rehabilitative objectives, and also posed the possibility of prisons becoming 'universities of crime'.

The emphasis on prison security was increased following the publication of the Woodcock Report (Home Office, 1994b) and the Learmont Report (Home Office, 1995a). The latter viewed custody as the primary purpose of prisons and put forward 127 recommendations; these included bringing all prisons up to minimum standards of security by strengthening perimeter fences and installing close-circuit television, replacing all dormitory accommodation with cells, introducing electronic and magnetic locking systems and making visitor searching more rigorous (Home Office, 1995a: 139–42). This approach was criticised for placing security considerations above the obligations of the Prison Service to treat prisoners humanely and to seek their rehabilitation. It was alleged that the Learmont philosophy pointed towards concentration camps and shooting prisoners who attempted to escape (Tumim, 1995).

The security situation might be ameliorated to some extent by reversing the policy of dispersal. Following an attempted breakout from Whitemoor in 1994 and an escape from Parkhurst in 1995 moves were undertaken to place the most dangerous prisoners in a smaller number of jails. The possibility of building a 'super-maximum' prison was also considered, since this would enable all dangerous prisoners to be concentrated in one institution (Home Office, 1995a: 132–8). Subsequently the Prison Service unveiled a £130 million anti-escape package, which included the use of sensitive alarms linked to perimeter fences, and additionally the number of prisons housing category A prisoners was reduced from 21 to 13.

The issue of security also exerted considerable influence over prison visits from family and friends. These are widely regarded as important influences on the behaviour of inmates while in prison: they also perform a major role in the subsequent rehabilitation and resettlement of prisoners. While it is important to stop visitors smuggling contraband into prisons, an over-emphasis on security considerations can greatly affect the quality of these visits and thus the useful consequences that derive from them.

It might be concluded that if increased emphasis was devoted to activities such as education and job training, which prisoners found useful, there would need to be less emphasis on security – at least in prisons housing low-risk offenders. The emphasis on security thus suggests that prisons are primarily designed as places of punishment rather than rehabilitation. In 1997, a Parliamentary committee recommended that improving the quantity and quality of purposeful activity should be the government's priority for the Prison Service, and suggested developing performance indicators and targets for purposeful activity (Home Affairs Committee, 1997).

Security in women's prisons

Although few women prisoners pose a serious threat to society, security also dominates the regime to which female offenders are subjected. In 1995, for example, an inspection team led by the Chief Inspector of Prisons, General Sir David Ramsbotham, abruptly terminated a visit to Holloway prison in reaction to what he regarded as overzealous security arrangements which involved women being locked in their cells for up to 23 hours a day.

Public outcry over security issues in women's prisons was occasioned by revelations in *The Guardian* on 11 January 1996 that a pregnant prisoner spent most of her labour in shackles, including being chained to a bed for ten hours. This eventually prompted the Home Secretary to amend its rules so that, in future, no woman who was taken to hospital to give birth would be restrained once she arrived there. However, in December 1996 a woman remand prisoner was handcuffed while attending hospital for breast cancer surgery. These incidents implied that security considerations could be used as a mechanism to humiliate prisoners.

A significant number of women prisoners are mothers of children below 18 (Caddle and Crisp, 1996). These need facilities such as mother-and-baby units and the ability to spend 'quality time' with their children. However, these requirements are unevenly provided for across the country. In 1999 a national review pointed out that only 64 mother-and-baby units were available in England, spread across four prisons, and called for the appointment of a national coordinator for such units (Review of Principles, Policies and Procedures on Mothers and Babies/Children in Prison, 1999). In 2000 there were only 72 places available, although in excess of 1,000 women prisoners had children under five.

Women in prison

Between 1993 and 1998, the average population of women in prison rose by almost 100 per cent, as against 45 per cent for men (Home Office, 1999: 1). In June 1998 there were 3,100 women in prison, which represented a percentage increase of 21 per cent compared to the figure 12 months previously. It was the first time since 1905 that the figure of 3,000 had been reached (Sparks, 1998b: 24). This figure subsequently rose to 4,529 in December 2005, justifying the development of prison regimes specific to the requirements of female prisoners.

The deaths in custody of eight women in Scottish prisons between 1995 and 1997 prompted a review by a team from the Prison and Social Work Services Inspectorate, concerning community disposals and the use of custody for women offenders in Scotland. The team found that the background of women in prison was marked by 'experience of abuse, drug misuse, low educational attainment, poverty, psychological distress and self-harm'. This made the prison experience for such women difficult to manage, increasing the risk of suicide (Sparks, 1998b: 24).

In 1997 the Chief Inspector of Prisons published the findings of a thematic review on women's prisons entitled *Prisons for Women in England and Wales*. In this report he challenged the view that the needs of women were the same as those of men and put forward 160 recommendations. These included:

- the establishment of a Director of Women's Prisons who would be in overall charge of the female establishment;
- staff working in women's prisons should have specific training to enable them to meet the special needs of female prisoners;
- particular care was required at the reception and induction stages since many women had not been in prison before and in excess of 50 per cent of women offenders had experienced sexual or physical abuse as either children or adults (Ablitt, 2000). This made searching procedures especially harrowing.

The 1997 Prison Service Review responded to the first of these recommendations by rejecting the desirability of functionally based Directorates to address the needs of specific groups of prisoners; instead it suggested that a Director of Regimes should be appointed onto the Prisons Board who would be supported by Assistant Directors with specific responsibilities for women, and also for young offenders, adult males, lifers and parole. Subsequently a Women's Policy Group was established in the Prison Service Headquarters.

A more fundamental reform, however, is to question the relevance of custodial sentences for most women offenders, few of whom have committed violent crimes. Female offenders are frequently 'victims of circumstances they have failed to cope with' (Neustatter, 2000), for whom community sentences may be more appropriate.

The sociology of imprisonment

Sociologies of imprisonment emphasise the impact that the prison environment has on the behaviour of its inmates. As will be discussed below, some of these accounts also include prison officers (Crawley, 2004) and some discuss the relationship between officers and prisoners, especially within the overall theme of the maintenance of order in these institutions.

Imprisonment has been described as entry to a 'total institution' (Goffman, 1961, 1968) in which all aspects of the lives of inmates are played out. Confinement involves a series of assaults upon the self that have the effect of contradicting or failing to corroborate previous self-conceptions (Cohen and Taylor, 1972). Prisoners are poorly prepared for the experiences they will face in prison and are forced to pick up the prison routine from other inmates (Ramsbotham, 2005: 5–6). They are subject to a number of basic deprivations (Matthews, 1999: 54) and attempts to compensate for the denials of liberty, access to goods and services, heterosexual relationships, autonomy and personal security have been argued to exert considerable influence over the behaviour of prisoners (Sykes, 1958). They have been depicted as 'lonely individuals' (Mathiesen, 1965: 12) in a position of psychological and material weakness, subordinate to the power wielded by prison staff which may give rise to anger, frustration, bewilderment, demoralisation or stress. Psychological disorders including anxiety, depression, withdrawal and self-injury may make reform or rehabilitation difficult to accomplish (Cooke et al., 1990: 55–66). Traditionally the Prison Service viewed mental illness as a disciplinary issue. Concern regarding the physical and psychological welfare of exceptional escape risk category A prisoners contained in Special Service Units was expressed by the human rights organisation, Amnesty International (Amnesty International, 1997).

Problems which include mental illness, inadequate care and treatment of those undergoing drug and alcohol detoxification programmes and the inability to adapt to prison regimes are major factors explaining prison suicides. On 30 January 2005, an editorial in *The Observer* newspaper stated that there had been 571 prison suicides since Labour came to power in 1997, and it has been argued that prisoners are seven times more likely to commit suicide than the general population, with young inmates being most at risk (Howard League for Penal Reform, 1993). A Suicide Awareness Unit was established in 1991 to help prepare a national strategy to combat this problem but its immediate impact was limited. In excess of 40 suicides occurred in both 1991 and 1992.

Depression, personality changes and psychological deterioration are influenced by factors that include whether a prisoner is given a fixed or indeterminate sentence and the length of time served. A study of the effects of long-term imprisonment on male life sentence prisoners in Durham's 'E' Wing drew attention to the fear of deterioration among such prisoners (Cohen and Taylor, 1972). Although this fear may exceed the actuality of the problem, it suggested that prisoners' energies were concentrated on matters such as survival rather than on self-improvement. The former may be achieved through coping strategies such as time management or adapting to the prison environment (which may result in 'institutionalisation' and the inability to adapt to life on the outside) (Goffman, 1961), by pursuing activities designed to aid the passing of the sentence (Sapsford, 1978), by prisoners cutting themselves off from their families (perhaps pretending that established relationships are over), or by fantasy (King and McDermott, 1995).

One problem in assessing whether or not deterioration occurs concerns the indicators that are used to measure it. Tests which seek to establish whether or not changes occur in a prisoner's intellectual or cognitive abilities may not reveal personality changes which make it difficult to subsequently adapt to the outside world. It is officially accepted that the fundamental nature of the prison environment tends to reduce an offender's self-reliance and feelings of responsibility. (Home Office, 1990). Aspects of the 1991 Criminal Justice Act (which included the requirement for enhanced prisoner participation in sentence planning in training prisons) were designed to offset these problems and were compatible with the desire to improve the individual.

In 1999 a survey into the mental health state of prisoners suggested that 95 per cent of male remand and sentenced prisoners displayed symptoms consistent with psychiatric disorders and almost all female remand and sentenced prisoners displayed symptoms common to one or more psychiatric disorders. Although some of these were evident prior to sentence, the high prevalence of psychiatric disorders could to some extent be related to the environment of prisons (Woolf, 1999).

Brutalisation

Prisons are violent places. Explicit violence gains credit for its perpetrators in both male and female prisons and a known capacity for such behaviour is the necessary currency for efficient and healthy survival (O'Dwyer and Carlen, 1985). This suggests that prisoners may either need to develop violent traits while in prison or risk being the victims of violence from other inmates. The latter is illustrated by the growth of bullying in the 1990s that may lead to suicide. Those subjected to violent treatment within prisons, especially if carried out by prison staff (or abetted should staff turn a blind eye to it), may leave prison with a grudge against society resulting in the commission of further, and more violent, criminal acts in the future. Although the Prison Service introduced a strategy to counter bullying in 1993, later research revealed that 'victimisation was pervasive'. A sample of young offenders and adult prisoners revealed that 46 per cent of the former and 30 per cent of the latter had been assaulted, robbed or threatened with violence the previous month (O'Donnell and Edgar, 1996: 1–2).

A recent aspect of this problem has been the rise of prison gangs who exert their control over other inmates through methods that include bullying, intimidation and, in some cases, murder. Much of this violence is associated with the prison drugs trade, but it may involve other aspects including racial violence (Thompson, 2005).

Violence by prison staff

Allegations of violence by prison staff towards inmates have been occasionally made. One problem is that such allegations are investigated by the Prison Service that may be seen as insufficiently independent to secure the confidence of prisoners in the system. In March 1998 a Coroner's Court jury determined that staff in a privately managed prison had unlawfully killed an inmate, Alton Manning. However, a particularly serious allegation of such brutality involving the systematic beating of inmates was made at Wormwood Scrubbs. In 1999, following a police investigation which entailed the biggest ever criminal investigation at a British jail examining allegations of assault and brutality mainly between January 1997 and May 1998, 25 prison officers were suspended in connection with assault-related allegations in 1999, 12 of whom were subsequently charged with assaulting inmates. A second investigation looking at cases that dated back to 1991 was also mounted.

The need for staff to show consideration towards those in their charge was referred to by the Chief Inspector of Prisons in 1999. He called for some older officers to end the 'old-style culture' which treated a prisoner as 'somebody who is subordinate to you' and argued that the culture of 'domination and intimidation' should give way to a situation in which officers should have 'the same responsibility of care for a prisoner that a nurse has for a patient in hospital' (HM Chief Inspector of Prisons, 1999).

'Universities of crime'

Prisons are sometimes popularly viewed as places in which relatively minor offenders learn the 'tricks of the trade' from seasoned inmates and thus return to society as more accomplished criminals. Prisons may thus constitute an expensive way of making bad people worse (Home Office, 1990). The current problem of prison overcrowding has tended to accentuate this problem by placing violent and dangerous prisoners in the same institutions as relatively minor offenders. The former may serve as role models for the latter in the absence of alternative influences. This was cited as the key explanation for the riot at Wymott prison in 1993 (HM Chief Inspector of Prisons, 1993).

One further explanation for prisons serving as institutions that 'educate' offenders in criminal habits is the negative image associated with it. The routine of prisons (which commences with routine removal of personal possessions, stripping and showering and – for men – being dressed in prison uniform) emphasises that society views prisoners as deviant and in need of a disciplined regime to remedy their personal failings. Such negativity may not be conducive to self-improvement. Additionally, the stigma of imprisonment may make it hard for prisoners to find gainful employment upon release. The knowledge of this (which is especially acute in periods of high unemployment) may serve to further isolate those who are already marginalised (Fleisher, 2003: 110) and perhaps encourage prisoners to make the best use of their time while inside to build contacts in the criminal underworld and learn skills which will better equip them for a life of crime upon release.

Purposeful activity

The term 'purposeful activity' describes a wide range of pursuits which include prison work, education and training courses, physical education, programmes to tackle substance abuse, anti-bullying initiatives, family visits and the taking of responsibilities in prison gardens and workshops (Home Affairs Committee, 2005). These are designed to provide prisoners with constructive use of their time while in prison and are integral to the maintenance of order within these institutions and an essential aid to the rehabilitation of inmates when released. Until 2004, a Prison Service Key Performance Indicator set a target of 24 hours a week to be spent in purposeful activities. However, targets of this nature did not measure the quality of the activities delivered in this period (Ramsbotham, 2005: 83). Additionally, the consistent failure of prisons to meet this target resulted in its abandonment from 2004/5 onwards and its subsequent downgrading to a Key Performance Target.

The inadequacy of the provision of purposeful activities in prisons was highlighted by the Home Affairs Select Committee in 2005. Based on data derived from a prison diaries project, it stated:

> … disturbingly high proportions of prisoners are engaged in little or no purposeful activity. Very few prisons provide for adequate amounts of purposeful activity across all, or most, of the main categories of such activities. The reasons for this include overcrowding and disruptions to education, vocational and treatment programmes caused by prisoner transfer, reducing prison staffing and generally poor administration. The consequences for prisoners are too many hours 'banged up' in their cells, with an adverse impact on their mental and physical health, and missed opportunities for rehabilitation.

The Committee thus urged the reinstatement of the 24 hours per week purposeful activity Key Performance Indicator (Home Affairs Committee, 2005).

The following section discusses some aspects of purposeful activity that have an obvious bearing on prisoners' reform and rehabilitation.

Treatment programmes

Therapeutic treatment is available for a limited number of violent psychiatric prisoners in specialist institutions such as Grendon or in therapeutic units in prisons such as Hull, where the traditional emphasis on work, education and physical exercise is replaced by therapeutic groupwork where prisoners are challenged to face up to their offending behaviour within a supportive environment in which doctors play a key role. Such regimes are costly but achieve success in terms of subsequent reconvictions of those with violent and sexual offences (Genders and Player, 1995), although there was a need for inmates to spend at least 18 months to achieve positive results that were evidenced by reconviction rates of around one-fifth to one-quarter (Marshall, 1997:1). Elsewhere accredited sex offender, anger control and drug rehabilitation programmes have been introduced to address the offending behaviour of offenders. This is especially important regarding sex offenders as programmes such as the Sex Offender Treatment Programme (SOTP) are designed to make them face up to the crimes for which they have been committed. However, programmes seeking to address all forms of offending behaviour are not universally available within the Prison Service which means that a number of prisoners are not able to benefit from them to aid their reform. Intensive programmes to combat alcohol abuse, for example, are, in general, poorly provided in prisons and psychiatric problems have traditionally been responded to by a heavy reliance being placed on drugs. In 1998 the Labour Home Secretary announced that further programmes directed at violent offenders and specifically at thieves and robbers would be developed (Straw, 1998).

Drug rehabilitation policy in prisons

It has been reported that 80 per cent of prisoners declare drug misuse prior to prison with around 55 per cent admitting to a serious drug problem (Home Office, 2004: 5). The prisons drug strategy of the Labour government was initiated in 1998, based upon the publication entitled *Tackling Drugs in Prison* (1998). This was formulated following a review of the Conservative government's 1995 policy document *Drug Misuse in Prisons*. This strategy embraced:

- action to prevent drugs being smuggled into prisons;
- clinical detoxification as the first step to help prisoners to get off drugs while in prison;
- the availability of drug rehabilitation programmes in prison and an increase in the number of therapeutic communities which offer intensive programmes to prisoners with severe dependency problems;
- the development of integrated counselling, assessment, referral, advice and throughcare services (termed CARATS);
- improved staff training on drugs issues;
- the provision of a wide range of incentives to encourage prisoners to avoid using drugs: this includes prisoners signing voluntary drug testing compacts to help them stay clean.

The Prison Service's Drug Strategy Unit commenced commissioning drug treatment programmes towards the end of 1998, and by 2000 all prisons provided access to some form of treatment programme. Drug rehabilitation was also aided by more general improvements in prison healthcare. In 2000 a formal partnership between the Prison Service and NHS was entered into to secure improved standards of healthcare in prisons and in April 2003 the Department of Health (and in Wales, the Welsh Assembly government) assumed national funding responsibility for prison health services. It was intended that the responsibility for commissioning health services for prisoners would be fully devolved to the local NHS by 2006 (Home Office, 2004: 6).

Education programmes

The rehabilitation of most prisoners, however, is heavily dependent on the acquisition of skills that will boost employment prospects upon release. However, prisons have not consistently offered medium- and long-term offenders meaningful educational or training opportunities. Education (which is essential not simply to boost employment prospects but also to enhance a prisoner's self-esteem) has traditionally been viewed as a privilege rather than a right whose provision varied from one prison to another. It was formerly provided by local authorities but since 1993 has been contracted out. The nature of the subjects taught might not necessarily be appropriate to prisoners, many of whom require basic skills in literacy and numeracy (Tumim, 1993). This issue was addressed by the 1997 Labour government that concentrated prison education resources on basic skills. In 2002/3 over 41,000 basic skills qualifications were gained by prisoners (Home Office, 2004: 4). In 1998 reforms introduced by the Labour Home Secretary included the introduction of targets against which education provision could be assessed for both the prison and prisoner, and the new draft of Prison Rules in 1999 specifically affirmed the right of a prisoner to be given reasonable facilities to improve their education by distance learning through courses offered by institutions such as the Open University.

Prison work and vocational skills programmes

Work conducted within prisons was traditionally associated with menial tasks that seemed more concerned with aiding the passage of time than with providing work-relevant skills. There was a traditional reluctance to expand this form of activity significantly as this might be perceived as rewarding prisoners and providing unfair benefits to those companies who are able to undercut their competitors by taking advantage of cheap prison labour. Accordingly, it was argued that 'production and manufacture in prison is likely to be inefficient and in many respects is "primitive" and "pre-capitalist"' (Matthews, 1999: 44). However, changes to this situation have been introduced. Initiatives were pursued during the 1990s enabling prisoners to earn above the average 'prison wage' by performing work for outside companies. (Examples of successful competition in the 1990s include the award to Coldingley Prison, Surrey, of contracts to provide laundry services for the NHS.) Developments of this nature were aided by the 1996 Prisoners' Earnings Act that provided for the payment of realistic wages.

Recent developments to aid prisoners to find work upon release have included the provision of facilities (both within prisons and the community) to obtain key work and training skills qualifications, and the Custody to Work initiative that was launched in 2000. By 2002/3 30 per cent of prisoners were released with a job or training place to go to. In excess of 14,000 unemployed prisoners attended their local Jobcentre on release under the Freshstart initiative and it was estimated that between April and October 2002, 14 per cent of those attending under Freshstart got a job within thirteen weeks of release from prison. Others received help from the New Deal or other training places (Home Office, 2004: 5).

Conclusion

In general, offending behaviour programmes, education facilities, and prison work and work experience programmes are most poorly provided in local prisons which are intended to house short-term prisoners and those remanded in custody. Additionally, the programmes available where these are on offer are influenced more by Key Performance Indicators rather than a prisoner's need: this may mean, for example, that courses offering anger therapy take precedence in securing resources over pre-release development courses. The success of such programmes is also likely to be most effective if backed up by courses available to prisoners on release. One example of such a programme is the Creative and Supportive Trust which was established by education officers at Holloway prison in 1982 which caters for women who have served a prison sentence or had been in drug or alcohol rehabilitation or psychiatric care. A key objective underpinning the formation of NOMS (a reform which is discussed below) was designed to ensure the continuity of measures designed to rehabilitate offenders conducted in prison and following release.

> What aspects of the prison environment make it difficult for these institutions to secure the rehabilitation of offenders?

The impact of privatisation

Privatisation was underpinned by an attempt to establish a purchaser–provider relationship between the Prison Service and private sector, and entailed subjecting the running of a prison to a process of competitive tender. Some of these (such as the running of Strangeways, Manchester) have been won by the Prison Service but private organisations have fared better in securing contracts to run newly built prisons. Additionally, the conduct of specific prison services at some or all prisons (which in 1999 included education, health, information technology, industries, catering and prison shops) may be transferred to the private sector.

The rationale for the running of prisons being placed in private hands was that they operate at lower running costs than those controlled by the Home Office to the detriment of the number of staff employed, staff wages, conditions of employment (especially pension entitlement) and working conditions (Planning Group Prison Service, 1998). It has been estimated that the running costs of private prisons are 15–25 per cent below those of state prisons (Tilt, 1995), a figure which was broadly endorsed by a review in 1997 which stated that on average privately run prisons offered an operational cost saving of 8–15 per cent. More recent research, however, has indicated that the gap between the running costs of private and publicly operated prisons was diminishing. Increased efficiencies in private sector prisons had led to 'a continuous narrowing in the operating cost saving offered by privately operated prisons'. The differential in 1994/5 of private prisons being 13–22 per cent cheaper had fallen by 1997/8 to –2–11 per cent (Woodbridge, 1999: 30).

A major concern with privatisation is that there will be increased emphasis placed on security to the detriment of attempts to reform or rehabilitate prisoners. This is especially so since performance measurements and sanctions in the contracts awarded to private prisons stipulate that an escape can contribute to a large fine being levied on the contractor. Between February 1994 and January 1999 fines that totalled £600,000 had been levied on private contractors due to performance failures (Prison Report 1999: 15).

A Parliamentary Select Committee considered the management of prisons in the public and private sectors in 1996/7. Its subsequent report delivered prior to the 1997 general election supported the expansion of the private sector (which in the view of the committee acted as a spur to efficiency in the public sector), although caution was urged in allowing the private sector to handle high-risk prisoners. It was concluded that private prisons were operating well in terms of quality of performance and that their overall performance was as good as, and in some cases better than, publicly administered prisons. It was believed that private prisons had delivered financial savings to the Prison Service although it was too early to be specific concerning the extent of these. The continued expansion of the private sector was urged in order for the full benefits of competition to be obtained (Home Affairs Committee, 1997). In 1999, an official report supported 'the maintenance, and where appropriate, the extension of contractorisation in terms of whole prisons, services and the relationship between Prison Service Headquarters and establishments' (Prison Service, 1999).

The involvement of the private sector in running prisons was intended to be a feature of the operation of NOMS (a reform which is discussed later in this chapter). The new term applied to this process is 'contestability', which entails the creation of a mixed economy of service delivery by the state, private and voluntary sectors.

The maintenance of order within prisons

As has been indicated above, the maintenance of order within prisons has formed an important emphasis in the sociology of imprisonment. Attention has been devoted to factors such as the role played by prison subcultures in providing stability (Clemmer, 1940) and the way in which prison officers shy away from coercive methods and instead develop strategies that seek to secure the cooperation of inmates (Sykes, 1958). Foucault put forward an 'analytics' of power as a framework within which to discuss the power relationships within prisons that give rise to control strategies within these institutions (Foucault, 1982).

This section discusses factors that may have a prejudicial impact on the maintenance of order within prisons.

Overcrowding

Overcrowding is not a new problem faced by the Prison Service and has resulted in a number of Home Secretaries introducing piecemeal interventions to solve particular crises. These included the 1982 Criminal Justice Act (which permitted the release of non-serious offenders up to six months before they had served their sentence), the introduction of changes in the parole system to facilitate the release of non-serious offenders (1984) and an increase in remission of sentence for good behaviour (1987).

Overcrowding may undermine order within prisons in a number of ways. Ecological theories related to the causes of crime suggest that aggression is likely to occur when large numbers of people are concentrated in small spaces. An excessive number of persons in one institution may thus aggravate this situation. Prisoners begin to squabble with each other and this could lead to rioting. Overcrowding also disrupts the prison routine and undermines the processes used to maintain order (Matthews, 1999: 68). Overcrowding has a number of detrimental effects on the prison environment. It may result in the cancellation of prisoners' association time, a denial of their access to communicating with those on the outside by telephone and the serving of meals at 'impossible' times (Ramsbotham, 2005: 7). This problem also hinders the effective delivery of rehabilitative programmes and has had a particularly detrimental effect on the nature and stability of the regime by creating a control problem and contributing towards a volatile prison atmosphere, one symptom of which was indiscipline. On 4 October 1994 *The Guardian* referred to figures issued by the Prison Service which indicated that in 1993, 100,000 offences against prison discipline were recorded, a rise of 13 per cent over the figures for the previous year. Overcrowding also resulted in prison officers having to devote much of their time to finding places for prisoners and escorting them around the system at the expense of providing constructive activities in workshops and classrooms, or developing relations with them to aid rehabilitation.

A further consequence of overcrowding was that minor offenders sent to local or community prisons found themselves being bussed to other institutions (termed the 'ship out') to make way for the latest influx from the courts. There were practical difficulties with this arrangement (for example, family visits became more difficult) and this sometimes led to violence whereby local offenders fought with inmates they regarded as 'outsiders' encroaching on 'their' prison. Prison officers also suffer adversely from this situation. They are required to work longer hours (in return for time off in lieu) and may regard the enhanced role played by control and security in their professional lives less rewarding than rehabilitative work.

Overcrowding may thus be an important explanation for disorders within prisons. The disturbance at Strangeways prison in 1990 occurred at a time when in excess of 1,600 prisoners occupied space designed for below 1,000.

The problem has been described as a 'corrosive influence' in the prison system (Woolf, 1994) which Lord Woolf sought to address in his 1991 report by suggesting that no establishment should exceed certified capacity by more than 3 per cent for more than seven days in any month save in exceptional circumstances. The level of overcrowding within Britain's prisons was significantly affected by the penal policy commenced by the Conservative government after 1993 and continued by their Labour successors. In April 2004 the prison population reached its highest-ever recorded level of 75,544 and in October of that year 82 of the 139 prisons in England and Wales were overcrowded (Home Affairs Committee, 2005).

Remand prisoners

Since the mid-1990s the number of prisoners on remand has steadily grown. The remand prison population rose by 20 per cent between 1985 and 1995 (Matthews, 1999: 87) and constituted around 12,000 prisoners at the start of Labour's period of government in 1997. Remand prisoners thus contribute significantly towards prison overcrowding. They included a number of juveniles aged 15–17 who (in spite of the intentions of the 1991 Criminal Justice Act) were remanded into Prison Service custody. Various factors account for this situation that include the delay in bringing an arrested person to trial and the overuse by the courts of custodial remands. The latter issue is a major problem since a small proportion of those detained in custody (less than half of males detained in custody and below one-third of females) (Shaw, 1997: 21) eventually secure a custodial sentence.

Composition of the prison population

Although it has been argued that the existence of an internal culture within prisons offsets disruption that may arise from the make-up of prison populations at any one point in time (Clemmer, 1940), the composition of individual prison populations has been advanced as a further factor influencing the maintenance of order. There is, however, no consensus as to the ideal make-up of such a population. The existence of a large number of short-term prisoners in one institution makes for a rapid turnover of inmates and has been identified as a possible cause of disturbance (Home Office, 1987). Alternatively, the 'toxic mix' of life sentence prisoners, politically motivated inmates and mentally disturbed persons in physically poor and insecure conditions has been cited as a major cause of the prison 'crisis' which may result in disorders (Evans, 1980). This problem was aggravated by initiatives embarked upon by Conservative governments between 1979 and 1997 (particularly 'Care in the Community') that resulted in mentally ill persons eventually finding their way into the prison system. By the early years of the twenty-first century it was estimated that 70 per cent of inmates in Britain's jails had mental health disorders and that a prime role of prison had become that of 'warehousing the sick' (Davies, 2004) or those who were unable to cope with life outside of prison (Ramsbotham, 2005: 72).

Overcrowding has also been blamed for unstable prison populations. The transfer of prisoners due to overcrowding disrupts the composition of the prison population. In 2003/4 there were 100,000 prison transfers (Home Affairs Committee, 2005). These undermine constructive sentence planning and disrupt a prisoner's participation in rehabilitative programmes. The official investigation into the Wymott riot suggested that overcrowding resulted in violent and volatile prisoners ending up in low security units as there was nowhere else for them to go. The design was inappropriate with too much freedom of movement being accorded to prisoners that enabled them to carry out acts of vandalism and display brutality towards other inmates. (HMCIP, 1993: 31–2). Similarly the disorders at Everthorpe prison in 1995 were partly attributed to category B prisoners having their security categorisation lowered in order to be accommodated at a jail designed for category C and D prisoners. Such prisoners were difficult to manage and proved to be a major control problem for the prison (Prison Reform Trust, 1995: 7).

Understaffing

Order within prisons may also be affected by staffing levels. Understaffing results in prison officers working overtime. The introduction of *Fresh Start* in 1987 sought to solve this problem by enabling prison officers to opt to work either 39 or 48 hours per week. Overtime would be eliminated in return for higher pay. However, it was alleged that partly due to budgets being allocated to individual prisons after 1985, insufficient prison officers were recruited to make good the shortfall of staffing which had previously been supplied through overtime (Cavadino and Dignan, 1992: 15). The disorder at Wymott prison in 1993, for example, took place at a time when seven members of staff supplemented by eleven auxiliary night staff (termed 'night patrols') were available to supervise in excess of 700 prisoners (HMCIP, 1993: 1–2).

Managerial weaknesses

The Prison Service has traditionally operated in a highly bureaucratic manner in which governors were effectively tied to their desks by the volume of paperwork generated from the Prison Service Headquarters to which they need to respond. This situation affected their abilities manage their prison staff and prisoners and may have contributed towards problems that undermined order in these institutions such as the abuse of prisoners (Ramsbotham, 2005: 105) or the development of a climate which fostered the constructive purpose of prisons. It has been argued that the emphasis placed by the Prison Service Headquarters on bureaucracy has been to the detriment of the provision of strategic and tactical direction to prison governors and this coupled with the government's preference for 'knee-jerk reactions' to problems rather than strategic planning (Ramsbotham, 2005: 112) had significantly contributed to the contemporary difficulties faced by prisons. These were especially acute in local prisons that were stated to be 'at the very centre of the Prison Service's problems'. It was argued that 'unless and until ministers and the Prison Service resolve the problems caused by their having to hold such a wide variety of prisoners, whose treatment requirements they cannot meet, they will not begin to meet their responsibilities for reducing re-offending' (Ramsbotham, 2005: 112).

Prison riots

Prison riots evidence the breakdown of order within these institutions. They have been defined as 'part of the continuum of practices and relationships inherent in prisons, which involves dissenting and/or protesting by individuals or groups of prisoners which interrupt their imprisonment, by means of which they take over all or part of the prison resources and either express one or more grievances or a demand for change, or both' (Adams, 1994: 13–14). This definition asserts that such events are not acts of mindless violence but are seen as purposeful actions by those involved in them. Numerous actions of this nature have occurred since 1945: a wave of riots occurred in 1961, 1972 and 1986 and major disturbances occurred at Parkhurst in 1969, Hull in 1976 and Gartree in 1978. Several disorders within prisons have occurred in the 1990s, including:

- a riot and subsequent siege at Strangeways Prison, Manchester, in 1990, which stretched over a period of 25 days;
- a riot in September 1993 at Wymott Prison which resulted in £20 million of damage and the loss of 800 prison places.

Such disturbances have been influenced by factors such as deteriorating conditions and the enhanced politicisation of prisoners (especially through the organisation Preservation of the Rights of Prisoners which was formed in 1972) who seek to establish their rights in an environment that has traditionally operated away from the public gaze. Various issues connected with the prison regime also help to account for such occurrences, which will be discussed below.

Lack of justice

The perception that inmates are treated unjustly either by the system itself or through the conduct of individual officers may result in disorder. Prison provides a disciplined regime whose regulations (contained in Prison Rules which were written in 1964) provide for a system of summary justice that may be regarded as overly harsh by prisoners. A particular source of concern in these Rules was the 'catch-all' provision that penalised conduct by a prisoner that 'in any way offends against good order and discipline'. This was, however, removed in the 1999 redrafting of these Rules. A system of punishments is necessary for the maintenance of control over prisoners but those on the receiving end may resent the imposition of this discipline upon them, particularly if they view it to be unfair or arbitrary. Perceptions of injustice may divert the energy of prisoners into rebellion while in prison.

Lord Woolf identified overcrowding and idleness as the two main causes of the Strangeways prison riot. To tackle these problems he argued there was the need for a balance to be struck within prisons between security, control and justice (Home Office, 1991a: 17). He argued that justice required prisoners to be treated fairly and humanely. Other accounts have emphasised the importance of legitimacy. It has been argued that 'a defensible and legitimated prison regime demands a dialogue in which prisoners' voices ... are registered and have a chance of being responded to'. Further, legitimacy demands reference 'to standards that can be defended externally in moral and political argument' (Sparks et al., 1996: 330).

Lord Woolf made a number of recommendations (Home Office, 1991a) to bring about the improvement of prisons. These included:

- the introduction of a national system of accredited standards for prisons;
- the establishment of a prison ombudsman as an ultimate court of appeal to safeguard prisoners' interests;
- the end of the practice of 'slopping out' through the provision of access to sanitation by all inmates by 1996;
- improved links with families (which might be achieved through the use of local prisons) coupled with more prison visits and the liberalisation of home leave and temporary release provisions;
- the introduction of contracts for each prisoner outlining their expectations and responsibilities;
- the improvement of conditions for remand prisoners, including lower security categorisations.

The government responded to this report with a White Paper that endorsed some of these recommendations. These included those related to contracts for prisoners, accredited standards and the establishment of an ombudsman (Home Office, 1991b). Following the publication of the report prisoners were given access to telephones (which enabled them to maintain contacts with families which was seen as an aid to rehabilitation) and the practice of 'slopping out' finally ended on 12 April 1996, although examples remained after that date (Sparks, 1997: 17), in particular in Scottish prisons.

Disruptive prisoners

Disruptive prisoners pose a particular problem for establishing a proper balance in prisons between control and justice. The introduction of Prison Service Headquarters circular Instruction 37/90 led to such prisoners being transferred from one prison to another at regular intervals. Subsequently a small number of special units (Close Supervision Centres) were opened in 1998 to replace this 'roundabout' scheme and deal with such prisoners. Their purpose was to enable seriously disruptive prisoners to be removed from high-security or training prisons and be contained in small highly supervised units where their behaviour could be stabilised in order for them to return to the mainstream prison system. However, the regime of these units is important. It is important that austerity (or a 'hard-line' approach) does not take precedence over therapeutic objectives, and there is a danger that already violent prisoners will feel themselves to be unjustly treated and become brutalised and made worse, especially if the criteria for being sent to such a unit is not clearly understood.

The prison ombudsman and prisoners' rights

The response to prisoners' complaints (individual or collective) has traditionally been poor. Neither the government nor the Prison Service seemed eager to remedy shortcomings when they were made aware of them (Ramsbotham, 2005: 8). The Inspectorate of Prisons was concerned with issues affecting efficiency and propriety but was not empowered to investigate grievances. Instead prisoners could utilise a variety of mechanisms to ventilate their problems including:

● making representations to Boards of Visitors for each prison;
● addressing petitions to the Home Secretary;
● presenting complaints to the Parliamentary Commissioner for Administration;
● pursuing prosecutions (dealing with issues such as seeking to assert the rights of the prisoner or seeking compensation for injuries suffered allegedly as the consequence of negligence by the authorities).

However, the absence of adequate institutionalised channels through which inmates could articulate their needs or grievances may legitimise disorder as the only available way to achieve such purposes. The introduction of a prison ombudsman was regarded as a particularly important mechanism to secure justice within prisons and thus avoid the occurrence of disorders by providing a mechanism through which grievances could be channelled. Five hundred cases were fully investigated in 1996.

There were, however, weaknesses associated with this innovation. The office was not based in statute and, additionally, there were areas that this official was not allowed to examine, which initially included complaints made by the families of those who had died while in custody. Thus the only public forum in which the death of a prisoner could be examined was that of the Coroner's Court Inquest whose remit extended only to the medical causes of death. Additionally, the ombudsman's terms of reference were redrawn in May 1996 to prevent the investigation of decisions made by a minister that formed the basis of a prisoner's complaint. He further lost unlimited access to Prison Service papers and was required to submit reports to the Prison Service prior to publication. Finally, recommendations made by the ombudsmen in response to complaints submitted by a prisoner can be rejected by the prison governor.

There are two main difficulties associated with attempts to ensure that prisoners' interests are properly safeguarded.

- *Opposition of prison staff.* The enhancement of prisoners' rights may evoke a 'crisis of authority' among prison officers who become concerned that their need to control and wield power over prisoners is threatened (Fitzgerald and Sim, 1982).
- *Political constraints.* The defence of prisoners' interests is likely to encounter political backlash from those who argue that prisons should be austere institutions where prisoners are treated as outlaws deprived of all civil rights.

Reforms introduced by post-1997 Labour governments helped to buttress the role of the ombudsman. In April 2004 he was given the responsibility for investigating suicides in prison and probation hostels in place of the former mechanism of a prisons inquiry.

The Prison Service and the Human Rights Act

The 1998 Human Rights Act made it expressly unlawful for public authorities to act in a way that was incompatible with the Convention and could serve to enhance the just treatment of prisoners. The implementation of this measure in October 2000 had significant repercussions for those in prison and seemed likely to result in the Prison Service facing increased legal challenges. The 1998 legislation posed a number of initial problems for this agency (Prison Reform Trust, 2000). These included:

- *The right to life* (Article 2). This implies a duty on the Prison Service to actively prevent suicides and the transmission of potentially fatal communicable diseases such as AIDS, and not to undertake actions likely to result in a prisoner being harmed (for example, placing a prisoner in a cell with another with a long record of violence or mental instability).
- *Outlawing torture, inhuman or degrading treatment* (Article 3). This might affect prison policies such as segregation, the use of restraints and alleged assaults by prison staff on inmates.

- *The right to a fair trial* (Article 6). Prisoners may allege that internal disciplinary proceedings before a governor (who is not legally qualified) empowered to increase the length of their sentence by up to 42 days, in which they are not legally represented, does not constitute an 'independent and impartial tribunal'. This situation was subsequently condemned by the European Court of Human Rights in 2002 in the case of *Ezeh and Connors* v. *United Kingdom*.
- *The right to privacy* (Article 8). This concerns issues such as correspondence between a prisoner and those on the outside world which may be subject to vetting.
- *The prohibition of all forms of discrimination* (Article 14). This could result in challenges to prison disciplinary procedures if these were felt to be unfair to members of minority groups.

The Prison Service will find it more difficult to win cases since it will be required to demonstrate 'necessity' for its actions as opposed to 'reasonableness' that was formerly the position.

The accountability of the Prison Service

The Prison Service is accountable to a number of external agencies including Parliament and the Treasury. Additionally, the scrutiny of individual establishments is carried out by the following:

- *Boards of Visitors*. These are responsible to the Prison Service. Their primary role is to prevent the abuse of prisoners and they have a duty under Prison Rules to inform the Secretary of State if they detect evidence of it. Until 1992 such bodies also handled the more serious disciplinary charges.

- *The Prison Inspectorate*. This is an independent body which was set up (following the May Report) in 1980 and whose chief inspector is selected from a person who does not come from the Prison Service. This reform was designed to break down the system of self-regulation which had existed in prisons since 1877. It seeks to visit each establishment (including those in the private sector) every five years (although unannounced inspections may also take place), and reports to the Home Secretary. A particular role of the Inspector is to consider the treatment of prisoners and conditions within prisons that includes the conditions of staff. Reports from this body tend to focus on outcomes rather than processes which are considered by alternative bodies including the Prison Service Audit Teams (Ramsbotham, 1998: 11).

The key development that occurred in the 1990s was the separation of policy planning and service delivery urged by the Ibbs Report, resulting in the establishment of agencies. These possessed a high degree of autonomy to provide services within guidelines, financial constraints and performance targets imposed by government departments to whom they were accountable and were the key vehicle for introducing the principles of new public management into the Prison Service which were designed both to raise the standards of the service (to promote economy, efficiency and effectiveness) and 'to provide additional incentives, responsibilities and opportunities for this lower down the organization' (Sparks et al., 1996: 20). Following the publication of the Lygo Report (1991), the Prison Service became an agency controlled by a Director General appointed by the Home Secretary in 1993, and this was followed by developments which included the provision of devolved budgets to individual prisons so that they had control on how money was spent in their institutions.

This reform implied a reduced rather than enhanced level of central government control in the operations of the Prison Service. However, two related issues emerged in 1995–96 that revealed this was not the case. The first was the extent to which it was possible to separate operations and policy issues, and the second was the extent to which the Home Secretary chose to play down the degree to which he intervened in operational matters by claiming that these were the responsibility of the Director General. This made it possible to assert that operational shortcomings such as prison escapes arose from administrative failures for which the minister was not personally responsible and thus could not be held accountable for them by Parliament. These issues were highlighted in the dismissal of Derek Lewis, the Director General of the Prison Service, in 1995. The independence of the Director General from government was further undermined when subsequent Labour Home Secretaries made this official a Permanent Secretary in the Home Office.

The Lewis dismissal

In 1994 six dangerous prisoners (including five IRA men) escaped from Whitemoor Prison in Cambridgeshire. The following month, January 1995, three high-risk prisoners escaped from Parkhurst prison. Following this latter breakout, the Home Secretary denied in Parliament on 10 January 1995 that he was responsible for prison operations such as security matters and appointed General Sir John Learmont to report into such issues. This report made a number of criticisms of the manner in which the Prison Service was being managed, stating that the Parkhurst escape revealed 'a chapter of errors at every level and a naivety that defies belief' (Home Office, 1995a: 72). The Home Secretary responded by sacking the Director General, Derek Lewis, although in March 1996 the High Court determined that he had been wrongfully dismissed.

The legitimacy of being able to draw a distinction between policy and operations underpinned the 'next steps' philosophy. Such a division has been described as 'hopeless' (Foster and Plowden, 1996: 172), and when applied to the Prison Service it has been argued that there will be some matters in which both policy and operations issues are unavoidably merged (Lloyd, 1995). The report into the Whitemoor attempted escape referred to the difficulties in discerning between operations and policy issues and additionally discussed the confusion surrounding the respective roles that ministers, the agency headquarters and individual governors exercised (Home Office, 1994b).

The accusation that the agency arrangement had resulted in increased political involvement in the affairs of the Prison Service was made by the Director General who claimed that his operational independence was undermined by having to report to the Home Secretary on a daily basis (Lewis, 1995) whose ability to intervene in such issues was aided by the formation of a Prison Service Monitoring Unit in December 1994. One key aspect of ministerial involvement centred on who had been responsible for insisting on the immediate suspension of the governor of Parkhurst, John Marriott, following the Parkhurst escape. The Home Secretary's evidence to the House of Commons Committee on Home Affairs on 25 January 1995 asserted that the suspension had been an operational matter whereas Lewis claimed it was a ministerial decision. Following the debate in the House of Commons on 19 October 1995, a leaked letter from the Prison Governors' Association to the Home Secretary was published in *The Observer* on 22 October 1995. This called for reduced ministerial involvement and claimed that such intervention in even 'minor operational matters' was causing bad management and lapses in security.

The division of responsibilities between the Home Secretary and the Director General made for ineffective accountability of the Prison Service and also posed the possibility of the Head of the Service being made a scapegoat for failures of a political nature. Solutions to this problem include making the Inspectorate (which currently conducts investigations of individual prisons) take charge of the entire service or for the Director General to become directly accountable to the Home Affairs Committee. This latter suggestion would involve this official accounting to the Select Committee for the agency's performance measured against annual targets set out in the framework document (Polidano, 1997: 14). This could be enhanced by the Committee's ability to conduct *ex post facto* examinations of key issues or problems affecting the Prison Service.

In 1997 the Prison Service Review emphasised the need to further develop the relationships between ministers and the Prison Service. It suggested this should be done not through formal structures (such as the Advisory Board advocated by Lygo in 1991) but through quarterly meetings between ministers, the Home Office and the Prisons Board. This report also suggested that a Deputy Director General should be appointed who would be responsible for the day-to-day management of the Prison Service (Prison Service Review, 1997).

Private prisons are subject to differing methods of accountability. Most (but not all) of the performance indicators of the Prison Service apply to private institutions and private institutions are subject to contract compliance audits which may result in the Prison Service deducting money if a private body fails to meet stipulated performance standards. It has also been suggested that private prisons should be accountable to a superintending body with powers to fine or impose other sanctions on such institutions (Harding, 1997).

Who runs the prisons?

The above section referred to the issue of control of the Prison Service and the relationship between the Home Secretary and Director General of the Service. There are, however, other dimensions to the issue of control in individual establishments.

Control by prisoners

It has been observed that it is impossible to run a prison around 'a simple dichotomy of coercion and consent' (Matthews, 1999: 79). 'Staff and prisoners live in a state of mutual dependence within prison' and prison officers are aware that they require the consent of prisoners to get them through the day (Liebling and Price, 2003: 79). Accordingly, prisons employ systems of reward and punishment to maintain order rather than relying on crude forms of coercion (Sykes, 1958). Prison officers often under-use the formal powers to control prisoners which they have at their disposal as this might undermine the 'order' or 'peace' which officers view as essential to the smooth running of these institutions (Liebling and Price, 2003: 88). Overcrowding enhances the need for prisoners to cooperate with the staff. However, the balance struck between enforcement and non-enforcement of prison rules to secure institutional harmony is a delicate one since an extreme version of this scenario would be that the prisoners effectively end up in charge of the prison, with prison staff being unwilling or unable to intervene in activities since this could lead to a major escalation of violence. In 1997 the Chief Inspector of Prisons, Sir David Ramsbotham, argued that this situation existed at HMP Lincoln, where one wing had effectively become a no-go area for prison officers.

Control by prison officers

It is has been argued that in some prisons the Prison Officers' Association (POA) rather than management was effectively in charge (Infield, 1997: 4). *Fresh Start*, introduced in 1987, sought to undermine the power of the POA, and it was also assumed that privatisation would reduce the power of this organisation (although in an attempt to counter this, in 1998 the POA resolved to seek members in private prison establishments). The first Director General of the Prison Service described the POA as the last bastion of 1960s trade unionism whose stubborn defence of restrictive practices coupled with its threatening and often belligerent demeanour resulted in deep public prejudice against prison officers and an image of a service rooted in the past (Lewis, 1997), and this view was repeated by a Chief Inspector of the Inspectorate of Prisons (Ramsbotham, 2005: 105 and 232–3). One of Lewis's reforms was to enforce a legal ban on the right of the POA to take industrial action. In 1999 a report by the Chief Inspector of Prisons condemned conditions at Exeter Prison as disgraceful and blamed the POA for causing the maximum disruption of the jail and for being responsible for actions which led to inmates being locked up several times a day. Ramsbotham stated that the situation was not industrial relations, but industrial anarchy (Ramsbotham, 1999).

Alternatives to prison

Alternatives to custodial sentences have long existed. There are two main categories of alternatives – those without any element of supervision and those that include this.

Sentences lacking supervision

There are a number of non-custodial sentences that lack supervision. These include the following.

Informal warning

This is given by a police officer and may apply to a relatively minor offence (such as a motorist who marginally exceeds the speed limit).

Cautioning

The cautioning system was initially introduced on an informal basis as a response to juvenile offending and was subsequently formalised in the 1982 Criminal Justice Act. Following the issuance of new guidelines in 1994 (Home Office, 1994c) it could be used for offenders of all ages. Formal cautions are given by a police officer in uniform and are recorded so that they can, if relevant, be cited to a court in the future if the offender is found guilty of a subsequent offence. The 1998 Crime and Disorder Act introduced important changes to the cautioning of juvenile offenders (which are discussed in Chapter 9). The 2003 Criminal Justice Act introduced a new penalty, that of conditional cautions, which are given to low-risk adult offenders, and the government intended to link this disposal to measures which included financial reparation to the victim and community work (Home Office, 2004: 12).

Conditional discharge

The conditional discharge was introduced by the 1948 Criminal Justice Act. It is a sentence of the court, non-compliance with which can lead the offender to being sent to prison. The requirement to attend court and be sentenced may have a preventive effect on an offender's future behaviour, although such a sentence is open to the charge that the offender has been allowed to escape meaningful penalty and has effectively been let off. The court may also dispense a suspended sentence that has a similar effect save that the threat of imprisonment seems more explicit. Such sentences are being decreasingly used.

Fines

Fines are the most common sentence of the court. The money extracted from offenders goes into the Treasury. Non-payment of fines traditionally resulted in prison sentences, although the 1914 Criminal Justice Administration Act introduced the ability to pay them in instalments. The major problem with fines was the failure to pay them and by 2002/3 the payment rate for these and similar imposition fell to 55 per cent (Home Office, 2004: 4). This prompted the Department of Constitutional Affairs to introduce reforms that included targeted interventions to improve performance in the worst court areas and new measures in the 2003 Courts Act that included automatic deductions from earnings or benefits from defaulters. Subsequently the collection of fines reached over 73 per cent in the first half of 2003, and it was anticipated that the creation of the Unified Courts Agency would make further improvements in this area of activity by providing for a national focus on, and management of, fine enforcement (Home Office, 2004: 4). It was envisaged that a revitalised fines system would replace 'a very substantial number' of community sentences which were currently given to low-risk offenders (Home Office, 2004: 12) which would be coupled with the extended use of fixed penalty notices to counter low-level criminal behaviour.

Binding over

The procedure of binding over originated in the 1361 Justice of the Peace Act. A verbal undertaking by an offender is sufficient to secure this penalty that is used, for example, in minor episodes of public disorder. Non-compliance with this undertaking will result in a financial forfeit.

Sentences which include supervision

There are numerous non-custodial sentences that include an element of supervision. These take the form of community-based interventions.

The vigorous advocacy of the use of alternatives to prison commenced in the 1970s, and this approach was developed by the emphasis that was placed on *punishment* within the community during the 1980s. The latter objective was boosted by the 1991 Criminal Justice Act. This sought to distinguish between those serious crimes (particularly involving violence against a person) which merited a loss of liberty, and those lesser offences which could be dealt with in ways which included discharges, financial penalties and what were termed 'community sentences', a generic term which was introduced by this legislation covering punishments which included attendance centre orders, probation orders, supervision orders, community service orders, combination orders and curfew orders. Further attempts to popularise community sentences were subsequently made in a Green Paper (Home Office, 1995b).

The operation of community sentences was significantly affected by the 2003 Criminal Justice Act that incorporated a number of existing community sentences as 'requirements' of the new community order introduced by this legislation. Community orders enabled sentencers to impose a combination of penalties on all offenders aged 18 and above. One intention of this approach was to enhance the demanding nature of community sentences since no restrictions were imposed on sentencers regarding the volume of penalties ('requirements') that they prescribed.

The following section discusses the development of sentences served in the community under supervision.

Probation orders

Community orders consist of community service (which is discussed below) and probation orders. The latter (which were retitled community rehabilitation orders by the 2000 Criminal Justice and Court Services Act) were historically viewed not as a form of punishment but, rather, as 'a form of conditional liberty ... a form of social work with offenders to help them overcome personal difficulties linked with offending' (Raynor and Vanstone, 2002: 1). Before the passage of the 1991 Criminal Justice Act they were legally viewed as an alternative to sentencing and, until 1997, the imposition of a probation order required the offender's approval. Since 1997 the offender's consent is only required in relation to probation conditions concerning treatment for a mental condition or drug/alcohol dependency.

These orders can be applied to a wide range of adult offenders and, since the passage of the 1991 Criminal Justice Act, may also be applied to any offender over the age of 16 (although 16- and 17-year-olds may alternatively be subject to the existing supervision order). The 'standard' probation order may be from six months to three years in duration and impose requirements on the offender which include being under the supervision of a probation officer, keeping in touch as instructed, and being of good behaviour and leading an industrious life. Additional conditions (known as 'probation plus') may be attached to the order, such as imposing a requirement on an offender to reside in a hostel or to undertake treatment programmes designed to confront the behaviour which resulted in an offence being committed. As with community service, probation orders are discharged within the framework of national standards.

The 1991 Criminal Justice Act for the first time permitted up to 100 hours of community service to be combined with a probation order in what was termed a 'combination order' (subsequently renamed community punishment and rehabilitation orders by the 2000 Criminal Justice and Court Services Act). This provision was initially targeted at the more serious offenders, but the use of combination orders has subsequently become more widespread (Whitfield, 1998: 81), rising from 1,400 in 1992 to 17,000 in 1996. Such an order, however, entails two different objectives (seeking help and advice and engaging in reparation) (Worrall, 1997: 93) and is supervised by two different sets of people who may possibly have different perspectives. There are other combined sentences available to the courts, including the payment of compensation and tagging.

The 2003 Criminal Justice Act transformed community rehabilitation orders into a supervision requirement of the new community order for those aged 18 and above.

Community service orders

Communitty service orders (CSOs) were introduced in England and Wales in 1973 under provisions of the 1972 Criminal Justice Act. These orders (and Day Training Centres which were also provided for in this legislation) were put forward as alternatives to custodial sentences and were supervised by the Probation Service (thus requiring good working relationships to be constructed between this agency and sentencers). CSOs were renamed community punishment orders by the 2000 Criminal Justice and Court Services Act. These orders were subsequently required to conform to national standards set by the Home Office that stipulated the criteria that placements should meet. CSOs were initially applied to adult offenders, but were extended to 16-year-olds by the 1982 Criminal Justice Act. In 2003, enhanced community punishment (ECP) was introduced so that all offenders placed on CSOs would be placed on an ECP scheme.

The ethos underpinning community service orders differed from that of probation orders by emphasising the concern to punish offenders rather than assisting them (Raynor and Vanstone, 2002: 2). Punishment administered within the community was an important aspect of the bifurcation principles that were introduced by the 1972 legislation that simultaneously proposed lengthier prison sentences for serious offences such as armed robbery. Community service orders required offenders to perform constructive tasks of unpaid work for a period of time that now ranges between 40 and 240 hours (the limit of 120 hours for 16-year-olds being scrapped by the 1991 Criminal Justice Act) that are designed to provide tangible benefits to the community. In this sense the orders are reparative. Breach of the CSO will result in the offender being returned to court. In 1997 around 52,000 of such orders were imposed which resulted in 17,000 individuals or groups being assisted from six million hours of unpaid activity (Whitfield, 1998: 22). Seventy-five per cent of CSOs are successfully completed (Whitfield, 1998: 78). Although it is sometimes perceived that such sentences are too soft on criminals, they could be developed into a more demanding response to minor criminal actions, a major advantage being that of cost: it has been estimated that according to 1996 figures each order cost £33 per offender (Whitfield, 1998: 81). Since the late 1990s some progress has been made to combine the work and discipline of a CSO with a basic vocational qualification.

The 2003 Criminal Justice Act transformed community punishment orders into an unpaid work requirement of the new community order.

Curfew orders and tagging

The origins of electronic monitoring date to the Home Office (1988) Green Paper *Punishment, Custody and the Community*, and tagging as a condition of bail was introduced on a trial basis in 1989/90. The 1991 Criminal Justice Act (as amended by the 1994 Criminal Justice and Public Order Act) introduced a new sentence of a curfew order enforced by tagging which was available for offenders aged 16 and above. This was initially implemented on a trial basis in three areas (Norfolk, Greater Manchester and Berkshire) in 1995.

The 1997 Labour government significantly extended the scheme by proposing the early release of short-term prisoners serving sentences between three months and less than four years (subject to an assessment of risk which involves prison, probation and police services) for the last two months of their sentence provided that they stayed at an approved address and agreed to a curfew (usually from 7 p.m. to 7 a.m.) monitored by an electronic tag. This would last for a minimum of 14 days and a maximum of 60 days. Those who breached the conditions of their curfew (including attempting to remove the tag) or who committed another offence while on curfew were returned to prison. This scheme, termed the 'Home Detention Curfew' (HDC), commenced in January 1999 and was operated by the private sector. While it is possible that offenders who are compelled to spend longer periods of times with their families may come to lead more structured lives, there are problems associated with the scheme. These include the unclear cost-effectiveness of this scheme and confusion over its objectives, especially whether it is an alternative to custody, an alternative to other forms of community punishment or merely a device to remedy prison overcrowding. The scheme may be combined with other sentences (including probation orders) designed to rehabilitate offenders.

Early evidence suggested that the failure rate of the scheme was a mere 5 per cent, partly because prison governors exercised considerable caution as to whom they released. The fairness of the scheme was, however, called into question as it was argued that a prisoner's chance of being accepted onto the HDC was less due to their perceived risk or home environment but was more influenced by the prison they were in (Shaw, 1999: 10).

The drug treatment and testing order

These were introduced in October 2000 and enabled offenders to address their drug problems through their participation in intensive community-based rehabilitation programmes. Regular tests are conducted to detect illicit drug use, and failure to comply with the order or testing positive will normally result in breach proceedings being taken. These orders are usually managed on behalf of the Probation Service by drug treatment agencies.

Assessment of community-based penalties

The 2001 Labour government sought to enhance the importance of community-based penalties. The 2005 Management of Offenders and Sentencing Bill proposed an overhaul of the system of fines, which included provisions whereby wealthy offenders would pay increased penalties. This put forward a modified version of the unit-fine system which had been abolished in 1993, whereby magistrates would decide fines by multiplying how many 'income units' the offence deserved based on its seriousness, multiplied by the offender's disposable income, up to a maximum of £75 a unit (Travis, 2005). This Bill also proposed to extend electronic tagging to persons serving community punishments.

The main advantages of community-based sentences include the following:

- *Cost.* The total spending of the government on the Prison Service was £1.6 billion in 1998/9 which was expected to increase to £2.0 billion in 2001/2.
- *Recidivism.* The use of alternatives to prison sentences could also be justified by research which suggested that the reconviction rates for imprisonment and community penalties were similar. Home Office

research suggested that sentenced prisoners who were reconvicted of a standard list offence within two years fluctuated between 51 and 57 per cent between 1987 and 1994 (Kershaw, 1999: 1) and it was argued that 'when adjustments are made to reconviction rates for community penalties to achieve comparability with prison, these have been within two percentage points of the figures for prison throughout the period 1987–1995' (Moxon, 1998: 90). In 1999, the two-year reconviction rate for those who had received a custodial sentence was 59 per cent. The figure was 56 per cent for those who had received a community penalty (Home Affairs Committee, 2005).

- *Reduced strain on the Prison Service.* By 2005 the size of the prison population had risen to 75,000 which justified the need to urgently search for alternative responses to crime to avoid the prison system becoming over-stretched beyond its capacity. The Sentencing Guidelines Council (whose role is discussed in Chapter 5) was given a duty to take into account the resources that are likely to be available which includes a consideration of the capacity of the Prison and Probation Services.

Political support for alternatives to custody

The importance of non-custodial sentences was emphasised by an investigation of the Home Affairs Committee in 1998. Its report, *Alternatives to Prison Sentences*, argued that the rise in the prison population witnessed over the previous five years was 'unsustainable' and thus argued that prisons should be reserved for dangerous and persistent offenders with other offenders being given non-custodial sentences. It estimated that the cost of keeping someone in prison totalled £24,000 exclusive of other costs (for example, the need for the prisoner's family to receive state aid) and that there was little to choose between custodial and non-custodial sentences in preventing further offending, although it drew adverse attention to the absence of research into the effectiveness of community sentences in preventing reoffending. It believed that community sentences possessed the potential to be more effective than prisons in reducing reoffending and that their effectiveness was enhanced when they adhered to a set of 'What Works?' principles which included matching the level of risk posed by an individual with the level of intervention and recognising that specific factors were associated with offending and that these should be treated separately from other needs. It was further alleged that if such sentences were to be credible with the public they had to be seen as stringently enforced. The Committee stated its view that in this respect it was unacceptable that local probation services on average took breach action in barely one-quarter of cases (Home Affairs Committee, 1998).

There are, however, difficulties associated with community-based penalties:

- *'Soft on crime'*. Public opinion views them as a 'soft option' which falls short of real punishment for criminal behaviour. In 1999 an organisation, Payback, was launched to counter this perception. A key aim of this organisation was to cut the prison population and it justified this by arguing that whereas it cost £24,000 to keep someone in prison for a year, a community service order cost a mere £1,700 and a probation order £2,200 (Payback, 1999). Additional sanctions for juvenile offending are discussed in Chapter 9.

- *Effectiveness*. Community-based penalties often offer ineffective responses to offending behaviour. It has been estimated that although drug treatment and testing orders are cheaper than custodial sentences (costing £6,000 per place as opposed to £30,000), they were relatively ineffective in securing sustained reduction in drug misuse and offending behaviour. Only 25 per cent of those who accepted the programme completed it successfully, with very wide variations across the country (Public Accounts Committee, 2005).

- *Laxity of enforcement*. Those who fail to adhere to the conditions of orders supervised by the Probation Service are deemed to be in breach of them and will be returned to court, although it has been asserted that 'probation officers are notoriously reluctant to institute 'breach proceedings' against offenders who fail to comply with the requirements of probation orders' (Worrall, 1997: 14; Home Affairs Committee, 1998: xxvi). This issue was tackled in successive editions of National Standards that sought to limit the discretion which probation officers exercised in connection with breaches (Raynor and Vanstone, 2002: 104). It has been subsequently argued that the establishment of the National Probation Service resulted in breach proceedings being undertaken in the majority of cases (Home Office, 2004: 3).

- *Lack of confidence by sentencers*. Sentencers are often reluctant to utilise community-based penalties as they lack confidence in them for reasons which have been discussed above. One consequence of this has been that sentencers have increasingly resorted to the use of short prison sentences: between 1989 and 1999 sentences of below 12 months for indictable offences committed by adults over 18 increased from 27,000 to 45,000, an overall increase of 67 per cent. (Halliday, 2001: 22). These alternatives to custodial sentences will only become widely used when the apparent scepticism of sentencers towards them has been overcome.

- *An extension of the controlled society*. The rise of what has been described as the 'decarcerated criminal' (Cohen, 1985) may arise through the use of community programmes. The main danger with this development is that:

  far from reducing the restrictions on criminals who might otherwise have been sent to prison, create a new clientele of criminals who are controlled by other mechanisms. The boundaries between freedom and confinement become blurred. The 'net' of social control is thus thrown ever wider into the community, its thinner mesh designed to entrap ever smaller 'fish'. Once caught in the net, the penetration of disciplinary intervention is ever deeper, reaching every aspect of the criminal's life. (Worrall, 1997: 25)

> Evaluate the strengths and weaknesses of responding to crime by non-custodial sentences.

The Probation Service

History

The origins of the Probation Service can be traced to a number of voluntary and ad hoc experiments conducted during the nineteenth century that were designed to provide a form of intervention designed not to punish offenders but to aid their rehabilitation. The most important of these were the police court missionaries first employed by the Church of England Temperance Society in 1876 to save people from the effects of drink and who numbered around 100 by 1900. Legislation to provide for a rehabilitative service occurred slowly. The 1887 Probation of Offenders Act was the first major piece of legislation in this field but contained no element of supervision. The key Act, therefore, was the 1907 Probation of Offenders Act. This placed probation work on a statutory footing by empowering the courts to appoint and pay probation officers whose role was to 'advise, assist and befriend' those being supervised. Probation was available to all courts and for almost all offences (murder and treason being exempted), provided the offender agreed and additionally consented to standard conditions. These embraced an undertaking to keep in touch with the probation officer as directed, leading an honest and industrious life and being of good behaviour and keeping the peace (quoted in Whitfield, 1998: 12–13). In 1925 the appointment of at least one probation officer to each court became a mandatory requirement (although this responsibility was sometimes discharged by part-timers).

The local nature of the service was amended in 1936, when as the result of a report by the Departmental Committee on Social Services in Courts of Summary Jurisdiction, the Home Office came to play a more significant role in terms of inspection and training and through the establishment of a Central Advisory Committee. The 1948 Criminal Justice Act repealed all earlier enactments relating to the Probation Service resulting in improved training, strengthened links with the courts, the organisation of new probation committees, and approved probation hostels and homes being brought within the scope of public funding. However, the organisation of the service in England and Wales remained local, being administered through 54 areas, each governed by a Probation Committee composed of magistrates, judges, local authority representatives and independent persons who managed the service in their area. This was answerable to the Home Office which controlled the Probation Service and supplied the bulk of its funding. Each Probation Committee produced its own plan of local objectives and priorities within the framework of the Home Office's national plan. Additionally, the early ethos of rehabilitation through religion gave way to a more secular form of professionalism whereby probation officers formulated interventions based on a social scientific evaluation of offenders on a one-to-one basis.

Milestones in the postwar development of the Probation Service

The following section briefly charts the key developments that have affected the development of the Probation Service.

- **1961** The Streatfield Report recommended greater use should be made of social inquiry reports in all courts (which were forerunners of pre-sentence reports).
- **1966** Work conducted in prisons became a main part of the work of the Probation Service.
- **1968** The introduction of parole whereby parolees were supervised by probation officers following their release from prison. Additionally, in Scotland, the Probation Service was incorporated into the newly created social services departments.
- **1973** The introduction of community service: such schemes were run by the Probation Service.
- **1984** The Probation Service was urged to participate in the multi-agency approach to crime prevention (Home Office, 1984). The first statement of national objectives and priorities was also issued by the Home Office.
- **1988** The Green Paper *Punishment, Custody and the Community* was issued, which was followed by the 1990 White Paper, *Crime, Justice and Protecting the Public*. This questioned the extensive use of custody (particularly for younger offenders) and suggested that greater use should be made of community-based options for offences that included burglary and theft. Such ideas were latterly incorporated into the 1991 Criminal Justice Act, which is discussed below.
- **1989** The Audit Commission's report, *The Probation Service – Promoting Value for Money*, produced 'a framework for probation intervention' that sought to provide a uniform system which incorporated the evaluation of programmes for dealing with offenders.
- **1991** The Criminal Justice Act promoted *punishment* in the community as an appropriate response to less serious offences that suggested that the focus of the Probation Service should be widened to include a retributive dimension and a concern to protect society from the consequences of crime.
- **1992** National Standards for the Probation Service were published setting out expected practice in both objectives and the process of supervision.

> ● **1999** The publication, *What Works: Reducing Re-Offending: Evidence Based Practice* (Home Office, 1999), put forward principles by which pathfinder projects would be evaluated. These would subsequently form the basis of standardised (or 'accredited') programmes through which offending behaviour would be addressed.
> ● **2002** Standardisation was developed regarding risk assessment through the use of the Offender Assessment System (OASys) to assess the level of risk of offenders over 18 and to provide for their needs from a repertoire of Pathfinder-agreed programmes. (Goodman, 2003: 211–212). A similar mechanism known as ASSET was developed by the Youth Justice Board for the use of YOTs in connection with offenders below 18.

Role of the Probation Service

The Probation Service performs a wide range of functions some of which (such as work in connection with divorces aimed at ensuring the welfare of the children or in connection with victims of crime following the publication of the *Victims Charter* in 1990) are not concerned with offenders. However, the main task of the service involves those who have committed crime. The aim of the Probation Service is to 'help offenders improve their personal and social situations ... ensuring court orders are observed, and ... helping to reduce the risk of re-offending' (Whitfield, 1998: 8). Specifically its functions are defined in the service's national statement of purposes which states that it serves the courts and public by:

● providing reports to the courts: these take the form of pre-sentence reports in which the needs of the offender are traditionally viewed as paramount;

● supervising offenders in the community;

● managing offender programmes to ensure offenders lead law-abiding lives in a way that minimises risk to the public;

● safeguarding the welfare of children in family proceedings;

● helping communities prevent crime and reducing its effects on victims.

These objectives translate into a number of specific tasks, some of which are detailed below, and which evidence a tension between 'caring for offenders and controlling their criminal behaviour' (Worrall, 1997: 67).

Crime prevention

Activities directed at high crime areas designed to prevent offending behaviour constitute a relatively small aspect of probation work, although it was anticipated that this might increase with the involvement of the service in multi-agency activities under the auspices of the 1998 crime and disorder legislation.

Preventing recidivism

One of the functions of the Probation Service is to work with offenders, seeking to transform their behaviour thereby minimising the risk of future reoffending. As has been discussed above, this was historically performed through individualised contact between probation officer and offender, but subsequently entailed probation officers directing offenders onto programmes deemed relevant to addressing the offender's behaviour. The extent to which programmes of this nature prevent recidivism has been questioned. It has been argued that 'some programmes *do* work and the best may reduce re-offending by around 25 per cent'. But to achieve this, programmes have to be clearly targeted on offending behaviour, consistently delivered by well trained staff, relevant to offenders' problems and needs, and equally relevant to the participants' learning styles (Whitfield, 1998: 16). Attempts to stimulate the replication of good practice were attempted by the work of the Probation Inspectorate that resulted in *Strategies for Effective Offender Supervision* (1998) and *Evidence Based Practice: A Guide to Effective Practice* (Chapman and Hough, 1998).

Determination of remand or bail

The service operates Bail Information Schemes, either 'first remand' or court-based schemes (which are carried out by probation officers) or 'second remand' or prison-based (which are carried out in conjunction with prison staff). These are designed to provide information to prosecutors, and also to suggest what extra conditions (such as living in a hostel run by the Probation Service) should be attached to a decision to grant bail pending a court hearing.

Sentencing

A key role of probation officers is to gather information and write reports for the courts in relation to offenders in order to inform sentencing decisions. These take the form of pre-sentence reports and specific sentence reports. Currently the Probation Service writes around 250,000 pre-sentence reports and in excess of 20,000 specific sentence reports each year. National Standards require that pre-sentence reports should be prepared within 15 working days, although in some probation areas are prepared only if custody or a community sentence are the likely outcomes (National Probation Service, 2004). Specific sentence reports are prepared more quickly and may be delivered verbally to the court. Additionally the probation service prepares over 20,000 bail information reports for the Crown Prosecution service.

Probation orders

These (since retitled community rehabilitation orders) are discussed above.

Prison work

Work undertaken by the Probation Service in prisons dates from the 1960 report of the Advisory Council, *The Organisation of Aftercare*, and involves taking over functions formerly carried out by prison welfare officers. It was initiated in 1966 and was enhanced by the introduction of parole in 1967, the supervision of those on parole becoming a responsibility of the Probation Service in 1968. The role of the Probation Service was particularly affected by the 'seamless sentence' provisions of the 1991 Criminal Justice Act which focused on activities undertaken both in prison and following release designed to address offending behaviour. This means that a prison sentence is partly served in prison and partly in the community involving prisoners being released on licence and supervised by the Probation Service. Serious offenders (including those sentenced to life imprisonment and some sex offenders) might be required to maintain long-term contact with the Probation Service.

One consequence of prison governors securing control over their own budgets was the decline in the number of prison probation officers (Home Office, 1998). Towards the end of the 1990s, over 500 probation officers were seconded to prisons (Whitfield, 1998: 23) who worked with prison staff in sentence planning, making plans for resettlement after release, liaising with probation staff in the offender's home area and running a range of programmes within the prison which seek to address the underlying causes of offending. Probation staff would often make assessments concerning release. The number of seconded probation officers working in prisons declined by 25 per cent between 1995 and 1997 (Whitfield, 1998: 91) but the introduction of the Home Detention Curfew increased demand for their services to assess those who could be eligible for the scheme. There was, however, the danger that the compiling of risk assessments would detract from the time available for probation officers to work with prisoners (Goodman, 1999: 28).

Changes affecting the Probation Service

The work of the Probation Service has been subjected to a number of important changes. These are discussed below.

The move away from providing individualised treatment

The 'nothing works' pessimism of the 1970s (Martinson, 1974) questioned the role performed by the Probation Service in dealing with offenders on a one-to-one basis, seeking to bring about a change in their behaviour and attitudes through individualised treatment. It was suggested that the role of the service should be reoriented away from treatment and towards the provision of appropriate help to offenders (Bottoms and McWilliams, 1979).

In 1984 the Probation Service was urged to participate in the multi-agency approach to crime prevention (Home Office, 1984). The first statement of national objectives and priorities was also issued by the Home Office that year. This sought to provide a unity of purpose to the work performed by over 50 largely autonomous probation areas through their incorporation into area plans. Both of these pronouncements attempted to move the probation service into activities other than working with individual offenders, in particular in connection with crime prevention. This change in role was subsequently emphasised when the Probation Service's first operational goal was stated to be 'reducing and preventing crime and the fear of crime by working in a partnership with others' (Home Office, 1992: 12).

This change in the role of the Probation Service was further influenced by two important developments that occurred during the 1990s. The first of these was the 'What Works?' movement. This had the effect of further moving the service away from individualised case work which sought to divert offenders from custody and towards the utilisation of structured programmes which were designed to alter behaviour patterns and whose ability to achieve this was capable of evaluation. Localised programmes (such as the Straight Thinking on Probation (STOP) programme which was introduced by the Mid Glamorgan Probation Service in 1990) could be more widely utilised once National Standards were introduced in 1992 that sought to disseminate examples of good practice. This approach was developed by later changes to scrutinise programmes that included the formation of a Joint Prison/Probation Accreditation Board in 1999. The centralised provision of programmes to address offending behaviour reflected an important departure from the perception of probation work being an aspect of social work.

National Standards established expected practice affecting objectives and the process of supervision. They covered a wide range of issues that included detailed instructions concerning the administration of order and were subsequently revised in 1995. It has been argued that National Standards sought to make probation officers more accountable to management which was in turn more accountable to the government – 'the overriding point about the introduction of National Standards was that they limited the discretion of the individual probation officer and focused on the management of supervision rather than on its content' (Worrall, 1997: 73). The target of National Standards was thus the individualised interventions conducted by probation officers: their new role was to be that of managing offenders through the term of their sentence rather than actually carrying out interventions themselves. The introduction of National Standards was therefore an important step in bringing changes to the role of probation officers whereby they became case managers as opposed to case workers (Goodman, 2003: 201). A third version of National Standards (published in April 2000) further reduced the discretion of probation officers regarding their interrelationship with offenders and changes to the way probation officers worked with offenders were subsequently published (National Probation Service, 2001).

Alterations to both the role and accountability of probation officers initiated by Conservative governments were coupled with other actions to broaden the base of recruitment and include persons with experience and skills deemed relevant to the nature of the work rather than those who had undertaken professional training. The aim of these changes was supplemented by the role of Her Majesty's Inspectorate of Probation that started to conduct thematic reviews and carry out the inspection of individual services after 1992. Its work included the advocacy of effective practice within the service.

The second development which took place during the 1990s affecting the role of the Probation Service was the rise of populist punitiveness at the expense of the rehabilitative commitment of what has been described as 'penal modernism' (Garland, 1985, 1990). The latter entailed 'the belief that crime could be reduced and criminals reformed by the application of scientific understanding and the development of appropriate "treatments"' (Raynor and Vanstone, 2002: 3). The service was required to redefine its purpose in line with the new philosophy of 'just deserts' whereby (in accordance with the spirit of the 1991 Criminal Justice Act) a 'twin-track' approach sought to promote *punishment* in the community as an appropriate response to less serious offences, suggesting that the focus of the Probation Service should be widened to include a retributive dimension and a concern to protect society from the consequences of crime. This change sought to shift the service 'centre stage' of the criminal justice system. Although the central role of the Probation Service was undermined by the appointment of Michael Howard as Home Secretary in 1993 (who desired to move prisons into the centre stage of the criminal justice system), it did entail a move away from the 'traditional social work basis and individual offender focus towards a more disciplinary correctionalist agency with a wider focus, incorporating victims' perspectives and public safety issues' (Crawford, 1999: 37).

Subsequent changes brought about by post-1997 Labour governments have further shifted the service away from its historic functions. It has been alleged that Labour tended to see the service in terms of a social control agency that should be concerned with punishment, control and surveillance (Goodman, 2003: 204). Increasingly the needs of the community dominated the probation work agenda: probation officers became concerned with assessing the risk which offenders posed.

These activities were at the expense of the individualistic treatment that probation officers formerly provided to offenders. It has been concluded that changes of this nature meant that 'the early ethos of 'advise, assist and befriend' has been put to rest and in its place are the central tasks of assessing and managing risk' (Goodman, 2003: 209). Risk assessment was at the heart of the role now performed by the service, 'supplanting ideologies of need, welfare or … rehabilitation' (Kemshall, 1998: 1). It marked the demise of the 'old penology' that emphasised the rehabilitation of individual offenders and its replacement by a 'new penology' based on the assessment of risk (Feeley and Simon, 1992; 1994) that was concerned with predicting future behaviour.

These changes to the Probation Service were subsequently formalised. The role of the Probation Service was stated to be that of protecting the public, promoting community safety and preventing crime. It would do this by evaluating information in order to make assessments and provide reports regarding risk and other matters of concern to organisations which used the service, by managing and enforcing court orders and licences, and by working directly with offenders to bring about changes in their behaviour that would reduce the impact of crime on the victim and the risk of harm being inflicted on other members of the community. The service would also manage and coordinate the contribution made by other services to work of this nature (Probation Officer Recruitment and Implementation Group, 1999: 1).

Offending behaviour programmes

In 1989 the Audit Commission published a report, *The Probation Service – Promoting Value for Money*, which produced 'a framework for probation intervention' designed to provide a uniform system that incorporated the evaluation of programmes for dealing with offenders.

The publication, *What Works: Reducing Re-Offending: Evidence Based Practice* (Home Office, 1999), put forward principles by which Pathfinder projects would be evaluated. These would subsequently form the basis of standardised (or 'accredited') programmes through which offending behaviour would be addressed. Standardisation was subsequently developed in 2002 regarding risk assessment whereby all offenders over 18 were assessed by the Offender Assessment System (OASys). Then, guided by the Joint Accreditation Panel/Correctional Services Accreditation Panel, probation officers slotted offenders into standardised programmes which were designed to tackle offending behaviour. An electronic version of this latter system (e-OASys) was subsequently developed to provide for enhanced connectivity within areas and between the probation system and the Prison Service (National Probation Service, 2004). The assessment of risk entailed reorienting the Probation Service's role whereby the protection of society was ranked above caring for the needs of offenders.

A key role of the Probation Service thus became that of managing the progress of offenders through accredited offending behaviour programmes: in 2004 there were 16 programmes of this nature either accredited or provisionally accredited for use. In 2003/4 13,136 offenders completed accredited programmes (National Probation Service, 2004). One advantage of the use of these programmes was that their success or otherwise could be evaluated. Risk assessment for those below 18 was carried out by YOTs using a system known as ASSET.

To what extent, and why, has the historic role of the Probation Service to 'advise, assist and befriend' offenders been subject to change in recent years?

Relationship with the Prison Service

Ideally the activities of the Probation and Prison Services would be closely intertwined, enabling the former to reinforce the rehabilitative activities of the latter. But this was not traditionally the case, and was unlikely to be achieved as long as 'one service continued to define its mission as saving people from the other' (Raynor and Vanstone, 2002: 62). The desirability of this cooperation underpinned the concept of 'throughcare' which was introduced in the 1970s, emphasising the importance of acquiring education and vocational skills while in prison, and as has been referred to above, the close cooperation of the two agencies was envisaged in the 'seamless sentence' provisions of the 1991 Criminal Justice Act. This legislation also coordinated the activities of the two agencies by reorienting the focus of community penalties, whereby they became regarded as forms of punishment rather than alternatives to custody (Raynor and Vanstone, 2002: 62). Further efforts to bring the two services closer together resulted in an attempt to spell out their respective roles in the 1993 document, *National Framework for Throughcare of Offenders in Custody to the Completion of Supervision in the Community*. However, the perception remained that the two services had different priorities, perspectives and structures. The extent of inter-agency cooperation was limited; for example, although many probation officers work inside prisons, the Prison Service computer was not able to exchange information with that of the Probation Service (Prison Report, 1998b: 3). Thus further initiatives to secure a more coordinated approach by the two agencies were required.

In 1997 a prisons–probation review was established, and in 1998 the Home Secretary urged the need for a closer working relationship between the two services (Straw, 1998). Additionally, in 1998 the Labour government published proposals related to these two agencies within the context of the government's comprehensive spending review whose proposals entailed granting an additional £127 million to the Probation Service. The issues raised in the review (Home Office, 1998: para. 4.12) included:

- replacing the 54 probation areas with a new national service;
- introducing joint planning between the Prison and Probation Services – this was urged in a number of areas which included common training, shared key performance indicators, joint accreditation of offender programmes, information sharing, a common approach to risk assessment and joint research projects;
- consideration of the renaming of the Probation Service in the belief that the present name was associated in the public eye with tolerance of crime. Among the alternatives put forward were the 'Justice Enforcement and Public Protection Service'.

A key problem posed by this document was that the Probation Service was likely to be moved further away from its initial role in connection with the reform and rehabilitation of offenders and to become increasingly immersed in the objective of safeguarding community security through the process of conducting risk assessments and exercising surveillance over those subject to community penalties. In this latter context it has been argued that probation officers may develop into 'soft cops' (Goodman, 2003: 219), an approach that has been conceptualised as 'polibation' (and is fully examined by Nash, 1999; 2004; and Mawby and Worrall, 2004).

The formation of the National Offender Management Service

The 2000 Criminal Justice and Court Services Act established the basis of a National Probation Service, which was set up in April 2001, under the control of the National Probation Directorate. Its organisational boundaries coincided with those utilised by the police service, the Crown Prosecution Service and the courts. It was subsequently observed that the creation of a national service brought greater consistency and innovation to a previously fragmented service and enabled a greater focus to be placed on performance management (Carter, 2003: 3 and 33). New programmes were introduced which were underpinned by joined-up government and risk management. These included Multi-Agency Public Protection Arrangements which required the police and the Probation Service (who were joined by the Prison Service following the enactment of the 2003 Criminal Justice Act) to assess the risks posed by high-risk sexual and violent offenders before they were released from prison and to manage that risk once they were released. The following year proposals were published to change the way in which the service would henceforth work with offenders (National Probation Service, 2001), which were subsequently incorporated into the service's strategic framework for 2001–4. The changes asserted the central role of the management of risk to the work of the Probation Service.

Although these reforms (and others which have been discussed previously) went some way towards reorientating the functions of the Probation Service, it was felt that further steps were needed 'in order to break down the silos of prison and probation and ensure a better focus on managing offenders' (Carter, 2003: 1). Arguments put forward to support this proposal included the allegations that information sharing between the two services was often poor (a difficulty compounded by organisational boundaries raising data protection issues), that programmes and interventions received in prison were not always followed up in the community and that no single organisation was ultimately responsible for the offender which meant 'there is no clear ownership on the front line for reducing re-offending' (Carter, 2003: 35).

Accordingly the merger of the Prison and Probation Services into a new body, the National Offender Management Service (NOMS), was called for which would focus on the management of offenders throughout the whole of their sentence, 'driven by information on what works to reduce offending' (Carter, 2003: 5). This was compatible with the appointment of a Commissioner for Correctional Services in 2003 to be responsible for managing and overseeing the government's targets for reducing reoffending. The new service would be charged with a clear responsibility to reduce reoffending (which would be measured two years after the end of the sentence), making use of a system based on improved information to provide for the risk-assessed use of scarce resources. It was also suggested that improved service delivery could be achieved through greater contestability, whereby contracts for programmes to prevent reoffending could be made the subject of competition by the public, private and voluntary sectors (Carter, 2003: 35). Contestability would enable value for money considerations to be applied to decisions related to the provision of services to aid offenders and protect the public and from which providers they should be purchased.

It was proposed that the two separate services should be restructured with a single chief executive accountable to ministers for the delivery of outcomes. One person (the National Offender Manager) would be responsible for the target to reduce reoffending, and would have complete control over the budget for managing offenders. This official's work would be aided by Regional Offender Managers (nine in England and one in Wales) who would be responsible for the end-to-end management of offenders in their region. Additionally they would eventually become responsible for fine collection in the region for which they were responsible. Their main work would be contracting with the providers of prison places, community punishment and interventions such as basic skills or health whether in the public, private or voluntary sectors. They would fund the delivery of specified services based on the evidence of what worked to reduce reoffending rather than leaving the services themselves to determine what should be delivered (Carter, 2003: 5 and 35–6). Under the new arrangements there would be a head of public sector prisons and an operational head in charge of community interventions and punishment. These officials would report directly to the chief executive and not be line-managed by the Regional Offender Managers, and would only be responsible to these officials for the delivery of contracts.

The task of supervising offenders would be carried out by offender managers who could be appointed from a range of providers in the public, private or voluntary sectors. Although it was envisaged that initially most offender managers would be from the public sector (chiefly probation officers – Blunkett, 2004: 2), it was anticipated that over time new providers would emerge (Carter, 2003: 37).

The government's response to the Carter Report was delivered in early 2004. This welcomed progress made by the Prison Service and National Probation Service in reducing the level of reoffending (which was in line with the 5 per cent reduction target set by the government), but it was argued that the establishment of a National Offender Management Service was also required to ensure that offenders were placed 'at the centre of a single system rather than falling in the gap between the two different services' (Blunkett, 2004: 2). The two objectives for this new service were to punish offenders and to reduce reoffending (Home Office, 2003: 10). It would provide 'end-to-end management of offenders, regardless of whether they are serving their sentences in prison, the community or both' (Home Office, 2004: 14). This was designed to ensure, for example, that an inmate who commenced a skills course while in prison would be able to continue with it upon release. To secure this reform, the government proposed the immediate appointment of a chief executive of NOMS who would set up the organisation and lead the new service (Home Office, 2004: 10) which was established on 1 June 2004. (In the event, the legal framework for the merger of the two services was provided in the 2005 Management of Offenders and Sentencing Bill. This Bill failed to become law before Parliament was dissolved on 11 April 2005, but the merger of the two services was prominently advocated in Labour's manifesto for the 2005 general election and was proceeded with following the Labour victory.)

Progress and effectiveness of reform

A common Offender Assessment System (OASys) will, when operational in 2006, become the key tool of end-to-end offender management and was conducted at the commencement of a sentence and at its end thus enabling changes to the offender to be assessed. This was an improvement on previous practice whereby separate OASys assessments were performed by both the Prison and Probation Services. The pursuance of a coordinated approach to the management of offenders also underpinned proposals to introduce a National Offender Management Information System (NOMIS) that is designed to be in place by July 2006. This consists of a database of offender profiles that will be available to all those who work with them and in November 2007 it is further intended to incorporate OASys into this system.

However, although the Prison Service had increasingly been involved in joined-up government in which the Chief Inspectors of Prisons, Probation, Social Services, the Constabulary, the CPS and the Magistrates' Courts Service began to unofficially meet to discuss issues of common concern (a development that was evidenced by a joint review published in 2000) (HM Inspectorates Review, 2000), the merger of the Prison and Probation Services posed a number of problems. The reform required 'a full integration of the hitherto independent Prison and Probation Services and the establishment of a regulated market place for independent (non-statutory) organizations to become increasingly involved in the delivery of services to offenders' (Pycroft, 2005: 135). A further difficulty affecting this reform was that the culture of the Prison and Probation Services was different. NOMS required the Probation Service to abandon its anti-incarceration stance and adopt a new one that viewed custodial sentences as an important aspect of rehabilitation (Gough, 2005: 91). The culture of the two agencies was also influenced by the Prison Service being nationally managed whereas the Probation Service was subject to local direction.

The logic of the government's reform was to scrap the 42 local boards and focus administration of the new service at the regional level whereby Regional Offender Managers would coordinate the work performed by the service. However, this reform was contentious. The Probation Service in particular desired to retain the existing structure, and in July 2004 the government decided to continue for the time being with the existing structure of 42 area boards. Although this decision could be justified by the desire to emphasise the relevance of the work performed by the Probation Service to community safety, and in particular the need to relate risk assessment to the attainment of local crime reduction targets, it was likely to have been based on political expediency. The retention of the 42 probation area boards had a considerable degree of political support that was evidenced in the adjournment debate held in the House of Commons on 6 April 2005, initiated by the Labour MP for Crosby, Mrs Claire Curtis-Thomas.

Resettlement

A significant number of those who receive custodial sentences (which in the mid-1990s comprised over half of adult offenders and around three-quarters of juveniles) (Home Office, 1996a) were reconvicted within two years. This implied that prisons were failing in their attempt to adjust the behaviour of offenders to that of 'respectable society' (Giddens, 1997: 187) but were alternatively serving as a mechanism to enhance the social exclusion of offenders, thereby increasing their commitment to offending behaviour (Matthews and Francis, 1996: 19). The rationale of NOMS was to tackle recidivism by reasserting the rehabilitative function of prisons. It was subsequently given the target of achieving a 10 per cent fall in the level of reoffending by 2010. This objective would be achieved by the new sentencing structure introduced by the 2003 Criminal Justice Act (which is discussed in Chapter 7), the improved management of offenders both within and outside of prisons, and the provision of effective programmes to address offending behaviour designed to secure the resettlement (the latter being the new term applied to 'throughcare' and 'aftercare') (Raynor and Vanstone, 2002: 111) of offenders within communities.

There are, however, difficulties associated with attaining resettlement. A previous scheme to facilitate resettlement, the Release on Temporary Licence (by which governors authorised prisoners to spend some time outside of prison), had been effectively abandoned after 1993 following public concern regarding the temporary release of criminals who went on to commit further crime. The new policy might result in dangerous criminals being released into communities who, if subject to insufficient supervision on release, could pose a danger to the public. This posed the question as to what was the nature and content of attention appropriate to this category of offender. Further, the effective resettlement of offenders within communities may not be easily attained. The behaviour of some offenders was shaped by their exclusion from local communities which they did not subsequently wish to rejoin (and in many cases ostracism would prevent this even if they wished to), and other aspects of post-1997 Labour policy (such as crime and disorder reduction partnerships) have been based, not on rehabilitation and resettlement, but, rather, on stigmatising and excluding those who perform criminal or disorderly acts.

There are additional factors that make resettlement into communities difficult to achieve in practice. Many offenders have a range of social problems that include drug dependency, low educational skills (which hinder future employment prospects), mental health problems and perhaps homelessness. Problems affecting ex-prisoners were identified by the Social Exclusion Unit as consisting of accommodation, education/training/employment, health, drugs/alcohol, finance/debt, children/family and attitudes/thinking and behaviour (Social Exclusion Unit, 2002). Thus resetttlement requires a range of social interventions to be directed at individual offenders to enable the range of problems that hinder resettlement into the community to be tackled. Regional Offender Managers are responsible for liaising with relevant local authorities, voluntary sector organisations and agencies such as drug action teams to secure help of this nature, but it may not be readily forth-coming, in particular if public sector bodies (such as local authority housing departments) prioritise resources for their 'traditional' clients rather than ex-offenders. It may also result in a fragmented approach being delivered by NOMS if case workers perform their work by directing offenders to a wide range of different service–providers.

A further difficulty concerns the impact that interventions designed to secure resettlement will have on individual offenders. Programmes will not produce standardised responses from their participants and case workers will need to address mental factors that influence an offender's propensity to desist from further crime. Literature that deals with an individual's transition from prison to the community (such as Zamble and Quinsey, 1997, and Immarigeon and Maruna, 2004) emphasise the importance of factors such as motivation and argue that this needs to be sustained (often in the face of set-backs) in order to achieve the goal of resettlement.

> What objectives did the Labour government seek to achieve by merging the Probation and Prison Services to create the National Offender Management Service (NOMS)? What problems is this reform likely to encounter?

Conclusion

This chapter has charted the development of the Prison Service since the publication of the Gladstone Report in 1895, and in particular has discussed the use of imprisonment in the policies pursued by post-1979 governments to combat crime. Particular attention has been devoted to the objective of rehabilitating offenders and it has been argued that key aspects of the prison environment have made it difficult for this objective to be achieved. The chapter has also considered the strategies used to maintain order in prisons.

In addition to prison, the chapter has considered the range of non-custodial disposals available to sentencers. In this context it considered the role of the Probation Service and has covered the historic role of this agency and the more recent changes that have served to reorientate its purpose. The chapter concluded with a discussion of the rationale of merging the Prison and Probation Services into one agency (the National Offender Management Service) in which the goal of reintegrating offenders in order to prevent recidivism is of paramount importance.

This chapter has focused on the range of custodial and non-custodial sentences related to adult offenders. Juvenile offenders (those below the age of 21) are dealt with separately in the following chapter which examines the principles that underpin the juvenile justice system and the manner in which it responds to juvenile criminality.

Further reading

There are many specialist texts that will provide an in-depth examination of the issues discussed in this chapter. These include:

Cavadino, M. and Dignan, J. (1997) *The Penal System: An Introduction*, 2nd edn. London: Sage.

Jewkes, Y. and Johnston, H. (2005) *Prison Readings*. Cullompton: Willan Publishing.

Matthews, R. (1995) *Doing Time: An Introduction to the Sociology of Imprisonment*. Basingstoke: Macmillan.

Ramsbotham, D. (2005) *Prisongate – The Shocking State of Britain's Prisons and the Need for Visionary Change*. London: The Free Press.

Raynor, P. and Vanstone, M. (2002) *Understanding Community Penalties: Probation, Policy and Social Change*. Buckingham: Open University Press.

Winstone, J. and Pakes, F. (eds), (2005) *Community Justice: Issues for Probation and Criminal Justice*. Cullompton: Willan Publishing.

Key events

- **1361** Enactment of the Justices of the Peace Act that established the basis of the procedure of binding over that is still used for minor cases of public disorder.
- **1779** Enactment of the Penitentiary Act. This measure promoted a new role for prisons as being concerned with reforming those who had committed crime.
- **1843** The first modern prison, Pentonville, was built in 1843 incorporating many of the features of Jeremy Bentham's panopticon design for prisons. Bentham's design entailed wings (which housed the prisoners) radiating from a central hub from which prison staff could observe and control all movement.
- **1898** Publication of Herbert Gladstone's report on prisons. The report's insistence that people were sent to prison *as* (rather than *for*) punishment influenced a move away from the harsh conditions that dominated the prison environment in the latter decades of the nineteenth century. Many of the report's recommendations were contained in the 1898 Prisons Act.
- **1907** Enactment of the Probation of Offenders' Act. This legislation placed probation work on a statutory footing that would be available in all courts for almost all crimes.
- **1948** Enactment of the Criminal Justice Act. It provided for a new organisational structure for the Probation Service and also introduced the conditional discharge.
- **1966** Publication of the report *Prison Escapes and Security*, written by Earl Louis Mountbatten. This made 52 recommendations, one of which was to introduce the A, B, C, D categorisation of prisoners.

- **1972** Enactment of the Criminal Justice Act. This measure sought to introduce the principle of bifurcation into sentencing policy by providing for harsher sentences for serious crimes and introducing the community service order as a non-custodial response to minor ones.
- **1980** Establishment of the Prison Inspectorate. The role of the Inspectorate is to visit individual institutions and to consider the treatment of prisoners and the conditions of the prison.
- **1982** Enactment of the Criminal Justice Act. This measure formalised cautioning that had previously been used informally in relation to juvenile offenders.
- **1990** A serious riot occurred at Strangeways prison, Manchester. This resulted in the appointment of Lord Woolf to write a report (published in 1991) that put forward a number of reforms that were designed to enable a balance to be struck between security, control and justice.
- **1991** Enactment of the Criminal Justice Act. This measure sought to promote bifurcation into sentencing policy and broaden the focus of the Probation Service. New disposals to deal with minor crimes were introduced consisting of the combination order (which provided for supervised community service coupled to a probation order) and curfew orders enforced by tagging. The latter were developed by post-1997 Labour governments that introduced the Home Detention Curfew in 1999 whereby some prisoners could be released early if they agreed to a curfew that was monitored by tagging.
- **1992** Introduction of National Standards for the Probation Service. This innovation began the reorientation of the work performed by probation officers into officials who were responsible for managing offenders rather than undertaking interventions themselves.
- **1993** Michael Howard became Home Secretary. He viewed prisons as the key mechanism to deliver his approach that sought to 'get tough with criminals'.
- **1993** The Prison Service became an executive agency of the Home Office. It is headed by a Director General, appointed by the Home Secretary.
- **1995** The contentious dismissal of Derek Lewis as Director General of the Prison Service by Home Secretary Michael Howard. This action occurred following a critical report of prison security written by General Sir John Learmont. In 1996 the High Court ruled that Lewis had been wrongfully dismissed.
- **1997** Enactment of the Crime (Sentences) Act. This measure introduced a range of mandatory sentences, thereby restricting the discretion of sentencers.
- **1999** Publication of *What Works? Reducing Re-offending: Evidence-based Practice*. This emphasised the importance of the use by the Probation Service of accredited programmes.
- **2000** Enactment of the Criminal Justice and Court Services Act. This measure established the basis of a national Probation Service under the control of a National Probation Directorate (which was set up in April 2001). The measure also renamed the existing community order, combination order and community service order, which respectively became known as the community rehabilitation order, community punishment and rehabilitation order and community penalty order.

- **2003** Publication of a report by Patrick Carter that recommended the amalgamation of the Prison Service and Probation Service into a new body, the National Offender Management Service.
- **2003** Enactment of the Criminal Justice Act. It sought to beef up the fine system by enabling deductions to be automatically taken from earnings or benefits, introduced the disposal of the conditional caution, and provided for Custody Plus and Custody Minus. It also introduced a new multifaceted community order, enabling sentencers to impose a wide range of conditions on a community sentence.

References

Ablitt, E. (2000) 'Community Penalties for Women – The Need for Evidence', *Criminal Justice Matters*, 39, Spring.

Adams, R. (1994) *Prison Riots in Britain and the USA*, 2nd edn. Basingstoke: Macmillan.

Amnesty International (1997) *Special Secure Units: Inhuman or Degrading Conditions.* London: Amnesty International.

Andrews, M. (2003) 'Punishment, Markets and the American Model: An Essay on a New American Dilemma', in S. McConville (ed.), *The Use of Punishment.* Cullompton: Willan Publishing.

Blunkett, D. (2004) 'Foreword', in Home Office, *Reducing Crime – Changing Lives: The Government's Plans for Transforming the Management of Offenders.* London: Home Office.

Bottoms, A. and McWilliams, W. (1979) 'A Non-Treatment Paradigm for Probation Practice', in *British Journal of Social Work*, 9 (2): 159–202.

Caddle, D. and Crisp, D. (1996) *Imprisoned Women and Mothers*, Home Office Research Study No. 162. London: HMSO.

Carter, P. (2003) *Managing Offenders, Reducing Crime: A New Approach.* London: Home Office Strategy Unit.

Cavadino, M. and Dignan, J. (1992) *The Penal System: An Introduction*, 1st edn. London: Sage.

Chapman, T. and Hough, M. (1998) *Evidence Based Practice: A Guide to Effective Practice.* London: Home Office, on behalf of Her Majesty's Inspectorate of Probation.

Clemmer, D. (1940) *The Prison Community.* New York: Holt, Rinehart & Winston.

Cohen, S. (1985) *Visions of Social Control.* Cambridge: Polity Press.

Cohen, S. and Taylor, L. (1972) *Psychological Survival: The Experience of Long-Term Imprisonment.* Harmondsworth: Penguin.

Cooke, D., Baldwin, P. and Howison, J. (1990) *Psychology in Prisons.* London: Routledge.

Crawford, A. (1999) *The Local Governance of Crime: Appeals to Community Partnerships.* Oxford: Oxford University Press.

Crawley, E. (2004) *Doing Prison Work: The Public and Private Lives of Prison Officers.* Cullompton: Willan Publishing.

Davies, N. (2004) 'Scandal of Society's Misfits Dumped in Jail', *Guardian*, 6 December.

Evans, P. (1980) *Prison Crisis.* London: George Allen & Unwin.

Feeley, M. and Simon, J. (1992) 'The New Penology: Notes on the Emerging Strategy of Correctionalism and Its Implications', *Criminology*, 30 (4): 449–74.

Feeley, M. and Simon, S. (1994) 'Actuarial Justice: The Emerging New Criminal Law', in D. Nelken (ed.), *The Future of Criminology.* London: Sage.

Fitzgerald, M. and Sim, M. (1980) 'Legitimating the Prison Crisis: A Critical Review of the May Report', *Howard Journal*, XIX: 73–84.

Fitzgerald, M. and Sim, M. (1982) *British Prisons*. Oxford: Blackwell.

Fleisher, M. (2003) 'Lost Youth and the Futility of Deterrence', in McConville, S. (ed.), *The Use of Punishment*. Cullompton: Willan Publishing.

Foster, C. and Plowden, F. (1996) *The State Under Stress: Can the Hollow State be Good Government?* Buckingham: Open University Press.

Foucault, M. (1982) 'The Subject of Power', in H. Dreyfus and P. Rainbow (eds), *Michel Foucault: Beyond Structuralism and Hermeneutics*. Brighton: Harvester.

Garland, D. (1985) *Punishment and Welfare: A History of Penal Strategies*. Aldershot: Gower.

Genders, E. and Player, E. (1995) *Grendon: Study of a Therapeutic Prison*. Oxford: Clarendon Press.

Giddens, A. (1997) *Sociology*. Cambridge: Polity Press.

Gladstone, H. (1895) *Report from the Departmental Committee on Prisons*, Sessional Paper 1895, c. 7702. London: HMSO.

Goffman, E. (1961) 'On the Characteristics of Total Institutions', in D. Cressey (ed.), *The Prison: Studies in Institutional Organization and Change*. New York: Holt, Rinehart & Winston.

Goffman, E. (1968) *Asylums*. Harmondsworth: Penguin.

Goodman, A. (1999) 'The Future of Probation', *Criminal Justice Matters*, 34: 28–9.

Goodman, A. (2003) 'Probation into the Millennium: The Punishing Service', in R. Matthews and J. Young (eds), *The New Politics of Crime and Punishment*. Collumpton: Willan Publishing.

Gough, D. (2005) ' "Tough on Probation": Probation Practice under the National Offender Management Service', in J. Winstone and F. Pakes (eds), *Community Justice: Issues for Probation and Criminal Justice*. Cullompton: Willan Publishing.

Halliday, J. (2001) *Making Punishments Work: Report of a Review of the Sentencing Framework for England and Wales*. London: Home Office.

Harding, R. (1997) *Prisons and Public Accountability*. Oxford: Oxford University Press.

Her Majesty's Chief Inspector of Prisons (1993) *Report of an Inquiry into the Disturbance at HM Prison Wymott on 6 September 1993*, Cm 2371. London: HMSO.

Her Majesty's Chief Inspector of Prisons (1999) *Annual Report*, 1999. London: TSO.

Her Majesty's Inspectorate of Probation (1998) *Strategies for Effective Offender Supervision: Report of the HMIP What Works? Project*. London: HMIP.

Her Majesty's Inspectorates' Review (2000) *Casework Information Needs within the Criminal Justice System, A Review by HM Inspectorates of Constabulary, the Crown Prosecution Service, Magistrates' Courts Service, Prisons, Probation Service and Social Service*. London: Chief Inspectors' Group.

Hick, J. and Allen, G. (1999) *A Century of Change: Trends in UK Statistics since 1900*, Research Paper 99/111. London: Social and General Statistics Section of the House of Commons Library.

Home Affairs Committee (1997) *The Management of the Prison Service (Public and Private)*, Second Report, Session 1996/7, House of Commons Paper 57.

Home Affairs Committee (1998) *Alternatives to Prison Sentences*, Third Report, Session 1997/8, House of Commons Paper 486.

Home Affairs Committee (2005) *Rehabilitation of Prisoners*, First Report, Session 2004/5, House of Commons Paper 193.

Home Office (1959) *Penal Practice in a Changing Society*. London: HMSO.

Home Office (1969) *People in Prisons*. London: HMSO.

Home Office (1979) *Committee of Inquiry into the United Kingdom Prison Service: Report*, Cm 7673 [The May Report]. London: HMSO.

Home Office (1984) *Probation Service in England and Wales: Statement of National Objectives and Priorities*. London: Home Office.

Home Office (1987) *Report of an Inquiry by HM Inspector of Prisons for England and Wales into the Disturbances in Prison Service Establishments in England between 29 April – 2 May, 1986*. London: HMSO.

Home Office (1988) *Punishment, Custody and the Community*, Cm 424. London: HMSO.

Home Office (1990) *Crime, Justice and Protecting the Public*, Cm 965. London: HMSO.

Home Office (1991a) *Prison Disturbances 1990: Report of an Inquiry by the Rt Hon Lord Justice Woolf (part I and II) and His Honour Judge Stephen Tumim (part II)*, Cm 1456 [The Woolf Report]. London: HMSO.

Home Office (1991b) *Custody, Care and Justice: The Way Ahead for the Prison Service in England and Wales*, Cm 1647. London: HMSO.

Home Office (1992) *Three Year Plan for the Probation Service, 1993–1996*. London: Home Office.

Home Office (1994b) *Report of the Inquiry into the Escape of Six Prisoners from the Special Security Unit at Whitemoor Prison, Cambridgeshire, on Friday 9th September 1994*, Cm 2741 [The Woodcock Report]. London: HMSO.

Home Office (1994c) *The Cautioning of Offenders*, Circular 18/94. London: Home Office.

Home Office (1995a) *Review of Prison Service Security in England and Wales and the Escape from Parkhurst Prison on Tuesday 3rd January 1995*, Cm 3020 [The Learmont Report]. London: HMSO

Home Office (1995b) *Strengthening Punishment in the Community*, Cm 2780. London: Home Office.

Home Office (1996a) *Prison Statistics England and Wales*, 1995. London: Home Office.

Home Office (1998) *Joining Forces to Protect the Public: Prisons-Probation: A Consultation Document*. London: Home Office.

Home Office (1999) *What Works: Reducing Re-offending: Evidence-Based Practice*. London: Home Office.

Home Office (2003) *The Prison Population in 2001: A Statistical Review*, Home Office Findings 195. London: Home Office Research, Development and Statistics Directorate.

Home Office (2004) *Reducing Crime – Changing Lives: The Government's Plans for Transforming the Management of Offenders*. London: Home Office.

Howard League for Penal Reform (1993) *Dying Inside*. London: Howard League for Penal Reform.

Howard, M. (1993a) Speech to the Conservative party conference, Blackpool, 6 October.

Howard, M. (1993b) Interview, *World at One*, BBC Radio, 15 October.

Howard, M. (1997) Special General Election Supplement, *Prison Report*, 38, Spring: 6–7.

Hudson, B. (1987) *Justice Through Punishment: A Critique of the 'Justice' Model of Corrections*. Basingstoke: Macmillan.

Immarigeon, R. and Maruna, S. (eds) (2004) *After Crime and Punishment: Ex-Offenders' Reintegration and Desistance from Crime*. Cullompton: Willan Publishing.

Infield, P. (1997) 'The Way We Were: How Wandsworth Has Been Transformed', *Prison Report*, 38, Spring: 4–5.

Kemshall, H. (1998) *Risk in Probation Practice*. Aldershot: Ashgate.

Kershaw, C. (1999) *Reconvictions of Offenders Sentenced or Discharged from Prison in 1994, England and Wales*, Home Office Statistical Bulletin, Issue 5/99. London: Home Office Research, Development and Statistics Directorate.

King, R. and McDermott, K. (1995) *The State of Our Prisons*. Oxford: Clarendon.

Lewis, D. (1995) Writ issued against the Home Secretary for wrongful dismissal and exemplary damages, 18 October, quoted in *Guardian*, 19 October.

Lewis, D. (1997) *Hidden Agendas*. London: Hamish Hamilton.

Liebling, A. and Price, D. (2003) 'Prison Officers and the Use of Discretion', in L. Gelsthorpe and N. Padfield (eds), *Exercising Discretion: Decision-Making in the Criminal Justice System and Beyond*. Cullompton: Willan Publishing.

Lloyd, P. (1995) 'Locked in a Jail Fiasco', *Guardian*, 18 October.

Marshall, P. (1997) *A Reconviction Study of HMP Grendon Therapeutic Community*, Research Findings No. 53. London: Home Office Research and Statistics Directorate.

Martinson, R. (1974) 'Questions and Answers about Prison Reform', *The Public Interest*, 34: 217–27.

Mathiesen, T. (1965) *The Defences of the Weak*. London: Tavistock.

Matthews, R. (1999) *Doing Time: An Introduction to the Sociology of Imprisonment*. Basingstoke: Macmillan.

Matthews, R. and Francis, P. (1996) *Prisons 2000: An International Perspective on the Current State and Future of Imprisonment*. Basingstoke: Macmillan.

Mawby, R. and Worrall, A. (2004) ' "Polibation" Revisited: Policing, Probation and Prolific Offender Projects', *International Journal of Police Science and Management*, 6 (2): 63–73.

Morris, N. (1974) *The Future of Imprisonment*. Chicago: University of Chicago Press.

Mountbatten of Burma, Earl (1966) Prison *Escapes and Security*, Cm 3175. London: HMSO.

Moxon, D. (1998) 'The Role of Sentencing Policy', in P. Goldblatt and C. Lewis (eds), *Reducing Offending: An Assessment of Research Evidence on Ways of Dealing with Offending Behaviour*, Research Study 187. London: Home Office Research and Statistics Directorate.

Nash, M. (1999) 'Enter the Polibation Officer', *International Journal of Police Science and Management*, 1 (4): 360–8.

Nash, M. (2004) 'Polibation Revisited – A Reply to Mawby and Worrall', *International Journal of Police Science and Management*, 6 (2): 74–6.

National Offender Management Service (2005) *Prison Population and Accommodation Briefing*, 9 December. London: NOMS.

National Probation Service (2001) *National Standards for the Supervision of Offenders in the Community*. London: Home office.

National Probation Service for England and Wales (2004) *Annual Report, 2003/04*. London: National Probation Service.

Neustatter, A. (2000) 'Jailed Because of Their Gender', *Guardian*, 4 April.

O'Donnell, I. and Edgar, K. (1996) *Victimisation in Prison*, Research Findings No. 37. London: Home Office Research and Statistics Directorate.

O'Dwyer, J. and Carlen, P. (1985) 'Josie: Surviving Holloway and Other Women's Prisons', in P. Carlen, *Criminal Women*. London: Polity Press.

O'Friel, B. (1995) Quoted in E. Brooker, 'Save Women from Our Jails', *Observer*, 18 June.

Padfield, N., Liebling, A. and Arnold, H. (2003) 'Discretion and the Release of Life Sentence Prisoners', in L. Gelsthorpe and N. Padfield (eds), *Exercising Discretion: Decision-Making in the Criminal Justice System and Beyond*. Cullompton: Willan Publishing.

Payback (1999) Quoted *Guardian*, 30 August.

Polidano, C. (1997) *'The Bureaucrat Who Fell Under a Bus': Ministerial Responsibility, Executive Agencies and the Derek Lewis Affair in Britain*, IDPM Public Policy and Management Working Paper No. 1. Manchester: Institute for Development Policy and Management.

Prison Reform Trust (1993) *Does Prison Work?* London: Prison Reform Trust.

Prison Reform Trust (1995) *The Prison Population Explosion*. London: Prison Reform Trust.

Prison Reform Trust (2000) *A Hard Act to Follow. Prisons and the Human Rights Act*. London: Prison Reform Trust.

Prison Report (1998a) 'Privatisation: Factfile 21', *Prison Report*, 42, Spring: 13–16.

Prison Report (1998b) 'Editorial', *Prison Report,* 44, Summer.

Prison Report (1999) 'Privatisation Factfile 26', *Prison Report*, 47, May.

Prison Service (1997) *Prison Service Review*, October. London: Home Office.

Prison Service (1999) *Quinquennial Review of the Prison Service, Prior Options Report*. London: Home Office.

Probation Officer Recruitment and Training Implementation Group (1999) *Probation Officer Recruitment and Training*. London: Home Office.

Public Accounts Committee (2004) *Youth Offending: The Delivery of Community and Custodial Sentences*. London: Public Accounts Committee, Fortieth Report, Session 2003/4, House of Commons Paper 307.

Pycroft, A. (2005) 'A New Chance for Rehabilitation: Multi-agency Provision and Potential under NOMS', in J. Winstone and F. Pakes (eds), *Community Justice: Issues for Probation and Criminal Justice*. Cullompton: Willan Publishing.

Ramsbotham, D. (1998) 'Sharper Teeth for the Tiger: A Fresh Direction for the Prisons Inspectorate', *Prison Report*, 43, June.

Ramsbotham, D. (1999) Quoted in *Guardian*, 12 August.

Ramsbotham, D. (2005) *Prisongate – The Shocking State of Britain's Prisons and the Need for Visionary Change*. London: Free Press.

Raynor, P. and Vanstone, M. (2002) *Understanding Community Penalties: Probation, Policy and Social Change*. Buckingham: Open University Press.

Review of Principles, Policies and Procedures on Mothers and Babies/Children in Prison (1999) Quoted in *Prison Report*, 48, August.

Rutherford, A. (1997) 'Criminal Policy and the Eliminative Ideal', *Social Policy and Administration*, 31: 116–35.

Sapsford, R. (1978) 'Life Sentence Prisoners: Psychological Changes During Sentence', *British Journal of Criminology*, 18: 128–45.

Scott, R. (1995) Quoted in *Observer*, 24 December.

Shaw, S. (1997) 'Remand Prisoners: Why There Are Too Many and How Numbers Could Be Reduced', *Prison Report*, 41, Winter.

Shaw, S. (1999) 'Home Detention Curfew: A Geographical Lottery', *Prison Report*, 48, August.

Social Exclusion Unit (2002) *Reducing Re-offending by Ex-Prisoners*. London: Cabinet Office.

Sparks, C. (1997) 'Slopping Out', *Prison Report*, 39, Summer: 17.

Sparks, C. (1998b) 'Women Prisoners – Scotland Takes the High Road', *Prison Report*, 44, Summer: 24–5.

Sparks, R., Bottoms, T. and Hay, W. (1996) *Prisons and the Problem of Order*. Oxford: Clarendon Press.

Straw, J. (1998) Prison Reform Trust Annual Lecture, London, 22 July.

Sykes, G. (1958) *The Society of Captives*. Princeton, NJ: Princeton University Press.

Tarling, R. (1993) *Analysing Offending: Data, Models and Interpretations*. London: HMSO.

Teers, R. (1997) 'Testing for Drugs in an Open Prison', *Prison Report*, 40, Autumn: 12–13.

Thompson, T. (2005) 'Gangs Bring Terror and Death to Jails', *Observer*, 23 January.

Tilt, R. (1995) Speech to a closed meeting of senior prison managers, December, quoted in *Guardian*, 20 December.

Travis, A. (2005) 'Sentencing Bill Seeks to Cut Prison Numbers', *Guardian*.

Tumim, S. (1993) Speech 28 December, quoted in *Guardian*, 29 December.

Tumim, S. (1995) Interview BBC Radio, 27 October, quoted in *Guardian*, 28 October.

White, P. (1998) *The Prison Population in 1997: A Statistical Review*, Home Office Research Finding 76. London: Home Office Information and Publications Group.

Whitfield, D. (1998) *Introduction to the Probation Service*, 2nd edn. Winchester: Waterside Press.

Woodbridge, J. (1999) *Review of Comparative Costs and Performance of Privately and Publicly-Owned Prisons 1997–98*, Home Office Statistical Bulletin, Issue 13/99. London: Home Office Research, Development and Statistics Directorate.

Woolf, Lord (1993) Quoted in *Today*, 14 October.

Woolf, Lord (1994) House of Lords Debates, 5 Series, Vol. 551, col. 1275, 2 February.

Woolf, N. (1999) *Psychiatric Morbidity among Prisoners in England and Wales*. London: Office of National Statistics.

Worrall, A. (1997) *Punishment in the Community: The Future of Criminal Justice*. Harlow: Longman.

Zamble, E. and Quinsey, V. (1997) *The Criminal Recidivism Process*. Cambridge, MA: Cambridge University Press.

9 Juvenile crime and the state's responsibility

This chapter examines the system that deals with crime committed by those below the age of 21. The age of criminal responsibility is ten years: a child below this age cannot be prosecuted although reforms introduced by post-1997 Labour governments make it possible for intervention (by bodies such as Youth Offending Teams) to be directed at the behaviour of children below this age. The 1933 Children and Young Persons Act classified persons below the age of 14 as 'children' and those aged 14–17 as 'young persons'. Those aged 18–20 are often referred to as 'young adults', although this designation is not derived from legislation. Until the enactment of the 1998 Crime and Disorder Act a presumption of *doli incapax* applied to those aged 10–13 whereby, in order to secure a conviction, it was necessary for the prosecution to prove that the child knew right from wrong in addition to establishing that he or she committed the crime with which they were charged.

This chapter examines the responses to crime committed by those aged 10–21. Specifically the chapter:

- charts the historical development of a specific system to deal with juvenile offending in England and Wales;
- considers changes made to the youth justice system between 1969 and 1997;
- analyses the rationale and content of changes introduced by Labour governments since 1997 to the operations of the youth justice system;
- analyses the strengths and weaknesses of reforms introduced to the youth justice system since 1997;
- considers the effectiveness of attempts made by post-1997 Labour governments to address the social causes of crime, an approach which has been especially directed at influencing the behaviour of young people.

The historical development of the youth justice system

Initially the English criminal justice system failed to draw any distinction between juvenile and adult offenders. Children were viewed as 'small adults', and treated and punished in a similar way to them. However, during the early years of the nineteenth century it began to be accepted that children could not be held entirely responsible for their criminal actions and that a set of arrangements should be introduced that differed from those used to respond to adult criminal behaviour. Early innovations of this nature included the 1838 Parkhurst Act (which provided the first state-run separate prison for juvenile offenders), the 1854 Youthful Offenders Act (which provided for a national network of juvenile reformatories) and the introduction of industrial schools in 1857. The latter catered for children aged between 7 and 14 who had been convicted of vagrancy.

The origins of the contemporary system for dealing with juvenile offenders date from the 1908 Children Act. This abolished imprisonment for offenders below 14, and permitted imprisonment for those aged 14 and 15 only in exceptional cases (for which the court had to issue an 'unruly' certificate). The legislation formally abolished the penalty of death against a child or young person and established a separate system of juvenile courts to deal with offenders aged 15 years and below. The concept of separate youth courts was pioneered by Chicago in 1899 and their role was to manage a new category of transgressor, the juvenile delinquent (Platt, 1969). Initially these courts also had powers to intervene in cases of child neglect.

Those who came before juvenile courts might be 'advised, assisted and befriended' by the Probation Service (which, newly established by the 1907 Probation of Offenders Act, had specific responsibilities for juvenile offenders) or, if they were aged between 16 and 21 they might be sent to borstal, an institution that was set up by the 1908 Crime Prevention Act. They were designed to provide training for juvenile criminals (initially aged 16–20, but the upper age limit was raised to 21 in 1936) in a craft or trade within the environment of a strict regime; the object was to enable trainees to secure employment and be more adequately equipped for life outside the institution. A semi-determinate sentence of between one and three years was served in these institutions, and on release this was followed by supervision by the Probation Service for a minimum period of six months. The 1908 legislation also placed industrial schools under Home Office control.

The operations of the juvenile justice system were further affected by the 1932 Children and Young Persons Act, whose powers were consolidated in the 1933 Children and Young Persons Act which ushered in what has been referred to as a period of 'penal modernism' (Garland, 2001) in which the welfare of young offenders assumed a centre-stage position. Offenders were viewed as disadvantaged or poorly socialised and the period witnessed a range of social and criminal justice policies which were designed to ameliorate the conditions which were regarded as conducive to crime with the Ministry of Health performing a significant role (Pitts, 2003: 76). In this period the focus of concern was on the needs, rather than the deeds, of young offenders (Pitts, 2003: 76–8).

The 1933 legislation provided for special panels of magistrates to determine juvenile cases throughout England and Wales who were encouraged to look beyond the offence and consider the longer-term development of the juvenile offender. A general duty was imposed on social workers (who performed much of the work with young offenders) to safeguard and promote the welfare of children in need. The Act raised the age of criminal responsibility to 8 years (which was subsequently raised to 10 years in the 1963 Children and Young Persons Act), and reformatories were renamed approved schools to cater for juvenile criminals aged between 10 and 15 years. Schedule One of this Act also listed a wide range of offences against children or young persons under the age of 18, and any person convicted of these offences (which include murder, manslaughter and rape) is designated a 'Schedule One Offender' regardless of the sentence imposed or the age of the person who commits the offence.

The 1948 Children and Young Persons Act established Children's Departments as an aspect of local authority social work provision and abolished corporal punishment. The legislation set up Detention Centres to provide for the more serious and persistent juvenile offenders (whereby youths aged 15–17 years could be detained in custody for up to three months) and introduced a new non-custodial disposal, the attendance centre. This was available for juvenile and young adult offenders and was designed to deprive them of their leisure time by requiring attendance for temporary periods of up to 48 hours; during this time they would participate in physical training and constructive hobby programmes.

The philosophy of the juvenile justice system

Aims and objectives of youth justice

There are a number of guiding principles that ought to be applied to a system of youth justice. These include:

- juveniles at risk of becoming criminals must be identified and aid provided to prevent this potential from being realised;
- juveniles who have offended must be subject to measures directed at preventing further (and more serious) manifestations of offending behaviour;
- juveniles who have offended must be given aid to accept community values so that they can be reintegrated into the community.

Why does a separate system for dealing with juvenile offenders exist in England and Wales? What principles underpin its operations?

The 1969 Children and Young Persons Act

The system for dealing with juvenile criminality has always been based upon a mixture of motives. In the nineteenth century it was influenced as much by the desire to protect society as it was by the wish to save children from the consequences of a future life of crime. For this reason it initially sanctioned taking juvenile offenders away from their family and community and placing them in an institutional setting. In the twentieth century a significant tension arose between the social welfare role of the juvenile justice system – which included enabling the state to undertake pre-emptive action and intervene in the lives of families whose children were deemed to have suffered neglect or abuse which might result in them turning to crime – and its role in ensuring that children who committed wrongdoings were adequately punished for their actions. A further difficulty was that the use of criminal justice processes to deliver welfare interventions could result in the denial of legal rights to those on the receiving end (Pitts, 1988: 1).

During the 1960s, the Labour party turned its attention to reforming the juvenile justice system. Its proposals were put forward against the background of 'the rediscovery of poverty' as a problem that affected 'families and neighbourhoods which have been unable to avail themselves of the opportunities offered by a prosperous technologically sophisticated society' (Pitts, 1988: 5). Crime was viewed as an aspect of this deprivation and Labour sought to transform juvenile criminal justice to 'a mechanism that dispensed welfare and treatment' (Pitts, 1998: 7). Initially Labour proposed (in its White Paper, *The Child, the Family and the Young Offender* (1965)) to transform the structure of the juvenile justice system in England and Wales, but it latterly contented itself (in the White Paper *Children in Trouble* (1968)) instead to transform its functioning (Pitts, 1988: 13–14). The resultant legislation was 1969 Children and Young Persons Act.

The 1969 Act unambiguously came down on the side of welfare and has been depicted as 'the highpoint of the 36-year struggle to construct a child-centred youth justice system, in which a concern for the "welfare" of the child, their needs rather than their deeds, was paramount' (Pitts, 2003: 78). The legislation sought (through the use of cautions and the involvement of other agencies) to encourage the diversion of young offenders from the courts (Gelsthorpe and Morris, 1994), and the new disposal of a supervision order, while not removing children completely from the criminal court system, was designed 'to assist in the development, maturation and welfare of children in trouble' (Raynor and Vanstone, 2002: 1). Local government was accorded a major role in the administration of the new system in which social workers gained powers at the expense of magistrates. This measure put forward a number of reforms that were designed to divert children from both the courts and custody sentences. These included the following:

- *The abolition of approved schools and remand homes*. These were replaced by community homes with residential and educational facilities.
- *The introduction of Intermediate Treatment (IT)*. This scheme was operated by local authorities and permitted them to introduce facilities for the use of

children and young persons who had offended or who were deemed to be at risk of offending (although at the point of intervention may not have actually done so). The aim of IT was to bring these young people into contact with constructive environments, although there was relatively little official guidance as to what should comprise such environments. IT could be a requirement of a supervision order, and it was anticipated that IT would eventually replace detention and attendance centres.

- *The redirection of the focus of juvenile courts towards welfare.* The remit of the juvenile courts was extended to civil as well as criminal matters; this enabled 'care proceedings' to be undertaken in respect of children whose upbringing or unsatisfactory socialisation within the family deemed them to be 'at risk' and thus in need of care or supervision to prevent this being realised. Care orders were issued by magistrates on the recommendation of social workers and could also be made in connection with criminal charges, whereby a juvenile could be placed in the care of a local authority which would then decide where the child was to be placed (which was typically in a CHE – a Community Home (with Education)). Limits were also placed on the circumstances under which juveniles could be subject to criminal proceedings: those aged 14–17 could be subject to criminal proceedings, but the police had first to consult with the local authority children's department before making an application to a magistrate. This provided a further example of the manner in which the legislation increased the role of social workers in the administration of the juvenile justice system.

The 1969 Children and Young Persons Act was based upon the 'welfare principle'. What do you understand by this term, and what are its main strengths and weaknesses?

The development of the youth justice system 1969–97

Tensions between the justice and welfare objectives of the juvenile justice system surfaced after 1969. Criticisms were voiced that juveniles who committed crime would not be sufficiently punished for their actions since the welfare aspects of the new system tended to focus attention away from the offence and towards the circumstances of the offender, as interpreted by social workers. For this latter reason many of the provisions of the 1969 Act were not implemented by the Conservative government which took office in 1970. The age of criminal responsibility was not raised from the age of 10 to 14, and in particular Intermediate Treatment failed to replace Attendance and

Detention Centres. It was asserted that by the mid-1970s, IT 'was being used as a catch-all for social compensation, compensatory education, personal growth, therapy, outdoor activity holidays for children with no money' (Pitts, 1988: 35) but did not develop into an alternative to the imprisonment of juveniles. Instead the 1970s witnessed an 'explosion' (Pitts, 1988: 22) in the imprisonment of juveniles. The main reason for this situation was that magistrates were sceptical of committing juvenile offenders into the care of social workers rather than probation officers with whose role they were familiar and thus adopted practices to avoid this. These practices included sending juveniles to the crown court for borstal sentencing that had the effect of releasing them to the Probation Service for 'after care' (Worrall, 1997: 69).

Reforms to the system of juvenile justice 1979–97

The response to juvenile crime was a major concern for government after 1979. This section seeks to examine the responses that were adopted in this period.

The new penology

The 1969 legislation was criticised from two perspectives. The first of these centred on the 'back to justice' argument which suggested that the involvement of the courts in the lives of young offenders (and in particular those young people who had committed no crimes) constituted a gross curtailment of civil liberties, as those subjected to this treatment were not provided with adequate legal protection. One aspect of this concern was finally resolved when the 1989 Children Act ended the involvement of Juvenile Courts in civil care proceedings. These were transferred to the family proceedings court, thus confining the attention of the Juvenile Court to criminal actions committed by children and young persons. A second concern with the 1969 legislation was that of cost and value for money, concerns that became accentuated following economic problems that surfaced after the 1983 general election.

These twin pressures gave rise to what has been referred to as 'radical non-intervention' (Schur, 1973) or 'progressive minimalism' (Pitts, 2003: 81–2). It was characterised by attempts to reduce the level of state intervention in response to all but the most serious juvenile offenders. One reason for this approach was the belief that much youth crime was of a transient nature, part of the process of growing up.

In 1979 the Black Committee on Children and Young Persons gave official recognition to the concern that intervention by the state in the life of a child at an early stage might speed up his or her progress through the criminal justice system. The committee argued that much juvenile crime was of a transient nature, and that for first – and second-time – juvenile offenders cautions were a more appropriate response than prosecutions that could result in custodial sentences. This approach (which was compatible with labelling theory discussed in Chapter 1) was sanctioned by the 1981 Royal Commission on Criminal Procedure, which noted that considerable differences existed between police forces over the use of cautions. Accordingly, the greater use of cautioning was endorsed by the Home Office (Home Office, 1985 and 1990), and clearer national guidelines which set out the criteria to be used for prosecution and cautioning were also issued (Home Office, 1985). A range of cautions were introduced during the 1980s, including warnings or 'informal cautions', formal cautions and 'caution plus' (which included an intervention element designed to make offenders face the consequence of their actions). One difficulty with this policy was that the use of cautions could result in 'net widening' (Ditchfield, 1976) whereby formal action was taken against minor offenders which would previously have had no action taken against them. However, it was argued that this problem was not realised in practice (Gelsthorpe and Morris, 1994: 978).

Additionally, alternatives to the imposition of custodial sentences for juvenile offenders were introduced after 1979. These were primarily viewed as forms of punishment, thus indicating a move away from the welfare principles underlying the 1969 legislation. The 1982 Criminal Justice Act made Community Service Orders available to 16-year-olds, and introduced new requirements that could be attached to supervision orders (which were young persons' equivalents of probation orders). This legislation further introduced statutory criteria for the imposition of a custodial sentence for offenders below the age of 21. Henceforth a court could not impose a custodial sentence on offenders below the age of 21 unless it was satisfied that there was no other appropriate method to deal with him or her. Imprisonment for those aged below 21 years of age was abolished, and henceforth custodial sentences imposed on those below this age would be discharged in a Youth Custody Centre (which replaced borstals) or a Detention Centre in which a short sentence of between four and six months would be served. The sentencing criteria were amended in the 1988 Criminal Justice Act whereby its application was related only to one offence even though the offender may have committed many others (Kemp and Gelsthorpe, 2003: 58). The 1991 Criminal Justice Act abolished custody for children below the age of 15, and introduced curfew orders for those aged 16 and above as an alternative to custody.

Other initiatives introduced in this period were also intended to divert young offenders from custodial sentences. These made prominent use of multi-agency responses to juvenile crime, an approach that has been dubbed 'corporatist' (Pratt, 1989). The main initiatives pursued were as follows:

- *Intensive Intermediate Treatment.* In 1983 the government sought, through the Department of Health and Social Security (DHSS) to put additional resources into IT which would be directed at the more serious and persistent young offenders and sought to avoid them being subject to custodial disposals. This would take the form of grants being made available to voluntary bodies 'in order to help the development of more intensive IT programmes designed specifically for those young people who would otherwise go to borstal or detention centres' (DHSS, 1983). Nonetheless, attendance centre orders retained their popularity with sentencers (Worrall,

1997: 99) which were available for juveniles and other young offenders aged 10–20. Combination orders (including attendance centre and supervision orders) could also be dispensed by the courts.

- *Multi-agency diversion panels.* Multi-agency responses to juvenile offending (which were a feature of Intermediate Treatment discussed above) were also implemented through diversion panels. Young offenders could be referred to these bodies as a condition of a police caution (the process of 'caution plus' referred to above). The key aim of these panels was the cost-effective management of young offenders as opposed to objectives seeking their rehabilitation or punishment (Pitts, 2003: 82).

- *Intensive Probation (IP.)* Although earlier research had suggested that offenders who were subject to intensive supervision reoffended at similar rates to those given ordinary supervision or none at all (Folkard et al., 1976; Phillpotts and Lancucki, 1979), new experiments were initiated in 1990 to provide IP for younger offenders aged 17–25 who had been charged with fairly serious offences such as burglary. An IP order was an alternative to a custodial sentence and comprised an individualised programme based on a personal action plan drawn up for the offender, which included the requirement of frequent contact with a project worker. The projects focused on confronting offending behaviour and used a multi-agency approach (Mair et al., 1994, ix–x).

The combination of progressive minimalist and corporatist approaches to juvenile crime has been referred to as 'the new penology' (Feeley and Simon, 1992). Its attempts to secure cost-effective interventions for all but the most serious offenders (who would be incapacitated) corresponded with the economic aims of the Conservative government to secure economy and value for money in the provision of public services (Pitts, 2003: 83).

Changes that were compatible with progressive minimalism and corporatism were also evident in reforms that were made to the procedures used for processing juvenile offenders. Under the 1991 Criminal Justice Act, Juvenile Courts were renamed Youth Courts whose jurisdiction was extended so that these courts catered for those aged between 10 and 17 years of age. Magistrates serving in these courts were to be drawn from a specialist Youth Court Panel. The desire to avoid incapacitation was emphasised in the requirement, imposed by the 1991 legislation, that Youth Courts should normally consider a pre-sentence report before passing a custodial sentence and imposing most forms of community orders. This was designed to make sentencers consider non-custodial alternatives. This report (which superseded the former social inquiry report) was prepared by agencies that included Social Services and the Probation Service, which might also draw upon the aid of other professionals such as teachers if the offender was at school. This requirement was slightly relaxed in the 1994 Criminal Justice and Public Order Act.

Benefits of the new penology

The approaches adopted by the Conservative government to juvenile justice had obvious political advantages. A caution was not classed as a conviction, and the process was less costly than an appearance before a Youth Court and any custodial sentence that it might impose. Accordingly, the number of young people in custody declined from 7,400 in 1980 to 1,400 in 1992, and the use of care orders in criminal proceedings declined from 2,700 to 100 in the same period (Whitfield, 1998: 115). The overall number of juveniles (aged 10–17) found guilty by the courts declined from 90,200 in 1980 to 24,700 in 1990, representing a 73 per cent decline in court caseloads in a decade (Rutherford, 1999: 47–8).

In conjunction with other procedural changes which were introduced at that time (including the creation of the Crown Prosecution Service which was initially loathe to prosecute juvenile shoplifters for minor offences) these statistics gave the appearance that the government had succeeded in securing a reduction in the level of juvenile crime. However, it has been argued that this situation was illusory, and that the apparent decline in the number of juvenile offenders occurred because the probability of being convicted or formally cautioned had decreased (Farrington, 1999: 4).

The rise of penal populism

A disproportionate amount of contemporary crime is committed by young people, mainly young males. In 1994, two out of every five known offenders were below the age of 21, and a quarter of which were under 18 (Audit Commission, 1996: 5). Most crime committed by young people aged between 14 and 17 was property-related, and the great bulk of this was carried out by a small group of prolific offenders so that approximately 5 per cent of offenders were responsible for 68 per cent of all offences (Audit Commission, 1996: 8). It was additionally estimated that the cost to society of crime committed by people under 21 was £13 billion a year, and that young men were not growing out of crime as they reached their late teens and early twenties (Bright, 1998: 15).

These statistics could be used to support the contention that the youth justice system was unduly lenient towards offenders and that a more punitive response to youth crime, in particular towards prolific juvenile offenders, was required. Accordingly, alongside the minimalist strategy pursued during the 1980s, a more punitive approach was adopted towards the most serious juvenile offenders. The absorption of borstals (which were renamed Youth Custody Centres) into the mainstream Prison Service was symbolised by staff reverting to wearing uniforms in 1983 (Pitts, 1988: 49), and the 1982 Criminal Justice Act introduced the 'short, sharp, shock' regime into four selected detention centres where inmates were subject to military style discipline in the belief that the toughness of the regime would deter youngsters from reoffending. However, this scheme had 'no discernible effect' on the reoffending rates of trainees and was phased out (Home Office, 1984: 243). One problem was that attempting to knock the criminal spirit out of young people might serve to brutalise them and result in further, more violent, transgressions of the law.

Additionally, the 1982 Criminal Justice Act provided for the possibility of harsher sentences for youth crime. This measure restricted the discretionary powers of social workers, and sought to ensure that decisions of Juvenile Courts were based on the hard facts concerning crimes rather than a subjective assessment of a child's welfare needs. The legislation gave Juvenile Court magistrates the power to impose custodial sentences on adolescents without referring him or her to the crown court for sentence, and allowed a Juvenile Court to impose a community service order on a defendant as young as 16. This Act also amended the care order procedure, enabling the courts to insist on a child's removal from his or her home for a period of up to six months. Subsequently, the 1988 Criminal Justice Act introduced the new sentence of detention in a Young Offenders Institution (YOI): this replaced detention centres and youth custody centres and was available for those aged 15–21.

The punitive aspects of the government's approach to youth crime were moved from the margins of the juvenile justice system (where it dealt with the most serious offenders) to centre stage during the 1990s. Concerns about the behaviour of young people were evidenced in rising crime rates in the late 1980s, the urban housing estate riots in 1991 and 1992 and the unruly behaviour of young people which included activities such 'joyriding', under-age drinking, 'acid house' parties and 'raves'. These concerns were climaxed with the murder by two children of James Bulger in 1993 and underwrote a new approach to the government's response to all crime, including that committed by juveniles. This was termed 'penal populism' (a term which has been discussed in Chapter 1). It heralded the abandonment of the minimalist tendencies contained in the 1991 Criminal Justice Act in favour of more punitive responses underpinned by retributive objectives that did little to provide help to young people who had offended. The new approach was based upon a belief that children could legitimately be held responsible for their criminal actions. Although training and educative functions continued to be performed by the incarcerative elements of the juvenile justice system, the rationale for the system increasingly became that of deterrence and punishment.

Youth crime became a specific target of the post-1992 Conservative government's law and order policies, an approach which was justified by figures suggesting the rise of crime coupled with the decrease in juvenile offending during the 1980s meant that the average juvenile offender was committing more crime (Farrington, 1999: 3). It was further perceived that those who did come before the courts were less likely to receive custodial sentences: this was especially so for those below the age of 15 since the only legislation which permitted custodial sentences (the 1933 Children and Young Persons Act) applied only to the most serious offences. Following the election, the then Home Secretary Kenneth Clarke promised to introduce measures to tackle 'nasty, persistent little offenders' (Clarke, 1993) and his successor as Home Secretary, Michael Howard, enthusiastically endorsed the penal populist approach to crime in his speech to the Conservative party conference in October 1993, thereby ensuring that law and order became a prominent political issue. The main changes which were introduced included the following:

- *The 1994 Criminal Justice Act and Public Order Act.* This Act increased the maximum sentence in a Youth Offender Institution from 12 months to 24. It proposed a new institution, the Secure Training Centre (or 'children's jail'). Children and young persons aged 12–14 who committed a minimum of three imprisonable offences would be subject to a Secure Training Order which would combine discipline with training. It has been argued that 'by striking at young offenders and focusing as much on previous record as immediate offence, secure training units marked the wholesale rejection of the underlying principles embedded in the Criminal Justice Act of 1991' (Rutherford, 1999: 55). Although the Conservative government failed to adopt this policy, this reform was implemented by the 1997 Labour government and the first Secure Training Centre opened at Cookham Wood in Kent.

- *'Boot camps'.* Innovations were introduced into regimes for older persistent juvenile offenders. These included the military-run corrective training centre at Colchester and the 'boot camp' regime at Thorn Cross Young Offenders Institution.

- *Restricted use of cautioning.* The government sought to restrict the use of cautions by stating that a second caution should be given only in exceptional circumstances (Home Office, 1994). It was estimated, however, that 70 per cent of first-time juvenile offenders who received a caution did not reoffend within two years (Audit Commission, 1996: 22).

Boot camps

The desire to reform and rehabilitate persistent older juvenile offenders underpinned the creation of the 'boot camp' regime that was conducted in selected YOIs at Colchester (which involved a joint programme with the Military Corrective Training Centre) and Thorn Cross. Here selected young offenders aged 18–21 were given what amounted to the 'last chance saloon'. They were subjected to 'high-intensity training', which was divided into five phases, each of five weeks. In the early phases the emphasis was placed on drill and physical education, but later phases introduced vocational training, therapy to aid the control of temper and anger, and sessions in which offenders discussed the nature of their offending and the impact of their crimes on the victims in order to prepare them for release. The fifth phase was a work placement away from the institution. The regime was relatively expensive, since a place at Thorn Cross cost around £22,700, or about £5,000 more than custody in a more traditional YOI regime (Prison Reform Trust, 1998), but it pointed to the constructive way in which a custodial environment could be used in contrast to institutions whose emphasis was more obviously punitive. In 1999 the Chief Inspector of Prisons, Sir David Ramsbotham, applauded the pilot scheme at Thorn Cross and suggested that a second one should be set up in Southern England. The Colchester 'boot camp' was closed in March 1998 but the Thorn Cross regime continued.

The youth justice system in the late 1990s

A number of deficiencies in the operations of the youth justice system were observed by the end of the 1990s. These were as follows:

- *Effectiveness*. The low detection rates for juvenile offences meant that very few offenders were processed by Youth Courts, and thus the vast majority of them received neither help nor punishment. Furthermore, the effectiveness of custodial sentences was questioned. Although the use of this form of punishment declined between 1984 and 1994 (and the average length of sentence was shorter), around 90 per cent of young males who were sentenced to custody for less than one year were reconvicted within two years of release (Audit Commission, 1996: 42).
- *Cost*. It cost the police £1,200 to identify a young offender, and a further £2,500 to prosecute him or her successfully. The total cost of dealing with offending by young people was around £1 billion a year (Audit Commission, 1996: 6 and 44). These figures suggested that the system provided poor value for money and that resources could be used more efficiently.
- *Speed*. A considerable period of time frequently elapsed between arrest and sentence – studies suggested that 'on average, the whole process can take from 70 days in some areas to 170 in others' (Audit Commission, 1996: 29–30). Excessive delay meant that the crime was not fresh in the mind of the juvenile offender who was thus less likely to be amenable to suggestions to mend his or her ways.
- *Lack of coordination*. The work of the different agencies which dealt with juveniles was poorly coordinated and their performance objectives were frequently dissimilar (Audit Commission, 1996: 59). It was argued that lack of jobs and inadequate nursery education and family centres to help young isolated mothers contributed to the level of youth crime. In particular, school exclusions (which had risen threefold between 1990/1 and 1994/5) were stated to have had a significant bearing on juvenile offending (Audit Commission, 1996: 66–7).

The 1998 Crime and Disorder Act

The Labour party had traditionally adopted an approach to crime which differed from that pursued by the Conservative party, believing that there was a need to tackle the problem at its roots rather than simply impose harsh actions against those who broke the law. Nonetheless, the party began to accept that the public expected those who committed crime to be appropriately punished for their actions. Accordingly, the notion of tough action against crime began to enter into Labour's law and order rhetoric alongside their concern to tackle its social causes. This was clearly articulated by the shadow Home Secretary, Tony Blair, in 1993 when he declared Labour's approach as 'tough on crime, tough on the causes of crime'.

In February 1993, in response to the government's pledge to tackle juvenile crime, the Labour party put forward a package of measures that included the provision of more secure places for persistent young offenders. Tough action was a prominent concern of a paper, *A Quiet Life: Tough Action on Criminal Neighbours*, published in 1995. In September 1997 the newly elected Labour government published three consultation papers to identify how it would use crime and disorder legislation to tackle youth crime, particularly that committed by a hard core of persistent juvenile offenders responsible for a disproportionate amount of crime. Subsequently a White Paper, *No More Excuses – A New Approach to Tackling Youth Crime in England and Wales*, was published in 1997, which led to the 1998 Crime and Disorder Act. This Act provided the youth justice system with a statutory aim ('to prevent offending by children and young persons') and proposed a comprehensive and wide-ranging reform of the youth justice system should be implemented, the key features of which are described below.

The multi-agency (or partnership) approach

The needs of young people were historically catered for by a range of public agencies. Their perspectives were different and they sometimes found it hard to work together effectively. The 1998 Crime and Disorder Act sought to tackle this fragmentation by providing a mechanism which would enable a multi-agency or partnership approach to be adopted towards preventing juvenile crime and dealing with juvenile offenders. This new mechanism was the Youth Offending Team (YOT).

The multi-agency approach to juvenile crime

The multi-agency or partnership approach was at the heart of the Labour government's policy for responding to crime and disorder. It was the under-pinning of drug action teams, youth offending teams, crime and disorder reduction partnerships (whose work is discussed in Chapters 2 and 4) and problem-oriented policing.

It was not, however, a novel response either to crime in general or to that committed by juveniles in particular. Inter-agency juvenile panels pre-dated the 1998 legislation. It was relatively common for the police to liaise with other agencies when juveniles committed criminal offences, and social services had to become involved when juveniles committed serious criminal offences that went before a court as they were responsible for drawing up pre-sentencing reports. Additionally, youths who came to the attention of the police (perhaps as the result of being called to a domestic dispute) and who were deemed by the police to be at risk of becoming victims of crime in the home would often be subject to some form of multi-agency intervention coordinated by a police Child Protection Department.

However, the nature of the multi-agency response varied both between police forces and also within them since youth justice departments were traditionally organised at divisional rather than force level. The 1998 Act thus sought to both formalise and standardise a multi-agency approach in which the police were not to be regarded as the lead agency or main instigator of a multi-agency solution. Additionally, whereas earlier multi-agency initiatives (such as multi-agency diversion panels) often sought to keep juveniles out of the criminal justice system, new developments (such as YOTs) had the effect of increasing the scope of interventions of this nature.

The government proposed that local authorities (which had exercised major responsibilities in connection with youth justice under the 1989 Children Act) should be given a statutory duty to ensure that appropriate youth justice services – including bail support – were provided and coordinated for their area through the mechanism of a YOT. The government considered that YOTs should involve professionals from a range of relevant agencies including social workers, probation officers, police officers, and education and health authority staff. All of these agencies were placed under a statutory duty to participate in local arrangements for YOTs. This new local partnership would work alongside other agencies, including Community Safety and Drug Action Teams. Each YOT would be responsible to a steering group of chief officers from the participating agencies. Its work would be directed by a manager responsible for purchasing and commissioning services that could be supplied from the public or voluntary sectors.

Additionally, the local authority was given a statutory duty to draw up, in consultation with other agencies, a strategic plan for youth justice work in the area (termed the Youth Justice Plan). This would provide information on the establishment, composition, funding and operation of YOTs, and indicate how youth justice work was linked to government objectives, local needs and the local crime and disorder reduction strategy. The Youth Justice Plan was designed to facilitate the devising of a coherent set of goals to shape policy, aid the planning and provision of services, and establish clear lines of accountability. In particular it would help to ensure that issues connected to youth justice were related to other local authority key strategic responsibilities. Subsequently, the government placed a duty on local authority chief executives to prepare a local preventative strategy for children and young people by April 2003 that typically involved identifying risk factors and targeting intervention at those young people who, on the basis of these factors, were deemed likely to exhibit offending behaviour. In Wales, the Welsh Assembly government played a key role in the development of a preventative youth offending strategy for the entire country (Welsh Assembly Government, 2004).

YOTs operate in accordance with national standards. Their day-to-day work includes assessing individuals and their offending behaviour at various stages in the juvenile justice process. They determine whether intervention (which may include family group conferencing) is required in support of the new police Final Warning Schemes in order to prevent further reoffending, and are responsible for the development and supervision of intervention programmes with the support and cooperation of other agencies. They pre-pare pre-sentence reports and other information required by the courts in connection with criminal proceedings against juveniles, liaise with victims and supervise community sentences imposed by the courts. It was initially noted, however, that in excess of 60 per cent of the workload undertaken by YOTs was devoted to activities which included attending meetings, training and completing administrative work rather than working directly with young people in order to address their offending behaviour (NACRO, 2003b: 3).

These duties added significantly to the responsibilities of the police service that formerly had no role in post-offending behaviour because this was viewed as the function of the Probation Service. They also indicated a move towards dealing with the causes rather than the symptoms of crime.

The government established a youth justice board to coordinate the youth justice system at national level. The Board was established on a statutory basis as a non-departmental public body accountable to the Home Secretary. The members of the Board are appointed by the Home Secretary whose responsibility is 'to give strategic direction, to set standards for, and measure the performance of the youth justice system as a whole' (Kemp and Gelsthorpe, 2003: 32). The Board's remit extends to YOTs (to ensure that comparable standards of efficiency and effectiveness exist across England and Wales which is measured against Youth Justice Board Performance Targets), the juvenile secure estate (which comprised local authority Community Homes (with education) (CHEs), Youth Offender Institutions, the Department of Health's Youth Training Centres and the Secure Training Centres set up under the auspices of the 1994 Criminal Justice and Public Order Act) and the youth court system. Initially it also awarded grants of a short-term, pump-priming nature to tackle specific crimes in particular localities. By March 2000 the Board had funded 450 local programmes covering parenting, reparation, restorative justice, mentoring, bail supervision, education and training, substance abuse and crime prevention initiatives (Warner, 2000). It has been argued that the functions performed by the Youth Justice Board marked 'a significant move towards a national system of youth justice in England and Wales' (Pitts, 2003: 89). The Labour government subsequently introduced market principles into the youth justice system, whereby after April 2000 the Youth Justice Board had a budget to purchase secure units from the Prison Service, local authorities or private providers.

Successful multi-agency intervention required a number of factors, one of which was that those who were party to cooperative arrangements enjoyed mutual trust. This was particularly important with regard to sharing informa-tion and relying on the parties involved not to unnecessarily divulge material gleaned through the cooperative process. There was also a need to devise performance indicators for YOTs, since those used by the individual participants did not include crime reduction targets.

New court orders

The 1998 Crime and Disorder Act blended preventive and punitive measures to combat crime. It sought to achieve the latter aim by the introduction of a range of court orders through which the penal populist objective of taking a tough line on crime would be achieved. These were not exclusively directed at juvenile crime and included provisions directed at sexual and racially aggravated offences. The following section discusses those court orders that clearly have implications for youth offending, although some of them have wider applications.

Anti-social behaviour orders

Anti-social behaviour is especially associated with young people. A study conducted in 2003 stated that 29 per cent of young people admitted to committing at least one act of anti-social behaviour in the previous year (Hayward and Sharp, 2005). Anti-social behaviour constituted an important source of public concern, considerably contributed to the public's fear of crime and was a drain on police resources. Yet it was alleged that the criminal justice system was unable to provide any effective remedy since behaviour such as 'shouting and swearing, hanging about and fooling around in groups, sometimes outside other people's homes' constituted nuisance rather than crime (Audit Commission, 1996: 13). The fact that young people were apparently able to behave in this manner with total impunity has been viewed as an aspect of the 'enforcement deficit' (Squires and Stephen, 2005: 26) within the criminal justice system that new Labour sought to address through the introduction of anti-social behaviour orders (ASBOs).

ASBOs built on the approach adopted in the 1997 Protection from Harassment Act and address the notion of nuisance in a form not previously catered for by legislation. The term 'anti-social behaviour' embraces an extremely wide range of activities 'from the dropping of litter on the streets at one end of the spectrum, through to the running of "crack houses" by drug dealers at the other' (Home Affairs Committee, 2005). ASBOs are issued by magistrates' courts at the behest of (initially) the police or a local authority that are required to consult on this issue. It was also anticipated that Crime and Disorder Reduction Partnerships and YOTs would be consulted in the process of applying for an ASBO, since YOTs might be required to provide services designed to combat further occurrences of anti-social behaviour. The civil standard of proof – the balance of probabilities – must be met to obtain an ASBO.

ASBOs may be directed at individuals or groups (such as families) and can be applied to children as young as ten as well as to teenagers and adults whose actions cause, or are likely to cause, 'harassment, alarm or distress to one or more persons not of the same household' but which fall short of actual criminal behaviour. ASBOs were perceived as a last resort when other forms of intervention (such as working with children and families) had failed to prevent misconduct.

ASBOs are issued after consideration by referral to a local authority community safety team. Initially the decision to apply for an ASBO was taken only after all other options had been considered and ASBOs were thus applied far sparingly. However, the upward trend in the number of ASBOs that have been issued suggests a move away from their use in this sparing fashion. It is unusual for courts to refuse a request for an ASBO. ASBOs last for a minimum of two years (with no upper limit) and breach of them is a criminal offence that is prosecuted by the CPS and could result in up to five years imprisonment for an adult or a detention and training order for a juvenile. Attaching the threat of a prison sentence to what is in effect a civil injunction blurs the distinction between civil and criminal law and provides a potentially easier route to prosecution. There is no need for the victims of anti-social behaviour to make a formal statement as the basis for action by the police or a local authority. Hearsay evidence and (in certain circumstances) video evidence is acceptable and, additionally, evidence provided by professional witnesses (such as council officials or police officers) may be used as the basis for obtaining these orders. The court which sanctions an ASBO on a young person aged under 18 years also has the discretion to impose a parenting order at the same time.

Assessment of ASBOs

New Labour's campaign against anti-social behaviour formed a crucial aspect of its objective to create 'strong and cohesive' communities (Home Office, 2004b). ASBOs provided a mechanism 'for addressing the collective and accumulating impact of harm and distress across a community' which traditional criminal justice interventions failed to provide (Squires and Stephen, 2005: 3) and ensured that people no longer had to face 'fear, harassment, intimidation and anti-social behaviour all alone' (Squires and Stephen, 2005: 27).

ASBOs sought to address behaviour that has been viewed as the starting point of future manifestations of criminal behaviour (Home Office, 1997). There are several strengths of ASBOs. They offer protection to vulnerable groups suffering harassment such as the elderly, the disabled, racial minorities, gays, and children on their way to and from school. They are relatively cheap to administer (unless the Court of Appeal becomes involves in which case costs rise significantly). A key advantage of these orders is that they are extremely flexible and can be applied to a very wide range of activities. They may prevent individuals visiting particular places or associating with designated persons. Practitioners will thus often view ASBOs as a useful tool with which to combat a wide range of behaviour which 'ordinary' members of the general public feel to be threatening or intimidating. Those most affected are not required to undertake civil proceedings (which may be costly) against those carrying out the offending behaviour, and their anonymity can be preserved by not having to attend court in connection with the ASBO application. In this sense, ASBOs provide an important aid to victims of anti-social behaviour.

However, ASBOs pose a number of problems. They provide a quantifiable measurement to show that action is being taken against anti-social behaviour regardless of the effectiveness of this approach. An important incentive for a local authority to be seen to be doing something about anti-social behaviour was initiated in 2005 whereby they would be assessed on their performance in tackling anti-social behaviour as part of their Comprehensive Performance Assessment. Inspections would focus on evidence that a local authority had contributed towards the successful responses in reducing anti-social behaviour through effective partnership work and had taken a strategic approach by integrating its response to tackling anti-social behaviour across all the services it delivered (Audit Commission, 2005).

There are several other difficulties associated with ASBOs. They deal with the symptoms of a problem and not the cause of unruly behaviour itself (Squires and Stephen, 2005: 7), and they may be an inappropriate response to disorder, especially when directed against those whose behaviour stems from factors such as mental illness. The term 'anti-social' is subjective and provides the possibility of the intolerant being able to sanction behaviour of which they disapprove. Because the term lacks precise definition it is prone to abuse. For example, ASBOs may be used in cases where there is insufficient evidence to substantiate a criminal charge, which opens the possibility of the orders being used in a vindictive manner against marginalised persons (in particular those with criminal records) who lack the means to adequately defend themselves. It has been argued that ASBOs perform a 'street cleaning function' (Burney, 2005: 101) since they are directed against certain types of 'problem people' (such as beggars, youths, prostitutes, drunkards and persons with mental disorders) who have been targeted 'simply by being in the street' (Burney, 2005: 36) thereby heightening their sense of social exclusion.

Critical criminologists see ASBOs as an unwarranted extension of the state's power to intervene which is directed against the marginalised on the basis of the existence of a problem which has been to a large extent exaggerated or artificially created (in the sense that it is directed against activities which 'should be ignored or written off as inevitable problems of everyday life and growing up' (Lemert, 2000), and which for many offenders constituted actions which were more akin to bad manners than incipient criminality) (Blaikie, 2004). The use to which ASBOs have been put accords to the concepts of 'net widening' and 'mesh thinning' associated with the 'dispersal of discipline thesis' (Cohen, 1985) whereby an increasing number of minor social transgressions become subject to new mechanisms of social control, an approach which is the antithesis of the strategy of 'radical non-intervention' (Schur, 1971). A further problem is that the use of ASBOs may increase the community's reliance on state intervention as opposed to the development of its own mechanisms of informal control over those acting in an unruly manner.

A local authority community safety team receives a report that a gang of youths are regularly causing a serious nuisance outside bungalows occupied by senior citizens. Evaluate the strengths and weaknesses of utilising ASBOs to curb the youths' behaviour.

Parenting orders

The belief that deficient parenting was an important underpinning to youth crime resulted in attempts to reinforce the role performed by the family as a controlling influence over children. The 1982 Criminal Justice Act aimed to make parents or guardians accept responsibility for their children's behaviour, and this approach was developed by post-1997 Labour governments. It was argued that 'strong families are the centre of peaceful and safe communities. Parents have a critical role in teaching their children the difference between right and wrong' (Home Office, 2003a: 8). The 1998 legislation introduced parenting orders that could be applied to a juvenile aged 10–17 who was convicted of a criminal offence. These orders instituted weekly support/guidance sessions over a three-month period which were designed to help parents control unruly children and to develop other parenting skills. Parents or guardians were also required to comply with any other provisions set out in the order for a period of up to 12 months, which could include an obligation to ensure that their children attended school. Failure to comply with the requirements laid down in an order could lead to a fine of up to £1,000. A National Parenting Hotline was also set up to offer advice and suggest local sources of help to parents in difficulty.

The 2003 Anti-social Behaviour Act amended the 1998 Act to increase the flexibility of parenting orders and widen the circumstances in which they could be obtained. A court making an ASBO to a person below the age of 16 was now required to make a parenting order against the child's parent(s) if it was believed that this course of action would prevent a repetition of the behaviour that had caused the ASBO to be issued. The 2003 Act also amended the 1996 Education Act to permit local education and school staff to issue fixed penalty notices in connection with cases of truancy. If parents refuse to pay this they may be taken to court for failing to ensure that their child attended school regularly.

Child safety orders

These are issued by Youth Courts at the request of local authorities. A child safety order applies to a child below the age of 10 years who:

- has committed an act which, if she or he were aged over 10, would constitute an offence;
- is deemed likely to commit such an act;
- has contravened a curfew notice;
- has acted in a manner which has caused (or was likely to cause) harassment, alarm or distress to one or more persons who are not in the child's household.

Child safety orders place the child under the supervision of a local authority or a member of a YOT or social services department for a period that would normally be of three months duration – although it could be extended in exceptional cases to 12 months. The civil law 'balance of probabilities' test is the required standard of proof needed to obtain this order.

Curfew notices

The 1998 legislation built on earlier initiatives that imposed curfews on individual offenders. Following consultation with the police and residents, local authorities are empowered to impose a curfew notice, the effect of which is to ban under tens from being out on the streets in a stipulated geographic area after a designated time (which may embrace any period between 9 p.m. and 6 a.m.) unless under the control of a parent or a responsible person aged 18 or over. A child found in breach of a curfew order may be returned to his or her home by a police officer who is further required to inform the local authority of the contravention of the ban. The local authority are responsible for investigating the matter, one of whose options is to seek to make the errant child the subject of a Child Safety Order.

The 2001 Criminal Justice and Police Act extended the operation of curfew notices to those below the age of 16.

Reparation orders

Reparation orders require young offenders to make amends for harm they have done to their victims (who could be individual or collective, such as a school). This order is granted only after consultation with a probation officer, social worker or member of a YOT, and the latter body is responsible for supervising the activities contained in that order.

Supervision orders

These were initially introduced in the 1969 Children and Young Persons Act and were strengthened in the 1998 legislation. Courts were enabled to instruct offenders to undertake reparative work for their victims. These orders apply to offenders aged 10–17 and may be of up to three years in duration. A residency requirement can be added to these orders at the discretion of the courts where it is assessed that the young person's living arrangements might contribute to non-compliance with the terms of the order or to further offending.

Reprimands and warnings

The 1998 Act introduced a new system of reprimands and warnings for offenders aged 10–17. Reprimands were similar to the old-style formal cautions (so that a record was kept which could be used if the youth committed a further offence) and provide an instant response to a minor instance of juvenile offending in cases where a reprimand or warning had not been given in the previous two years. The YOT is not involved in the reprimand process. A warning is issued if a further offence is committed by someone who has been reprimanded, provided that the offender admitted the offence and it was not sufficiently serious to be referred to the courts. If a young person has received a warning in the previous two years he or she would have to be referred to the courts if a further offence was committed, thus ending the old system of repeat cautioning which had been viewed as an ineffective approach to juvenile crime. A warning may also be given as an initial intervention in connection with a serious offence without a reprimand being first issued.

The decision to issue a reprimand or warning is made by the police based on a gravity factor matrix developed by ACPO that takes into account the seriousness of the crime and the offending history of the youth. However, although the police remain responsible for determining what course of action should be taken against a young offender, they are required to refer the youth issued with a warning to the YOT where he or she is assessed according to the criteria laid down in Assessment Structure Screening Evaluation Target (ASSET) which is designed to stop further reoffending. The YOT may then decide to intervene, although they will not do so in all cases. In 2002/3, 74 per cent of young people warned by the police and assessed by YOTs took part in intervention programmes designed to reduce reoffending (Home Office, 2004a: 6). If the YOT intervenes, it becomes responsible for designing any intervention programmes that it thinks necessary.

Action plan orders

These are court orders applied in respect of offenders aged 10–17 following consideration of a report from a YOT. Action plan orders provide for an intensive three-month programme to address the causes of offending that is supervised by a probation officer, social worker or member of a YOT. The programmes that are provided under this order may include a wide range of measures including educational arrangements, a prohibition from a particular locality, a requirement to be present at an attendance centre and reparative provisions. It is, however, open to question whether three months is sufficient to achieve this purpose unless there is funding to continue the process of reform and rehabilitation after the action plan order has ended.

Detention and training orders

Detention and training orders are applied to serious offences committed by offenders aged 12–17 (but could, at the Home Secretary's discretion, be applied to children as young as 10, giving rise to the accusation that the state was creating 'baby prisons'). The new detention and training orders comprise a mixture of 50 per cent detention in secure accommodation (which could include Young Offenders Institutions, Secure Training Centres, local authority secure accommodation, youth treatment centres and, in extreme cases, adult prisons). The remaining 50 per cent is supervised in the community (the supervision being conducted by a probation officer, a social worker or a member of a YOT). The court can require a young person to take part in an Intensive Supervision and Surveillance Programme as a condition of the community part of the sentence. The minimum sentence is four months and the maximum is two years.

Developments after 1998

This section discusses further initiatives to tackle youth crime that were put forward following the 1998 Crime and Disorder Act.

Anti-social behaviour

The tackling of anti-social behaviour became a key aspect of Labour's approach towards crime and disorder from 1997, one reason for this being the scale of the problem. In September 2003 the Home Office conducted a one-day count of anti-social behaviour to get a snapshot of the problem. Participating organisations (which embraced local authorities and the police and fire services) reported 66,000 incidents in England and Wales. The Home Office estimated that this was equivalent to 13.5 million reports per year, or one every two seconds (Home Office, 2003b). One Labour MP and former minister declared that anti-social behaviour was indicative of the breakdown in the social contract: he laid the main cause of 'the rise and rise of yobbery and anti-social behaviour' at the door of an increasing number of families who were 'failing to impart ... social skills to their offspring' (Field, 2004). Action to tackle this behaviour was based on the assumption that it generates a 'broken windows' syndrome (as discussed by Kelling and Wilson, 1982), although there is no hard quantitative evidence to support this (Whitehead, Stockdale and Razza, 2003).

In addition to ASBOs, other measures to tackle anti-social behaviour have also been pursued. An extra-statutory development, the Acceptable Behaviour Contract (ABC), was introduced to combat anti-social behaviour and may be used by Crime and Disorder Reduction Partnerships to tackle anti-social behaviour, especially that committed by those between 10 and 18 years of age. ABCs (sometimes referred to as Acceptable Behaviour Agreements) are voluntary agreements entered into by a person committing anti-social behaviour and public bodies which include the police, housing departments, schools or registered social landlords. They rely on multi-agency responses to combat the unruly behaviour and may be used to warn an offender to change their ways or face a court hearing at which an ASBO could be issued. ABCs were initially developed in the London Borough of Islington during the 1990s where they were applied to anti-social behaviour committed by those aged 10–17 but now also apply throughout England and Wales.

The 2002 Police Reform Act initiated important developments in connection with ASBOs. Henceforth they could be valid throughout the country, and the courts could impose an ASBO when convicting an offender for any criminal offence at a youth, magistrates' or crown court. This procedure (variously referred to as 'ASBO bolt-ons' or Criminal Anti-Social Behaviour Order (CRASBOs) could be made to commence following release from a custodial sentence if this was the sentence imposed by the courts for the initial offence (NACRO, 2003a: 5). This Act further enabled registered social landlords and the British Transport Police to apply for ASBOs.

Further measures to tackle anti-social behaviour were contained in the 2001 Criminal Justice and Police Act that introduced Penalty Notices for Disorder (PNDs) across England and Wales. These imposed fixed penalty fines for various forms of disorderly behaviour (the list of offences covered by the legislation being extended by delegated legislation in July 2004) committed by persons over 18 years of age. In January 2003 the Home Office established an Anti-Social Behaviour Unit, and the 2003 Anti-social

Behaviour Act extended the fixed penalty scheme to cover disorderly behaviour (which included noise nuisance, truancy and graffiti) committed by those aged 16–17 years of age. PNDs could be handed out by police and police community support officers. Some 40,000 of these were issued between April 2004 and the end of the year (Travis, 2004b). Additionally, a pilot scheme commencing in December 2004 that operated in seven police forces was introduced whereby juveniles aged 10–15 could be fined up to £40 for anti-social activities such as vandalism and underage drinking. This scheme would operate for a year and entailed extending existing fixed penalty fines to those below the age of 16. The aim of this initiative was to make parents or guardians (who faced prison sentences if the fines were not paid) accept responsibility for the behaviour of their children.

The 2003 Anti-social Behaviour Act also introduced the new power of dispersal orders. These would be applied to areas that suffered from persistent and serious anti-social behaviour that justified the issuance of an authorisation notice by a senior police officer (to which the local authority had to consent) that lasted for a period of up to six months. The authorisation notice provided the police (or police community support officers) with powers to remove groups consisting of two or more persons from the designated area and also to return unsupervised persons below the age of 16 in a public place between the hours of 9 p.m. and 6 a.m. to their place of residence. This power would be applied when it was reasonable for a police officer to believe that members of the public had been 'intimidated, alarmed or distressed' by the presence of the group. One danger with this approach is that it may merely displace a problem to another area unless accompanied with strategies designed to divert youths from anti-social behaviour, and in this sense has been described as 'an excellent tool to protect middle-class areas from trouble overflowing from nearby estates' (Pakes and Winstone, 2005: 9).

Other measures to tackle anti-social behaviour, including attempts to make the drinks industry be mindful of its responsibilities regarding the consequences of excessive alcohol consumption, were put forward in early 2005. A package of measures was put forward which included closing pubs that persistently served underage drinkers, and introducing 'alcohol disorder zones' in which publicans would be given eight weeks to deal with the problem of disorder or foot the bills for the consequent expenditure incurred by public services including the police, street cleaning and the NHS (Home Office et al., 2005). Additionally, the 2005 Clean Neighbourhoods and Environment Act also contained provisions to counter anti-social behaviour such as graffiti.

In December 2004 a new 'community justice court' was opened in Liverpool to deal with lower level crime and anti-social behaviour. It was modelled on a community court which was set up in the Red Hook area of Brooklyn and would adopt a holistic approach to those appearing before it, whereby several agencies (including probation officers, drug counsellors and mental health workers) would be involved in the proceedings (Gillan, 2004).

A feature of the operations of this court was that residents were consulted to ensure that the court's punishments were tailored to improve their quality of life (Travis, 2004a).

Action directed at anti-social behaviour was a key aspect of the 'respect agenda' of the third term of the Labour government. This was promoted by the Prime Minister who argued that action against anti-social behaviour was a progressive cause and an important aspect of the government's attempts to 'rebuild the bonds of community for a modern age'. Particular attention was devoted to families who were 'out of control and in crisis' (Blair, 2006). The Prime Minister proposed that the range of agencies empowered to issue parenting orders woud be expanded, the ability to evict for anti-social behaviour would be extended to the private sector, and new intervention schemes would be introduced for those who truanted or who had been excluded from schools. The enforcement aspect of this approach was balanced with a raft of preventive measures that included targeting disadvantaged young people though sport and art, expanding the Youth Opportunity Fund and providing professional counselling and family support for disruptive families to which they agreed to abide by a strict code of behaviour.

Referral Orders

Reparation, supervision and action plan orders and interventions following a final warning are important aspects of what is termed 'restorative justice' (a concept which is discussed in more detail below). This was further developed in the 1999 Youth Justice and Criminal Evidence Act.

This legislation (which was subsequently consolidated in the 2000 Powers of the Criminal Courts (Sentencing) Act) established Youth Offender Panels (YOPs) to which first-time offenders aged between 10 and 17 years old who pleaded guilty – and whose crime was sufficiently serious not to warrant an absolute discharge but which did not justify a custodial (or a hospital) sentence – would be referred through the mechanism of a referral order issued by a youth court. It is a mandatory sentence that lasts between three and 12 months, one advantage of which is that many young offenders who would previously have been given a conditional discharge (or perhaps a fine) will now receive a programme that is designed to help prevent reoffending. This reform was also designed to help speed up the operations of the youth justice system since the YOP would convene soon after the referral had been made, ideally within the 15 working days laid down by the national standard (Newburn et al., 2002: vi). Referral Orders envisage that YOPs will operate according to the principles of restorative justice (Young and Hoyle, 2003: 203) (an issue that is explored in Chapter 7 since this approach is not confined to the youth justice system). YOPs contain one member from the YOT and at least two other participants drawn from the local community (termed 'community panel members' or CPMs), one of whom acts as a facilitator. Meetings of the YOP must include the offender, his or her parents and, ideally, the victim or a representative of the community.

A key function of YOPs is to formulate a programme of action (termed a 'youth offender contract') that may include reparative provisions (such as community reparation or written apologies). If it proves impossible to reach an agreement on an appropriate contract, the offender will be referred back to the court for sentencing. Resentencing by the courts will also occur if the offender fails to comply with the requirements imposed on him or her by the referral order. The contract is considered by further progress panel meetings, and the YOT (which implements the requirements imposed by the contract) also monitors its progress. When the youth offender contract has been completed the conviction is regarded as 'spent' under the provisions of the 1974 Rehabilitation of Offenders Act and thus does not have to be declared save in exceptional circumstances.

Referral orders are relatively inexpensive. An evaluation of YOPs in 11 pilot areas estimated that the mean cost per referral order was £630 outside London, or (if London was included) £690 per order (Newburn et al., 2002: x). However, some initial difficulties have been encountered with the operations of YOPs. It has been argued that the contractual language of referral orders masks their compulsory and potentially authoritarian nature (Wonnacott, 1999). Further, although the involvement of victims is an important aspect of the process of restorative justice, initial evidence suggested that they did not always attend YOPs. Their involvement depended on factors such as the priority accorded to victim contact, and in some cases victims were not offered the opportunity to attend a YOP (Newburn et al., 2002: viii).

Youth Community Orders

The 2003 Criminal Justice Act provided for the consolidation of a number of existing sanctions directed at crime committed by 16–17-year-old persons (including attendance centre orders, action plan orders and supervision orders) and replaced some of the existing penalties such as community punishment and rehabilitation orders. However, the implementation of this legislation was suspended for this category of offenders pending the introduction of new legislation affecting the youth justice system. Community orders thus apply only to those aged 18 and above.

Secure accommodation

Changes were also made since 1997 in the use of secure accommodation. Until June 1999, 12–14-year-old boys and 12–16-year-old girls who were refused bail were remanded into the care of the local authority, which would then decide how that child should be accommodated. If it seemed likely the child would either abscond or would injure him/herself or others, the local authority could apply for a secure accommodation order. Otherwise the child would be kept in some other form of accommodation.

After 1 June 1999, however, the courts were given the power to remand 12–14-year-old boys and 12–16-year-old girls into secure accommodation if bail had been refused and they had consulted with the local authority. This applies to any child who:

- is charged with, or convicted of, a violent or sexual offence or an offence for which an adult could receive a sentence of 14 years or more;
- had a recent history of absconding from local authority accommodation;
- is a serious danger to the public.

Boys aged 15 and 16 could also be subject to this process, provided the court believed that Prison Service accommodation was inappropriate and that secure accommodation was available.

The content of programmes designed to tackle offending behaviour

Many of the court orders utilised against juvenile offenders require them to undertake programmes to address their behaviour. An important example of this is the Intensive Supervision and Surveillance Programme (ISSP) that is directed at offenders aged 10–17. These are either prolific offenders or serious offenders whose participation in the programme is recommended to the court by the YOT in a pre-sentence report. ISSP was piloted by the Youth Justice Board in 2001 and was seen as a potential alternative to short-term custodial sentences that were viewed as ineffective since around eight out of ten of young offenders who received a short custodial sentence were reconvicted within two years (Public Accounts Committee, 2004). ISSP presents a multi-dimensional response to offending behaviour and targets the risk factors that contribute to crime. It requires a young offender to attend rehabilitation and other activities (such as work or training) for a minimum of 25 hours a week for the first three months and for a minimum of five hours a week in the second period of three months. The offender is additionally subjected to surveillance which includes curfews enforced by electronic means. The length of ISSP was extended from six to 12 months by the 2003 Criminal Justice Act. However, an evaluation of this programme suggested that over half of those placed on it failed to meet its requirements, and about one in four failed to the extent that they were given a custodial sentence (Public Accounts Committee, 2004).

The Intensive Change and Control Programme (ICCP) was piloted in 2003/4 and is directed at offenders aged 18–20. ICCP is a community-based sentence for offenders who would otherwise be liable for a prison sentence of up to 12 months. It is administered by the Probation Service and those on the programme are required to spend 25 hours a week on targeted educational and offending behaviour work and are also subject to police and electronic surveillance and home visits. A further example of a programme directed at serious offenders is Intensive Supervision and Monitoring (ISM) that may be developed into an alternative to prison sentences for first-time low-risk offenders (Home Office, 2004a: 13).

Programmes designed to tackle offending behaviour have been increasingly subjected to the rigour of a 'what works' evaluation (for example, Lipsey 1992, 1995). This analysis enables guidelines to be produced to improve the effectiveness of programmes. These embrace matching programmes to the seriousness of offending and the risk that offenders will commit further offences, ensuring that programmes focus on the factors that support or contribute to an offender's behaviour, and providing programmes that are structured with the learning styles of offenders and staff being compatible. The most successful programmes are multi-dimensional (in the sense of seeking to address a variety of factors that influence a person's disposition to offend, and are skills orientated. The length and intensity of programmes need to be flexible, adjusted in accordance to the nature (or threat) of an individual's offending behaviour. Research has also suggested that community-based programmes are more effective in addressing offending behaviour than are custodial sentences. All programmes should be subjected to monitoring and evaluation (McGuire and Priestley, 1995; see also Raynor and Vanstone, 2002: 88).

A considerable degree of attention has been devoted to attempts seeking to identify the risk factors which influence offending and reoffending behaviour (Farrington, 1996). These include socio-economic conditions, educational attainment, family background, the strength of community, the influence exerted by peer groups and individual factors such as hyperactivity and impulsivity (Utting and Vennard, 2000: 23–4).

New Youth Court procedures

It has been observed that the public had little confidence in the Youth Court (Kilpatrick, 2001). To tackle this a Demonstration Project was launched which ran from October 1998 to March 2000 in Rotherham and five courts in Leicestershire which sought to explore how cultural changes within the court (which were underpinned by close inter-agency cooperation) to secure greater openness, direct engagement with the offender and his or her family, feedback on the effectiveness of sentencing (to provide details about matters which included breaches and reconviction rates) and a less adversarial setting (to assist the young defendant to understand and participate in the proceedings) could be used to support statutory provisions and promote confidence in the system (Home Office/Lord Chancellor's Department, 2001: 4). Following evaluation of this project (Allen et al., 2000), all Youth Courts were asked to review their own practices and to adopt those developed in the project areas wherever possible (Home Office/Lord Chancellor's Department, 2001: 5). In both project areas the essentially private nature of Youth Court proceedings was revised to enable persons with a legitimate interest (in particular victims) to attend, and it was suggested that mechanisms should be put in place to accommodate those victims who wanted to be in court (Home Office/Lord Chancellor's Department, 2001: 12).

Analyse the extent to which the approach adopted to deal with juvenile crime has been driven by penal populist principles since 1979.

Assessment of Labour's reforms to the juvenile justice system

Juvenile crime is an important contributor to the overall level of crime in society. It has been suggested that one quarter of boys aged 14–17 and around 13 per cent of teenage girls could be classified as 'serious or prolific' offenders (defined as those who committed six or more offences in the previous year), and that around 40 per cent of boys aged 14–17 were active offenders (having committed one offence in the previous year) (Budd and Sharp, 2005). The above account has identified the multifaceted nature of the policies Labour introduced to combat juvenile crime and disorder. These were underpinned by a number of principles that included:

- an acceptance that juvenile crime and disorder could not be tackled by the actions of the police alone, or, alternatively, the pursuance of an approach based on the partnership of a number of public sector bodies which would adopt a joined-up approach at local level to tackle these problems;

- the introduction of a wide range of court orders which responded to crime and disorder with punitive sanctions: these were also designed to demonstrate to public opinion that the government was adopting a tough line against anti-social and criminal activities committed by juveniles. It has been argued that the Labour government's endorsement of penal populism resulted in 'a range of penalties that aimed to hold young offenders to their responsibilities, replaced rehabilitation with correctionalism, and repackaged youth imprisonment as a valuable correctional resource' (Pitts, 2003: 95–6). In contrast to the earlier approach of progressive minimalism, Labour's approach also vastly extended the capacity of the criminal justice system to respond to juvenile crime;

- a move away from a juvenile justice system based mainly on retributive principles to one which sought to enable offenders to make amends for their actions and enable their reintegration into society;

- the adoption of managerialist solutions to juvenile crime, based on an assumption that initiatives such as performance targets, the use of evidence-based solutions to problems and the enhanced coordination of agencies involved with young people will make a substantial contribution to reducing the level of juvenile criminality;

- an acknowledgement that social disadvantage was a significant underpinning to juvenile criminality. Thus managerialist responses to juvenile crime have been augmented by a number of long-term social reforms (which are discussed in the next section of this chapter). The depiction of social policy as a means to tackle crime (rather than the advancement of greater equality as a desirable goal in itself) was designed to persuade 'middle England' voters/taxpayers of the rightfulness of Labour's social reforms;

- risk assessment: the perception that social problems such as truancy and school exclusion, drug and alcohol abuse and family breakdown were multiple risk factors which had important consequences for youth offending highlighted the importance of multifaceted interventions (Liddle and Solanki, 2002: 1). An important aspect of the work performed by YOTs was to ensure that the needs of offenders were adequately catered for by the programmes which were available. A structured needs and risk assessment tool, ASSET, was introduced to ensure that a good match was provided between need and provision (NACRO, 2003a: 3);

- the involvement of local people and local communities in response to juvenile crime and disorder: crime was viewed as both a cause and a consequence of communal disintegration and Labour's approach was especially directed at re-establishing order in socially disorganised communities.

Advantages of Labour's approach to crime and disorder

This section evaluates the main advantages derived from the government's approach to juvenile crime.

The multi-agency approach

The new arrangements concerned with juvenile justice placed a prominent emphasis on coordination. The 1998 Act required each local authority that exercised social services and education responsibilities to establish a YOT in partnership with local police, probation and health services. It was intended that via youth offender teams, local government would be responsible for coordinating youth justice systems. A significant feature of Labour's multi-agency approach was that local government was in the 'driving seat'. Earlier initiatives involving multi-agency approaches had sometimes foundered because they were perceived as police-driven. The 1998 Act ensured that local government (which unlike the police service was directly accountable for its actions to local people) would play a prominent role in youth justice matters and enable a strategy for youth justice to be coordinated with other local authority key strategic responsibilities such as children's services planning, family support, economic regeneration, drug action, community safety initiatives and anti-poverty strategies. The enhanced cooperation between agencies facilitated the devising of a coherent set of goals to shape policy and aid the planning and provision of services.

Speeding up the operations of the youth justice system

When Labour entered office it was estimated that cases involving juveniles were taking, on average, around 4.5 months from arrest to completion (Home Office, 1997: 23). During the 1997 election, the Labour party pledged to halve this period, arguing that delays of this length angered, frustrated and distressed victims, and did not help young offenders as they were not immediately made to face up to what they had done, or given the opportunity to participate in programmes to divert them from crime.

Accordingly, section 44 of the 1998 Crime and Disorder Act aimed to speed up the operations of the youth justice system by enabling the Secretary of State to make regulations governing the maximum period which could elapse in the case of an accused person below 18 years of age between arrest and the initial court appearance, and between conviction and the imposition of sentence. By the end of 1998 the gap between arrest and sentence had been reduced to an average of 106 days. This reform enabled intervention by agencies such as YOTs to be initiated more speedily.

Making juvenile offenders take responsibility

The 1998 Crime and Disorder Act and the 1999 Youth Justice and Criminal Evidence Act sought to make juvenile offenders (and their parents) take responsibility for their actions so that they would learn a valuable moral lesson and take the first step towards rehabilitation. This was designed to end what the excuse culture of the youth justice system implied: that young people could not help their behaviour. It was argued that 'rarely are they confronted with their behaviour and helped to take more personal responsibility for their actions. The system allows them to go on wrecking their own lives as well as disrupting their families and communities' (Straw, 1997).

Disadvantages of Labour's approach to crime and disorder

The approach adopted by the Labour government has been subject to a number of criticisms. These are discussed below.

Initial reluctance to use the new court orders

Labour's approach to juvenile crime was hampered by the initial reluctance of agencies concerned with the juvenile justice process to use the new orders with which they had been provided. One reason for this was that local authorities preferred to use mediation schemes or improved housing management as a response to nuisance neighbours. This situation prompted the Home Secretary, Jack Straw, to issue a 'sharp reminder' to councils to start using curfews and also anti-social behaviour orders to curb crime and disorder. On 2 June 2000 he issued new guidelines to encourage wider use of anti-social behaviour orders. Further initiatives to use these orders included the Anti-Social Behaviour Action Plan and the Together Campaign, both of which were launched in 2003 to tackle anti-social behaviour.

Although child safety orders and curfew notices are rarely used, greater use has been made of ASBOs which are extremely flexible and can be applied to a wide range of unsocial actions ranging from racial abuse to the threat or use of violence. Accordingly, by August 2004, 2,400 ASBOs were issued across England and Wales, with 1,323 being taken out in the year to March 2004 (Home Office, 2004b).

Unnecessary severity

The tendency to view children as 'small adults' who were normally capable of being held responsible for their actions was most obviously displayed in removing the common law presumption of *doli incapax*, whereby the prosecution had to prove that children aged 10 to 13 knew the difference between right and wrong. This reform would enable children to be prosecuted in court (although the age of criminal responsibility would remain at 10). A related problem is concerned with anti-social behaviour orders. The Act failed to treat children differently from adults in the issue of these orders since applications for them against children are heard in magistrates' courts rather than youth courts. This procedure was contrary to the ruling of the European Court of Human Rights in the James Bulger case.

Labour's proposals could also increase the number of custodial sentences for juvenile offenders, for example by abolishing *doli incapax* and making it theoretically possible for 10-year-olds to be placed in custody. In November 1998 there were 11,500 young offenders aged 15–20 in prisons (NACRO, 1999b). This is a problem since incarcerating young people deprives them of the chance to learn basic life skills within the family. It could possibly lead to persistent offending and a view of prison as a refuge from worldly pressures.

Young offenders in custodial regimes

Although the level of youth crime (as measured by 'known offending') is falling (with the number of persons aged 10–17 convicted or cautioned for indictable offences falling by 17 per cent in the decade 1988–98) (NACRO, 2002: 1), increasing numbers of young people are being given custodial sentences and the length of these sentences is increasing: between 1993 and 1998 the number of persons aged 15–20 given custodial sentences rose by 42 per cent, and the average sentence given to boys aged 15–17 rose from 5.6 months in 1989 to 10.3 months in 1997 (NACRO, 2002: 3–4). The introduction of the detention and training order in April 2000 exacerbated this trend (NACRO, 2000: 1), which has been attributed to factors that include poor pre-sentence reports (in the sense of failing to make any clear proposal) or the advocacy of a custodial order in these reports (NACRO, 2000: 3). The cost of custody for young offenders is expensive (the cost of locking up 15–17-year-old boys in 1998/9 being £26,113) (Her Majesty's Prison Service, 1999) but reconviction rates are high, with 76 per cent of males aged 14–20 who were discharged from custody in 1996 being reconvicted within two years (NACRO, 2002: 5). However, the Labour government has continued to the use custodial sentences to combat youth crime. The 2003 Criminal Justice Act provided additional custodial provisions for young offenders – detention for the public protection and extended detention. These new sentences apply to young offenders convicted of sexual or violent crimes.

In 1998 the Chief Inspector of Prisons published a report, *Young Prisoners: A Thematic Review by Her Majesty's Chief Inspector of Prisons for England and Wales*. This emphasised the importance of the rehabilitation of young offenders. It endorsed the objective of diverting young people from custody wherever possible, and asserted that the pre-eminent objective of custodial sentences for young offenders was to change their attitudes. This required education and opportunities for personal growth delivered by very skilled staff. He proposed a number of reforms to the young offender estate, the key suggestions being as follows:

- The Prison Service should relinquish responsibility for all children under the age of 18. Local authorities should pay the costs of all children held in custody, and should ensure that all the conditions of custody adhere to clear principles such as those contained in the 1989 Children Act.
- All criminal justice and community organisations should be organised within a single unified framework, responsible for the custody of children and the support of families and schools to prevent children growing up as offenders.
- Young Offender Institution Rules should be rewritten to ensure that the regimes address the particular needs of adolescents.
- A new Director of Young Prisoners should be appointed, whose role would include developing properly accredited programmes to tackle the offending behaviour and social problems of young offenders and to ensure that criminal justice and community agencies work effectively with the Prison Service.

Subsequently a number of initiatives were developed to advance the principles outlined in this report. In 1999 the Youth Justice Board assumed operational control for custodial facilities used exclusively by persons below the age of 18. A mentor scheme was introduced at Feltham YOI, whereby young offenders were brought into contact with a person with experience in the world of work who would serve as a role model. In September 1999 the then Prisons Minister, Paul Boateng, announced his intention to bring forward legislation to enable more than 6,500 prisoners below the age of 21 to be placed in adult prisons. This was viewed as the first step in creating specialist institutions for those aged from 18 to the mid-20s, in which courses could be introduced to teach numeracy and literacy, combat drug abuse and criminal behaviour.

However, the assertion of Lord Chief Justice Woolf in 2000 that the atmosphere of YOIs was so corrosive that the child killers of James Bulger would be unable to cope cast a doubt over the effectiveness of these institutions.

Ineffectiveness

Some of the innovations that were introduced in the 1998 crime and disorder legislation may prove to be ineffective. For example, curfew notices are based on the belief that controlling the hours when young people are in a public place will limit their opportunities to engage in anti-social behaviour. However, there is no reliable evidence to suggest that curfews reduce juvenile delinquency (McDowell et al., 2000). Studies have suggested that although juvenile arrest rates declined during the hours of a curfew they increased at other times, so that the net impact of this policy on the level of juvenile offending was nil (Hunt and Weiner, 1977). Schemes of this nature also rely on rigorous enforcement that may not be easily accomplished.

Consistency with other aspects of government policy

The government has also been accused of pursuing policies that undermine some of its other initiatives to tackle crime. In July 2002, Keith Hellawell (who had served as the UK Anti-drugs Coordinator) resigned as he believed the government's decision to reclassify cannabis sent out mixed messages and was not helpful in the fight against drugs.

This has especially been the case regarding attempts to respond to anti-social behaviour. The presumption of anonymity for children involved in criminal proceedings (provided for by the 1933 Children and Young Persons Act) may be prejudiced if an ASBO is 'bolted onto' a criminal conviction since this often requires publicity to enable the general public to be aware of the existence of the order and against whom it has been made (NACRO, 2003b: 6). It has been argued that ASBOs and restorative justice are 'informed by different values and principles', the first having an underpinning of social exclusion and the latter that of social inclusion (Young and Hoyle, 2003: 210).

It has also been alleged that aspects of Labour's approach are contrary to the 1998 Human Rights Act. For example, although young offenders may have legal representation at YOP meetings, no legal aid is available to pay for this and in practice very few offenders are represented (Young and Hoyle, 2003: 215). The accusation that ASBOs conflict with the government's human rights legislation provoked the fury of the then Home Secretary, Jack Straw, who claimed legal experts had been running a campaign against anti social-behaviour orders, suggesting (in his view 'ludicrously') that they contravened the European Convention on Human Rights. He urged those who espoused the principles of justice and liberty to remember the justice and liberty of those citizens who were subject to appalling behaviour, and suggested there was an element of hypocrisy in a situation in which lawyers represented those who perpetrated such crimes 'and then get into their BMWs and drive off into areas where they are immune from such crime' (Straw, 1999).

Changes to the legislation regulating anti-social behaviour also provoked further criticisms of this nature. Section 30 of the 2003 Anti-social Behaviour Act gave the police powers to pick up any group of two or more young people or children who were outdoors after 9 p.m., regardless of their behaviour, in places where a dispersal order was in force. Officers then take these children to their homes and they are required to remain there until 6 a.m. In 2004, the civil rights group Liberty announced it intended to mount a challenge in the European Court of Human Rights to blanket orders of this nature on the grounds that they contravened the right to free movement and assembly of those who were subject to them.

Complexity

The 1998 Crime and Disorder Act created a number of disposals available to the youth courts that seem complex (and apparently overlapping) to those charged with administering them. For example, in order to apply a parenting order to a child below the age of 10, it is first necessary to obtain a child safety order. The new administrative arrangements may also pose a number of problems: some of the new developments require the coordination of local authority services, which may be hindered by departmentalism.

Additional problems are faced by the police service, which has to liaise with a number of different YOTs whose operations and working practices may vary. These bodies may also adopt different philosophies, in particular as to whether the participants are expected to gel into one agency or whether each should bring its own agency perspectives and professional expertise to bear on the issues that come before them.

Fairness

The reforms introduced by Labour governments entailed a wide degree of decentralisation to permit community involvement in the youth justice process. It is important, however, that innovations such as Youth Offender Panels are socially representative to ensure that all sections of society view them as legitimate. Further, the criteria governing decisions such as the content of referral orders may be subject to wide variation across the country, giving rise to perceptions of unfairness.

Mixed motives

Labour's approach towards juvenile crime has been underpinned by a mixture of motives that are not necessarily compatible. A number of provisions contained in the 1998 legislation (such as parenting orders and reparation provisions) seemed to be geared towards reducing the crime and damage caused by juvenile offenders rather than aiding their rehabilitation or addressing the social causes of crime. This approach has been dubbed 'new correctionalism' which was designed to appeal to middle England voters (Pitts, 2000).

A particular discrepancy arose between the penal populist desire to be seen as tough on crime and the policies that sought to tackle its social causes. The government's policies increasingly moved in the former direction, as exemplified by the Prime Minister's speech at Tübingen in June 2000 when he suggested the use of on-the-spot fines for hooligans who would be marched by the police to the nearest cashpoint to pay them. Subsequently, in July 2000, a number of chief constables and local authority chief executives attended a summit on crime, at which late-night inner-city crime and disorder was discussed. The measures considered included empowering senior police officers to temporarily close down clubs and public houses with a history of violence and prohibiting drinking in public places. In September 2000 the government issued a consultation paper to deal with loutish behaviour, whose suggestions included the use of fixed penalty notices to tackle a range of disorderly actions (Home Office, 2000b) which were introduced in the 2001 Criminal Justice and Police Act. The 2000 Football Disorder Act gave magistrates the power to ban persons from travelling abroad if it was believed that they had committed or contributed to an action in the United Kingdom or elsewhere which would constitute a criminal offence in the United Kingdom.

Insufficient protection for the rights of the accused

The civil liberties of those who are subject to the sanctions contained in the 1998 Crime and Disorder Act are not always adequately protected. A tendency has been noted for the police to issue a final warning rather than a reprimand for a first offence (Holdaway et al., 2001: 61) which may pose the problem of accelerating a young person's progress through the juvenile justice system. ASBOs are issued by magistrates' courts (not youth courts even when applied to children and young persons) thus undermining the anonymity normally provided to young defendants by the 1933 Children and Young Persons Act since measures can be taken to publicise those who are subject to ASBOs. Further, although ASBOs are granted on the civil law test of 'the balance of probabilities', breach of them constitutes a criminal act. Child safety orders are issued on the civil law test of the balance of probabilities rather than the criminal proof test of beyond reasonable doubt. Those subject to these sanctions do not have any right to cross-examine prosecution witnesses. Reprimands or warnings may be cited in subsequent criminal proceedings as if the young person had actually been convicted of an offence.

Applications for child safety orders (for the under tens) might be more appropriately made through the Family Proceedings Court rather than the youth court, since the latter effectively places a child below the age of criminal responsibility within the remit of a court established to deal with criminal activity. It may further be questioned as to whether the rights of children who find themselves in this position are properly safeguarded.

Resource implications

The innovations contained in the 1998 legislation have considerable resource implications in terms of staff training, staff time and the development of new programmes and bail support facilities. For example, those who staff YOTs need to possess a broad range of skills and expertise to deal with issues such as children under 10, parenting skills and victim mediation. Additionally, action plan orders require significant resources. The government was initially unwilling to provide the funding required for these new arrangements, as it believed that the necessary money would be found by redistributing existing finances in the mainstream budgets of the agencies which implement the 1998 legislation.

The financing of Youth Offending Teams

In the financial year that commenced in April 2000, the 155 YOTs planned to spend £140 million. This figure was derived as follows:

- 60 per cent from the budgets of social services departments;
- 13 per cent from police budgets;
- 12 per cent from Probation Service budgets;
- 8 per cent from education budgets;
- 7 per cent from health service budgets.

Additionally, central government money was contributed via project grants and through the Youth Justice Board which contributed around £30 million for YOT programmes. From April 2000 pooled budgeting arrangements could be used.

However, the funding arrangements of YOTs (and in particular the existence of pooled budgets) were subject to wide variation. It was concluded that 'budgets will continue to be a thorny issue until there is proper responsibility for YOT budgets at governmental level, each participating ministry having a clear requirement to work with young offenders and with a related budget to cede to YOTs' (NACRO, 2003b: 6).

Parental responsibility

There is insufficient provision of structured parenting programmes for the parents of older children in connection with the parenting order. Offending by young persons may not be due to bad parenting, but may arise from factors such as the impact of deprivation, boredom and the absence of recreational facilities or peer group pressure on a child's behaviour that may overcome the efforts of the best parents (Pitts, 2000). Furthermore, the fine of £1,000 for a breach of a parenting order would in many cases be unrealistic. Enhanced support to families delivered outside of the youth justice system that seeks to prevent dysfunctional family units might be a more effective measure compared to an attempt, contained in the Act, to 'demonise parents'.

What, according to the 1996 Audit Commission report, *Misspent Youth*, was wrong with the operations of the youth justice system? How successfully did the 1998 Crime and Disorder Act remedy these deficiencies?

'Tough on the causes of crime'

The 1997 Labour government was more willing than its Conservative predecessors to endorse an approach that sought to temper the operations of free market capitalism with state intervention to aid those who adversely suffered from its operations. This was referred to as the 'Third Way'. However, social policy was justified not because it would create a more egalitarian society, but, rather, on the beneficial impact social policy (which at some stage implied increased spending) would have on crime and disorder. What has been termed the 'criminalisation of social policy' (Squires and Stephen, 2005: 121) refers to the priority accorded to crime and disorder management in these policies. In 1998, the Home Secretary, Jack Straw, outlined a £250 million crime reduction strategy as part of the government's Comprehensive Spending Review that was to be directed at the social causes of crime. This accepted that social conditions could result in crime – something which previous Conservative governments had been unwilling to acknowledge. The initiatives additional to the Crime and Disorder Act that were put forward were mainly (but not exclusively) directed at juvenile crime, and along with the 1998 legislation provided a coherent package of measures to tackle crime.

Tackling social exclusion

In 1996 the Audit Commission drew attention to the fact that lack of jobs, inadequate nursery education and insufficient family centres to help young isolated mothers contributed to the level of youth crime. A later report observed that 25 per cent of young male prisoners were homeless (or were living in insecure accommodation) prior to imprisonment, over half of those under 18 receiving custodial sentences had been in care, and over half of this category of offender had been excluded from school. It was further reported that nearly two-thirds of young male offenders had no qualifications, two-thirds were unemployed prior to imprisonment, almost two-thirds misused drugs or had alcohol problems, one in six admitted to having been abused and one in ten admitted to self-harm (Social Exclusion Unit, 2000).

Labour sought to address problems of this nature by mounting an attack on social exclusion. In December 1997 the Social Exclusion Unit was set up in the Cabinet Office. This was overseen by the Deputy Prime Minister and operated across existing government departments in order to facilitate a coordinated or 'joined-up' approach within Whitehall to tackle this problem by developing programmes to tackle the "background" socio-structural factors' (Pitts, 2001: 146) which were perceived as contributing to crime. These included promoting social improvement and encouraging local economic initiatives to create jobs. Joined-up government also underpinned the establishment of a cross-departmental review of crime reduction that was conducted in association with the 2000 Comprehensive Spending Review. This put forward targets for reducing truancy and exclusion, improving literacy levels and tackling the crime rates of children in care.

Labour's attack on social exclusion embraced a wide range of policies designed to tackle social problems such as unemployment and income inequality. Tackling poverty assumed a prominent position in the government's agenda. Between 1979 and 1997, the number of people living in poverty had increased from 5 to 14 million, and the government set itself the objective of abolishing child poverty within 20 years (Piachaud, 1999).

Labour's approach to social exclusion further reflected the belief that children who were exposed to multiple risks were more likely to offend (Graham and Bowling, 1995).

The main initiatives that were designed to both prevent social exclusion in the future and to reintegrate those who had previously been excluded are briefly outlined below.

'Welfare to work'

The entry (or re-entry) to work was viewed as a major route out of social exclusion (Young and Matthews, 2003: 20). In April 1998 the New Deal programme for the young long-term unemployed aged 18–24 was initiated. This offered four options: a job, full-time education or training, voluntary work or work with the government's environmental task force. This scheme was extended to those aged over 25 in the 2000 budget, and was made permanent in the 2000 Comprehensive Spending Review. The government subsequently committed itself to offering apprenticeship places to all 16–18 year olds who chose not to enter further education. The scheme latterly incorporated a 'rapid response' New Deal programme to help areas affected by severe job losses, and also embraced the 'New Deal for Lone Parents' that used personal advisers to aid single parents to find employment. The objective of reducing the number of lone parents on benefits was also advanced by government funding of childcare facilities, which aimed to provide a childcare place for every lone parent living in a disadvantaged area by 2004. In 2005 the government proposed that lone parents with children over the age of 11 would be required to attend interviews in order to receive a work search premium of £20 a week on top of their income support.

The reintegrative aspects of Labour's policies to combat social exclusion were also specifically directed at those whose exclusion was based on the stigmatisation experienced by those who had offended. The rehabilitation of young offenders was addressed in a pilot 'welfare to work' scheme (initially covering around 2,000 young people aged 18–24 in eleven YOIs and prisons). This concentrated on courses providing job preparation skills, training and employment advice, and aimed to improve the work skills of young prisoners and to give them a better chance when they entered the job market thereby reducing the likelihood of their reoffending.

Aid to poorer families

The main aim of directing help to poor families was to tackle child poverty. Labour's approach to poverty placed considerable emphasis on employment (or 'the obligation to work') (Lund, 2002: 196) as the means to achieve this objective. The 1998 National Minimum Wage Act imposed a statutory floor on wages and was especially designed to promote 'work-seeking behaviour' (Lund, 2002: 194). The Working Families Tax Credit was launched in 1999 to replace Family Credit; it aimed to increase state aid to those in work on low incomes, guaranteeing a minimum income of £200 per week for a family with one full-time worker, who, additionally, would not pay income tax on earnings of less than £235 a week. Ministers envisaged that the scheme would lift 800,000 children out of poverty, or a total of around 1.5 million parents and children (Elliott, 1999). Additionally, the 2000 budget announced the introduction of the Integrated Child Credit. All families would continue to receive child benefit, but additional aid would be directed at poor families. A key objective of this initiative was to raise the level of incomes for single people in work.

Labour's policies towards poor families were particularly directed at single parents. It involved a carrot and stick approach. The National Childcare Strategy (which was launched in 1998) sought to boost the number of nurseries in deprived areas. In 2001, all single parents were required to attend 'gateway' interviews to discuss work options. Failure to do so resulted in a reduction in the adult rate of benefit (Lund, 2002: 194).

Additional aid was also provided to enhance the security of those no longer able to work. This included the new Minimum Income Guarantee for pensioners that replaced means tested Income Support.

Education

The Labour government made conspicuous use of the education system to combat juvenile crime and disorder. This was reflected in the compulsory introduction of citizenship in the school curriculum in 2002 that sought to educate young people in civic involvement. A project launched by the Howard League for Penal Reform in 1998 specifically applied citizenship to the issues of crime and disorder. It was directed at 11,000 London schoolchildren aged 13–14 and sought to reduce crime and disorder by fostering a sense of citizenship.

The government also undertook actions to raise educational standards, to combat the problem of bullying and to tackle the issues of truancy and school exclusion. A key objective was to prevent young people becoming alienated from education. The initiatives which were put forward included the Sure Start programme, which was modelled on the American Head Start programme. This targeted the parents of every child below the age of 4 in the most deprived areas of the United Kingdom, offering them advice on parenting and their children's health, and providing access to play centres and childcare. Investment in this scheme was doubled in the 2000 Comprehensive Spending Review.

In 1999, intensive nursery schemes supplemented the Sure Start programme. These were allocated to high-crime areas and directed at children whose upbringing led them to be perceived as potential future offenders. The aim of these schemes was to encourage children of pre-school age how to think ahead and organise their lives. It was anticipated that that this would produce observable benefits by the time the child reached the age of 10, measured by indicators which included improved school behaviour and achievement and fewer signs of criminality. There were, however, considerable problems attached with accurately assessing those at risk, including the possibility of self-fulfilling prophecies.

A further initiative to improve educational standards was the announcement, in March 1999, that extra resources would be allocated to improving the educational attainment of children attending inner-city comprehensive schools. Some of this aid would be spent on providing 'masterclasses' at specialist schools for the ablest children, and the number of specialist and beacon schools would be greatly expanded.

Truancy and school exclusions were regarded as major factors in juvenile crime. One estimate suggested that in London 40 per cent of robberies, 25 per cent of burglaries and 20 per cent of thefts were committed by children aged 10–16: most of these offences, which accounted for 5 per cent of all crime in London, occurred during school hours (Metropolitan Police, 1998). Accordingly, the Excellence in Cities programme provided money to help prevent school exclusions (for example, by extending school-based learning support units whereby troublesome children could be dealt with in schools). This programme also funded mentoring schemes that were designed to address the problem of children who were excluded from schools and those who left with no qualifications. This approach was coupled with punitive measures to tackle truancy: on 1 December 1998 new powers (derived from section 16 of the 1998 Crime and Disorder Act) came into force whereby police officers could remove truants from public places to 'designated premises'. The 2000 Criminal Justice and Court Services Act latterly introduced penalties for parents who failed to make their truanting children attend school.

Other educational policies included the Fresh Start programme, which was designed to rescue chronically failing schools by reopening them under different names with new management and staffing arrangements. In March 2000, the Secretary of State for Education and Employment proposed to develop the previous Conservative City Technology Colleges initiative by establishing a network of City Academies. This reform was initiated in 2002. Academies operate outside the control of local authorities and involve business and voluntary sector sponsors and education partners. They replace underperforming schools in addition to providing new educational facilities. The 2000 Comprehensive Spending Review increased the overall size of the education budget and established the cross-departmental Children's Fund. This is operated by voluntary organisations and was designed to identify and provide services for children who are manifesting signs of difficulty.

Although Labour's policies sought to improve educational standards for all children, there arose the possibility that aspects of them would intensify social divisions by aiding educational attainment, and ultimately social mobility, only for a gifted minority while intensifying perceptions of social disadvantage for the remainder. The spectre of low-level or 'dead-end' jobs for the lower achievers might not be sufficient to induce conformity from rebellious children and eliminate problems such as truancy and school exclusion.

Neighbourhood regeneration

Post-1997 Labour governments devoted considerable attention to the revival of neighbourhoods: 'the goal must be to reduce that gap between the poorest neighbourhoods and the rest of the country and bring them for the first time in decades up to an acceptable level' (Social Exclusion Unit, 1998: 10). The targeting of initiatives at deprived areas formed an important aspect of an anti-crime strategy. The 'New Deal for Communities', which was launched in 1998, aimed to tackle poverty in urban areas by measures which included targeting a number of 'pathfinder' districts (initially 17) with resources, developing a regeneration programme in which the private community and the voluntary sectors worked in partnership, and securing a more effective coordination of the activities pursued by various government departments. Areas of acute social need also qualified to bid for aid from the Single Regeneration Budget, which was designed to aid regeneration.

Additionally, research was initiated in 1998 by 18 Policy Action Teams (PATs) acting under the auspices of the Social Exclusion Unit. This resulted in the publication of a wide-ranging urban renewal strategy in 2000 that was directed at addressing the crime rates, unemployment levels, mortality rates and skill shortages in the poorest 44 districts in Britain, embracing 3,000 communities which were dubbed by *The Guardian* on 13 April 2000 as 'concentration camps in the midst of civilised society'. This was followed by a long-term national strategy which was designed to close the gap between the poorest neighbourhoods and the rest of the country over the next 10–20 years (Social Exclusion Unit, 2001b). Multi-agency Local Strategic Partnerships (LSPs) played an important role in delivering the national strategy. Also in 2001 a Community Empowerment Fund was established by the Department of Transport, Local Government and the Regions with the ability to spend £36 million over three years in the 88 most deprived localities in England. As with the work performed by the LSPs, community involvement was an essential aspect of regeneration schemes financed from this fund. Latterly a Neighbourhood Renewal Fund was set up to target resources to the most deprived neighbourhoods, and a Neighbourhood Development Unit was established in the Office of the Deputy Prime Minister to monitor and coordinate local regeneration activities.

The government's policies were predicated on the assumption that reducing crime was the prerequisite for achieving neighbourhood regeneration (Social Exclusion Unit, 2001b). However, this is not the sole explanation for neighbourhood decline that is, instead, influenced by a multiplicity of interacting factors (Hancock, 2003: 133–4). It has also been argued that despite attempts to involve local people in regeneration projects, the success of programmes designed to combat youth crime, disorder and vandalism depended on the extent to which *young* people were actively involved (Local Government Information Unit, 2000).

Drugs

The strongest predictor of crime among boys and men is drugs use (Home Office, 2000a). It has been calculated that offenders feeding their drug habits commit one in three burglaries and street robberies, and further account for a high amount of crack-related violence and prostitution. The estimated cost of drug-driven crime was £3–4 billion a year, and it was alleged that the punishments imposed on drug users rarely stopped their drug use (NACRO, 1999a).

The 1995 White Paper, *Tackling Drugs Together*, resulted in the establishment of drug action teams (DATs) to provide the strategic coordination of local action against drug misuse. DATs utilised multi-agency approaches to combat drug and drug-related crime, and police forces became important participants in DATs. Arrest referral schemes were also introduced to arrange treatment for arrested drug users, and the police became involved in education programmes in schools that were designed to discourage youngsters from becoming involved with drugs in the first place.

The Labour government aimed to build on these earlier approaches with the appointment of Keith Hellawell as the UK Anti-drugs Coordinator in charge of the UK Anti-Drug Coordination Unit (UKADCU). In 1998 UKADCU published its ten-year plan for tackling drug misuse, *Tackling Drugs to Build a Better Britain*. Its aims were to help young people resist drug abuse, to protect communities from drug-related anti-social and criminal behaviour, to enable people with drug problems to overcome them and to stifle the availability of illegal drugs (UKADCU, 2000).

Heavy emphasis was devoted in the government's approach to treatment, education and prevention as opposed to the traditional approach which gave priority to the enforcement of the drug laws: its ten-year strategy included an additional £217 million over the following three years for treatment and support services for drug misusers, treatment programmes in prisons, education and prevention programmes and extra funding for the treatment-based court sentence (the treatment and testing order) which was introduced in the 1998 Crime and Disorder Act. Additional money was also provided for arrest referral schemes.

Labour's approach attached considerable importance to multi-agency cooperation. It was augmented by the establishment of the National Treatment Agency for Substance Misuse in 2001 as a joint initiative of the Home Office and Department of Health. This imposes national standards for treatment and rehabilitation on local drug action teams and voluntary and charitable drug treatment centres, and acts as a clearing-house providing residential rehabilitation places for the toughest cases involving long-term addicts.

This preventive approach was balanced against more punitive proposals that were put forward in the 2000 Criminal Justice and Court Services Act. This introduced a new drug abstinence order whereby the courts could order a convicted user of a Class A drug to stay clean and be regularly tested, with non-observance attracting a further penalty. This Act also empowered the courts to order the drug testing of defendants charged with property crime, robbery and Class A drug offences, or with any other crime which was suspected of being linked to the misuse of heroin or cocaine/crack. The results of these tests are used to inform bail decisions.

The effectiveness of Labour's attempts to address the social causes of crime

The above account has suggested that since 1997 Labour has pursued a range of social and economic policies to address crime that was seen as both a cause and also as a product of social exclusion (Young and Matthews, 2003: 8).

However, the effectiveness of Labour's policies as a remedy to social exclusion has been subjected to criticisms that are discussed below.

Failure to tackle social inequality

It has been argued that Labour policies tended to focus on contemporary factors such as the contribution made by globalisation to the decline of manufacturing industry. Their approach sought to provide those who became unemployed or unemployable in the old economic order with the necessary skills to enable them to exploit the new opportunities arising in a post-industrial society (in particular associated with service industries). In this sense their approach (which was especially evidenced in policies concerned with employment and education) sought to enable people to help themselves rather than relying on a passive welfare state to provide them with benefits (Social Exclusion Unit, 2001a: 37). In some cases the approach adopted by the government went beyond encouragement to find work and embraced a more forceful approach as was evidenced by proposals put forward in 2005 whereby incapacity benefit would be split in two, and the majority of the less sick claimants would suffer financial penalties if they did not attend interviews which were designed to enable them to return to work.

However, it has been argued that this approach was not based on an analysis of the class structure in society entailing an appreciation of how globalisation had exacerbated *existing* divisions in society. It has thus been argued that New Labour's third way diluted its social justice and equality agenda (Powell, 2002: 19) by failing to address the fundamental causes of inequality in society. The new goal of eliminating exclusion was substituted for the old socialist objectives of the pursuit of equality and the advancement of social justice (Lund, 2002: 200; Young and Matthews, 2003: 17–20) and inclusion became the chief way through which New Labour's goal of equality would be delivered (Powell, 2002: 25). The new approach placed considerable emphasis on encouraging individuals to avail themselves of opportunities in areas such as education, training and employment at the expense of policies designed to secure the redistribution of wealth, and in this sense it might be argued that Labour's policies to combat social exclusion directed attention to the personal characteristics of the excluded rather than the structural causes of this problem (Lund, 2002: 206). Arguments of this nature thus conclude that these policies (which included forcing the poor to accept low-paid jobs) offered no long-term remedy to entrenched social divisions that were the basic cause of social inequality.

A further aspect of this argument focuses on the approach underpinning the work of the Social Exclusion Unit that has emphasised the importance of joined-up government in the delivery of programmes to aid the socially disadvantaged. However, it has been argued that this approach sought to remedy social problems by adopting a managerialist solution rather than a transformative one (Pitts, 2001: 147), that is the solution to social exclusion is seen as one of more efficiently managing existing resources expended by government departments rather than attempting to bring about a fundamental redistribution of wealth and resources in favour of the poor.

Social reform and public spending

Labour's initial desire to adhere to Conservative spending plans and not to raise taxes to tackle social disadvantages meant that expenditure on state welfare services declined in real terms from £262 billion in 1996 to £257 billion in 1999 (Office for National Statistics, 2001: 112). The impact of this meant that major social disadvantages such as child poverty, the gap between the rich and poor, and urban decline were not remedied. In 1997, the United Kingdom had one of the worst records of child poverty in the industrialised world. An editorial in *The Guardian* on 25 August 1999 argued that although the government intended to take around 1.2 million children out of child poverty by 2002, this would leave 4 million children still in poverty because of the way in which two decades of Conservative government massively increased inequality. It was subsequently stated that after seven years of Labour government, 3.5 million children were living below the breadline and the government had failed to achieve its first child poverty target, that of reducing it by one-quarter in 2004–5 (Carvel and Elliott, 2005).

The inadequacies of Labour's approach to tackling social inclusion were further evidenced in its failure to address inequality. Although the level of absolute poverty declined, the gap between rich and poor increased in Labour's early years (Lund, 2002: 208–10). Similarly, Labour's policies to achieve urban regeneration were also criticised for failing to advance policies which included redressing regional imbalances and the inadequate tax base of Britain's major cities which serve a geographic area which goes beyond their administrative boundaries.

The 2000 Comprehensive Spending Review responded to criticisms of this nature by proposing a £43 billion spending package over three years which would be directed at policy areas including education, employment, housing, the National Health Service and crime.

The family and marginalisation

Labour's social policies have been criticised for their failure to address the exclusion of marginalised groups (a problem which is exacerbated by the discriminatory practices associated with the criminal justice process) (Young and Matthews, 2003: 20–1). Instead, Labour has consistently emphasised the importance of the family unit and has used the rhetoric of the remoralisation of society that had been associated with the Conservative party. This was forcibly articulated in the Prime Minister's call for a moral crusade following media attention on two 12-year-old girls in South Yorkshire becoming pregnant, one by a 14-year-old boy. Blair urged 'a partnership between Government and the country to lay the foundations of that moral purpose' (Blair, 1999). This placed considerable emphasis on the role of the family in teaching children right from wrong and was backed up by provisions in the 1998 Crime and Disorder Act such as curfew notices and the provision of effective sex education to prevent teenage pregnancies. Boys who fathered children were to be targeted by the Child Support Agency, and forced to accept responsibility for the upkeep of their children by contributing from their earnings or bene-fit. The government also considered the possibility of introducing legislation to require teachers to emphasise the benefits of marriage and the traditional family unit when discussing moral or sexual issues.

Success of programmes

Schemes concerned with tackling the social causes of crime have been criti-cised for being ineffective. Initial findings suggested that large numbers were dropping out of the education and training courses of the New Deal pro-gramme, and that most of those who successfully completed them were not finding work but were being recycled into the other options of the scheme (Morgan, 2000). It was also impossible to assess the extent to which eco-nomic growth as opposed to the contents of the New Deal programme contributed towards enhancing the employment prospects of those who par-ticipated in this scheme.

Lack of coherence

Labour's response to juvenile crime embraced the reforms to criminal justice policy and processes and social reforms that have been discussed in this and the previous section of this chapter. Labour sought to address what had been put forward as key indicators of future criminality – socio-economic depriva-tion, poor parenting, criminal and anti-social families, low intelligence and school failure, hyperactivity/impulsivity/attention deficiency, and anti-social behaviour (such as drinking and the use of drugs) (Farrington and West; 1990; Farrington, 1996). However, it has been argued that there was no inherent coherence in these approaches, and it has been concluded that by the end of the 1990s the youth justice system was offering neither welfare, nor diversion, nor progressive justice to those who came before it (Goldson, 2000). Instead the system stood accused of seeking to prevent offending 'by any pragmatic means possible. The viability of such means primarily rested on prior assessments of risk' (Muncie, 2002: 145).

> Evaluate the strengths and weaknesses of policies put forward since 1997 that have sought to tackle the social causes of crime.

Conclusion

This chapter has considered the response adopted by the state towards crime committed by young people. It has examined the principles underpinning the existence of a separate youth justice system and has charted the way in which this system has developed. Particular attention was devoted to the tensions that exist as to whether a youth justice system should place prime emphasis on the welfare of young offenders or on the safety of society and on the rationale for changes introduced by post-1997 governments that have had the effect of making the youth justice system more punitive.

The chapter has discussed contemporary juvenile justice policy in some detail. It examined the problems associated with the operation of this system in the late 1990s and considered the response of the 1997 Labour government to youth crime that was contained in the 1998 Crime and Disorder Act and the 1999 Youth Justice and Criminal Evidence Act. The chapter evaluated the strengths and weaknesses of the approach that was adopted, in particular with reference to innovations such as anti-social behaviour orders. Finally, the chapter analysed the policies pursued by post-1997 governments to address the social causes of crime that were especially directed at influencing the behaviour of young people.

This chapter concludes the examination that has been presented of the operations of the key agencies in the criminal justice process whose role is to respond to crime. In order for the operations of these bodies to be seen as legitimate throughout society, it is necessary that all citizens should be treated equally. The following chapter examines the extent to which racial discrimination influences the operations of agencies discussed in the previous chapters.

Further reading

There are many specialist texts that will provide an in-depth examination of the issues discussed in this chapter. These include:

Burney, E. (2005) *Making People Behave: Anti-social Behaviour, Politics and Policy*. Cullompton: Willan Publishing.

Matthews, R. and Young, J. (eds), (2003) *The New Politics of Crime and Punishment*. Cullompton: Willan Publishing.

McDowell, G. and Smith, J. (editors), (1999) *Juvenile Delinquency in the US and the UK*, 2nd edn. Basingstoke: Macmillan.

Muncie, J. (2004) *Youth and Crime*, 2nd edn. London: Sage, 2004.

Pitts, J. (2001) *The New Politics of Youth Crime*. Basingstoke: Palgrave.

Squires, P. and Stephen, D. (2005) *Rougher Justice: Anti-social Behaviour and Young People*. Cullompton: Willan Publishing.

Key events

- **1838** Enactment of the Parkhurst Act. This provided for the first state-run prison catering for juvenile offenders.
- **1854** Enactment of the Youthful Offenders Act. This measure created a nationwide network of juvenile reformatories.
- **1908** Enactment of the Children Act. This Act abolished imprisonment for offenders below the age of 14 and removed the death penalty for children and young persons. It also created a separate system of courts (termed juvenile courts) to deal with offenders aged 15 years and below.
- **1908** Enactment of the Crime Prevention Act. This legislation established borstals to house serious offenders between the ages of 16 and 20 (the upper limit being raised to 21 in 1936). Training was emphasised in the borstal regime.
- **1932** Enactment of the Children and Young Persons Act. This made the welfare of young offenders a key policy objective and provided the basis for a number of subsequent social and criminal justice policies that sought to tackle the conditions that were viewed as conducive to crime. The key provisions of this Act were consolidated in the 1933 Children and Young Persons Act that also raised the age of criminal responsibility to 8 years (increased to 10 years by the 1963 Children and Young Persons Act) and created special panels of magistrates to deal with juvenile cases.
- **1948** Enactment of the Children and Young Persons Act. This provided for a Children's Department to play an important role in local authority social work provision, and also established detention centres to cater for persistent juvenile offenders aged 15–17 years of age.
- **1969** Enactment of the Children and Young Persons Act. This Act emphasised the importance of the welfare principle to govern the state's intervention in the lives of young people. Social workers were provided with a key role in administering the new system that emphasised the desirability of diverting young offenders from custody.
- **1979** Publication of the Black Committee on Children and Young Persons. This criticised the use of custodial sentences for youth offenders and helped to popularise the increased role of cautioning as a response to youth crime.
- **1982** Enactment of the Criminal Justice Act. This Act abolished imprisonment for offenders below the age of 21 years. Short custodial sentences imposed on offenders below this age would henceforth be carried out in a youth custody centre (which replaced borstals) or a detention centre.
- **1988** Enactment of the Criminal Justice Act. This measure established Young Offender Institutions to replace detention centres and youth custody centres.
- **1989** Enactment of the Children Act. This measure ended the involvement of youth courts in civil care proceedings.
- **1991** Enactment of the Criminal Justice Act. This legislation renamed juvenile courts as youth courts to cater for offenders aged between 10 and 17 years of age, abolished custodial sentences for persons below 15 years of age and also emphasised the desirability of avoiding custodial

sentences for young offenders. Curfews for those aged 16 and over were introduced by this measure.

- **1993** The murder of the toddler, Jamie Bulger, by two children. This tragic event helped to project a penal populist approach to youth crime into the government's crime-fighting agenda.
- **1993** Speech by the then shadow Home Secretary, Tony Blair, when he announced the policy of the Labour party to be 'tough on crime, tough on the causes of crime'. This soundbite formed the basis of the approach of post-1997 Labour governments to crime, combining penal populist responses to crime and disorder with attempts to tackle the social roots of this behaviour.
- **1994** Enactment of the Criminal Justice and Public Order Act. This legislation provided for the creation of Secure Training Centres to cater for serious offenders aged between 12 and 14 years of age.
- **1996** Publication by the Audit Commission of *Misspent Youth*. This report put forward a number of criticisms of the operations of the youth justice system, and paved the way for reforms which were provided for in the 1998 Crime and Disorder Act.
- **1997** Establishment of the Social Exclusion Unit. This body was set up to promote a joined-up approach in Whitehall to tackle the wide range of problems that contributed to social exclusion.
- **1998** Enactment of the Crime and Disorder Act. This measure put forward a number of new court orders to respond to youth crime, some of which (such as ASBOs) could be applied to crime committed by adults. Multi-agency (or partnership) work was placed on a statutory footing by the creation of Crime and Disorder Reduction Partnerships and Youth Offending Teams.
- **1998** Initiation of the New Deal programme for the long-term unemployed and the launch of the New Deal for Communities to tackle urban poverty.
- **1999** Enactment of the Youth Justice and Criminal Evidence Act. This legislation created Youth Offender Panels as mechanisms to enable members of communities to participate in the sentencing of young offenders. It also considerably advanced the principle of restorative justice as a response to youth crime.
- **1999** Launch of the Working Families Tax Credit. This was an important aspect of the government's policies to provide aid to poorer families.
- **2001** Enactment of the Criminal Justice and Police Act. This legislation introduced Penalty Notices for Disorder that constituted fixed penalty fines for various forms of disorderly behaviour committed by persons aged 18 years and over.
- **2002** Enactment of the Police Reform Act. This measure further developed ASBOs, in particular by enabling them to be added (bolted-on) to a specific offence for which a person was convicted.
- **2003** Enactment of the Anti-social Behaviour Act. This measure introduced dispersal orders, whereby the police could remove two or more young people who were outdoors after 9 p.m. in an area in which such an order was in place. The Act also extended Penalty Notices for Disorder to those aged 16 and 17 years of age.

References

Allen, C., Crow, I. and Cavadino, M. (2000) *Evaluation of the Youth Court Demonstration Project*, Home Office Research Study 214. London: Home Office.

Audit Commission (1996) *Misspent Youth*. London: Audit Commission.

Audit Commission (2005) *Comprehensive Performance Assessment 2005: Keyline Enquiry for Corporate Assessment (Practitioner Version)*. London: Audit Commission.

Blaikie, T. (2004) 'It's About Manners, Stupid', *The Independent*, 28 November.

Blair, T. (1999) 'My Moral Manifesto for the 21st Century', *Observer*, 5 September.

Blair, T. (2006) Respect Action Plan launch speech, 10 January.

Bright, J. (1998) 'Preventing Youth Crime', *Criminal Justice Matters*, 33, Autumn.

Budd, T. and Sharp, C. (2005) *Offending in England and Wales: First Results from the 2003 Crime and Justice Survey*, Home Office Research, Development and Statistics Directorate Findings 244. London: Home Office.

Burney, E. (2005) *Making People Behave: Anti-social Behaviour, Politics and Policy*. Cullompton: Willan Publishing.

Carvel, J. and Elliott, L. (2005) 'Child Poverty Defies Government Targets', *Guardian*, 31 March.

Clarke, K. (1993) Interview, BBC Radio *The World This Weekend*, 21 February, quoted in *Guardian*, 23 February.

Cohen, S. (1985) *Visions of Social Control*. Cambridge: Polity Press.

Department of Health and Social Security (1983) *Further Development of Intermediate Treatment*, Local Authority Circular LAC (83) 3, 26 January.

Ditchfield, J. (1976) *Police Cautioning in England and Wales*, Home Office Research Study 37. London: Home Office.

Elliott, L. (1999) 'Labour Widens War on Child Poverty', *Guardian*, 8 September.

Farrington, D. (1996) *Understanding and Preventing Youth Crime*, Social Policy Research Findings 93. York: Rowntree Foundation.

Farrington, D. (1999) 'Predicting Persistent Young Offenders', in G. McDowell and J. Smith (eds), *Juvenile Delinquency in the US and the UK*. Basingstoke: Macmillan.

Farrington, D. and West, D. (1990) 'The Cambridge Study in Delinquent Development', in H. Kerner and G. Kaiser (eds), *Criminality: Personality, Behaviour and Life History*. Berlin: Springer-Verlag.

Feeley, M. and Simon, J. (1992) '"The New Penology": Notes on the Emerging Strategy of Corrections and Its Implementation', *Criminology*, 30 (4): 452–74.

Field, F. (2004) Lecture at Liverpool University, 9 December.

Folkard, M., Smith, D. and Smith, D. (1976) *IMPACT: Intensive Matched Probation and After-Care Treatment*, Home Office Research Study 36. London: HMSO.

Garland, D. (2001) *The Culture of Control*. Oxford: Oxford University Press.

Gelsthorpe, L. and Morris, A. (1994) 'Juvenile Justice 1994–1992', in M. Maguire, R. Morgan and R. Reiner (eds), *The Oxford Handbook of Criminology*. Oxford: Clarendon Press.

Gillan, A. (2004) 'Late Arrivals and No Shows – But New Court's Friendly Judge Keeps Smiling', *Guardian*, 10 December.

Goldson, B. (2000) 'Whither Diversion? Interventionism and the New Youth Justice', in B, Goldson, *Youth Justice: Contemporary Policy and Practice*. Aldershot: Ashgate.

Graham, J. and Bowling, B. (1995) *Young People and Crime*, Home Office Research Study 145. London: Home Office Research and Statistics Directorate.

Hancock, L. (2003) 'Urban Regeneration and Crime Reduction: Contradictions and Dilemmas', in R. Matthews and J. Young (eds), *The New Politics of Crime and Punishment*. Collumpton: Willan Publishing.

Hayward, R. and Sharp, C. (2005) *Young People, Crime and Antisocial Behaviour*, Home Office Research, Development and Statistics Directorate, Findings 245. London: Home Office.

Her Majesty's Chief Inspector of Prisons (1998) *Young Prisoners: A Thematic Review by Her Majesty's Chief Inspector of Prisons for England and Wales*. London: HMSO.

Her Majesty's Prison Service (1999) *Annual Report and Accounts 1998 to March 1999.* London: TSO.

Holdaway, S. et al. (2001) *New Strategies to Address Youth Offending: The National Evaluation of the Pilot Youth Offending Teams,* Home Office Occasional Paper Number 69. London: Home Office.

Home Affairs Committee (2005) *Anti-Social Behaviour.* London: Home Affairs Select Committee, Fifth Report, Session 2004/5, House of Commons Paper 80–1.

Home Office (1984) *Tougher Regimes in Detention Centres: Report of an Evaluation by the Young Offender Psychology Unit.* London: HMSO.

Home Office (1985) *The Cautioning of Offenders,* Circular 14/1985. London: Home Office.

Home Office (1990) *The Cautioning of Offenders,* Circular 59/90. London: Home Office.

Home Office (1994) *The Cautioning of Offenders,* Circular 181994. London: Home Office.

Home Office (1997) *No More Excuses – A New Approach to Tackling Youth Crime in England and Wales,* Cm 3809. London: TSO.

Home Office (2000a) *Youth Crime. Findings from the Youth Lifestyle Study.* London: Home Office.

Home Office (2000b) *Reducing Public Disorder: The Role of Fixed Penalty Notices.* London: Home Office.

Home Office (2003a) *Respect and Responsibility: Taking a Stand Against Anti-Social Behaviour,* Cm 5778. London: TSO.

Home Office (2003b) *Anti-social Behaviour Day Count.* London: Home Office (available at: www.homeoffice.gov.uk/docs/ASB_Day_Count_Summary.pdf).

Home Office (2003c) *Restorative Justice: The Government's Strategy: A Consultative Document on the Government's Strategy on Restorative Justice.* London: Home Office.

Home Office (2004a) *Reducing Crime – Changing Lives: The Government's Plans for Transforming the Management of Offenders.* London: Home Office.

Home Office (2004b) *Confident Communities in a Secure Britain: The Home Office Strategic Plan 2004–2008.* London: Home Office.

Home Office, Department of Culture, Media and Sport and Office of the Deputy Prime Minister (2005) *Drinking Responsibly: The Government's Proposals.* London: Home Office, Department of Culture, Media and Sport and Office of the Deputy Prime Minister.

Home Office/Lord Chancellor's Department (2001) *The Youth Court 2001 – The Changing Culture of the Youth Court: Good Practice Guide.* London: Home Office/Lord Chancellor's Department.

Hunt, L. and Weiner, K. (1977) 'The Impact of a Juvenile Curfew', *Journal of Police Science and Administration,* 5: 407–12.

Kelling, G. and Wilson, J. (1982) 'Broken Windows: The Police and Neighbourhood Safety', *Atlantic Monthly,* 249: 29–38.

Kemp, V. and Gelsthorpe, L. (2003) 'Youth Justice: Discretion in Pre-Court Decision-Making', in L. Gelsthorpe and N. Padfield (eds), *Exercising Discretion: Decision-Making in the Criminal Justice System and Beyond.* Cullompton: Willan Publishing.

Kilpatrick, A. (2001) 'Foreword', in Home Office/Lord Chancellor's Department (2001) *The Youth Court 2001 – The Changing Culture of the Youth Court: Good Practice Guide.* London: Home Office/Lord Chancellor's Department.

Lemert, E. (2000) 'Dilemmas of Intervention', in C. Lemert and M. Winter (eds), *Crime and Deviance: Essays and Innovations of Edwin M. Lemert.* Boston: Rowman & Littlefield.

Liddle, M. and Solanki, A.-R. (2002) *Persistent Young Offenders: Research on Individual Backgrounds and Life Experiences,* Research Briefing 1. London: NACRO.

Lipsey, M. (1992) 'Juvenile Delinquency Treatment: A Meta-analytic Inquiry into the Variability of Effects', in T. Cook et al. (eds), *Meta-Analysis for Explanation: A Casebook.* New York: Russell Sage Foundation.

Lipsey, M. (1995) 'What Do We Learn from 400 Research Studies on the Effectiveness of Treatment with Juvenile Delinquents?', in J. McGuire (ed.), *What Works? Reducing Re-offending.* Chichester: John Wiley.

Local Government Information Unit (2000) *Taking Part.* London: Local Government Information Unit.

Lund, B. (2002) *Understanding State Welfare: Social Justice or Social Exclusion?* London: Sage.

Mair, G., Lloyd, C., Nee, C. and Sibbitt, R. (1994) *Intensive Probation in England and Wales: An Evaluation*, Home Office Research Study 133. London: HMSO.

McDowell, D., Lottin, C. and Wiersema, B. (2000) 'The Impact of Youth Curfew Laws on Juvenile Crime Rates', *Crime and Delinquency*, 46 (1): 76–91.

McGuire, J. and Priestley, J. (1995) 'Reviewing "What Works?" Past, Present and Future', in J. McGuire, (ed.), *What Works? Reducing Re-offending*. Chichester: John Wiley.

Metropolitan Police (1998) *Performance Information Bureau*. London: Metropolitan Police Service.

Morgan, O. (2000) 'Drop Out Crisis Hits New Deal for Jobless', *Observer*, 2 April.

Muncie, J. (2002) 'A New Deal for Youth? Early Intervention and Correctionalism', in G. Hughes, E. McLaughlin and J. Muncie, *Crime Prevention and Community Safety: New Directions*. London: Sage.

NACRO (1999a) *Drug Driven Crime*. London: NACRO.

NACRO (1999b) *Wasted Lives*. London: NACRO.

NACRO (2000) *Pre-Sentence Reports and Custodial Sentencing*. London: NACRO.

NACRO (2002) *Some Facts About Young Offender*, Youth Crime Section Factsheet. London: NACRO.

NACRO (2003a) *Anti-social Behaviour Orders and Associated Measures (Part 1)*, Youth Crime Briefing. London: NACRO.

NACRO (2003b) *Lessons from Pilots: A Summary of the National Evaluation of the Pilot Youth Offending Teams*. London: NACRO.

Newburn, T. et al. (2002) *The Introduction of Referral Orders into the Youth Justice System: Final Report*, Home Office Research Study 242. London: Home Office Research, Development and Statistics Directorate.

Office for National Statistics (2001) *Social Trends 31*. London: TSO.

Pakes, F. and Winstone, J. (2005) 'Community Justice: The Smell of Fresh Bread', in J. Winstone and F. Pakes (eds), *Community Justice: Issues for Probation and Criminal Justice*. Cullompton: Willan Publishing.

Phillpotts, G. and Lancucki, L. (1979) *Previous Convictions, Sentence and Reconvictions*, Home Office Research Study 53. London: HMSO.

Piachaud, D. (1999) 'Wealth by Stealth', *Guardian*, 1 September.

Pitts, J. (1998) *The Politics of Juvenile Crime*. London: Sage.

Pitts, J. (2000) 'New Youth Justice, New Youth Crime', *Criminal Justice Matters*, 38.

Pitts, J. (2001) *The New Politics of Youth Crime*. Basingstoke: Palgrave.

Pitts, J. (2003) 'Youth Justice in England and Wales', in R. Matthews and J. Young (eds), *The New Politics of Crime and Punishment*. Cullompton: Willan Publishing.

Platt, A. (1969) *The Child Savers: The Intervention of Delinquenc*. Chicago: University of Chicago Press.

Powell, M. (ed.) (2002) *Evaluating New Labour's Welfare Reforms*. Bristol: Policy Press.

Pratt, J. (1989) 'Corporatism: the Third Model of Juvenile Justice', *British Journal of Criminology*, 29 (3): 236–54.

Prison Reform Trust (1998) *Prison Report*, Issue 42, Spring.

Public Accounts Committee (2004) *Youth Offending: The delivery of Community and Custodial Sentences*, Fortieth Report, Sessions 2003–4, House of Commons Paper 307.

Raynor, P. and Vanstone, M. (2002) *Understanding Community Penalties: Probation, Policy and Social Change*. Buckingham: Open University Press.

Rutherford, A. (1999) 'The New Political Consensus on Youth Justice in Britain', in G. McDowell and J. Smith (eds), *Juvenile Delinquency in the US and the UK*. Basingstoke: Macmillan.

Schur, E. (1971) *Labeling Deviant Behaviour*. New York: Random House.

Schur, E. (1973) *Radical Non-intervention*. Englewood Cliffs, NJ: Prentice Hall.

Social Exclusion Unit (1998) *Bringing Britain Together: A National Strategy for Neighbourhood Renewal*, Cm 4045. London: TSO.

Social Exclusion Unit (2000) *Report of Policy Action Team 12: Young People*. London: Social Exclusion Unit.

Social Exclusion Unit (2001a) *Preventing Social Exclusion*. London: Social Exclusion Unit.

Social Exclusion Unit (2001b) *A New Commitment to Neighbourhood Renewal: National Strategy Action Plan*. London: Social Exclusion Unit.

Squires, P. and Stephen, D. (2005) *Rougher Justice: Anti-social Behaviour and Young People*. Cullompton: Willan Publishing.

Straw, J. (1997) Preface to *No More Excuses – A New Approach to Tackling Youth Crime in England and Wales*, Cm 3809. London: TSO.

Straw, J. (1999) Speech to the Police Superintendents Association Conference, Chester, 13 September.

Travis, A. (2004a) 'Neighbours to Decide Punishment', *Guardian*, 8 December.

Travis, A. (2004b) 'Ten-Year-Olds Face Instant Fines', *Guardian*, 27 December.

United Kingdom Anti-Drug Coordination Unit (2000) *Tackling Drugs to Build a Better Britain – The Government's 10-Year Strategy for Tackling Drug Misuse*. London: TSO.

Utting, D. and Vennard, J. (2000) *What Works with Young Offenders in the Community?* Ilford, Essex: Barnardo's.

Warner, Lord (2000) 'Tackling Root Causes', *Guardian*, 29 March.

Welsh Assembly Government (2004) *All Wales Youth Offending Strategy*. Cardiff: Welsh Assembly Government.

Whitehead, C., Stockdale, J. and Razza, G. (2003) *The Economic and Social Costs of Anti-social Behaviour: A Review*. London: London School of Economics.

Whitfield, D. (1998) *Introduction to the Probation Service*. Winchester: Waterside Press.

Wonnacott, C. (1999) 'The Counterfeit Contract: Reform, Pretence and Muddled Principles in the New Referral Order', *Child and Family Law Quarterly*, 11 (3): 271–87.

Worrall, A. (1997) *Punishment in the Community: The Future of Criminal Justice*. Harlow: Longman.

Young, J. and Matthews, R. (2003) 'New Labour, Crime Control and Social Exclusion', in R. Matthews and J. Young (eds), *The New Politics of Crime and Punishment*. Collumpton: Willan Publishing.

Young, R. and Hoyle, C. (2003) 'Restorative Justice and Punishment' in S. McConville (ed.), *The Use of Punishment*. Cullompton: Willan Publishing.

10 Race and the criminal justice system

This chapter will examine the manner in which accusations of racism made against agencies operating within the criminal justice process have been addressed. Particular attention will be devoted to the content and implementation of two key reports that were written by Lord Scarman (Scarman, 1981) and Sir William Macpherson (Macpherson, 1999). The content of this chapter will reflect the considerable degree of attention devoted to the police service in both reports. Specifically this chapter:

- considers the background to, and the content of, the 1981 Scarman Report and its subsequent impact on the police service;
- discusses accusations of racial injustice levelled against other agencies in the criminal justice process;
- evaluates the background to, and content of, Sir William Macpherson's 1999 report;
- analyses the implementation of the recommendations put forward by Sir William Macpherson;
- identifies the impact made by the Macpherson Report on the operations of a number of agencies within the criminal justice process;
- considers impediments to the progress of the reforms proposed in the Macpherson Report, devoting particular attention to the police service.

The Scarman Report

Many of the urban disorders that occurred in 1980 and 1981 took place following some form of police intervention in a community. This perhaps suggested that poor police–public relationships contributed towards these events, and this perception was given official recognition in Lord Scarman's report that focused on the Brixton disorders in April 1981 but included similar events which took place elsewhere in Britain later that year. Although this report was specifically concerned with the police service, it brought into public debate the way in which the operations of the criminal justice system in general could contribute to feelings of alienation felt by disaffected groups and result in outbreaks of disorder.

Scarman's investigation was an inquiry constituted under the 1964 Police Act and the bulk of his report was concerned with proposals that were designed to improve police–public relationships, in particular with minority ethnic communities. He noted that the police had failed to adapt themselves adequately to operate in these areas, and that existing training arrangements were inadequate to prepare officers for policing a multi-racial society (Scarman, 1981: 79). To address problems of this nature he suggested the modification of police training programmes to incorporate an increased emphasis on community relations. He further proposed that the composition of police forces should become more reflective of the society they served, although he rejected a quota system or the lowering of entry standards as mechanisms to achieve this ideal (Scarman, 1981: 76–7). He argued that racially prejudiced or discriminatory behaviour should become a specific disciplinary offence which, if substantiated, would normally lead to an officer's dismissal from the police service, and he put forward amendments to the procedures involved for handling complaints against police officers, which included the introduction of a conciliation process for minor issues (Scarman, 1981: 115–20).

Scarman reinforced the recommendation of the Royal Commission on Criminal Procedure in 1981 that stop and search powers should be rationalised across England and Wales and their use governed by the introduction of a number of safeguards, thus enabling their usage by individual officers to become more effectively monitored (Scarman, 1981: 84–7, 113). He also argued that there should be enhanced consultation with the general public, provided that this did not undermine the principle of constabulary independence (Scarman, 1981: 63–4). He proposed that the emphasis on law enforcement as the prime role of the police service should be reconsidered since law enforcement could jeopardise the maintenance of public tranquillity that he regarded as the priority of police work (Scarman, 1981: 62–3). In this respect he attached considerable importance to community policing and the activities performed by home beat officers (Scarman, 1981: 88–92).

Implementation of the Scarman Report

The police service was receptive to the introduction of reforms in the wake of the 1980 and 1981 disorders. Other pressures at this time to reform police practices included the examination of policing in London by the Policy Studies Institute (Smith and Gray, 1983). Some developments (such as community policing initiatives which were designed to bring the police and public closer together and thus undo some of the damage associated with unit beat policing – an issue which is explored more fully in Chapter 2) preceded Scarman but received increased attention within the police service in the early 1980s, especially since one study suggested that this style of policing could operate effectively in multi-ethnic inner-city areas such as Handsworth in Birmingham (Brown, 1982).

Following the publication of the Scarman Report, increased attention was placed on interviewing procedures in an attempt to ensure that recruits who harboured racist sentiments did not gain entry to the service. Vigorous attempts were also made to increase the number of police officers drawn from minority ethnic communities. In July 1981 the House of Commons Home Affairs Committee recommended that police forces should take 'vigorous steps' to recruit minority ethnic officers (Home Affairs Committee, 1981) following which a Home Office circular stated that police forces in areas with substantial minority ethnic communities 'should keep in mind the need to attract recruits from those minorities' (Home Office, 1982a).

In July 1982 a Home Office Study Group made suggestions for improved publicity about police work and the prospects it offered to be directed at minority communities (Home Office, 1982b). This embodied moves in the direction of positive discrimination with the suggestion that chief officers should use their discretion to accept otherwise suitable candidates who were below the national minimum height limit, and that black or Asian applicants who failed the educational tests should be given advice in order to help them successfully re-apply. The report recommended that chief officers should scrutinise their force selection procedures and that HM Inspectors of Constabulary should monitor the progress made in this direction by individual forces (Home Office, 1982b). Following the publication of this report, the height requirement was formally abandoned. Further pressure by the Home Office to increase the level of minority ethnic recruitment was exerted in Circular 87/1989 (which concerned equal opportunities within the police service) (Home Office, 1989), and Circular 33/1990. The latter suggested that chief constables should consider a number of matters related to the recruitment of officers from minority ethnic groups including setting targets for the level of minority ethnic representation in each force, devising performance indicators for force policy on minority ethnic recruitment and establishing a programme of special recruitment initiatives (Home Office, 1990).

Reforms were also introduced into training programmes. Scarman had made a number of criticisms of the Metropolitan Police Service's probationer training course (Scarman, 1981: 81–2) that resulted in significant changes. The length of the initial training period was extended and the role performed by tutor constables was upgraded. In 1982 the Metropolitan Police introduced a course in human awareness training for recruits. This involved devoting about one-quarter of the 20-week initial training course to three broad areas of study (interpersonal skills, self-awareness and community relations) that was designed to improve the social skills and street wisdom of police officers. The effectiveness of the course was, however, challenged, a significant number of participants believing that human awareness training was inadequate or unsatisfactory to prepare them to perform their duties as police officers. It was observed that once initial training had ended officers underwent experiences that tended to make them police in ways that were not compatible with its philosophy. However, fewer complaints were made against officers who had received human awareness training, which suggested that it possessed some beneficial consequences (Bull and Horncastle, 1983).

In 1982 probationer training throughout England and Wales in race relations was scrutinised, with attention being drawn to the detrimental impact that police culture and experiences on the streets could exert on its long-term value (Southgate, 1982). In 1983 a more comprehensive examination of community and race relations training was published (Police Training Council Working Party, 1983). This made a number of criticisms concerning arrangements then in place for providing training in these areas, including a tendency to teach these issues academically and in a manner which failed to integrate them into mainstream police activities. Accordingly, it was recommended that future training in community and race relations should be provided to all officers up to the rank of chief superintendent and be delivered at regular intervals throughout an officer's career, closely related to the responsibilities of each rank.

Following the publication of this report, the Home Office established a Centre for the Study of Community and Race Relations to provide police trainers with appropriate skills, knowledge and awareness and to aid police training schools to develop relevant curricula. This was closed in 1988 and replaced in 1989 by a Home Office specialist support unit that also provided courses for police trainers. Additionally, four short courses in racism and human awareness training were sponsored by the Home Office in the autumn of 1983. Their objective was to develop a heightened awareness of the nature of racism in society and also within the individual. However, it was concluded that problems arose concerning the unclear objectives of these courses, which resulted in trainers and participants having different expectations. The emphasis that was placed on an individual discussing their personal experiences and attitudes at the expense of participants being given information by trainers was generally unpopular, and it was further observed that some of the tutors displayed hostile attitudes towards the police (Southgate, 1984).

Further reforms that were designed to improve the relationship between the police service and the general public (especially in the inner-city areas) included the introduction of a range of safeguards in the 1984 Police and Criminal Evidence Act. In particular these sought to regulate the use of stop and search powers by requiring officers to record their use of these powers that could then be monitored by supervisors. The 1984 legislation also reformed the police complaints system by introducing the Police Complaints Authority with the power to supervise the investigation of serious complaints made against police officers. (This reform is discussed more fully in Chapter 4.) Mechanisms to improve the liaison between police and public were also introduced. These included the establishment of local consultative committees (which were made compulsory by section 106 of the 1984 Act) and a number of police initiatives such as the setting up of community contact departments and the permanent allocation of police officers to specific neighbourhoods.

The limited impact of the Scarman Report on the police service

The reasons for the apparent failure of the Scarman Report to secure improved relationships between police and public (especially minority ethnic communities) are considered below.

Recruitment

In 1981 there were 132 black officers serving in the Metropolitan Police Service (0.5 per cent of the force's strength) and 326 in all English and Welsh forces (0.3 per cent of the total number of police officers) (Scarman, 1981: 76). Scarman envisaged that the recruitment of more officers from minority ethnic communities was a key reform to both changing the attitudes and habits of police officers and to provide the service with legitimacy within minority communities. However, changes in the racial make-up of Britain's police forces proved very difficult to achieve and there was no striking success in making the service more socially representative. The expenditure of £1 million to attract recruits into the Metropolitan Police from minority ethnic communities resulted in only a small increase in the number of these officers (467, or less than 2 per cent of the force's strength) by 1990. At the end of 1993 there were 1,814 police officers of minority ethnic origins in England and Wales, which represented around 1.5 per cent of the total number of officers employed by these forces. Recruitment rates indicated a slightly improved position, whereby 3.8 per cent of appointments to English and Welsh forces in 1993 were from persons drawn from minority ethnic groups (Oakley, 1996: 13–14).

An important explanation for the continued under-representation of members of minority ethnic groups in the police service was the assumption that improved relationships between the police service and these communities could be secured by the employment of more minority ethnic officers. However, the negative image of the police service which was held within these communities (a problem which was specifically acknowledged by the then Home Office Minister, Douglas Hogg, in a speech delivered to a National Conference of Police Recruiting Officers in Derby in 1986) meant that persons from minority ethnic groups who joined the service ran the risk of rejection by their own peers and the possibility of being subjected to racial prejudice from white officers who constituted the bulk of Britain's police officers. This situation explained both the low numbers of recruits from minority ethnic backgrounds who joined the police service and the relatively high wastage rates of these recruits. In 1993, 66 minority ethnic officers in England and Wales left the service (a figure which constituted around 32 per cent of the numbers who were appointed that year) (Oakley, 1996: 14).

Training

A number of attempts were made after 1981 to reform police training programmes (in particular those received by probationer constables) in order to improve the relationship between the service and minority ethnic groups. But these failed to secure any dramatic changes in police sensitivity towards racial issues. In addition to matters that were raised above in connection with the discussion of the various initiatives that were brought forward, a particular problem concerned the philosophy that underpinned the approaches that were adopted. A considerable difference exists between multicultural and anti-racist training programmes. The former suggests that the problems that sometimes occur between races are based on misunderstandings and can be remedied by providing information on the history, cultures and backgrounds of minority communities. Anti-racist training, however, insists that racial intolerance will only be remedied when members of the dominant culture become aware of their own racism. This makes them receptive to suggestions put forward to remedy their own acknowledged defects. The approach required by this latter form of training is challenging, especially when programmes of this type were delivered by non-police personnel.

The discriminatory use of police powers

Allegations of the persistence of abuses by the police towards members of minority ethnic groups continued to be made. An important aspect of this was the manner in which powers to stop and search persons and vehicles were used in a discriminatory fashion (Institute of Race Relations, 1987: 1–55). One explanation for the persistence of this situation was that the safeguards that were introduced in the 1984 Police and Criminal Evidence Act relating to the use of these powers were contained in Codes of Practice accompanying this legislation rather than in the Act itself. This meant that an officer who chose to disregard the new constraints on his or her use of stop and search powers was not guilty of a criminal offence although he/she might be the subject of a disciplinary charge. Accordingly, the influence that these safeguards exerted over the conduct of officers 'on the streets' was partially dependent on their willingness to abide by them and by the stance that judges adopted towards breaches in cases that subsequently came to court (Joyce, 2001: 324). The amended stop and search provisions of the 1994 Criminal Justice and Public Order Act (which removed the requirement of reasonableness that a prohibited article would be found) could result in intensified perceptions of racism within the police service unless the use of these powers was effectively monitored.

Police – community liaison

Although a number of initiatives were introduced after 1981 to enhance the level of police–community contact, their effect was limited. In particular, formal consultation with the community (introduced by section 106 of the 1984 Act) failed to produce any substantial improvement in police–community relationships (Morgan and Maggs, 1985). One reason for this was that consultation merely entails the right to be heard and thus did not alter the power relationship between police and public to ensure that 'those to whom power is delegated account for the way they have used it' (Simey, 1985: 3). It has been noted above that initiatives were also introduced to enhance the level of contact between the police service and minority ethnic communities.

By the late 1980s most police forces had established discrete units concerned with race and community relations, typically based at force headquarters and divisional levels. These, however, failed to permeate all aspects of policing, and their existence perhaps implied that issues affecting race relations were of concern only to a small number of specialist officers.

Policing methods

Following the Scarman Report, most police forces introduced some form of community policing arrangements into multi-ethnic, inner-city areas. However, these failed to secure any significant improvement in police–public relationships in these areas, in particular because of the relatively lowly status of these officers in the police service. This problem raised questions about 'issues such as pay and career progression to ensure that good officers were attracted to, and retained, in this role' (Home Office, 2001: 41) as opposed to the prevailing situation whereby those who saw this as their long-term function in the service were viewed as lacking ambition.

Additionally, the support which the public were willing to give to the police service because of the role performed by area police officers tended to be offset by the use of complementary police methods (Gifford et al., 1989: 163–71) which involved an often aggressive response based on the presumption that black people were violent and in need of coercive treatment. This was an important aspect of what has been depicted as the move towards paramilitary policing in urban areas, involving the 'application of (quasi) military training, equipment, philosophy and organisation to questions of policing' (Jefferson, 1990: 374). It led to the deterioration of police–public relationships arising from the increased tendency to apply confrontational tactics to respond to threats (actual or real) posed to law and order enforcement in inner-city areas. This method of policing (which emphasised the law enforcement role of the police above the performance of service functions) is discussed in more detail in Chapter 2.

Failure to address police culture

A particular weakness of Lord Scarman's Report was the treatment of racism within the police service. He defined institutional racism as a policy that received official endorsement from the police hierarchy and argued that 'the direction and policies of the Metropolitan Police are not racist' and he 'totally and unequivocally' rejected criticisms that had been presented to him as evidence to his inquiry relating to the 'integrity and impartiality of the senior direction of the force'. In a similar vein he asserted that racially prejudiced behaviour by officers below the level of the senior direction of the force was not common, although he accepted that racial prejudice 'does manifest itself occasionally in the behaviour of a few officers on the streets' (Scarman, 1981: 64). He thus denied the existence of institutional racism and alternatively put forward reforms directed at weeding out the few 'rotten apples in the barrel'. These included pursuing current initiatives that were designed to identify evidence of racial prejudice (particularly among new recruits) through the use of scientific methods (Scarman, 1981: 78–9) and by the introduction of a specific offence into the Police Disciplinary Code whereby racially prejudiced or discriminatory behaviour by an officer would normally result in his or her dismissal from the service (Scarman, 1981: 87). This reform was introduced by the Police (Discipline) Regulations 1985.

> Why did the Scarman Report fail to make any significant improvement to the relationship between the police service and minority ethnic communities?

The persistence of problems affecting police–public relations

Although (as has been indicated above) a considerable number of reforms were made to policing in the wake of the publication of Lord Scarman's report, these did not significantly improve the relationship between police and public, especially in areas with large minority ethnic communities. In 1985 a riot occurred in Handsworth, Birmingham, in the wake of a number of confrontational situations between the police and young black people. In the same year the police shooting of Cherry Groce resulted in a major riot in Brixton, and a major disorder occurred in Haringey's Broadwater Farm Estate after the death of Cynthia Jarrett from a heart attack which followed a police raid on her house in connection with inquiries related to her son. Many of the riots that took place in the 1990s were triggered by police interventions, even in areas without significant minority ethnic groups. The Meadow Well Estate riot in Tyneside in 1991, for example, occurred following a police chase that resulted in the death of a 'joyrider', and the disorders that took place on Oxford's Blackbird Leys Estate followed an attempt by the police to clamp down on 'hotting'. A report into the 1995 Bradford disorders drew attention to an 'inadequate relationship between the police and the people of Manningham', which created a disposition to violence (Allen and Barratt, 1996: 15).

The main reasons for the persistence of friction between the police service and minority ethnic communities are briefly discussed below.

The 'black youth – crime' linkage

The link between race and crime was asserted in 1995 when the Metropolitan Commissioner, Sir Paul Condon, stated that 80 per cent of 'muggings' in high-crime areas including Harlesden, Stoke Newington and Lambeth were carried out by young black men. This statement implied that the colour of a person's skin and not socio-economic factors such as poverty and high unemployment were responsible for certain types of crime. Such negative views of black people served to weaken the trust which these communities had of the police, particularly when crimes of racial violence failed to receive the same priority given to criminal actions alleged to be committed by black persons.

Stop and search powers

'PACE stop/searches have important symbolic significance in the context of the "race" and crime debate' (Fitzgerald and Sibbitt, 1997: ix). A Home Office study based on ten police forces stated that black people were five times more likely to be stopped and searched by the police. In 1997/8, 1 million stop and searches were carried out under PACE; 11 per cent of those stopped were black and 5 per cent were Asian, both groups accounting for 166,000 stops and searches (Home Office, 1998: 13). A fuller picture based on a detailed analysis of stop, search and arrest figures from all 43 police forces in England and Wales concluded that black people were 7.5 times more likely to be stopped and searched by the police than white people aged 10 and over (Statewatch, 1999: 2). This suggested that such powers continued to be disproportionately used against black people and were rarely justified by the legal requirement of reasonable suspicion (Fitzgerald, 1999).

Arrest of black people

The Commission for Racial Equality (CRE) investigated accusations that black juveniles were more likely to be referred by the police for prosecution rather than being cautioned or diverted from the courts in some other way. It was concluded that there was a higher prosecution rate for minority ethnic young offenders that did not arise from the seriousness of offences committed or past record (CRE, 1992: 7 and 25).

In 1998 a study of arrest rates observed 'staggering' differences between police forces in England and Wales (Statewatch, 1998: 16). A subsequent report stated that black people were 4.4 times more likely to be arrested than white people, and that in 16 of the 43 police forces in England and Wales the proportion of black people aged over 10 who had been arrested stood at one in five or more. Merseyside police had one of the highest rates, with 298 black arrests per thousand (Statewatch, 1999: 2). A further report stated that in 1998/9 there were 1.3 million arrests: 7 per cent of these were African-Caribbean (who constituted around 2 per cent of the population), 4 per cent were Asians (3 per cent of the population), and 1 per cent were from other minority ethnic groups. However, the percentage of minority ethnic detainees actually charged was the same as the percentage of whites charged: 59 per cent (Howard League for Penal Reform, 2000).

Deaths in custody

A serious problem affecting minority ethnic groups was the perception that excessive force was sometimes used by the police towards those being arrested and those who were detained but that the absence of witnesses made it possible to mask the conduct of the officers concerned. This departed from the principle of minimum force (Bowling and Phillips, 2002: 132) and sometimes included the use of oppressive control techniques (Institute of Race Relations, 1991).

Deaths in custody resulted in a subsequent 'long struggle ... to get those in authority to acknowledge their lack of care, their failure of custodianship' (Institute of Race Relations, 1991: 5). The acquittal in 1995 of police officers involved in the death of Joy Gardner, who choked on her own vomit while restrained in a body-belt, led Bernie Grant MP to articulate the sense of outrage of many black people when he stated in *The Guardian* on 17 June 1995 that the tendency for the deaths of black people in custody to go unpunished suggested that 'a black life is worth nothing'.

Between 1990 and 1999, 1,350 persons died in police custody. In 1998, there were 65 deaths, a rise of 41 per cent compared to 1995. Nine per cent of those who died were black and 1.5 per cent Asian: a total of 10.5 per cent which was more than double the African-Caribbean/Asian percentage of the national population (around 5 per cent). This prompted the Police Complaints Authority to warn the police service against handcuffing the hands of detainees behind their backs while they were lying on the ground in order to prevent positional asphyxia that had led to the deaths of a number of black people in police custody during the previous three years. The report emphasised, however, that the 147 persons who had died in police custody in this period included only 12 blacks (Police Complaints Authority, 1999). This report led to some forces altering their procedures by measures that included the installation of closed-circuit television and the provision of basic first-aid training to custody officers (Police Complaints Authority, 2000).

The police treatment of racial violence

The attitude of the police service to the specific problem of racial violence has a crucial bearing on its relationship with minority ethnic communities in general since perceived indifference to racial violence by the police is viewed as indicative that those on the receiving end are officially regarded as second-class citizens: 'inactivity by the police may be the most serious failure of the state to protect all its citizens equally' (Wilson, 1983: 8).

Numerous allegations were made of alleged police indifference to black victims of racial violence following the publication of the Scarman Report (Bowling, 1998). An early report criticised the failure of the police to protect black people and accused the police themselves of attacking and harassing them (Hunte, 1965). It was subsequently alleged that police responses to these actions involved a denial that there was any racial motive to such incidents, a desire to avoid official intervention in favour of treating the incident as a civil dispute between neighbours, the provision of misleading advice or hostility towards victims, and delays in responding to requests for help from victims of these attacks (Bethnal Green and Stepney Trades

Council, 1978: 7–8; Gordon, 1983: 48; Independent Committee of Inquiry into Policing in Hackney, 1989: 235). A particular problem with the police handling of these incidents was that the alleged perpetrators were frequently interviewed before those who were the victims of such violence. Those subject to racial violence were instructed by the police to look after themselves by undertaking actions such as 'using reinforced plastic to replace glass windows which were constantly being smashed, keeping a dog and never walking home alone at night' (Metropolitan Police Community Relations Branch, 1987: 6–9).

Police Monitoring Groups that emerged during the early part of the 1980s scrutinised racial attacks and the police response to them. It was further alleged that attempts by communities to protect themselves against racial attacks have been met with an unsympathetic police response which resulted in prosecutions of the 'Bradford 12' in 1982 and the 'Newham 8' in 1983, seeking to criminalise the right of self-defence (Wilson, 1983: 8). A similar problem arose in 1994 when an Asian, Lakhbir Deol, was charged with murder when he sought to defend himself and his property against a racial attack. Accusations of police indifference to black victims of racial violence have also included the allegation of the reluctance of the police to identify crimes in which race was a factor. A report by the Crown Prosecution Service stated that in 1997/8 only 37 per cent of incidents with a racial element were flagged up as such by the police (Kirkwood: 1998).

Explanations of police attitudes towards racial violence

One key explanation for the stance adopted by the police towards racial attacks is the negative attitude which officers allegedly had of black people because of their association with crime such as mugging, drugs, prostitution (Gutzmore, 1983: 27; Tompson, 1988: 21) and disorder. The acceptance of the relationship between crime and the colour of a person's skin by the police service made it difficult for officers to view black youths as the victims of crime and also accounts for other practices that discriminate against ethnic minorities.

There are, however, alternative opinions that question police bias in dealing with racial violence. It might be argued that the random nature of many racial attacks made it hard for the police to mount effective operations designed to combat them, even when the violence was clustered in certain areas. Additionally, the frequent absence of corroborating evidence was an impediment to the successful detection of those involved in racial attacks and securing their subsequent conviction.

Reforms directed at the police handling of racial violence

In order to respond to criticisms that have been referred to above, the Association of Chief Police Officers (ACPO) published *Racial Attacks – ACPO Guiding Principles* in 1985. The following year a common reporting and monitoring system for these incidents was established, supervised by the Inspectorate. Although problems arose with the practices that were adopted (especially the degree of subjectivity involved in assessing whether an incident had been racially motivated) this initiative indicated a desire on the part of the police hierarchy to take positive action on this issue. However, in 1986 the Home Affairs Committee argued that the police had failed to make racial attacks a priority and urged that this should be done, and it was recommended that the police should receive special training in handling racial violence (Home Affairs Committee, 1986). In 1988 the Home Office required all police forces to record details of 'racial incidents'. However, this approach was criticised for relating to any incident of an inter-racial nature rather than only to violence perpetrated by white persons on members of ethnic minorities (Gordon, 1996: 21).

Individual police forces pursued additional initiatives which included the establishment of specialist race attack squads in some North London police stations, the setting up of victim 'hot lines' and attempts to improve the relationship between police and public by transforming community contact work into mainstream policing. This approach involved the abandonment of discrete community contact departments and the enhanced use of area constables in multi-ethnic, urban areas. Additionally the emphasis of the Home Office on a multi-agency response to racial violence and harassment (which was formalised with the establishment of the Inter-Departmental Government Working Party in 1987) resulted in police involvement in a range of local-level initiatives designed to tackle these problems. One difficulty with such approaches, however, is that they may result in individual agencies absolving themselves of their own responsibilities (Gordon, 1983: 174–5).

In 1993 the newly installed Metropolitan Commissioner of Police indicated that his force had to be 'totally intolerant' of racially motivated attacks and of those who used racial hatred for political ends (Condon, 1993). Problems including the low clear-up rate for incidents of this nature prompted a Parliamentary committee to assert that while progress had been made by the police service in dealing with this type of crime, it was necessary for the Home Office to re-emphasise to all chief constables that tackling racial incidents should be regarded as a priority task (Home Affairs Committee, 1994: 11). Subsequent initiatives included the involvement of CRE officers with the Police Staff College at Bramshill in 1995 to develop and deliver a two-and-a-half day training course for police officers on the policing of racial incidents, and cooperation between the CRE and ACPO in 1996 to develop management standards for police forces around the country concerning responses to racial harassment.

Police – minority ethnic group relationships post Scarman: conclusion

The above discussion has indicated that although reforms to police practices were introduced following the Scarman Report, they failed to significantly improve the relationship between the police service and minority ethnic communities. In 1995 the Inspectorate conducted an equal opportunity inspection of 13 police forces and subsequently accepted aid from the CRE for this area of work. A key problem with this approach is the absence of positive discrimination legislation making it impossible to change the composition of police forces by methods that include the use of employment quotas. Police forces could have pursued a more active role to eliminate racism by making greater usage of the sanction in section 101 of the 1984 Police and Criminal Evidence Act whereby Police Disciplinary Regulations were amended to provide for a specific disciplinary offence of racially discriminatory behaviour, one penalty for which was dismissal from the police service. This sanction could have been directed at police behaviour both towards their colleagues as well as towards members of the public. However, police officers were rarely punished for this behaviour.

The progress of reform was fully investigated by the Inspectorate in 1997. Its report highlighted a number of shortcomings. Concerns were particularly expressed in connection with the police handling of racial violence, the report arguing that many officers remained unaware of the definition of a racial incident initially laid down by ACPO in 1985, and that there were widely different interpretations of what it meant among those who believed that they did know (HMIC, 1997: 30). It was argued that there was continuing evidence of 'inappropriate language and behaviour by police officers', which was unchecked by sergeants and inspectors (HMIC, 1997: 9), and that the links constructed between the police and minority ethnic communities were limited in scope and relied heavily on 'formal links with a narrow (and possibly unrepresentative) section of the minority community' (HMIC, 1997: 26). It was thus recommended that all forces should undertake a community and race relations audit, that sensitivity to community and race relations should be positively recognised in the recruitment, promotion, appraisal, the posting and deployment of staff, and that a community and race relations dimension should be explicitly included in all relevant training (HMIC, 1997: 59).

These criticisms prompted ACPO to establish a task force to examine issues surrounding police/race relations in 1998, and the Metropolitan Police to set up a Racial and Violent Crimes Task Force in the same year whose work was aided by the formation of Community Safety Units at borough level. Nonetheless, a follow-up report by the Inspectorate in 1999 revealed that only limited progress had been made in implementing the recommendations made in its earlier report. It was asserted that 'there has been a general improvement but the overall picture is patchy. There is a lack of consistency and the pockets of good work identified tend to be the product of a committed few rather than representing corporate endeavour' (HMIC, 1999: 3). Only eleven forces had conducted any form of community and race relations audit (HMIC, 1999: 40) and only 16 forces reported that they had a community and race relations strategy (or equivalent) in place, with a further ten forces in the developmental stage (HMIC, 1999: 37). The officer who led the inspection commented that 'we were disappointed to find that progress has been less than satisfactory, with many of the original recommendations largely ignored and few forces placing the issue high on their agenda' (Crompton: 1999).

> Why has the use of stop and search powers by the police been an emotive issue that has adversely affected the relationship between the police service and minority ethnic communities?

The response of other agencies in the criminal justice system to racism before 1999

In addition to the police service, accusations of racism were directed against other agencies that operate in the criminal justice process. Some examples of this problem are discussed below as a background to criticisms voiced in the Macpherson Report (1999).

The Crown Prosecution Service

Allegations of racism were directed against the CPS. However, progress in improving the image of this organisation was hampered by allegations that it discriminated against its own minority ethnic employees. On 5 May 1996 *The Observer* stated that only 2.8 per cent of CPS staff were African-Caribbean yet the rate at which they were sacked was about ten times this figure. In total, 25 per cent of those who were dismissed by the CPS for inefficiency were black, and one-sixth of those on extended probation were African-Caribbean. Perceptions of unjust treatment resulted in the CRE meeting the Director of Public Prosecutions, Barbara Mills, in July 1995 to urge comprehensive ethnic monitoring of CPS decisions. Limited advances were also made in equal opportunity training for CPS managers and staff during 1995. On 9 December 1998, however, the head of the CPS was reported in *The Guardian* as stating that minority ethnic staff faced a promotion 'glass ceiling' with few black or Asian lawyers holding senior positions within the organisation.

The organisation's handling of racial violence posed a particular problem. Perceptions that the CPS had a poor record in dealing with racist violence led the House of Commons Home Affairs Committee in 1989 to recommend the introduction of a comprehensive scheme of monitoring racial incident cases; this would include the proportion of cases discontinued (or in which charges were downgraded) by the CPS and the reasons for these actions. However, this advice was not immediately acted upon. In 1992 the Code for Crown Prosecutors was amended so that a clear racial motive would be regarded as an aggravating feature when assessing whether a prosecution was required in the public interest. The following year the CPS began monitoring racial incident cases, and in 1995 set up the Racial Incident Monitoring Scheme to track racial crime. One benefit of this approach was that the CPS was more able to discern a racial motivation to a crime even if the police had failed to identify this as an element.

The courts and racism

There were accusations of inappropriate conduct by members of the judiciary towards minority ethnic defendants. Between 1997 and 1999, the Lord Chancellor disciplined five judges for making offensive racial comments and the launch of the Equal Treatment Bench Book in 1999 was aimed to increase the sensitivity of the judiciary to race. There are two important dimensions to allegations of racism within the judiciary – sentencing policy and the attitude that was taken towards racial violence. These are discussed more fully below.

Sentencing policy

A number of accusations of racial bias were made in connection with actions undertaken by the courts:

- cautioning was used less frequently for black people than for whites (Statewatch, 1999: 2–4);
- decisions to remand prisoners were biased against ethnic minority groups, so that on 30 June 1996, 24 per cent of black male prisoners were held on remand compared with 21 per cent of white males (Shaw, 1997: 20);
- in 1997 there were 11,200 people from minority ethnic groups in Prison Service establishments. Minority ethnic groups accounted for 18 per cent of the male and 25 per cent of the female prison populations (Home Office, 1998: 31);
- black people served longer prison sentences on average than whites: 61 per cent of black prisoners served sentences of more than four years compared with 47 per cent of white prisoners (Statewatch, 1999: 4).

The inference of bias in the sentencing policies of the courts may, however, be challenged. A study of crown courts in the West Midlands suggested that the main explanations for the difference between the proportion of black males in the general population and their proportion in the prison system were the greater number of black offenders who appeared for sentencing at these courts, and the nature and circumstances of the crimes with which they were charged.

One issue (which could be viewed as indirect discrimination) was the tendency of black offenders to plead not guilty and thus not be entitled to receive the discount on sentence which a guilty plea would attract. Additionally, those refusing to plead guilty were less likely to secure the benefit of a Social Inquiry Report formerly prepared by social workers (Hood, 1992: 203–5) or a pre-sentence report compiled by probation officers or YOTs. The manner in which reports of this nature were prepared for the courts might give rise to perceptions of biased treatment by the judiciary (Kirk, 1996).

Racial violence

The following examples suggested that members of minority ethnic groups were sometimes treated unfairly by the courts when they were both defendants and victims of crime.

- In 1993, two youths who subjected an Asian teenager to an attack that left him partly blinded in one eye were jailed for only three and a half years. According to *The Independent* on 22 September 1993, the trial judge admitted that 'we are going to kill you, you smelly Paki' constituted racial undertones but did not amount to an 'aggravating feature'.

- In 1994 Richard Edmonds, a leading member of the British National Party, received a derisory three-month prison sentence for his part in an attack on a black man which left him scarred for life.

- In 1998 a judge imposed a sentence of two years probation and 100 hours community service on two white youths who launched an unprovoked attack on a black teenager, breaking his nose and calling him a 'stinking nigger'. The judge expressed his view that there was 'no deep-seated racist attitude or hatred' on the part of the defendants.

However, the attitude of the courts in dealing with cases related to racial violence was not totally biased. There were examples of those found guilty of racial attacks being given severe sentences. In 1993, for example, two men were jailed for life for the racist killing of as Asian minicab driver, Fiaz Mirza. The judge recommended that one of these men should serve a minimum sentence of 22 years in prison. A report by the Crown Prosecution Service indicated that in 1997/8, 1,506 defendants in England and Wales were charged with an offence that constituted a racial incident, an increase of 161 on the previous year. Eighty-three per cent of those prosecuted were convicted. However, it was observed that sentencers remained reluctant to impose additional sentences on those convicted of crimes when evidence of racial motivation was brought to the court's attention (Kirkwood, 1998).

Additionally, in 1994 Lord Chief Justice Taylor (in *R. v. Ribbans, Duggan and Ridley*) ruled that although the law did not have any specific offence of racial violence, a proven racial motive in any crime of violence could lead the judge to exercise discretion and give an increased sentence. The 1998 Crime and Disorder Act introduced a range of provisions to deal with racially aggravated offences of assault, criminal damage, harassment and public order offences. It was perceived that the stiffer sentences provided for racially motivated crime under the 1998 Crime and Disorder Act would have a significant effect on how offenders are prosecuted and sentenced. Even if a person is not charged with an offence under this legislation, the court is required to impose an increased penalty if it is satisfied that race was an aggravating factor in the crime.

The Prison Service

The over-representation of black people in prison meant that the nature of the prison environment was of particular importance. Accusations of racial harassment, based on a perception that black prisoners posed particular problems of control, led to all prisons being required to appoint race relations liaison officers and a race relations management team. In 1995 the CRE and

Prison Service published a report on the *Management of Race Relations in Prison Establishments*. This resulted in a revised draft of the Prison Service's *Race Relations Manual* and racial abuse became a specific disciplinary offence for prison staff. It has, however, been argued that racism has been largely unchallenged within the prison environment: 'you would be hard pressed to find a report from a Board of Visitors which does not remark on the absence of racial tension. Similarly, in nearly twenty years, the Prisons Inspectorate has had little or nothing to say on race issues' (*Prison Report*, 1998: 3).

One indicator of racism within prisons was the number of racial incidents. In 1991 there were 106 of these, rising to 141 in 1993. Between 1992 and 1998, seven prisoners died while being restrained. Six of these were black and the seventh was of mixed race. The then Director General of the Prison Service, Richard Tilt, stated in 1998 that this situation could be attributed to physiological differences.

The Stephen Lawrence murder: a catalyst for change

The murder of the black teenager Stephen Lawrence in 1993 eventually provided the impetus to change the way in which the criminal justice system responded to ethnic minorities in general and to racially motivated violence in particular. This agenda for change was provided in a report written by Sir William Macpherson (Macpherson, 1999). The background to this report, its main recommendations and their implementation are discussed in this section.

Racist murders in the 1990s

The key issue underpinning the manner in which the investigation into the racist murder of Stephen Lawrence was the police handling of crime when members of minority groups were the victims. On 24 February 1999, *The Guardian* published a list of 25 black and Asian people (in addition to Stephen Lawrence who is discussed in more detail below) who had been murdered in racially motivated attacks since 1991. The police response to this extreme form of racial violence, however, seemed inappropriate. It was argued that murderers of black people were less likely to be caught than those of white or other ethnic groups: in 1996/7 and 1997/8 'there was a much higher proportion (40 per cent) of homicides with black victims where there was no suspect than for white (10 per cent) or Asian (13 per cent) victims' (Home Office, 1998: 27).

A particular criticism levelled against the police service in connection with serious cases of this kind was that officers were often disinclined to view any racial motive in murders involving members of ethnic minority communities. In one case (involving the death of Michael Menson in 1997), the Metropolitan Police failed for 18 months to perceive the incident as murder at all, alternatively viewing the attack as a self-inflicted injury. Similarly, in the case of 'Ricky' Reel, in 1997 the Metropolitan Police insisted that his death had been a tragic accident and vetoed the PCA's decision that the Surrey Police (who were investigating a complaint regarding the Metropolitan Police Service's handling of the incident) should also investigate the death itself. In November 1999 an inquest jury formally rejected the Metropolitan Police's argument that his death had been an accident by recording an open verdict.

However, the murder of Stephen Lawrence on 22 April 1993 in South London proved to be a major catalyst that emphasised the need for change in the way in which the criminal justice system, and especially the Metropolitan Police, responded to racially motivated violence. Criticisms of the manner in which the subsequent investigation was handled included officers at the scene failing to assess any racial factor in the murder and the delay in arresting suspects. The first arrests occurred on 7 May, although important information regarding the identity of the murderers had been received by the investigating team soon after the murder had taken place. Two persons were subsequently charged with murder but the CPS dropped the charges on 29 July on the grounds of insufficient evidence. In 1994 the CPS again declined to prosecute on the grounds of insufficient evidence. The Lawrence family subsequently initiated a private prosecution against three youths allegedly involved in the attack that broke down in 1996 when the trial judge ruled that the identification of two of the defendants by a person who had been attacked with Lawrence was 'contradictory' and 'contaminated'. In 1997 an inquest jury returned a unanimous verdict that 'Stephen Lawrence was unlawfully killed in a completely unprovoked racist attack by five white youths'.

In March 1997, the Police Complaints Authority initiated an investigation into the manner in which the Metropolitan Police Service had handled the investigation. The full report was published in February 1998, and concluded that there was no evidence to support the allegation of racist conduct by any Metropolitan Police officer who had been involved in the investigation of the murder of Stephen Lawrence. However, the remit of this investigation (which arose out of a complaint by the Lawrence family into the manner in which their son's murder had been handled) was confined to complaints made in relation to the conduct of individual officers, and in July 1997 the Labour government's newly appointed Home Secretary, Jack Straw, established a far more wide-ranging inquiry which was empowered to examine allegations of racism within the Metropolitan Police Service. It was headed by a retired High Court Judge, Sir William Macpherson, whose work was aided by three advisors, Tom Cook, the Rt Revd John Sentamu and Dr Richard Stone.

> 'The botched investigation by the Metropolitan Police Service into the murder of Stephen Lawrence was indicative of the inadequate manner in which racially motivated violence was responded to by the police service.' To what extent do you agree with this statement and how do you account for this situation?

The Macpherson Report

In the hearings that were held in connection with this investigation, Ian Johnston, the Assistant Commissioner of the Metropolitan Police apologised to the Lawrence family for their shortcomings regarding the investigation into the murder of their son. In 1999, Macpherson's report was fiercely critical of the police handling of this matter (Macpherson, 1999). He examined three specific allegations in connection with it – that the Metropolitan Police were

- incompetent;
- racist;
- corrupt.

Macpherson judged that the Metropolitan Police Service was guilty of the first two accusations, enabling it to draw cold comfort from the fact that he did not endorse the charge of corruption. Sir William stated that the investigation had been fundamentally flawed and 'marred by a combination of professional incompetence, institutional racism, and a failure of leadership by senior officers' (Macpherson, 1999: 317). Sir William believed that the police were guilty of gross negligence in their investigation of Stephen's murder, an accusation that hinged on the failure of the police to make early arrests which was stated to be 'the most fundamental fault in the investigation of this murder' (Macpherson, 1999: 95).

Institutional racism

The concept of institutional racism was developed in the struggles of black Americans for civil rights. Despite court-room victories and the enactment of legislation such as the 1965 Civil Rights Act and 1965 Voting Act, the condition of most black Americans failed to change for the better. This gave rise to the term 'institutional racism' which suggested that racism should be analysed not only from the perspective of an individual act of prejudice but at the level of a racist power structure within society. It was argued that institutional racism was akin to a system of internal colonialism in which black people stood as colonial subjects in relation to white society (Carmichael and Hamilton, 1967). This term was subsequently defined to embrace established laws, customs and practices that systematically reflected and produced racial inequalities and the interactions of various spheres of social life to maintain an overall pattern of opression (Blauner, 1972).

It has been argued above that Lord Scarman's report in 1981 endorsed the 'bad apple' explanation of racism (Crowther, 2000: 98) which attributed this problem to personal attitudes which were held by a minority of officers who knowingly and intentionally discriminated against persons from minority ethnic groups. Macpherson, however, disagreed with this, effectively arguing that racism existed throughout the Metropolitan Police and that the problem was organisational rather than one that affected a small number of individuals. This directed attention towards the existence of institutional racism that had been previously defined as 'racial prejudice and discrimination generated by the way institutions function, intentionally or otherwise, rather than by the individual personalities of their members' (Lee, 1986). Macpherson's definition of 'institutional racism' in his report pointed to

> the collective failure of an organisation to provide an appropriate and professional service to people because of their colour, culture or ethnic origin. It can be seen or detected in processes, attitudes and behaviour which amount to discrimination through unwitting prejudice, ignorance, thoughtlessness and racist stereotyping which disadvantage minority ethnic people. (Macpherson, 1999: 28)

Although this term has been criticised for being 'almost incoherent' (Tonry, 2004: 76), for sidestepping questions of causality and for asserting racism to be the sole or primary cause of black disadvantage (thus ignoring other processes relating to class and gender), it is useful as it directed attention to how 'racist discourses can be embodied within the structures and organisations of society' (Singh, 2000: 29 and 38) and provided explanations for practices which derive from either unwitting or uncritical racism (Smith, 1989: 101). Further, although Macpherson did not specifically address police culture (Rowe, 2004: 43), the impact of his report directed considerable attention to this issue.

Reforms proposed by the Macpherson Report

Macpherson's report suggested a number of reforms (70 in total) which were designed to ensure that the criminal justice system (and especially the police service to which 60 of the recommendations applied in whole or in part) operated in a manner which was perceived to be fairer to minority ethnic communities by addressing racism and enhancing the effectiveness of measures to combat racial violence. The main recommendations and the significance of these proposals are discussed below.

- *A drive to rebuild the confidence of the ethnic minority communities in policing.* The proposal that a Ministerial Priority 'to increase trust and confidence in policing amongst minority ethnic communities' (Macpherson, 1999: 327) should be established for all police forces (using powers given to the Home Secretary in the 1994 Police and Magistrates' Courts Act) was Macpherson's first recommendation. This emphasised the government's role in bringing about improved relationships between the police service and minority ethnic communities, and was designed to counter bureaucratic inertia which may arise when large organisations are left to their own devices to implement far-reaching reform programmes. It was proposed that the performance indicators which could be used to monitor the implementation of this priority included the nature, extent and achievement of racism awareness training, the levels of recruitment, retention and progression of minority ethnic recruits (an issue which is discussed more fully below), levels of complaint of racist behaviour by officers and their outcomes, the existence and application of strategies for the recording, investigation and prosecution of racist incidents, measures to encourage incidents of this kind to be reported and the extent of multi-agency cooperation and information exchange.

- *Definition of racist incidents.* Macpherson observed that a key shortcoming of the Metropolitan Police Service's investigation into Stephen Lawrence's murder was the failure of the first investigating team 'to recognise and accept racism and race relations as central feature of their investigation ... a substantial number of officers of junior rank would not accept that the murder of Stephen Lawrence was simply and solely "racially motivated"' (Macpherson, 1999: 23). Macpherson believed that the then current definition of racial incident (which was defined as 'any incident in which it appears to the reporting or investigating officer that the complaint involves an element of racial motivation made by any person') was potentially confusing and should be made crisper. Recommendation 12 of his report thus proposed that a racist incident should be defined as 'any incident which is perceived to be racist by the victim or any other person', and the term should be understood to include both crimes and non-crimes in policing terms. Both should be recorded and investigated with equal commitment. This recommendation was designed to make the police service victim-orientated.

- *The recruitment of more black and Asian police officers.* In 1998 the minority ethnic population comprised 5.6 per cent of the total population. However, there were only 2,483 black or Asian police officers in all English and Welsh police forces (which constituted below 2 per cent of the total personnel of 124,798) (Home Office, 1998: 37). This was a particular problem in London where minority ethnic communities comprised around one-quarter of the population but the Metropolitan Police Service contained only 3.4 per cent of its 26,411 officers from these communities (although minority ethnic groups were more adequately represented in the Special Constabulary and the civilian support staff) (HMIC, 2000: 8). Research also revealed that rates for resignation and dismissal from the police service were higher for minority ethnic officers than for white officers (Bland et al., 1999) and that in March 1999 only 14 per cent of minority ethnic officers had been promoted compared to 23 per cent of white officers (Bowling and Phillips, 2002: 218). As has been noted above, Macpherson thus proposed that the Home Secretary and Police Authorities' policing plans should include targets for recruitment, progression and retention of minority ethnic staff (Macpherson, 1999: 334).

- *Stop and search powers.* It has been observed above that stop and search is a major cause of friction between the police service and minority ethnic communities. Like Lord Scarman, Macpherson accepted the rationale for these powers in the prevention and detection of crime but wished to improve the level of protection of those who were subjected to them. He thus proposed that records should be kept by police officers of all non-statutory (or voluntary) 'stops' in addition to 'stops and searches' made under any legislation. Only stops and searches conducted under the 1984 Police and Criminal Evidence Act were subject to safeguards, so that other legislation (such as section 60 of the 1994 Criminal Justice and Public Order Act) that authorised the use of powers of this nature was exempt from scrutiny (Rowe, 2004: 95–8). This reform was designed to make the use by officers of their discretionary powers capable of being more effectively monitored by police supervisors.

- *Racial awareness training.* Although Lord Scarman had proposed changes to police training programmes which were designed to prepare officers for policing a multiracial society, these courses had been progressively scaled down in most forces so that they were primarily directed at officers who had dealings with minority organisations and communities and would not be expected to exert any significant impact on the overall culture of the police service. Macpherson pointed out that 'not a single officer questioned before us in 1998 had received any training of significance in racism awareness and race relations throughout the course of his career', and he proposed that there should be an immediate review and revision of racism awareness training within police forces and that all officers, including detectives and civilian staff, should be trained in racism awareness and valuing cultural diversity. It was also proposed that the police service should consider promoting joint training with other organisations and professions (Macpherson, 1999: 30).

- *To consider whether the use of racist language and behaviour and the possession of offensive weapons in a private place should become a criminal offence.* This recommendation was prompted by evidence obtained from a police surveillance video of those suspected of Stephen Lawrence's murder which showed them acting in a violent manner and using racist language. It would extend the scope of the criminal law into the home and to other venues such as clubs and meeting places. This course of action, however, raised problems as it would inevitably lead to accusations of Britain having a 'thought police'.

- *Freedom of information legislation should extend to most areas of policing.* Disclosure would be withheld subject only to the test of 'substantial harm'. This proposal was designed to make allegations of incompetence and prejudice easier to prove in the future, and went further than the recommendation in the 1998 White Paper on this subject which included documents relating to the administrative functions of the police while excluding material related to their investigation and prosecution responsibilities.

- *Reform of the 1976 Race Relations Act.* This reform was designed to combat institutional racism. It was designed to bring the entire public sector within the scope of the legislation. It would enable the CRE to launch investigations into individual police forces, thus enhancing their degree of accountability to outside agencies.

- *To consider the abolition of double jeopardy.* Double jeopardy ensures that defendants are not subject to repeated trials and encourages the police and prosecutors to be diligent at the outset of a case. This reform was designed to enable the Court of Appeal to permit a person to be retried, having initially been acquitted, if fresh and viable evidence subsequently became available.

- *The introduction of a tougher police disciplinary regime.* It was proposed that racist words or actions should lead to disciplinary proceedings which would normally result in an officer's dismissal from the service. Scarman had put forward a similar proposal in 1981 but although section 101 of the 1984 Police and Criminal Evidence Act Act required Police Discipline Regulations to be amended to make racially discriminatory behaviour a specific disciplinary offence, resistance from the police service prevented it from being acted upon. It was also proposed that disciplinary action should be available for at least five years after an officer had retired. This latter suggestion was especially influenced by the fact that four senior officers whose conduct with regard to the Lawrence investigation had been criticised by the PCA had retired from the police service and were thus unable to face neglect of duty charges. Only one officer subsequently faced a disciplinary hearing over the investigation and in July 1999, following a tribunal ruling that he had been guilty of two counts of neglect of duty, received the lightest sentence possible (a caution for each of the two counts).

Evaluate the significance of policies put forward in the Macpherson Report that were designed to improve the relationship between the police service and minority ethnic communities.

Responses to the Macpherson Report

The damning nature of the criticisms made of the criminal justice system in general and of the police service in particular regarding its need to improve its relationships with minority ethnic groups ensured that the recommendations made by Sir William Macpherson would be acted upon. This section discusses the nature of the reforms that were introduced by key agencies within the criminal justice system after 1999.

The courts

Crown courts

One important development that was concerned with attempts to alter the culture and working practices of the judiciary took place in 1999 when an Equal Treatment Bench Book was launched by the Lord Chancellor and the Lord Chief Justice. This aimed to increase the sensitivity of judges to issues of race and their awareness of Britain's multicultural society. Every judge in England and Wales was to be issued with this guide which advised them to avoid gaffes such as referring to black people as 'coloured', stereotyping particular communities as 'crime-prone' and asking followers of minority religions for their 'christian' names. They were told never to use terms which included 'Paki', 'negro', 'ethnics' or 'half-caste'. The guide provided judges with a brief history of the main ethnic minorities in Britain including their religions, customs, festivals, special apparel and dietary rules (Equal Treatment Advisory Committee of the Judicial Studies Board, 1999). A similar publication was latterly prepared for Scottish judges by an Equal Treatment Working Party of the Judicial Studies Committee. This also pointed out that the words 'Coloured', 'Ethnics', 'Paki', 'Negro', 'Negroid', 'Oriental', 'Half-caste' and 'Tink' 'were unacceptable to use in referring to people' as they are 'considered to be offensive' (Equal Treatment Working Party of the Judicial Studies Committee for Scotland, 2002: chapter 2, p. 9).

Magistrates' courts

Following the Macpherson Report, the Joint Liaison Group (which is composed of members of organisations which are represented in the Magistrates' Courts Service) set up the Magistrates' Courts Service Race Issues Group whose aim was to assist the response of the Magistrates' Courts Service to the report. This Group sought to develop a strategy to tackle institutional racism covering both the formal and informal levels of organisational culture. This comprised an examination of existing policies, procedures, practices, behaviour and outcomes to identify and acknowledge the existence of this problem, following which an action plan to eradicate institutional racism throughout the organisation would be developed and implemented (Magistrates' Courts Service Race Issues Group, 2000: 7). The importance of inter-agency liaison at national, regional and local level was also stressed to improve public confidence in the fairness of the criminal justice system, in particular with regard to issues which included stop and/or search, arrest, charge/summons, prosecution, bail, legal aid, discontinuance, conviction and sentence (Magistrates' Courts Service Race Issues Group, 2000: 8). It was particularly emphasised that since Black and Asian people represented a far higher proportion of the prison population than their population in Britain, magistrates' courts should examine court processes to ensure that defendants from minority ethnic groups received fair treatment (Magistrates' Courts Service Race Issues Group, 2000: 10).

It was also proposed to counter criticisms that black and Asian people had low rates of satisfaction with the response from the criminal justice agencies when dealing with racially motivated crimes through measures which included providing victims and witnesses from minority ethnic groups with adequate information in a format which was understandable and acceptable. One proposed way to achieve this was that magistrates' courts committees should consult with local minority ethnic communities to identify their needs and draw up local policies to meet them (Magistrates' Courts Service Race Issues Group, 2000: 11). The importance of a comprehensive complaints procedure in each magistrates' courts committee was emphasised to deal with race equality issues both internally and externally (Magistrates' Courts Service Race Issues Group, 2000: 13).

Organisational culture was depicted as a key area in connection with tackling institutional racism. The need to 'eliminate institutional barriers both formal and informal to employment and to discourage a club mentality or initiation process' was emphasised. It was argued that the recruitment of people from minority ethnic backgrounds would not in itself change the organisational culture and nor could these new recruits 'be expected to thrive in a hostile or excluding culture'. Reforms which were proposed included the development of mentoring schemes, the facilitation of support structures for magistrates and staff from minority ethnic groups, the development of positive action training for staff and the adoption of a code of conduct covering aspects of behaviour and standards which were expected (Magistrates' Courts Service Race Issues Group, 2000: 14).

The Magistrates' New Training Initiative introduced several competences for magistrates that covered their knowledge and treatment of defendants and other court users from diverse backgrounds and disadvantaged groups. It was proposed to further this philosophy by encouraging magistrates' courts committees to adopt a code of conduct providing a clear indication of acceptable and unacceptable behaviour for all who took part in the work of the courts which would provide a framework within which all training would then take place. It was also suggested that national standards of performance for the Magistrates' New Training Initiative should be implemented to enable magistrates to be adequately appraised on those competences which related to equal treatment and diversity issues (Magistrates' Courts Service Race Issues Group, 2000: 16). It was noted that current training provision in race and diversity issues for staff employed in magistrates' courts tended to be 'fragmented and lacking in consistency', and that it was not always clear what was the objective of training in this area, with outcomes seldom being identified or measured. To remedy this, it was suggested that a national review of training should be commissioned which would identify all current race equality training for staff employed in the Magistrates' Courts Service. Other recommendations included that all trainers and facilitators should possess basic skills/awareness in order to be able to consider/incorporate race equality issues in all training programmes, and that compulsory training in race and equality issues should be provided for all staff (Magistrates' Courts Service Race Issues Group, 2000: 17).

The police service

This section examines the responses made to this report by the police service and the Labour government.

The police service's response

Following the publication of the Macpherson Report, a package of measures entitled *Protect and Respect* was announced by the Metropolitan Police Service. These included the following:

- *Random testing of officers to assess racist attitudes.* This reform involved the use of black undercover officers to ensure that officers behaved in a courteous and correct fashion regardless of the colour of a complainant or witness.
- *The fast-tracking of racially motivated crimes through the forensic system.* This recommendation was designed to improve the investigation of these crimes and heighten the possibility of securing the convictions of those responsible for them.
- *Improved reporting rates of racially motivated crime.* An important aspect of the attempt to improve the level of reporting of these incidents was for officers to be more aware of what constituted such an incident.

In March 1999, the Metropolitan Police Service published a report, *A Police Service for All the People*, that put forward a 15-point plan designed to tackle institutional racism. One objective was to have a fifth of senior posts held by minority ethnic officers that would be achieved by introducing a special career development scheme for officers of the rank of inspector and above. In 1999, only four of the 873 minority ethnic officers in this force were of superintendent rank. The issue of recruitment was addressed through suggestions that fellowships could be made available to minority ethnic students in their final year of study to encourage them to join the police service following graduation, and the retention of these officers was to be tackled by establishing network groups of 30–35 ethnic minority officers across London, each with career development officers attached to them. Mentoring schemes would also be introduced to aid ethnic minority officers. Other developments which were pursued nationwide included the joint development by Centrex (the Central Police Training and Development Authority) and the National Black Police Association of a leadership course to help retain minority ethnic officers and boost their promotion prospects (Rowe, 2004: 32).

The government's response

In March 1999 the then Home Secretary, Jack Straw, announced the government's response to the proposals of the Macpherson Report which were contained in an 'action plan'. This was presented to the House of Commons on 23 March 1999 and included the issues that are discussed below.

Recruitment, retention and promotion

Jack Straw had formerly endorsed proposals for a national target of 7 per cent for minority ethnic officers, which would be exceeded in inner-city areas. In the wake of the Macpherson inquiry, he formally committed himself to imposing targets governing recruitment, promotion and retention of black and Asian officers at a speech delivered to the Black Police Association in October 1998. In March 1999 the Home Office published *The Home Secretary's Employment Targets*, which related to the recruitment, retention and progression of minority ethnic officers and staff. This required the police service to incrementally increase the proportion of staff from minority ethnic communities from the present 2 per cent to 7 per cent by 2009, with each force being set individual targets to attain by that date which would reflect the proportion of persons from minority ethnic backgrounds living in the force area. Thus the Metropolitan Police Service would be required to achieve a target figure of 25 per cent by 2009. This would in total amount to in excess of 8,000 officers from minority ethnic communities over the next ten years in order to kick-start 'the police service attaining a proper ethnic balance' (Straw: 1999a). Targets for retention and progression were set at parity with white officers, although progression targets were staged over time and rank.

Attention was also paid to screening applicants, in particular with regard to racist views and attitudes. Prior to 2002 no national scheme existed for the recruitment and selection of constables by individual police forces, although general guidance was provided by the Home Office. In 2002, the Home Office commissioned Centrex to develop a method of selection, the National Recruitment Standards Assessment Centre (or 'assessment centre', also known as SEARCH (Selection Entrance Assessment for Recruiting Constables Holistically)) based on job-related exercises for the use of all police forces. The centre (which was designed in line with British Psychological Society Guidance) uses a combination of interviews, tests and role-plays to assess seven competencies. These are: teamwork; personal responsibility; community and customer focus; effective communication; problem-solving; resilience; and respect for diversity. In each SEARCH process the candidate is required to undergo four role-playing exercises, two written exercises, two psychometric ability tests and one structured interview (Calvert-Smith, 2005: 51). A candidate's attitude towards race and diversity is tested across all exercises in the new assessment centre, including the interview. One of these competencies was 'respect for race and diversity' (Calvert-Smith, 2004: 21). Any candidate scoring below 50 per cent on this competence was rejected. Additionally, assessors were trained to be alert for any inappropriate speech or behaviour by candidates 'for example, swearing, disrespect, aggression or the expression of racist, sexist or homophobic sentiments, whether within the exercises or without them'. If behaviour of this nature arose, it was noted and the quality assurors then decided if it warranted a reduction in the marks awarded for the respect for diversity competence (Calvert-Smith, 2005: 52).

'It is important that the composition of the police service should reflect that of the society it polices.' To what extent do you agree with this statement, and why has it proved difficult to realise this objective?

Definition of racist incidents

Macpherson's definition of a racist incident (Macpherson, 1999: 328) was accepted by the government, although this would only be used in the initial reporting of an incident and would not determine the issue of racial motivation when someone was charged and tried.

Race relations legislation

The government introduced legislation in 1999 to bring the police service within the scope of the Race Relations Act. Initially it was proposed to make direct racism alone challengeable in the courts which is notoriously hard to substantiate. However, in February 2000 the Home Secretary amended his Bill to include indirect discrimination. The 2000 Race Relations (Amendment) Act placed a duty on the entire public sector (including the police, prisons and immigration services) to promote race equality. In order to help public authorities achieve this goal, the Home Secretary was empowered to impose specific duties upon them. The 2000 legislation further enabled chief constables to be found liable for the discriminatory acts of one officer against another – a situation that the Court of Appeal ruled (in the case of *Chief Constable of Bedfordshire* v. *Liversidge* [2002]) was not possible under the 1976 legislation.

Freedom of information legislation

The Home Secretary's 2000 Freedom of Information Act did not include many of Macpherson's recommendations. Information obtained during police investigations was exempt from release, subject to the force's discretion. Other policing agencies consisting of MI5, MI6 and GCHQ (whose work is discussed in the concluding chapter) were exempt from the provisions of this Act. The measure also contained no powers whereby the Information Commissioner could order the disclosure of information in the exempt categories (including criminal investigations) on public interest grounds.

Racism awareness training

In 1994 the Police Training Council had put forward proposals for the delivery of community and race relations training. These had not been fully or effectively implemented by all forces. It was thus proposed by the government that all forces should positively respond to the 1994 proposals. In October 1999 new training courses of this nature were introduced by the Metropolitan Police, and the Home Office set a target date of December 2002 by which time all 'front-line' staff were expected to have received training in race and diversity issues.

Police discipline

In April 1999 the Police Disciplinary Code was replaced by a Code of Conduct. This set out standards of behaviour that were expected from officers and embraced the requirement of politeness and tolerance that embraced the need to avoid 'unreasonable discrimination' (a term which was not, however, defined in the Code). The absence of a specific offence of racially discriminatory behaviour (which had existed before 1999) meant that statistics dealing with racial discrimination would not be automatically generated. Although each case is dealt with on its merits, it was anticipated that racist behaviour by officers would normally result in their dismissal. Under the new procedure, officers lost their right of silence in connection with disciplinary hearings, and the standard of proof was lowered to the civil law test of the balance of probabilities. The proposal that disciplinary action should be available for five years after an officer retired was to be considered by the Home Secretary, and he also agreed to consider legislation that would enable forfeiture of police pensions for serious disciplinary offences. ACPO also agreed that any officer who became a member of the BNP would be subject to a misconduct investigation (Calvert-Smith, 2004: 40).

Stops and stop and search

The Home Secretary agreed to consider whether a written record with reasons for all stops should be given to those searched. It was subsequently agreed that to ensure this reform did not place an unacceptable burden on police officers, the introduction of the recording of 'stops' would be phased in and the results monitored (Home Office, 2002: 22).

An independent complaints system

The government was sympathetic to an independent system for investigating complaints against the police, and a feasibility study was conducted into the costs of such a system. Proposals were subsequently put forward by the Home Secretary to introduce a stronger independent element into the system of investigating complaints against the police (Home Office, 2000b), and a subsequent White Paper promised legislation to replace the Police Complaints Authority with an Independent Police Complaints Commission (IPCC) that would investigate the serious complaints independently (Home Office, 2001: 24). As has been discussed in Chapter 4, this reform was introduced in the 2002 Police Reform Act. Although a formal complaint by one officer against a fellow officer is normally referred to the force's grievance procedure, the IPCC has a broader role than that of the PCA in examining internal disciplinary matters, and it is likely that most allegations of racism brought by serving police officers will be investigated by the new body.

Double jeopardy

The issue of reforming double jeopardy was referred for review to the Law Commission which published an interim consultation paper in 1999 which suggested that exceptions might be made to this rule in exceptional circumstances as when new evidence emerged which was substantially stronger and could not have been obtained before the first trial. This change would apply only to serious offences punishable by at least three years imprisonment and where there was a strong likelihood of obtaining a conviction. All retrials would require the permission of the High Court with the right of appeal to the Court of Appeal. In 2000 the Home Affairs Committee lent its support for the relaxation of this rule for offences that carried a life sentence and where new evidence emerged that made the previous acquittal unsafe. It also proposed that the relaxation of this rule should be retrospective. The 2003 Criminal Justice Act enacted this reform.

The effectiveness of the Macpherson Report

The criminal justice system

This section considers the effectiveness of reforms that have been introduced since the Macpherson Report which were designed to ensure that the criminal justice system treated persons from minority ethnic groups fairly.

The Crown Prosecution Service

In the wake of the Macpherson Report, particular attention was devoted to the manner in which the CPS dealt with racial violence. The Macpherson Report recommended that the police service and CPS should ensure that care was taken at all stages of a prosecution to recognise and include reference to any evidence of racial motivation. In particular it should be the duty of the CPS to ensure that this evidence was referred to at both the trial and in the sentencing process. Additionally, the CPS and counsel should ensure that this evidence should not be excluded as the consequence of 'plea bargaining'. It was also proposed that the CPS should ensure that all decisions to discontinue a prosecution should be carefully and fully recorded in writing (Macpherson, 1999: 331). In 1999/2000, 2,417 defendant cases involving racist incidents were identified by the CPS. One thousand eight hundred and thirty-four of these (76 per cent) were prosecuted: most defendants pleaded guilty (66 per cent) and the overall conviction rate, including not guilty pleas, was 79 per cent (Home Office, 2000a: 49). Additionally, it has been observed that defendants of African, Caribbean and Asian origin were more likely to have their cases terminated by the CPS either because the evidence presented by the police was weak or because it was against the public interest to prosecute (Bowling and Phillips, 2002: 239).

However, accusations of racism within the CPS had an adverse impact on the image of this organisation and its desire to be seen as pursuing a rigorous approach towards racial violence. Between 1993 and 2000, 22 claims by minority ethnic lawyers alleging racial discrimination by the CPS were launched, and in February 2000 an employment tribunal awarded £30,000 to an minority ethnic crown prosecutor, stating that the organisation's conduct had fallen below the standards which would have been expected from a corner shop. In October 1999 a tribunal made the third finding of race discrimination against the CPS in less than a year and in December 1999 the Commission for Racial Equality proposed a formal investigation into allegations of racism within the CPS in connection with decisions to prosecute and its employment (including promotion) policies. The CPS was able to have this investigation suspended by initiating an independent investigation in January 2000 conducted by Sylvia Denman.

The conclusions of Denman's report stated that the CPS had responded slowly to modern equal opportunities legislation and practices and that although ethnic minority staff were well represented overall they were 'seriously under-represented in both the higher administrative grades and the higher lawyer grades' because barriers to ethnic minority recruitment and progression persisted. It was reported that 'a significant number' of ethnic minority staff had experienced race discrimination at one time or another within the CPS although most failed to report it, and that the concept of institutional racism was not generally understood or acknowledged. It was, however, accepted that 'modest progress' had been made during the period of the inquiry in seeking to ensure that the CPS developed a national culture which embraced all sections of the community and that there was 'a very clear commitment to change at the most senior levels' (Denman, 2001: 13–14). It was thus recommended that positive action should be taken to redress the current under-representation of minority ethnic staff at the lower and middle management grades and that monitoring should be used to achieve change in the CPS, especially in relation to setting targets. It was proposed that external investigation of equal opportunity complaints should be immediately implemented and that an external mediation service should be available to all staff (Denman, 2001: 15).

Additionally, the CRE launched its own separate, formal, investigation into allegations that staff at Croydon, Surrey, were working in racially segregated teams. The subsequent report argued that separation on racial lines had occurred at this office (race being 'a not insignificant factor' in accounting for this situation), and additionally that the few internal complaints of discrimination that were made were inadequately investigated or not dealt with within a reasonable period of time. It was concluded, however, that these facts did not support a finding of unlawful segregation within the meaning of the 1976 Race Relations Act as there was no evidence that the CPS had acted to keep staff apart on racial lines or that this situation was maintained or supported by specific acts of direct discrimination. It was accepted, however, that had the 2000 Race Relations (Amendment) Act been in force during the period under investigation the outcome could have been different since the CPS might have been in breach of its statutory obligation to pursue actions to bring about race equality, end unlawful discrimination and promote better race relations (CRE, 2001: 6).

There were, however, signs of subsequent improvement. It was reported that 13.9 per cent of staff came from black and minority ethnic communities, the Commission for Racial Equality commended the CPS review of its Race Equality Scheme and recognised the CPS Equality Plan as a model (Office for Criminal Justice Reform, 2004: 53).

The courts

Following the publication of the Macpherson Report, more strenuous action was pursued against judges whose behaviour regarding racial issues was deemed to be inappropriate. According to *The Guardian* on 29 September

1999, between May 1997 and September 1999 five judges were disciplined by the Lord Chancellor for making offensive racial remarks.

The sentencing practices of the courts were also scrutinised for racial bias. It was argued that the introduction of racial awareness training for judges and magistrates had yielded dividends and that only one in five black defendants in crown court trials, one in ten in magistrates' courts trials and one in eight Asian defendants in both tiers of court felt that they had been subjected to unfair treatment as a result of racial bias. The main complaint was that the sentence was higher than that which a white person would have received for a similar offence. However, it was revealed that black solicitors were likely to perceive racism within the courts and were more likely to have witnessed racism affecting the system. Only 43 per cent of black lawyers said that ethnic minorities were always treated fairly and with equal respect by the criminal courts. It was thus concluded there was a need for an increased degree of minority ethnic involvement in the administration of the judicial process (Hood et al., 2003).

Further, problems remained in connection with the manner in which the courts dealt with racial violence. The perception that the courts were insufficiently sympathetic to minority ethnic victims of racial violence was evidenced in April 2001 in trials involving two Leeds United footballers who had been accused of attacking an Asian student, Sarfraz Najeib. The first trial collapsed following the publication of an article in the *Sunday Mirror* based on an interview with the victim's father that the trial judge held to make it impossible for the jury to reach an unbiased decision. Although the Crown Prosecution Service had previously decided not to pursue racism as a motive for the attack, the trial judge, Mr Justice Poole, went out of his way when delivering his judgement to abort the trial, to criticise the recommendation contained in the Macpherson Report regarding the definition of a racial incident. In the second trial, one of the two footballers was found guilty of affray (the other being acquitted of all charges by the all-white jury) and sentenced to 100 hours community service. Although another participant was jailed for six years, the lenient sentence given by the judge to the footballer was illjudged to discourage others from carrying out violence of this nature. Perceptions that the action taken to protect members of minority ethnic communities from violence remained insufficient should be seen in the context that on conviction black people were more likely to receive custodial sentences which were longer for black and Asian persons than for whites (Bowling and Phillips, 2002: 240).

The police service and the Macpherson Report

The recommendations of the Macpherson Report were especially directed at the police service. This section evaluates the initial effectiveness of these reforms.

The confidence of ethnic minorites in the police

The government responded to Macpherson's recommendation that a Ministerial Priority should be put forward to rebuild the confidence of minority ethnic groups in the police service by making this a police national objective in 2000/1. However, a major problem with achieving this aim was the image of the police. In 1999 a *Guardian*/ICM poll showed that one in four members of the general public believed that the police were racist, 31 per cent of the 18–24 year old age group believed that most police officers were racist or very racist, 33 per cent of respondents believed that the police failed to treat black or Asian people fairly, while only 45 per cent disagreed with this proposition. It might be concluded that unless the image of the police dramatically improved, targets to increase recruitment of ethnic minority officers would inevitably fail.

The recruitment of police officers from minority ethnic communities

Progress in recruiting more police officers drawn from African-Caribbean and Asian communities was initially slow. Detailed information on recruitment was compiled by *The Guardian* from answers to Parliamentary questions put by the Liberal Democrat MP, Simon Hughes, and published on 3 August 2000. This indicated that in the two years from March 1998 to March 2000, the number of minority ethnic officers had increased from 2,483 to 2,754. However, police forces were required to recruit 826 officers from minority ethnic communities each year for ten years to meet the Home Secretary's target. Progress in key forces was limited. In West Yorkshire the overall number of minority ethnic officers declined in this two-year period and the Metropolitan Police (which needed to recruit 566 ethnic minority officers each year over ten years) succeeded in attracting only 125 between March 1999 and March 2000. By early 2002, this force had 1,205 officers drawn from minority ethnic communities, 4.42 per cent of the total (Hopkins, 2002), and the global figure for England and Wales stood at 3,386 (2.6 per cent of the total) (Home Office, 2002: 27).

One difficulty with attaining this objective was the financial constraints imposed on police forces that compelled some (including West Yorkshire which policed multi-ethnic Bradford) to scale down recruitment. An additional problem was the wastage rate of minority ethnic officers who were twice as likely to resign and three times more likely to be dismissed than their white peers. The then Home Secretary argued that ways had to be found to stop this 'exodus' (Straw, 1999b). Additionally, a survey conducted by *The Guardian* that was published in 24 February 2000 also revealed that 20 forces had no tests in place to measure whether officers had racist attitudes and that only 17 forces had complied with Macpherson's suggestion that all officers should be trained in racial awareness and cultural diversity.

Further problems in connection with recruitment subsequently arose. There was a perception that the need to hit Home Office targets for recruitment resulted in the risk that 'undeserving candidates' might be hired. This problem was regarded as particularly acute in London where the MPS was required to achieve a target of 25 per cent of its members from minority ethnic communities by 2009. Current progress meant that up to 80 per cent of new recruits would have to be black or Asian, a situation that the president of the National Black Police Association described as 'ridiculous'. He stated that this resulted in ordinary officers being 'confused and suspicious' by the MPS's tactics, and he expressed support for reducing targets in favour of working on a sustainable environment for black officers within the police (Powell, 2004). The promotion of minority ethnic officers also led to resentment from their white colleagues and resulted in a record number of white officers resorting to employment tribunals alleging that their prospects had been hindered by racial discrimination (Hinsliff, 2004).

Training

The Police Training Council responded to the comments made in the Stephen Lawrence Inquiry Report on training by developing a number of initiatives (some of which were implemented in anticipation of the report). The race equality duty imposed on forces by the 2000 Race Relations (Amendment) Act required all forces to train their staff on the general duty to promote race equality. The diversity element of the initial residential element of the Probationer Constable Training Programme (which was delivered at Hendon for recruits into the Metropolitan Police Service and at a Centrex centre for recruits to other forces) was extended into a module lasting from three to five days. All forces introduced a post-probationary programme that was composed of compulsory Community and Race Relations workshops that most officers and staff had attended by the end of 2003 (Calvert-Smith, 2004: 25). Diversity issues were incorporated into specialist training that included stop and search courses and senior command courses. Additionally, a three-day Personal Leadership Programme was developed by Centrex in partnership with the National Black Police Association at which around 700 minority ethnic staff had attended by the middle of 2004 (Calvert-Smith, 2004: 25). Individual force initiatives (such as Community and Race Relations workshops delivered in 24 of London's 32 boroughs in 2001/2) were also pursued following the Macpherson Report.

Stop and search

The Home Secretary's commitment to consider the recommendations made by the Macpherson Report regarding stop and search led to a 'scoping' study (prior to the introduction of national pilots) being mounted by the Home Office Policing and Reducing Crime Unit. This study revealed several problems with existing procedures which included the use made of 'voluntary' searches, the monitoring by officers of the use of stop and search powers (which in all forces which participated in the study had been developed relatively recently), the issue of 'how best to manage officers suspected, through improved monitoring, of using stop and search unlawfully or unfairly' (Quinton and Bland, 1999: 2), and the definition that should be accorded to 'stops' (as distinct, for example, from exploratory questioning).

The importance which stops and searches played in police work was queried by a further Home Office study which pointed to the substantial variations among forces in the extent to which searches were used even by those with similar characteristics and crime rates and queried the effectiveness of stops and searches in areas which included the detection of offenders for the range of crimes they addressed and the direct disruptive impact which they made on crime by intercepting those who were going out to commit offences. It was argued that it was not clear to what extent searches undermined criminal activity by securing the arrest and conviction of prolific offenders and that there was little solid evidence that searchers had a deterrent effect on crime (Miller et al., 2000: 5–6).

Initially, there remained concerns about the disproportionate rates of attention paid by police officers to persons from minority ethnic backgrounds (especially concerning the use of stop and search powers) and a lack of confidence in policing, particularly in connection with the service received by persons from minority communities (Clancy et al., 2001). A number of well-publicised episodes occurred regarding the treatment of Asian and African-Caribbean persons by the police that seemed to go beyond the aberrant actions of a few officers and suggested that institutional racism remained a problem for the service, especially the Metropolitan Police. In October 1999, a lay advisory group which had been set up following the Macpherson Report suspended its work after claims that two of its members were racially abused by police officers when they attended the scene of the Paddington rail disaster to counsel the families of black and Asian victims. Complaints were also voiced that senior officers had failed to attend the group's meetings.

Further problems occurred following the attack on the World Trade Center in September 2001 that was attributed to Muslim fundamentalists. The subsequent emphasis that was placed on security by the Home Secretary became translated into the disproportionate use of stop and search powers against persons from these communities under the pretext of counter-terror measures. The problem became sufficiently serious for the Independent Police Complaints Commission to announce in January 2005 that it would investigate all complaints regarding arrests under the legislation and not confine itself to serious grievances (Cowan, 2005). It undertook this decision because it believed that the use of police anti-terrorist powers against Muslims had damaged their confidence in the police.

Between 2001/2 and 2002/3, police stops and searches of Asian persons under the provisions of the 2000 Terrorism Act increased by 302 per cent (Home Affairs Committee, 2005: 19). Although the great bulk of those stopped and searched under these powers were white persons (rising from 14,429 in 2002/3 to 20,637 in 2003/4, a 43 per cent increase), the number of black people stopped and searched increased in the same period by 55 per cent (from 1,745 to 2,704) and the number of Asian people rose by 22 per cent (from 2,989 to 3,668) (Dodd and Travis, 2005). However, additional statistics which revealed that the proportion of Asian persons stopped and searched under all legislation (the 1984 Police and Criminal Evidence Act, the 1994 Criminal Justice and Public Order Act and the 2000 Terrorism Act) remained constant at 7 per cent of the total in 2002/3 and 2003/4 (Home Affairs Committee, 2005: 19) contributed towards the Home Affairs Committee's conclusion that the Asian community was not being unreasonably targeted by stop and search powers. However, it accepted that Muslims did not perceive this to be the case and thus recommended that the police and government should make special efforts to reassure them and proposed that the Muslim community should be involved in the independent scrutiny of police intelligence (Home Affairs Committee, 2005: 5). Any comfort which the Muslim community might derive from this Committee's report was tempered by the remarks of the Home Office Minister, Hazel Blears, who according to *The Guardian* newspaper on 2 March 2005 informed this Committee the previous day that Muslims would have to accept that they would be stopped and searched by the police more often than the rest of the public.

Problems of this nature highlight the difficulty of enforcing rules governing the behaviour of officers 'on the streets', behaviour which in carrying out this highly emotive aspect of policing is underpinned by police occupational culture. Changing this is thus a prerequisite for alterations in the use made by police officers of stop and search powers.

The police service and racial violence

One important indicator of a change in police attitudes towards minority ethnic groups concerned the service's response to racial violence. One aspect of this response to the Macpherson Report was the formation of specialist victim-orientated Community Safety Units. Some forces, most notably the Metropolitan Police, secured success in achieving convictions in a number of high-profile cases of this nature. However, statistics suggested that racial violence was on the increase following the publication of the Macpherson Report. The total of racist incidents in 1997/8 was 13,878 (HMIC, 1999: 27). Throughout England and Wales there were 47,814 racist incidents reported to and recorded by the police in 1999/2000, compared to 23,049 in the previous year. This included 21,750 offences created by the 1998 Crime and Disorder Act (Home Office, 2000a: 49). Serious acts of racial violence included the murder of the ten-year old school boy, Damilola Taylor, in November 2000, for which four youths were arrested but acquitted in June 2001 when the evidence of the prosecution's key witness, a 14-year-old girl, was thrown out by the judge who criticised the actions of the police who had offered her inducements to give evidence. Three other boys were subsequently arrested for this murder in January 2005. These figures suggest a significant rise in racial crimes that has been affected by the adoption of Macpherson's suggestion to record offences as race crimes when the victim used this designation. However, recording methods (whereby one incident may generate several offences or several incidents one offence) have also influenced these statistics.

The effectiveness of changes to police procedures to deal with racial violence in London was questioned in a report by the Inspectorate. This praised the role performed by officers in specialist units but argued that more needed to be done to win over the hearts and minds of non-specialist police officers. Reference was made to 'a pervasive feeling ... among some staff that what is seen as special treatment to the victims of racial attacks can only be delivered by prejudicing service to the broader community'. The report thus urged that this issue should be addressed in community and race relations training courses (HMIC, 2000: 6). This opinion was underpinned by resentment felt by many rank-and-file officers that they had been effectively 'sold down the river' by senior management accepting Macpherson's view that the service was institutionally racist which they did not believe was the case (an issue which is discussed below).

Accusations of inadequate police response to racially motivated violence where members of minority ethnic groups were the victims continued to be made. Disorder at Oldham in 2001 occurred against the background of assertions of police indifference to racist attacks in which Asians were the victims coupled with allegations made by the local police commander in June 2001 that Asians committed the majority of incidents of racial violence. This resulted in the formation of self-defence groups. The inquest into the death of Errol McGowan (who had been found hanged in Telford in July 1999) in 2001 heard evidence that he believed a campaign of harassment and threats had been directed against him but that the West Mercia police had failed to provide him with an effective remedy. In 1999 Jay Abatan was the victim of a racial attack in Sussex. No person has been convicted of this crime. Two suspects had charges of manslaughter dismissed before the case could go to court and a year later lesser charges were also dismissed. Subsequently a report into the way in which the Sussex police handled the investigation was conducted by the Essex Police. This drew attention to 57 inconsistencies, failures and inexplicable decisions taken by the Sussex force, following which it made a public apology to the family of the murder victim.

The reform of police culture

The reform of police culture underpins the ability of the police service to move positively in the direction outlined in the Macpherson Report. Before the publication of the report, some senior officers expressed support for root and branch reform of the police service to restore public confidence in it: Ian Blair (then the Chief Constable of Surrey) called for the modernisation of the 'homogenous and traditional' police culture, which he believed was old-fashioned and had to be changed in order for the police to serve a multicultural and modern nation. He particularly drew attention to minority ethnic officers feeling that they had to adopt the 'mores of a white culture' (Blair, 1999).

A key initiative to affect the working environment of police forces had already been initiated by minority ethnic police officers. In 1994 a Black Police Association was launched within the Metropolitan Police that might serve as a means to tackle aspects of the occupational subculture of the police service that marginalised minority ethnic officers (Rowe, 2004: 43–4). It is 'a rankless, gradeless organisation', whose function was to perform 'a welfare and support role within the Met Police, but also to echo the concerns and issues of the black community that we are a part of' (Logan, 2004). This 'may strengthen the racialised identity of its members and, realising their collective strength, unite them through both a shared experience of social exclusion ... and ... a positive commitment to policing' (Holdaway, 1996: 196). Critics, however, believe that this might have divisive consequences, diverting energy into internal police affairs perhaps to the detriment of the provision of a service to the public (Broughton and Bennett, 1994) or by aggravating conflict between this organisation and the Police Federation.

Following the Macpherson Report a number of significant changes were made in police forces to respond to the criticisms which were put forward, in particular that of institutional racism. In the Metropolitan Police area the slogan of 'protect and respect' was adopted in order to indicate changed police attitudes towards ethnic minority communities and specialist community safety units were set up in each division to investigate complaints of racial crimes. In line with Macpherson's recommendation that the police service should adhere to the victim's view that a crime was of a racist nature, the ethos of these community safety units was victim-oriented. Aided by changes spearheaded by community safety units, the reporting and arrests for racial crime increased as did intelligence on these crimes. Additionally, the Metropolitan Police established an Understanding and Responding to Race Hate Crime project whose role was to analyse and review data to give the force a clearer understanding of the issue.

Changing police culture was deemed by Macpherson as an integral aspect of eliminating racist attitudes within the police service (and throughout the criminal justice process in general) but this may be a difficult goal to achieve since 'not only is the police culture responsible for racist attitudes and abusive behaviour, but it also forms part the basis of secrecy and solidarity among police officers, so that deviant practices are covered up and rationalised' (Chan, 1997: 225). It was in this respect that the screening of the television programme *The Secret Policeman* (which is discussed below) in 2003 made an important contribution to attempts to purge institutional racism from the police service.

The Probation Service

Minority ethnic groups are significantly over-represented in the prison population: the incarceration rate for black people in 1998 was 1,245 per 100,000 population compared to 185 for white people. There was, however, no evidence of differential rates of offending between these two groups (Howard League for Penal Reform, 2000). A major function of the Probation Service is to prepare pre-sentence reports. Discriminatory practices in this activity could have an important bearing on the level of imprisonment for minority ethnic defendants.

A review of pre-sentence reports estimated that while 60 per cent of those prepared for white defendants were satisfactory, the figure for African/ African-Caribbean defendants was only 49 per cent. It was argued that a higher proportion of pre-sentence reports written for these minority groups contained a clear proposal for custody or indicated that custody was a likely option than reports prepared for white defendants. This difference did not reflect differentials in the seriousness of the offences committed by different ethnic groups since it was estimated that a community sentence was a realistic option in over half of the reports prepared on African/African-Caribbean offenders (Her Majesty's Inspectorate of Probation, 2000).

The Probation Service may have to deal with those found guilty of racially motivated crimes. Towards the end of the 1990s the West Midlands Probation Service pioneered anti-racism offending behaviour programmes which were directed at convicted racists. This scheme, entitled *Murder to Murmur: Working with Racially Motivated and Racist Offenders*, sought to expose racist offenders and tackle their attitudes and behaviour in order to prevent further acts of violence. Probation officers were enjoined to be observant of, and to challenge, racism wherever they observed it. However, a subsequent report into the operations of the probation services stated that few had produced detailed guidelines for working with racially motivated offenders and that no commonly accepted definition of what constituted a racially motivated offender existed across the services (HMIP, 2000).

The Probation Service made advances in the wake of Macpherson in connection with race equality and diversity. In 2004 it was reported that all probation areas had exceeded their targets for the employment of minority ethnic staff, and that a shadowing scheme had been implemented to provide five minority ethnic area managers with the opportunity to learn about strategic leadership at the highest level (National Probation Service, 2004). Efforts have also been made to address the needs of offenders from minority ethnic backgrounds through the development of specialised programmes. It has been argued that these must focus on the negative feelings that derive from racism, discrimination and socio-economic inequality and provide for 'the exploration of self-identity, the challenging of negative views of the self and the wider community, the re-framing of the offender perception from that of the victim to agent, and facilitating the development and exploration of pro-social (and pro-community) choices. (Williams, 2006: 159–160). The issue of racially motivated offenders was addressed in a report by the Chief Inspector of Probation who alluded to the absence of a strategic approach towards racially motivated offenders at either national or local probation board level and he urged the need to improve the way in which the Probation Service dealt with this category of offenders (Bridges, 2005: 5). He also suggested that the ban on prison officers being active members of the far right political organisations such as the British National Party should be extended to the Probation Service in order for it to retain the confidence of ethnic minority communities (Bridges, 2005: 40).

The Prison Service

In 1998 the Labour Home Secretary, Jack Straw, addressed the Prison Service Conference and urged the need for an effective anti-discriminatory policy and for the recruitment, retention and promotion of black members of staff. The new *Aims, Objectives and Principles of the Prison Service* included a commitment to promote equality of opportunity for all and to combat discrimination which gave rise to the service's new race equality for staff and prisoners (RESPOND) programme. In 1999 the Prison Service appointed a Muslim adviser following an increase in the number of Muslim prisoners in England and Wales to 4,355, whose role included educating prison staff and ensuring that Muslim prisoners had proper opportunities to practise their religion, access to Halal food and links with the outside Muslim community.

A report by NACRO in 1996 had stated that in the Prison Service, five governor grades out of 1,013 and 467 of the total 19,325 prison officers were black. In the wake of the Macpherson Report, targets were set by the Home Office in 1999 for ethnic minority recruitment into the Prison Service. These sought to increase the percentage of ethnic minority officers from 3.2 per cent to the figure of 7 per cent by 2009. Between 1999 and 2003, the percentage of minority ethnic staff rose to 5 per cent (Office for Criminal Justice Reform, 2004: 53).

The number of racist incidents in prison in 1998/9 was 293 for prisoner on prisoner, 379 for prisoner on staff and 218 for staff on prisoner. In February 2000, the Prison Service adopted the definition of a racist incident provided in the Macpherson Report and from August 2000 four new racially aggravated offences were introduced into Prison Rules (Home Office, 2000a: 50).

However, major problems persisted with the ability of the Prison Service to deal with the problem of racial violence in their institutions and it has been argued that the 'stereotyping of black people as "violent" and "dangerous" legitimises violence against them, and allows their mental and physical health needs to be overlooked when in the care of the police and prison services' (Bowling and Phillips, 2002: 241). In March 2001, Zahid Mubarek (whose crime was that of minor theft and interfering with a motor vehicle) was made to share a cell with a racist psychopath with a history of violence at Feltham Young Offenders Institution. Mubarek was murdered by this inmate, and at a subsequent inquiry into his death previously confidential documents were revealed which highlighted a catalogue of racist abuse and discrimination at this YOI by officers, three of whom had been disciplined (but not dismissed) for their part in an earlier attack on a minority ethnic inmate (al Yafai, 2005). A witness statement to this inquiry by the Prison Service's first race equality adviser, Judy Clements, referred to a 'deeply ingrained culture of prejudice' at this institution whereby 'allegations of serious violence against black prisoners were not investigated, and inmates who reported racist incidents found themselves disciplined by the authorities' (Asthana and Bright, 2005).

In a separate incident, in 2004 the Commission for Racial Equality condemned the delay in dismissing two prison officers (one of whom worked at Holloway prison and the other at Pentonville jail) who had been suspended on full pay for three years for allegedly intimidating black staff. A subsequent police raid on their house discovered a collection of Nazi memorabilia, neo-fascist literature and Ku Klux Klan-inspired material. The Prison Service was amenable to the return to work of this married couple when the police decided not to proceed with charges against them (Bright, 2004).

> Evaluate the impact of the Macpherson Report on the subsequent operations of the criminal justice system.

The impediments to reform

In the early years of the twenty-first century, the perception arose that the momentum in achieving the objectives contained in the Macpherson Report was slowing down. There are a number of reasons that might explain this situation that are discussed below in specific relation to the police service whose failings were infamously revealed in a BBC television programme, *The Secret Policeman*, which was screened on 21 October 2003. This used covert observation of officers in the early stages of their careers who were undergoing training at the Police National Training Centre at Bruche, Warrington, which was used by ten forces in the North of England and Wales. Some of these recruits articulated racist language and sentiments that in the wake of Macpherson totally beggared belief and called into question the extent to which the police service had meaningfully taken Macpherson's recommendations on board. The situation was appropriately summarised by the chair of the CRE who stated that 'these men were not teenagers on the razzle after a drunken night out. They were in their twenties and thirties, they consistently displayed this behaviour over a period of months and they were absolutely confident that no-one would challenge them, much less report or punish them' (Phillips, 2003).

The following section seeks to suggest reasons why the police service had failed to counter institutional racism and what further steps might remedy this situation.

Police reservations concerning the conclusions of Macpherson

Institutions such as the police service are often resistant to change, and reforms are most likely to be achieved if those pressing it can secure the support of all members (not just the leaders) of the organisation. This was clearly not attempted in respect of the Macpherson Report and the police service where it was assumed that branding the service as institutionally racist would secure compliance to reforms, but this was clearly not the case. A large number of rank-and-file officers rejected the acceptance by some of their leaders that the forces they headed were institutionally racist (albeit they primarily defined this as unintentional racism). It has been argued that 'the fundamental problem with terms such as "institutional racism" is that they are polar words, conversation stoppers rather than conversation starters. To say that someone is racist ... is to accuse them of something hateful. Not surprisingly, people don't like to be accused of acting hatefully, and often they respond by taking offence, stalking away, or vehemently denying the accusation.' For such reasons terms such as 'institutional insensitivity' or 'racial insensitivity' may have been more appropriate to describe the situation that Macpherson sought to reform (Tonry, 2004: 76–7).

Resistance by those in the police service took many forms, one of which was to deny the validity of Macpherson's claims that the service was institutionally racist. In contrast to many of the heads of criminal justice agencies who queued up in 2001–2 to declare their organisations to be institutionally racist (Tonry, 2004: 76), the Deputy Chief Constable of Kent Robert Ayling (who had headed a PCA-supervised inquiry into the Metropolitan Police's handling of the Lawrence murder investigation in 1993) asserted in *The Guardian* on 9

March 1999 that the evidence to support the charge of institutional racism was limited. This view is underpinned by an assertion that it is difficult to discern '*collective* failure' based on the behaviour of a *few* officers concerned with the investigation of Stephen Lawrence's murder (Lea, 2003: 50–1).

The resistance of some officers to this view was also displayed in advice to white victims of crime involving members of minority ethnic groups that theirs was a racial crime, even if the victim did not perceive it as such. Accordingly, since the publication of the Macpherson Report, there has been a rise in the number of white persons who have been victims of such attacks: according to the figures published in *The Guardian* on 11 May 2001, between 1997 and 1998 the Metropolitan Police recorded 27 per cent of victims of racial attacks as white, 27 per cent as black and 37 per cent as Asian, but between 1999 and 2000 the number of black victims rose to 29 per cent and the number of white victims to 31 per cent. Similarly there has been an increase in the number of black suspects of racial incidents. Between 1997 and 1998, 71 per cent of suspects of racial incidents were white. This figure fell to 67 per cent between 1999 and 2000, and during the same period the percentage of black suspects rose from 16 to 20 per cent. This has led to suggestions that this is perverse reporting by officers actively conniving in a white backlash against the recommendations of the Macpherson Report (Fitzgerald, 2001). It has also had the consequence of overloading community safety units with casework.

Other forms of rejection included looking for reasons other than institutional racism to explain the inability of the Metropolitan Police Service to apprehend and successfully prosecute Stephen Lawrence's murderers. These included assertions that Macpherson underestimated the complexity of murder inquiries. The chair of the Metropolitan Police Federation argued that the real issue was not institutional racism but deficiencies in management whereby a review of the murder inquiry ordered by the then senior officers of the area was 'signed off, accepted as correct, passed up the chain of command and then relied upon as a shield to deflect criticism. That single act has let down every single Metropolitan officer' (Smyth, 1999).

A subsequent report which alluded to problems affecting murder investigations in the Metropolitan Police Service also implied that institutional racism might not be the full explanation for failures by the Metropolitan Police to apprehend perpetrators of serious crimes. It was revealed that murder investigations did not have a specific priority in that force. The report asserted that the lower than average rate for the detection of murders in the ten-year period 1989–98 (84 per cent compared to the national average of 92 per cent) was 'largely attributable to the level of resources assigned to investigation rather than to the expertise or competence of detective officers' (HMIC, 2000: 11–12). It thus recommended that the Metropolitan Police should carefully consider the maximum caseload appropriate for senior investigating officers to manage, having regard to the varying complexity of cases (HMIC, 2000: 161). Poor liaison with the CPS in the early stages of a murder investigation was also highlighted. It was asserted that close cooperation between the police and this agency was required to ensure that the investigation was steered along the correct path so that the best evidence was available in court. It was recommended that a structure for formal liaison between the Metropolitan Police and the CPS should be established as a matter of urgency (HMIC, 2000: 12 and 162).

Macpherson's recommendations were inadequate to produce reform

It has been argued that the Macpherson Report lacked precision in key areas to enable it to serve as an agenda for effective reform. In particular, the discussion of institutional racism 'fails to locate with sufficient precision its roots within the structure of operational policing and in the relationship between police and minority communities' (Lea, 2003: 48): that is, it is necessary to identify precisely what it is about day-to-day police work which generates and sustains an occupational culture supportive of racism (Lea, 2003: 51). Thus to address this issue fully would require a reform agenda broader than that set by Macpherson.

One explanation which has been put forward for the initial failure of the Macpherson Report to effectively tackle institutional racism is the lack of political clout possessed by communities on the receiving end of police practices (in particular the excessive use made of stop and search powers) which evidence the existence of institutional racism.

Institutional racism is founded on the assumption that minority ethnic groups constitute the 'dangerous class' in society that needs to be controlled (Lea, 2003: 62–4) in order to combat the criminal and disorderly activities with which politically and economically marginalised groups are stereotypically associated. The perception that minority ethnic groups lack the power to either 'cause problems' for the police or to help them achieve their crime-fighting goals is put forward as an explanation for the hostile police attitude towards them (Reiner, 1992: 137; Lea, 2003: 54–5). To redress this would require a major redistribution of economic and political resources to alter the power relationship between the police service and such marginalised groups.

There are various ways whereby the power relationship between police and minority ethnic communities could be altered to the advantage of the latter. On 24 February 1999, Jonathan Freedland, writing in *The Guardian*, suggested it would have been inconceivable that the Stephen Lawrence investigation would have been handled so incompetently had the Commissioner of Police been accountable to the voters of London with its 25 per cent minority ethnic electorate. He stated that 'if he had to face the voters, as police chiefs do in some of America's biggest cities, would he not have realised his job was on the line?' He further suggested that if, alternatively, the Commissioner was accountable to a mayor (as is the case in New York) this episode would not have arisen either since the mayor would have sacked the police chief in order to keep his own job. Although it is unlikely that reforms of this nature would be introduced, there are other ongoing developments that subject the police to an increased degree of external control and might serve as the basis for further developments to secure democratic control over policing.

These include Crime and Disorder Reduction Partnerships (which may serve as vehicles for minority groups to reorientate policing to address their specific needs and concerns) (Lea, 2003: 56). In London, reforms which include the appointment of a police authority under the provisions of the 1999 Greater London Assembly Act (to replace the control wielded over policing since 1829 by the Home Secretary) and the direct election of a mayor (the first of whom was Ken Livingstone, elected in 2000 and re-elected in 2004) present the possibility of increased accountability of the police to their local public, although there are limits to the effectiveness of these reforms to London government. The Metropolitan Police Authority is not subject to direct democratic control or accountability and the London mayor does not appoint the Commissioner of the Metropolitan Police Service. Other reforms introduced by post-1997 Labour governments which included the reform of the Race Relations Act and the endorsement of an independent system for investigating complaints against the police also erode the autonomy of the police service and make it more susceptible to the views and opinions of the general public.

The government's commitment to reform

A further obstacle hindering the progress of Macpherson's reforms has been the perception that the government began to lose interest in the subject. The 2001 general election witnessed the Labour and Conservative parties articulating negative sentiments towards asylum seekers (Joyce, 2002: 146) and the essentially racist nature of this populist agenda was subsequently displayed in the interest shown by Jack Straw's successor as Home Secretary, David Blunkett, into security measures which were predicated on the need to combat terrorism, a concern which was accentuated following Britain's involvement in the 2003 war in Iraq and the bombings that took place in London in 2005. Blunkett was accused of 'downgrading racism issues' (Lawrence, 2003) and was effectively seeking to bury the Macpherson Report.

Other relevant issues include the retirement of John Grieve whose determination in seeking to convict racists was an important factor in the initial response of the Metropolitan Police Service to its failures that were referred to in Macpherson's report.

Some reforms not fully implemented

Some of the recommendations contained in, or promoted in response to, Macpherson's report were not immediately implemented. These included the changes to the interview procedures and the monitoring of all stops and stops and searches that is a crucial requirement to oversee the behaviour of officers working on the streets.

The initial interview process is crucial to ensure that those with racist views and opinions do not enter the service in the first place. No amount of anti-racist training will ever succeed in altering entrenched racist views.

Reforms to achieve this (in particular the adoption by all forces of the National Recruitment Standards Assessment Centre) have been put in place. This programme included an assessment process that was designed to test candidates' attitudes towards race and diversity through interviews, role-play and written assessment and was designed to weed out racists. Changes were also introduced to the way in which probationer training was delivered whereby the focus of training was moved away from training schools and became orientated towards practice-based training within local communities.

Changes to stop and stop and search procedures have also been subsequently introduced. The 2003 Criminal Justice Act extended police powers to stop and search to cover situations in which a constable reasonably suspects that a person is carrying an article that he intends to use to cause criminal damage (such as graffiti). From 1 April 2005, all police forces were required to have mechanisms in place to ensure that anyone who was asked by an officer to account for themselves in a public place regarding their actions, behaviour, presence or items in their possession was provided with a record of the encounter. This form of police intervention was now referred to as a 'stop and account' as opposed to a 'stop'. The Codes of Practice for PACE introduced in 2004 placed a new responsibility on supervisors to monitor and detect what was referred to as 'disproportionatlity' in the searches conducted by officers. Disproportionality regarding the use of stop and search powers would also be measured within the PPAF (which is discussed in Chapter 4). The Police Federation, however, was critical of this development concerning disproportionality, arguing that 'the Home Office and Chief Officers readily admit they do not understand the term' (Police Federation, 2005).

It might thus be argued that the culture of the police service will change following the adoption of reforms in the important areas that have been identified above.

Existing law prevents progress

A key problem with attempts to achieve targets set by the Home Secretary regarding recruitment, retention and progression was that it implied the need to adopt positive discrimination that is contrary to sections 1(1)(a) and 4(1) of the Race Relations Act (Calvert-Smith, 2005: 46). In a period in which there was a surplus of successful candidates and thus the need to draw up waiting lists, it was found that some forces had adopted policies which included offering appointments to successful minority ethnic candidates more speedily than was the case with white applicants (HMIC: 2004). This was likely to constitute a breach of the existing law which permitted 'positive action' without breaching the principle of equality of opportunity (Calvert-Smith, 2005: 46 and 49). One way to redress this problem would be to amend the law to permit positive discrimination to regularise the practices that some forces were allegedly pursuing (that is, 'queue-jumping' the waiting lists of successful applicants), but this might provoke a backlash both within and beyond the police service (Calvert-Smith, 2005: 48).

Failure by the service to put its own house in order

Attempts to eradicate racism within police forces had been traditionally directed at the external issue of police–public relationships. Key pronouncements regarding quality of service expressed concern with ensuring that members of the public did not receive less favourable treatment from the police 'on the grounds of race, colour, nationality, or national or ethnic origins or were disadvantaged by conditions or requirements which could not be shown to be justifiable' (ACPO/CRE, 1993: 9). However, 'absolutely no critical attention is given to the features of the occupational culture that redefine what ... are "good" and desirable features of a work environment ... but exclude minority ethnic officers from full and active membership' (Holdaway, 1996: 171).

An alternative approach is to focus on the internal characteristics of the police service. This involves an examination of police culture, one core characteristic of which is alleged to be racial prejudice (Reiner, 1985: 100–3) that mobilises the lower ranks of the police service to resist progressive change. This approach goes beyond attempts designed to stop the use of racialist language (Holdaway, 1996: 168) and addresses the manner in which the key features of police occupational culture 'construct and sustain racialised relations within the police' (Holdaway, 1996: 169). Tackling those processes which cause and reproduce racism (particularly the marginalisation of black officers) within police forces is seen as an indispensable requirement for eliminating the public display of such behaviour towards members of minority ethnic communities. This approach will ensure that reforms to police recruitment and training policies were advanced within an organisational climate that was supportive of initiatives to eradicate racism.

It might thus be argued that one reason for the failure of the Macpherson Report to produce an immediate and dramatic improvement in the relationship of the police service with minority ethnic communities was that its energies were overly focused on its external relations to the detriment of adequate attention to its internal procedures, in particular the experience which employment in the police service offered to members of minority ethnic groups. This deficiency was subsequently tackled in further reports.

The Commission for Racial Equality Interim Report

This programme prompted the chair of the Commission for Racial Equality to order a formal investigation of the police service in England and Wales in December 2003. The Commission for Racial Equality Scotland also ordered a separate review of policing and race relations in Scotland. It was headed by the then Director of Public Prosecution, David Calvert-Smith, and examined three areas – the recruitment, training and management of police officers, the monitoring of these areas by the police service and police inspectorates, and the way in which police authorities and police forces were meeting the statutory general duty of promoting race equality. The focus of the investigation was on the experience of minority ethnic groups within the police service. An interim report was issued in June 2004.

Although it was observed that recruits from the Greater Manchester Police, Cheshire Constabulary and North Wales Police had not been subject to the National Recruitment Standards Assessment Centre (as these forces had not at that stage adopted SEARCH) (Calvert-Smith, 2004: 22), this report expressed its disappointment in the overall quality of the race equality schemes which had been produced by police forces and police authorities and the arrangements which had been made to monitor employment. These functions derived from specific duties placed upon police authorities and forces by the Race Relations Act 1976 (Statutory Duties) Order 2001. The interim report recommended that the CRE should initiate enforcement action against police authorities and forces whose race equality and employment arrangements failed to meet the CRE's minimum standards required to meet these specific duties. It was also proposed that the Audit Commission should ensure that the auditing and inspection of police authorities included an assessment of how each authority was meeting the race equality duty (Calvert-Smith, 2004: 15–20).

The report devoted particular attention to the screening of job applicants, which was described as 'one of the most important questions raised following the broadcast of *The Secret Policeman*' (Calvert Smith, 2004: 21). The report expressed dissatisfaction that the new screening procedure for police recruits (which was supposed to be mandatory) had not been universally adopted (Calvert-Smith, 2004: 23). The report also observed that for those forces which used the National Recruitment Standards Assessment Centre, the rejection rate on the criterion of the Respect for Race and Diversity Competence was, ironically, 'significantly and sometimes substantially lower for white than for ethnic minority candidates'. The report stated that this pattern was 'disturbing' since the procedure had been designed to screen out racists of the kind depicted in *The Secret Policeman* (Calvert-Smith, 2005: 52) and called for further research into the assessment methods and scoring systems (Calvert-Smith, 2004: 22–3).

The report recognised that it was difficult to assess the kind of training that was appropriate for police officers in the area of racial equality issues. However, the aim of training of this nature (delivered on both probationer and post-probationer courses) was within the general context of seeking to ensure that 'everyone working in the police service develops the Knowledge, Understanding, Skills, Attitudes and Behaviour (KUSAB) required to meet the present and future needs of the police service' (HMIC, 2002: para. 4.9 and HMIC, 2003a: para. 1.30). Particular scrutiny was directed at the extent to which initial probationary training achieved these objectives. In 2002 it was observed that the diversity element of probationer training tended to focus on information relating to race and gender and that 'the amount of attitudinal and behavioural development ... is inadequate' (HMIC, 2002: paras 2.23 and 4.21). The following year it was observed that there was little community involvement in diversity training and that some staff displayed behaviour that was inappropriate (HMIC, 2003b: para. 3.28). Post-probationer training was also criticised for reasons that included the inability of many officers who were interviewed following the training 'to demonstrate any real understanding of the terms 'institutional racism' and 'institutional discrimination', and how they are manifested in the police service' (HMIC, 2003a: para. 8.30).

The progress which was made in implementing changes recommended by HMIC reports into training in general and diversity training in particular had been slow and the CRE report concluded that training at probationer level had failed to address many of the earlier criticisms. It was argued that such training 'barely ... touched' the development of 'understanding, skills and attitudes on matters concerning racial equality' (Calvert-Smith, 2004: 27), a problem which was partly attributed to the method of delivery and level of knowledge of, and commitment to, diversity issues by instructors, most of whom were white, and the dominant 'bar culture' of training schools which was alleged to have 'reinforced macho and anti-diversity attitudes and excluded participants from minority groups who abjured alcohol or heavy drinking' (Calvert-Smith, 2004: 27–8). It was concluded that 'ethnic minority trainees and trainers often feel isolated and vulnerable, in the absence of effective provision of pastoral care, and a safe complaints process for probationary trainees' (Calvert-Smith, 2004: 35). Post-probationary training was also criticised for reasons that included the reluctance of trainers to challenge racist attitudes that were expressed in the classroom and for failing to identify and meet separately the learning needs of different ranks and roles (Calvert-Smith, 2004: 29 and 36).

The CRE report also examined disciplinary and grievance procedures within the service and racial discrimination claims in employment tribunals. It was asserted that the definition of what constituted misconduct was subject to considerable variation across police forces and that forces were using a wide range of sanctions (ranging from words of advice to dismissal) in cases of racial misconduct (Calvert-Smith, 2004: 40–1). Grievance procedures relating to complaints by an officer against a fellow officer(s) were regarded as inadequate, resulting in many racial discrimination complaints being alternatively referred to an employment tribunal at considerable cost to the complainant (Calvert-Smith, 2004: 44–5 and 46–7). The CRE report also drew attention to the findings of a report which stated that black and Asian officers in the Metropolitan Police Service were one-and-a-half to two times more likely to be subjected to internal investigations and written warnings than their white counterparts (Ghaffur, 2004) and asserted that evidence which suggested the disproportionate use of the disciplinary process against minority ethnic officers would be examined in the second stage of the CRE's examination (Calvert-Smith, 2004: 42).

The Morris Inquiry

A further inquiry into professional standards and employment matters in the Metropolitan Police Service was established by the Metropolitan Police Authority. This was prompted by a number of high-profile cases involving ethnic minority officers who had been falsely accused of offences and focused on the way in which the police service handled complaints, grievances and allegations against individuals and conflict within the workplace.

It was chaired by the former General Secretary of the Transport and General Workers' Union, Sir Bill Morris, and reported in 2004.

The report expressed concern that although extensive work had been undertaken to develop diversity policies within the Metropolitan Police Service, there was 'no common understanding of diversity within the organisation' and that it was 'not embedded within the culture of the MPS. We fear that it remains, at worse, a source of fear and anxiety and, at best, a process of ticking boxes' (Morris, 2004: 13). One aspect of this problem was discrimination in the way in which black and minority ethnic officers were treated in relation to the management of their conduct. It was argued that this reflected the lack of confidence of some managers to manage black and minority ethnic officers without being affected by their race. The inquiry proposed to refer this issue to both the IPCC and CRE for their consideration.

The issue of how the Metropolitan Police Service handled matters related to professional standards accordingly received prominent attention in the report. Two approaches were discussed.

The first of these was the recommendation that employment law should be extended to police officers within the framework of the office of constable which would be achieved by replacing the current regulatory framework for dealing with complaints and allegations of misconduct against police officers with a disciplinary procedure based upon the ACAS Code of Practice on Disciplinary and Grievance Procedures to cover all workplace conflicts.

The second approach was to recommend that the MPS improve the way in which it handled complaints within the framework of the existing system.

Concern was expressed regarding the manner in which the MPS's Directorate of Professional Standards managed investigations, and it was recommended that the Commissioner should personally oversee a fundamental review of the way in which this Directorate operated, including consideration as to how officers were appointed to it. This was designed to ensure that senior managers were effectively accountable for the conduct and management of disciplinary investigations. Additionally, a new model of case management was put forward which included input from outside the Directorate to ensure that it was effectively held to account for investigations, especially where officers were suspended (Morris, 2004: 15–16).

Additional recommendations were made in connection with the conduct of police personnel. The MPS was urged to take active steps to remain vigilant and monitor the culture at Hendon and to ensure that all staff and recruits were aware of what constituted inappropriate behaviour (such as bullying and discrimination). Formal support mechanisms were also advocated to cover all recruits (Morris, 2004: 26).

The report also made some specific recommendations related to race. It was urged that the MPS should take urgent steps to eliminate the discriminatory management practice which had led to a disproportionate number of investigations of black and minority ethnic officers. The MPS was also recommended to give adequate priority to all aspects of diversity, especially in the light of the Framework Equal Treatment Directive 2000. Consideration should also be given to extending the Diversity Excellence Model to other Operational Command Units and directorates (Morris, 2004: 20–1).

Reference was also made to the 'high-profile' cases of Superintendent Dizaei and Sergeant Virdi. Dizaei had been subject to two investigations for dishonesty. He was ultimately cleared of this offence at the Old Bailey in September 2003 and awarded £80,000. Virdi was sacked for allegedly sending himself hate mail, but reinstated after a tribunal hearing. A full independent case review (in which race would form a part) of the case involving Superintendent Dizaei was also urged in order to do justice to those who were involved, and the Metropolitan Police Authority was urged to convene and chair a case conference involving the Commissioner and other relevant stakeholders to establish what progress had been made in implementing the recommendations of the Virdi Inquiry Report and to determine what, if any, further action should be taken (Morris, 2004: 21).

The Commission for Racial Equality Final Report

Sir David Calvert-Smith's final report was published in March 2005 and contained 125 recommendations to deal with the problems that emerged in relation to the inquiry's remit. In order to pursue the race equality duty, it was recommended that chief officers should ensure that their forces put in place requisite arrangements under the employment monitoring duty and that both the arrangements and the monitoring information gathered should be readily available for regular inspection and scrutiny. In connection with recruitment, it was recommended that all chief officers should review their positive action steps concerning the recruitment and retention of under-represented racial groups and that the Home Secretary should add an annual intake target to the existing employment targets which the inquiry regarded to be 'a more immediate and direct measure of performance regarding ethnic minority recruiting' (Calvert-Smith, 2005). Centrex was required to report concerning race differences in recruitment and selection, and it was suggested that it should review the scripted interview to see how its content could be made more race specific (Calvert-Smith, 2005).

In connection with training, chief officers and police authorities that had not developed a race and diversity training strategy were enjoined to do so and it was recommended that ACPO and the Association of Police Authorities should develop and publish guidelines on a force/authority race and diversity training strategy which would draw on existing good practice. It was further recommended that Centrex and chief constables should make the completion of the Race and Diversity Trainers' Programme (or its equivalent) a mandatory requirement for all in-force race and diversity trainers (Calvert-Smith, 2005).

Particular attention was devoted to discipline and grievance procedures. The proposals of the Morris Inquiry were echoed in the recommendation that the Home Office should consider giving police officers wider employment rights and making them subject to a non-statutory disciplinary procedure incorporated in their terms and conditions, preserving the office of constable. The Home Office and/or HMIC were recommended to urgently commission research across the police service on the nature and extent of any disproportionate impact on minority ethnic officers that might exist in the operation of the police disciplinary procedure, and it was suggested that chief officers should have a system in place to record management information about low-level and informal action taken to deal with the actuality or allegations of racial misconduct. The Home Office was urged to amend the Code of Conduct in line with the Code of Ethics that applied to the Northern Ireland Police Service to create a single code containing standards of conduct and practice for police officers in relation to non-discrimination on racial grounds. It was also recommended that draft written guidance on understanding racial discrimination and comprehensive guideline sanctions for racial misconduct should be prepared to become part of the police service disciplinary policy for police officers. It was also proposed that the Home Office should consider extending the guardianship role of the Independent Police Complaints Commission to cover the operation of the disciplinary procedure for police officers (Calvert-Smith, 2005).

The report recommended that the Home Office should determine a nationally agreed grievance procedure for the police service which should be assessed by the Home Office for its impact on race equality and chief officers were required to ensure that responsibility for operating the formal grievance procedure rested with staff who were independent of the complainant's line management. Chief officers were also recommended to implement safeguards to protect police officers from racial victimisation and to enable such victimisation to be promptly and effectively dealt with either through discipline or through the grievance procedure. Managers should be trained on the handling of race grievances and their performance and development reviews should include the measurement of their performance in resolving disputes of this nature. It was also suggested that the Home Office might consider giving police officers the right to complain directly to the IPCC about racism, provided that where possible they had initially used the appropriate internal procedure. Chief officers were also encouraged to promote the use of confidential reporting for racism and police authorities were urged to scrutinise their force's use of disciplinary actions against police officers to enable them to monitor whether there was any disproportionate adverse impact on minority ethnic officers and to require their forces to report to them on their confidential reporting facility. It was also proposed that police authorities should receive a report following every employment tribunal case detailing the wider race equality impact of the case, the lessons that the force had learned and an action plan to address any changes in policy or practices as a result (Calvert-Smith, 2005).

In connection with officers' performance development reviews (PDRs), it was suggested that the Home Office should require evidence-based reporting for core competencies such as fostering or promoting respect for race and diversity, and chief officers should ensure that the outcome of any disciplinary tribunals for racial misconduct were recorded within the PDR. It was recommended that HMIC and police authorities should inspect and scrutinise forces thoroughly to ensure that they adopted a consistent and coherent PDR system that dealt effectively with racist behaviour (Calvert-Smith, 2005).

The report made recommendations related to governance and accountability, which included the recommendation that police authorities should ensure that lawful steps were taken to encourage minority ethnic participation in their work, and that they should carry out regular staff satisfaction surveys on race-related issues (Calvert-Smith, 2005).

> What do you understand by the term 'institutional racism'? Why has this proved to be a difficult problem for the police service to tackle effectively?

Further reforms

The BBC programme and subsequent revelations highlighted that there remained an urgent need to tackle institutional racism within the police service. In addition to the prospect of matters improving with the adoption of National Occupational Standards aligned to the National Competency Framework (HMIC, 2003a: 5), one or two issues which might be examined in this reappraisal are briefly discussed below (Joyce, 2004: 16–17).

Further reforms to the selection process might be contemplated. These include extending the role of lay advisors to participate in the initial interview procedure, and also to provide for procedures during the residential aspects of the probationary period whereby applicants' views can be monitored, if necessary by the use of covert methods as were employed by the BBC.

The retention and promotion of suitably qualified staff from minority ethnic backgrounds also needs to be seriously addressed. The actuality or perception of unfairness in promotion would be alleviated if the service was required to hand over the recruiting and selection of candidates for promotion to senior ranks (perhaps that of inspector and above) to an outside agency which would impartially measure an officer's *curriculum vitae* against the person and job specification. This would guard against the bias inherent in the 'old boy' network and might also be applied to applications for specialist areas of police work such as the CID that contain relatively few officers from minority ethnic backgrounds. Race and diversity issues should also become key components of police promotion examinations, assessments and interviews.

The delivery of anti-racist training must be re-evaluated. The purpose of courses of this nature must be spelled out to participants at the outset to secure their support (including, but extending beyond, the pragmatic considerations set out in HMIC, 2003a: 13), and effective ways must also be devised to monitor their subsequent impact by devising measurable outcomes. A further development to measure racist conduct would be the use of machinery at BCU level whereby the use made by individual officers of stop and search powers is regularly and routinely monitored by police managers, and ultimately by both BCU commanders and the Police Authority. A particular advantage of this reform would be to secure the involvement of sergeants and inspectors in securing organisational objectives. Consideration should also be given to the appropriateness of using stops and searches as individual performance indicators where this is the case.

There are additional reforms that can be directed at altering the culture of the service. The image of force departments dealing with complaints, discipline and grievance procedures would be improved if they contained an appropriate number of officers from minority ethnic groups to ensure that accusations of racist conduct either by members of the public or by serving officers were handled by those who are fully aware of the impact of these actions on the individual who is subjected to them. The involvement of lay advisors in disciplinary panels where race is an issue might improve the image of this aspect of the disciplinary process although it raises important issues such as the access of independent and lay advisors to documentation. Additionally, police forces and industrial tribunals should adopt fast-tracking procedures to deal with complaints of racial misconduct and organisational discrimination made by members of the public or serving police officers.

It is also important that the service develops appropriate responses to use against those found guilty of racial misconduct. This is especially relevant when dealing with problems derived from unwitting racism where, as the Police Complaints Authority's guidelines for investigating complaints of racism stated (Travis, 2003), the sanction of dismissal may not be appropriate. Adequate retraining should become available so that officers who are guilty of racial misconduct have the opportunity to understand why their actions were wrong and become aware of how they should conduct themselves in the future. This could incorporate an assessable distance-learning component to augment classroom-based training.

Ultimately, however, coercive means have an important role to play in influencing the culture of the service. The penalty of dismissal for severe cases of racial misconduct must be consistently applied. It was only in response to the BBC programme that the sanction of loss of employment became utilised and in all cases those who stood accused of racist misconduct were allowed to resign from the service rather than being dishonourably dismissed from it. If the service is serious about combating racism, dismissal rather than resignation is the only appropriate penalty that should be routinely applied to severe transgressions of this nature such as those revealed in the BBC programme.

Conclusion

This chapter focuses on the issue of racial discrimination within the criminal justice system. The attention devoted to the police service reflects the weight of literature dealing with this topic at the present time.

The chapter considered the background to the Scarman Report and the recommendations that were contained within it. It evaluated why this report failed to make any significant improvement to the relationship between minority ethnic communities and the police service. It further considered accusations of racial discrimination that were levelled against other agencies operating within the criminal justice process before the publication of the Macpherson Report in 1999.

The chapter then assessed the importance of the botched murder investigation mounted by the Metropolitan Police into the murder of the black teenager, Stephen Lawrence, as the catalyst for change. It considered the contents of this report and the significance of the proposals that were put forward, drawing particular attention to the definition of institutional racism that was offered. It analysed the responses made by various agencies in the criminal justice process and by the government to Macpherson's proposals and considered the impediments to their implementation. Further reports that sought to combat racial discrimination especially in the police service were considered in this context.

Further reading

There are many specialist texts that will provide an in-depth examination of the issues discussed in this chapter. These include:

Bowling, B. and Phillips, C. (2002) *Racism, Crime and Justice*. Harlow: Longman.

Chan, J. (1997) *Changing Police Culture: Policing in a Multicultural Society*. Cambridge: Cambridge University Press.

Sir W. Macpherson, (1999) *The Stephen Lawrence Inquiry: Report of an Inquiry by Sir William Macpherson of Cluny*. London: TSO, Cm 4262.

Marlow A. and Loveday, B. (editors) *After Macpherson*. Dorset: Russell House Publishing.

Rowe, M. (2004) *Policing, Race and Racism*. Cullompton: Willan Publishing.

Key events

- **1981** Publication of the Scarman Report into a series of disturbances that occurred throughout England. His report made a number of suggestions to improve the relationship between the police service and minority ethnic communities.
- **1984** Enactment of the Police and Criminal Evidence Act. This measure sought to reconstruct the concept of policing by consent and introduced safeguards governing matters such as the use of stop and search powers by the police and the treatment of suspects in police stations.
- **1993** Murder of the black teenager Stephen Lawrence in South London. The inability of the Metropolitan Police to secure the conviction of those responsible for his death resulted in the 1997 Labour government instigating a report that was written by the retired judge, Sir William Macpherson.
- **1998** Enactment of the Crime and Disorder Act that introduced a range of provisions to deal with racially motivated crime.

- **1999** Publication of Sir William Macpherson's report into the botched investigation conducted by the Metropolitan Police Service into the murder of Stephen Lawrence. He accused the police service of being institutionally racist and made a number of recommendations that were designed to eliminate this problem from the operations of the criminal justice system.
- **1999** Launch of the *Equal Treatment Bench Book* by the Lord Chancellor and Lord Chief Justice that sought to increase the sensitivity of judges to race issues.
- **1999** Replacement of the Police Disciplinary Code with the Code of Conduct that established standards of behaviour expected from all police officers.
- **2000** Enactment of the Race Relations (Amendment) Act. This measure had been recommended in the Macpherson Report and imposed a race equality duty on all agencies working in the criminal justice process.
- **2001** Publication of the Denman Report into the operations of the Crown Prosecution Service. This argued that the CPS had responded slowly to contemporary equal opportunities legislation and practices.
- **2002** Enactment of the Police Reform Act. This set up a new system of investigating complaints against police officers that included the independent investigation of serious accusations.
- **2003** Screening of the programme *The Secret Policeman* that revealed the articulation of offensive racist sentiments by some police probationers at the police training college at Bruche in North Western England.
- **2003** Enactment of the Criminal Justice Act. The provisions of this legislation included the recommendation put forward in the Macpherson Report that double jeopardy could be abandoned in certain exceptional circumstances.
- **2004** Publication of an interim report commissioned by the Commission for Racial Equality and written by David Calvert-Smith that focused on the experience of minority ethnic officers in the police service. The final report was published in March 2005 and contained 125 recommendations.
- **2004** Report by Sir Bill Morris into professional standards and employment matters in the Metropolitan Police Service. This report was commissioned by the Metropolitan Police Authority.

References

ACPO/CRE (1993) *Policing and Racial Equality*. London: Association of Chief Police Officers and the Commission for Racial Equality.

al Yafai, F. (2005) 'Feltham Officers Disciplined for Race Attack', *Guardian*, 18 January.

Allen, S. and Barratt, J. (1996) *The Bradford Commission Report: Report of an Inquiry into the Wider Implications of Public Disorders which Occurred on 9, 10 and 11 June 1995*. London: HMSO.

Asthana, A. and Bright, M. (2005) 'Racism "Ingrained into Prison Culture"', *Observer*, 30 January.

Bethnal Green and Stepney Trades Council (1978) *Blood on the Streets: A Report by the Bethnal Green and Stepney Trades Council on Racial Attacks in East London*. London: Bethnal Green and Stepney Trades Council.

Blair, I. (1999) *Speech to the Social Market Foundation*, London, 18 Febuary, quoted in *Guardian*, 19 February.

Bland, N., Mundy, G., Russell, J. and Tuffin, R. (1999) *Career Progression of Ethnic Minority Police Officers*, Home Office Police Research Series Paper 107. London: Home Office Research, Development and Statistics Directorate.

Blauner, R. (1972) *Racial Oppression in America*. New York: Harper & Row.

Bowling, B. (1998) *Violent Racism: Victimisation, Policing and Social Context*. Oxford: Oxford University Press.

Bowling, B. and Phillips, C. (2002) *Racism, Crime and Justice*. Harlow: Longman.

Bridges, A. (2005) *I'm Not Racist But … An Inspection of National Probation Service Work with Racially Motivated Offenders*. London: Home Office.

Bright, M. (2004) 'Failure to Sack Racist Prison Staff Condemned', *Observer*, 26 September.

Broughton, F. and Bennett, M. (1994) Quoted in *Guardian*, 27 September.

Brown, J. (1982) *Policing by Multi-Racial Consent: The Handsworth Experience*. London: Bedford Square Press.

Bull, R. and Horncastle, P. (1983) *Metropolitan Police Recruit Training: An Independent Evaluation*. London: Police Foundation.

Calvert-Smith, D. (2004) *A Formal Investigation of the Police Service in England and Wales: An Interim Report*. London: Commission for Racial Equality.

Calvert-Smith, D. (2005) *A Formal Investigation of the Police Service in England and Wales: Final Report*. London: Commission for Racial Equality.

Carmichael, S. and Hamilton, C. (1967) *Black Power*. New York: Vintage.

Chan, J. (1997) *Changing Police Culture: Policing in a Multicultural Society*. Cambridge: Cambridge University Press.

Clancy, A., Hough, M., Aust, R. and Kershaw, C. (2001) *Crime, Policing and Justice: The Experience of Ethnic Minorities*, Home Office Research Study 223, Findings from the 2000 British Crime Survey. London: Home Office.

Commission for Racial Equality (1992) *A Question of Judgement: Race and Sentencing*. London: Commission for Racial Equality.

Commission for Racial Equality (2001) *The Crown Prosecution Service, Croydon Branch: Report of a Formal Investigation*. London: Commission for Racial Equality.

Condon, P. (1993) Quoted in *Guardian*, 1 March.

Cowan, R. (2005) 'Police Watchdog to Examine All Terror Arrest Complaints', *Guardian*, 25 January.

Crompton, D. (1999) Quoted in *Guardian*, 2 March.

Crowther, C. (2000) *Policing Urban Poverty*. Basingstoke: Macmillan.

Denman, S. (2001) *Race Discrimination in the Crown Prosecution Service: Final Report*. London: Crown Prosecution Service.

Dodd, V. and Travis, A. (2005) 'Muslims Face Increased Stop and Search', *Guardian*, 2 March.

Equal Treatment Advisory Committee of the Judicial Studies Board (1999) *Equal Treatment Bench Book: Guidance for the Judiciary*. London: Judicial Studies Board.

Equal Treatment Working Party of the Judicial Studies Committee for Scotland (2002) *Equal Treatment Bench Book: Guidance for the Judiciary*. Edinburgh: Judicial Studies Commission for Scotland.

Fitzgerald, M. (1999) *Searches in London under Section 1 of the Police and Criminal Evidence Act*. London: Metropolitan Police Service.

Fitzgerald, M. (2001) 'Ethnic Minorities and Community Safety', in R. Matthews and J. Pitts (eds), *Crime, Disorder and Community Safety: A New Agenda*. London: Routledge.

Fitzgerald, M. and Sibbitt, R. (1997) *Ethnic Monitoring in Police Forces: A Beginning*, Research Study 173. London: Home Office, Research and Statistics Directorate.

Ghaffur, T. (2004) *Thematic Review of Race and Diversity Training in the Metropolitan Police Service*. London: Metropolitan Police Service.

Gifford, T. et al. (1989) *Loosen the Shackles: First Report of the Liverpool 8 Enquiry into Race Relations in Liverpool*. London: Karia Press.

Gordon, P. (1983) *White Law: Racism in the Police, the Courts and Prisons*. London: Pluto Press.

Gordon, P. (1996) 'The Racialisation of Statistics', in R. Skellington (ed.), *'Race' in Britain Today*, 2nd edn. London: Sage.

Gutzmore, C. (1983) 'Capital, Black Youth and Crime', *Race and Class*, XXV (2): 13–30.

Her Majesty's Inspectorate of Constabulary (1997) *Winning the Race: Policing Plural Communities, HMIC Thematic Report on Police Community and Race Relations 1996/97*. London: Home Office.

Her Majesty's Inspectorate of Constabulary (1999) *Winning the Race: Policing Plural Communities Re-visited: A Follow Up to the Thematic Report on Police, Community and Race Relations, 1998/9*. London: Home Office.

Her Majesty's Inspectorate of Constabulary (2000) *Policing London: 'Winning Consent', a Review of Murder Investigation, Community and Race Relations Issues in the Metropolitan Police Service*. London: Home Office.

Her Majesty's Inspectorate of Constabulary (2002) *Training Matters: Report of an Inspection of Police Probationer Training*. London: Home Office.

Her Majesty's Inspectorate of Constabulary (2003a) *Diversity Matters: HM Inspectorate of Constabulary Thematic Inspection, Executive Summary*. London: Home Office.

Her Majesty's Inspectorate of Constabulary (2003b) *CENTREX: Central Police Training and Development Authority: Inspection Report*. London: Home Office.

Her Majesty's Inspectorate of Constabulary (2004) *National Recruitment Standards, Thematic Inspection Report*. London: Home Office.

Her Majesty's Inspectorate of Probation (2000) *Towards Racial Equality: A Thematic Inspection*. London: Home Office.

Hinsliff, G. (2004) 'White Police Claim Racism', *Observer*, 22 August.

Holdaway, S. (1996) *The Racialisation of British Policing*. Basingstoke: Macmillan.

Home Affairs Committee (1981) *Racial Disadvantage*, Fifth Report, Session 1981/2, House of Commons Paper 424.

Home Affairs Committee (1986) *Racial Attacks and Harassment*, Third Report, Session 1985/6, House of Commons Paper 409.

Home Affairs Committee (1994) *Racial Attacks and Harassment*, Third Report, Session 1994/5 House of Commons Paper 71, Volume 1.

Home Affairs Committee (2005) *Terrorism and Community Relations*, Sixth Report, Session 2004/5, House of Commons Paper 165.

Home Office (1982a) *Ethnic Minority Recruitment*, Circular 5982. London: Home Office.

Home Office (1982b) *Report of a Study Group: Recruitment into the Police Service of Members of Ethnic Minorities*. London: HMSO.

Home Office (1989) *Equal Opportunities in the Police Service*, Circular 87/89. London: Home Office.

Home Office (1990) *Ethnic Minority Recruitment into the Police Service*, Circular 33/90. London: Home Office.

Home Office (1998) *Statistics on Race and the Criminal Justice System*. London: Home Office, Research and Statistics Directorate.

Home Office (2000a) *Statistics on Race and the Criminal Justice System*. London: Home Office Research, Development and Statistics Directorate.

Home Office (2000b) *Complaints Against the Police: A Consultative Paper*. London: Home Office Police Operational Unit.

Home Office (2000c) *Policing a New Century: A Blueprint for Reform*, Cm 5236. London: TSO.

Home Office (2001) *Building Cohesive Communities: A Report of the Ministerial Group on Public Order and Community Concern*. London: Home Office.

Home Office (2002) *The National Policing Plan 2003–2006*. London: Home Office Communications Directorate.

Hood, R. in collaboration with Cordovil, G. (1992) *Race and Sentencing*. Oxford: Oxford University Press.

Hood, R., Shute, S. and Seemungel, F. (2003) *Ethnic Minorities in the Criminal Courts: Perceptions of Fairness and Equality of Treatment*, Research Department Report 2/2003. London: Department for Constitutional Affairs.

Hopkins, N. (2002) 'Met Winning the Battle Against Prejudice', *Guardian*, 22 February.

Howard League for Penal Reform (2000) *Ethnic Minorities in the Criminal Justice System*, Factsheet 9. London: Howard League for Penal Reform.

Hunte, J. (1965) *Nigger Hunting in London?* London: West Indian Standing Conference.

Independent Committee of Inquiry Commissioned by the Roach Family Support Committee (1989) *Policing in Hackney 1945–1984*. London: Karia Press.

Institute of Race Relations (1987) *Policing Against Black People*. London: Institute of Race Relations.

Institute of Race Relations (1991) *Deadly Silence: Black Deaths in Custody*. London: Institute of Race Relations.

Jefferson, T. (1990) *The Case Against Paramilitary Policing*. Milton Keynes: Open University Press.

Joyce, P. (2001) 'The Governance of the Police in England and Wales, 1964–1988', *Police Practice and Research*, 2 (4): 315–44.

Joyce, P. (2002) *The Politics of Protest*. Basingstoke: Palgrave.

Joyce, P. (2004) 'Raising the Race Question', *Policing Today*, 10 (1): 15–17.

Kirk, B. (1996) *Negative Images: A Simple Matter of Black and White*. Aldershot: Avebury.

Kirkwood, A. (1998) *Crown Prosecution Service: Racial Incident Monitoring, Annual Report 1997–1998*. York: Crown Prosecution Service, amended version.

Lawrence, D. (2003) Speech at the Unite Against Racism Conference, London, 22 February, cited in *Institute of Race Relations News*, February.

Lea, J. (1986) 'Police Racism: Some Theories and Their Policy Implications', in R. Matthew and J. Young (eds), *Confronting Crime*. London: Sage.

Lea, J. (2003) 'Institutional Racism in Policing: The Macpherson Report and Its Consequences', in R. Matthews and J. Young (eds), *The New Politics of Crime and Punishment*. Collumpton: Willan Publishing.

Logan, L. (2004) Evidence submitted to the Morris Inquiry, 1 April 2004 (available at: www.morrisinquiry.gov.uk/transcripts/2004-04-01-2-mbpa.htm).

Macpherson, Sir W. (1999) *The Stephen Lawrence Inquiry: Report of an Inquiry by Sir William Macpherson of Cluny*, Cm 4252. London: TSO.

Magistrates Courts' Service Race Issues Group (2000) *Justice in Action*. London: Magistrates' Courts Service Race Issues Group.

Metropolitan Police Community Relations Branch (1987) *Racial Harassment Action Guide*. London: Metropolitan Police Service.

Miller, J., Bland, N. and Quinton, P. (2000) *The Impact of Stops and Searches on Crime and the Community*, Police Research Service Paper 127. London: Home Office Police and Reducing Crime Unit, Research, Development and Statistics Directorate.

Morgan, R. and Maggs, C. (1985) *Setting the PACE: Police–Community Consultative Arrangements in England and Wales*, Bath Social Policy Paper 4. Bath: University of Bath.

Morris, Sir W. (2004) *The Case for Change: People in the Metropolitan Police Service – The Report of the Morris Inquiry*. London: Morris Inquiry.

National Probation Service for England and Wales (2004) *Annual Report 2003/04*. London: National Probation Service.

Oakley, R. (1996) *Race and Equal Opportunities in the Police Service*. London: Commission for Racial Equality.

Office for Criminal Justice Reform (2004) *Cutting Crime, Delivering Justice: A Strategic Plan for Criminal Justice 2004–08*. London: TSO.

Phillips, T. (2003) Speech to the Metropolitan Black Police Association, 30 October, quoted in D. Calvert-Smith (2004) *A Formal Investigation of the Police Service in England and Wales: An Interim Report*. London: Commission for Racial Equality, p. 5.

Police Complaints Authority (1999) *Deaths in Police Custody*. London: TSO.

Police Complaints Authority (2000) *One Year On – Deaths in Police Custody*. London: TSO.

Police Federation (2005) *Stop and Search* (available at: www.polfed.org/we_stand_stop_search.asp).

Police Training Council Working Party (1983) *Community and Race Relations Training for the Police*. London: Home Office.

Powell, R. (2004) Quoted in *Observer*, 22 August.

Prison Report (1998) 'Firm within a Firm', editorial, no. 43.

Quinton, P. and Bland, N. (1999) *Modernising the Tactic: Improving the Use of Stop and Search*, Briefing Note No. 2/99. London: Home Office Research, Development and Statistics Directorate, Police and Reducing Crime Unit.

Reiner, R. (1985) *The Politics of the Police*, 1st edn. Brighton: Harvester Press.

Reiner, R. (1992) *The Politics of the Police*, 2nd edn. Toronto: University of Toronto Press.

Rowe, M. (2004) *Policing, Race and Racism*. Cullompton: Willan Publishing.

Scarman, Lord (1981) *The Brixton Disorders, Report of an Inquiry by the Rt. Hon. The Lord Scarman, OBE*, Cmnd 8427. London: HMSO.

Shaw, S. (1997) 'Remand Prisoners: Why There Are Too Many and How Numbers Could Be Reduced', *Prison Report*, no. 41.

Simey, M. (1985) *Government by Consent: The Principle and Practice of Accountability in Local Government*. London: Bedford Square Press.

Singh, G. (2000) 'The Concept and Content of Institutional Racism', in A. Marlow and B. Loveday (eds), *After Macpherson*. Lyme Regis: Russell House.

Smith, D. and Gray, J. (1983) *Police and People in London*, 4 vols. London: Policy Studies Institute.

Smith, S. (1989) *The Politics of 'Race' and Residence: Citizenship, Segregation and White Supremacy in Britain*. Cambridge: Polity.

Smyth, G. (1999) Letter to *Guardian*, 10 February.

Southgate, P. (1982) *Police Probationer Training in Race Relations*, Paper 8. London: Home Office Research and Planning Unit.

Southgate, P. (1984) *Racism Awareness Training for the Police*, Paper 8. London: Home Office, Research and Planning Unit.

Statewatch (1998) 'UK: Stop and Search and Arrest and Racism', *Statewatch*, 8 (3 and 4).

Statewatch (1999) 'The Cycle of UK Racism – Stop, Search, Arrest and Imprisonment', *Statewatch*, 9 (1).

Straw, J. (1999a) Speech at Gloucester, 1 March, quoted in *Guardian*, 2 March.

Straw, J. (1999b) Speech to a conference of chief constables, Southampton, 14 April.

Tompson, K. (1988) *Under Siege: Racial Violence in Britain Today*. Harmondsworth: Penguin.

Tonry, M. (2004) *Punishment and Politics: Evidence and Emulation in the Making of English Crime Control Policy*. Cullompton: Willan Publishing.

Travis, A. (2000) 'Police Racism Need Not Lead to Dismissal', *Guardian*, 11 August.

Williams, P. (2006) 'Designing and Delivering Programmes for Minority Ethnic Offenders' in S. Lewis, P. Raynor, D. Smith and A. Wardak. *Race and Probation*. Cullompton: Willan Publishing.

Wilson, A. (1983) 'Conspiracies to Assault', *New Statesman*, 105 (2710), 22 February.

Conclusion

Although the criminal justice system comprises a number of different agencies, their contemporary operations have been influenced by a number of themes that have been identified in the previous chapters.

The first of these is an appreciation that the scope of crime and disorder in contemporary western societies ensures that the operations of the criminal justice system is a key political issue. In the United States it was estimated that the annual burden of crime was around $1 trillion: this figure included items such as the costs of the legal system and crime prevention agencies, losses occasioned by victims, the opportunity costs of victims', criminals' and prisoners' time, the fear of being victimised and the cost of deterrence (Anderson, 1999). A comparative annual estimate for the United Kingdom was £60 billion, or around £1,000 for every man, woman and child. Governments need to demonstrate effectiveness in combating these problems or else risk suffering at the hands of the electorate. This means that the various agencies of the criminal justice system operate within a political environment in which governments seek to influence their objectives and operating practices. This may be achieved in various ways.

Governments may initiate legislation that seeks to impose controls over the activities of criminal justice agencies. Examples of this include the 1994 Police and Magistrates' Courts Act and the 1997 Crime (Sentencing) Act (which was revised by the 2000 Powers of the Criminal Courts (Sentencing) Act), which are discussed in Chapters 4 and 5 respectively. Legislation of this nature erodes the discretion previously exercised by criminal justice practitioners such as police officers, magistrates and judges. This approach raised concerns that governments introducing such innovations were seeking to politicise the criminal justice system. These arguments were forcibly voiced by those opposed to the 1994 Police and Magistrates' Courts Act. However, the key rationale for the new mechanisms of central control was to ensure that public money was spent efficiently rather than to further a government's political ambitions.

A further way in which governments have sought to impose central control and direction over agencies within the criminal justice process has been to focus concern on activities performed by these bodies and especially the manner in which they discharge them. Chapter 4 referred to this approach as 'marketability' (Jones, 2003).

Commencing in the 1980s this approach entailed subjecting the criminal justice system to what was termed managerialism or 'new public management'. Managerialism 'refers to the implementation of a variety of techniques, generally borrowed from the private sector within a culture of cost efficiency and service effectiveness' (James and Raine, 1998: 31). It seeks to operate public services as businesses, since 'with their bureaucratic tendencies' they were viewed as 'inherently inefficient' and the professionals working in them were perceived as 'self-serving' (James and Raine, 1998: 33).

New public management

New public management was associated with a number of reforms to the operations of public sector bodies that:

- emphasised the need for public services to be driven by concerns of efficiency, value for money and quality of service. This would be secured by methods that included the use of management methods associated with the private sector such as setting targets and performance indicators;
- sought to transform citizens into consumers whose power rested not on the political sanction of accountability but, rather, on their ability to shop around and go elsewhere if a service was not being provided efficiently;
- entailed organisational goals being set by central government while giving agency heads a considerable degree of freedom as to how these were attained: this approach is sometimes referred to as the 'steering/rowing' analogy;
- led to public policy being implemented by a range of bodies rather than being the preserve of agencies that functioned as arms of the state: this goal was achieved by the processes of 'hiving off' and compulsory competitive tendering.

Accordingly, the organisational (and to some extent the managerial) structure of the criminal justice system was increasingly influenced by reforms (Raine and Wilson, 1997) that emphasised value for money and efficiency in the delivery of services. Methods to achieve this included the introduction of targets, performance indicators and business plans. These had a number of consequences that included agency heads being required to display managerial and budgetary control skills as opposed to leadership qualities (McDonnell, 2000: 13), and a shift of emphasis towards the attainment of objectives at the expense of compliance with bureaucratic rules and procedures (Hood, 1994: 129).

The emphasis on efficiency, value for money and quality of service were integral aspects of new public management which sought to transform citizens into consumers whose power rested not upon the political sanction of accountability but, rather, upon the consumers' ability to shop around and go elsewhere if a public service was being provided inefficiently. This reflected the importance attached by the new right to the free market, which emphasised competition between service providers in order to enhance the level of consumer choice.

This objective was implemented in a number of ways. It resulted in privatisation whereby the private sector competed for the right to deliver services which were formerly solely associated with the public sector (such as the management of prisons) through the process of contracting out. Attempts were also made to develop internal markets (through policies which included compulsory competitive tendering) to further the objective of competition.

One further consequence of this approach was to require agencies implementing public policy to justify which aspects of their work should remain in the public sector and transferring the remainder to the private sector. As is discussed in Chapter 4, this resulted in attempts to define what are the 'core' tasks of policing and what other (termed 'ancillary') functions could be offloaded elsewhere.

The policies that were associated with furthering consumer choice led to the fragmentation of government, with public policy being implemented by a range of agencies rather than being the preserve of bodies that functioned as arms of the state. The spread of this approach across the Western world reflected an international trend in public administration that was a consequence of globalisation.

New public management was also identified with the twin forces of centralisation and decentralisation. One aspect of this reform was the establishment of autonomous agencies under the 'Next Steps' programme. (This reform is discussed in connection with the Prison Service in Chapter 8.) Elsewhere, the goals of established agencies within the criminal justice system became set by central government while leaving their attainment to agency heads who possessed a considerable operational freedom while functioning within a budget which was also centrally determined. Agencies were, however, subjected to increased forms of scrutiny (imposed by bodies such as the Audit Commission and new forms of central inspection) and agency heads were required to generate considerable volumes of statistics for central headquarters in order that their performance could be assessed.

A number of criticisms have been levelled at new public management. It required agencies such as the police to devote much of their resources to activities (mainly associated with crime fighting) which were able to be quantifiably measured at the expense of service functions which were essential in cementing a good police–public relationship but which did not lend themselves as easily to this form of assessment.

This approach has also been criticised for concentrating on outcomes as opposed to outputs. Outputs are concerned with an assessment as to whether stated objectives have been met whereas outcomes are concerned with the impact which the methods used to attain an objective have on the service's key stakeholders. For example, the vigorous use of stop and search powers may help to attain an objective which seeks a reduction in the level of street crime but may have a disastrous impact on the relationship between the police and those members of the public who feel themselves to be unfairly singled out for police attention of this nature.

Post-1997 Labour governments did not abandon the managerialist reforms of their Conservative predecessors. These were, instead, further developed through an approach that is termed 'new managerialism' (discussed by Flynn, 2000: 5–6).

New managerialism

The managerial reforms pursued by Labour governments after 1997 embraced the following approaches:
- the retention of performance targets and indicators;
- the introduction of best value as a process to assess efficiency and effectiveness in service delivery and to enhance the quality of service: best value replaced the Conservative's compulsory competitive tendering procedures and was the key reform of the 1997–2001 Labour government;
- the extension of centralised direction of the criminal justice process in areas that included the delivery of services and managerial processes;
- the involvement of the criminal justice system in evidence-based activities that attaches importance to evaluation of activities;
- the promotion of joined-up government, an approach that considerably extended earlier initiatives in multi-agency working;
- the development of a new emphasis on localism that (as Chapter 4 discusses), resulted in developments that include neighbourhood policing;
- the creation of a mixed economy of service delivery whereby criminal justice services are provided by the public, private and voluntary sectors: this approach derived from privatisation and is referred to as contestability.

The emphasis placed by previous Conservative governments on targets and performance indicators was maintained and substantially enhanced in connection with best-value targets and public service agreements. Best value (whose application to the police service is discussed in Chapter 4) focused on efficiency, effectiveness and quality of service and replaced the former Conservative policy of compulsory competitive tendering.

Agencies within the criminal justice process remained subject to central inspection and monitoring which Labour governments extended beyond service delivery to embrace managerial processes.

New Labour also emphasised the importance of evidence-based solutions to problems facing the criminal justice system (based on the 'what works?' philosophy) and of joined-up government. Both of these approaches have had important consequences for the way in which the criminal justice process operates.

The issue of 'what works?' enhanced the importance attached to evaluation as a concern of practitioners working in the criminal justice process and to criminology in general. Various models exist which outline the processes which evaluation entails (such as SARA – scanning, analysis, response and assessment). The importance attached to evaluation is displayed through the initiation of pilot schemes or projects whose impact can be analysed before a policy is rolled out nationally, thereby seeking to ensure that public policy is fashioned on the basis of informed decisions. The aim of evaluation of this nature is to assess both the outputs and outcomes of a particular intervention with a view to improving its effectiveness and enabling the dissemination of good practice where this is found. Evaluation can also be an important tool to enhance the accountability of agencies to their stakeholders.

There are, however, a number of problems associated with good evaluation. Data can be manipulated by evaluators to produce the results wanted by those who commission it. It is also an extremely complex and costly undertaking to conduct rigorously, often beyond the means or capacity of those seeking assessment of their activities.

Other problems connected with evaluation include issues arising from the cause and effect dilemma – a desirable effect may have happened regardless of the specific intervention that is being assessed in the evaluation process. For example, a project aiming to reduce the level of street crime through the installation of CCTV may claim success if the level of crime of this nature falls in the locality where this intervention occurred. However, good evaluation requires data from other localities to be included in the assessment to guard against the possibility that there was a downward national trend in crime of this nature and that the installation of CCTV in a selected neighbourhood made little or no difference to the reduction of this form of crime. Random control trials have thus been utilised to guard against problems of this nature.

Further difficulties arise in connection with attempts to more widely apply the benefits arising from what has been evaluated as a successful intervention in a specific area. It cannot be assumed that because something has worked successfully in one area that it will work equally effectively elsewhere. There may have been unique factors affecting the success of an intervention that will be difficult to repeat in other localities. For example, if evaluation discovers that the establishment of a youth club had a significant effect in reducing the level of juvenile crime and anti-social behaviour in a specific area, it cannot be deduced with any certainty that this form of intervention will be universally as effective. It may be that the success of this intervention derived from the calibre of the staff working in that youth club as opposed to the formation of a youth club per se. Similarly, there may have been characteristics peculiar to a particular locality to explain the success of an intervention there and it may not thus be capable of wider replication. Evaluation thus needs to go beyond an assessment as to whether something has 'worked' to provide an understanding as to *why* this beneficial effect has arisen.

Nor can it be assumed that a similar activity will consistently produce similar results or reactions. It may be possible to assert, on the basis of evaluation, that an intervention had worked but it cannot be concluded from this with any degree of certainty that what has worked today will necessarily work next week, next month or next year.

The emphasis on 'what works?' places evaluation centre stage of the crime-fighting agenda. Good evaluation is perhaps seen as the means to find the magic bullet that will solve the crime problem. However, as is argued in Chapter 1, there are numerous explanations that seek to suggest why persons commit crime. This discussion suggested that there is no one universal 'cause' of crime, and it may be further deduced from this that the occurrence of crime is governed by a wide and complex set of factors whose existence and interrelationships, may be unique to particular localities or even to specific individuals. It may thus be concluded that the quest for an all-embracing solution to crime derived from evaluation is likely to be as unfruitful as the quest for the Holy Grail.

A further development associated with new managerialism has been that of joined-up government. The aim of this was to enhance the level of coordination between the various agencies whose work was of relevance to crime and disorder. It suggested that crime could be reduced not by structural reforms seeking to achieve a greater level of social equality but by managerial improvements. These reforms were in part derived from the assumption that deficiencies in the criminal justice system were derived from 'system failures' which could be solved by removing 'the gaps and limitations of friction and conflict' to ensure the smooth running of the system (Crawford, 1999: 66). The underpinnings of this approach were 'coherence, coordination and integration' (Blumstein, 1986).

The compartmentalised way in which agencies working in the criminal justice process traditionally operated often made a coordinated approach towards crime and disorder difficult to achieve: the police service, for example, has historically been more concerned with serving the victims of crime through the arrest and prosecution of offenders whereas the Probation Service's prime historic responsibility was to cater for the care and long-term interests of those who had offended. Although reforms (such as the establishment of the Criminal Justice Consultative Council in 1991) were put forward to promote a greater sense of common purpose between agencies in the criminal justice process, they failed to promote a unified approach to tackle crime. Chapter 9, for example, refers to the problems that were identified by the Audit Commission (1996) as arising in the juvenile justice system from the lack of coordination between agencies concerned with young people.

Traditionally it was assumed that the potential for securing an integrated criminal justice system was limited since 'it is important to recognise the existence of interaction between the different parts of the system, that the "output" of one stage provides the "input" for another, and that for the system to be "rational" there would need to be an overall goal towards which each and every part was directed'. It was argued that 'the complex socio-political nature of crime and society's response to criminal behaviour seems to rule out the possibility of any real integration or "rationality" throughout the penal process' (Bottomley, 1973: 225). It was in the sense of the lack of coordination between various agencies that the term 'process' was justified rather than 'system' being applied, the latter suggesting a degree of coordination and the existence of shared goals that were historically absent. Accordingly, the emphasis placed by post-1997 Labour governments on coordinated activity to achieve shared goals is compatible with an attempt to 'systematise' the criminal justice 'process' (Loveday, 2000: 23).

Labour governments have avidly pursued reforms that sought to bring about joined-up government in a number of ways and at a number of levels of government. Structures to achieve coordination of agencies within the criminal justice system at national level have been set up. The National Criminal Justice Board was established in April 2003 on which ministers of the Home Office, Department for Constitutional Affairs and Law Officers' Departments sit alongside heads of the main criminal justice agencies, ACPO, the Association of Police Authorities and a representative of the judiciary. Criminal justice ministers are jointly responsible for the delivery of public service agreement targets relating to bringing offenders to justice and raising public confidence in the criminal justice system. The Board 'monitors progress towards these targets, holds agencies and areas to account where performance falls short, and where problems arise that cannot be overcome at local level, makes sure that solutions are found' (Office for Criminal Justice Reform, 2004: 15). It is advised on criminal justice reform by the Criminal Justice Council that is designed to provide 'an objective, external perspective on the role and workings of the system' (Home Office, Department for Constitutional Affairs and Attorney General, 2002: 147).

Additionally, the Office for Criminal Justice Reform was set up in 2004. This is a cross-departmental body that reports to the Home Office, the Department for Constitutional Affairs and the Law Officers' Department and seeks to promote cooperation between all criminal justice agencies.

The theme of coordination was especially apparent in the government's publication of a strategic plan for the entire criminal justice system in which a range of performance indicators and targets were set for all agencies in order to secure a coordinated effort in which the growth and fear of crime and the level of disorder was diminished (Home Office, 1999a). In July 2004 a further strategic plan for criminal justice was published by the Office for Criminal Justice Reform which focused on 'how we will bring more criminals to justice, improve the way different agencies are working together, and give victims and witnesses better services' (Blunkett et al., 2004: 7). It was envisaged that in 2008, 150,000 more offences would be brought to justice, the detection rate would be improved from 19 per cent to at least 25 per cent, and that the top 15–20 most prolific offenders in each CDRP area would be 'relentlessly' targeted (Office for Criminal Justice Reform, 2004: 10).

These aims would be accomplished through improvements which included additional investment in information technology to enable 'all criminal justice staff … to communicate swiftly and efficiently through a single IT infrastructure'. Additionally, the relationship between the criminal justice departments was strengthened by the creation of a trilateral centre for the Criminal Justice System (Office for Criminal Justice Reform, 2004: 11). The 2006 Police and Justice legislation will further the aim of coordination by creating a new HM Chief Inspector for Justice, Community Safety and Custody to replace the existing criminal justice agency Inspectorates.

Coordination has also been advanced in connection with the development of common skills across the criminal justice sector. The organisation Skills for Justice seeks to assess the skills that are required by all criminal justice agencies and to put forward an action plan to provide for training and workforce development.

The objective of securing joined-up government at national level has also involved the merger of previously separate services. An important example of this has been the creation of a single correctional service, NOMS, involving the merger of the Probation and Prison Services. This reform (which is discussed in Chapter 8) was driven by the desire to reduce the level of recidivism through improved mechanisms to reintegrate offenders into their communities.

In addition to attempts to secure coordination at the national level, attempts have been made to further this objective locally. When the Labour government first entered office in 1997 there existed a number of conflicting boundaries – 'there were 43 police forces; 13 CPS areas; 96 Magistrates' Courts Committees, covering around 460 Magistrates' Courts, and there were six Crown Court circuits' (Blunkett et al., 2004). Subsequent rationalisation eliminated these differences resulting in key criminal justice agencies operating across similar geographic areas. Additionally, police divisional boundaries became aligned with those of local government.

The objective of securing closer cooperation at local level was further advanced in 2003 when the government established 42 Local Criminal Justice Boards for England and Wales. These were designed to coordinate the activities of the criminal justice system at the local level by bringing chief officers of each criminal justice agency together at a local level with a prime aim of bringing more offenders to justice. National targets were set for key areas of criminal justice work which included the number of offenders 'brought to justice' (which entails an offender being either convicted, cautioned, given a street warning for the possession of cannabis, receiving a penalty notice for disorder or having offences taken into consideration in a court), ineffective trials, public confidence in the criminal justice system bringing offenders to justice, fine enforcement and the time between arrest and sentence, and the performance of each area in meeting these targets was published quarterly (CJS Online, 2004).

Specific areas of criminal justice were also subjected to the joined-up approach at the local level. Initial progress in this direction affected the operations of the juvenile justice system (an issue which is discussed in Chapter 9) through the establishment of multi-agency Youth Offending Teams. In addition to formalised machinery to achieve an enhanced level of inter-agency cooperation at the local level, this objective has also been furthered through other means. Agencies have frequently been enjoined to cooperate with other bodies to solve specific crime-related problems, and, as Chapter 3 describes, the development of problem-oriented policing is underpinned by a multi-agency approach.

The joined-up approach extended beyond criminal justice agencies to embrace other bodies in the public, private and voluntary sectors that were enjoined to consider how their work related to the fight against crime. The health service became involved in the operations of crime and disorder reduction partnerships and local government came to perform a key role in community safety issues (a matter that is discussed more fully below). The contemporary emphasis placed on curbing the level of recidivism has resulted in a number of government departments being required to contribute to the resettlement of offenders into communities.

In addition to attempts that have been made to coordinate the operations of the criminal justice system both nationally and locally, efforts have also been made to address the social causes of crime by this approach. In particular the work performed by the Social Exclusion Unit has sought to secure a joined-up approach at the local level to address social problems that are perceived to have an important bearing on crime. As is discussed more fully in Chapter 2, local strategic partnerships (LSPs) perform a key role in delivering neighbourhood renewal. They seek to bring together the public, private, voluntary and community sectors to tackle complex problems requiring multi-agency responses. LSPs devise targets known as local public service agreements which are agreements between local and central government to attain specified targets. Crime and disorder reduction partnerships are an important delivery mechanism of LSPs.

A further theme underpinning reforms to the criminal justice process identified by this work has been the enhanced role of the community in criminal justice matters. There are a number of time-honoured ways whereby individual members of local communities can be involved in matters of this nature (for example through the Special Constabulary, neighbourhood watch schemes or the lay magistracy). These avenues have been extended by legislation such as the 1999 Youth Justice and Criminal Evidence Act which enabled local persons to become involved in the sentencing of young offenders through their involvement in Youth Offender Panels.

However, the approach adopted by post-1997 Labour governments went beyond seeking to foster personal involvement in criminal justice matters to embrace attempts to galvanise community feeling and to use this in the fight against crime and disorder. Initially, as Chapter 2 argues, this took the form of involving local government in crime-related issues. Subsequently, this approach extended beyond local government to involving neighbourhoods and communities in aspects related to community safety. This approach underpinned the introduction of local crime audits by the 1998 Crime and Disorder Act that in theory enabled communities to place their concerns on the crime-fighting agenda. The objective of seeking to resurrect 'community' or 'neighbourhood' as a quasi-tier of government may make further inroads into the autonomy of state-employed professionals.

An important related theme affecting community safety has been the enhanced concern attached to the assessment of risk. This places the concern of safety at the forefront of criminal justice policy. 'In modernity, risk, in its purely technical meaning, came to rely upon conditions in which the probability estimates of an event are able to be known or knowable' (Lupton, 1999: 7). Agencies operating within the criminal justice system have increasingly formulated their interventions by seeking to predict future behaviour and, as is argued in Chapter 8, this has become an increasingly important function of the Probation Service. However, the emphasis given to risk assessment has been criticised. It has been argued that 'despite its claims to objectivity, risk analysis is an unreliable tool and provides an inconsistent and largely ineffective way of identifying, filtering and judging offenders. Its thinly disguised subjectivism serves neither to address the reasons for offending, nor does it make much contribution to protecting the public' (Goodman, 2003: 244).

This work has also identified the extent to which the crime-fighting agenda has been increasingly driven by penal populist impulses in recent years in which governments seek to display their credentials of 'being tough on criminals'. Although this approach has been tempered by other policies (such as attempts to tackle the social causes of crime, an issue that is discussed in Chapter 9), it has dominated the crime-fighting agenda. This was especially evidenced in the 2005 general elections when both major parties sought to 'talk up' their own toughness on this issue and berate the 'softness' of their opponents (Joyce, 2004: 21–3). The effect of this approach has included the increased presence of various forms of uniformed personnel in communities, a consistently high prison population and attempts to regulate a wide variety of behaviour labelled as anti-social. These issues are explored in Chapters 3, 8 and 9.

A final theme affecting the operations of the criminal justice system has been directed at the perception of racism. The proposals that were directed at the police service by Lord Scarman's report in 1981 (Home Office, 1981) failed to secure any significant improvement in the relationship between the police and ethnic minority communities. This failure was most evident in the 1990s in the attitude adopted by police forces (and the judicial system in general) towards racially motivated attacks. The botched investigation by the Metropolitan Police into the murder of Stephen Lawrence in 1993 prompted the 1997 Labour government to initiate an inquiry undertaken by a retired judge, Sir William Macpherson. The recommendations contained in his 1999 report (especially his view concerning institutionalised racism) (Home Office, 1999b) set the agenda for the reform of the entire criminal justice system in the twenty-first century.

One illustration of the improved manner in which racially motivated violence has subsequently been dealt with occurred in Liverpool in 2005 when a young black teenager, Anthony Walker, was murdered. The Merseyside Police immediately branded his killing as racist and on 1 August 2005, three days after the killing, named two suspects whom they wished to interview. These suspects (who were by now in Holland) were arrested on their return to Britain and charged with Anthony's murder on 5 August. One subsequently pleaded guilty and the other was found guilty by a jury following an eleven-day trial. Both received life sentences. The trial judge, Mr Justice Lawson, confirmed that the murder was racially motivated which had the effect of raising the tariff that both were required to serve. One murderer was required to serve 24 years and the other 18 years.

This work has also identified a number of problems in connection with the reforms that have been introduced into the criminal justice process. One of these is that of incompatibility – certain reforms have conflicted with other innovations. Chapter 4 examined one of these in connection with reforms introduced into policing which created the potential for tensions arising between the increased level of central control exerted over the service since 1994 and the importance subsequently attached to the devising of locally determined priorities.

One attempt to solve tensions of this nature and further the objective of joined-up working across the tiers of government has been the introduction of local area agreements (LAAs). This initiative was announced by the Office of the Deputy Prime Minister in 2004, a main aim of which was to redefine the relationship between central and local government and simplify the funding stream from central government. Under these proposals, local government (which represents a range of bodies including the LSP) and central government (represented by the regional office) fashion an agreement (the LAA). The LAA formulates plans in three priority areas (safer/stronger communities, children/young people and healthier communities/older people) comprising a package of central and local area targets. The local priorities derive from the local authority's (or local authorities' if the LAA includes more than one such authority) community strategy and the objectives of the LSP and their constituent bodies, such as CDRPs. The LAA budget is derived from the mainstream budgets of the participating agencies and from money obtained from the Neighbourhood Renewal Fund and the Safe and Stronger Communities Fund (which is intended to be rolled out nationally in 2005/6).

Accusations of incompatible criminal justice policy have also been made in connection with the campaign waged by recent Labour governments against anti-social behaviour. One aspect of this argument is the way in which the use of fixed penalty notices to combat various aspects of such behaviour undermines interventions designed to nip criminal behaviour in the bud, as was put forward, for example, in the procedure introduced by the 1998 Crime and Disorder legislation whereby a warning issued by a police officer to an offender aged 10–17 would result in that youth automatically being referred to the YOT. The use of one-off responses to anti-social behaviour is at odds with attempts to tackle the root causes of actions of this nature.

A further example of incompatibility concerns attempts to limit the discretion of sentencers. As Chapter 5 argues, this objective was implemented in the Conservative government's 1997 Crime (Sentences) Act that (as revised by the 2000 Powers of the Criminal Courts (Sentencing) Act) introduced a range of mandatory sentences. This approach was continued through the work of the Sentencing Guidelines Council when established in 2000. However, the objective of securing consistency in sentencing is at odds with attempts to involve members of local communities in activities of this nature (for example, through their involvement in Youth Offender Panels, the role of which is considered in Chapter 9) since this approach can result in different sanctions being applied to very similar crimes.

It has been also been argued that the emphasis placed by post-1997 Labour governments on human rights has conflicted with other aspects of government policy. Government policies that include the 2002 Proceeds of Crime Act and the use of fixed penalty notice fines under anti-social behaviour legislation have reversed the burden of proof and require the suspect to prove their innocence. Chapter 8 discussed the concept of the risk society in which the calculation of the extent to which an individual's future behaviour will have an adverse impact on the safety of the community assumes a key position in penal policy. This approach has given rise to suggestions of incarcerating those with severe personality disorders even if they have not committed any crime and imposing extended surveillance over those convicted of crimes such as sexual offences.

Chapter 9 provided further examples of this conflict by referring to arguments alleging that Anti-social Behaviour Orders (which play a key part in the government's law and order strategy) might be challenged under the human rights legislation since these are technically civil orders that may be obtained on the basis of 'hearsay' evidence that would be unacceptable in a criminal trial. However, breach of an ASBO is a criminal offence. This might be argued to be contrary to Articles 6 (the right to a fair trial) and 7 (no punishment without law) (Afzal and Schuller, 2001: 7–8). Disputes of this nature have also given rise to arguments that link the enjoyment of rights with the exercise of responsibility (Giddens, 2000) – rights are only available to those who fulfil their social responsibilities. This situation was emphasised by the Prime Minister in his launch of the Respect Action Plan (Blair, 2006).

A more significant conflict challenging the government's commitment to human rights has arisen in connection with their policies to combat terrorism. Security policy assumed enhanced importance in the wake of attacks in America on 11 September 2001, the invasion of Iraq in 2003 and terrorist attacks in London in July 2005.

The balance between security and liberty is a fine one to draw, and allegations have been made that some of the policies put forward, such as the detention of foreign nationals without trial (under the 2001 Anti-terrorism, Crime and Security Act), the exclusion or deportation from the UK of non-UK citizens whose actions were deemed to glorify or encourage terrorism (accomplished by orders introduced in 2005 based on powers granted by the 1971 Immigration Act) and, the acknowledged use of a 'shoot to kill' policy against suspected terrorists by the Metropolitan Police (which resulted in the death of an innocent Brazilian young man who was mistaken for a suicide bomber in July 2005), were in contravention of the government's commitment to human rights. In 2005 the head of MI5, Dame Eliza Manningham-Buller, warned in a speech delivered at the Hague in Holland that civil liberties might have to be eroded in order to prevent future terrorist attacks in Britain. She was especially concerned with the practical application of information based upon intelligence (in areas such as control orders and deportations) which fell short of hard evidence and which might prejudice the civil rights of those subject to actions of this nature.

In seeking to chart the development of criminal justice policy, this book has emphasised that this area of public policy is constantly changing. The following 'Keeping up to date' section seeks to enable readers to keep abreast of contemporary developments by providing information on what can be obtained from a wide range of bodies which initiate criminal justice policy or who exert influence over its content once firm ideas have been put forward.

References

Afzal, S. and Schuller, N. (2001) *Getting It Right: A Guide to the Human Rights Act 1998 for Community Safety Partnerships*. London: NACRO, Crime and Social Policy Briefing.

Anderson, D. (1999) 'The Aggregate Burden of Crime', *Journal of Law and Economics*, XLII (2): 611–42.

Audit Commission (1996) *Misspent Youth*. London: Audit Commission.

Blair, T. (2006) Respect Action Plan launch speech, 10 January.

Blumstein, A. (1986) 'Coherence, Coordination and Integration in the Administration of Criminal Justice', in J. van Dijk et al. (eds), *Criminal Law in Action: An Overview of Current Issues in Western Societies*. Arnhem: Gouda Quint.

Blunkett, D., Falconer, Lord C. and Goldsmith, Lord I. (2004) 'Preface' in Home Office, Department for Constitutional Affairs and Attorney General, *Cutting Crime, Delivering Justice: A Strategic Plan for Criminal Justice 2004–08*, Cm 6288. London: TSO.

Bottomley, K. (1973) *Decisions in Penal Process*, London: Martin Robertson.

Crawford, A. (1999) *The Local Governance of Crime: Appeals to Community Partnerships*. Oxford: Oxford University Press.

Criminal Justice System Online (2004) *Local Criminal Justice Board Performance* (available at: www.cjsonline.org/news/2004/july/cjs_stats2.html).

Flynn, N. (2000) 'The Government's Approach to Performance Management', *Criminal Justice Matters*, 40, Summer: 5–6.

Giddens, A. (2000) *The Third Way and its Critics,* Cambridge: Polity Press.

Goodman, A. (2003) 'Probation into the Millennium: The Punishing Service', in R. Matthews and J. Young (eds), *The New Politics of Crime and Punishment*. Cullompton: Willan Publishing.

Home Office (1981) *The Brixton Disorders 10–12 April 1981, Report of an Inquiry by the Rt Hon. Lord Scarman, OBE*, Cm 8427. London: HMSO.

Home Office (1999a) *Criminal Justice System Strategic Plan 1999–2002*. London: TSO.

Home Office (1999b) *The Stephen Lawrence Inquiry: Report of an Inquiry by Sir William Macpherson of Cluny*, Cm 4262. London: TSO.

Home Office, Department for Constitutional Affairs and Attorney General (2002) *Justice for All*, Cm 5563. London: TSO.

Hood, C. (1994) *Explaining Economic Policy Reversals*. Buckingham: Open University Press.

James, A. and Raine, J. (1998) *The New Politics of Criminal Justice*. Harlow: Longman.

Jones, T. (2003) 'The Governance and Accountability of Policing', in T. Newburn (ed.), *Handbook of Policing*. Cullompton: Willan Publishing.

Joyce, P. (2004) 'Crime, Policing and the Parties', *Policing Today*, 10 (4): 21–3.

Loveday, B. (2000) 'Policing Performance', *Criminal Justice Matters*, no. 40, Summer: 23–4.

Lupton, D. (1999) *Risk*. London: Routledge.

McDonnell, D. (2000) 'Managerialism, Privatisation and the Prison Scene', *Criminal Justice Matters*, no. 40, Summer: 13–14.

Office for Criminal Justice Reform (2004) *Cutting Crime, Delivering Justice: A Strategic Plan for Criminal Justice 2004–08*, Cm 6288. London: TSO.

Raine, J. and Wilson, M. (1997) 'Beyond Managerialism in Criminal Justice', *Howard Journal*, 36 (1): 80–95.

Keeping up to date

The response to crime is constantly changing and students of criminology and criminal justice policy need to keep abreast of these alterations.

The following provides a list of key organisations whose work is relevant to the operations of the criminal justice process. The website addresses of these organisations are also provided. However, website addresses do change and if the one given here fails to work you are advised to enter the name of the organisation into a search engine.

Acts of Parliament

(www.opsi.gov.uk/acts.htm)
Much of the work performed within the criminal justice process is governed by Acts of Parliament. These may, for example, provide for the creation of agencies operating in this process and give them powers with which to conduct their work. Legislation affecting the criminal justice process is contained in Public General Acts and they are available on-line from 1988 onwards at this website.

Association of Chief Police Officers (ACPO)

(www.acpo.police.uk)
ACPO originates from the County Chief Constables Club (formed in 1858) and the Chief Constables' Association of England and Wales (which was established to represent city and borough police forces in 1896). It assumed its present form in 1948, and the Royal Ulster Constabulary was incorporated in 1970. ACPO consists of the most senior ranks of the police service (chief constables, deputy chief constables and assistant chief constables or their equivalents in the 44 police forces of England, Wales and Northern Ireland, together with the most senior ranks from national policing agencies, the Isle of Man and the Channel Islands and a small number of senior non-police staff). These numbered 312 in 2005. Initially ACPO served as both a staff association for these senior ranks and also acted as the central focus for the development of police policy. The staff association role was taken over by the Chief Police Officers' Staff Association in 1996 enabling ACPO to concentrate on policy formulation. Its website contains on-line copies of the Annual Report since 2000 and ACPO policies on a very wide range of activities concerned with the internal and external operations of the police service.

Association of Police Authorities (APA)

(www.apa.police.uk)
The APA represents the 44 police authorities in England, Wales and Northern Ireland. This body was established in April 1997 to promote the concerns of these bodies both locally and nationally and to seek to influence police policy. On-line material on its website includes responses to consultative documents related to police reform and material connected with police policy such as stop and search powers. The APA Views section provides up-to-date statements on contemporary police issues and the APA's annual report is available from 2002/3.

Audit Commission

(www.audit-commission.gov.uk)
The Audit Commission was initially created in 1983 to regulate the external auditors of local authorities in England and Wales and its remit was subsequently extended to a wide range of bodies that spend public money. It seeks to aid those responsible for delivering public services to achieve a high level of quality by attaining the three 'Es' of economy, efficiency and effectiveness. On-line reports relevant to criminal justice matters are to be found within the Criminal Justice sector of the website. This includes reports on the police and probation services, cross-sector working and the criminal justice system. Additionally, the Inspection Report section of the website contains investigations of areas that include community safety. It is useful to occasionally check the Commission's website for details of their current investigations.

Bar Council

(www.barcouncil.org.uk)
The General Council of the Bar was established in 1894 to represent the interests of barristers in England and Wales. It is the governing body of the Bar and seeks to promote and improve its services and functions and represent its interests on all matters related to the profession. It also serves as the disciplinary body for barristers. It is composed of in excess of 115 barristers who are elected and represent the Inns of Court and interest groups. The Bar Council's website contains on-line copies of its annual reports since 2001 and a range of material relevant to the operations of the criminal justice process such as consultation papers. Much of the work of the Bar Council is discharged by committees and reports by these (covering issues such as equality and diversity) are also available on-line.

Commission for Judicial Appointments (CJA)

(www.cja.gov.uk)
The CJA was established in 2001 to review the process whereby judges and Queen's Counsel are appointed and to investigate complaints in connection with either of these processes. It has no role, however, in the actual appoint-

ment process. It submits an annual report to the Lord Chancellor which is available on-line since 2002. The CJA's website also has on-line copies of its reports into the judicial appointments over which it exercises scrutiny and the agency's responses to consultation papers published by the Department for Constitutional Affairs.

Commission for Racial Equality (CRE)

(www.cre.gov.uk)
The CRE was established by the 1976 Race Relations Act with the aim of working towards the elimination of racial discrimination and the promotion of equality of opportunity. The remit of the CRE was extended by the 2001 Race Relations (Amendment) Act whereby all public services were given the statutory responsibility of promoting racial equality. For the first time, agencies within the criminal justice process that included the police service and the Prison Service were brought under the scope of race relations legislation.

The CRE's website contains on-line material which includes the Code of Practice and Guidance to give practical help to authorities to meet the race equality duty. It also provides access to CRE publications, some of which are available on-line.

Courts Service

(www.hmcourts-service.gov.uk)
In 2005 Her Majesty's Courts Service was set up as an executive agency of the Department of Constitutional Affairs to provide for unified organisation and administration of the civil, family and criminal courts in England and Wales. Its website provides on-line information on the work of the Service, and access to Crown Court Annual Reports since 2000/1 and County Court Annual Reports since 2002/3.

Crime and Disorder Reduction Partnerships (CDRPs)

(www.crimereduction.gov.uk/partnerships)
CDRPs (or Community Safety Partnerships) were established by the 1998 Crime and Disorder Act (as amended by the 2002 Police Reform Act) to provide for multi-agency cooperation to reduce the level of local crime and disorder. The legislation places a statutory obligation on what are termed 'responsible authorities' (namely police forces, local authorities, fire authorities, police authorities, health authorities in Wales and primary care trusts in England) to cooperate in identifying local crime and disorder issues and to develop strategies to cope with them. CDRPs work closely with drug action teams (DATs) and integrate the latter's work in unitary local authorities in 2004. The CDRP website provides on-line access to the local crime and disorder reduction strategy of each of the 376 CDRPs in England and Wales.

Crime Info

(www.crimeinfo.org.uk)
This extremely informative website is operated by the Centre for Crime and Justice Studies at King's College London and provides up-to-date information on a wide range of topics affecting the study of crime and the criminal justice system. The site includes a discussion forum, an interactive exercise in which you can discover what it is like to be a judge and a topic of the month. Additionally, a highly useful dictionary section provides readily understandable definitions of complex technical terms.

Criminal Cases Review Commission (CCRC)

(www.ccrc.gov.uk)
This body was established by the 1995 Criminal Appeal Act to investigate suspected miscarriages of justice in England, Wales and Northern Ireland and determine whether to refer a conviction or a sentence to the Court of Appeal. It became operational in March 1997. Its website contains an on-line case library that contains information on the cases handled by the CCRC, and for some of these a full copy of the Appeal Court's judgement is available at www.casetrack.com (although this is a subscription service). The CCRC website also contains a small publications list, some of which (including the annual report) are available on-line.

Crown Prosecution Service (CPS)

(www.cps.gov.uk)
The CPS was established by the 1985 Prosecution of Offenders Act and became operational in 1986. It is responsible for prosecuting persons charged by the police with a criminal offence in England and Wales. Specifically, it advises the police on prosecutions, reviews cases submitted to it by the police and prepares and presents cases at court. It is headed by the Director of Public Prosecutions who is responsible to the Attorney General. Its website includes on-line Annual Reports since 2000/1 and business plans and provides access to material prepared by the 42 CPS areas. Additionally, the Code for Crown Prosecutors is available on-line together with CPS guidance on prosecution policy in connection with specific criminal offences including racist and religious crimes.

The work of the CPS is monitored by the CPS Inspectorate, the CPSI. (www.hmcpsi.gov.uk). The role of the CPSI is to promote improvements in the efficiency, effectiveness and fairness of the prosecution service within the framework of a joined-up criminal justice process through the processes of inspection, evaluation and dissemination of good practice. Its website includes on-line Annual Reports since 2000/1 and reports of thematic and joint reviews, and provides access to reports prepared by the CPS areas and branches.

Department for Constitutional Affairs (DCA)

(www.dca.gov.uk)
This department (formerly known as the Lord Chancellor's Department) was established in June 2003 and is headed by the Lord Chancellor. Its role is to 'uphold justice, rights and democracy' which entails a range of tasks including running the courts and improving the justice system. The DCA website provides a range of on-line reports and consultation papers on issues connected with the operations and administration of the criminal justice process. The website also contains on-line publications prepared by the DCA Research Unit relevant to research undertaken in behalf of the department, and by the DCA's Economic and Statistics Directorate whose task is to coordinate statistics across the department.

Europol

(www.europol.eu.int)
Officially known as the European Police Office, the creation of Europol was sanctioned by the 1992 Maastricht Treaty. It commenced limited operations as the European Drugs Unit (EDU) in 1994 and became fully operational in 1999. It is based in the Hague (Holland) and is funded by the EU member countries. Its main purpose is to support law enforcement agencies in EU countries by gathering and analysing information and intelligence in connection with terrorism, drug trafficking and other forms of international organised criminal activity. Its website contains on-line reports on organised crime, specific aspects of serious crime and the annual report.

Home Affairs Committee

(www.parliament.uk/parliamentary_committees/home_affairs_committee.cfm)
The Home Affairs Committee is a Select Committee of the House of Commons that conducts periodic investigations into services administered by, and issues connected with, the Home Office. Many of these are concerned with the criminal justice process and it is worth while periodically investigating this website to see what the Committee is currently examining. Evidence submitted to the Committee during its investigations is published in addition to the Committee's final report. The latter can be found by clicking onto 'Reports and Publications' and these are available on-line from the 1997/8 Parliamentary Session onwards.

Home Office

(www.homeoffice.gov.uk)
The Home Office plays a key role in the operations of the criminal justice process and its website provides immediate access to a vast amount of up-to-date information that is available on-line. The website is organised into a

number of headings, the key ones of which include Community and Race, Crime and Policing, and Justice and Victims.

The Research, Development and Statistics Directorate (RDS) publishes a wealth of information relevant to students of criminal justice which is available on-line at www.homeoffice.gov.uk/rds. This includes the British Crime Survey, crime statistics and the annual publication *Statistics on Race and the Criminal Justice System*. This publication provides a range of up-to-date information and statistics on criminal justice issues affecting minority ethnic communities. These include the police use of stop and search powers, racist incidents and crimes, prosecution and sentencing policy and complaints against the police.

The RDS also publishes Home Office Research Studies (which were formerly published by the Research and Planning Unit). These consist of reports undertaken by or on behalf of the Home Office on the areas over which the Home Secretary exercises responsibility and are available on-line from 1969. This unit also publishes research findings, Statistical publications and miscellaneous papers, all of which contain valuable information on the operations of aspects of the criminal justice process.

Home Office Circulars

(www.circulars.homeoffice.gov.uk)
Home Office circulars provide a considerable volume of information on the operations of those aspects of the criminal justice process that are controlled by the Home Office. Circulars give instructions on issues that include the implementation of legislation and policy administered by this department. Circulars are available on-line from 1944 onwards.

Howard League for Penal Reform

(www.howardleague.org)
The Howard League is a penal reform charity, established in 1866. It seeks to reform the penal system through education and campaigns in support of its core beliefs, one of which expresses support for community sentences. In addition to the *Howard Journal for Criminal Justice*, it publishes a wide range of material on issues connected with the criminal justice process that includes prisons, restorative justice, sentencing and victims.

Independent Police Complaints Commission (IPCC)

(www.ipcc.gov.uk)
This body is responsible for managing or supervising police investigations into complaints made by members of the public against police officers and can independently investigate the most serious cases of this nature. It replaced the Police Complaints Authority and was established by the 2002 Police Reform Act. It commenced work on 1 April 2004. The IPCC publishes

periodic reports into important issues affecting police–public relations (such as deaths in police custody and stop and search powers) and also conducts a research programme. Current issues under consideration include public confidence in the complaints system and the local resolution of complaints. The IPCC website also includes statistical information on issues such as deaths during or following police contact in England and Wales since 1997/8.

Justice

(www.justice.org.uk)
Justice is an influential legal and human rights organisation that was established in 1957. It seeks to improve the legal system and quality of justice by advocating improvements to all aspects of the operations of the criminal justice process, in particular by promoting human rights. It conducts research and issues policy briefings. A list of publications are available on its website. Many of these have to be purchased, although some material is available on-line.

Law Society

(www.lawsociety.org.uk)
The Law Society of England and Wales is the regulatory and supervisory body for solicitors in England and Wales. It was formed in 1825 (replacing the London Law Institutions which had been formed in 1823), although it did not officially adopt the title of 'Law Society' until 1903. Its charter was granted in 1843. It represents the interests of solicitors and also seeks to influence the process of law reform. Its website contains on-line copies of its Annual Report since 1999/2000 and publications on a range of issues affecting the profession. The website also contains an on-line copy of the publications produced by the Law Society Strategic Research Unit that are available for purchase.

Legal Action Group (LAG)

(www.lag.org.uk)
The LAG is a charity that was established in 1972 which seeks to promote equal access to justice for all members of society. The LAG produces a journal, *Legal Action*, which is available on-line, and provides information on its publications which cover areas that include crime, criminal justice, human rights, legal aid and the legal profession. These are available for purchase.

Legal Services Commission (LSC)

(www.legalservices.gov.uk)
The LSC is an executive non-departmental body sponsored by the Department of Constitutional Affairs whose role is to administer the legal aid system. It was created by the 1999 Access to Justice Act and became operational in April 2000.

It is responsible for two legal aid schemes – the Community Legal Service (through which civil legal aid and advice is delivered) and the Criminal Defence Service (which funds defence services for those involved in criminal investigations and proceedings). The LSC website includes a number of useful on-line public information leaflets related to its operations.

Liberty

(www.liberty-human-rights.org.uk)
This body was established in 1934 and was originally called the National Council for Civil Liberties. It is an important human rights and civil liberties organisation that aims to secure equal rights for everyone and opposes abuses or the excessive use of state power against its citizens. Its activities include lobbying Parliament, providing advice to the public and expert opinion, and conducting research and publishing reports on a wide range of issues that have human rights or civil liberties implications. Currently, these include ASBOs, curfews, police powers, the 1998 Human Rights Act and internment and are available on-line.

National Association for the Care and Resettlement of Offenders (NACRO)

(www.nacro.org.uk)
NACRO is a crime-related charity that was established in 1966. It funds a large number of projects which seek to provide ex-offenders, disadvantaged persons and deprived communities with practical help in areas such as education, employment and housing. Detailed information on the services with which NACRO is involved are available on-line at its website which also provides access to the organisation's publications catalogue which covers areas such as youth crime, mental health, race and criminal justice and crime reduction. Some of these are available on-line and others can be purchased.

National Offender Management Service (NOMS)

(www.noms.gov.uk)
NOMS was created in 2004. It amalgamated the prison and probation services into a single correctional service and was designed to oversee the end-to-end management of offenders and to design interventions and services for offenders in order to reduce reoffending and conviction rates and to protect the public. It is headed by a chief executive who is responsible for strategic policy. A national offender manager controls offender management and national commissioning and ten regional offender managers control most of the expenditure of the service. Its website contains a number of on-line policy and consultation papers, and other useful publications that include a copy of *The Prison Discipline Manual* and Business Plans from 2005/6.

Office for Criminal Justice Reform (OCJR)

(www.cjsonline.gov.uk/the_cjs/departments_of_the_cjs/ocjr)
The OCJR is a cross-departmental team which is designed to promote the principle of joined-up government in the criminal justice process by coordinating the relevant activities performed by the Home Office, the Department for Constitutional Affairs and the Office of the Attorney General, thereby providing an improved service to the public. The team reports to the Home Secretary, Lord Chancellor and the Law Officers' Department. The process of reform is driven at national level by the National Criminal Justice Board that is headed by the same three government departments. The National Board is responsible for attaining the criminal justice system's public service agreements and to do this it sets delivery targets for the 42 local criminal justice boards that were set up in 2003. These are composed of agencies responsible for delivering criminal justice system targets – the police, CPS, magistrates and crown courts, YOTs, and Prison and Probation Services. The OCJR website provides on-line information on the operations of the criminal justice process and key publications related to the goal of a joined-up approach to criminal justice, including the 2002 White Paper, *Justice for All*, and the document *Cutting Crime, Delivering Justice: A Strategic Plan for Criminal Justice 2004/8*.

Information related to operations of the National Criminal Justice Board can be obtained from its website, www.cjsonline.org.uk/working/stats/ncjb.html. Information of the operations of the 42 local boards can be accessed through www.cjsonline.org.uk/working/lcjb.html.

Parliament

(www.parliament.uk)
Key issues affecting criminal justice that require legislation are discussed in the House of Commons and the House of Lords and these deliberations provide excellent sources to enable the pros and cons of measures to be considered. General issues are considered in the Second Reading of Bills and detailed issues are discussed at the Committee stage.

Debates in the House of Commons are recorded in the publication, *Hansard*, which is available on-line at www.parliament.uk/hansard/hansard.cfm. You will then be able to click on to daily debates (which are concerned with current legislation), bound volume debates (which provide details of legislation considered in previous Sessions of Parliament) and Standing Committees considering Bills. On-line bound volume debates commence in the 1988/9 Parliamentary Session in the House of Commons and 1994/5 Parliamentary Session in the House of Lords. On-line debates in House of Commons Standing Committees commence in the 1997/8 Parliamentary Sessions.

Parole Board

(www.paroleboard.gov.uk)
The Parole Board was set up by the 1967 Criminal Justice Act and became operational the following year. It became an independent non-departmental board in 1996 under the provisions of the 1994 Criminal Justice and Public Order Act. Its current operations are governed by the 2003 Criminal Justice Act that makes the release of most prisoners automatic once they have served one-half of their specified sentence. The Parole Board's main role is to judge requests for release by serious offenders who have been convicted of violent or sexual offences, although it may consider decisions to recall to prison those given determinate sentences and regularly reviews those given extended sentences who have been released into community supervision. The Parole Board's website contains on-line copies of its Annual Report since 1997/8 and its Business and Corporate Plan since 2001/2. The site also contains information leaflets related to the Board's work and policy statements dealing with areas that include risk assessment and race.

Police Federation of England and Wales

(www.polfed.org)
This organisation was established by the 1919 Police Act and provided with a statutory duty to represent its members (which comprise all officers below the rank of superintendent) on issues related to their welfare and efficiency. Its work includes negotiating on pay and conditions and campaigning on a wide range of issues affecting the police service. It is also consulted on the formulation of police regulations. Its journal is *Police* magazine, and editions published since 2003 are available on-line.

Police forces

(www.police.uk)
There are 43 police forces in England and Wales, each with their own website. Access to specific force websites can be obtained through the above website address and clicking onto 'Police Forces'. This will provide an alphabetical list of forces and their individual websites. The online information available includes matters such as performance statistics, matters of current importance and news updates to provide for communication between the police force and the public that it serves.

The activities performed by police forces in England and Wales are subject to scrutiny by Her Majesty's Inspectorate of Constabulary (HMIC). The office was first established by the 1856 County and Borough Police Act, and the current duties are contained in the 1996 Police Act. Initially, Inspectors were required to have a background in policing, but since 1993 a lay element has been introduced. The HMIC website (www.homeoffice.gov.uk/hmic/hmic.htm) provides access to on-line reports concerned with force inspections, inspections of basic command units, thematic inspections and best-value reviews of specific activities conducted by individual forces. The Annual Report of the Chief Inspector of Constabulary (HMCIC) is available on-line from 1998/9.

Scotland has eight police forces, maintained by either a police authority or a joint board. On-line information on all eight forces is available through the Scottish Police Forces website, www.scottish.police.uk. This provides information on individual force organisation and policy and access to material including annual reports and performance indicators.

Policing in Northern Ireland is provided by the Police Service of Northern Ireland (PSNI). This force was established as a successor to the Royal Ulster Constabulary in November 2001 as an aspect of the Belfast Agreement. Its website, www.psni.police.uk, provides on-line access to RUC/PSNI Annual Reports since 1995/6 and an archive of press releases since January 2001. The PSNI is supervised by the Northern Ireland Policing Board, whose website, www.nipolicingboard.org.uk, provides on-line access to a wide range of literature related to policing including the Board's Annual Report since 2001/2, the current Corporate Plan and the Police Plan since 2002–5.

Political parties

(www.labour.org.uk)
(www.conservatives.com)
(www.libdems.org.uk)
Crime is an important political issue that is accorded considerable attention during election contests. Political parties devote much attention to crime and their websites include policy statements that put forward their own intentions in this area and criticise the policies of their opponents. It is worthwhile consulting the websites of the main parties for up-to-date information on their respective anti-crime measures which are contained in reports and also in speeches and press statements by leading politicians with responsibilities for home affairs.

Prison Reform Trust (PRT)

(www.prisonreformtrust.org.uk)
The PRT is a charity established in 1981. It seeks to create a just, humane and effective penal system and to this end offers advice and assistance to a range of persons (including prisoners and their families, prison and probation staff and academics) and conducts research on all aspects of imprisonment. Some information is available on-line, and the PRT website also contains a list of publications available for purchase. The website supplies further links to other websites operated by organisations whose work is concerned with imprisonment. The PRT issues a quarterly journal, *Prison Report*, which is available to Friends of the PRT (who make an annual gift to this charity).

Prison Service

(www.hmprisonservice.gov.uk)
The main objectives of the Prison Service are to hold prisoners securely, to reduce the risk of prisoners reoffending and to provide safe and well-ordered establishments in which prisoners are treated humanely, decently and lawfully. In order to achieve these aims, the Prison Service works in close partnership with other agencies in the criminal justice system. The website of the Prison Service for England and Wales contains on-line copies of Annual Reports (since 2001), the Business Plan (since 2000/1) and publications and documents on issues such as prison performance standards and Prison Service statistics (such as the size of the prison population). There is also an on-line prison virtual tour. The *Prison Service Journal* discusses issues of relevance to the Prison Service. This is a subscription journal, but articles in the most current issue are available on-line. A compatible publication, *Prison Service News*, is available on-line since November 2003.

Separate prison services exist for Scotland and Northern Ireland whose websites contain similar material to that of the site for England and Wales. The Scottish Prison Service (www.sps.gov.uk) is an executive agency of the Scottish Executive and is responsible for Scotland's 16 custodial establishments. The Northern Ireland Prison Service (www.niprisonservice.gov.uk) is an executive agency of the Northern Ireland Executive and controls Northern Ireland's three custodial institutions.

Her Majesty's Inspectorate of Prisons provides independent scrutiny of the conditions for, and treatment of, prisoners and other detainees held in prisons, young offender institutions and immigration removal centres. Contracted-out prisons also fall within this official's remit. It is headed by a Chief Inspector of Prisons and seeks to promote the concept of a 'healthy prison' in which staff work effectively to support prisoners and detainees to reduce reoffending or achieve other agreed outcomes. Its website (www.homeoffice.gov.uk/justice/prisons/inspprisons) contains on-line reports of inspections of specific institutions, thematic reviews and research publications. The annual report is also available from 1996/7 and the HMIP Business Plan since 2004/5.

The Prison Service and Probation Service were amalgamated into the National Offender Management Service in 2004. The work of this new agency is discussed elsewhere in this section.

National Probation Service (NPS)

(www.probation.homeoffice.gov.uk)
The Probation Service was created by the 1907 Probation of Offenders Act. The service was administered through local probation areas until the enactment of the 2000 Criminal Justice and Court Services Act when a national service was created, organised into 42 operational areas. The service aims to protect the public, reduce the level of reoffending, provide for the secure punishment of offenders in the community, ensure offenders are aware of

the impact of their crimes on the victims and general public and to secure the rehabilitation of offenders. Its key responsibilities include supervising offenders serving community sentences and those who have been released from prison on licence with a statutory period of community supervision and running probation hostels. The NPS website includes on-line news/update and briefing sections which provide up-to-date information on a wide range of issues affecting the service. It also includes a list of local probation areas, and access to some area websites.

The NPS is inspected by Her Majesty's Inspectorate of Probation (HMIP). HMIP reports directly to the Home Secretary on the performance of the NPS and Youth Offending Teams, in particular on the effectiveness of their work in relation to individual offenders, children and young people which aims to reduce reoffending and protect the public. The HMIP's website (www.homeoffice. gov.uk/justice/probation/inspprob) contains on-line reports of inspections of specific probation areas and activities performed by the NPS.

The Probation Service and Prison Service were amalgamated into the National Offender Management Service in 2004. The work of this new agency is discussed elsewhere in this section.

Public Accounts Committee (PAC)

(www.parliament.uk/parliamentary_committees/committee_of_public_accounts.cfm)
The PAC was established in 1861, and made permanent the following year. Its task is to examine 'the accounts showing the appropriation of the sums granted by Parliament to meet the public expenditure, and [since 1934] of such other accounts laid before Parliament as the committee may think fit'. Its website contains reports, oral and written evidence and government responses to PAC reports. Reports cover a wide range of subject areas, and include matters connected with the criminal justice process. These are available on-line commencing in the 1997/8 Parliamentary Session, and it is worthwhile periodically checking this website for details of current investigations into criminal justice affairs.

Scottish Executive

(www.scotland.gov.uk)
In Scotland, the Scottish Executive constitutes the devolved government for Scotland. The Justice Department of the Scottish Executive is responsible for a wide range of activities concerned with the criminal justice process. These include the police service, the administration of the courts and legal aid. There are two executive agencies attached to the Justice Department, the Scottish Prison Service and the Scottish Courts Service. The website of the Scottish Prison Service (www.scotland.gov.uk/Topics/Justice/Prisons) contains on-line information concerning headquarters policy statements and research publications. Copies of the Annual Report and Accounts are available from

1999/2000. The website of the Scottish Courts Service (www.scotcourts.gov.uk) provides on-line access to the agency's 2002/5 Corporate Plan, the Annual Report and Accounts since 2002/3 and information leaflets related to its work.

Security Industry Authority (SIA)

(www.the-sia.org.uk/home)
The SIA was established by the 2001 Private Security Industry Act to manage the operations of the private security industry, to raise standards of professionalism and skill in the private security industry and to promote the spread of best practice. Its website includes general publications, information on specific licensing sectors and financial and strategic information related to the agency.

Security Service (MI5)

(www.mi5.gov.uk)
MI5 was established in 1909 to combat spying activities undertaken in Britain on behalf of Germany. Its role was subsequently extended to counter all covert threats to national security. Until the enactment of the 1989 Security Service Act, MI5 had no statutory basis. The role of MI5 was broadened during the 1990s. In 1992 it was given the lead role of countering terrorism on mainland Britain and the 1996 Security Service Act allocated the agency the responsibility to combat 'serious' crime (which was defined as an offence which carried a sentence of three years or more on first conviction or any offence involving conduct by a number of persons in pursuit of a common purpose). MI5's website contains much on-line information on the detailed activities of the organisation and also on security advice.

Sentencing Guidelines Council (SGC)

(www.sentencing-guidelines.gov.uk)
The SGC was established by the 2003 Criminal Justice Act and took over the responsibility for formulating sentencing guidelines from the Magistrates' Association and the Court of Appeal. In doing so it takes advice from the Sentencing Advisory Panel which gives advice to the SGC on particular offences or categories of offences and other sentencing issues. Its website contains a wide range of online material which includes guidelines and draft guidelines and consultation papers and research reports related to aspects of crime and sentencing. The SGC's newsletter, *The Sentence*, and the body's annual reports are also available electronically.

Serious Organised Crime Agency (SOCA)

(no website as yet)
SOCA was established by the 2005 Serious Organised Crime and Police Act to combat organised crime. It brought together under one roof a number of existing bodies – the National Criminal Intelligence Service, the National Crime Squad, the investigative and intelligence work performed by HM Customs and Excise in relation to serious drug trafficking and the recovery of criminal assets and the responsibilities exercised by the Home Office for organised immigration crime.

Social Exclusion Unit (SEU)

(www.socialexclusionunit.gov.uk)
This body was set up in 1997, initially within the Cabinet Office. It was transferred to the Office of the Deputy Prime Minister in May 2002 and works closely with other agencies within that Office, including the Neighbourhood Renewal Unit and the Housing Support Directorate. The emphasis placed by post-1997 Labour governments on tackling the social causes of crime (such as unemployment, family background, substance misuse and low educational attainment) through a joined-up approach at the local level has meant that the work of the SEU is of considerable importance to criminology. The SEU website contains on-line reports on issues such as neighbourhood renewal, groups experiencing social exclusion, anti-social behaviour and neighbourhood wardens. Much of this is prepared by the SEU's Policy Action Teams (PATs).

Statewatch

(www.statewatch.org)
Statewatch monitors state and civil liberties throughout the EU and seeks to identify developments which threaten to encroach or erode civil and political liberties. Its website contains on-line briefings on issues that include changes/projected alternations to state powers in connection with protest and developments affecting EU-wide policing. It also provides an extremely useful on-line link to UK legislation of relevance to the concerns of Statewatch. Statewatch publishes *Statewatch Bulletin*. This is available by subscription, but a sample issue is available on-line.

Victim Support

(www.victimsupport.org.uk)
Victim Support is an independent charity that seeks to help people cope with the effects of crime. It provides counselling and information on matters such as court procedures and compensation, and also campaigns on behalf of victims and witnesses. It operates through local branches that can be accessed

through the organisation's websites. The website related to England and Wales contains on-line information related to the work of Victim Support. This includes leaflets and reports related to specific categories of crime, the Annual Report and Accounts (available since 2000) and the National Strategy 2005–8. The magazine *Victim and Witness View*, launched in November 2004, is also available on-line.

Willan Publishing

(www.willanpublishing.co.uk)
Willan is a specialist criminology publisher whose catalogue includes a very wide range of material in key areas of the criminal justice process, such as crime and crime prevention, sentencing and punishment, probation, policing, prisons, youth justice, criminal justice history and criminal behaviour. This website contains full details of current and forthcoming publications and includes a title, author and search facility and secure ordering facilities.

Youth Justice Board

(www.yjb.gov.uk)
The main purpose of the Youth Justice Board for England and Wales is to prevent offending by children and young persons below the age of 18. It became operational in September 1998 and performs a number of specific functions which include advising the Home Secretary on the operations of the youth justice system, monitoring the performance of the youth justice system, purchasing places for children and young people remanded in or sentenced to custody, identifying and disseminating good practice, and commissioning and publishing research. The website of the Youth Justice Board provides up-to-date information on the organisation's activities and also provides access to publications related to its work. Many of these reports and publications are available on-line, others can be purchased. The website also includes on-line copies of the Annual Report and Annual Statistics since 2003/4.

The Youth Justice Board website also provides access to information relating to the operations of the 155 Youth Offending Teams in England and Wales. On-line information includes the Annual Reports since 2004 and copies of the programme of inspections into specific YOTs that commenced in 2003.

Key terms in crime and criminal justice policy

Accountability This is a mechanism whereby a person or agency is required to answer to other people or agencies in respect of the actions they have undertaken. Accountability is often of an *ex post facto* nature, whereby an action may be undertaken but is subsequently subject to scrutiny and the possible deployment of sanctions if improprieties have been committed by those who have taken it.

Anomie Anomie refers to a state of social indiscipline in which the socially approved way of obtaining goals is subject to widespread challenge resulting in the law being unable to effectively maintain social cohesion. The concept was developed by Emile Durkheim and subsequently advanced by Robert Merton.

Best value Best value is a process designed to assess efficiency and effectiveness in the delivery of services by public sector bodies and also to enhance the quality of service: best value replaced the Conservative's compulsory competitive tendering procedures and was introduced into the public sector by the 1997–2001 Labour government.

Bifurcation This refers to sentencing policy that seeks to sharply differentiate between serious and non-serious crime. It embraces a 'twin-track' approach whereby serious offences receive severe penalties (such as long terms of imprisonment) and less serious crimes are responded to leniently (by responses such as non-custodial sentences served in the community).

Broken windows This refers to a view, put forward by Kelling and Wilson in 1982, that it is necessary to take firm action to enforce the law against low level crime (characterised by vandalism and graffiti) which has a detrimental impact on neighbourhood cohesion. Nipping behaviour of this nature in the bud may prevent the development of more serious manifestations of criminality.

Classicist criminology This approach to the study of crime emphasised the importance of free will and viewed a criminal act as one that had been consciously carried out by its perpetrator having rationally weighed up the advantages and disadvantages of undertaking the action. The main focus of classicist criminology was on the operations of the criminal justice system. They believed that if this operated in a consistent and predictable fashion it would eliminate crime committed by those who felt that they would 'get away with it'.

Code for Crown Prosecutors The Code for Crown Prosecutors is prepared by the Director of Public Prosecutions and gives guidance to solicitors working for the Crown Prosecution Service concerning the general principles to be followed when making decisions concerning whether or not to prosecute. These emphasise the need for there to be a realistic prospect of securing a conviction (the evidential test) and whether the public interest is served by pursuing a prosecution (the public interest test). The Code for Crown Prosecutors further puts forward guidelines to aid decisions as to what precise charge should be brought against a person who is being proceeded against.

Community sentences These embrace non-custodial responses to crime that are served by offenders within their communities. The 2000 Criminal Justice and Court Services Act provided for a range of such disposals – community punishment orders, community rehabilitation orders and community punishment and rehabilitation orders – and the 2003 Criminal Justice Act provided for community orders that enabled sentencers to proscribe a wide range of requirements to address an individual's offending behaviour.

Crime and disorder reduction partnerships (CDRPs) The 1998 Crime and Disorder Act placed a statutory duty on police forces and local authorities (termed 'responsible authorities') to act in cooperation with police authorities, health authorities and probation committees in multi-agency bodies which became known as crime and disorder reduction partnerships (CDRPs), although this designation did not appear in the legislation. In Wales CDRPs are termed community safety partnerships. The role of these partnerships was to develop and implement a strategy for reducing crime and disorder in each district and unitary local authority in England and Wales. They act as the driving force for community safety initiatives.

'Cuffing' The practice of 'cuffing' entails a police officer either not recording a crime that has been reported or downgrading a reported crime to an incident which can be excluded from official statistics. The decision to do this was initially motivated by a desire to avoid the time-consuming practice of filling out a crime report for minor incidents, but the introduction of performance indicators for the police service in 1992 intensified pressures on the police to avoid recording all offences notified to them. Crime statistics were a key source of evidence of police performance, so increased levels of reported crimes could imply inefficiency.

Cybercrime This term broadly refers to crime involving the use of computers. There are two main forms of computer-related crime – computer-assisted crime involving the use of computers to perform crimes that pre-dated their existence such as fraud or theft, and computer-focused crime that refers to the emergence of new crimes such as hacking and viruses as the result of computer technology.

'Dark figure' of crime This term refers to the gap between the volume of crime that is actually committed in society and that which enters into official crime statistics. This discrepancy is explained by the nature of the process of crime reporting which consists of a number of stages, each of which acts as a filtering process progressively reducing the number of crimes that are officially reported.

Department for Constitutional Affairs This department was created in June 2003 and is responsible for the administration of the courts, human rights and constitutional issues. It replaced the functions previously carried out by the Lord Chancellor's Department. The first minister to head this new department was Lord Falconer, although as Parliament failed to endorse the government's intention to abolish the post of Lord Chancellor, his official title is that of 'Secretary of State for Constitutional Affairs and Lord Chancellor'.

Deviancy This refers to actions committed by individuals that society disapproves of but which are not illegal. Those who carry them out may thus encounter hostility from their fellow citizens resulting in their ostracism from society.

Director of Public Prosecutions (DPP) This office was created by the 1879 Prosecution of Offences Act. The role of this official was to initiate and carry out criminal proceedings and to advise and assist other officials (such as police officers) concerning the prosecution of offences. The 1985 Prosecution of Offences Act made the DPP head of the newly created Crown Prosecution Service that henceforth became responsible for the conduct of criminal proceedings.

Discretion Discretion refers to the ability of an official, organisation or individual to utilise their independent judgement to determine a course of action or inaction to be pursued. Discretion is frequently exercised in the context of an encounter between an individual and criminal justice practitioner.

Doli incapax This term applies to those who have committed crime but, because of their age, are not held responsible for it because they are considered insufficiently mature to be able to discern right from wrong. Currently, children below the age of 10 (the age of criminal responsibility) are deemed to be in this situation. Formerly children aged 10–13 were also in this position, but this presumption was ended by the 1998 Crime and Disorder Act.

Economic crime This term refers to a range of activities that include bribery, corruption, cybercrime, money laundering and various forms of fraud that are associated with white-collar crime, middle-class crime and organised crime and which particularly impose a burden on business enterprise.

Home detention curfew In January 1999 the government introduced this procedure that provided for the early release of short-term prisoners serving sentences between three months and less than four years for the last two months of their sentence provided that they stayed at an approved address and agreed to a curfew (usually from 7 p.m. to 7 a.m.) monitored by an electronic tag. This would last for a minimum of 14 days and a maximum of 60 days. Those who breached the conditions of their curfew (including attempting to remove the tag) or who committed another offence while on curfew were returned to prison.

Home Secretary This minister is in charge of a wide range of matters affecting the internal affairs of the United Kingdom. This includes exercising ultimate responsibility for the police and Prison Service and the maintenance of national security.

Human rights These consist of basic entitlements that should be available to all human beings in every country. Unlike civil rights (that are specific to individual countries), human rights are universal in application. A full statement of human rights is to be found in the European Convention for the Protection of Human Rights and Fundamental Freedoms (1950). It includes entitlements such as the right to a fair trial and the freedom of thought, conscience, expression and religion, and prohibits torture and inhuman and degrading treatment. The declaration is ultimately enforced by the European Court of Human Rights but its incorporation into UK law by the 1998 Human Rights Act means that accusations that public bodies (including the government) have breached an individual's human rights will be initially heard in domestic courts.

Institutional racism This refers to the use of discriminatory practices against members of minority ethnic groups by an organisation. The term is capable of a number of definitions that include a deliberate organisational policy to discriminate or discrimination that is derived unwittingly from an organisation's working practices.

Joined-up government This approach seeks to enhance the level of coordination between the various agencies whose work is of relevance to crime and disorder. It entails developments such as the use by all agencies of the same organisational boundaries and the construction of mechanisms to provide for multi-agency working. Joined-up government suggests that crime can be reduced not by structural reforms seeking to achieve a greater level of social equality but by managerial improvements affecting the way in which the criminal justice system operates.

Judicial review This is a legal procedure whereby the court is able to strike down an action undertaken by any public body, including the executive branch of government, on the grounds that it has failed to follow the correct procedures that are laid down in law.

Justice model This refers to an approach to the punishment of offenders that is underpinned by reductivist rather than rehabilitative ideals. In particular it seeks to ensure that punishments reflect the seriousness of the crime that has been committed, thereby ensuring that offenders get their 'just deserts' for their actions. Other features of the justice model emphasise the desirability of consistent sentences (especially by curbing the discretion of officials working in criminal justice agencies) and the need for the criminal justice process to effectively protect the accused's rights.

Mandatory sentence This imposes an obligation on sentencers (magistrates or judges) to hand out a pre-determined response to those convicted of crimes that are subject to this provision. Murder, for example, carries a mandatory sentence of life imprisonment. Judges are required to administer this penalty, regardless of the circumstances surrounding the crime. The present raft of mandatory sentences was considerably added to in the 1997 Crime (Sentences) Act and subsequent legislation.

Moral panic This refers to a process in which a specific type of crime is focused upon by the media in order to whip up public hysteria against those who are identified as the perpetrators. The aim of this is to secure widespread public approval for the introduction of sanctions directed against the targeted group.

New deviancy This approach to the study of crime and deviancy rejected the existence of consensual values within society, and asserted that it functioned in the interests of the powerful who were able to foist their attitudes throughout society because of the control they exerted over the state's ideological apparatus (such as religion, education and the mass media), its political system and its coercive machinery (especially the police and courts). Deviancy was viewed as behaviour that was defined as 'bad' or 'unacceptable' by this powerful group of people who were able to utilise their power to stigmatise actions of which they did not approve. New deviancy theory thus concentrated on social intervention and social reaction to activities which were labelled as 'deviant' rather than seeking to discover their initial causes. Labelling theory is an important aspect of new deviancy theory.

New managerialism This term refers to the approach adopted by post-1997 Labour governments towards the performance culture of the public sector. Performance targets and indicators were retained, and within the criminal justice process were subjected to central inspection and monitoring which was extended beyond service delivery to embrace managerial processes. However, compulsory competitive tendering gave way to a process of best value, whereby agencies were required to justify why they were required to deliver a specific service and to ascertain the best way to deliver it.

New public management This approach towards the delivery of services by the public sector was identified with the new right. It emphasised the importance of public sector organisations providing value for money and sought to reorganise the operations of public sector agencies through the use of management techniques associated with the private sector such as the use of performance indicators and business plans. This approach was associated with a shift towards organisations attaining centrally determined objectives at the expense of compliance with bureaucratic rules and procedures.

OASys OASys is the Offender Assessment System that is designed to assess the level of risk posed by all offenders aged 18 and over. It is used by both the Prison and Probation Services.

Panopticon In 1791 Jeremy Bentham wrote a three-volume work, *The Panopticon*, in which he devised a blueprint for the design of prisons which would enable them to bring about the transformation of the behaviour of offenders. Central to his idea was the principle of surveillance whereby an observer was able to monitor prisoners without them being aware when they were being watched. The design of Millbank Penitentiary and Pentonville Prison adopted many of the features of Bentham's panopticon.

Penal populism The terms 'penal populism' or 'populist punitiveness' were coined during the 1990s and this approach was especially directed at the rise of persistent young offenders. It denies the relevance of any social explanation for crime and emphasises the need to adopt a harsh approach towards those who carry out such actions. It is characterised by factors that include the use of 'hard' policing methods, longer sentences and the increased size of the prison population, and harsher prison conditions. Governments following this course of action do so as they believe that the approach of 'getting tough with criminals' is viewed favourably by the general public.

Penology This term refers to the study of the way in which society responds to crime. It covers the wide range of processes that are concerned with the prevention of crime, the punishment, management and treatment of offenders and the measures concerned with reintegrating them into their communities.

Plural policing This entails an enhanced role for organisations other than the police service in performing random patrol work. Those performing this work effectively constitute a second tier of police service providers and the organisations supplying work of this nature may be located in either the public or private sectors.

Police authority This body was initially established by the 1964 Police Act. It was composed of local councillors and magistrates and its role was to maintain 'an adequate and efficient' police force for their area. The make-up of police authorities was subsequently altered by the 1994 Police and Magistrates' Courts Act. They are composed of 17 members – nine local councillors, three magistrates and five persons appointed by the Home Secretary.

Police Code of Conduct This sets out the standards of professional behaviour expected of police officers, the breach of which constitutes a disciplinary offence that in extreme cases can result in dismissal from the police service.

Political spectrum This model places different political ideologies in relationship to each other, thereby enabling their differences and similarities to be identified. Ideologies are placed under the broad headings of 'left', 'right' and 'centre', indicating the stances they adopt towards political, economic and social change – the right opposes this, the left endorses it and the centre wishes to introduce changes of this nature gradually within the existing framework of society.

Positivist criminology This approach to the study of crime adopts a deterministic approach whereby offenders are seen as being propelled into committing criminal acts by forces (that may be biological, psychological or sociological) over which they have no control. Common to all forms of positivist criminology is the belief that society rests on consensual values and offenders should be treated rather than punished for their actions. Positivist criminology also insists that theories related to why crime occurs should derive from scientific analysis.

Pre-sentence report This is a report that provides information to sentencers regarding the background of an offender and the circumstances related to his or her commission of a crime. It is designed to ensure that a sentence of the court is an appropriate response to the criminal action that has been committed. Pre-sentence reports are prepared by the Probation Service which also prepares specific sentence reports for minor offences.

Privatisation This policy was favoured by new right governments and was consistent with their belief in the free market. It entails services previously performed by the public sector being transferred to private sector organisations. These services are either totally divorced from government henceforth, or are contracted out and are thus periodically subject to a process of competitive tendering by bodies wishing to deliver them.

Problem-oriented policing This is a method of policing that seeks to direct police action to recurrent problems as opposed to an approach that reacts to them after they have taken place. It emphasises the importance of identifying and analysing recurrent problems and formulating action to stop them from occurring in the future. Problem-oriented policing emphasises the multi-agency approach to curbing crime, whereby activities directed at crime involve actions undertaken by a range of agencies and not by the police alone.

Reactive policing This is a style of policing (that has also been dubbed 'fire brigade policing') in which the police respond to events rather than seeking to forestall them. This method of policing tends to isolate the police from the communities in which they work and tends to promote the use of police powers in a random way based on stereotypical assumptions. This style of policing was widely regarded to have been a significant factor in the riots that occurred in a number of English cities in 1981.

Recidivism This refers to the reconviction of those who have previously been sentenced for committing a crime. It is an important measurement of the extent to which punishment succeeds in reforming the habits of those who have broken the law.

Reductivism This term refers to methods of punishment that seek to prevent offending behaviour in the future. Punishment is designed to bring about the reform and rehabilitation of criminals so that they do not subsequently indulge in criminal actions.

Responsibilisation This entails governments shifting the task of crime control from the central state to the local level where it is carried out by a range of actors including local government, private and voluntary sector bodies and the general public. Crime and disorder reduction partnerships are an important example of this process in operation.

Retributivism This term embraces responses to crime that seek to punish persons for the actions they have previously committed. Punishment is justified on the basis that it enables society to 'get its own back' on criminals, regardless of whether this has any impact on their future behaviour.

Risk This term refers to the important role that criminal justice policy accords to public safety. Agencies operating within the criminal justice system have increasingly formulated their interventions on the basis of predictions regarding the extent to which the future behaviour of offenders was likely to jeopardise communal safety. This approach has given rise to actuarial penal techniques seeking to assess the future risk posed by offenders.

Rule of law This constitutional principle asserts the supremacy of the law as an instrument governing the actions of individual citizens in their relationships with each other and also controls the conduct of the state towards them. In particular it suggests that citizens can only be punished by the state using formalised procedures when they have broken the law, and that all citizens will be treated in the same way when they commit wrongdoings.

Sentencers This term applies to officials who deliver society's response to crime through the courts over which they preside. In the criminal justice system these comprise judges and magistrates.

Sentencing tariff The tariff sets the level of penalty that should normally be applied by sentencers to particular crimes. In the case of murder, the tariff was the period that had to be served in prison in order to meet the requirements of retribution and deterrence. In 2002 the Sentencing Advisory Panel recommended that the phrase 'minimum term' should be substituted for 'the tariff' in these cases.

Separation of powers This concept suggests that each of the three branches of government (the executive, legislature and judiciary) should perform a defined range of functions, possess autonomy in their relationship with the other two and be staffed by personnel different from that of the others. This principle was first advocated by Baron Montesquieu in his work *De l'Esprit des Lois*, written in 1748, whose main concern was to avoid the tyranny that he believed arose when power was concentrated in the executive branch of government. Although total separation of the three branches of government is unworkable in practice, the judiciary in England and Wales have historically enjoyed a considerable degree of autonomy and may overrule governments through procedures that include judicial review and their implementation of the 1998 Human Rights Act.

Situational crime prevention This approach to crime prevention entails measures directed at highly specific forms of crime that involve manipulating the immediate environment to increase the effort and risks of crime and reduce the rewards to those who might be tempted to carry out such activities. The situational approach is heavily reliant on primary prevention methods and is contrasted with social methods of crime prevention that seek to tackle the root causes of criminal behaviour, typically through social policy.

Social disorganisation This approach to the study of crime was associated with the Chicago School of Human Ecology. It suggests that crime was an ever-present feature of a specific geographic area of a city that Ernest Burgess in 1925 had termed 'zone two' or the 'zone of transition'. It was characterised by rapid population change, dilapidation and conflicting demands made upon land use. New immigrants would initially settle in this zone (or ghetto) as rented residential property was cheapest here, but would move outwards into the other residential zones when their material conditions improved, being replaced by further immigrants. The absence of effective informal mechanisms of social control was viewed as the main reason for this area of the city being a constant crime zone.

Social methods of crime prevention Social crime prevention is based upon the belief that social conditions such as unemployment, poor housing and low educational achievement have a key bearing on crime. It thus seeks to tackle what are regarded as the root causes of crime by methods that seek to alter social environments.

Social strain theory This explanation of crime was developed by Robert Merton whose ideas were originally put forward in 1938. He asserted that anomie arose from a mismatch between the culturally induced aspirations to strive for success (which he asserted in western societies was the pursuit of wealth) and the structurally determined opportunities to achieve it. Social inequality imposed a strain on an individual's commitment to society's success goals and the approved way of attaining them, and resulted in anomie which was characterised by rule-breaking behaviour by those who were socially disadvantaged.

Taken into consideration (TIC) This term (that is also referred to as 'write-offs') entails an offender who has been apprehended for committing a crime confessing to others. He or she is not specifically charged with these additional offences and may suffer no further penalty for these admissions. The system has been criticised for being a means whereby police officers artificially boost their force's detection rates through confessions from criminals that are not always reliable.

Tripartite system of police control and accountability This term denotes a three-way division in the exercise of responsibility over police affairs shared between police authorities, the Home Secretary and chief constables. This system was initially provided for in the 1964 Police Act.

Victimology This aspect of criminology concerns the study of victims of crime. In particular it seeks to establish why certain people become victims of crime and how personal lifestyles influence the risk of victimisation.

White-collar crime As initially defined by Edwin Sutherland, this term referred to crimes committed by respectable persons within the environment of the workplace. Subsequent definitions have differentiated between illegal actions carried out in the workplace that are designed to benefit the individual performing them, illicit actions that are intended to further the interests of a commercial concern carried out by its employees, and criminal activities by persons of 'respectable' social status to further their own interests but which are not performed in the workplace (such as tax evasion and insurance fraud).

Zero tolerance This approach is most readily identified with a style of policing that emphasises the need to take an inflexible attitude towards law enforcement. It is especially directed against low level crime and seeks to ensure that the law is consistently applied against those who commit it. Unlike problem-oriented policing, it does not require the involvement of agencies other than the police to implement.

Index